W9-BYZ-976

THIRD EDITION

Computer Networking
A Top-Down Approach Featuring the Internet

James F. Kurose

University of Massachusetts, Amherst

◆

Keith W. Ross

Polytechnic University, Brooklyn

PEARSON

Addison
Wesley

Boston   San Francisco   New York
London Toronto Sydney Tokyo Singapore Madrid
Mexico City Munich Paris Cape Town Hong Kong Montreal

Managing Editor	Patty Mahtani
Executive Editor	Susan Hartman Sullivan
Assistant Editor	Elizabeth Paquin
Marketing Manager	Michelle Brown
Production Supervisor	Marilyn Lloyd
Project Management	Argosy Publishing, Inc.
Composition	Argosy Publishing, Inc.
Art	Pat Rossi Calkin and Argosy Publishing, Inc.
Art Development	Janet Theurer
Text and Cover Design	Joyce Cosentino Wells
Prepress and Manufacturing	Caroline Fell
Cover Photo:	©2004 Photodisc

Access the latest information about Addison-Wesley Computing titles from our World Wide Web site: http://www.aw-bc.com/computing

The programs and applications presented in this book have been included for their instructional value. They have been tested with care, but are not guaranteed for any particular purpose. The publisher does not offer any warranties or representations, nor does it accept any liabilities with respect to the programs or applications.

If you purchased this book within the United States or Canada you should be aware that it has been wrongfully imported without the approval of the Publisher or the Author.

Copyright © 2005 by Pearson Education, Inc.

All rights reserved. No part of this publication may be reproduced, stored in a retrieval system, or transmitted, in any form or by any means, electronic, mechanical, photocopying, recording, or otherwise, without the prior written permission of the publisher. Printed in the United States of America.

ISBN 0-321-26976-4

1 2 3 4 5 6 7 8 9 10-CRW-08 07 06 05 04

CONGRATULATIONS!

Thank you for purchasing a new copy of *Computer Networking: A Top-Down Approach Featuring the Internet*, Third Edition. Your textbook includes six months of prepaid access to the book's Companion Website. This prepaid subscription provides you with full access to all student support areas, including:

- Six new hands-on Ethereal labs.
- Six programming labs, including two new labs.
- Java applets illustrating key networking concepts.
- Interactive quizzes to help you assess your basic understanding of the material.
- Links to relevant material.

To Activate Your Prepaid Subscription:

You will need to register online using a computer with an Internet connection and a Web browser. The process takes just a couple of minutes and only needs to be completed once.

1. Go to http://www.aw-bc.com/kurose_ross.

2. Click the "Register" button.

3. Use a coin to scratch off the gray coating below and reveal your student access code.* Do not use a knife or other sharp object which can damage the code.

4. On the registration page, enter your student access code. Do not type the dashes. You can use lowercase or uppercase letters.

5. Follow the on-screen instructions. If you need help at any time during the online registration process, simply click the **Need Help?** icon.

6. Once your personal Login Name and Password are confirmed, you can begin using the *Computer Networking: A Top-Down Approach Featuring the Internet* Companion Website!

To log into this Website after you've registered:

You only need to register for this Companion Website once. After that, you can access the site by going to http://www.aw-bc.com/kurose_ross, clicking "Student Resources," and providing your Login Name and Password when prompted.

*IMPORTANT: The Access Code on this page can only be used once to establish a subscription to the *Computer Networking: A Top-Down Approach Featuring the Internet*, Third Edition Companion Website. This subscription is valid for six months upon activation, and is not transferable. If this access code has already been scratched off, it may no longer be valid. If this is the case, you can purchase a subscription by going to http://www.aw-bc.com/kurose_ross and clicking "Register."

About the Authors

Jim Kurose

Jim Kurose is a professor of Computer Science at the University of Massachusetts, Amherst.

Dr. Kurose has received a number of recognitions for his educational activities including Outstanding Teacher Awards from the National Technological University (eight times), the University of Massachusetts, and the Northeast Association of Graduate Schools. He received the IEEE Taylor Booth Education Medal and was recognized for his leadership of Massachusetts' Commonwealth Information Technology Initiative. He has been the recipient of a GE Fellowship, an IBM Faculty Development Award, and a Lilly Teaching Fellowship.

Dr. Kurose is a former Editor-in-Chief of the IEEE Transactions on Communications and of the IEEE/ACM Transactions on Networking. He has been active in the program committees for IEEE Infocom, ACM SIG-COMM, and ACM SIGMETRICS for a number of years and has served as Technical Program Co-Chair for those conferences. He is a Fellow of the IEEE and the ACM. His research interests include network protocols and architecture, network measurement, sensor networks, multimedia communication, and modeling and performance evaluation. He holds a Ph.D. in Computer Science from Columbia University.

Keith Ross

Keith Ross is the Leornard J. Shustek Professor in Computer Science at Polytechnic University in Brooklyn. From 1985 to 1998 he was a professor in the Department of Systems Engineering at the University of Pennsylvania. From 1998 to 2003 he was a professor in the Multimedia Communications Department at Institute Eurecom in France. Keith Ross is also the principal founder and original CEO of Wimba, which develops voice-over-IP technologies for e-learning markets.

Dr. Ross has published numerous research papers and has written two books. He has served on editorial boards on many major journals, including IEEE/ACM Transactions on Networking, and on numerous programming committees, including ACM SIGCOMM and IEEE Infocom. He has supervised 15 Ph.D. theses. His research and teaching interests include P2P systems, multimedia networking, network protocols, and stochastic networks. He received his Ph.D. from the University of Michigan.

To Julie and our three precious
ones—Chris, Charlie, and Nina
JFK

To my wonderful wife, Véronique,
(she's such a great cook among other things!),
and our three daughters, Cécile, Claire, and Katie
KWR

Preface

Welcome to the third edition of *Computer Networking: A Top-Down Approach Featuring the Internet.* Since the publication of the first edition four years ago, our book has been adopted for use at hundreds of colleges and universities, translated into more than 10 languages, and used by over one-hundred thousand students and practitioners worldwide. We've heard from many of these readers and have been overwhelmed by the positive response.

We think one important reason for this success has been that the book offers a fresh approach to computer networking instruction. Why is a fresh approach needed? In recent years we have witnessed two revolutionary changes in the field of networking – changes not reflected in books based on a 1980's or early-to-mid 1990's approach towards networking. First, the Internet has taken over computer networking. Any serious discussion about computer networking today has to be done with the Internet in mind. Second, the biggest "growth area" in the field of networking has arguably been in networking services and applications, as evidenced by the emergence of the Web, ubiquitous e-mail use, audio and video streaming, Internet phone, instant messaging, peer-to-peer applications, and online commerce.

What's new in the third edition?

We've made changes in this third edition, but we've also kept unchanged what we believe (and the instructors and students who have used our book have confirmed) to be the most important aspects of this book: its top-down approach, its focus on the Internet, its attention to both principles and practice, and its accessible style and approach toward learning about computer networking.

Nevertheless, we have made many significant changes in the third edition, including a **new chapter on wireless and mobile networks**. We are currently witnessing a major shift in how users access the Internet and its services. Untethered users now access the Internet wirelessly from offices, homes, and public places. They do so while on the road and on the move, via an array of devices including laptops, phones, PDAs and more. Our new chapter on wireless and mobility includes in-depth coverage of 802.11, an overview of cellular Internet access, and a comprehensive discussion of mobility in the Internet and in cellular networks. With the addition of this new chapter, the textbook now contains four advanced, specialty chapters: wireless and mobile networks; multimedia networks; network security; and network management.

A second major addition is a set of **hands-on Ethereal labs**. Ethereal is free, public-domain packet sniffing and analysis tool that can be run on all popular operating systems, including the most common Windows operating systems. It has rich functionality that includes an intuitive user interface and the ability to analyze nearly 400 protocols. In addition to the existing and new programming assignments, our book now has six Ethereal labs that are coordinated with the material in the text and that can be done on a student's own personal computer. (We'll also be creating additional Ethereal labs over the upcoming years.) In these labs, students can observe network protocols in action, seeing how protocol entities running in their computers interact and exchange messages with protocol entities executing elsewhere in the Internet. Students learn by doing. We have also added **two new socket programming assignments**: a UDP assignment and a proxy Web server assignment.

And that is not all. The third edition has been updated to reflect rapid changes in the field of networking over the last few years. It includes new and expanded material on peer-to-peer networking, BGP, MPLS, network security, broadcast routing, and Internet addressing and forwarding. We have also restructured Chapter 4, exposing more clearly the roles of forwarding and routing, and their interplay within the network layer.

Audience

This textbook is for a first course on computer networking. It can be used in both computer science and electrical engineering departments. In terms of programming languages, the book assumes only that the student has experience with C, C++, or Java (and even then only in a few places). Although this book is more precise and analytical than many other introductory computer networking texts, it rarely uses any mathematical concepts that are not taught in high school. We have made a deliberate effort to avoid using any advanced calculus, probability, or stochastic process concepts. The book is therefore appropriate for undergraduate courses and for first-year graduate courses. It should also be useful to practitioners in the telecommunications industry.

What Is Unique about This Textbook?

The subject of computer networking is enormously complex, involving many concepts, protocols, and technologies that are woven together in an intricate manner. To cope with this scope and complexity, many computer networking texts are often organized around the "layers" of a network architecture. With a layered organization, students can see through the complexity of computer networking—they learn about the distinct concepts and protocols in one part of the architecture while seeing the big picture of how all parts fit together. From a pedagogical perspective, our personal experience has been that such a layered approach is indeed highly desirable. Nevertheless, we have found the traditional approach of teaching— bottom up, that is, from the physical layer towards the application layer—is not the best approach for a modern course on computer networking.

A Top-Down Approach

Our book broke new ground 4 years ago by treating networking in a top-down manner —that is, by beginning at the application layer and working its way down toward the physical layer. The top-down approach has several important benefits. First, it places emphasis on the application layer (a "high growth area" in networking). Indeed, many of the recent revolutions in computer networking— including the Web, peer-to-peer file sharing, and media streaming—have taken place at the application layer. An early emphasis on application-layer issues differs from the approaches taken in most other texts, which have only a small (or nonexistent) amount of material on network applications, their requirements, application-layer paradigms (e.g., client/server), and application programming interfaces.

Second, our experience as instructors (and that of many instructors have used this text) has been that teaching networking applications near the beginning of the course is a powerful motivational tool. Students are thrilled to learn about how networking applications work—applications such as email and the Web, which most students use on a daily basis. Once a student understands the applications, the student can then understand the network services needed to support these applications. The student can then, in turn, examine the various ways in which such services might be provided and implemented in the lower layers. Covering applications early thus provides motivation for the remainder of the text.

Third, a top-down approach enables instructors to introduce network application development at an early stage. Students not only see how popular applications and protocols work, but also learn how easy it is to create their own network applications and application-level protocols. With the top-down approach, students get early exposure to the notions of application programming interfaces (APIs), service models, and protocols—important concepts that resurface in all subsequent layers. By providing socket programming examples in Java, we highlight the central ideas without confusing students with complex code. Undergraduates in electrical engineering and computer science should not have difficulty following the Java code.

An Internet Focus

As indicated by the title, this textbook features the Internet, and uses the Internet's architecture and protocols as primary vehicles for studying fundamental computer networking concepts. Of course, we also include concepts and protocols from other network architectures. But the spotlight is clearly on the Internet, a fact reflected in our organizing the book around the Internet's five-layer architecture: the application, transport, network, link, and physical layers.

Another benefit of spotlighting the Internet is that most computer science and electrical engineering students are eager to learn about the Internet and its protocols. They've heard that the Internet is a revolutionary and disruptive technology and can see that it is profoundly changing our world. Given the enormous relevance of the Internet, students are naturally curious about what is "under the hood." Thus, it is easy for an instructor to get students excited about basic principles when using the Internet as the guiding focus.

Addressing Principles

Two of the unique features of the book—its top-down approach and its focus on the Internet—appear in the subtitle of this book. If we could have squeezed a *third* phrase into the subtitle, it would have contained the word *principles*. The field of networking is now mature enough that a number of fundamentally important issues can be identified. For example, in the transport layer, the fundamental issues include reliable communication over an unreliable network layer, connection establishment/teardown and handshaking, congestion and flow control, and multiplexing. Two fundamentally important network-layer issues are determining "good" paths between two routers and interconnecting a large number of heterogeneous networks. In the data link layer, a fundamental problem is sharing a multiple access channel. In network security, techniques for providing confidentiality, authentication, and message integrity are all based on cryptographic fundamentals. This text identifies fundamental networking issues and studies approaches towards addressing these issues. The student learning these principles will gain knowledge with a long "shelf life;" long after today's network standards and protocols have been become obsolete, the principles they embody will remain important and relevant. We believe that the combination of using the Internet to get the student's foot in the door and then emphasizing fundamental issues and solution approaches will allow the student to quickly understand just about any networking technology.

The Web Site

Purchasing this textbook grants each reader six months of access to a companion Web site for all book readers at http://www.aw.com/kurose-ross, which includes:

♦ *Interactive learning material.* The site contains interactive Java applets, illustrating key networking concepts. It also provides direct access to the programs such as the Traceroute program (through your browser) that shows the path that packets follow in the Internet. Professors can use these interactive features as mini labs. The Web site also provides direct access to search engines for Internet Drafts and to a newsgroup in which topics of this book are discussed. Finally, the site also makes available interactive quizzes that permit students to check their basic understanding of the subject matter.

◆ *Links to relevant on-line material.* We've made an effort to include Web URLs for as many of the book's references as possible. The bibliography is online and will be updated as links change, and as new material becomes available. We've also added links to some of our own favorite Web sites. The links point not only to RFCs and journal and conference articles, but also to sites that are more pedagogical in nature, including home-brewed pages on particular aspects of Internet technology and articles appearing in online trade magazines. Professors can assign the material behind the links as supplementary or even required reading.

◆ *Laboratory assignments.* The Web site also provides a number of detailed programming assignments and Ethereal lab assignments. The programming assignments include building a multithreaded Web server, building an e-mail client with a GUI interface, programming the sender and receiver sides of a reliable data transport protocol, programming a distributed routing algorithm, and more. The Web site also provides the details of the hands-on Ethereal Labs discussed above.

Pedagogical Features

We have each been teaching computer networking for nearly 20 years. We bring to this text more than combined 35 years of teaching experience to over 3,000 students. We have also been active researchers in computer networking during this time. (In fact, Jim and Keith first met each other as master's students in a computer networking course taught by Mischa Schwartz in 1979 at Columbia University.) We think all this gives us a good perspective on where networking has been and where it is likely to go in the future. Nevertheless, we have resisted temptations to bias the material in this book towards our own pet research projects. We figure you can visit our personal Web sites if you are interested in our research. Thus, this book is about modern computer networking—it is about contemporary protocols and technologies as well as the underlying principles behind these protocols and technologies. We also believe that learning (and teaching!) about networking can be fun. A sense of humor, use of analogies, and real-world examples in this book will hopefully make this material more fun.

Historical Sidebars and Principles in Practice

The field of computer networking has a rich and fascinating history. We have made a special effort in the text to tell the history of computer networking. This is done with a special historical section in Chapter 1 and with about a dozen historical sidebars sprinkled throughout the chapters. In these historical pieces, we cover the invention of packet switching, the evolution of the Internet, the birth of major networking giants such as Cisco and 3Com, and many other important events. Students will be stimulated by these historical pieces. We include special sidebars that highlight important principles in computer networking. These sidebars will help students appreciate some of the fundamental concepts being applied in modern networking.

Interviews

We have included yet another original feature that should inspire and motivate students—interviews with renowned innovators in the field of networking. We provide interviews with Len Kleinrock, Tim Berners-Lee, Sally Floyd, Vint Cerf, Simon Lam, Charlie Perkins, Henning Schulzrinne, Steven Bellovin, and Jeff Case.

Supplements for Instructors

We provide a complete supplements package to aid instructors in teaching this course. All of this material is available on the instructor's Web site, http://www.aw.com/kurose-ross. Access to this portion of the WWW site is available to instructors by contacting your Addison-Wesley sales representative or by sending an email message to aw.cs@aw.com.

- *Powerpoint slides.* The course Web site provides PowerPoint® slides for all nine chapters. The slides cover each chapter in detail. They use graphics and animations (rather than relying only on monotonous text bullets) to make the slides interesting and visually appealing. We provide the original PowerPoint slides so you can customize them to best suit your own teaching needs. Some of these slides have been contributed by other instructors who have taught from our book.
- *Homework Solutions.* The Web site provides a solutions manual for the homework problems in the text.
- *Discussion group and contributions from other instructors.* The Web site also includes a section where instructors can post comments, questions, and replies. We have also included instructional material contributed by other instructors using our book.

Chapter Dependencies

The first chapter of this text presents a self-contained overview of computer networking. Introducing many key concepts and terminology, this chapter sets the stage for the rest of the book. All of the other chapters directly depend on this first chapter. We recommend that, after completing Chapter 1, instructors cover Chapters 2 through 5 in sequence, thereby teaching according to the top-down philosophy. Each of these five chapters leverages material from the preceding chapters.

After completing the first five chapters, the instructor has quite a bit of flexibility. There are no interdependencies among the last four chapters, so they can be taught in any order. However, each of the last four chapters depends on the material in the first five chapters. Many instructors teach the first five chapters and then teach one of the last for four chapters for dessert.

One Final Note: We'd Love to Hear from You

We encourage instructors and students to create new Java applets that illustrate the concepts and protocols in this book. If you have an applet that you think would be appropriate for this text, please submit it to the authors. If the applet (including notation and terminology) are appropriate, we will be happy to include it on the text's Web site, with an appropriate reference to the authors of the applet. As noted above, we also encourage instructors to send us new homework problems (and solutions) that would complement the current homework problems. We will post these on the instructor-only portion of the Web site.

We also encourage students and instructors to e-mail us about any comments they might have about our book. It's been wonderful for us to hear from so many instructors and students from around the world about our first two editions. Feel free to send us interesting URLs, to point out typos, to disagree with any of our claims, and to tell us what works and what doesn't work. Tell us what you think should or shouldn't be included in the next edition. Send your e-mail to kurose@cs.umass.edu and ross@poly.edu

Acknowledgements

Since we began writing this book in 1996, many people have given us invaluable help and have been influential in shaping our thoughts on how to best organize and teach a networking course. We want to say A BIG THANKS to everyone who has helped. We are also very thankful to the hundreds of readers from around the world—students, faculty, practitioners—who have sent us thoughts and comments on earlier editions of the book and suggestions for future editions of the book. Special thanks go out to:

Al Aho (Columbia University)
Pratima Akkunoor (Arizona State University)
Paul Amer (University of Delaware)

Shamiul Azom (Arizona State University)
Paul Barford (University of Wisconsin)
Bobby Bhattacharjee (University of Maryland)
Steven Bellovin (AT&T Research)
Pravin Bhagwat (Wibhu)
Supratik Bhattacharyya (Sprint)
Shahid Bokhari (University of Engineering & Technology, Lahore)
Ernst Biersack (Eurécom Institute)
Daniel Brushteyn (former University of Pennsylvania student)
Ken Calvert (University of Kentucky)
Evandro Cantu (Federal University of Santa Catarina)
Jeff Case (SNMP Research International)
Vinton Cerf (MCI WorldCom)
Byung Kyu Choi (Michigan Technological University)
John Daigle (University of Mississippi)
Edmundo A. de Souza e Silva (Federal University of Rio de Janiero)
Philippe Decuetos (Eurécom Institute)
Christophe Diot (Sprint)
Michalis Faloutsos (University of California at Riverside)
Wu-chi Feng (Oregon Graduate Institute)
Charles M. Fleckenstein (Sprint)
David Flessas (Sprint)
Sally Floyd (ICIR, University of California at Berkeley)
Paul Francis (Cornell)
Lixin Gao (University of Massachusetts)
JJ Garcia-Luna-Aceves (University of California at Santa Cruz)
Mario Gerla (University of California at Los Angeles)
David Goodman (Polytechnic University)
Tim Griffin (AT&T Research)
Max Hailperin (Gustavus Adolphus College)
Bruce Harvey (Florida A&M University, Florida State University)
Carl Hauser (Washington State University)
Phillipp Hoschka (INRIA/W3C)
Albert Huang (former University of Pennsylvania student)
Esther A. Hughes (Virginia Commonwealth University)
Jobin James (University of California at Riverside)
Sugih Jamin (University of Michigan)
Shivkumar Kalyanaraman (Rensselaer Polytechnic Institute)
Jussi Kangasharju (University of Darmstadt)
Sneha Kasera (University of Utah)
Hyojin Kim (former University of Pennsylvania student)
Leonard Kleinrock (University of California at Los Angeles)
David Kotz (Dartmouth College)

Beshan Kulapala (Arizona State University)
Miguel A. Labrador (University of South Florida)
Steve Lai (Ohio State University)
Tim-Berners Lee (World Wide Web Consortium)
Brian Levine (University of Massachusetts)
William Liang (former University of Pennsylvania student)
Willis Marti (Texas A&M University)
Deep Medhi (University of Missouri, Kansas City)
Bob Metcalfe (International Data Group)
Sue Moon (KAIST)
Erich Nahum (IBM Research)
Christos Papadopoulos (University of Southern California)
Craig Partridge (BBN Technologies)
Radia Perlman (Sun Microsystems)
Jitendra Padhye (Microsoft Research)
Kevin Phillips (Sprint)
George Polyzos (University of California at San Diego)
Sriram Rajagopalan (Arizona State University)
Ken Reek (Rochester Institute of Technology)
Martin Reisslein (Arizona State University)
Jennifer Rexford (AT&T Research)
Sumit Roy (University of Washington)
Avi Rubin (Johns Hopkins University)
Dan Rubenstein (Columbia University)
Despina Saparilla (Lucent Bell Labs)
Henning Schulzrinne (Columbia University)
Mischa Schwartz (Columbia University)
Harish Sethu (Drexel University)
K. Sam Shanmugan (University of Kansas)
Prashant Shenoy (University of Massachusetts)
Clay Shields (Georgetown University)
Subin Shrestra (University of Pennsylvania)
Peter Steenkiste (Carnegie Mellon University)
Tatsuya Suda (University of California at Irvine)
Kin Sun Tam (State University of New York at Albany)
Don Towsley (University of Massachusetts)
David Turner (California State University, San Bernardino)
David Wetherall (University of Washington)
Ira Winston (University of Pennsylvania)
Raj Yavatkar (Intel)
Yechiam Yemini (Columbia University)
Ellen Zegura (Georgia Institute of Technology)
Hui Zhang (Carnegie Mellon University)

Lixia Zhang (University of California at Los Angeles)
ZhiLi Zhang (University of Minnesota)
Lixia Zhang (University of California at Los Angeles)
Shuchun Zhang (former University of Pennsylvania student)
Phil Zimmermann (independent consultant)

We also want to thank the entire Addison-Wesley team, who have done an absolutely outstanding job (and who have put up with two very finicky authors!): Marilyn Lloyd, Susan Hartman Sullivan, Patty Mahtani and Beth Paquin. Thanks also to the artists, Janet Theurer and Patrice Rossi Calkin, for their work on the beautiful figures in the second and third editions of this book, and to Nancy Kotary and Daniel Rausch for their wonderful production work on this edition. Finally, a most special thanks go to Susan, our editor at Addison-Wesley. This book would not be what it is (and may well not have been at all) without her graceful management, constant encouragement, nearly infinite patience, good humor, and perseverance.

Table of Contents

Chapter 7   Multimedia Networking   565

Computer Networking

A Top-Down Approach Featuring the Internet

Third Edition

1

Computer Networks and the Internet

From Web browsers in cellular telephones to cafes with public wireless Internet access, from home networks with high-speed broadband access to traditional workplace IT infrastructure with a networked PC on every desk, to networked cars, to networked environmental sensors, to the interplanetary Internet—just as it seems that computer networks are essentially ubiquitous, exciting new applications are developed that extend the reach of today's networks even further. It seems that computer networks are everywhere! This book will provide you with a modern introduction to the dynamic field of computer networking, giving you the principles and practical insights you'll need to understand not only today's networks, but tomorrow's as well.

This first chapter presents an overview of computer networking and the Internet. Our goal here is to paint a broad picture, to see the forest through the trees. We'll cover a lot of ground in this introductory chapter and discuss a lot of pieces of a computer network, without losing sight of the big picture. The chapter lays the groundwork for the rest of the book.

We'll structure our overview of computer networks in this chapter as follows. After introducing some basic terminology and concepts, we'll first examine the basic hardware and software components that make up a network. We'll begin at the network's edge and look at the end systems and network applications running in the network. We'll consider the transport services provided to these applications. We'll then explore the core of a computer network, examining the links and the switches that transport data, as well as the access networks and physical media that connect end systems to the network core. We'll learn that the Internet is a network of networks, and we'll learn how these networks connect with each other.

After having completed this overview of the edge and core of a computer network, we'll take the broader and more abstract view in the second half of this chapter. We'll examine the causes of data-transfer delay and loss in a computer network, and provide simple quantitative models for end-to-end delay, models that take into account transmission, propagation, and queuing delays. We'll then introduce some of the key architectural principles in computer networking, namely protocol layering and service models. Finally, we'll close this chapter with a brief history of computer networking.

1.1   What Is the Internet?

In this book we use the public Internet, a specific computer network, as our principal vehicle for discussing computer networks and their protocols. But what is the Internet? We would like to be able to give you a one-sentence definition of the Internet, a definition that you can take home and share with your family and friends. Alas, the Internet is very complex and ever changing, both in terms of its hardware and software components, as well as in the services it provides.

1.1.1 A Nuts-and-Bolts Description

Instead of giving a one-sentence definition, let's try a more descriptive approach. There are a couple of ways to do this. One way is to describe the nuts and bolts of the Internet, that is, the basic hardware and software components that make up the Internet. Another way is to describe the Internet in terms of a networking infrastructure that provides services to distributed applications. Let's begin with the nuts-and-bolts description, using Figure 1.1 to illustrate our discussion.

The public Internet is a worldwide computer network, that is, a network that interconnects millions of computing devices throughout the world. Not too long ago, these computing devices were primarily traditional desktop PCs, UNIX-based workstations, and so-called servers that store and transmit information such as Web pages and e-mail messages. Increasingly, however, nontraditional Internet end systems such as personal digital assistants (PDAs), TVs, mobile computers, cell phones, automobiles, environmental sensing devices, picture frames, home electrical and security systems, Web cams, and even toasters are being connected to the Internet [BBC 2001]. Indeed, the term *computer network* is beginning to sound a bit dated, given the many nontraditional devices being hooked up to the Internet. In Internet jargon, all of these devices are

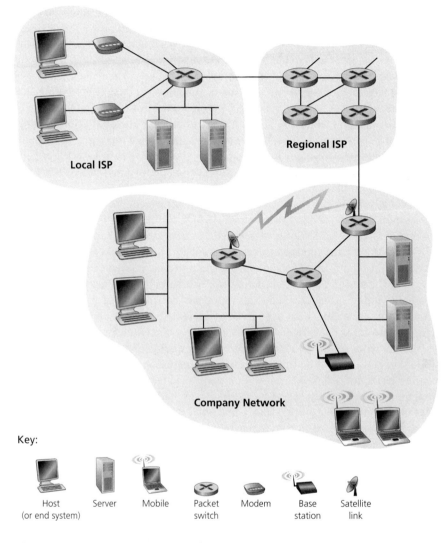

Key:

Host (or end system)	Server	Mobile	Packet switch	Modem	Base station	Satellite link

Figure 1.1 ♦ Some pieces of the Internet

called **hosts** or **end systems**. As of January 2003 there were more than 233 million end systems using the Internet, and this number continues to grow rapidly [ISC 2004].

End systems are connected together by **communication links**. We'll see in Section 1.4 that there are many types of communication links, which are made up of different types of physical media, including coaxial cable, copper wire, fiber optics, and radio spectrum. Different links can transmit data at different rates, with the **transmission rate** of a link measured in bits/second.

End systems are not usually directly attached to each other via a single communication link. Instead, they are indirectly connected to each other through intermediate switching devices known as **packet switches**. A packet switch takes a chunk of information arriving on one of its incoming communication links and forwards that chunk of information on one of its outgoing communication links. In the jargon of computer networking, the chunk of information is called a **packet**. Packet switches come in many shapes and flavors, but the two most prominent types in today's Internet are **routers** and **link-layer switches**. Both types of switches forward packets toward their ultimate destinations. We'll examine routers in detail in Chapter 4 and link-layer switches in detail in Chapter 5.

From the sending end system to the receiving end system, the sequence of communication links and packet switches traversed by a packet is known as a **route** or **path** through the network. Rather than provide a *dedicated* path between communicating end systems, the Internet uses a technique known as **packet switching** that allows multiple communicating end systems to share a path, or parts of a path, at the same time. The first packet-switched networks, created in the 1970s, are the earliest ancestors of today's Internet. The exact amount of traffic being carried in today's Internet is the subject of some debate [Odylsko 2003], but conservative estimates put the monthly traffic rate on long-distance US-based networks at roughly 100,000 terabytes per month, with the amount of traffic approximately doubling every year.

End systems access the Internet through **Internet Service Providers (ISPs)**, including residential ISPs such as AOL or your local telephone or cable company; corporate ISPs; university ISPs; and ISPs such as T-Mobile that provide wireless access in airports, hotels, coffee shops, and other public places. Each ISP is a network of packet switches and communication links. ISPs provide a variety of types of network access to the end systems, including 56 kbps dial-up modem access, residential broadband access such as cable modem or DSL, high-speed LAN access, and wireless access. ISPs also provide Internet access to content providers, connecting Web sites directly to the Internet. To allow communication among Internet users and to allow users to access worldwide Internet content, these lower-tier ISPs are interconnected through national and international upper-tier ISPs, such as AT&T and Sprint. An upper-tier ISP consists of high-speed routers interconnected with high-speed fiber-optic links. Each ISP network, whether upper-tier or lower-tier, is managed independently, runs the IP protocol (see below), and conforms to certain naming and address conventions. We'll examine ISPs and their interconnection more closely in Section 1.5.

End systems, packet switches, and other pieces of the Internet, run **protocols** that control the sending and receiving of information within the Internet. The **Transmission Control Protocol (TCP)** and the **Internet Protocol (IP)** are two of the most important protocols in the Internet. The IP protocol specifies the format of the packets that are sent and received among routers and end systems. The Internet's principal protocols are collectively known as **TCP/IP**. We'll begin looking into protocols in this introductory chapter. But that's just a start—much of this book is concerned with computer network protocols!

Given the importance of protocols to the Internet, it's important that everyone agree on what each and every protocol does. This is where standards come into play. **Internet standards** are developed by the Internet Engineering Task Force (IETF)[IETF 2004]. The IETF standards documents are called **requests for comments (RFCs)**. RFCs started out as general requests for comments (hence the name) to resolve architecture problems that faced the precursor to the Internet. RFCs tend to be quite technical and detailed. They define protocols such as TCP, IP, HTTP (for the Web), and Simple Mail Transfer Protocol (SMTP) (for open-standards e-mail). The IETF has also standardized what protocols must be run by an Internet host [RFC 1122; RFC 1123] and an Internet router [RFC 1812]. There are more than 3,500 RFCs. Other bodies also specify standards for network components, most notably for network links. The IEEE 802 LAN/MAN Standards Committee [IEEE 802 2004], for example, specifies the Ethernet and wireless Wi-Fi standards.

The public Internet (that is, the global network of networks discussed above) is the network that one typically refers to as *the* Internet. There are also many private networks, such as many corporate and government networks, whose hosts cannot exchange messages with hosts outside of the private network (unless the messages pass through so-called firewalls, which restrict the flow of messages to and from the network). These private networks are often referred to as **intranets**, as they use the same types of hosts, routers, links, and protocols as the public Internet.

1.1.2 A Service Description

The preceding discussion has identified many of the pieces that make up the Internet. Let's now leave the nuts-and-bolts description and take a service-oriented view.

♦ The Internet allows **distributed applications** running on its end systems to exchange data with each other. These applications include Web surfing, instant messaging, audio and video streaming, Internet telephony, distributed games, peer-to-peer (P2P) file sharing, remote login, electronic mail, and much, much more. It is worth emphasizing that the Web is not a separate network but rather just one of many distributed applications that use the communication services provided by the Internet.

♦ The Internet provides two services to its distributed applications: a **connection-oriented reliable service** and a **connectionless unreliable service**. Loosely speaking, the connection-oriented reliable service guarantees that data transmitted from a sender to a receiver will eventually be delivered to the receiver in order and in its entirety. The connectionless unreliable service does not make any guarantees about eventual delivery. Typically, a distributed application makes use of one or the other (but not both) of these two services.

♦ Currently, the Internet does not provide a service that makes promises about *how long* it will take to deliver the data from sender to receiver. And except for increasing your access transmission rate to your Internet service provider, you currently cannot obtain better service (for example, bounded delays) by paying more—a state of affairs that some (particularly Americans!) find odd. We'll take a look at state-of-the-art Internet research that is aimed at changing this situation in Chapter 7.

This second description of the Internet—that is, in terms of the services it provides to distributed applications—is an important one. Increasingly, advances in the nuts-and-bolts components of the Internet are being driven by the needs of new applications. So it's important to keep in mind that the Internet is an infrastructure in which new applications are being constantly invented and deployed.

We have just given two descriptions of the Internet, one in terms of its hardware and software components, the other in terms of the services it provides to distributed applications. But perhaps you are still confused as to what the Internet is. What are packet switching, TCP/IP, and connection-oriented service? What are routers? What kinds of communication links are present in the Internet? What is a distributed application? How can a toaster or a weather sensor be attached to the Internet? If you feel a bit overwhelmed by all of this now, don't worry—the purpose of this book is to introduce you to both the nuts and bolts of the Internet, as well as the principles that govern how and why it works. We'll explain these important terms and questions in the following sections and chapters.

1.1.3 What Is a Protocol?

Now that we've got a bit of a feel for what the Internet is, let's consider another important buzzword in computer networking: *protocol*. What is a protocol? What does a protocol do? How would you recognize a protocol if you met one?

A Human Analogy

It is probably easiest to understand the notion of a computer network protocol by first considering some human analogies, since we humans execute protocols all of the time. Consider what you do when you want to ask someone for the time of day. A typical exchange is shown in Figure 1.2. Human protocol (or good manners, at least) dictates that one first offer a greeting (the first "Hi" in Figure 1.2) to initiate communication with someone else. The typical response to a "Hi" is a returned "Hi" message. Implicitly, one then takes a cordial "Hi" response as an indication that one can proceed and ask for the time of day. A different response to the initial "Hi" (such as "Don't bother me!" or "I don't speak English," or some unprintable reply) might indicate an unwillingness or inability to communicate. In this case, the human protocol would be not to ask for the time of day. Sometimes one gets no response at all to

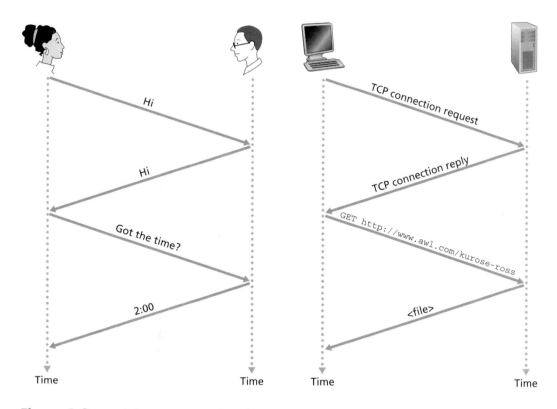

Figure 1.2 ♦ A human protocol and a computer network protocol

a question, in which case one typically gives up asking that person for the time. Note that in our human protocol, *there are specific messages we send, and specific actions we take in response to the received reply messages or other events (such as no reply within some given amount of time).* Clearly, transmitted and received messages, and actions taken when these messages are sent or received or other events occur, play a central role in a human protocol. If people run different protocols (for example, if one person has manners but the other does not, or if one understands the concept of time and the other does not) the protocols do not interoperate and no useful work can be accomplished. The same is true in networking—it takes two (or more) communicating entities running the same protocol in order to accomplish a task.

Let's consider a second human analogy. Suppose you're in a college class (a computer networking class, for example!). The teacher is droning on about protocols and you're confused. The teacher stops to ask, "Are there any questions?" (a message that is transmitted to, and received by, all students who are not sleeping). You raise your hand (transmitting an implicit message to the teacher). Your teacher acknowledges you with a smile, saying "Yes . . ." (a transmitted message encouraging you to ask your question—teachers *love* to be asked questions), and you then ask your question (that is, transmit your message to your teacher). Your teacher hears your question (receives your question message) and answers (transmits a reply to you). Once again, we see that the transmission and receipt of messages, and a set of conventional actions taken when these messages are sent and received, are at the heart of this question-and-answer protocol.

Network Protocols

A network protocol is similar to a human protocol, except that the entities exchanging messages and taking actions are hardware or software components of some device (for example, computer, router, or other network-capable device). All activity in the Internet that involves two or more communicating remote entities is governed by a protocol. For example, hardware-implemented protocols in the network interface cards of two physically connected computers control the flow of bits on the "wire" between the two network interface cards; congestion-control protocols in end systems control the rate at which packets are transmitted between sender and receiver; protocols in routers determine a packet's path from source to destination. Protocols are running everywhere in the Internet, and consequently much of this book is about computer network protocols.

As an example of a computer network protocol with which you are probably familiar, consider what happens when you make a request to a Web server, that is, when you type the URL of a Web page into your Web browser. The scenario is illustrated in the right half of Figure 1.2. First, your computer will send a connection request message to the Web server and wait for a reply. The Web server will eventually receive your connection request message and return a connection reply message. Knowing that it is now OK to request the Web document, your computer then sends the name of the Web page it wants to fetch from that Web server in a GET message. Finally, the Web server returns the Web page (file) to your computer.

Given the human and networking examples above, the exchange of messages and the actions taken when these messages are sent and received are the key defining elements of a protocol:

> A **protocol** *defines the format and the order of messages exchanged between two or more communicating entities, as well as the actions taken on the transmission and/or receipt of a message or other event.*

The Internet, and computer networks in general, make extensive use of protocols. Different protocols are used to accomplish different communication tasks. As you read through this book, you will learn that some protocols are simple and straightforward, while others are complex and intellectually deep. Mastering the field of computer networking is equivalent to understanding the what, why, and how of networking protocols.

1.2 The Network Edge

In the previous sections we presented a high-level overview of the Internet and networking protocols. We are now going to delve a bit more deeply into the components of a computer network (and the Internet, in particular). We begin in this section at the edge of a network and look at the components with which we are most familiar—namely, the computers that we use on a daily basis. In the next section we'll move from the network edge to the network core and examine switching and routing in computer networks. Then in Section 1.4 we'll discuss the actual physical links that carry the signals sent between computers and switches.

1.2.1 End Systems, Clients, and Servers

In computer networking jargon, the computers connected to the Internet are often referred to as **end systems**. They are referred to as end systems because they sit at the edge of the Internet, as shown in Figure 1.3. The Internet's end systems include desktop computers (e.g., desktop PCs, Macs, and UNIX-based workstations), servers (e.g., Web and e-mail servers), and mobile computers (e.g., portable computers, PDAs, and phones with wireless Internet connections). Furthermore, an increasing number of alternative devices, such as thin clients and household appliances [Thinplanet 2002], Web TVs and set-top boxes [Nesbitt 2002], digital cameras, home appliances, factory floor equipment, and environmental sensors, are being attached to the Internet as end systems (see sidebar).

End systems are also referred to as *hosts* because they host (that is, run) application programs such as a Web browser program, a Web server program, an e-mail reader program, or an e-mail server program. Throughout this book we will use the terms hosts and end systems interchangeably; that is, host = end system. Hosts are sometimes further divided into two categories: **clients** and **servers**. Informally, clients tend to be desktop and mobile PCs, PDAs, and so on, whereas servers tend to be more powerful machines that store and distribute Web pages, stream video, relay e-mail, and so on.

In the context of networking software, there is another definition of a client and server, a definition that we'll refer to throughout this book. A **client program** is a program running on one end system that requests and receives a service from a **server program** running on another end system. Studied in detail in Chapter 2, this client-server model is undoubtedly the most prevalent structure for Internet applications. The Web, e-mail, file transfer, remote login (for example, Telnet), newsgroups, and many other popular applications adopt the client/server model. Since a client program typically runs on one computer and the server program runs on another computer, client/server Internet applications are, by definition, **distributed applications**. The client program and the server program interact by sending each other messages over the Internet. At this level of abstraction, the routers, links, and other nuts and bolts of the Internet serve as a black box that transfers messages

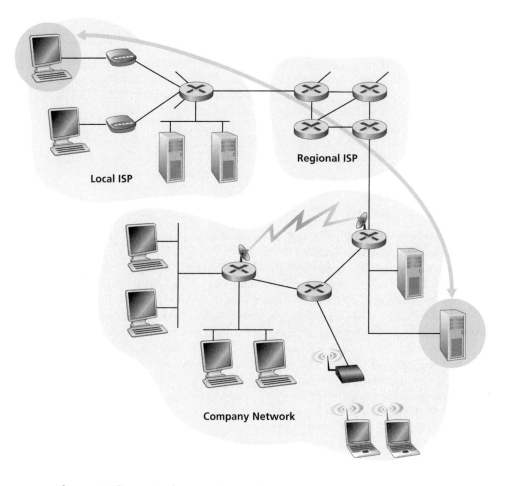

Figure 1.3   ♦   End-system interaction

between the distributed, communicating components of an Internet application. This is the level of abstraction depicted in Figure 1.3.

Not all Internet applications today consist of pure client programs interacting with pure server programs. For example, in popular P2P file-sharing applications (such as KaZaA) the P2P application in the user's end system acts as both a client program and a server program. The program running in a peer (that is, a user's machine) acts as a client when it requests a file from another peer; and the program acts as a server when it sends a file to another peer. In Internet telephony, the two communicating parties interact as peers; there is no sense in which one party requests service from another. We'll compare and contrast client-server and P2P architectures in detail in Chapter 2.

CASE HISTORY

A DIZZYING ARRAY OF INTERNET END SYSTEMS

Not too long ago, the end-system devices connected to the Internet were primarily traditional computers such as desktop machines and powerful servers. Beginning in the late 1990's and continuing today, a wide range of interesting devices of increasing diversity are being connected to the Internet. These devices share the common feature of needing to send and receive digital data to and from other devices. Given the Internet's ubiquity, its well-defined (standardized) protocols, and the availability of Internet-ready commodity hardware, it's natural to use Internet technology to connect these devices together.

Some of these devices seem to have been created purely for fun. A desktop IP-capable picture frame [Ceiva 2004] downloads digital photos from a remote server and displays them in a device that looks like a traditional picture frame; an Internet toaster downloads meteorological information from a server and burns an image of the day's forecast (e.g., mixed clouds and sun) on your morning toast [BBC 2001]. Other devices provide useful information—webcams display current traffic and weather conditions or monitor a location of interest; Internet-connected washing machines have been developed that can be monitored remotely via a Web browser and that generate e-mail when a load of wash is done. IP-enabled cell phones put Web browsing, e-mail, and messaging at your fingertips. A new class of networked sensor systems promise to revolutionize how we observe and interact with our environment. Networked sensors that are embedded into the physical environment allow monitoring of buildings, bridges, and other man-made structures [Elgamal 2001]; seismic activity [CISN 2004]; wildlife habitats [Mainwaring 2002]; river estuaries [Baptista 2003]; biomedical function [Schwiebert 2001]; winds and meteorological hazards in the lower boundary layer of the atmosphere [CASA 2004]—and make this information available to remote users. The Center for Embedded Networked Sensing at UCLA [CENS 2004] is an NSF Science & Technology Center whose goal is to apply embedded sensor network technology to critical scientific and social applications.

1.2.2 Connectionless and Connection-Oriented Service

End systems use the Internet to communicate with each other. Specifically, end-system programs use the services of the Internet to send messages to each other. The links, routers, and other pieces of the Internet provide the means to transport these messages between the end-system programs. But what are the characteristics of the communication services that the Internet provides to its end systems?

TCP/IP networks, and in particular the Internet, provide two types of services to end-system applications: **connectionless service** and **connection-oriented**

service. A developer creating an Internet application (for example, an e-mail application, a file transfer application, a Web application, or an Internet phone application) must design the application to use one of these two services. We now briefly describe these two services. (We'll discuss these two services in much more detail in Chapter 3, which covers transport-layer protocols.)

Connection-Oriented Service

When an application uses the connection-oriented service, the client program and the server program (residing in different end systems) send control packets to each other before sending packets with the actual data to be transferred. This so-called handshaking procedure alerts the client and server, allowing them to prepare for an onslaught of data packets. Once the handshaking procedure is finished, a connection is said to be established between the two end systems.

It is interesting to note that this initial handshaking procedure is similar to the protocol used in human interaction. The exchange of "Hi's" we saw in Figure 1.2 is an example of a human handshaking protocol (even though handshaking is not literally taking place between the two people). For the Web interaction also shown in Figure 1.2, the first two messages exchanged are also handshaking messages. The subsequent two messages—the GET message and the response message containing the file—include real data and are sent only after the connection has been established.

Why the terminology *connection-oriented service* and not just *connection service*? This terminology is due to the fact that the end systems are connected in a very loose manner. In particular, only the end systems themselves are aware of this connection; the packet switches within the Internet are completely oblivious to the connection. Indeed, a connection in the Internet consists of nothing more than allocated buffers and state variables in the end systems; the intervening packet switches do not maintain any connection-state information.

The Internet's connection-oriented service comes bundled with several other services, including reliable data transfer, flow control, and congestion control. By **reliable data transfer**, we mean that an application can rely on the connection to deliver all of its data without error and in the proper order. Reliability in the Internet is achieved through the use of acknowledgments and retransmissions. To get a preliminary feel for how the Internet implements the reliable transport service, consider an application that has established a connection between end systems A and B. When end system B receives a packet from A, it sends an acknowledgment; when end system A receives the acknowledgment, it knows that the corresponding packet has definitely been received. When end system A doesn't receive an acknowledgment, it assumes the packet it sent wasn't received by B and thus retransmits the packet. **Flow control** makes sure that neither side of a connection overwhelms the other side by sending too many packets too fast. We'll see in Chapter 3 that the Internet implements the flow-control service by using sender and receiver buffers in the communicating end systems. The Internet's congestion-control service helps prevent the Internet from entering a state of gridlock. When a packet switch becomes congested, its buffers can overflow and packet loss can occur. In such circumstances, if every pair of communicating end systems continues to pump packets into the network as fast as they can, gridlock sets in and few packets are delivered to their destinations. The Internet avoids this problem by forcing end systems to decrease the rate at which they send packets into the network during periods of congestion. End systems are alerted to the existence of severe congestion when they stop receiving acknowledgments for the packets they have sent.

We emphasize here that although the Internet's connection-oriented service comes bundled with reliable data transfer, flow control, and congestion control, these three features are by no means essential components of a connection-oriented service. A different type of computer network may provide a connection-oriented service to its applications without bundling in one or more of these features. Indeed, any protocol that performs handshaking between the communicating entities before transferring data is a connection-oriented service [Iren 1999].

The Internet's connection-oriented service has a name—**Transmission Control Protocol (TCP)**; the initial version of the TCP protocol is defined in the Internet Request for Comments RFC 793 [RFC 793]. The services that TCP provides to an application include reliable transport, flow control, and congestion control. TCP provides a **byte-steam abstraction**, reliably delivering a stream of bytes from the sender to the receiver. It is important to note that an application need only care about the services that are provided; it need not worry about *how* TCP actually implements reliability, flow control, or congestion control. We, of course, are *very* interested in how TCP implements these services, and we'll cover these topics in detail in Chapter 3.

Connectionless Service

There is no handshaking with the Internet's connectionless service. When one side of an application wants to send packets to the other side of the application, the sending program simply sends the packets. Since there is no handshaking procedure prior to data packet transmission, data can be delivered sooner. This makes connectionless service ideal for simple transaction-oriented applications. But there is no reliable data transfer either, so a source never knows for sure which packets have arrived at the destination. Moreover, the Internet's connectionless service makes no provision for flow control or congestion control. The Internet's connectionless service is called **User Datagram Protocol (UDP)**; UDP is defined in the Internet Request for Comments RFC 768.

Most of the more familiar Internet applications use TCP, the Internet's connection-oriented service. These applications include Telnet (for remote login), SMTP (for e-mail), FTP (for file transfer), and HTTP (for the Web). Nevertheless, UDP, the Internet's connectionless service, is used by many applications, including many of the emerging multimedia applications, such as Internet phone and video conferencing.

1.3 The Network Core

Having examined the end systems and end-end transport service model of the Internet, let us now delve more deeply inside the network. In the next section we study the network core—the mesh of routers that interconnect the Internet's end systems. Figure 1.4 highlights the network core with thick, shaded lines.

1.3.1 Circuit Switching and Packet Switching

There are two fundamental approaches to building a network core: **circuit switching** and **packet switching**. In circuit-switched networks, the resources needed along

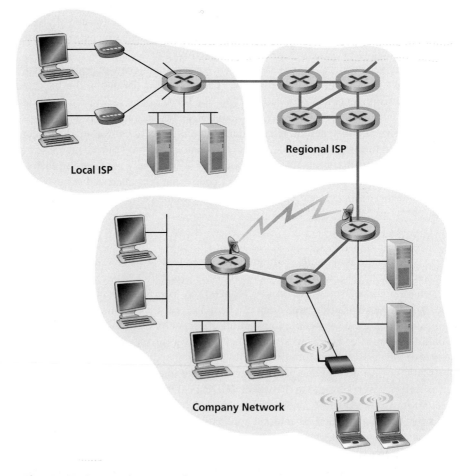

Figure 1.4 ◆ The network core

a path (buffers, link transmission rate) to provide for communication between the end systems are *reserved* for the duration of the communication session. In packet-switched networks, these resources are *not* reserved; a session's messages use the resources on demand, and as a consequence, may have to wait (that is, queue) for access to a communication link. As a simple analogy, consider two restaurants, one that requires reservations and another that neither requires reservations nor accepts them. For the restaurant that requires reservations, we have to go through the hassle of calling before we leave home. But when we arrive at the restaurant we can, in principle, immediately communicate with the waiter and order our meal. For the restaurant that does not require reservations, we don't need to bother to reserve a table. But when we arrive at the restaurant, we may have to wait for a table before we can communicate with the waiter.

The ubiquitous telephone networks are examples of circuit-switched networks. Consider what happens when one person wants to send information (voice or fac-simile) to another over a telephone network. Before the sender can send the infor-mation, the network must establish a connection between the sender and the receiver. In contrast with the TCP connection that we discussed in the previous sec-tion, this is a bona fide connection for which the switches on the path between the sender and receiver maintain connection state for that connection. In the jargon of telephony, this connection is called a **circuit**. When the network establishes the cir-cuit, it also reserves a constant transmission rate in the network's links for the dura-tion of the connection. Since bandwidth has been reserved for this sender-to-receiver connection, the sender can transfer the data to the receiver at the *guaranteed* constant rate.

Today's Internet is a quintessential packet-switched network. Consider what happens when one host wants to send a packet to another host over the Internet. As with circuit switching, the packet is transmitted over a series of communication links. But with packet switching, the packet is sent into the network without reserv-ing any bandwidth whatsoever. If one of the links is congested because other pack-ets need to be transmitted over the link at the same time, then our packet will have to wait in a buffer at the sending side of the transmission link, and suffer a delay. The Internet makes its *best effort* to deliver packets in a timely manner, but it does not make any guarantees.

Not all telecommunication networks can be neatly classified as pure circuit-switched networks or pure packet-switched networks. Nevertheless, this fundamen-tal classification into packet- and circuit-switched networks is an excellent starting point in understanding telecommunication network technology.

Circuit Switching

This book is about computer networks, the Internet, and packet switching, not about telephone networks and circuit switching. Nevertheless, it is important to under-stand why the Internet and other computer networks use packet switching rather than the more traditional circuit-switching technology used in the telephone networks. For this reason, we now give a brief overview of circuit switching.

Figure 1.5 illustrates a circuit-switched network. In this network, the four circuit switches are interconnected by four links. Each of these links has *n* circuits, so that each link can support *n* simultaneous connections. The hosts (for example, PCs and workstations) are each directly connected to one of the switches. When two hosts want to communicate, the network establishes a dedicated **end-to-end connection** between two hosts. (Conference calls between more than two devices are, of course, also possible. But to keep things simple, let's suppose for now that there are only two hosts for each connection.) Thus, in order for Host A to send messages to Host B, the network must first reserve one circuit on each of two links. Because each link has *n* circuits, for each link used by the end-to-end connection, the connection gets a fraction 1/*n* of the link's bandwidth for the duration of the connection.

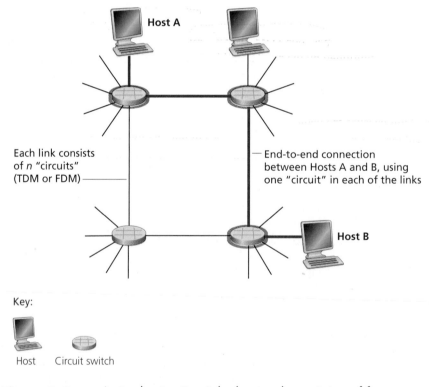

Host A

Each link consists
of *n* "circuits"
(TDM or FDM)

End-to-end connection
between Hosts A and B, using
one "circuit" in each of the links

Host B

Key:

Host   Circuit switch

Figure 1.5   ◆   A simple circuit-switched network consisting of four
switches and four links

Multiplexing in Circuit-Switched Networks

A circuit in a link is implemented with either **frequency-division multiplexing (FDM)** or **time-division multiplexing (TDM)**. With FDM, the frequency spectrum of a link is shared among the connections established across the link. Specifically, the link dedicates a frequency band to each connection for the duration of the connection. In telephone networks, this frequency band typically has a width of 4 kHz (that is, 4,000 Hertz or 4,000 cycles per second). The width of the band is called, not surprisingly, the **bandwidth**. FM radio stations also use FDM to share the frequency spectrum between 88 MHz and 108 MHz.

For a TDM link, time is divided into frames of fixed duration, and each frame is divided into a fixed number of time slots. When the network establishes a connection across a link, the network dedicates one time slot in every frame to the connection. These slots are dedicated for the sole use of that connection, with a time slot available for use (in every frame) to transmit the connection's data.

Figure 1.6 illustrates FDM and TDM for a specific network link supporting up to four circuits. For FDM, the frequency domain is segmented into four bands, each of bandwidth 4 kHz. For TDM, the time domain is segmented into frames, with four time slots in each frame; each circuit is assigned the same dedicated slot in the revolving TDM frames. For TDM, the transmission rate of a circuit is equal to the frame rate multiplied by the number of bits in a slot. For example, if the link transmits 8,000 frames per second and each slot consists of 8 bits, then the transmission rate of a circuit is 64 kbps.

Proponents of packet switching have always argued that circuit switching is wasteful because the dedicated circuits are idle during **silent periods**. For example, when one person in a telephone call stops talking, the idle network resources (frequency bands or slots in the links along the connection's route) cannot be used by other ongoing connections. As another example of how these resources can be underutilized, consider a radiologist who uses a circuit-switched network to remotely access a series of x-rays. The radiologist sets up a connection, requests an image, contemplates the image, and then requests a new image. Network resources are wasted during the radiologist's contemplation periods. Proponents of packet switching also enjoy pointing out that establishing end-to-end circuits and reserving end-to-end bandwidth is complicated and requires complex signaling software to coordinate the operation of the switches along the end-to-end path.

Before we finish our discussion of circuit switching, let's work through a numerical example that should shed further insight on the topic. Let us consider how long it takes to send a file of 640,000 bits from Host A to Host B over a circuit-switched network. Suppose that all links in the network use TDM with 24 slots and have a bit rate of 1.536 Mbps. Also suppose that it takes 500 msec to establish an end-to-end circuit before Host A can begin to transmit the file. How long does it take to send the file? Each circuit has a transmission rate of (1.536 Mbps)/24 = 64 kbps, so it takes (640,000 bits)/(64 kbps) = 10 seconds to transmit the file. To this 10 seconds we add

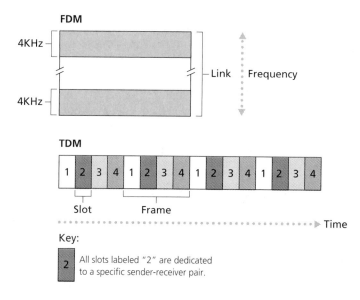

Figure 1.6 ♦ With FDM, each circuit continuously gets a fraction of the bandwidth. With TDM, each circuit gets all of the bandwidth periodically during brief intervals of time (that is, during slots).

the circuit establishment time, giving 10.5 seconds to send the file. Note that the transmission time is independent of the number of links: The transmission time would be 10 seconds if the end-to-end circuit passed through one link or a hundred links. (The actual end-to-end delay also includes a propagation delay; see Section 1.6.)

Packet Switching

We saw in Section 1.1 that applications exchange **messages** in accomplishing their task. Messages can contain anything the protocol designer wants. Messages may perform a control function (for example, the "Hi" messages in our handshaking example) or can contain data, such as an e-mail message, a JPEG image, or an MP3 audio file. In modern computer networks, the source breaks long messages into smaller chunks of data known as **packets**. Between source and destination, each of these packets travels through communication links and **packet switches** (for which there are two predominant types, **routers** and link-layer switches). Packets are transmitted over each communication link at a rate equal to the *full* transmission rate of the link. Most packet switches use **store-and-forward transmission** at the inputs to the links. Store-and-forward transmission means that the switch must receive the entire packet before it can begin to transmit the first bit of the packet onto the outbound link. Thus store-and-forward packet switches introduce a store-and-forward delay at the input to each link along the packet's route. This delay is proportional to the packet's length in bits. In particular, if a packet consists of L bits, and the packet is to be forwarded onto an outbound link of R bps, then the store-and-forward delay at the switch is L/R seconds.

Each packet switch has multiple links attached to it. For each attached link, the packet switch has an **output buffer** (also called an **output queue**), which stores packets that the router is about to send into that link. The output buffers play a key role in packet switching. If an arriving packet needs to be transmitted across a link but finds the link busy with the transmission of another packet, the arriving packet must wait in the output buffer. Thus, in addition to the store-and-forward delays, packets suffer output buffer **queuing delays**. These delays are variable and depend on the level of congestion in the network. Since the amount of buffer space is finite, an arriving packet may find that the buffer is completely filled with other packets waiting for transmission. In this case, **packet loss** will occur—either the arriving packet or one of the already-queued packets will be dropped. Returning to our restaurant analogy from earlier in this section, the queuing delay is analogous to the amount of time you spend waiting at the restaurant's bar for a table to become free. Packet loss is analogous to being told by the waiter that you must leave the premises because there are already too many other people waiting at the bar for a table.

Figure 1.7 illustrates a simple packet-switched network. In this and subsequent figures, packets are represented by three-dimensional slabs. The width of a slab represents the number of bits in the packet. In this figure, all packets have the same width and hence the same length. Suppose Hosts A and B are sending packets to Host E. Hosts A and B first send their packets along 10 Mbps Ethernet links to the first packet switch. The packet switch directs these packets to the 1.5 Mbps link. If the arrival rate of packets to the switch exceeds the rate at which the switch can forward packets across the 1.5 Mbps output link, congestion will occur as packets queue in the link's output buffer before being transmitted onto the link.

Let's now consider how long it takes to send a packet of L bits from one host to another host across a packet-switched network. Let's suppose that there are Q links between the two hosts, each of rate R bps. Assume that queuing delays and end-to-end propagation delays are negligible and that there is no connection establishment. The packet must first be transmitted onto the first link emanating from Host A; this takes L/R seconds. It must then be transmitted on each of the $Q - 1$ remaining links; that is, it must be stored and forwarded $Q - 1$ times. Thus the total delay is QL/R.

Packet Switching Versus Circuit Switching; Statistical Multiplexing

Having described circuit switching and packet switching, let us compare the two. Critics of packet switching have often argued that packet switching is not suitable for real-time services (for example, telephone calls and video conference calls) because of its variable and unpredictable end-to-end delays (due primarily to

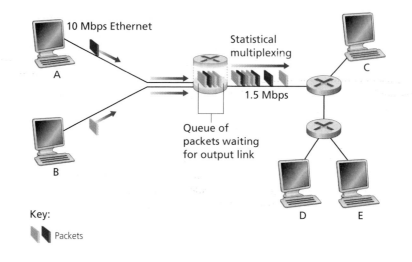

Figure 1.7 ♦ Packet switching

variable and unpredictable queuing delays). Proponents of packet switching argue that (1) it offers better sharing of bandwidth than circuit switching and (2) it is simpler, more efficient, and less costly to implement than circuit switching. An interesting discussion of packet switching versus circuit switching is [Molinero-Fernandez 2002]. Generally speaking, people who do not like to hassle with restaurant reservations prefer packet switching to circuit switching.

Why is packet switching more efficient? Let us look at a simple example. Suppose users share a 1 Mbps link. Also suppose that each user alternates between periods of activity, when the user generates data at a constant rate of 100 kbps, and periods of inactivity, when the user generates no data. Suppose further that the user is active only 10 percent of the time (and is idly drinking coffee during the remaining 90 percent of the time). With circuit switching, 100 kbps must be *reserved* for *each* user at all times. For example, with circuit-switched TDM, if a one-second frame is divided into 10 time slots of 100 ms each, then each user would be allocated one time slot per frame.

Thus, the link can support only 10 (= 1Mbps/100 kbps) simultaneous users. With packet switching, the probability that a specific user is active is 0.1 (that is, 10 percent). If there are 35 users, the probability that there are 11 or more simultaneously active users is approximately 0.0004. (Homework Problem 8 outlines how this probability is obtained.) When there are 10 or fewer simultaneously active users (which happens with probability 0.9996), the aggregate arrival rate of data is less than or equal to 1 Mbps, the output rate of the link. Thus, when there are 10 or fewer active users, users' packets flow through the link essentially without delay, as is the case with circuit switching. When there are more than 10 simultaneously active users, then the aggregate arrival rate of packets exceeds the output capacity of the link, and the output queue will begin to grow. (It continues to grow until the aggregate input rate falls back below 1 Mbps, at which point the queue will begin to diminish in length.) Because the probability of having more than 10 simultaneously active users is minuscule in this example, packet switching provides essentially the same performance as circuit switching, *but does so while allowing for more than three times the number of users.*

Let's now consider a second simple example. Suppose there are 10 users and that one user suddenly generates one thousand 1,000-bit packets, while other users remain quiescent and do not generate packets. Under TDM circuit switching with 10 slots per frame and each slot consisting of 1,000 bits, the active user can only use its one time slot per frame to transmit data, while the remaining nine times slots in each frame remain idle. It will be 10 seconds before all of the active user's one million bits of data has been transmitted. In the case of packet-switching, the active user can continuously send its packets at the full link rate of 1 Mbps, since there are no other users generating packets that need to be multiplexed with the active user's packets. In this case, all of the active user's data will be transmitted within 1 second.

The above examples illustrate two ways in which the performance of packet switching can be superior to that of circuit switching. They also highlight the crucial difference between the two forms of sharing a link's transmission rate among multiple data streams Circuit switching preallocates use of the transmission link regardless of demand, with allocated but unneeded link time going unused. Packet switching on the other hand allocates link use *on demand*. Link transmission capacity will be shared on a packet-by-packet basis only among those users who have packets that need to be transmitted over the link. Such on-demand (rather than preallocated) sharing of resources is sometimes referred to as the **statistical multiplexing** of resources.

Although packet switching and circuit switching are both prevalent in today's telecommunication networks, the trend is certainly in the direction of packet switching. Even many of today's circuit-switched telephone networks are slowly migrating toward packet switching. In particular, telephone networks often use packet switching for the expensive overseas portion of a telephone call.

1.3.2 Packet-Switched Networks: Datagram Networks and Virtual-Circuit Networks

There are two broad classes of packet-switched networks: datagram networks and virtual-circuit networks. They differ in whether their switches use destination addresses or so-called virtual-circuit numbers to forward packets toward their destinations. We'll call any network that forwards packets according to host destination addresses a **datagram network**. The routers in the Internet forward packets according to host destination addresses; hence the Internet is a datagram network. We'll call any network that forwards packets according to virtual-circuit numbers a

virtual-circuit network. Examples of packet-switching technologies that use virtual circuits include X.25, frame relay, and asynchronous transfer mode (ATM). While the difference between using destination addresses and virtual-circuit numbers may seem minor, the choice has a huge impact on how routes are set up and how routing is managed, as we'll see below.

Virtual-Circuit Networks

As the name suggests, a **virtual circuit (VC)** can be thought of as a virtual connection between a source and destination host. Importantly, setting up and maintaining this VC will involve not only the two end systems but each and every switch along the VC's source-to-destination path. A **virtual-circuit identifier (VC ID)** will be assigned to a VC when a VC is first established between source and destination. Any packet that is part of the VC has the VC ID in its header. Each packet switch has a table that maps VC IDs to outbound links. When a packet arrives to a packet switch, the switch examines the packet's VC ID, indexes its table, and forwards the packet to the designated outbound link. Note that with VCs, the source and destination of a VC are only indirectly identified through the VC ID; the actual addresses of the source and destination end systems are not needed to perform switching. This means that packet switching can be performed quickly (by looking up a VC ID of the incoming packet in the small VC translation table, rather than by looking up a destination address in a potentially large address space).

As noted above, a switch in a VC network maintains **state information** for its ongoing connections. Specifically, each time a new connection is established across a switch, a new connection entry must be added to the switch's translation table; and each time a connection is released, an entry must be removed from the table. Even if there is no VC ID translation, it is still necessary to maintain state information that associates VC numbers to output interface numbers. The issue of whether or not a packet switch maintains state information for each ongoing connection is a crucial one—one that we return to shortly below.

Datagram Networks

Datagram networks are analogous in many respects to the postal service. When a sender mails a letter to a destination, the sender wraps the letter in an envelope and writes the destination address on the envelope. This destination address has a hierarchical structure. For example, letters sent to a location in the United States include the country (USA), the state (for example, Pennsylvania), the city (for example, Philadelphia), the street (for example, Walnut Street), and the number of the house on the street (for example, 421). The postal service uses the address on the envelope to route the letter to its destination. For example, if the letter is sent from France, then a postal office in France will first forward the letter to a postal center in the United States. This postal center in the United States will then forward the letter to a postal center in Philadelphia. Finally, a mail carrier working in Philadelphia will deliver the letter to its ultimate destination.

In a datagram network, each packet traversing the network contains in its header the address of the packet's destination. As with postal addresses, this address has a hierarchical structure. When a packet arrives at a packet switch in the network, the packet switch examines a portion of the packet's destination address and forwards the packet to an adjacent switch. More specifically, each packet switch has a forwarding table that maps destination addresses (or portions of the destination addresses) to an outbound link. When a packet arrives at a switch, the switch examines the address and indexes its table with this destination address to find the appropriate outbound link. The switch then directs the packet to this outbound link.

The end-to-end routing process is also analogous to a car driver who does not use maps but instead prefers to ask for directions. For example, suppose Joe is driving from Philadelphia to 156 Lakeside Drive in Orlando, Florida. Joe first drives to his neighborhood gas station and asks how to get to 156 Lakeside Drive in Orlando, Florida. The gas station attendant extracts the Florida portion of the address and tells Joe that he needs to get onto the interstate highway I-95 South, which has an entrance just next to the gas station. He also tells Joe that once he enters Florida he should ask someone else there. Joe then takes I-95 South until he gets to Jacksonville, Florida, at which point he asks another gas station attendant for directions. The attendant extracts the Orlando portion of the address and tells Joe that he should continue on I-95 to Daytona Beach and then ask someone else. In Daytona Beach another gas station attendant also extracts the Orlando portion of the address and tells Joe that he should take I-4 directly to Orlando. Joe takes I-4 and gets off at the Orlando exit. Joe goes to another gas station attendant, and this time the attendant extracts the Lakeside Drive portion of the address and tells Joe the road he must follow to get to Lakeside Drive. Once Joe reaches Lakeside Drive, he asks a kid on a bicycle how to get to his destination. The kid extracts the 156 portion of the address and points to the house. Joe finally reaches his ultimate destination.

We will be discussing packet forwarding in datagram networks in great detail in this book. But for now we mention that, in contrast with VC networks, *datagram networks do not maintain connection-state information in their switches*. In fact, a packet switch in a pure datagram network is completely oblivious to any flows of traffic that may be passing through it. A packet switch in a datagram network makes forwarding decisions based upon a packet's destination address, not upon the connection to which the packet belongs. Because VC networks must maintain connection-state information—information that must be installed and removed as virtual-circuits come and go, and cleaned up (removed) should a VC terminate abnormally—VC networks require potentially complex state-maintenance protocols not found in datagram networks

How would you actually like to see the end-to-end route that packets take in the Internet? We now invite you to get your hands dirty by interacting with the Traceroute program, by visiting the site http://www.traceroute.org. (See a discussion of Trace-route in Section 1.6.)

Network Taxonomy

We have now introduced several important networking concepts: circuit switching, packet switching, virtual circuits, connectionless service, and connection-oriented service. How does it all fit together?

First, in our simple view of the world, a telecommunication network either employs circuit switching or packet switching (see Figure 1.8). A link in a circuit-switched network can employ either FDM or TDM. Packet-switched networks are either virtual-circuit networks or datagram networks. Switches in virtual-circuit networks forward packets according to the packets' VC numbers, and they maintain connection state. Switches in datagram networks forward packets according to the packets' destination addresses and do not maintain connection state.

1.4 Access Networks and Physical Media

In Sections 1.2 and 1.3 we examined the roles of end systems and packet switches in a computer network. In this section we consider **access networks**—the physical link(s) that connect an end system to its **edge router,** which is the first router on a path from the end system to any other distant end system. The access network thus provides the infrastructure to connect the so-called customer premises into the

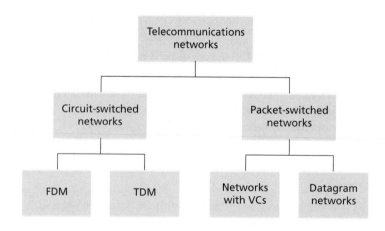

Figure 1.8 ◆ Taxonomy of telecommunication networks

network infrastructure. Figure 1.9 shows several types of access links from end
system to edge router; the access links are highlighted in thick, shaded lines. Since
access network technology is closely tied to physical media technology (fiber, coaxial pair, twisted-pair telephone wire, radio spectrum), we consider these two topics
together in this section.

1.4.1 Access Networks

Access networks can be loosely classified into three categories:

♦ **Residential access**, connecting home end systems into the network

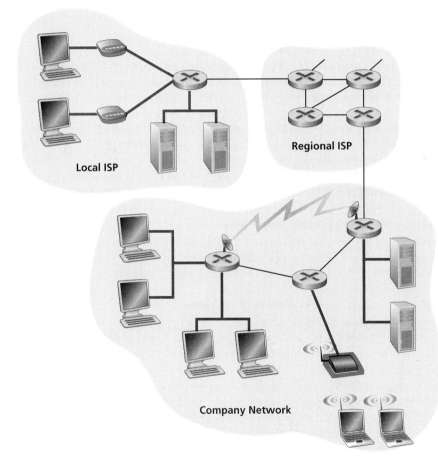

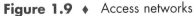

Figure 1.9 ♦ Access networks

♦ **Company access**, connecting end systems in a business or educational institution into the network

♦ **Wireless access**, connecting end systems (that are often mobile) into the network

These categories are not hard and fast—for example, some company end systems may use the access technology that we ascribe to residential access, and vice versa. The following descriptions are meant to hold for the common cases.

Residential Access

Residential access refers to connecting a home end system (typically a PC, but increasingly a home network, see below) to an edge router. One form of residential access is the **dial-up modem** over an ordinary analog telephone line into a residential ISP (such as America Online). The home modem converts the digital output of the PC into analog format for transmission over the analog phone line. This analog phone line is made of twisted-pair copper wire and is the same telephone line used to make ordinary phone calls. (We will discuss twisted pair later in this section.) At the other end of the analog phone line, a modem in the ISP converts the analog signal back into digital form for input to the ISP router. Thus, the access network is simply a pair of modems along with a point-to-point dial-up phone line. Today's modem speeds allow dial-up access at rates up to 56 kbps. However, due to the poor quality of the twisted-pair line between many homes and ISPs, many users get an effective rate significantly less than 56 kbps.

Many residential users find a dial-up modem's 56 kbps access to be excruciatingly slow. For example, it takes approximately eight minutes to download a single three-minute MP3 song over a 56 kbps dial-up modem. Moreover, dial-up modem access ties up a user's ordinary phone line—while a residential user uses a dial-up modem to surf the Web, the user cannot receive and make ordinary phone calls over the phone line. Fortunately, new broadband access technologies are providing residential users higher bit rates; and they are also providing a means for users to access the Internet and talk on the phone at the same time. There are two common types of broadband residential access: **digital subscriber line (DSL)** [DSL 2004] and **hybrid fiber-coaxial cable (HFC)** [Cable Labs 2004].

As of 2003, broadband residential access was much less prevalent than 56 kbps dial-up modem access: The number of broadband lines per 100 population was approximately 23 in South Korea, 13 in Canada, and 7 in the United States, with most European countries also having less that 10 percent penetration [Point Topic 2003]. However, DSL and HFC are being rapidly deployed throughout the world, with HFC being generally more prevalent in the United States and DSL being generally more prevalent in Europe and Asia.

DSL access is typically provided by a telephone company (for example, Verizon or France Telecom), sometimes in partnership with an independent ISP. Conceptually similar to dial-up modems, DSL is a new modem technology again running over existing twisted-pair telephone lines. But by restricting the distance between user and ISP modem, DSL can transmit and receive data at much higher rates. The data rates are typically asymmetrical in the two directions, with a higher rate from ISP router to home than from the home to ISP router. The asymmetry in the data rates reflects the belief that a home user is more likely to be a consumer of information (bringing data into the home) than a producer of information. In theory, DSL can provide rates of more than 10 Mbps from ISP to home and more than 1 Mbps from home to ISP. However, in practice the rates offered by DSL providers are much less. As of 2004, typical downstream rates are 1 to 2 Mbps; and typical upstream rates are in the hundreds of kbps.

DSL uses frequency division multiplexing, as described in the previous section. In particular, DSL divides the communication link between the home and the ISP into three nonoverlapping frequency bands:

♦ A high-speed downstream channel, in the 50 kHz to 1 MHz band

♦ A medium-speed upstream channel, in the 4 kHz to 50 kHz band

♦ An ordinary two-way telephone channel, in the 0 to 4 kHz band

The actual downstream and upstream transmission rate available to the user is a function of the distance between the home modem and the ISP modem, the gauge of the twisted-pair line, and the degree of electrical interference, among other considerations. Engineers have explicitly designed DSL, unlike dial-up modems, for short distances between residential and ISP modems, allowing for substantially higher transmission rates than dial-up access.

While DSL and dial-up modems use ordinary phone lines, HFC access networks are extensions of the current cable network used for broadcasting cable television. In a traditional cable system, a cable head end broadcasts through a distribution network of coaxial cable and amplifiers to residences. As illustrated in Figure 1.10, fiber optics connect the cable head end to neighborhood-level junctions, from which traditional coaxial cable is then used to reach individual houses and apartments. Each neighborhood junction typically supports 500 to 5,000 homes.

As with DSL, HFC requires special modems, called **cable modems**. Companies that provide cable Internet access require their customers to either purchase or lease a modem. Typically, the cable modem is an external device and connects to the home PC through a 10-BaseT Ethernet port. (We will discuss Ethernet in great detail in Chapter 5.) Cable modems divide the HFC network into two channels, a downstream and an upstream channel. As with DSL, the downstream channel is typically allocated more transmission rate than the upstream channel.

One important characteristic of HFC is that it is a shared broadcast medium. In particular, every packet sent by the head end travels downstream on every link to every home; and every packet sent by a home travels on the upstream channel to the head end. For this reason, if several users are simultaneously downloading MP3s on

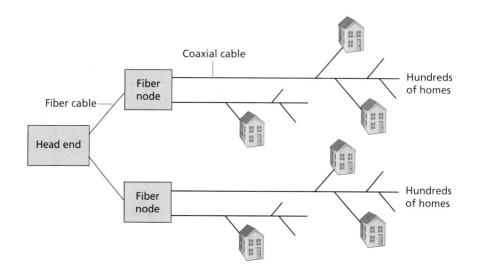

Figure 1.10 ◆ A hybrid fiber-coaxial access network

the downstream channel, the actual rate at which each user receives its MP3 will be significantly less than the downstream rate. On the other hand, if there are only a few active users and they are all Web surfing, then each of the users may actually receive Web pages at the full downstream rate, because users will rarely request a Web page at exactly the same time. Because the upstream channel is also shared, a distributed multiple access protocol is needed to coordinate transmissions and avoid collisions. (We'll discuss this collision issue in some detail when we discuss Ethernet in Chapter 5.) Advocates of DSL are quick to point out that DSL is a point-to-point connection between the home and ISP, and therefore all the DSL transmission rate is dedicated rather than shared. Cable advocates, however, argue that a reasonably dimensioned HFC network provides higher transmission rates than DSL. The battle between DSL and HFC for high-speed residential access has clearly begun.

One of the attractive features of DSL and HFC is that the services are **always on**; that is, the user can leave his or her computer on and remain permanently connected to an ISP while simultaneously making and receiving ordinary telephone calls.

Company Access

On corporate and university campuses, a local area network (LAN) is typically used to connect an end system to the edge router. As we will see in Chapter 5, there are many types of LAN technology. However, Ethernet technology is currently by far the most prevalent access technology in company networks. Ethernet operates at 10 Mbps or 100 Mbps (and now even at 1 Gbps and 10 Gbps). It uses either twisted-pair copper wire or coaxial cable to connect a number of end systems with each other and with an edge router. The edge router is responsible for routing packets that have destinations outside of that LAN. Like HFC, Ethernet uses a shared medium, so that end users share the transmission rate of the LAN. More recently, shared Ethernet technology has been migrating toward switched Ethernet technology. Switched Ethernet uses multiple twisted-pair Ethernet segments connected at a "switch" to allow the full transmission rate of an Ethernet to be delivered to different users on the same LAN simultaneously. We will explore shared and switched Ethernet in detail in Chapter 5.

Wireless Access

Accompanying the current Internet revolution, the wireless revolution is also having a profound impact on the way people work and live. Today, more people in Europe have a mobile phone than had a PC or a car. And the wireless trend is continuing, with many analysts predicting that wireless (and often mobile) handheld devices—such as mobile phones and PDAs—will overtake wired computers as the dominant Internet access devices throughout the world. Today, there are two broad types of wireless Internet access. In a **wireless LAN**, wireless users transmit/receive packets to/from a base station (also known as a wireless access point) within a radius of a few tens of meters. The base station is typically connected to the wired Internet and thus serves to connect wireless users to the wired network. In **wide-area wireless access networks**, the base station is managed by a telecommunications provider and serves users within a radius of tens of kilometers.

Wireless LANs, based on IEEE 802.11 technology (also known as wireless Ethernet and Wi-Fi), are currently enjoying rapid deployment in university departments, business offices, coffee cafes, and homes. For example, both of the authors' universities have installed IEEE 802.11 base stations on their campuses. Using this wireless LAN infrastructure, students send and receive e-mail or surf the Web from anywhere on campus (for example, library, dorm room, classroom, or outdoor campus bench). The 802.11 technology, which we'll discuss in detail in Chapter 6, provides a shared transmission rate of 11 Mbps.

Today many homes are combining broadband residential access (that is, cable modems or DSL) with inexpensive wireless LAN technology to create powerful home networks. Figure 1.11 shows a schematic of a typical home network (actually, this is the home network setup of both authors). This home network consists of a roaming laptop as well as three stationary PCs (two wired, one wireless); a base station (the wireless access point) which communicates with the wireless PCs; a cable modem, providing broadband access to the Internet; and a router, which interconnects the base station and the stationary PC with the cable modem. This network allows household members to have broadband access to the Internet, with one member roaming from the kitchen to the backyard to the bedrooms. The total fixed cost for such a network is less than $250 (including the cable/DSL modem).

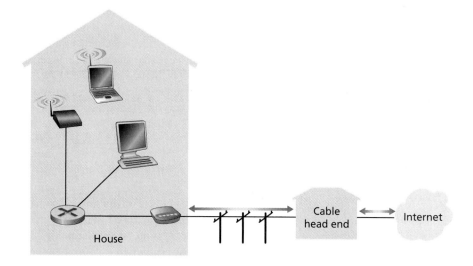

Figure 1.11 ◆ A schematic of a typical home network

When you access the Internet through wireless LAN technology, you typically need to be within a few tens of meters of a base station. This is feasible for home access, coffee shop access, and, more generally, access within and around a building. But what if you are on the beach or in your car and you need Internet access? For such wide-area access, roaming Internet users make use of the portable phone infrastructure, accessing base stations that are up to tens of kilometers away.

WAP (wireless access protocol, version 2) [WAP 2004], widely available in Europe, and i-mode, widely available in Japan, are two technologies that allow for Internet access over the portable phone infrastructure. Resembling ordinary wireless phones but with somewhat bigger screens, WAP phones provide low-to-medium speed Internet access as well as portable phone service. Instead of HTML, WAP phones use a special markup language— WAP Markup Language (WML)—that has been optimized for small screens and low-speed access. In Europe, the WAP protocol runs on top of Europe's highly successful GSM wireless telephony infrastructure, with WAP 2.0 operating over a TCP/IP protocol stack. The proprietary i-mode technology, which is similar in concept and functionality to WAP, has been a huge success in Japan.

Telecommunications companies are currently making enormous investments in Third Generation (3G) wireless, which provides packet-switched wide-area wireless Internet access at speeds in excess of 384 kbps [Kaaranen 2001] [Korhonen 2003]. 3G systems provide high-speed access to the Web and interactive video, and should provide voice quality that is better than that of an ordinary wired telephone. The first

3G systems have been deployed in Japan. With such huge investments being made in 3G technology, infrastructure, and licenses, many analysts (and investors!) wonder whether 3G will be the great success that it is hyped to be. Will it instead lose out to competing technologies such as IEEE 802.11? Or will 802.11 and 3G technologies be combined to provide ubiquitous but heterogeneous access. The jury is still out. (See [Weinstein 2002] and the case history in Section 6.2.) We'll cover both 802.11 and 3G in detail in Chapter 6.

1.4.2 Physical Media

In the previous subsection, we gave an overview of some of the most important network access technologies in the Internet. As we described these technologies, we also indicated the physical media used. For example, we said that HFC uses a combination of fiber cable and coaxial cable. We said that dial-up 56 kbps modems and ADSL use twisted-pair copper wire. And we said that mobile access networks use the radio spectrum. In this subsection we provide a brief overview of these and other transmission media that are commonly employed in the Internet.

In order to define what is meant by a physical medium, let us reflect on the brief life of a bit. Consider a bit traveling from one end system, through a series of links and routers, to another end system. This poor bit gets transmitted many, many times! The source end system first transmits the bit, and shortly thereafter the first router in the series receives the bit; the first router then transmits the bit, and shortly thereafter the second router receives the bit; and so on. Thus our bit, when traveling from source to destination, passes through a series of transmitter-receiver pairs. For each transmitter-receiver pair, the bit is sent by propagating electromagnetic waves or optical pulses across a **physical medium**. The physical medium can take many shapes and forms and does not have to be of the same type for each transmitter-receiver pair along the path. Examples of physical media include twisted-pair copper wire, coaxial cable, multimode fiber-optic cable, terrestrial radio spectrum, and satellite radio spectrum. Physical media fall into two categories: **guided media** and **unguided media**. With guided media, the waves are guided along a solid medium, such as a fiber-optic cable, a twisted-pair copper wire, or a coaxial cable. With unguided media, the waves propagate in the atmosphere and in outer space, such as in a wireless LAN or a digital satellite channel.

But before we get into the characteristics of the various media types, let us say a few words about their costs. The actual cost of the physical link (copper wire, fiber-optic cable, and so on) is often relatively minor compared with other networking costs. In particular, the labor cost associated with the installation of the physical link can be orders of magnitude higher than the cost of the material. For this reason, many builders install twisted pair, optical fiber, and coaxial cable in every room in a building. Even if only one medium is initially used, there is a good chance that another medium could be used in the near future, and so money is saved by not having to lay additional wires in the future.

Twisted-Pair Copper Wire

The least expensive and most commonly used guided transmission medium is twisted-pair copper wire. For over a hundred years it has been used by telephone networks. In fact, more than 99 percent of the wired connections from the telephone handset to the local telephone switch use twisted-pair copper wire. Most of us have seen twisted pair in our homes and work environments. Twisted pair consists of two insulated copper wires, each about 1 mm thick, arranged in a regular spiral pattern. The wires are twisted together to reduce the electrical interference from similar pairs close by. Typically, a number of pairs are bundled together in a cable by wrapping the pairs in a protective shield. A wire pair constitutes a single communication link. **Unshielded twisted pair (UTP)** is commonly used for computer networks within a building, that is, for LANs. Data rates for LANs using twisted pair today range from 10 Mbps to 1 Gbps. The data rates that can be achieved depend on the thickness of the wire and the distance between transmitter and receiver.

When fiber-optic technology emerged in the 1980s, many people disparaged twisted pair because of its relatively low bit rates. Some people even felt that fiber-optic technology would completely replace twisted pair. But twisted pair did not give up so easily. Modern twisted-pair technology, such as category 5 UTP, can achieve data rates of 100 Mbps for distances up to a few hundred meters. Even higher rates are possible over shorter distances. In the end, twisted pair has emerged as the dominant solution for high-speed LAN networking.

As discussed in the section on access networks, twisted pair is also commonly used for residential Internet access. We saw that dial-up modem technology enables access at rates of up to 56 kbps over twisted pair. We also saw that DSL (digital subscriber line) technology has enabled residential users to access the Internet at rates in excess of 6 Mbps over twisted pair (when users live close to the ISP's modem).

Coaxial Cable

Like twisted pair, coaxial cable consists of two copper conductors, but the two conductors are concentric rather than parallel. With this construction and a special insulation and shielding, coaxial cable can have high bit rates. Coaxial cable is quite common in cable television systems. As we saw earlier, cable television systems have recently been coupled with cable modems to provide residential users with Internet access at rates of 1 Mbps or higher. In cable television and cable Internet access, the transmitter shifts the digital signal to a specific frequency band, and the resulting analog signal is sent from the transmitter to one or more receivers. Coaxial cable can be used as a guided **shared medium**. Specifically, a number of end systems can be connected directly to the cable, and all the end systems receive whatever is sent by the other end systems.

Fiber Optics

An optical fiber is a thin, flexible medium that conducts pulses of light, with each pulse representing a bit. A single optical fiber can support tremendous bit rates, up to tens or even hundreds of gigabits per second. They are immune to electromagnetic interference, have very low signal attenuation up to 100 kilometers, and are very hard to tap. These characteristics have made fiber optics the preferred long-haul guided transmission media, particularly for overseas links. Many of the long-distance telephone networks in the United States and elsewhere now use fiber optics exclusively. Fiber optics is also prevalent in the backbone of the Internet. However, the high cost of optical devices—such as transmitters, receivers, and switches—has hindered their deployment for short-haul transport, such as in a LAN or into the home in a residential access network. [IEC Optical 2003] [Goralski 2001], [Ramaswami 1998], and [Mukherjee 1997] provide coverage of various aspects of optical networking. Optical link speeds can reach into the tens of gigabits per second.

Terrestrial Radio Channels

Radio channels carry signals in the electromagnetic spectrum. They are an attractive medium because they require no physical wire to be installed, can penetrate walls, provide connectivity to a mobile user, and can potentially carry a signal for long distances. The characteristics of a radio channel depend significantly on the propagation environment and the distance over which a signal is to be carried. Environmental considerations determine path loss and shadow fading (which decrease the signal strength as the signal travels over a distance and around/through obstructing objects), multipath fading (due to signal reflection off of interfering objects), and interference (due to other radio channels or electromagnetic signals).

Terrestrial radio channels can be broadly classified into two groups: those that operate in local areas, typically spanning from ten to a few hundred meters; and those that operate in the wide area, spanning tens of kilometers. The wireless LAN products described in Section 1.4.1 use local-area radio channels; WAP, i-mode, and 3G technologies, also discussed in Section 1.4.1, use wide-area radio channels. See [Dornan 2001] for a survey and discussion of the technology and products. We'll discuss radio channels in detail in Chapter 6.

Satellite Radio Channels

A communication satellite links two or more Earth-based microwave transmitter/receivers, known as ground stations. The satellite receives transmissions on one frequency band, regenerates the signal using a repeater (discussed below), and transmits the signal on another frequency. Satellites can provide transmission rates in the gigabit per second range. Two types of satellites are used in communications: **geostationary satellites** and **low-altitude satellites**.

Geostationary satellites permanently remain above the same spot on Earth. This stationary presence is achieved by placing the satellite in orbit at 36,000 kilometers above Earth's surface. This huge distance from ground station through satellite back to ground station introduces a substantial signal propagation delay of 250 milliseconds. Nevertheless, satellite links, which can operate at speeds of hundreds of Mbps, are often used in telephone networks and in the backbone of the Internet.

Low-altitude satellites are placed much closer to Earth and do not remain permanently above one spot on Earth. They rotate around Earth just as the Moon does. To provide continuous coverage to an area, many satellites need to be placed in orbit. There are currently many low-altitude communication systems in development. Lloyd's satellite constellation Web page [Wood 2004] provides and collects information on satellite constellation systems for communications. Low-altitude satellite technology may be used for Internet access sometime in the future.

1.5 ISPs and Internet Backbones

We saw earlier that end systems (user PCs, PDAs, Web servers, mail servers, and so on) connect into the Internet via an access network. Recall that the access network may be a wired or wireless local area network (for example, in a company, school, or library) or may be a residential ISP (for example, AOL or MSN) that is reached via dial-up modem, cable modem, or DSL. But connecting end users and content providers into access networks is only a small piece of solving the puzzle of connecting the hundreds of millions of users and hundreds of thousands of networks that make up the Internet. The Internet is a *network of networks*—understanding this phrase is the key to solving this puzzle.

In the public Internet, access networks situated at the edge of the Internet are connected to the rest of the Internet through a tiered hierarchy of ISPs, as shown in Figure 1.12. Access ISPs (for example, residential ISPs such as AOL, and company ISPs using LANs) are at the bottom of this hierarchy. At the very top of the hierarchy is a relatively small number of so-called **tier-1 ISPs**. In many ways, a tier-1 ISP is the same as any network—it has links and routers and is connected to other networks. In other ways, however, tier-1 ISPs are special. Their link speeds are often 622 Mbps or higher, with the larger tier-1 ISPs having links in the 2.5 to 10 Gbps range; their routers must consequently be able to forward packets at extremely high rates. Tier-1 ISPs are also characterized by being:

♦ Directly connected to *each* of the other tier-1 ISPs

♦ Connected to a large number of tier-2 ISPs and other customer networks

♦ International in coverage

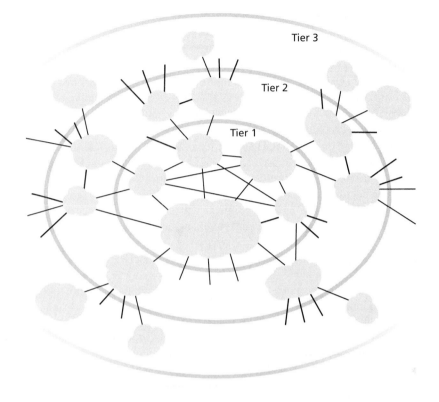

Figure 1.12 ♦ Interconnection of ISPs

Tier-1 ISPs are also known as **Internet backbone** networks. These include Sprint, MCI (previously UUNet/WorldCom), AT&T, Level3 (which acquired Genuity), Qwest, and Cable & Wireless. In mid-2002, WorldCom was by far the largest tier-1 ISP—more than twice as big as its nearest rival according to several measures of size [Teleography 2002]. Interestingly, no group officially sanctions tier-1 status; as the saying goes—if you have to ask if you are a member of a group, you're probably not.

A tier-2 ISP typically has regional or national coverage, and (importantly) connects to only a few of the tier-1 ISPs (see Figure 1.12). Thus, in order to reach a large portion of the global Internet, a tier-2 ISP needs to route traffic through one of the tier-1 ISPs to which it is connected. A tier-2 ISP is said to be a **customer** of the tier-1 ISPs to which it is connected, and the tier-1 ISP is said to be a **provider** to its customer. Many large companies and institutions connect their enterprise's network directly into a tier-1 or tier-2 ISP, thus becoming a customer of that ISP. A provider

ISP charges its customer ISP a fee, which typically depends on the transmission rate of the link connecting the two. A tier-2 network may also choose to connect directly to other tier-2 networks, in which case traffic can flow between the two tier-2 networks without having to pass through a tier-1 network. Below the tier-2 ISPs are the lower-tier ISPs, which connect to the larger Internet via one or more tier-2 ISPs. At the bottom of the hierarchy are the access ISPs. Further complicating matters, some tier-1 providers are also tier-2 providers (that is, vertically integrated), selling Internet access directly to end users and content providers, as well as to lower-tier ISPs. When two ISPs are directly connected to each other, they are said to **peer** with each other. An interesting study [Subramanian 2002] seeks to define the Internet's tiered structure more precisely by studying the Internet's topology in terms of customer-provider and peer-peer relationships.

Within an ISP's network, the points at which the ISP connect to other ISPs (whether below, above, or at the same level in the hierarchy) are known as **Points of Presence (POPs)**. A POP is simply a group of one or more routers in the ISP's network at which routers in other ISPs or in the networks belonging to the ISP's customers can connect. A tier-1 provider typically has many POPs scattered across different geographical locations in its network, with multiple customer networks and other ISPs connecting into each POP. For a customer network to connect to a provider's POP, the customer typically leases a high-speed link from a third-party telecommunications provider and directly connects one of its routers to a router at the provider's POP. Two tier-1 ISPs can also peer with each other by connecting together a pair of POPs, one from each of the two ISPs. Furthermore, two ISPs may have multiple peering points connecting with each other at two or more pairs of POPs.

In addition to connecting to each other at private peering points, ISPs often interconnect at **Network Access Points (NAPs)**, each of which can be owned and operated by either some third-party telecommunications company or by an Internet backbone provider. NAPs exchange huge quantities of traffic among many ISPs. However, increasingly, tier-1 ISPs are bypassing the NAPs and are interconnecting directly at private peering points [Kende 2000]. The trend is for the tier-1 ISPs to interconnect with each other directly at private peering points, and for tier-2 ISPs to interconnect with other tier-2 ISPs and with tier-1 ISPs at NAPs. Because the NAPs relay and switch tremendous volumes of traffic, they are in themselves complex high-speed switching networks, often concentrated in a single building.

In summary, the topology of the Internet is complex, consisting of dozens of tier-1 and tier-2 ISPs and thousands of lower-tier ISPs. The ISPs are diverse in their coverage, with some spanning multiple continents and oceans, and others limited to narrow regions of the world. The lower-tier ISPs connect to the higher-tier ISPs, and the higher-tier ISPs interconnect at (typically) private peering points and NAPs. Users and content providers are customers of lower-tier ISPs, and lower-tier ISPs are customers of higher-tier ISPs.

We conclude this section by mentioning that any one of us can become an access ISP as soon as we have an Internet connection. All we need to do is purchase the necessary equipment (for example, router and modem pool) to allow other users to connect to us. Thus new tiers and branches can be added to the Internet topology just as a new piece of Lego can be attached to an existing Lego construction.

1.6 Delay and Loss in Packet-Switched Networks

Having now briefly considered the major pieces of the Internet architecture—the applications, end systems, end-to-end transport protocols, routers, and links—let us now look at what can happen to a packet as it travels from its source to its destination. Recall that a packet starts in a host (the source), passes through a series of routers, and ends its journey in another host (the destination). As a packet travels from one node (host or router) to the subsequent node (host or router) along this path, the packet suffers from several types of delays at *each* node along the path. The most important of these delays are the **nodal processing delay, queuing delay, transmission delay,** and **propagation delay**; together, these delays accumulate to give a **total nodal delay**. In order to acquire a deep understanding of packet switching and computer networks, we must understand the nature and importance of these delays.

1.6.1 Types of Delay

Let's explore these delays in the context of Figure 1.13. As part of its end-to-end route between source and destination, a packet is sent from the upstream node through router A to router B. Our goal is to characterize the nodal delay at router A. Note that router A has an outbound link leading to router B. This link is preceded by a queue (also known as a buffer). When the packet arrives at router A from the upstream node, router A examines the packet's header to determine the appropriate outbound link for the packet and then directs the packet to the link. In this example, the outbound link for the packet is the one that leads to router B. A packet can be transmitted on a link only if there is no other packet currently being transmitted on the link and if there are no other packets preceding it in the queue; if the link is currently busy or if there are other packets already queued for the link, the newly arriving packet will then join the queue.

Processing Delay

The time required to examine the packet's header and determine where to direct the packet is part of the **processing delay**. The processing delay can also include other factors, such as the time needed to check for bit-level errors in the packet that occurred in transmitting the packet's bits from the upstream node to router A. Processing delays in high-speed routers are typically on the order of microseconds or less. After this

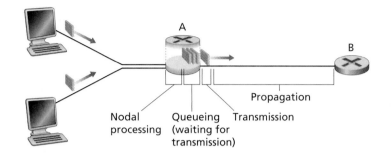

Figure 1.13 ♦ The nodal delay at router A

nodal processing, the router directs the packet to the queue that precedes the link to router B. (In Chapter 4 we'll study the details of how a router operates.)

Queuing Delay

At the queue, the packet experiences a **queuing delay** as it waits to be transmitted onto the link. The length of the queuing delay of a specific packet will depend on the number of earlier-arriving packets that are queued and waiting for transmission across the link. If the queue is empty and no other packet is currently being transmitted, then our packet's queuing delay will be zero. On the other hand, if the traffic is heavy and many other packets are also waiting to be transmitted, the queuing delay will be long. We will see shortly that the number of packets that an arriving packet might expect to find is a function of the intensity and nature of the traffic arriving at the queue. Queuing delays can be on the order of microseconds to milliseconds in practice.

Transmission Delay

Assuming that packets are transmitted in a first-come-first-served manner, as is common in packet-switched networks, our packet can be transmitted only after all the packets that have arrived before it have been transmitted. Denote the length of the packet by L bits, and denote the transmission rate of the link from router A to router B by R bits/sec. The rate R is determined by the transmission rate of the link to router B. For example, for a 10 Mbps Ethernet link, the rate is $R = 10$ Mbps; for a 100 Mbps Ethernet link, the rate is $R = 100$ Mbps. The **transmission delay** (also called the store-and-forward delay, as discussed in Section 1.3) is L/R. This is the amount of time required to push (that is, transmit) all of the packet's bits into the link. Transmission delays are typically on the order of microseconds to milliseconds in practice.

Propagation Delay

Once a bit is pushed onto the link, it needs to propagate to router B. The time required to propagate from the beginning of the link to router B is the **propagation delay**. The bit propagates at the propagation speed of the link. The propagation speed depends on the physical medium of the link (that is, fiber optics, twisted-pair copper wire, and so on) and is in the range of

$$2 \cdot 10^8 \text{ meters/sec to } 3 \cdot 10^8 \text{ meters/sec} \quad = \text{ prop speed } = S.$$

which is equal to, or a little less than, the speed of light. The propagation delay is the distance between two routers divided by the propagation speed. That is, the propagation delay is d/s, where d is the distance between router A and router B and s is the propagation speed of the link. Once the last bit of the packet propagates to node B, it and all the preceding bits of the packet are stored in router B. The whole process then continues with router B now performing the forwarding. In wide-area networks, propagation delays are on the order of milliseconds.

Comparing Transmission and Propagation Delay

Newcomers to the field of computer networking sometimes have difficulty understanding the difference between transmission delay and propagation delay. The difference is subtle but important. The transmission delay is the amount of time required for the router to push out the packet; it is a function of the packet's length and the transmission rate of the link, but has nothing to do with the distance between the two routers. The propagation delay, on the other hand, is the time it takes a bit to propagate from one router to the next; it is a function of the distance between the two routers, but has nothing to do with the packet's length or the transmission rate of the link.

An analogy might clarify the notions of transmission and propagation delay. Consider a highway that has a tollbooth every 100 kilometers. You can think of the highway segments between tollbooths as links and the tollbooths as routers. Suppose that cars travel (that is, propagate) on the highway at a rate of 100 km/hour (that is, when a car leaves a tollbooth, it instantaneously accelerates to 100 km/hour and maintains that speed between tollbooths). Suppose next that 10 cars, traveling together as a caravan follow each other in a fixed order. You can think of each car as a bit and the caravan as a packet. Also suppose that each tollbooth services (that is, transmits) a car at a rate of one car per 12 seconds, and that it is late at night so that the caravan's cars are the only cars on the highway. Finally, suppose that whenever the first car of the caravan arrives at a tollbooth, it waits at the entrance until the other nine cars have arrived and lined up behind it. (Thus the entire caravan must be stored at the tollbooth before it can begin to be forwarded.) The time required for the tollbooth to push the entire caravan onto the highway is (10 cars)/(5 cars/minute)

= 2 minutes. This time is analogous to the transmission delay in a router. The time required for a car to travel from the exit of one tollbooth to the next tollbooth is 100 km/(100 km/hour) = 1 hour. This time is analogous to propagation delay. Therefore, the time from when the caravan is stored in front of a tollbooth until the caravan is stored in front of the next tollbooth is the sum of transmission delay and propagation delay—in this example, 62 minutes.

Let's explore this analogy a bit more. What would happen if the tollbooth service time for a caravan were greater than the time for a car to travel between tollbooths? For example, suppose now that the cars travel at the rate of 1,000 km/hour and the tollbooth services cars at the rate of one car per minute. Then the traveling delay between two tollbooths is 6 minutes and the time to serve a caravan is 10 minutes. In this case, the first few cars in the caravan will arrive at the second tollbooth before the last cars in the caravan leave the first tollbooth. This situation also arises in packet-switched networks—the first bits in a packet can arrive at a router while many of the remaining bits in the packet are still waiting to be transmitted by the preceding router.

If we let d_{proc}, d_{queue}, d_{trans}, and d_{prop} denote the processing, queuing, transmission, and propagation delays, then the total nodal delay is given by

$$d_{nodal} = d_{proc} + d_{queue} + d_{trans} + d_{prop}$$

The contribution of these delay components can vary significantly. For example, d_{prop} can be negligible (for example, a couple of microseconds) for a link connecting two routers on the same university campus; however, d_{prop} is hundreds of milliseconds for two routers interconnected by a geostationary satellite link, and can be the dominant term in d_{nodal}. Similarly, d_{trans} can range from negligible to significant. Its contribution is typically negligible for transmission rates of 10 Mbps and higher (for example, for LANs); however, it can be hundreds of milliseconds for large Internet packets sent over low-speed dial-up modem links. The processing delay, d_{proc}, is often negligible; however, it strongly influences a router's maximum throughput, which is the maximum rate at which a router can forward packets.

1.6.2 Queuing Delay and Packet Loss

The most complicated and interesting component of nodal delay is the queuing delay, d_{queue}. In fact, queuing delay is so important and interesting in computer networking that thousands of papers and numerous books have been written about it [Bertsekas 1991; Daigle 1991; Kleinrock 1975, 1976; Ross 1995]. We give only a high-level, intuitive discussion of queuing delay here; the more curious reader may want to browse through some of the books (or even eventually write a PhD thesis on the subject!). Unlike the other three delays (namely, d_{proc}, d_{trans}, and d_{prop}), the queuing delay can vary from packet to packet. For example, if 10 packets arrive at an empty queue at the same time, the first packet transmitted will suffer no queuing delay, while the last packet transmitted will suffer a relatively large queuing delay (while it waits for the other nine packets to be transmitted). Therefore, when characterizing queuing delay, one typically uses statistical measures, such as average queuing delay, variance of queuing delay, and the probability that the queuing delay exceeds some specified value.

When is the queuing delay large and when is it insignificant? The answer to this question depends on the rate at which traffic arrives at the queue, the transmission rate of the link, and the nature of the arriving traffic, that is, whether the traffic arrives periodically or whether it arrives in bursts. To gain some insight here, let a denote the average rate at which packets arrive at the queue (a is in units of packets/sec). Recall that R is the transmission rate; that is, it is the rate (in bits/sec) at which bits are pushed out of the queue. Also suppose, for simplicity, that all packets consist of L bits. Then the average rate at which bits arrive at the queue is La bits/sec. Finally, assume that the queue is very big, so that it can hold essentially an infinite number of bits. The ratio La/R, called the **traffic intensity**, often plays an important role in estimating the extent of the queuing delay. If $La/R > 1$, then the average rate at which bits arrive at the queue exceeds the rate at which the bits can be transmitted from the queue. In this unfortunate situation, the queue will tend to increase without bound and the queuing delay will approach infinity! Therefore, one of the golden rules in traffic engineering is: *Design your system so that the traffic intensity is no greater than 1.*

Now consider the case $La/R \leq 1$. Here, the nature of the arriving traffic impacts the queuing delay. For example, if packets arrive periodically—that is, one packet arrives every L/R seconds—then every packet will arrive at an empty queue and there will be no queuing delay. On the other hand, if packets arrive in bursts but periodically, there can be a significant average queuing delay. For example, suppose N packets arrive simultaneously every $(L/R)N$ seconds. Then the first packet transmitted has no queuing delay; the second packet transmitted has a queuing delay of L/R seconds; and more generally, the nth packet transmitted has a queuing delay of $(n - 1)L/R$ seconds. We leave it as an exercise for you to calculate the average queuing delay in this example.

The two examples described above of periodic arrivals are a bit academic. Typically, the arrival process to a queue is *random;* that is, the arrivals do not follow any pattern and the packets are spaced apart by random amounts of time. In this more realistic case, the quantity La/R is not usually sufficient to fully characterize the delay statistics. Nonetheless, it is useful in gaining an intuitive understanding of the extent of the queuing delay. In particular, if traffic intensity is close to zero, then packet arrivals are few and far between and it is unlikely that an arriving packet will find another packet in the queue. Hence, the average queuing delay will be close to zero. On the other hand, when the traffic intensity is close to 1, there will be intervals of time when the arrival rate exceeds the transmission capacity (due to the burstiness of arrivals), and a queue will form. As the traffic intensity approaches 1, the average queue length gets larger and larger. The qualitative dependence of average queuing delay on the traffic intensity is shown in Figure 1.14.

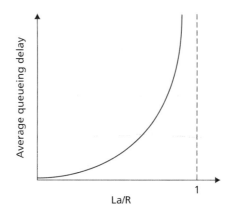

Figure 1.14 ♦ Dependence of average queuing delay on traffic intensity

One important aspect of Figure 1.14 is the fact that as the traffic intensity approaches 1, the average queuing delay increases rapidly. A small percentage increase in the intensity will result in a much larger percentage-wise increase in delay. Perhaps you have experienced this phenomenon on the highway. If you regularly drive on a road that is typically congested, the fact that the road is typically congested means that its traffic intensity is close to 1. If some event causes an even slightly larger-than-usual amount of traffic, the delays you experience can be huge.

Packet Loss

In our discussions above, we have assumed that the queue is capable of holding an infinite number of packets. In reality a queue preceding a link has finite capacity, although the queuing capacity greatly depends on the switch design and cost. Because the queue capacity is finite, packet delays do not really approach infinity as the traffic intensity approaches 1. Instead, a packet can arrive to find a full queue. With no place to store such a packet, a router will **drop** that packet; that is, the packet will be **lost**. From an end-system viewpoint, this will look like a packet having been transmitted into the network core but never emerging from the network at the destination. The fraction of lost packets increases as the traffic intensity increases. Therefore, performance at a node is often measured not only in terms of delay, but also in terms of the probability of packet loss. As we'll discuss in the subsequent chapters, a lost packet may be retransmitted on an end-to-end basis, either by the application or by the transport layer protocol.

End-to-End Delay

Our discussion up to this point has been focused on the nodal delay, that is, the delay at a single router. Let us conclude our discussion by briefly considering the delay from source to destination. To get a handle on this concept, suppose there are $N-1$ routers between the source host and the destination host. Let us also suppose that the network is uncongested (so that queuing delays are negligible), the processing delay at each router and at the source host is d_{proc}, the transmission rate out of each router and out of the source host is R bits/sec, and the propagation on each link is d_{prop}. The nodal delays accumulate and give an end-to-end delay,

$$d_{end\text{-}end} = N\,(d_{proc} + d_{trans} + d_{prop})$$

where, once again, $d_{trans} = L/R$, where L is the packet size. We leave it to you to generalize this formula to the case of heterogeneous delays at the nodes and to the presence of an average queuing delay at each node.

1.6.3 Delay and Routes in the Internet

To get a hands-on feel for the delay in a computer network, we can make use of the Traceroute diagnostic program. Traceroute is a simple program that can run in any Internet host. When the user specifies a destination hostname, the program in the source host sends multiple, special packets toward that destination. As these packets work their way toward the destination, they pass through a series of routers. When a router receives one of these special packets, it sends a short message back to the source. This message contains the name and address of the router.

More specifically, suppose there are $N-1$ routers between the source and the destination. Then the source will send N special packets into the network, with each packet addressed to the ultimate destination. These N special packets are marked *1* through *N*, with the first packet marked *1* and the last packet marked *N*. When the *n*th router receives the *n*th packet marked *n*, the router does not forward the packet toward its destination, but instead sends a message back to the source. When the destination host receives the *N*th packet, it too returns a message back to the source. The source records the time that elapses between when it sends a packet and when it receives the corresponding return message; it also records the name and address of the router (or the destination host) that returns the message. In this manner, the source can reconstruct the route taken by packets flowing from source to destination, and the source can determine the round-trip delays to all the intervening routers. Traceroute actually repeats the experiment just described three times, so the source actually sends *3 • N* packets to the destination. RFC 1393 describes Traceroute in detail.

Here is an example of the output of the Traceroute program, where the route was being traced from the source host gaia.cs.umass.edu (at the University of Massachusetts) to cis.poly.edu (at Polytechnic University in Brooklyn). The output has six columns: the first column is the *n* value described above, that is, the number of the router along the route; the second column is the name of the router; the third column is the address of the router (of the form xxx.xxx.xxx.xxx); the last three columns are the round-trip delays for three experiments. If the source receives fewer than three messages from any given router (due to packet loss in the network), Traceroute places an asterisk just after the router number and reports fewer than three round-trip times for that router.

```
1  cs-gw (128.119.240.254) 1.009 ms 0.899 ms 0.993 ms
2  128.119.3.154 (128.119.3.154) 0.931 ms 0.441 ms 0.651 ms
3  border4-rt-gi-1-3.gw.umass.edu (128.119.2.194) 1.032 ms 0.484 ms 0.451 ms
4  acr1-ge-2-1-0.Boston.cw.net (208.172.51.129) 10.006 ms 8.150 ms 8.460 ms
5  agr4-loopback.NewYork.cw.net (206.24.194.104) 12.272 ms 14.344 ms 13.267 ms
6  acr2-loopback.NewYork.cw.net (206.24.194.62) 13.225 ms 12.292 ms 12.148 ms
7  pos10-2.core2.NewYork1.Level3.net (209.244.160.133) 12.218 ms 11.823 ms 11.793 ms
8  gige9-1-52.hsipaccess1.NewYork1.Level3.net (64.159.17.39) 13.081 ms 11.556 ms 13.297 ms
9  p0-0.polyu.bbnplanet.net (4.25.109.122) 12.716 ms 13.052 ms 12.786 ms
10 cis.poly.edu (128.238.32.126) 14.080 ms 13.035 ms 12.802 ms
```

In the trace above there are nine routers between the source and the destination. Most of these routers have a name, and all of them have addresses. For example, the name of Router 3 is border4-rt-gi-1-3.gw.umass.edu and its address is 128.119.2.194. Looking at the data provided for this same router, we see that in the first of the three trials the round-trip delay between the source and the router was 1.03 msec. The round-trip delays for the subsequent two trials were 0.48 and 0.45 msec. These round-trip delays include all of the delays just discussed, including transmission delays, propagation delays, router processing delays, and queuing delays. Because the queuing delay is varying with time, the round-trip delay of packet n sent to a router n can actually be longer than the round-trip delay of packet $n+1$ sent to router $n+1$. Indeed, note in the example above that the delays to Router 6 appear to be larger than the delays in Router 7. Note that this is an artifact of the measurement process—any packet going to Router 7 must necessarily pass through Router 6.

Want to try out Traceroute for yourself? We *highly* recommended that you visit http://www.traceroute.org, which provides a Web interface to an extensive of list of sources for route tracing. You choose a source and supply the hostname for any destination. The Traceroute program then does all the work.

1.7 Protocol Layers and Their Service Models

From our discussion thus far, it is apparent that the Internet is an *extremely* complicated system. We have seen that there are many pieces to the Internet: numerous applications and protocols, various types of end systems and connections between end systems, routers, and various types of link-level media. Given this enormous complexity, is there any hope of organizing network architecture, or at least our discussion of network architecture? Fortunately, the answer to both questions is yes.

1.7.1 Layered Architecture

Before attempting to organize our thoughts on Internet architecture, let's look for a human analogy. Actually, we deal with complex systems all the time in our everyday life. Imagine if someone asked you to describe, for example, the airline system. How would you find the structure to describe this complex system that has ticketing agents, baggage checkers, gate personnel, pilots, airplanes, air traffic control, and a worldwide system for routing airplanes? One way to describe this system might be to describe the series of actions you take (or others take for you) when you fly on an airline. You purchase your ticket, check your bags, go to the gate, and eventually get loaded onto the plane. The plane takes off and is routed to its destination. After your plane lands, you deplane at the gate and claim your bags. If the trip was bad, you complain about the flight to the ticket agent (getting nothing for your effort). This scenario is shown in Figure 1.15.

Already, we can see some analogies here with computer networking: You are being shipped from source to destination by the airline; a packet is shipped from source host to destination host in the Internet. But this is not quite the analogy we are after. We are looking for some *structure* in Figure 1.15. Looking at Figure 1.15, we note that there is a ticketing function at each end; there is also a baggage function for already-ticketed passengers, and a gate function for already-ticketed and

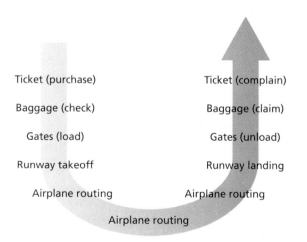

Figure 1.15 ♦ Taking an airplane trip: actions

already-baggage-checked passengers. For passengers who have made it through the gate (that is, passengers who are already ticketed, baggage-checked, and through the gate), there is a takeoff and landing function, and while in flight, there is an airplane-routing function. This suggests that we can look at the functionality in Figure 1.15 in a *horizontal* manner, as shown in Figure 1.16.

Figure 1.16 has divided the airline functionality into layers, providing a framework in which we can discuss airline travel. Note that each layer, combined with the layers below it, implements some functionality, some *service*. At the ticketing layer and below, airline-counter-to-airline-counter transfer of a person is accomplished. At the baggage layer and below, baggage-check-to-baggage-claim transfer of a person and bags is accomplished. Note that the baggage layer provides this service only to an already-ticketed person. At the gate layer, departure-gate-to-arrival-gate transfer of a person and bags is accomplished. At the takeoff/landing layer, runway-to-runway transfer of people and their bags is accomplished. Each layer provides its service by (1) performing certain actions within that layer (for example, at the gate layer, loading and unloading people from an airplane) and by (2) using the services of the layer directly below it (for example, in the gate layer, using the runway-to-runway passenger transfer service of the takeoff/landing layer).

A layered architecture allows us to discuss a well-defined, specific part of a large and complex system. This simplification itself is of considerable value by providing modularity, making it much easier to change the implementation of the service provided by the layer. As long as the layer provides the same service to the layer above it, and uses the same services from the layer below it, the remainder of the system remains unchanged when a layer's implementation is changed. (Note that changing the implementation of a service is very different from changing the service itself!) For example, if the gate functions were changed (for instance, to have people board and disembark by height), the remainder of the airline system would remain unchanged since the gate layer still provides the same function (loading and unloading people); it simply implements that function in a different manner after the change. For large and complex systems that are constantly being updated, the ability to change the implementation of a service without affecting other components of the system is another important advantage of layering.

Protocol Layering

But enough about airlines. Let's now turn our attention to network protocols. To provide structure to the design of network protocols, network designers organize protocols—and the network hardware and software that implement the protocols—in **layers**. Each protocol belongs to one of the layers, just as each function in the airline architecture in Figure 1.16 belonged to a layer. We are again interested in the **services** that a layer offers to the layer above—the so-called **service model** of a layer. Just as in the case of our airline example, each layer provides its service by (1) performing certain actions within that layer and by (2) using the services of the

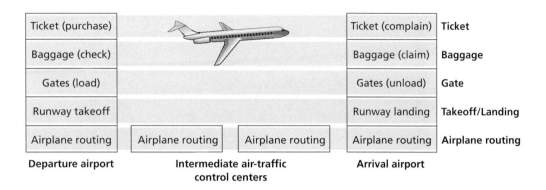

Figure 1.16 ♦ Horizontal layering of airline functionality

layer directly below it. For example, the services provided by layer *n* may include reliable delivery of messages from one edge of the network to the other. This might be implemented by using an unreliable edge-to-edge message delivery service of layer *n* –1, and adding layer *n* functionality to detect and retransmit lost messages.

A protocol layer can be implemented in software, in hardware, or in a combination of the two. Application-layer protocols—such as HTTP and SMTP—are almost always implemented in software in the end systems; so are transport-layer protocols. Because the physical layer and data link layers are responsible for handling communication over a specific link, they are typically implemented in a network interface card (for example, Ethernet or Wi-Fi interface cards) associated with a given link. The network layer is often a mixed implementation of hardware and software. Also note that just as the functions in the layered airline architecture were distributed among the various airports and flight control centers that make up the system, so too is a layer *n* protocol *distributed* among the end systems, packet switches and other components that make up the network. That is, there's often a piece of a layer *n* protocol in each of these network components.

Protocol layering has conceptual and structural advantages. As we have seen, layering provides a structured way to discuss system components. Modularity makes it easier to update system components. We mention, however, that some researchers and networking engineers are vehemently opposed to layering [Wakeman 1992]. One potential drawback of layering is that one layer may duplicate lower-layer functionality. For example, many protocol stacks provide error recovery on both a link basis and an end-to-end basis. A second potential drawback is that functionality at one layer may need information (for example, a timestamp value) that is present only in another layer; this violates the goal of separation of layers.

When taken together, the protocols of the various layers are called the **protocol stack**. The Internet protocol stack consists of five layers: the physical, link, network, transport, and application layers, as shown in Figure 1.17.

Application Layer

The application layer is where network applications and their application-layer protocols reside. The Internet's application layer includes many protocols, such as the HTTP protocol (which provides for Web document request and transfer), SMTP (which provides for the transfer of e-mail messages), and FTP (which provides for the transfer of files between two end systems). We'll see that certain network functions, such as the translation of human-friendly names for Internet end systems like gaia.cs.umass.edu to a 32-bit network address, are also done with the help of an application-layer protocol, the domain name system (DNS).We'll see in Chapter 2 that it is very easy to create our own new application-layer protocols.

Recall from our definition of a protocol in Section 1.1 that messages are exchanged between the distributed entities implementing a protocol. In this book, we'll refer to these messages as application-layer messages

Transport Layer

The Internet's transport layer transports application-layer messages between the client and server sides of an application. In the Internet there are two transport protocols, TCP and UDP, either of which can transport application-layer messages. TCP provides a connection-oriented service to its applications. This service includes guaranteed delivery of application-layer messages to the destination and flow control (that is, sender/receiver speed matching). TCP also breaks long messages into shorter segments and provides a congestion-control mechanism, so that a source throttles its transmission rate when the network is congested. The UDP protocol provides its applications a connectionless service, which (as we saw in Section 1.2) is very much a no-frills service. In this book, we'll refer to a transport layer packet as a **segment**.

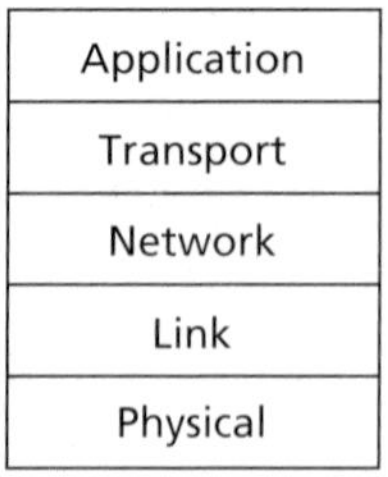

| Application |
| Transport |
| Network |
| Link |
| Physical |

Figure 1.17 ◆ The Internet protocol stack

Network Layer

The Internet's network layer is responsible for moving network-layer packets known as *datagrams* from one host to another. The Internet transport layer protocol (TCP or UDP) in a source host passes a transport-layer segment and a destination address to the network layer, just as you would give the postal service a letter with a destination address. The network layer then provides the service of delivering the segment to the transport layer in the destination host.

The Internet's network layer has two principal components. It has a protocol that defines the fields in the datagram as well as how the end systems and routers act on these fields. This protocol is the celebrated IP protocol. There is only one IP protocol, and all Internet components that have a network layer must run the IP protocol. The Internet's network layer also contains routing protocols that determine the routes that datagrams take between sources and destinations. The Internet has many routing protocols. As we saw in Section 1.5, the Internet is a network of networks, and within a network, the network administrator can run any routing protocol desired. Although the network layer contains both the IP protocol and numerous routing protocols, it is often simply referred to as the IP layer, reflecting the fact that IP is the glue that binds the Internet together.

Link Layer

The Internet's network layer routes a datagram through a series of packet switches (called *routers*, in the Internet) between the source and destination. To move a packet from one node (host or packet switch) to the next node in the route, the network layer relies on the services of the link layer. In particular, at each node, the network layer passes the datagram down to the link layer, which delivers the datagram to the next node along the route. At this next node, the link layer passes the datagram up to the network layer.

The services provided by the link layer depend on the specific link-layer protocol that is employed over the link. For example, some protocols provide reliable delivery on a link basis, that is, from transmitting node, over one link, to receiving node. Note that this reliable delivery service is different from the reliable delivery service of TCP, which provides reliable delivery from one end system to another. Examples of link layers include Ethernet and the Point-to-Point Protocol (PPP). As datagrams typically need to traverse several links to travel from source to destination, a datagram may be handled by different link-layer protocols at different links along its route. For example, a datagram may be handled by Ethernet on one link and by PPP on the next link. The network layer will receive a different service from each of the different link-layer protocols. In this book, we'll refer to the link-layer packets as **frames**.

Physical Layer

While the job of the link layer is to move entire frames from one network element to an adjacent network element, the job of the physical layer is to move the *individual bits* within the frame from one node to the next. The protocols in this layer are again link dependent and further depend on the actual transmission medium of the link (for example, twisted-pair copper wire, single-mode fiber optics). For example, Ethernet has many physical layer protocols: one for twisted-pair copper wire, another for coaxial cable, another for fiber, and so on. In each case, a bit is moved across the link in a different way.

If you examine the Table of Contents, you will see that we have roughly organized this book using the layers of the Internet protocol stack. We take a **top-down approach**, first covering the application layer and then proceeding downward.

1.7.2 Layers, Messages, Segments, Datagrams, and Frames

Figure 1.18 shows the physical path that data takes down a sending-end system's protocol stack, up and down the protocol stacks of an intervening link-layer switch and router, and then up the protocol stack at the receiving-end system. As we discuss later in this book, routers and link-layer switches are both packet-switches. Similar to end systems, routers and link-layer switches organize their networking hardware and software into layers. But routers and link-layer switches do not implement *all* of the layers in the protocol stack; they typically implement only the bottom layers. As shown in Figure 1.18, link-layer switches implement layers 1 and 2; routers implement layers 1 through 3. This means, for example, that Internet routers are capable of implementing the IP protocol (a layer 3 protocol), while link-layer switches are not. We'll see later that while link-layer switches do not recognize IP addresses, they are capable of recognizing layer 2 addresses, such as Ethernet addresses. Note that hosts implement all five layers; this is consistent with the view that the Internet architecture puts much of its complexity at the edges of the network.

Figure 1.18 also illustrates the important concept of **encapsulation**. At the sending host, an **application-layer message** (M in Figure 1.18) is passed to the transport layer. In the simplest case, the transport layer takes the message and appends additional information (so-called transport-layer header information, H_t in Figure 1.18) that will be used by the receiver-side transport layer. The application-layer message and the transport layer header information together constitute the **transport-layer segment**. The transport-layer segment thus encapsulates the application-layer message. The added information might include information allowing the receiver-side transport layer to deliver the message up to the appropriate application, and error-detection bits that allow the receiver to determine whether bits in the message have been changed in route. The transport layer then passes the segment to the network layer, which adds network-layer header

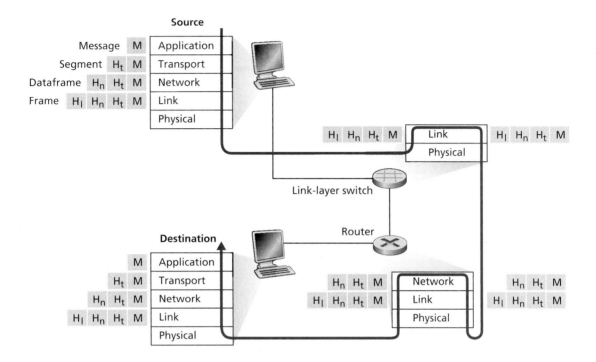

Figure 1.18 ◆ Hosts, routers, and link-layer switches; each contains a different set of layers, reflecting their differences in functionality

information (H_n in Figure 1.18) such as source and destination-end system addresses, creating a **network-layer datagram**. The datagram is then passed to the link layer, which (of course!) will add its own link-layer header information and create a **link-layer frame**.

A useful analogy here is the sending of an interoffice memo via the public postal service. The memo itself is the application-layer message. The memo is put in an interoffice memo envelope with the memo recipient's name and department written on the front of the envelope. This information will help the mailroom at the receiving office direct the memo to the correct individual. The interoffice envelope, which contains header information (the recipient's name and department number) and encapsulates the application-layer message (the memo) is analogous to the transport layer segment. The sending office mailroom takes the interoffice memo, puts it inside an envelope suitable for sending through the public postal service, writes the postal address of the sending and receiving company office on the postal envelope, and adds a stamp. Here, the postal envelope is analogous to the datagram—it encapsulates the transport-layer segment (the interoffice envelope and contents), which encapsulates the original message (the memo). The post office delivers the postal envelope to the receiving office's mailroom, where it is opened and the interoffice memo removed. The interoffice memo is then forwarded to the appropriate individual, who opens the envelope and removes the memo.

The process of encapsulation can be more complex than that described above. For example, a large message may be divided into multiple transport-layer segments (which might themselves each be divided into multiple network-layer datagrams). At the receiving end, such a segment must then be reconstructed from its constituent datagrams.

1.8 History of Computer Networking and the Internet

Sections 1.1 through 1.7 presented an overview of the technology of computer networking and the Internet. You should know enough now to impress your family and friends! However, if you really want to be a big hit at the next cocktail party, you should sprinkle your discourse with tidbits about the fascinating history of the Internet [Segaller 1998].

1.8.1 The Development of Packet Switching: 1961–1972

The field of computer networking and today's Internet trace their beginnings back to the early 1960s, when the telephone network was the world's dominant communication network. Recall from Section 1.3 that the telephone network uses circuit switching to transmit information from a sender to a receiver—an appropriate choice given that voice is transmitted at a constant rate between sender and receiver. Given the increasing importance (and great expense) of computers in the early 1960s and the advent of timeshared computers, it was perhaps natural (at least with perfect hindsight!) to consider the question of how to hook computers together so that they could be shared among geographically distributed users. The traffic generated by such users was likely to be *bursty*—intervals of activity, such as the sending of a command to a remote computer, followed by periods of inactivity while waiting for a reply or while contemplating the received response.

Three research groups around the world, each unaware of the others' work [Leiner 1998], began inventing packet switching as an efficient and robust alternative to circuit switching. The first published work on packet-switching techniques was that of Leonard Kleinrock [Kleinrock 1961; Kleinrock 1964], then a graduate student at MIT. Using queuing theory, Kleinrock's work elegantly demonstrated the effectiveness of the packet-switching approach for bursty traffic sources. In 1964, Paul Baran [Baran 1964] at the Rand Institute had begun investigating the use of packet switching for secure voice over military networks, and at the National

Physical Laboratory in England, Donald Davies and Roger Scantlebury were also developing their ideas on packet switching.

The work at MIT, Rand, and the NPL laid the foundations for today's Internet. But the Internet also has a long history of a let's-build-it-and-demonstrate-it attitude that also dates back to the early 1960s. J. C. R. Licklider [DEC 1990] and Lawrence Roberts, both colleagues of Kleinrock's at MIT, went on to lead the computer science program at the Advanced Research Projects Agency (ARPA) in the United States. Roberts published an overall plan for the ARPAnet [Roberts 1967], the first packet-switched computer network and a direct ancestor of today's public Internet. The early packet switches were known as **interface message processors (IMPs),** and the contract to build these switches was awarded to the BBN company. On Labor Day in 1969, the first IMP was installed at UCLA under Kleinrock's supervision, and three additional IMPs were installed shortly thereafter at the Stanford Research Institute (SRI), UC Santa Barbara, and the University of Utah (Figure 1.19). The fledgling precursor to the Internet was four nodes large by the end of 1969. Kleinrock recalls the very first use of the network to perform a remote login from UCLA to SRI, crashing the system [Kleinrock 2004].

By 1972, ARPAnet had grown to approximately 15 nodes and was given its first public demonstration by Robert Kahn at the 1972 International Conference on Computer Communications. The first host-to-host protocol between ARPAnet end systems, known as the network-control protocol (NCP), was completed [RFC 001]. With an end-to-end protocol available, applications could now be written. Ray Tomlinson at BBN wrote the first e-mail program in 1972.

1.8.2 Proprietary Networks and Internetworking: 1972–1980

The initial ARPAnet was a single, closed network. In order to communicate with an ARPAnet host, one had to be actually attached to another ARPAnet IMP. In the early to mid-1970s, additional packet-switching networks besides ARPAnet came into being:

♦ ALOHAnet, a microwave network linking universities on the Hawaiian islands [Abramson 1970], as well as DARPA's packet-satellite [RFC 829] and packet-radio networks [Kahn 1978]

♦ Telenet, a BBN commercial packet-switching network based on ARPAnet technology

♦ Cyclades, a French packet-switching network pioneered by Louis Pouzin [Think 2002]

♦ Time-sharing networks such as Tymnet and the GE Information Services network, among others in the late 1960s and early 1970s [Schwartz 1977]

♦ IBM's SNA (1969–1974), which paralleled the ARPAnet work [Schwartz 1977]

Figure 1.19   ♦   An early interface message processor (IMP) and
L. Kleinrock (Mark J. Terrill, AP/Wide World Photos)

The number of networks was growing. With perfect hindsight we can see that the time was ripe for developing an encompassing architecture for connecting networks. Pioneering work on interconnecting networks, (under the sponsorship of the Defense Advanced Research Projects Agency (DARPA)), in essence creating a *network of networks,* was done by Vinton Cerf and Robert Kahn [Cerf 1974]; the term *internetting* was coined to describe this work.

These architectural principles were embodied in TCP. The early versions of TCP, however, were quite different from today's TCP. The early versions of TCP combined a reliable in-sequence delivery of data via end-system retransmission (still part of today's TCP) with forwarding functions (which today are performed by IP). Early experimentation with TCP, combined with the recognition of the importance of an unreliable, non-flow-controlled end-end transport service for applications such as packetized voice, led to the separation of IP out of TCP and the development of the UDP protocol. The three key Internet protocols that we see today—TCP, UDP, and IP—were conceptually in place by the end of the 1970s.

In addition to the DARPA Internet-related research, many other important networking activities were underway. In Hawaii, Norman Abramson was developing ALOHAnet, a packet-based radio network that allowed multiple remote sites on the Hawaiian Islands to communicate with each other. The ALOHA protocol [Abramson 1970] was the first multiple-access protocol, allowing geographically distributed users to share a single broadcast communication medium (a radio frequency). Metcalfe and Boggs built on Abramson's multiple-access protocol work when they developed the Ethernet protocol [Metcalfe 1976] for wire-based shared broadcast networks; see Figure 1.20. Interestingly, Metcalfe and Boggs' Ethernet protocol was motivated by the need to connect multiple PCs, printers, and shared disks [Perkins 1994]. Twenty-five years ago, well before the PC revolution and the explosion of networks, Metcalfe and Boggs were laying the foundation for today's PC LANs. Ethernet technology represented an important step for internetworking as well. Each Ethernet local area network was itself a network, and as the number of LANs proliferated, the need to internetwork these LANs together became increasingly important. We'll discuss Ethernet, ALOHA, and other LAN technologies in detail in Chapter 5.

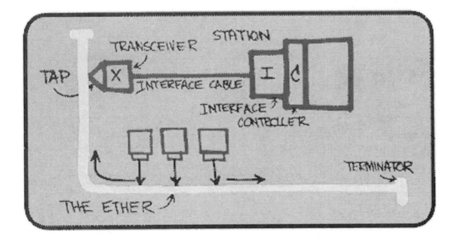

Figure 1.20 ♦ Metcalfe's original conception of the Ethernet

1.8.3 A Proliferation of Networks: 1980–1990

By the end of the 1970s, approximately two hundred hosts were connected to the ARPAnet. By the end of the 1980s the number of hosts connected to the public Internet, a confederation of networks looking much like today's Internet, would reach a hundred thousand. The 1980s would be a time of tremendous growth.

Much of that growth resulted from several distinct efforts to create computer networks linking universities together. BITNET provided e-mail and file transfers among several universities in the Northeast. CSNET (computer science network) was formed to link university researchers who did not have access to ARPAnet. In 1986, NSFNET was created to provide access to NSF-sponsored supercomputing centers. Starting with an initial backbone speed of 56 kbps, NSFNET's backbone would be running at 1.5 Mbps by the end of the decade and would be serving as a primary backbone linking regional networks.

In the ARPAnet community, many of the final pieces of today's Internet architecture were falling into place. January 1, 1983 saw the official deployment of TCP/IP as the new standard host protocol for ARPAnet (replacing the NCP protocol). The transition [RFC 801] from NCP to TCP/IP was a flag day event—all hosts were required to transfer over to TCP/IP as of that day. In the late 1980s, important extensions were made to TCP to implement host-based congestion control [Jacobson 1988]. The DNS, used to map between a human-readable Internet name (for example, gaia.cs .umass.edu) and its 32-bit IP address, was also developed [RFC 1034].

Paralleling this development of the ARPAnet (which was for the most part a US effort), in the early 1980s the French launched the Minitel project, an ambitious plan to bring data networking into everyone's home. Sponsored by the French government, the Minitel system consisted of a public packet-switched network (based on the X.25 protocol suite, which uses virtual circuits), Minitel servers, and inexpensive terminals with built-in low-speed modems. The Minitel became a huge success in 1984 when the French government gave away a free Minitel terminal to each French household that wanted one. Minitel sites included free sites—such as a telephone directory site—as well as private sites, which collected a usage-based fee from each user. At its peak in the mid 1990s, it offered more than 20,000 services, ranging from home banking to specialized research databases. It was used by over 20 percent of France's population, generated more than $1 billion in revenue each year, and created 10,000 jobs. The Minitel was in a large proportion of French homes 10 years before most Americans had ever heard of the Internet.

1.8.4 The Internet Explosion: The 1990s

The 1990s were ushered in with a number of events that symbolized the continued evolution and the soon-to-arrive commercialization of the Internet. ARPAnet, the progenitor of the Internet, ceased to exist. MILNET and the Defense Data Network had grown in the 1980s to carry most of the US Department of Defense–related traffic and NSFNET had begun to serve as a backbone network connecting regional networks in the United States and national networks overseas. In 1991, NSFNET lifted its restrictions on the use of NSFNET for commercial purposes. NSFNET itself would be decommissioned in 1995, with Internet backbone traffic being carried by commercial Internet service providers.

The main event of the 1990s, however, was to be the emergence of the World Wide Web, which brought the Internet into the homes and businesses of millions of people worldwide. The Web also served as a platform for enabling and deploying hundreds of new applications, including online stock trading and banking, streamed multimedia services, and information retrieval services. For a brief history of the early days of the Web, see [W3C 1995].

The Web was invented at CERN by Tim Berners-Lee between 1989 and 1991 [Berners-Lee 1989], based on ideas originating in earlier work on hypertext from the 1940s by Bush [Bush 1945] and since the 1960s by Ted Nelson [Ziff-Davis 1998]. Berners-Lee and his associates developed initial versions of HTML, HTTP, a Web server, and a browser—the four key components of the Web. The original CERN browsers provided only a line-mode interface. Around the end of 1992 there were about two hundred Web servers in operation, this collection of servers being just a harbinger of what was about to come. At about this time several researchers were developing Web browsers with GUI interfaces, including Marc Andreesen, who led the development of the popular GUI browser Mosaic. In 1994 Marc Andreesen and Jim Clark formed Mosaic Communications, which later became Netscape Communications Corporation [Cusumano 1998; Quittner 1998]. By 1995, university students were using Mosaic and Netscape browsers to surf the Web on a daily basis. At about this time companies—big and small—began to operate Web servers and transact commerce over the Web. In 1996, Microsoft started to make browsers, which started the browser war between Netscape and Microsoft, which Microsoft won a few years later [Cusumano 1998].

The second half of the 1990s was a period of tremendous growth and innovation for the Internet, with major corporations and thousands of startups creating Internet products and services. Internet e-mail continued to evolve with feature-rich mail readers providing address books, attachments, hot links, and multimedia transport. By the end of the millennium the Internet was supporting hundreds of popular applications, including four killer applications:

♦ E-mail, including attachments and Web-accessible e-mail

♦ The Web, including Web browsing and Internet commerce

♦ Instant messaging, with contact lists, pioneered by ICQ

♦ Peer-to-peer file sharing of MP3s, pioneered by Napster

Interestingly, the first two killer applications came from the research community, whereas the last two were created by a few young entrepreneurs.

The period from 1995 to 2001 was a roller-coaster ride for the Internet in the financial markets. Before they were even profitable, hundreds of Internet startups made initial public offerings and started to be traded in a stock market. Many companies were valued in the billions of dollars without having any significant revenue streams. The Internet stocks collapsed in 2000–2001, and many startups shut down. Nevertheless, a number of companies emerged as big winners in the Internet space (even if their stock prices suffered in the crash), including Microsoft, Cisco, AOL, Yahoo, e-Bay, and Amazon.

During the 1990s, networking research and development also made significant advances in the areas of high-speed routers and routing (Chapter 4) and LANs (Chapter 5). The technical community struggled with the problems of defining and implementing an Internet service model for traffic requiring real-time constraints, such as continuous media applications (Chapter 7). The need to secure and manage Internet infrastructure (Chapters 8 and 9) also became of paramount importance as e-commerce applications proliferated and the Internet became a central component of the world's telecommunications infrastructure.

1.8.5 Recent Developments

Innovation in computer networking continues at a rapid pace. Advances are being made on all fronts, including deployment of new applications, content distribution, Internet telephony, higher transmission speeds in LANs, and faster routers. But three developments merit special attention: a proliferation of high-speed access networking (including wireless access), security, and P2P networking.

As discussed in Section 1.4, increasing penetration of broadband residential Internet access via cable modem and DSL is setting the stage for a wealth of new multimedia applications, including streaming high-quality video-on-demand and high-quality interactive video conferencing. The increasing ubiquity of high-speed (11 Mbps and higher) public Wi-Fi networks and medium-speed (hundred's of kbps) Internet access of cellular telephony networks are not only making it possible to remain constantly connected, but also enabling an exciting new set of location-specific services. We'll cover wireless and mobile networks in Chapter 6.

Following a series of denial-of-service attacks on prominent Web servers in the late 1990's and the proliferation of worm attacks (e.g., the Blaster worm) that infect end systems and clog the network with traffic, network security has become an immensely important topic. These attacks have resulted in the development of intrusion detection systems to provide early warning of an attack, the use of firewalls to filter out unwanted traffic before it enters the network, and the use of IP traceback to pinpoint the origin of attacks. We'll cover a number of important security-related topics in Chapter 8.

The last innovation of which we take special note is P2P networking. A P2P networking application exploits the resources in users' computers—storage, content, CPU cycles, and human presence—and has significant autonomy from central servers. Typically, the users' computers (i.e., the peers) have intermittent connectivity. As if this writing, KaZaA is the most popular P2P file-sharing system. Its network typically has more than 4 million connected end systems and its traffic constitutes 20 to 50 percent of all Internet traffic [Sariou 2002].

1.9 Summary

In this chapter we've covered a tremendous amount of material! We've looked at the various pieces of hardware and software that make up the Internet in particular and computer networks in general. We started at the edge of the network, looking at end systems and applications, and at the transport service provided to the applications running on the end systems. Using network-based distributed applications as examples, we introduced the notion of a protocol—a key concept in networking. We then dove deeper inside the network, into the network core, identifying packet switching and circuit switching as the two basic approaches for transporting data through a telecommunication network, and we examined the strengths and weaknesses of each approach. We then looked at the lowest (from an architectural standpoint) parts of the network—the link-layer technologies and physical media typically found in the access network. We also examined the structure of the global Internet, learning that the Internet is a network of networks. We saw that the Internet's hierarchical structure, consisting of higher- and lower-tier ISPs, has allowed it to scale to include thousands of networks.

In the second part of this introductory chapter, we examined several topics central to the field of computer networking. We first examined the causes of delay and packet loss in a packet-switched network. We developed simple quantitative models of transmission, propagation, and queuing delays; we will make extensive use of these delay models in the homework problems throughout this book. Next we examined protocol layering and service models, key architectural principles in networking that we will also refer back to throughout this book. We finished our introduction to networking with a brief history of computer networking. The first chapter in itself constitutes a mini-course in computer networking.

So, we have indeed covered a tremendous amount of ground in this first chapter! If you're a bit overwhelmed, don't worry. In the following chapters we'll revisit all of these ideas, covering them in much more detail (that's a promise, not a threat!). At this point, we hope you leave this chapter with a still-developing intuition for the pieces that make up a network, a still-developing command of the vocabulary of networking (don't be shy about referring back to this chapter), and an ever-growing desire to learn more about networking. That's the task ahead of us for the rest of this book.

Road-Mapping This Book

Before starting any trip, you should always glance at a road map in order to become familiar with the major roads and junctures that lie ahead. For the trip we are about to embark on, the ultimate destination is a deep understanding of the how, what, and why of computer networks. Our road map is the sequence of chapters of this book:

1. Computer Networks and the Internet
2. Application Layer
3. Transport Layer
4. Network Layer
5. Link Layer and Local Area Networks
6. Wireless and Mobility
7. Multimedia Networking
8. Security in Computer Networks
9. Network Management

Chapters 2 through 5 are the four core chapters of this book. You should notice that these chapters are organized around the top four layers of the five-layer Internet protocol stack, one chapter for each layer. Further note that our journey will begin at the top of the Internet protocol stack, namely, the application layer, and will work its way downward. The rationale behind this top-down journey is that once we understand the applications, we can understand the network services needed to support these applications. We can then, in turn, examine the various ways in which such services might be implemented by a network architecture. Covering applications early thus provides motivation for the remainder of the text.

The second half of the book—Chapters 6 through 9—zooms in on four enormously important (and somewhat independent) topics in modern computer networking. In Chapter 6, we examine wireless and mobility, including Wi-Fi LANs, GSM, and mobile IP. In Chapter 7 (Multimedia Networking) we examine audio and video applications such as Internet phone, video conferencing, and streaming of stored media. We also look at how a packet-switched network can be designed to provide consistent quality of service to audio and video applications. In Chapter 8 (Security in Computer Networks), we first look at the underpinnings of encryption and network security, and then we examine how the basic theory is being applied in a broad range of Internet contexts. The last chapter (Network Management) examines the key issues in network management as well as the primary Internet protocols used for network management.

Homework Problems and Questions

Chapter 1 Review Questions

SECTIONS 1.1–1.5

1. What is the difference between a host and an end system? List the types of end systems. Is a Web server an end system?

2. The word *protocol* is often used to describe diplomatic relations. Give an example of a diplomatic protocol.

3. What is a client program? What is a server program? Does a server program request and receive services from a client program?

4. What are the two types of transport services that the Internet provides to its applications? What are some characteristics of each of these services?

5. It has been said that flow control and congestion control are equivalent. Is this true for the Internet's connection-oriented service? Are the objectives of flow control and congestion control the same?

6. Provide a brief, high-level description of how the Internet's connection-oriented service provides reliable transport.

7. What advantage does a circuit-switched network have over a packet-switched network? What advantages does TDM have over FDM in a circuit-switched network?

8. Why is it said that packet switching employs statistical multiplexing? Contrast statistical multiplexing with the multiplexing that takes place in TDM.

9. Suppose there is exactly one packet switch between a sending host and a receiving host. The transmission rates between the sending host and the switch and between the switch and the receiving host are R_1 and R_2, respectively. Assuming that the switch uses store-and-forward packet switching, what is the total end-to-end delay to send a packet of length L? (Ignore queuing, propagation delay, and processing delay.)

10. What is meant by connection state information in a virtual-circuit network? If in a switch in a VC network, connections are established and torn down at a rate of one connection per millisecond (on average), at what rate does the forwarding table in the switch need to be modified?

11. Suppose you are developing the standard for a new type of packet-switched network. You need to decide whether your network will use VCs or datagram routing. What are the pros and cons for using VCs?

12. List six access technologies. Classify each one as residential access, company access, or mobile access.

13. What is the key distinguishing difference between a tier-1 ISP and a tier-2 ISP?

14. What is the difference between a POP and a NAP?

15. Is HFC transmission rate dedicated or shared among users? Are collisions possible in a downstream HFC channel? Why or why not?

16. What is the transmission rate of Ethernet LANs? For a given transmission rate, can each user on the LAN continuously transmit at that rate?

17. What are some of the physical media that Ethernet can run over?

18. Dial-up modems, HFC, and ADSL are all used for residential access. For each of these access technologies, provide a range of transmission rates and comment on whether the transmission rate is shared or dedicated.

SECTIONS 1.6–1.8

19. Consider sending a packet from a sending host to a receiving host over a fixed route. List the delay components in the end-to-end delay. Which of these delays are constant and which are variable?

20. List five tasks that a layer can perform. Is it possible that one (or more) of these tasks could be performed by two (or more) layers?

21. What are the five layers in the Internet protocol stack? What are the principal responsibilities of each of these layers?

22. What is an application-layer message? A transport-layer segment? A network-layer datagram? A link-layer frame?

23. Which layers in the Internet protocol stack does a router process? Which layers does a link-layer switch process? Which layers does a host process?

Problems

1. Design and describe an application-level protocol to be used between an automatic teller machine and a bank's centralized computer. Your protocol should allow a user's card and password to be verified, the account balance (which is maintained at the centralized computer) to be queried, and an account withdrawal to be made (that is, money disbursed to the user). Your protocol entities should be able to handle the all-too-common case in which there is not enough money in the account to cover the withdrawal. Specify your protocol by listing the messages exchanged and the action taken by the automatic teller machine or the bank's centralized computer on transmission and receipt of messages. Sketch the operation of your protocol for the case of a simple withdrawal with no errors, using a diagram similar to that in Figure 1.2. Explicitly state the assumptions made by your protocol about the underlying end-to-end transport service.

2. Consider an application that transmits data at a steady rate (for example, the sender generates an N-bit unit of data every k time units, where k is small and fixed). Also, when such an application starts, it will continue running for a relatively long period of time. Answer the following questions, briefly justifying your answer:

   a. Would a packet-switched network or a circuit-switched network be more appropriate for this application? Why?

   b. Suppose that a packet-switched network is used and the only traffic in this network comes from such applications as described above. Furthermore, assume that the sum of the application data rates is less than the capacities of each and every link. Is some form of congestion control needed? Why?

3. Consider the circuit-switched network in Figure 1.5. Recall that there are n circuits on each link.

   a. What is the maximum number of simultaneous connections that can be in progress at any one time in this network?

   b. Suppose that all connections are between the switch in the upper-left-hand corner and the switch in the lower-right-hand corner. What is the maximum number of simultaneous connections that can be in progress?

4. Review the car-caravan analogy in Section 1.6. Again assume a propagation speed of 100 km/hour.

   a. Suppose the caravan travels 200 km, beginning in front of one tollbooth, passing through a second tollbooth, and finishing just before a third tollbooth. What is the end-to-end delay?

   b. Repeat (a), now assuming that there are seven cars in the caravan instead of ten.

5. Consider sending a packet of F bits over a path of Q links. Each link transmits at R bps. The network is lightly loaded so that there are no queuing delays. Propagation delay is negligible.

   a. Suppose the network is a packet-switched virtual-circuit network. Denote the VC setup time by t_s seconds. Suppose the sending layers add a total of h bits of header to the packet. How long does it take to send the file from source to destination?

   b. Suppose the network is a packet-switched datagram network and a connectionless service is used. Now suppose each packet has $2h$ bits of header. How long does it take to send the packet?

   c. Finally, suppose that the network is a circuit-switched network. Further suppose that the transmission rate of the circuit between source and destination is R bps. Assuming t_s setup time and h bits of header appended to the packet, how long does it take to send the packet?

6. This elementary problem begins to explore propagation delay and transmission delay, two central concepts in data networking. Consider two hosts, A and B, connected by a single link of rate R bps. Suppose that the two hosts are separated by m meters, and suppose the propagation speed along the link is s meters/sec. Host A is to send a packet of size L bits to Host B.

    a. Express the propagation delay, d_{prop}, in terms of m and s.

    b. Determine the transmission time of the packet, d_{trans}, in terms of L and R.

    c. Ignoring processing and queuing delays, obtain an expression for the end-to-end delay.

    d. Suppose Host A begins to transmit the packet at time $t = 0$. At time $t = d_{trans}$, where is the last bit of the packet?

    e. Suppose d_{prop} is greater than d_{trans}. At time $t = d_{trans}$, where is the first bit of the packet?

    f. Suppose d_{prop} is less than d_{trans}. At time $t = d_{trans}$, where is the first bit of the packet?

    g. Suppose $s = 2.5 \cdot 10^8$, $L = 100$ bits, and $R = 28$ kbps. Find the distance m so that d_{prop} equals d_{trans}.

7. In this problem we consider sending voice from Host A to Host B over a packet-switched network (for example, Internet phone). Host A converts analog voice to a digital 64 kbps bit stream on the fly. Host A then groups the bits into 48-byte packets. There is one link between Host A and B; its transmission rate is 1 Mbps and its propagation delay is 2 msec. As soon as Host A gathers a packet, it sends it to Host B. As soon as Host B receives an entire packet, it converts the packet's bits to an analog signal. How much time elapses from the time a bit is created (from the original analog signal at Host A) until the bit is decoded (as part of the analog signal at Host B)?

8. Suppose users share a 1 Mbps link. Also suppose each user requires 100 kbps when transmitting, but each user transmits only 10 percent of the time. (See the discussion Packet Switching Versus Circuit Switching in Section 1.3.)

    a. When circuit switching is used, how many users can be supported?

    b. For the remainder of this problem, suppose packet switching is used. Find the probability that a given user is transmitting.

    c. Suppose there are 40 users. Find the probability that at any given time, exactly n users are transmitting simultaneously. (*Hint*: Use the binomial distribution.)

    d. Find the probability that there are 11 or more users transmitting simultaneously.

9. Consider the discussion in Section 1.3 under the heading of Packet Switching Versus Circuit Switching, in which an example is provided with a 1 Mbps link.

Users are generating data at a rate of 100 kbps when busy, but are busy generating data only with probability $p = 0.1$. Suppose that the 1 Mbps link is replaced by a 1 Gbps link.

a. What is N, the maximum number of users that can be supported simultaneously under circuit switching?

b. Now consider packet switching and a user population of M users. Give a formula (in terms of p, M, N) for the probability that more than N users are sending data.

10. Consider the queuing delay in a router buffer (preceding an outbound link). Suppose all packets are L bits, the transmission rate is R bps, and that N packets simultaneously arrive at the buffer every LN/R seconds. Find the average queuing delay of a packet. (*Hint*: The queuing delay for the first packet is zero; for the second packet L/R; for the third packet $2L/R$. The Nth packet has already been transmitted when the second batch of packets arrives.)

11. Consider the queuing delay in a router buffer. Let I denote traffic intensity; that is, $I = La/R$. Suppose that the queuing delay takes the form IL/R $(1 - I)$ for $I < 1$.

a. Provide a formula for the total delay, that is, the queuing delay plus the transmission delay.

b. Plot the total delay as a function of L/R.

12. a. Generalize the end-to-end delay formula in Section 1.6 for heterogeneous processing rates, transmission rates, and propagation delays.

b. Repeat (a), but now also suppose that there is an average queuing delay of d_{queue} at each node.

13. Perform a Traceroute between source and destination on the same continent at three different hours of the day.

a. Find the average and standard deviation of the round-trip delays at each of the three hours.

b. Find the number of routers in the path at each of the three hours. Did the paths change during any of the hours?

c. Try to identify the number of ISP networks that the Traceroute packets pass through from source to destination. Routers with similar names and/or similar IP addresses should be considered as part of the same ISP. In your experiments, do the largest delays occur at the peering interfaces between adjacent ISPs?

d. Repeat the above for a source and destination on different continents. Compare the intracontinent and intercontinent results.

14. Suppose two hosts, A and B, are separated by 10,000 kilometers and are connected by a direct link of $R = 1$ Mbps. Suppose the propagation speed over the link is $2.5 \cdot 10^8$ meters/sec.

a. Calculate the bandwidth-delay product, $R \cdot t_{prop}$.

b. Consider sending a file of 400,000 bits from Host A to Host B. Suppose the file is sent continuously as one big message. What is the maximum number of bits that will be in the link at any given time?

c. Provide an interpretation of the bandwidth-delay product.

d. What is the width (in meters) of a bit in the link? Is it longer than a football field?

e. Derive a general expression for the width of a bit in terms of the propagation speed s, the transmission rate R, and the length of the link m.

15. Referring to problem 14, suppose we can modify R. For what value of R is the width of a bit as long as the length of the link?

16. Consider problem 14 but now with a link of $R = 1$ Gbps.

a. Calculate the bandwidth-delay product, $R \cdot t_{prop}$.

b. Consider sending a file of 400,000 bits from Host A to Host B. Suppose the file is sent continuously as one big message. What is the maximum number of bits that will be in the link at any given time?

c. What is the width (in meters) of a bit in the link?

17. Refer again to problem 14.

a. How long does it take to send the file, assuming it is sent continuously?

b. Suppose now the file is broken up into 10 packets with each packet containing 40,000 bits. Suppose that each packet is acknowledged by the receiver and the transmission time of an acknowledgment packet is negligible. Finally, assume that the sender cannot send a packet until the preceding one is acknowledged. How long does it take to send the file?

c. Compare the results from (a) and (b).

18. Suppose there is a 10 Mbps microwave link between a geostationary satellite and its base station on Earth. Every minute the satellite takes a digital photo and sends it to the base station. Assume a propagation speed of $2.4 \cdot 10^8$ meters/sec.

a. What is the propagation delay of the link?

b. What is the bandwidth-delay product, $R \cdot t_{prop}$?

c. Let x denote the size of the photo. What is the minimum value of x for the microwave link to be continuously transmitting?

19. Consider the airline travel analogy in our discussion of layering in Section 1.7, and the addition of headers to protocol data units as they flow down the protocol stack. Is there an equivalent notion of header information that is added to passengers and baggage as they move down the airline protocol stack?

20. In modern packet-switched networks, the source host segments long, application-layer messages (for example, an image or a music file) into smaller packets and

sends the packets into the network. The receiver then reassembles the packets back into the original message. We refer to this process as *message segmentation*. Figure 1.21 illustrates the end-to-end transport of a message with and without message segmentation. Consider a message that is $7.5 \cdot 10^6$ bits long that is to be sent from source to destination in Figure 1.21. Suppose each link in the figure is 1.5 Mbps. Ignore propagation, queuing, and processing delays.

a. Consider sending the message from source to destination *without* message segmentation. How long does it take to move the message from the source host to the first packet switch? Keeping in mind that each switch uses store-and-forward packet switching, what is the total time to move the message from source host to destination host?

b. Now suppose that the message is segmented into 5,000 packets, with each packet being 1,500 bits long. How long does it take to move the first packet from source host to the first switch? When the first packet is being sent from the first switch to the second switch, the second packet is being sent from the source host to the second switch. At what time will the second packet be fully received at the first switch?

c. How long does it take to move the file from source host to destination host when message segmentation is used? Compare this result with your answer in part (a) and comment.

d. Discuss the drawbacks of message segmentation.

21. Experiment with the message-segmentation Java applet at the book's Web site. Do the delays in the applet correspond to the delays in the previous question? How do link propagation delays affect the overall end-to-end delay for packet switching (with message segmentation) and for message switching?

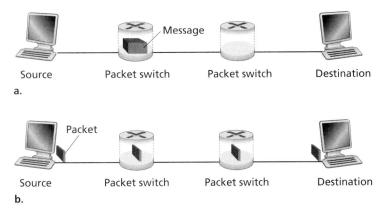

Figure 1.21 ♦ End-to-end message transport: (a) without message segmentation; (b) with message segmentation.

22. Consider sending a large file of F bits from Host A to Host B. There are two links (and one switch) between A and B, and the links are uncongested (that is, no queuing delays). Host A segments the file into segments of S bits each and adds 40 bits of header to each segment, forming packets of $L = 40 + S$ bits. Each link has a transmission rate of R bps. Find the value of S that minimizes the delay of moving the file from Host A to Host B. Disregard propagation delay.

Discussion Questions

1. What types of wireless cellular services are available in your area?

2. Using the 802.11 wireless LAN technology, design a home network for your home or your parents' home. List the specific product models in your home network along with their costs.

3. What is PC-to-phone? Find some of the Web sites of companies that are in the PC-to-phone business.

4. What is Short Message Service (SMS)? Is this service popular in any part of the world, and if so, where and how popular? Is it possible to send an SMS message from a Web site to a portable phone?

5. What is streaming of stored audio? Describe some of the existing products for Internet audio streaming. Find some of the Web sites of companies that are in the Internet audio-streaming business.

6. What is Internet video conferencing? Describe some of the existing products for Internet video conferencing. Find some of the Web sites of companies that are in the Internet video-conferencing business.

7. Find five companies that provide P2P file-sharing services. For each company, what kind of files (that is, content) do they handle?

8. What is instant messaging? Are there any products that allow you to access an instant messaging service through a handheld device?

9. Who invented ICQ, the first instant messaging service? When was it invented and how old were the inventors? Similarly, who invented Napster? When was it invented and how old were the inventors?

10. Compare and contrast Wi-Fi wireless Internet access and 3G wireless Internet access. What are the bit rates of the two services? What are the costs? Discuss roaming and access ubiquity.

11. Why has Napster ceased to exist? What is the RIAA and what measures is it taking to limit P2P file sharing of copyrighted content? What is the difference between direct and indirect copyright infringement?

12. Do you think that 10 years from now there will still be widespread sharing of copyrighted files over computer networks? Why or why not? Elaborate.

Ethereal Lab 1

"Tell me and I forget. Show me and I remember. Involve me and I understand."
Chinese proverb

One's understanding of network protocols can often be greatly deepened by seeing them in action and by playing around with them—observing the sequence of messages exchanged between two protocol entities, delving into the details of protocol operation, and causing protocols to perform certain actions, and observing these actions and their consequences. This can be done in simulated scenarios or in a real network environment such as the Internet. The Java applets in the textbook Web site take the first approach. In the Ethereal labs, we'll take the latter approach. You'll run network applications in various scenarios using a computer on your desk, at home, or in a lab. You'll observe the network protocols in your computer, interacting and exchanging messages with protocol entities executing elsewhere in the Internet. Thus, you and your computer will be an integral part of these live labs. You'll observe—and you'll learn—by doing.

The basic tool for observing the messages exchanged between executing protocol entities is called a **packet sniffer**. As the name suggests, a packet sniffer passively copies (sniffs) messages being sent from and received by your computer; it also displays the contents of the various protocol fields of these captured messages. A screenshot of the Ethereal packet sniffer is shown in Figure 1.22. Ethereal is a free packet sniffer that runs on Windows, Linux/Unix, and Mac computers. In Chapters 1 through 5, you will find Ethereal labs that allow you to explore a number of the protocols studied in the chapter. In this first Ethereal lab, you'll obtain and install a copy of Ethereal, access a Web site, and capture and examine the protocol messages being exchanged between your Web browser and the Web server.

You can find full details about this first Ethereal lab (including instructions about how to obtain and install Ethereal) at the Web site http://www.awl.com/kurose-ross.

command memo

listing of captured packets

details of selected packet header

packet **content** in hexadecimal and ASCII

```
<capture> - Ethereal                                                    _ □ X
File  Edit  Capture  Display  Tools                                        Help

No. .  Time       Source            Destination       Protocol  Info
28  11.620320  192.168.1.105    165.193.123.224   HTTP    GET /kurose-ross HTTP/1.1
30  11.664644  165.193.123.224  192.168.1.105     HTTP    HTTP/1.1 302 Moved Temporarily
34  11.690459  192.168.1.105    165.193.123.218   HTTP    GET /kurose-ross HTTP/1.1
36  11.717668  165.193.123.218  192.168.1.105     HTTP    HTTP/1.1 302 Moved Temporarily
40  11.740930  192.168.1.105    165.193.123.218   HTTP    GET /kurose-ross/ HTTP/1.1
42  11.773356  165.193.123.218  192.168.1.105     HTTP    HTTP/1.1 200 OK
43  11.773602  165.193.123.218  192.168.1.105     HTTP    Continuation
52  11.855518  192.168.1.105    209.202.161.132   HTTP    GET /aw_kurose_network_2/ HTTP/1.1
56  11.889120  209.202.161.132  192.168.1.105     HTTP    HTTP/1.1 304 Not Modified
58  11.921507  192.168.1.105    209.202.161.132   HTTP    GET /aw_kurose_network_2/0,7240,227080-top,00.h
61  11.950999  192.168.1.105    209.202.161.132   HTTP    GET /aw_kurose_network_2/0,7240,227080-main,00.
62  11.970119  209.202.161.132  192.168.1.105     HTTP    HTTP/1.1 304 Not Modified
63  11.984506  192.168.1.105    209.202.161.132   HTTP    GET /wps/media/styles/20/_wps_style/space.gif H
65  12.003191  209.202.161.132  192.168.1.105     HTTP    HTTP/1.1 304 Not Modified
66  12.017287  192.168.1.105    209.202.161.132   HTTP    GET /wps/media/styles/20/_wps_style/logoaw.jpg
67  12.019972  209.202.161.132  192.168.1.105     HTTP    HTTP/1.1 304 Not Modified

⊞ Frame 30 (250 bytes on wire, 250 bytes captured)
⊞ Ethernet II, Src: 00:06:25:da:af:73, Dst: 00:08:74:4f:36:23
⊞ Internet Protocol, Src Addr: 165.193.123.224 (165.193.123.224), Dst Addr: 192.168.1.105 (192.168.1.105)
⊞ Transmission Control Protocol, Src Port: http (80), Dst Port: 4621 (4621), Seq: 3337260317, Ack: 3624086792, Len
⊟ Hypertext Transfer Protocol
    HTTP/1.1 302 Moved Temporarily\r\n
    Server: Netscape-Enterprise/3.6 SP3\r\n
    Date: Mon, 11 Aug 2003 02:17:06 GMT\r\n
    Location: http://www.aw-bc.com/kurose-ross\r\n
    Content-length: 0\r\n
    Content-type: text/html\r\n
    \r\n

0000  00 08 74 4f 36 23 00 06  25 da af 73 08 00 45 00   ..tO6#.. %..s..E.
0010  00 ec 2a cd 40 00 32 06  39 8c a5 c1 7b e0 c0 a8   ..*.@.2. 9...{...
0020  01 69 00 50 12 0d c6 ea  8d 1d d8 03 2d 08 50 18   .i.P.... ....-.P.
0030  fd 5c 49 3d 00 00 48 54  54 50 2f 31 2e 31 20 33   .\I=..HT TP/1.1 3
0040  30 32 20 4d 6f 76 65 64  20 54 65 6d 70 6f 72 61   02 Moved Tempora

Filter: http                                      / Reset Apply File: <capture> Drops: 0
```

Figure 1.22 ♦ An Ethereal screen shot

Leonard Kleinrock

Leonard Kleinrock is a professor of computer science at the University of California, Los Angeles. In 1969, his computer at UCLA became the first node of the Internet. His creation of packet-switching principles in 1961 became the technology behind the Internet. Leonard is also the chairman and founder of Nomadix, Inc., a company whose technology provides greater accessibility of broadband Internet service. He received his B.E.E. from the City College of New York (CCNY) and his masters and PhD in electrical engineering from MIT.

What made you decide to specialize in networking/Internet technology?

As a PhD student at MIT in 1959, I looked around and found that most of my classmates were doing research in the area of information theory and coding theory. At MIT, there was the great researcher, Claude Shannon, who had launched these fields and had solved most of the important problems already. The research problems that were left were hard and of lesser consequence. So I decided to launch out in a new area that no one else had yet conceived of. Remember that at MIT I was surrounded by lots of computers, and it was clear to me that soon these machines would need to communicate with each other. At the time, there was no effective way for them to do so, so I decided to develop the technology that would permit efficient data networks to be created.

What was your first job in the computer industry? What did it entail?

I went to the evening session at CCNY from 1951 to 1957 for my bachelor's degree in electrical engineering. During the day, I worked first as a technician and then as an engineer at a small, industrial electronics firm called Photobell. While there, I introduced digital technology to their product line. Essentially, we were using photoelectric devices to detect the presence of certain items (boxes, people, etc.) and the use of a circuit known then as a *bistable multivibrator* was just the kind of technology we needed to bring digital processing into this field of detection. These circuits happen to be the building blocks for computers, and have come to be known as *flip-flops* or *switches* in today's vernacular.

What was going through your mind when you sent the first host-to-host message (from UCLA to the Stanford Research Institute)?

The first host-to-host message was a bit of an anticlimax. In my mind, the more impressive first event took place on September 2, 1969, when the first piece of networking equipment (the IMP) connected to the first operational system in the outside world (my host computer at UCLA). That's when the Internet was born. Earlier that year, I was quoted in a UCLA press release saying that once the network was up and running, it would be possible to gain access to computer utilities from our homes and offices as easily as we gain access to electricity and telephone connectivity. So my vision at that time was that the Internet would be ubiquitous, always on, always available, anyone with any device could connect from any location, and it would be invisible. However, I never anticipated that my 94-year-old mother would be on the Internet today—and indeed she is!

What is your vision for the future of networking?

The clearest part of my vision is that of nomadic computing and smart spaces. The availability of lightweight, inexpensive, high-performance, portable computing devices plus the ubiquity of the Internet has enabled us to become nomads. *Nomadic computing* refers to the technology that enables end users who travel from place to place to gain access to Internet services in a transparent fashion, no matter where they travel. However, nomadic computing is only one step. The next step will enable us to move out from the netherworld of cyberspace to the physical world of smart spaces. Our environments (desks, walls, vehicles, watches, belts, and so on) will come alive with technology, through actuators, sensors, logic, processing, storage, cameras, microphones, speakers, displays, and communication. This embedded technology will allow our environment to provide the IP services we want. When I walk into a room, the room will know I entered. I will be able to communicate with my environment naturally, as in spoken English; my requests will generate replies that present Web pages to me from wall displays, through my eyeglasses, as speech, holograms, and so forth.

Looking a bit further out, I see a networking future that includes the following additional key components. I see intelligent software agents deployed across the network whose function it is to mine data, act on that data, observe trends, and carry out tasks dynamically and adaptively. I see considerably more network traffic generated not so much by humans, but by these embedded devices and these intelligent software agents. I see large collections of self-organizing systems controlling this vast, fast network. I see huge amounts of information flashing across this network instantaneously with this information undergoing enormous processing and filtering. The Internet will essentially be a pervasive global nervous system. I see all these things and more as we move headlong through the twenty-first century.

What people have inspired you professionally?

By far, it was Claude Shannon from MIT, a brilliant researcher who had the ability to relate his mathematical ideas to the physical world in highly intuitive ways. He was on my Ph.D. thesis committee.

Do you have any advice for students entering the networking/Internet field?

The Internet and all that it enables is a vast new frontier, full of amazing challenges. There is room for great innovation. Don't be constrained by today's technology. Reach out and imagine what could be and then make it happen.

2

Application Layer

Network applications are the *raisons d'etre* of a computer network. If we couldn't conceive of any useful applications, there wouldn't be any need to design networking protocols to support them. Over the past 35 years, numerous ingenious and wonderful network applications have been created. These applications include the classic text-based applications that became popular in the 1980s: text e-mail, remote access to computers, file transfers, newsgroups, and text chat. They include the killer application of the mid-1990s: the Web. They include many multimedia applications, such as streaming video, Internet radio, Internet telephony, and video conferencing. And they include the two killer applications introduced at the end of the millennium—instant messaging with contact lists, and peer-to-peer (P2P) file sharing.

In this chapter we study the conceptual and implementation aspects of network applications. We begin by defining key application-layer concepts, including application-layer protocols, clients and servers, processes, sockets, and transport-layer interfaces. We then examine several network applications in detail, including the Web, e-mail, DNS, and P2P file sharing.

We then cover network application development, over both TCP and UDP. In particular, we study the socket API and walk through some simple client-server applications in Java. As an example, we explore how a simple Web server can be created in Java. We also provide several fun and interesting socket programming assignments at the end of the chapter.

The application layer is a particularly good place to start our study of protocols. It's familiar ground. We're acquainted with many of the applications that rely on the protocols we will study. It will give us a good feel for what protocols are all about and will introduce us to many of the same issues that we'll see again when we study transport, network, and link layer protocols.

2.1 Principles of Network Applications

Let's begin by listing examples of popular network applications:

- Electronic mail
- The Web
- Instant messaging
- Login into a remote computer such as Telnet and SSH
- P2P file sharing
- File transfer between two accounts on two computers, such as FTP
- Multi-user networked games
- Streaming stored video clips
- Internet phone
- Real-time video conferencing

We'll discuss many of these applications in varying levels of detail in this book. For example, in this chapter we'll cover e-mail, the Web, and P2P file sharing. In Chapter 7, which covers multimedia networking, we'll cover video streaming and Internet telephony.

Now suppose you have a great idea for a new network application. Perhaps this application will be a great service to humanity, or will please your professor, or will bring you great wealth, or will simply be fun to develop. Whatever your motivation may be, let's now examine how you transform the idea into a real-world network application.

At the core of network application development is writing programs that run on different end systems and communicate with each other over the network. For example, in the Web application there are two distinct programs that communicate with each other: the browser program running in the user's host (desktop, laptop, PDA, cell phone, and so on); and the Web server program running in the Web server host. As another example, in a P2P file-sharing system there is a program in each host that participates in the file-sharing community. In this case, the programs in each of the hosts may be similar or identical.

Thus, when developing your new application, you need to write software that will run on multiple machines. Importantly, you do not need to write software that runs on network-core devices, such as routers or Ethernet switches. Even if you wanted to write application software for the network-core devices, you wouldn't be able to do so. As we learned in Chapter 1, and as shown earlier in Figure 1.18, network-core devices do not function at the application layer; they function at lower layers, specifically at the network layer and below. This basic design—namely, confining the application software to the end systems—as shown in Figure 2.1, has facilitated the rapid development and deployment of a vast array of Internet applications.

2.1.1 Network Application Architectures

When building a new network application, you'll first need to decide on the application's architecture. Indeed, before diving into software coding, you should have a broad architectural plan for your application. Keep in mind that an application's architecture is distinctly different from the network architecture (e.g., the five-layer Internet architecture discussed in Chapter 1). From the application developer's perspective, the network architecture is fixed and provides a specific set of services to applications. The **application architecture**, on the other hand, is designed by the application developer and dictates how the application is organized over the various end systems. In choosing the application architecture, an application developer will likely draw on one of the three predominant architectures used in modern network applications: the client-server architecture, the P2P architecture, and a hybrid of the client-server and P2P architectures.

In a **client-server architecture**, there is an always-on host, called the *server*, which services requests from many other hosts, called *clients*. The client hosts can be either sometimes-on or always-on. A classic example is the Web application for which an always-on Web server services requests from browsers running on client hosts. When a Web server receives a request for an object from a client host, it responds by sending the requested object to the client host. Note that with the client-server architecture, clients do not directly communicate with each other; for example, in the Web application, two browsers do not directly communicate. Another characteristic of the client-server architecture is that the server has a fixed, well-known address, called an IP address (which we'll discuss soon). Because the server has a fixed, well-known address, and because the server is always on, a client can always contact the server by sending a packet to the server's address. Some of the better-known applications with a client-server architecture include the Web, file transfer, remote login, and e-mail. This client-server architecture is shown in Figure 2.2(a).

Often in a client-server application, a single server host is incapable of keeping up with all the requests from its clients. For example, a popular news Web site can quickly become overwhelmed if it has only one server handling all of its requests.

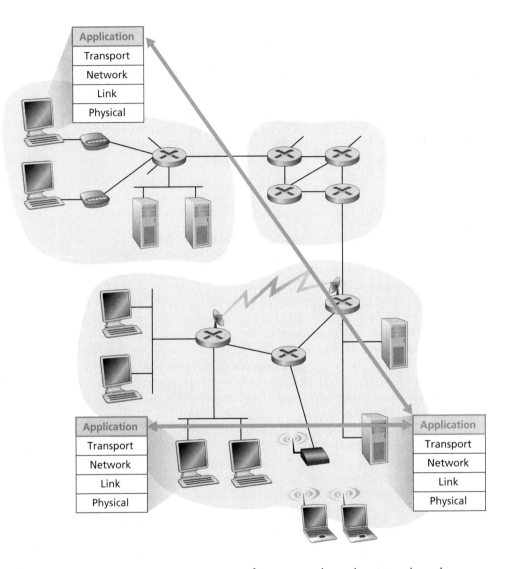

Figure 2.1   ♦   Communication for a network application takes place between end systems at the application layer.

For this reason, clusters of hosts—sometimes referred to as a **server farm**—are often used to create a powerful virtual server in client-server architectures.

In a pure **P2P architecture**, there isn't an always-on server at the center of the application. Instead, arbitrary pairs of hosts, called *peers*, communicate directly with each other. Because the peers communicate without passing through some special server, the architecture is called peer-to-peer. In the P2P architecture, none of the participating hosts is required to be always on; in addition, a participating host may change its IP address each time it comes on. A nice example of an application that has a pure P2P architecture is Gnutella [Gnutella 2004], an open-source P2P file-sharing application. In Gnutella, any host can request files, send files, query to find where a file is located, respond to queries, and forward queries. We'll examine Gnutella in more detail in Section 2.6. The P2P architecture is illustrated in Figure 2.2 (b).

One of the greatest strengths of the P2P architecture is its scalability. For example, in a P2P file-sharing application, millions of peers may participate in the file-sharing community, with each one functioning as a server and contributing resources to the community. Thus, while each peer will generate workload by requesting files, each peer also adds service capacity to the system by responding to the requests of other peers. Thus, in principle, P2P file sharing is intrinsically scalable—each additional peer not only increases demand but also increases service capacity. In today's Internet, P2P file-sharing traffic accounts for a major fraction of all traffic [Saroiu 2002].

On the other hand, because of the highly distributed and decentralized nature of P2P applications, they can be difficult to manage. For example, one peer may have the only copy of an important file, and that peer can drop out of the community at

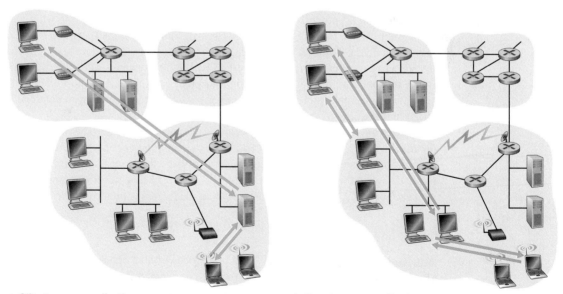

a. Client-server application   **b. Peer-to-peer application**

Figure 2.2 ♦ (a) Client-server architecture; (b) P2P architecture.

any time. It remains an open question whether it is possible to build industrial-strength P2P solutions for enterprise applications [Adya 2004].

Client-server and P2P are two common architectures for network applications. However, many applications are organized as **hybrids** of the client-server and P2P architectures. One such example is now defunct Napster, which was the first of the popular MP3 file-sharing applications. Napster is P2P in the sense that MP3 files are exchanged directly among peers, without passing through dedicated, always-on servers; but Napster is also client-server in the sense that a peer queries a central server to determine which currently-up peers have a desired MP3 file. (The Napster architecture is covered in more detail in Section 2.6.) Another application that uses a hybrid architecture is instant messaging. In instant messaging, the chatting between two users is typically P2P; that is, the text sent between the two users does not pass through an always-on, intermediate server. However, when Alice launches her instant messaging application, she registers herself at a central server; and when Bob wants to chat with someone on his buddy list, his instant messaging client contacts the central server to find out which buddies are currently online and available.

2.1.2 Processes Communicating

Before building your network application, you also need a basic understanding of how the programs, running in multiple end systems, communicate with each other. In the jargon of operating systems, it is not actually programs but **processes** that are communicating. A process can be thought of as a program that is running within an end system. When communicating processes are running on the same end system, they communicate with each other using interprocess communication. The rules for interprocess communication are governed by the end system's operating system. But in this book we are not interested in how processes on the same host communicate, but instead in how processes running on *different* end systems (with potentially different operating systems) communicate.

Processes on two different end systems communicate with each other by exchanging **messages** across the computer network. A sending process creates and sends messages into the network; a receiving process receives these messages and possibly responds by sending messages back. Figure 2.1 illustrates that processes communicate with each other by using the application layer of the five-layer protocol stack.

Client and Server Processes

A network application consists of pairs of processes that send messages to each other over a network. For example, in the Web application a client browser process exchanges messages with a Web server process. In a P2P file-sharing system, a file is transferred from a process in one peer to a process in another peer. For each pair of communicating processes, we typically label one of the two processes as the **client** and the other process as the **server**. With the Web, a browser is a client process and a Web server is a server process. With P2P file sharing, the peer that is downloading the file is labeled as the client, and the peer that is uploading the file is labeled as the server.

You may have observed that in some applications, such as in P2P file sharing, a process can be both a client and server. Indeed, a process in a P2P file-sharing system can both upload and download files. Nevertheless, in the context of any given communication session between a pair of processes, we can still label one process as the client and the other process as the server. We define the client and server processes as follows:

> *In the context of a communication session between a pair of processes, the process that initiates the communication (that is, initially contacts the other process at the beginning of the session) is labeled as the **client**. The process that waits to be contacted to begin the session is the **server**.*

In the Web, a browser process initializes contact with a Web server process; hence the browser process is the client and the Web server process is the server. In P2P file sharing, when Peer A asks Peer B to send a specific file, Peer A is the client and Peer B is the server in the context of this specific communication session. When there's no confusion, we'll sometimes also use the terminology "client side and server side of an application." At the end of this chapter, we'll step through simple code for both the client and server sides of network applications.

There is one point in our terminology that may need some clarification. In Section 2.1.1 we classified applications as having client-server, P2P, or hybrid architectures. The classification is useful, as it provides a general framework for architecting network applications. However, we need to keep in mind that most network applications—including applications with the P2P architecture—consist of multiple pairs of communicating processes; as part of a communication session between a pair of processes, one process is labeled as the client and the other is labeled as the server.

Sockets

As noted above, most applications consist of pairs of communicating processes, with the two processes in each pair sending messages to each other. Any message sent from one process to another must go through the underlying network. A process sends messages into, and receives messages from, the network through its **socket**. Let's consider an analogy to help us understand processes and sockets. A process is analogous to a house and its socket is analogous to its door. When a process wants to send a message to another process on another host, it shoves the message out its door (socket) and into the network. This sending process assumes that there is a transportation infrastructure on the other side of its door that will transport the message across the network to the door of the destination process. Once the message arrives at the destination host, the message passes through the receiving process's door (socket), and the receiving process then acts on the message.

Figure 2.3 illustrates socket communication between two processes that communicate over the Internet. (Figure 2.3 assumes that the underlying transport protocol is TCP, although the UDP protocol could be used as well in the Internet.) As shown in this figure, a socket is the interface between the application layer and the transport layer within a host. It is also referred to as the **application programming interface (API)** between the application and the network, since the socket is the programming interface with which network applications are built in the Internet. The application developer has control of everything on the application-layer side of the socket but has little control of the transport-layer side of the socket. The only control that the application developer has on the transport-layer side is (1) the choice of transport protocol and (2) perhaps the ability to fix a few transport-layer parameters such as maximum buffer and maximum segment sizes. Once the application developer chooses a transport protocol (if a choice is available), the application is built using the transport-layer services provided by that protocol. We'll explore sockets in some detail in Sections 2.7 and 2.8.

Addressing Processes

In order for a process on one host to send a message to a process on another host, the sending process must identify the receiving process. To identify the receiving process, two pieces of information need to be specified: (1) the name or address of the host and (2) an identifier that specifies the receiving process in the destination host.

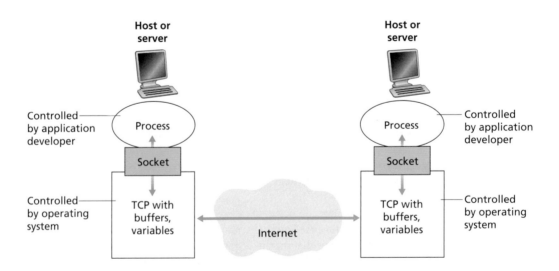

Figure 2.3   ◆   Application processes, sockets, and underlying transport protocol

Let us first consider host addresses. In Internet applications, the destination host is identified by its **IP address**. We'll discuss IP addresses in great detail in Chapter 4. For now, it suffices to know that the IP address is a 32-bit quantity that *uniquely* identifies the host (more precisely, it uniquely identifies the network interface that connects that host to the Internet). Since the IP address of any host connected to the public Internet must be *globally* unique, the assignment of IP addresses must be carefully managed, as discussed in Chapter 4.

In addition to knowing the address of the host to which a message is destined, the sending host must also identify the receiving process running in the host. This information is needed because in general a host could be running many network applications. A destination **port number** serves this purpose. Popular applications have been assigned specific port numbers. For example, a Web server is identified by port number 80. A mail server process (using the SMTP protocol) is identified by port number 25. A list of well-known port numbers for all Internet standard protocols can be found at http://www.iana.org. When a developer creates a new network application, the application must be assigned a new port number. We'll examine port numbers in detail in Chapter 3.

2.1.3 Application-Layer Protocols

We have just learned that network processes communicate with each other by sending messages into sockets. But how are these messages structured? What are the meanings of the various fields in the messages? When do the processes send the messages? These questions bring us into the realm of application-layer protocols. An **application-layer protocol** defines how an application's processes, running on different end systems, pass messages to each other. In particular, an application-layer protocol defines:

♦ The types of messages exchanged, for example, request messages and response messages

♦ The syntax of the various message types, such as the fields in the message and how the fields are delineated

♦ The semantics of the fields, that is, the meaning of the information in the fields

♦ Rules for determining when and how a process sends messages and responds to messages

Some application-layer protocols are specified in RFCs and are therefore in the public domain. For example, the Web's application-layer protocol, HTTP (the Hyper-Text Transfer Protocol [RFC 2616]), is available as an RFC. If a browser developer follows the rules of the HTTP RFC, the browser will be able to retrieve Web pages from any Web server that has also followed the rules of the HTTP RFC. Many other application-layer protocols are proprietary and intentionally not available in the public domain. For example, many of the existing P2P file-sharing systems use proprietary application-layer protocols.

It is important to distinguish between network applications and application-layer protocols. An application-layer protocol is only one piece (albeit, a big piece) of a network application. Let's look at a couple of examples. The Web is a client-server application that allows users to obtain documents from Web servers on demand. The Web application consists of many components, including a standard for document formats (that is, HTML), Web browsers (for example, Netscape Navigator and Microsoft Internet Explorer), Web servers (for example, Apache, Microsoft, and Netscape servers), and an application-layer protocol. The Web's application-layer protocol, HTTP, defines the format and sequence of the messages that are passed between browser and Web server. Thus, HTTP is only one piece of the Web application. As another example, consider the Internet e-mail application. Internet electronic mail also has many components, including mail servers that house user mailboxes; mail readers that allow users to read and create messages; a standard for defining the structure of an e-mail message; and application-layer protocols that define how messages are passed between servers, how messages are passed between servers and mail readers, and how the contents of certain parts of the mail message (for example, a mail message header) are to be interpreted. The principal application-layer protocol for electronic mail is SMTP (Simple Mail Transfer Protocol) [RFC 2821]. Thus, e-mail's principal application-layer protocol, SMTP, is only one piece (albeit, a big piece) of the e-mail application.

2.1.4 What Services Does an Application Need?

Recall that a socket is the interface between the application process and the transport-layer protocol. The application at the sending side pushes messages through the door. At the other side of the door, the transport-layer protocol has the responsibility of getting the messages to the door at the receiving process.

Many networks, including the Internet, provide more than one transport-layer protocol. When you develop an application, you must choose one of the available transport-layer protocols. How do you make this choice? Most likely, you would study the services that are provided by the available transport-layer protocols, and you would pick the protocol that has the services that best match the needs of your application. The situation is similar to choosing either train or airplane transport for travel between two cities. You have to choose one or the other, and each transportation mode offers different services. (For example, the train offers downtown pickup and drop-off, whereas the plane offers shorter travel time.)

What services might a network application need from a transport-layer protocol? We can broadly classify an application's service requirements along three dimensions: data loss, bandwidth, and timing.

Reliable Data Transfer

Some applications, such as electronic mail, instant messaging, file transfer, remote host access, Web document transfers, and financial applications require fully reliable data transfer, that is, no data loss. In particular, a loss of file data, or data in a financial transaction, can have devastating consequences (in the latter case, for either the bank or the customer!). Other **loss-tolerant applications**, most notably multimedia applications such as real-time audio/video or stored audio/video, can tolerate some amount of data loss. In these multimedia applications, lost data might result in a small glitch in the played-out audio/video—not a crucial impairment. The effects of such loss on application quality, and actual amount of tolerable packet loss, will depend strongly on the application and the coding scheme used.

Bandwidth

Some applications must be able to transmit data at a certain rate in order to be effective. For example, if an Internet telephony application encodes voice at 32 kbps, then it must be able to send data into the network and have data delivered to the receiving application at this rate. If this amount of bandwidth is not available, the application needs to encode at a different rate (and receive enough bandwidth to sustain this different coding rate) or it should give up, since receiving half of the needed bandwidth is of no use to such a **bandwidth-sensitive application**. Many current multimedia applications are bandwidth sensitive, but future multimedia applications may use adaptive coding techniques to encode at a rate that matches the currently available bandwidth. While bandwidth-sensitive applications require a given amount of bandwidth, **elastic applications** can make use of as much or as little bandwidth as happens to be available. Electronic mail, file transfer, and Web transfers are all elastic applications. Of course, the more bandwidth, the better. There's an adage that says that one cannot be too rich, too thin, or have too much bandwidth!

Timing

The final service requirement is that of timing. Interactive real-time applications, such as Internet telephony, virtual environments, teleconferencing, and multiplayer games require tight timing constraints on data delivery in order to be effective. For example, many of these applications require that end-to-end delays be on the order of a few hundred milliseconds or less. (See Chapter 7, [Gauthier 1999; Ramjee 1994].) Long delays in Internet telephony, for example, tend to result in unnatural pauses in the conversation; in a multiplayer game or virtual interactive environment, a long delay between taking an action and seeing the response from the environment (for example, from another player at the end of an end-to-end connection) makes the application feel less realistic. For non-real-time applications, lower delay is always preferable to higher delay, but no tight constraint is placed on the end-to-end delays.

Figure 2.4 summarizes the reliability, bandwidth and the timing requirements of some popular and emerging Internet applications. Figure 2.4 outlines only a few of the key requirements of the more popular Internet applications. Our goal here is not to provide a complete classification, but simply to identify some of the most important axes along which network application requirements can be classified.

2.1.5 Services Provided by the Internet Transport Protocols

The Internet (and, more generally, TCP/IP networks) makes two transport protocols available to applications, UDP and TCP. When you (as a software developer) create a new network application for the Internet, one of the first decisions that you must make is whether to use UDP or TCP. Each of these protocols offers a different service model to the invoking applications.

TCP Services

The TCP service model includes a connection-oriented service and a reliable data transfer service. When an application invokes TCP for its transport protocol, the application receives both of these services from TCP.

♦ *Connection-oriented service:* TCP has the client and server exchange transport-layer control information with each other *before* the application-level messages begin to flow. This so-called handshaking procedure alerts the client and server, allowing them to prepare for an onslaught of packets. After the handshaking phase, a **TCP connection** is said to exist between the sockets of the two

Application	Data Loss	Bandwidth	Time-Sensitive
File transfer	No loss	Elastic	No
E-mail	No loss	Elastic	No
Web documents	No loss	Elastic (few kbps)	No
Real-time audio/video	Loss-tolerant	Audio: few kbps–1 Mbps Video: 10 kbps–5 Mbps	Yes: 100s of msec
Stored audio/video	Loss-tolerant	Same as above	Yes: few seconds
Interactive games	Loss-tolerant	Few kbps–10 kbps	Yes: 100s of msec
Instant messaging	No loss	Elastic	Yes and no

Figure 2.4 ♦ Requirements of selected network applications

processes. The connection is a full-duplex connection in that the two processes can send messages to each other over the connection at the same time. When the application is finished sending messages, it must tear down the connection. The service is referred to as a "connection-oriented" service rather than a "connection" service because the two processes are connected in a very loose manner. In Chapter 3 we'll discuss connection-oriented service in detail and examine how it is implemented.

♦ *Reliable transport service:* The communicating processes can rely on TCP to deliver all data sent without error and in the proper order. When one side of the application passes a stream of bytes into a socket, it can count on TCP to deliver the same stream of bytes to the receiving socket, with no missing or duplicate bytes.

TCP also includes a congestion-control mechanism, a service for the general welfare of the Internet rather than for the direct benefit of the communicating processes. The TCP congestion-control mechanism throttles a sending process (client or server) when the network is congested between sender and receiver. As we will see in Chapter 3, TCP congestion control aslo attempts to limit each TCP connection to its fair share of network bandwidth.

The throttling of the transmission rate can have a very harmful effect on real-time audio and video applications that have a minimum required bandwidth constraint. Moreover, real-time applications are loss-tolerant and do not need a fully reliable transport service. For these reasons, developers of real-time applications usually run their applications over UDP rather than TCP.

Having outlined the services provided by TCP, let us say a few words about the services that TCP does *not* provide. First, TCP does not guarantee a minimum transmission rate. In particular, a sending process is not permitted to transmit at any rate it pleases; instead the sending rate is regulated by TCP congestion control, which may force the sender to send at a low average rate. Second, TCP does not provide any delay guarantees. In particular, when a sending process passes data into a TCP socket, the data will eventually arrive at the receiving process, but TCP guarantees absolutely no limit on how long the data may take to get there. As many of us have experienced with the "world wide wait," one can sometimes wait tens of seconds or even minutes for TCP to deliver a message (containing, for example, an HTML file) from Web server to Web client. In summary, TCP guarantees delivery of all data, but provides no guarantees on the rate of delivery or on the delays experienced.

UDP Services

UDP is a no-frills, lightweight transport protocol with a minimalist service model. UDP is connectionless, so there is no handshaking before the two processes start to communicate. UDP provides an unreliable data transfer service—that is, when a process sends a message into a UDP socket, UDP provides *no* guarantee that the message will ever reach the receiving process. Furthermore, messages that do arrive to the receiving process may arrive out of order.

UDP does not include a congestion-control mechanism, so a sending process can pump data into a UDP socket at any rate it pleases (although not all the data may make it to the receiving socket). Because real-time applications usually can tolerate some loss but require a minimal rate, developers of real-time applications often choose to run their applications over UDP, thereby circumventing TCP's congestion control and packet overheads. Similar to TCP, UDP provides no guarantee on delay.

Figure 2.5 indicates the transport protocols used by some popular Internet applications. We see that e-mail, remote terminal access, the Web, and file transfer all use TCP. These applications have chosen TCP primarily because TCP provides a reliable data transfer service, guaranteeing that all data will eventually get to its destination. We also see that Internet telephony typically runs over UDP. Each side of an Internet phone application needs to send data across the network at some minimum rate (see real-time audio in Figure 2.4); this is more likely to be possible with UDP than with TCP. Also, Internet phone applications are loss-tolerant, so they do not need the reliable data transfer service provided by TCP.

As noted earlier, neither TCP nor UDP offers timing guarantees. Does this mean that time-sensitive applications cannot run in today's Internet? The answer is clearly no—the Internet has been hosting time-sensitive applications for many years. These applications often work fairly well because they have been designed to cope, to the greatest extent possible, with this lack of guarantee. We'll investigate several of these design tricks in Chapter 7. Nevertheless, clever design has its limitations when delay is excessive, as is often the case in the public Internet. In summary, today's Internet can often provide satisfactory service to time-sensitive applications, but it cannot provide any timing or bandwidth guarantees. In Chapter 7, we'll also discuss

Applications	Application-Layer Protocol	Underlying Transport Protocol
Electronic mail	SMTP [RFC 2821]	TCP
Remote terminal access	Telnet [RFC 854]	TCP
Web	HTTP [RFC 2616]	TCP
File transfer	FTP [RFC 959]	TCP
Remote file server	NFS [McKusik 1996]]	UDP or TCP
Streaming multimedia	Often proprietary (e.g., Real Networks)	UDP or TCP
Internet telephony	Often proprietary (e.g., Net2phone)	Typically UDP

Figure 2.5 ♦ Popular Internet applications, their application-layer protocols, and their underlying transport protocols

emerging Internet service models that provide new services, including guaranteed delay service for time-sensitive applications.

2.1.6 Network Applications Covered in This Book

New public domain and proprietary Internet applications are being developed every day. Rather than covering a large number of Internet applications in an encyclopedic manner, we have chosen to focus on a small number of applications that are both pervasive and important. In this chapter we discuss five important applications: the Web, file transfer, electronic mail, directory service, and P2P file sharing. We first discuss the Web, not only because it is an enormously popular application, but also because its application-layer protocol, HTTP, is straightforward and easy to understand. After covering the Web, we briefly examine FTP, because it provides a nice contrast to HTTP. We then discuss electronic mail, the Internet's first killer application. E-mail is more complex than the Web in the sense that it makes use of not one but several application-layer protocols. After e-mail, we cover DNS, which provides a directory service for the Internet. Most users do not interact with DNS directly; instead, users invoke DNS indirectly through other applications (including the Web, file transfer, and electronic mail). DNS illustrates nicely how a piece of core network functionality (network-name to network-address translation) can be implemented at the application layer in the Internet. Finally, we discuss P2P file sharing, which by some measures (e.g., network traffic) is the most popular class of applications in the Internet today.

2.2 The Web and HTTP

Until the 1990s the Internet was used primarily by researchers, academics, and university students to log in to remote hosts, to transfer files from local hosts to remote hosts and vice versa, to receive and send news, and to receive and send electronic mail. Although these applications were (and continue to be) extremely useful, the Internet was essentially unknown outside of the academic and research communities. Then, in the early 1990s, a major new application arrived on the scene—the World Wide Web [Berners-Lee 1994]. The Web is the Internet application that caught the general public's eye. It dramatically changed how people interact inside and outside their work environments. It elevated the Internet from just one of many data networks (including online networks such as Prodigy, America Online, and CompuServe, national data networks such as Minitel/ Transpac in France, private X.25, and frame relay networks) to essentially the one and only data network.

History is sprinkled with the arrival of electronic communication technologies that have had major societal impacts. The first such technology was the telephone, invented in the 1870s. The telephone allowed two persons to communicate orally in real time without being in the same physical location. The next significant electronic communication technology was broadcast radio/television, which arrived in the 1920s and 1930s. Broadcast radio/television allowed people to receive vast quantities of audio and video information. The Internet is yet another electronic communication technology with a major societal impact. E-mail and the Web, two of its most popular applications, have revolutionized how we live and work. We'll discuss e-mail in Section 2.4. We'll cover the Web and its application-later protocol in this section.

Perhaps what appeals the most to users is that the Web operates *on demand*. Users receive what they want, when they want it. This is unlike broadcast radio and television, which force users to tune in when the content provider makes the content available. In addition to being available on demand, the Web has many other wonderful features that people love and cherish. It is enormously easy for any individual to make information available over the Web–everyone can become a publisher at extremely low cost. Hyperlinks and search engines help us navigate through an ocean of Web sites. Graphics stimulate our senses. Forms, Java applets, and many other devices enable us to interact with pages and sites. And more and more, the Web provides a menu interface to vast quantities of audio and video material stored in the Internet—multimedia that can be accessed on demand.

2.2.1 Overview of HTTP

The **HyperText Transfer Protocol (HTTP)**, the Web's application-layer protocol, is at the heart of the Web. It is defined in [RFC 1945] and [RFC 2616]. HTTP is implemented in two programs: a client program and a server program. The client program and server program, executing on different end systems, talk to each other by exchanging HTTP messages. HTTP defines the structure of these messages and how the client and server exchange the messages. Before explaining HTTP in detail, we should review some Web terminology.

A **Web page** (also called a document) consists of objects. An **object** is simply a file—such as an HTML file, a JPEG image, a GIF image, a Java applet, an audio clip, and so on—that is addressable by a single URL. Most Web pages consist of a **base HTML file** and several referenced objects. For example, if a Web page contains HTML text and five JPEG images, then the Web page has six objects: the base HTML file plus the five images. The base HTML file references the other objects in the page with the objects' URLs. Each URL has two components: the host name of the server that houses the object and the object's path name. For example, the URL

```
http://www.someSchool.edu/someDepartment/picture.gif
```

has `www.someSchool.edu` for a host name and `/someDepartment/picture.gif` for a path name. A **browser** is a user agent for the Web; it displays the requested Web page to the user and provides numerous navigational and configuration features. Because Web browsers also implement the client side of HTTP, in the context of the Web, we will use the words *browser* and *client* interchangeably.

Popular Web browsers include Netscape Communicator and Microsoft Internet Explorer. A **Web server** houses Web objects, each addressable by a URL. Web servers also implement the server side of HTTP. Popular Web servers include Apache and Microsoft Internet Information Server. (Netcraft provides a nice survey of Web server penetration [Netcraft 2004].)

HTTP defines how Web clients (for example, browsers) request Web pages from Web servers and how servers transfer Web pages to clients. We discuss the interaction between client and server in detail later, but the general idea is illustrated in Figure 2.6. When a user requests a Web page (for example, clicks on a hyperlink), the browser sends HTTP request messages for the objects in the page to the server. The server receives the requests and responds with HTTP response messages that contain the objects. Through 1997 essentially all browsers and Web servers implemented version HTTP/1.0, which is defined in RFC 1945. Beginning in 1998, Web servers and browsers began to implement version HTTP/1.1, which is defined in RFC 2616. HTTP/1.1 is backward compatible with HTTP/1.0; a Web server running 1.1 can "talk" with a browser running 1.0, and a browser running 1.1 can "talk" with a server running 1.0. Because HTTP/1.1 is now dominant, henceforth when we refer to HTTP we are referring to HTTP/1.1.

HTTP uses TCP as its underlying transport protocol (rather than running on top of UDP). The HTTP client first initiates a TCP connection with the server. Once the connection is established, the browser and the server processes access TCP through their socket interfaces. As described in Section 2.1, on the client side the socket interface is the door between the client process and the TCP connection; on the server side it is the door between the server process and the TCP connection. The

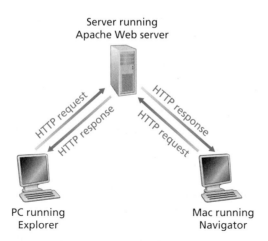

Server running
Apache Web server

HTTP request

HTTP response

HTTP response

HTTP request

PC running
Explorer

Mac running
Navigator

Figure 2.6 ♦ HTTP request-response behavior

client sends HTTP request messages into its socket interface and receives HTTP response messages from its socket interface. Similarly, the HTTP server receives request messages from its socket interface and sends response messages into its socket interface. Once the client sends a message into its socket interface, the message is out of the client's hands and is "in the hands" of TCP. Recall from Section 2.1 that TCP provides a reliable data transfer service to HTTP. This implies that each HTTP request message emitted by a client process eventually arrives intact at the server; similarly, each HTTP response message emitted by the server process eventually arrives intact at the client. Here we see one of the great advantages of a layered architecture—HTTP need not worry about lost data or the details of how TCP recovers from loss or reordering of data within the network. That is the job of TCP and the protocols in the lower layers of the protocol stack.

It is important to note that the server sends requested files to clients without storing any state information about the client. If a particular client asks for the same object twice in a period of a few seconds, the server does not respond by saying that it just served the object to the client; instead, the server resends the object, as it has completely forgotten what it did earlier. Because an HTTP server maintains no information about the clients, HTTP is said to be a **stateless protocol**.

We also remark that the Web uses the client-server application architecture, as described in Section 2.1. A Web server is always-on, with a fixed IP address, and it services requests from potentially millions of different browsers.

2.2.2 Nonpersistent and Persistent Connections

HTTP can use both nonpersistent connections and persistent connections. Although HTTP uses persistent connections in its default mode, HTTP clients and servers can also be configured to use non-persistent connections instead. We'll examine both non persistent and persistent HTTP connections in this subsection.

Nonpersistent Connections

Let us walk through the steps of transferring a Web page from server to client for the case of nonpersistent connections. Suppose the page consists of a base HTML file and 10 JPEG images, and that all 11 of these objects reside on the same server. Suppose the URL for the base HTML file is

```
http://www.someSchool.edu/someDepartment/home.index
```

Here is what happens:

1. The HTTP client process initiates a TCP connection to the server
   `www.someSchool.edu` on port number 80, which is the default port number for HTTP.

2. The HTTP client sends an HTTP request message to the server via its socket associated with the TCP connection. The request message includes the path name /someDepartment/home.index. (We will discuss the HTTP messages in some detail below.)

3. The HTTP server process receives the request message via its socket associated with the connection, retrieves the object /someDepartment/home.index from its storage (RAM or disk), encapsulates the object in an HTTP response message, and sends the response message to the client via its socket.

4. The HTTP server process tells TCP to close the TCP connection. (But TCP doesn't actually terminate the connection until it knows for sure that the client has received the response message intact.)

5. The HTTP client receives the response message. The TCP connection terminates. The message indicates that the encapsulated object is an HTML file. The client extracts the file from the response message, examines the HTML file, and finds references to the 10 JPEG objects.

6. The first four steps are then repeated for each of the referenced JPEG objects.

As the browser receives the Web page, it displays the page to the user. Two different browsers may interpret (that is, display to the user) a Web page in somewhat different ways. HTTP has nothing to do with how a Web page is interpreted by a client. The HTTP specifications ([RFC 1945] and [RFC 2616]) define only the communication protocol between the client HTTP program and the server HTTP program.

The steps above illustrate the use of nonpersistent connections, where each TCP connection is closed after the server sends the object—the connection does not persist for other objects. Note that each TCP connection transports exactly one request message and one response message. Thus, in this example, when a user requests the Web page, 11 TCP connections are generated.

In the steps described above, we were intentionally vague about whether the client obtains the 10 JPEGs over 10 serial TCP connections, or whether some of the JPEGs are obtained over parallel TCP connections. Indeed, users can configure modern browsers to control the degree of parallelism. In their default modes, most browsers open 5 to 10 parallel TCP connections, and each of these connections handles one request-response transaction. If the user prefers, the maximum number of parallel connections can be set to one, in which case the 10 connections are established serially. As we'll see in the next chapter, the use of parallel connections shortens the response time.

Before continuing, let's do a back-of-the-envelope calculation to estimate the amount of time that elapses from when a client requests the base HTML file until the entire file is received by the client. To this end, we define the **round-trip time (RTT)**, which is the time it takes for a small packet to travel from client to server and then back to the client. The RTT includes packet-propagation delays, packet-queuing delays in intermediate routers and switches, and packet-processing delays.

(These delays were discussed in Section 1.6.) Now consider what happens when a user clicks on a hyperlink. As shown in Figure 2.7, this causes the browser to initiate a TCP connection between the browser and the Web server; this involves a "three-way handshake"—the client sends a small TCP segment to the server, the server acknowledges and responds with a small TCP segment, and, finally, the client acknowledges back to the server. The first two parts of the three-way handshake take one RTT. After completing the first two parts of the handshake, the client sends the HTTP request message combined with the third part of the three-way handshake (the acknowledgment) into the TCP connection. Once the request message arrives at the server, the server sends the HTML file into the TCP connection. This HTTP request/response eats up another RTT. Thus, roughly, the total response time is two RTTs plus the transmission time at the server of the HTML file.

Persistent Connections

Nonpersistent connections have some shortcomings. First, a brand-new connection must be established and maintained for *each requested object*. For each of these

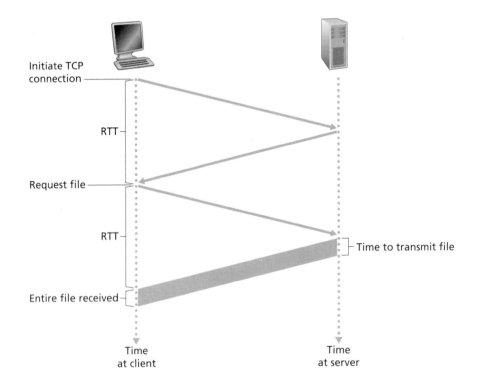

Figure 2.7   ♦   Back-of-the-envelope calculation for requesting an HTML file

connections, TCP buffers must be allocated and TCP variables must b
the client and server. This can place a serious burden on the Web serv
be serving requests from hundreds of different clients simultaneou
we just described, each object suffers a delivery delay of two RT⁷
establish the TCP connection and one RTT to request and receive a'

With persistent connections, the server leaves the TCP conn
sending a response. Subsequent requests and responses between the .
server can be sent over the same connection. In particular, an entire Web page .
the example above, the base HTML file and the ten images) can be sent over a single persistent TCP connection. Moreover, multiple Web pages residing on the same
server can be sent from the server to the same client over a single persistent TCP
connection. Typically, the HTTP server closes a connection when it isn't used for a
certain time (a configurable timeout interval).

There are two versions of persistent connections: **without pipelining** and **with
pipelining**. For the version without pipelining, the client issues a new request only
when the previous response has been received. In this case, the client experiences
one RTT in order to request and receive each of the referenced objects (the 10
images in the example above). Although this is an improvement over nonpersistent's
two RTTs per object, the RTT delay can be further reduced with pipelining. Another
disadvantage of no pipelining is that after the server sends an object over the persistent TCP connection, the connection idles—does nothing—while it waits for
another request to arrive. This idling wastes server resources.

The default mode of HTTP uses persistent connections with pipelining. With
pipelining, the HTTP client issues a request as soon as it encounters a reference.
Thus the HTTP client can make back-to-back requests for the referenced objects;
that is, it can make a new request before receiving a response to a previous request.
When the server receives the back-to-back requests, it sends the objects back-to-
back. With pipelining, it is possible for only one RTT to be expended for all the referenced objects (rather than one RTT per referenced object when pipelining isn't
used). Furthermore, the pipelined TCP connection remains idle for a smaller fraction of time. We'll quantitatively compare the performance of nonpersistent and persistent connections in the homework problems of Chapters 2 and 3. You are also
encouraged to see [Heidemann 1997; Nielsen 1997].

2.2.3 HTTP Message Format

The HTTP specifications [RFC 2616]) include the definitions of the HTTP message
formats. There are two types of HTTP messages, request messages and response
messages, both of which are discussed below.

HTTP Request Message

Below we provide a typical HTTP request message:

```
GET /somedir/page.html HTTP/1.1
Host: www.someschool.edu
Connection: close
User-agent: Mozilla/4.0
Accept-language: fr
```

We can learn a lot by taking a close look at this simple request message. First of all, we see that the message is written in ordinary ASCII text, so that your ordinary computer-literate human being can read it. Second, we see that the message consists of five lines, each followed by a carriage return and a line feed. The last line is followed by an additional carriage return and line feed. Although this particular request message has five lines, a request message can have many more lines or as few as one line. The first line of an HTTP request message is called the **request line**; the subsequent lines are called the **header lines**. The request line has three fields: the method field, the URL field, and the HTTP version field. The method field can take on several different values, including GET, POST, and HEAD. The great majority of HTTP request messages use the GET method. The GET method is used when the browser requests an object, with the requested object identified in the URL field. In this example, the browser is requesting the object /somedir/page.html. The version is self-explanatory; in this example, the browser implements version HTTP/1.1.

Now let's look at the header lines in the example. The header line Host: www.someschool.edu specifies the host on which the object resides. You might think that this header line is unnecessary, as there is already a TCP connection in place to the host. But, as we'll see in Section 2.2.6, the information provided by the host header line is required by Web proxy caches. By including the Connection: close header line, the browser is telling the server that it doesn't want to bother with persistent connections; it wants the server to close the connection after sending the requested object. The User-agent: header line specifies the user agent, that is, the browser type that is making the request to the server. Here the user agent is Mozilla/4.0, a Netscape browser. This header line is useful because the server can actually send different versions of the same object to different types of user agents. (Each of the versions is addressed by the same URL.) Finally, the Accept-language: header indicates that the user prefers to receive a French version of the object, if such an object exists on the server; otherwise, the server should send its default version. The Accept-language: header is just one of many content negotiation headers available in HTTP.

Having looked at an example, let us now look at the general format of a request message, as shown in Figure 2.8. We see that the general format closely follows our earlier example. You may have noticed, however, that after the header lines (and the additional carriage return and line feed) there is an "entity body." The entity body is empty with the GET method, but is used with the POST method. An HTTP client often uses the POST method when the user fills out a form—for example, when a user provides search words to a search engine. With a POST message, the user is still requesting a Web page from the server, but the specific contents of the Web page depend on what the user entered into the form fields. If the value of the method field is POST, then the entity body contains what the user entered into the form fields.

We would be remiss if we didn't mention that a request generated with a form does not necessarily use the POST method. Instead, HTML forms often use the GET method and include the inputted data (in the form fields) in the requested URL. For example, if a form uses the GET method, has two fields, and the inputs to the two fields are monkeys and bananas, then the URL will have the structure www.somesite.com/animalsearch?monkeys&bananas. In your day-to-day Web surfing, you have probably noticed extended URLs of this sort.

The HEAD method is similar to the GET method. When a server receives a request with the HEAD method, it responds with an HTTP message but it leaves out the requested object. Application developers often use the HEAD method for debugging.

The HTTP/1.0 specification allows for only three types of methods: GET, POST, and HEAD. In addition to these three methods, the HTTP/1.1 specification allows for several additional methods, including PUT and DELETE. The PUT method is often used in conjunction with Web publishing tools. It allows a user to upload an object to a specific path (directory) on a specific Web server. The PUT method is also used by applications that need to upload objects to Web servers. The DELETE method allows a user, or an application, to delete an object on a Web server.

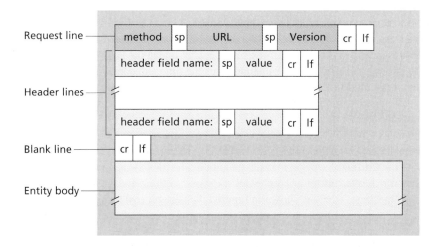

Figure 2.8 ◆ General format of a request message

HTTP Response Message

Below we provide a typical HTTP response message. This response message could be the response to the example request message just discussed.

```
HTTP/1.1 200 OK
Connection: close
Date: Thu, 03 Jul 2003 12:00:15 GMT
Server: Apache/1.3.0 (Unix)
Last-Modified: Sun, 5 May 2003 09:23:24 GMT
Content-Length: 6821
Content-Type: text/html

(data data data data data ...)
```

Let's take a careful look at this response message. It has three sections: an initial **status line**, six **header lines**, and then the **entity body**. The entity body is the meat of the message—it contains the requested object itself (represented by `data data data data data ...`). The status line has three fields: the protocol version field, a status code, and a corresponding status message. In this example, the status line indicates that the server is using HTTP/1.1 and that everything is OK (that is, the server has found, and is sending, the requested object).

Now let's look at the header lines. The server uses the `Connection: close` header line to tell the client that it is going to close the TCP connection after sending the message. The `Date:` header line indicates the time and date when the HTTP response was created and sent by the server. Note that this is not the time when the object was created or last modified; it is the time when the server retrieves the object from its file system, inserts the object into the response message, and sends the response message. The `Server:` header line indicates that the message was generated by an Apache Web server; it is analogous to the `User-agent:` header line in the HTTP request message. The `Last-Modified:` header line indicates the time and date when the object was created or last modified. The `Last-Modified:` header, which we will soon cover in more detail, is critical for object caching, both in the local client and in network cache servers (also known as proxy servers). The `Content-Length:` header line indicates the number of bytes in the object being sent. The `Content-Type:` header line indicates that the object in the entity body is HTML text. (The object type is officially indicated by the `Content-Type:` header and not by the file extension.)

Having looked at an example, let us now examine the general format of a response message, which is shown in Figure 2.9. This general format of the response message matches the previous example of a response message. Let's say a few additional words about status codes and their phrases. The status code and associated phrase indicate the result of the request. Some common status codes and associated phrases include:

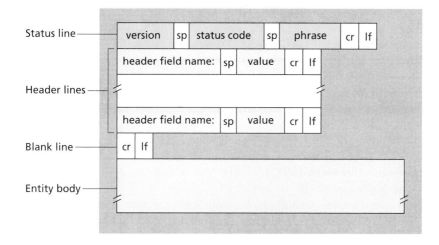

Figure 2.9 ♦ General format of a response message

♦ **200 OK:** Request succeeded and the information is returned in the response.

♦ **301 Moved Permanently:** Requested object has been permanently moved; new URL is specified in **Location:** header of the response message. The client software will automatically retrieve the new URL.

♦ **400 Bad Request:** This is a generic error code indicating that the request could not be understood by the server.

♦ **404 Not Found:** The requested document does not exist on this server.

♦ **505 HTTP Version Not Supported:** The requested HTTP protocol version is not supported by the server.

How would you like to see a real HTTP response message? This is highly recommended and very easy to do! First Telnet into your favorite Web server. Then type in a one-line request message for some object that is housed on the server. For example, if you have access to a command prompt, type:

```
telnet cis.poly.edu 80
```

```
GET /~ross/ HTTP/1.1
Host: cis.poly.edu
```

(Press the carriage return twice after typing the last line.) This opens a TCP connection to port 80 of the host **cis.poly.edu** and then sends the HTTP request message. You should see a response message that includes the base HTML file of

Professor Ross's homepage. If you'd rather just see the HTTP message lines and not receive the object itself, replace GET with HEAD. Finally, replace /~ross/ with /~banana/ and see what kind of response message you get.

In this section we discussed a number of header lines that can be used within HTTP request and response messages. The HTTP specification defines many, many more header lines that can be inserted by browsers, Web servers, and network cache servers. We have covered only a small number of the totality of header lines. We'll cover a few more below and another small number when we discuss network Web caching in Section 2.2.6. A highly readable and comprehensive discussion of the HTTP protocol, including its headers and status codes, is given in [Krishnamurty 2001]; see also [Luotonen 1998] for a developer's view. An excellent introduction to the Web is [Yeager 1996].

How does a browser decide which header lines to include in a request message? How does a Web server decide which header lines to include in a response message? A browser will generate header lines as a function of the browser type and version (for example, an HTTP/1.0 browser will not generate any 1.1 header lines), the user configuration of the browser (for example, preferred language), and whether the browser currently has a cached, but possibly out-of-date, version of the object. Web servers behave similarly: There are different products, versions, and configurations, all of which influence which header lines are included in response messages.

2.2.4 User-Server Interaction: Cookies

We mentioned above that an HTTP server is stateless. This simplifies server design and has permitted engineers to develop high performance Web servers that can handle thousands of simultaneous TCP connections. However, it is often desirable for a Web site to identify users, either because the server wishes to restrict user access or because it wants to serve content as a function of the user identity. For these purposes, HTTP uses cookies.

Cookies, defined in the RFC 2109, allow sites to keep track of users. Although not all sites use cookies, most major portal (for example, Yahoo), e-commerce (for example, Amazon), and advertising (for example, DoubleClick) sites make extensive use of cookies.

Cookie technology has four components: (1) a cookie header line in the HTTP response message; (2) a cookie header line in the HTTP request message; (3) a cookie file kept on the user's end system and managed by the user's browser; (4) a back-end database at the Web site. Let's walk through an example of how cookies are used. Suppose Susan, who always accesses the Web using Internet Explorer from her home PC, contacts an e-commerce site for the first time, and this site uses cookies. When the request comes into the Web server, the Web site creates a unique identification number and creates an entry in its back-end database that is indexed by the identification number. The server then responds to Susan's browser, including in the

HTTP response a `Set-cookie:` header, which contains the identification number. For example, the header line might be:

```
Set-cookie: 1678453
```

When Susan's browser receives the HTTP response message, it sees the `Set-cookie:` header. The browser then appends a line to the special cookie file that the browser manages. This line includes the host name of the server and the identification number in the `Set-cookie:` header. As Susan continues to browse this e-commerce site, each time she requests a Web page, her browser consults her cookie file, extracts her identification number for this site, and puts in the HTTP request a cookie header line that includes the identification number. Specifically, each of her HTTP requests to the e-commerce server includes the header line:

```
Cookie: 1678453
```

In this manner, the Web site is able to track Susan's activity at the Web site. Although the Web site does not necessarily know Susan's name, it knows exactly which pages user 1678453 visited, in which order, and at what times! The e-commerce site could then use cookies to provide a shopping cart service—during a particular session with the site, the site can maintain a list of all of Susan's purchases, so that she can pay for them collectively at the end of the session.

If Susan returns to the site, say, one week later, her browser will continue to put the header line `Cookie: 1678453` in the request messages. The e-commerce site can recommend products to Susan based on Web pages she has visited at the site in the past. If Susan also registers herself with the site—providing full name, e-mail address, postal address, and credit card information—the e-commerce site can then include this information in its database, thereby associating Susan's name with her identification number (and all of the pages she has visited at the site in the past!). This is how some e-commerce sites provide "one-click shopping"—when Susan chooses to purchase an item during a subsequent visit, she doesn't need to re-enter her name, credit card number, or address.

From this discussion we see that cookies can be used to identify a user. The first time a user visits a site, the user can provide a user identification (possibly his or her name). The browser then passes a cookie header to the server during all subsequent visits to the site, thereby identifying the user to the server. We also see from this discussion that cookies can be used to create a user session layer on top of stateless HTTP. For example, when a user logs into a Web-based e-mail application, the browser sends cookie information to the server, permitting the server to identify the user throughout the user's session with the application.

Although cookies often simplify the Internet shopping experience for the user, they remain highly controversial because they can also be considered as an infringement on a user's privacy. As we just saw, using a combination of cookies and user-supplied account information, a Web site can learn a lot about a user and potentially sell what it knows to some third party. Furthermore, cookies can also be used to gather information about a particular user's behavior *across* a large number of Web sites. Indeed, Web pages that display banner ads use HTTP request messages to obtain the banner ads (which are GIFs or JPEGs) from the HTTP server of an advertising agency. Each of the requests to the advertising agency's HTTP server can contain a cookie that is managed by the advertising agency. Because major Internet advertising agencies supply banner ads to many Web sites, the agency can build a profile about an individual's browsing patterns across multiple sites.

We conclude by pointing the reader to Persistent Client State HTTP Cookies [Netscape Cookie 1999], which provides an in-depth but readable introduction to cookies. We also recommend Cookie Central [Cookie Central 2004], which includes extensive information on the cookie controversy.

2.2.5 HTTP Content

Throughout this chapter we have tacitly assumed that the data carried in HTTP response messages are objects from Web pages, that is, HTML files, GIFs, JPEGs, Java applets, and so on. We have presented HTTP in the context of the Web in order to give an example with a concrete and familiar application—namely, Web surfing. But we would be remiss not to mention that HTTP is often used to transfer many other sorts of files.

For example, HTTP is often used today in electronic commerce applications to transfer XML files from one machine to another, with neither of these machines involving a browser or a user. Banks often use XML to structure banking information (such as customer account information), and banking machines often use HTTP to exchange this XML structured information. (A discussion of XML is beyond the scope of this book. We will just say here that a typical XML document provides structured data and an indication of the meaning of the data; typically, it does not provide formatting indications, as does HTML.) HTTP is also used to transfer VoiceXML, WML (the WAP markup language), and other XML document types. Moreover, as we'll see at the end of this chapter, HTTP is often used as the file transfer protocol for P2P file sharing. And as we'll see in Chapter 7, HTTP is frequently used for streaming stored audio and video content.

2.2.6 Web Caching

A **Web cache**—also called a **proxy server**—is a network entity that satisfies HTTP requests on the behalf of an origin Web server. The Web cache has its own disk storage and keeps copies of recently requested objects in this storage. As shown in Figure 2.10, a user's browser can be configured so that all of the user's HTTP requests are first directed to the Web cache. Once a browser is configured, each browser request for an object is first directed to the Web cache. As an example, suppose a browser is requesting the object `http://www.someschool.edu/ campus.gif`. Here is what happens:

1. The browser establishes a TCP connection to the Web cache and sends an HTTP request for the object to the Web cache.
2. The Web cache checks to see if it has a copy of the object stored locally. If it does, the Web cache forwards the object within an HTTP response message to the client browser.
3. If the Web cache does not have the object, the Web cache opens a TCP connection to the origin server, that is, to `www.someschool.edu`. The Web cache then sends an HTTP request for the object into the TCP connection. After receiving this request, the origin server sends the object within an HTTP response to the Web cache.
4. When the Web cache receives the object, it stores a copy in its local storage and forwards a copy, within an HTTP response message, to the client browser (over the existing TCP connection between the client browser and the Web cache).

Note that a cache is both a server and a client at the same time. When it receives requests from and sends responses to a browser, it is a server. When it sends requests to and receives responses from an origin server, it is a client.

Typically a Web cache is purchased and installed by an ISP. For example, a university might install a cache on its campus network and configure all of the campus browsers to point to the cache. Or a major residential ISP (such as AOL) might

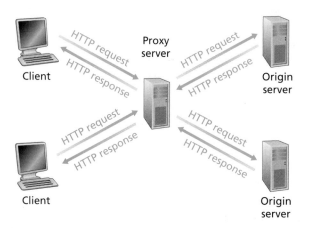

Figure 2.10 ♦ Clients requesting objects through a Web cache

install one or more caches in its network and preconfigure its shipped browsers to point to the installed caches.

Web caching has seen deployment in the Internet for two reasons. First, a Web cache can substantially reduce the response time for a client request, particularly if the bottleneck bandwidth between the client and the origin server is much less than the bottleneck bandwidth between the client and the cache. If there is a high-speed connection between the client and the cache, as there often is, and if the cache has the requested object, then the cache will be able to deliver the object rapidly to the client. Second, as we will soon illustrate with an example, Web caches can substantially reduce traffic on an institution's access link to the Internet. By reducing traffic, the institution (for example, a company or a university) does not have to upgrade bandwidth as quickly, thereby reducing costs. Furthermore, Web caches can substantially reduce Web traffic in the Internet as a whole, thereby improving performance for all applications.

To gain a deeper understanding of the benefits of caches, let's consider an example in the context of Figure 2.11. This figure shows two networks—the institutional network and the rest of the public Internet. The institutional network is a high-speed LAN. A router in the institutional network and a router in the Internet are connected by a 1.5 Mbps link. The origin servers are attached to the Internet but are located all over the globe. Suppose that the average object size is 100,000 bits and that the average request rate from the institution's browsers to the origin servers is 15 requests per second. Suppose that the HTTP request messages are negligibly small and thus create no traffic in the networks or in the access link (from institutional router to Internet router). Also suppose that the amount of time it takes from when the router on the Internet side of the access link in Figure 2.11 forwards an HTTP request (within an IP datagram) until it receives the response (typically within many IP datagrams) is two seconds on average. Informally, we refer to this last delay as the "Internet delay."

The total response time—that is, the time from the browser's request of an object until its receipt of the object—is the sum of the LAN delay, the access delay (that is, the delay between the two routers), and the Internet delay. Let's now do a very crude calculation to estimate this delay. The traffic intensity on the LAN (see Section 1.6) is

$$(15 \text{ requests/sec}) \cdot (100 \text{ kbits/request})/(10 \text{ Mbps}) = 0.15$$

whereas the traffic intensity on the access link (from the Internet router to institution router) is

$$(15 \text{ requests/sec}) \cdot (100 \text{ kbits/request})/(1.5 \text{ Mbps}) = 1$$

A traffic intensity of 0.15 on a LAN typically results in, at most, tens of milliseconds of delay; hence, we can neglect the LAN delay. However, as discussed in

Section 1.6, as the traffic intensity approaches 1 (as is the case of the access link in Figure 2.11), the delay on a link becomes very large and grows without bound. Thus, the average response time to satisfy requests is going to be on the order of minutes, if not more, which is unacceptable for the institution's users. Clearly something must be done.

One possible solution is to increase the access rate from 1.5 Mbps to, say, 10 Mbps. This will lower the traffic intensity on the access link to 0.15, which translates to negligible delays between the two routers. In this case, the total response time will roughly be two seconds, that is, the Internet delay. But this solution also means that the institution must upgrade its access link from 1.5 Mbps to 10 Mbps, which can be very costly.

Now consider the alternative solution of not upgrading the access link but instead installing a Web cache in the institutional network. This solution is illustrated in Figure 2.12. Hit rates—the fraction of requests that are satisfied by a

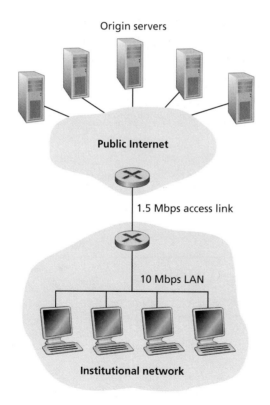

Figure 2.11 ♦ Bottleneck between an institutional network and the Internet

cache—typically range from 0.2 to 0.7 in practice. For illustrative purposes, let us suppose that the cache provides a hit rate of 0.4 for this institution. Because the clients and the cache are connected to the same high-speed LAN, 40 percent of the requests will be satisfied almost immediately, say, within 10 milliseconds, by the cache. Nevertheless, the remaining 60 percent of the requests still need to be satisfied by the origin servers. But with only 60 percent of the requested objects passing through the access link, the traffic intensity on the access link is reduced from 1.0 to 0.6. Typically, a traffic intensity less than 0.8 corresponds to a small delay, say, tens of milliseconds, on a 1.5 Mbps link. This delay is negligible compared with the two-second Internet delay. Given these considerations, average delay therefore is

$$0.4 \cdot (0.01 \text{ seconds}) + 0.6 \cdot (2.01 \text{ seconds})$$

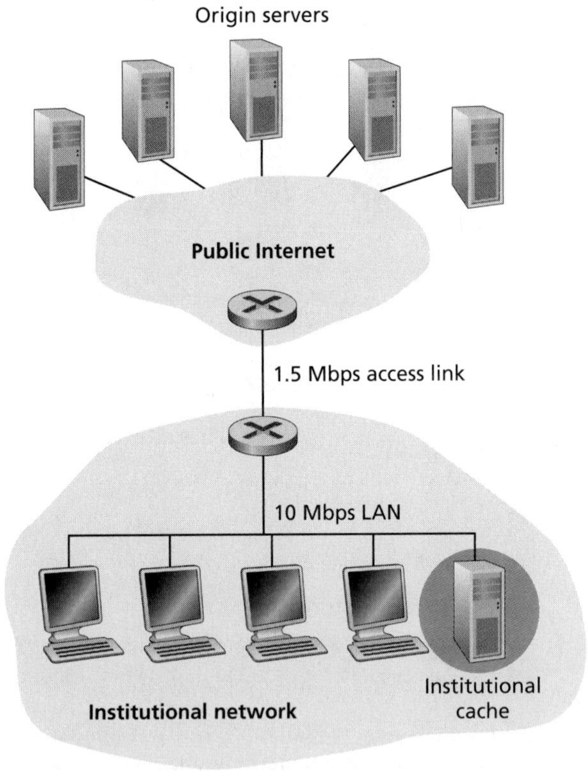

Figure 2.12 ♦ Adding a cache to the institutional network

which is just slightly greater than 1.2 seconds. Thus, this second solution provides an even lower response time than the first solution, and it doesn't require the institution to upgrade its link to the Internet. The institution does, of course, have to purchase and install a Web cache. But this cost is low—many caches use public-domain software that runs on inexpensive PCs.

2.2.7 The Conditional GET

Although caching can reduce user-perceived response times, it introduces a new problem—the copy of an object residing in the cache may be stale. In other words, the object housed in the Web server may have been modified since the copy was cached at the client. Fortunately, HTTP has a mechanism that allows a cache to verify that its objects are up to date. This mechanism is called the **conditional GET**. An HTTP request message is a so-called conditional GET message if (1) the request message uses the `GET` method and (2) the request message includes an `If-Modified-Since:` header line.

To illustrate how the conditional GET operates, let's walk through an example. First, on the behalf of a requesting browser, a proxy cache sends a request message to a Web server:

```
GET /fruit/kiwi.gif HTTP/1.1
Host: www.exotiquecuisine.com
```

Second, the Web server sends a response message with the requested object to the cache:

```
HTTP/1.1 200 OK
Date: Mon, 7 Jul 2003 15:39:29
Server: Apache/1.3.0 (Unix)
Last-Modified: Wed, 2 Jul 2003 09:23:24
Content-Type: image/gif

(data data data data data ...)
```

The cache forwards the object to the requesting browser but also caches the object locally. Importantly, the cache also stores the last-modified date along with the object. Third, one week later, another browser requests the same object via the cache, and the object is still in the cache. Since this object may have been modified at the Web server in the past week, the cache performs an up-to-date check by issuing a conditional GET. Specifically, the cache sends:

```
GET /fruit/kiwi.gif HTTP/1.1
Host: www.exotiquecuisine.com
If-modified-since: Wed, 2 Jul 2003 09:23:24
```

Note that the value of the `If-modified-since:` header line is exactly equal to the value of the `Last-Modified:` header line that was sent by the server one week ago. This conditional GET is telling the server to send the object only if the object has been modified since the specified date. Suppose the object has not been modified since 2 Jul 2003 09:23:24. Then, fourth, the Web server sends a response message to the cache:

```
HTTP/1.1 304 Not Modified
Date: Mon, 14 Jul 2003 15:39:29
Server: Apache/1.3.0 (Unix)
```

(*empty entity body*)

We see that in response to the conditional GET, the Web server still sends a response message but does not include the requested object in the response message. Including the requested object would only waste bandwidth and increase user-perceived response time, particularly if the object is large. Note that this last response message has in the status line 304 Not Modified, which tells the cache that it can go ahead and forward its cached copy of the object to the requesting browser.

2.3 File Transfer: FTP

In a typical FTP session, the user is sitting in front of one host (the local host) and wants to transfer files to or from a remote host. In order for the user to access the remote account, the user must provide a user identification and a password. After providing this authorization information, the user can transfer files from the local file system to the remote file system and vice versa. As shown in Figure 2.13, the user interacts with FTP through an FTP user agent. The user first provides the hostname of the remote host, causing the FTP client process in the local host to establish a TCP connection with the FTP server process in the remote host. The user then provides the user identification and password, which get sent over the TCP connection as part of FTP commands. Once the server has authorized the user, the user copies one or more files stored in the local file system into the remote file system (or vice versa).

HTTP and FTP are both file transfer protocols and have many common characteristics; for example, they both run on top of TCP. However, the two application-layer protocols have some important differences. The most striking difference is that FTP uses two parallel TCP connections to transfer a file, a **control connection** and

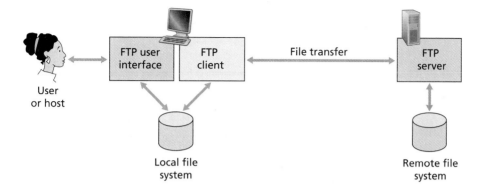

Figure 2.13 ◆ FTP moves files between local and remote file systems

a **data connection**. The control connection is used for sending control information between the two hosts—information such as user identification, password, commands to change remote directory, and commands to "put" and "get" files. The data connection is used to actually send a file. Because FTP uses a separate control connection, FTP is said to send its control information **out-of-band**. In Chapter 7 we'll see that the RTSP protocol, which is used for controlling the transfer of continuous media such as audio and video, also sends its control information out-of-band. HTTP, as you recall, sends request and response header lines into the same TCP connection that carries the transferred file itself. For this reason, HTTP is said to send its control information **in-band**. In the next section we'll see that SMTP, the main protocol for electronic mail, also sends control information in-band. The FTP control and data connections are illustrated in Figure 2.14.

When a user starts an FTP session with a remote host, the client side of FTP (user) first initiates a control TCP connection with the server side (remote host) on server port number 21. The client side of FTP sends the user identification and password over this control connection. The client side of FTP also sends, over the control connection, commands to change the remote directory. When the server side receives over the control connection a command for a file transfer (either to, or from, the remote host), the server side initiates a TCP data connection to the client side. FTP sends exactly one file over the data connection and then closes the data connection. If, during the same session, the user wants to transfer another file, FTP opens another data connection. Thus, with FTP, the control connection remains open throughout the duration of the user session, but a new data connection is created for each file transferred within a session (that is, the data connections are nonpersistent).

Throughout a session, the FTP server must maintain **state** about the user. In particular, the server must associate the control connection with a specific user account,

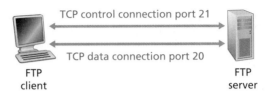

Figure 2.14 ♦ Control and data connections

and the server must keep track of the user's current directory as the user wanders about the remote directory tree. Keeping track of this state information for each ongoing user session significantly constrains the total number of sessions that FTP can maintain simultaneously. Recall that HTTP, on the other hand, is stateless—it does not have to keep track of any user state.

2.3.1 FTP Commands and Replies

We end this section with a brief discussion of some of the more common FTP commands. The commands, from client to server, and replies, from server to client, are sent across the control connection in 7-bit ASCII format. Thus, like HTTP commands, FTP commands are readable by people. In order to delineate successive commands, a carriage return and line feed end each command. Each command consists of four uppercase ASCII characters, some with optional arguments. Some of the more common commands are given below:

♦ **USER username:** Used to send the user identification to the server.

♦ **PASS password:** Used to send the user password to the server.

♦ **LIST:** Used to ask the server to send back a list of all the files in the current remote directory. The list of files is sent over a (new and nonpersistent) data connection rather than the control TCP connection.

♦ **RETR filename:** Used to retrieve (that is, get) a file from the current directory of the remote host. Triggers the remote host to initiate a data connection and to send the requested file over the data connection.

♦ **STOR filename:** Used to store (that is, put) a file into the current directory of the remote host.

There is typically a one-to-one correspondence between the command that the user issues and the FTP command sent across the control connection. Each command is followed by a reply, sent from server to client. The replies are three-digit numbers, with an optional message following the number. This is similar in structure to the status code and phrase in the status line of the HTTP response message;

the inventors of HTTP intentionally included this similarity in the HTTP response messages. Some typical replies, along with their possible messages, are as follows:

- `331 Username OK, password required`
- `125 Data connection already open; transfer starting`
- `425 Can't open data connection`
- `452 Error writing file`

Readers who are interested in learning about the other FTP commands and replies are encouraged to read RFC 959.

2.4 Electronic Mail in the Internet

Electronic mail has been around since the beginning of the Internet. It was the most popular application when the Internet was in its infancy [Segaller 1998], it has become more and more elaborate and powerful over the years, and it continues to evolve. It is one of the Internet's most important killer applications to date.

As is ordinary postal mail, e-mail is an asynchronous communication medium—people send and read messages when it is convenient for them, without having to coordinate with other people's schedules. In contrast with postal mail, electronic mail is fast, easy to distribute, and inexpensive. Modern e-mail has many powerful features. Using mailing lists, e-mail messages and spam can be sent to thousands of recipients at a time. Modern e-mail messages often include attachments, hyperlinks, HTML-formatted text, and photos. For the most part, e-mail has been text-centric, but it can also be used as a platform for asynchronous voice and video messaging [Ross 2003].

In this section we examine the application-layer protocols that are at the heart of Internet e-mail. But before we jump into an in-depth discussion of these protocols, let's take a high-level view of the Internet mail system and its key components.

Figure 2.15 presents a high-level view of the Internet mail system. We see from this diagram that it has three major components: **user agents**, **mail servers**, and the **Simple Mail Transefer Protocol (SMTP)**. We now describe each of these components in the context of a sender, Alice, sending an e-mail message to a recipient, Bob. User agents allow users to read, reply to, forward, save, and compose messages. (User agents for electronic mail are sometimes called *mail readers,* although we generally avoid this term in this book.) When Alice is finished composing her message, her user agent sends the message to her mail server, where the message is placed in the mail server's outgoing message queue. When Bob wants to read a message, his user agent retrieves the message from his mailbox in his mail server. In the late 1990s, graphical user interface (GUI) user agents became popular, allowing users to view and compose multimedia messages. Currently, Eudora, Microsoft's Outlook, and Netscape's Messenger are among the popular GUI user agents for e-mail. There are also many text-based e-mail user interfaces in the public domain, including mail, pine, and elm.

Mail servers form the core of the e-mail infrastructure. Each recipient, such as Bob, has a **mailbox** located in one of the mail servers. Bob's mailbox manages and maintains the messages that have been sent to him. A typical message starts its journey in the sender's user agent, travels to the sender's mail server, and travels to the recipient's mail server, where it is deposited in the recipient's mailbox. When Bob wants to access the messages in his mailbox, the mail server containing his mailbox authenticates Bob (with usernames and passwords). Alice's mail server must also deal with failures in Bob's mail server. If Alice's server cannot deliver mail to Bob's server, Alice's server holds the message in a **message queue** and attempts to transfer the message later. Reattempts are often done every 30 minutes or so; if there is no success after several days, the server removes the message and notifies the sender (Alice) with an e-mail message.

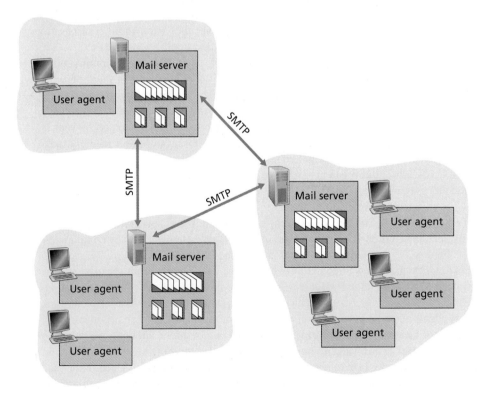

Figure 2.15   ♦   A high-level view of the Internet e-mail system

SMTP is the principal application-layer protocol for Internet electronic mail. It uses the reliable data transfer service of TCP to transfer mail from the sender's mail server to the recipient's mail server. As with most application-layer protocols, SMTP has two sides: a client side, which executes on the sender's mail server, and a server side, which executes on the recipient's mail server. Both the client and server sides of SMTP run on every mail server. When a mail server sends mail to other mail servers, it acts as an SMTP client. When a mail server receives mail from other mail servers it acts as an SMTP server.

CASE HISTORY

HOTMAIL

In December 1995, Sabeer Bhatia and Jack Smith visited the Internet venture capitalist Draper Fisher Jurvetson and proposed developing a free Web-based e-mail system. The idea was to give a free e-mail account to anyone who wanted one, and to make the accounts accessible from the Web. With Web-based e-mail, anyone with access to the Web—say, from a school or community library—could read and send e-mails. Furthermore, Web-based e-mail would offer great mobility to its subscribers. In exchange for 15 percent of the company, Draper Fisher Jurvetson financed Bhatia and Smith, who formed a company called Hotmail. With three full-time people and 12 to 14 part-time people who worked for stock options, they were able to develop and launch the service in July 1996. Within a month after launch they had 100,000 subscribers. The number of subscribers continued to grow rapidly, with all of their subscribers being exposed to advertising banners while reading their e-mail. In December 1997, less than 18 months after launching the service, Hotmail had over 12 million subscribers and was acquired by Microsoft, reportedly for $400 million dollars.

The success of Hotmail is often attributed to its "first-mover advantage" and to the intrinsic "viral marketing" of e-mail. Hotmail had a first-mover advantage because it was the first company to offer Web-based e-mail. Other companies, of course, copied Hotmail's idea, but Hotmail had a six-month lead on them. The coveted first-mover advantage is obtained by having an original idea, and then developing it quickly and secretly. A service or a product is said to have viral marketing if it markets itself. E-mail is a classic example of a service with viral marketing—the sender sends a message to one or more recipients, and then all the recipients become aware of the service. Hotmail demonstrated that the combination of first-mover advantage and viral marketing could produce a killer application. Perhaps some of the students reading this book will be among the new entrepreneurs who conceive and develop first-mover Internet services with inherent viral marketing.

2.4.1 SMTP

SMTP, defined in RFC 2821, is at the heart of Internet electronic mail. As mentioned above, SMTP transfers messages from senders' mail servers to the recipients' mail servers. SMTP is much older than HTTP. (The original SMTP RFC dates back to 1982, and SMTP was around long before that.) Although SMTP has numerous wonderful qualities, as evidenced by its ubiquity in the Internet, it is nevertheless a legacy technology that possesses certain archaic characteristics. For example, it restricts the body (not just the headers) of all mail messages to simple 7-bit ASCII. This restriction made sense in the early 1980s when transmission capacity was scarce and no one was e-mailing large attachments or large image, audio, or video files. But today, in the multimedia era, the 7-bit ASCII restriction is a bit of a pain—it requires binary multimedia data to be encoded to ASCII before being sent over SMTP; and it requires the corresponding ASCII message to be decoded back to binary after SMTP transport. Recall from Section 2.2 that HTTP does not require multimedia data to be ASCII encoded before transfer.

To illustrate the basic operation of SMTP, let's walk through a common scenario. Suppose Alice wants to send Bob a simple ASCII message.

1. Alice invokes her user agent for e-mail, provides Bob's e-mail address (for example, bob@someschool.edu), composes a message, and instructs the user agent to send the message.
2. Alice's user agent sends the message to her mail server, where it is placed in a message queue.
3. The client side of SMTP, running on Alice's mail server, sees the message in the message queue. It opens a TCP connection to an SMTP server, running on Bob's mail server.
4. After some initial SMTP handshaking, the SMTP client sends Alice's message into the TCP connection.
5. At Bob's mail server, the server side of SMTP receives the message. Bob's mail server then places the message in Bob's mailbox.
6. Bob invokes his user agent to read the message at his convenience.

The scenario is summarized in Figure 2.16.

It is important to observe that SMTP does not normally use intermediate mail servers for sending mail, even when the two mail servers are located at opposite ends of the world. If Alice's server is in Hong Kong and Bob's server is in St. Louis, the TCP connection is a direct connection between the Hong Kong and St. Louis servers. In particular, if Bob's mail server is down, the message remains in Alice's mail server and waits for a new attempt—the message does not get placed in some intermediate mail server.

Let's now take a closer look at how SMTP transfers a message from a sending mail server to a receiving mail server. We will see that the SMTP protocol has many

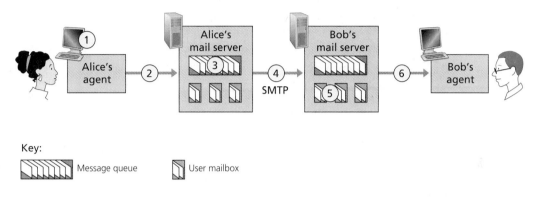

Key:

Message queue   User mailbox

Figure 2.16 ◆ Alice sends a message to Bob

similarities with protocols that are used for face-to-face human interaction. First, the client SMTP (running on the sending mail server host) has TCP establish a connection on port 25 to the server SMTP (running on the receiving mail server host). If the server is down, the client tries again later. Once this connection is established, the server and client perform some application-layer handshaking—just as humans often introduce themselves before transferring information from one to another, SMTP clients and servers introduce themselves before transferring information. During this SMTP handshaking phase, the SMTP client indicates the e-mail address of the sender (the person who generated the message) and the e-mail address of the recipient. Once the SMTP client and server have introduced themselves to each other, the client sends the message. SMTP can count on the reliable data transfer service of TCP to get the message to the server without errors. The client then repeats this process over the same TCP connection if it has other messages to send to the server; otherwise, it instructs TCP to close the connection.

Let's next take a look at an example transcript of messages exchanged between an SMTP client (C) and an SMTP server (S). The host name of the client is `crepes.fr` and the host name of the server is `hamburger.edu`. The ASCII text lines prefaced with `C:` are exactly the lines the client sends into its TCP socket, and the ASCII text lines prefaced with `S:` are exactly the lines the server sends into its TCP socket. The following transcript begins as soon as the TCP connection is established.

```
S: 220 hamburger.edu
C: HELO crepes.fr
```

```
S: 250 Hello crepes.fr, pleased to meet you
C: MAIL FROM: <alice@crepes.fr>
S: 250 alice@crepes.fr ... Sender ok
C: RCPT TO: <bob@hamburger.edu>
S: 250 bob@hamburger.edu ... Recipient ok
C: DATA
S: 354 Enter mail, end with "." on a line by itself
C: Do you like ketchup?
C: How about pickles?
C: .
S: 250 Message accepted for delivery
C: QUIT
S: 221 hamburger.edu closing connection
```

In the example above, the client sends a message ("Do you like ketchup? How about pickles?") from mail server crepes.fr to mail server hamburger.edu. As part of the dialogue, the client issued five commands: HELO (an abbreviation for HELLO), MAIL FROM, RCPT TO, DATA, and QUIT. These commands are self-explanatory. The client also sends a line consisting of a single period, which indicates the end of the message to the server. (In ASCII jargon, each message ends with CRLF.CRLF, where CR and LF stand for carriage return and line feed, respectively.) The server issues replies to each command, with each reply having a reply code and some (optional) English-language explanation. We mention here that SMTP uses persistent connections: If the sending mail server has several messages to send to the same receiving mail server, it can send all of the messages over the same TCP connection. For each message, the client begins the process with a new MAIL FROM: crepes.fr, designates the end of message with an isolated period, and issues QUIT only after all messages have been sent.

It is highly recommended that you use Telnet to carry out a direct dialogue with an SMTP server. To do this, issue

```
telnet serverName 25
```

where serverName is the name of a local mail server. When you do this, you are simply establishing a TCP connection between your local host and the mail server. After typing this line, you should immediately receive the 220 reply from the server. Then issue the SMTP commands HELO, MAIL FROM, RCPT TO, DATA, CRLF.CRLF, and QUIT at the appropriate times. It is also highly recommended that you do Programming Assignment 2 at the end of this chapter. In that assignment, you'll build a simple user agent that implements the client side of SMTP. It will allow you to send and e-mail message to an arbitrary recipient via a local mail server.

2.4.2 Comparison with HTTP

Let us now briefly compare SMTP with HTTP. Both protocols are used to transfer files from one host to another: HTTP transfers files (also called objects) from a Web server to a Web client (typically a browser); SMTP transfers files (that is, e-mail messages) from one mail server to another mail server. When transferring the files, both persistent HTTP and SMTP use persistent connections. Thus, the two protocols have common characteristics. However, there are important differences. First, HTTP is mainly a **pull protocol**—someone loads information on a Web server and users use HTTP to pull the information from the server at their convenience. In particular, the TCP connection is initiated by the machine that wants to receive the file. On the other hand, SMTP is primarily a **push protocol**—the sending mail server pushes the file to the receiving mail server. In particular, the TCP connection is initiated by the machine that wants to send the file.

A second difference, which we alluded to earlier, is that SMTP requires each message, including the body of each message, to be in 7-bit ASCII format. If the message contains characters that are not 7-bit ASCII (for example, French characters with accents) or contains binary data (such as an image file), then the message has to be encoded into 7-bit ASCII. HTTP data does not impose this restriction.

A third important difference concerns how a document consisting of text and images (along with possibly other media types) is handled. As we learned in Section 2.2, HTTP encapsulates each object in its own HTTP response message. Internet mail, as we'll discuss in greater detail below, places all of the message's objects into one message.

2.4.3 Mail Message Formats and MIME

When Alice writes an ordinary snail-mail letter to Bob, she may include all kinds of peripheral header information at the top of the letter, such as Bob's address, her own return address, and the date. Similarly, when an e-mail message is sent from one person to another, a header containing peripheral information precedes the body of the message itself. This peripheral information is contained in a series of header lines, which are defined in RFC 822. The header lines and the body of the message are separated by a blank line (that is, by `CRLF`). RFC 822 specifies the exact format for mail header lines as well as their semantic interpretations. As with HTTP, each header line contains readable text, consisting of a keyword followed by a colon followed by a value. Some of the keywords are required and others are optional. Every header must have a `From:` header line and a `To:` header line; a header may include a `Subject:` header line as well as other optional header lines. It is important to note that these header lines are *different* from the SMTP commands we studied in Section 2.4.1 (even though they contain some common words such as "*from*" and "*to*"). The commands in that section were part of the SMTP handshaking protocol; the header lines examined in this section are part of the mail message itself.

A typical message header looks like this:

```
From: alice@crepes.fr
To: bob@hamburger.edu
Subject: Searching for the meaning of life.
```

After the message header, a blank line follows; then the message body (in ASCII) follows. You should use Telnet to send a message to a mail server that contains some header lines, including the `Subject:` header line. To do this, issue `telnet serverName 25`.

The MIME Extension for Non-ASCII Data

While the message headers described in RFC 822 are satisfactory for sending ordinary ASCII text, they are not sufficiently rich for multimedia messages (for example, messages with images, audio, and video) or for carrying non-ASCII text formats (for example, characters used by languages other than English). To send content other than ASCII text, the sending user agent must include additional headers in the message. These extra headers are defined in RFC 2045 and RFC 2046, the (Multipurpose Internet Mail Extensions (MIME) extensions to RFC 822.

The two key MIME headers for supporting multimedia are the `Content-Type:` header and the `Content-Transfer-Encoding:` header. The `Content-Type:` header allows the receiving user agent to take an appropriate action on the message. For example, by indicating that the message body contains a JPEG image, the receiving user agent can direct the message body to a JPEG decompression routine. To understand the need for the `Content-Transfer-Encoding:` header, recall that non-ASCII text messages must be encoded to an ASCII format that isn't going to confuse SMTP. The `Content-Transfer-Encoding:` header alerts the receiving user agent that the message body has been ASCII-encoded and indicates the type of encoding used. Thus, when a user agent receives a message with these two headers, it first uses the value of the `Content-Transfer-Encoding:` header to convert the message body to its original non-ASCII form, and then uses the `Content-Type:` header to determine what actions it should take on the message body.

Let's take a look at a concrete example. Suppose Alice wants to send a JPEG image to Bob. To do this, Alice invokes her user agent for e-mail, specifies Bob's e-mail address, specifies the subject of the message, and inserts the JPEG image into the message body of the message. (Depending on the user agent Alice uses, she might insert the image into the message as an attachment.) When Alice finishes composing her message, she clicks on "Send." Alice's user agent then generates a MIME message, which might look something like this:

```
From: alice@crepes.fr
To: bob@hamburger.edu
```

```
Subject: Picture of yummy crepe.
MIME-Version: 1.0
Content-Transfer-Encoding: base64
Content-Type: image/jpeg

(base64 encoded data .....
.........................
......base64 encoded data)
```

We observe from the above MIME message that Alice's user agent encoded the JPEG image using base64 encoding. This is one of several encoding techniques standardized in MIME [RFC 2045] for conversion to an acceptable 7-bit ASCII format. Another popular encoding technique is quoted-printable content-transfer-encoding, which is typically used to convert an 8-bit ASCII message (possibly containing non-English characters) to 7-bit ASCII.

When Bob reads his mail with his user agent, his user agent operates on this same MIME message. When Bob's user agent observes the `Content-Transfer-Encoding: base64` header line, it proceeds to decode the base64-encoded message body. The message also includes a `Content-Type: image/jpeg` header line; this indicates to Bob's user agent that the message body should be JPEG decompressed. Finally, the message includes the `MIME-Version:` header, which, of course, indicates the MIME version that is being used. Note that the message otherwise follows the standard RFC 822/SMTP format. In particular, after the message header there is a blank line and then the message body.

The Received Message

We would be remiss if we didn't mention another class of header lines that are inserted by the SMTP *receiving* server. The receiving server, upon receiving a message with RFC 822 and MIME header lines, appends a `Received:` header line to the top of the message; this header line specifies the name of the SMTP server that sent the message (from), the name of the SMTP server that received the message (by), and the time at which the receiving server received the message. Thus, the message seen by the destination user takes the following form:

```
Received: from crepes.fr by hamburger.edu; 12 Oct 98 15:27:39 GMT
From: alice@crepes.fr
To: bob@hamburger.edu
Subject: Picture of yummy crepe.
MIME-Version: 1.0
Content-Transfer-Encoding: base64
Content-Type: image/jpeg
```

```
base64 encoded data .......
..........................................
.......base64 encoded data
```

Almost everyone who has used electronic mail has seen the `Received:` header line (along with the other header lines) preceding e-mail messages. (This line is often directly seen on the screen or when the message is sent to a printer.) You may have noticed that a single message sometimes has multiple `Received:` header lines and a more complex `Return-Path:` header line. This is because a message may be forwarded to more than one SMTP server in the path between sender and recipient. For example, if Bob has instructed his e-mail server `hamburger.edu` to forward all of his messages to `sushi.jp`, then the message read by Bob's user agent would begin with something like:

```
Received: from hamburger.edu by sushi.jp; 3 Jul 01 15:30.01 GMT
Received: from crepes.fr by hamburger.edu; 3 Jul 01 15:17:39 GMT
```

These header lines provide the receiving user agent a trace of the SMTP servers visited as well as timestamps of when the visits occurred.

2.4.4 Mail Access Protocols

Once SMTP delivers the message from Alice's mail server to Bob's mail server, the message is placed in Bob's mailbox. Throughout this discussion we have tacitly assumed that Bob reads his mail by logging onto the server host and then executing a mail reader that runs on that host. Up until the early 1990s this was the standard way of doing things. But today, mail access uses a client-server architecture—the typical user reads e-mail with a client that executes on the user's end system, for example, on an office PC, a laptop, or a PDA. By executing a mail client on a local PC, users enjoy a rich set of features, including the ability to view multimedia messages and attachments.

Given that Bob (the recipient) executes his user agent on his local PC, it is natural to consider placing a mail server on his local PC as well. With this approach, Alice's mail server would dialogue directly with Bob's PC. There is a problem with this approach, however. Recall that a mail server manages mailboxes and runs the client and server sides of SMTP. If Bob's mail server were to reside on his local PC, then Bob's PC would have to remain always on, and connected to the Internet, in order to receive new mail, which can arrive at any time. This is impractical for many Internet users. Instead, a typical user runs a user agent on the local PC but accesses its mailbox stored on an always-on shared mail server. This mail server is shared with other users and is typically maintained by the user's ISP (for example, university or company).

Now let's consider the path an e-mail message takes when it is sent from Alice to Bob. We just learned that at some point along the path the e-mail message needs to be deposited in Bob's mail server. This could be done simply by having Alice's user agent send the message directly to Bob's mail server. And this could be done with SMTP—indeed, SMTP has been designed for pushing e-mail from one host to another. However, typically the sender's user agent does not dialogue directly with the recipient's mail server. Instead, as shown in Figure 2.17, Alice's user agent uses SMTP to push the e-mail message into her mail server, then Alice's mail server uses SMTP (as an SMTP client) to relay the e-mail message to Bob's mail server. Why the two-step procedure? Primarily because without relaying through Alice's mail server, Alice's user agent doesn't have any recourse to an unreachable destination mail server. By having Alice first deposit the e-mail in her own mail server, Alice's mail server can repeatedly try to send the message to Bob's mail server, say every 30 minutes, until Bob's mail server becomes operational. (And if Alice's mail server is down, then she has the recourse of complaining to her system administrator!) The SMTP RFC defines how the SMTP commands can be used to relay a message across multiple SMTP servers.

But there is still one missing piece to the puzzle! How does a recipient like Bob, running a user agent on his local PC, obtain his messages, which are sitting in a mail server within Bob's ISP? Note that Bob's user agent can't use SMTP to obtain the messages because obtaining the messages is a pull operation, whereas SMTP is a push protocol. The puzzle is completed by introducing a special mail access protocol that transfers messages from Bob's mail server to his local PC. There are currently a number of popular mail access protocols, including **Post Office Protocol—Version 3 (POP3)**, **Internet Mail Access Protocol (IMAP)**, and HTTP.

Figure 2.17 provides a summary of the protocols that are used for Internet mail: SMTP is used to transfer mail from the sender's mail server to the recipient's mail server; SMTP is also used to transfer mail from the sender's user agent to the sender's mail server. A mail access protocol, such as POP3, is used to transfer mail from the recipient's mail server to the recipient's user agent.

POP3

POP3 is an extremely simple mail access protocol. It is defined in RFC 1939, which is short and quite readable. Because the protocol is so simple, its functionality is rather limited. POP3 begins when the user agent (the client) opens a TCP connection to the mail server (the server) on port 110. With the TCP connection established, POP3 progresses through three phases: authorization, transaction, and update. During the first phase, authorization, the user agent sends a username and a password (in the clear) to authenticate the user. During the second phase, transaction, the user agent retrieves messages; also during this phase, the user agent can mark messages for deletion, remove deletion marks, and obtain mail statistics. The

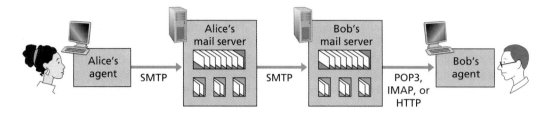

Figure 2.17 ♦ E-mail protocols and their communicating entities

third phase, update, occurs after the client has issued the `quit` command, ending the POP3 session; at this time, the mail server deletes the messages that were marked for deletion.

In a POP3 transaction, the user agent issues commands, and the server responds to each command with a reply. There are two possible responses: +OK (sometimes followed by server-to-client data), used by the server to indicate that the previous command was fine; and −ERR, used by the server to indicate that something was wrong with the previous command.

The authorization phase has two principal commands: `user <user name>` and `pass <password>`. To illustrate these two commands, we suggest that you Telnet directly into a POP3 server, using port 110, and issue these commands. Suppose that `mailServer` is the name of your mail server. You will see something like:

```
telnet mailServer 110
+OK POP3 server ready
user bob
+OK
pass hungry
+OK user successfully logged on
```

If you misspell a command, the POP3 server will reply with an −ERR message.

Now let's take a look at the transaction phase. A user agent using POP3 can often be configured (by the user) to "download and delete" or to "download and keep." The sequence of commands issued by a POP3 user agent depends on which of these two modes the user agent is operating in. In the download-and-delete mode, the user agent will issue the `list`, `retr`, and `dele` commands. As an example, suppose the user has two messages in his or her mailbox. In the dialogue below, **C:** (standing for client) is the user agent and **S:** (standing for server) is the mail server. The transaction will look something like:

```
C: list
S: 1 498
```

```
S: 2 912
S: .
C: retr 1
S: (blah blah ...
S: ................
S: .........blah)
S: .
C: dele 1
C: retr 2
S: (blah blah ...
S: ................
S: .........blah)
S: .
C: dele 2
C: quit
S: +OK POP3 server signing off
```

The user agent first asks the mail server to list the size of each of the stored messages. The user agent then retrieves and deletes each message from the server. Note that after the authorization phase, the user agent employed only four commands: `list`, `retr`, `dele`, and `quit`. The syntax for these commands is defined in RFC 1939. After processing the quit command, the POP3 server enters the update phase and removes messages 1 and 2 from the mailbox.

A problem with this download-and-delete mode is that the recipient, Bob, may be nomadic and want to access his mail messages from multiple machines, for example, his office PC, his home PC, and his portable computer. The download-and-delete mode partitions Bob's mail messages over these three machines; in particular, if Bob first reads a message on his office PC, he will not be able to reread the message from his portable at home later in the evening. In the download-and-keep mode, the user agent leaves the messages on the mail server after downloading them. In this case, Bob can reread messages from different machines; he can access a message from work and access it again later in the week from home.

During a POP3 session between a user agent and the mail server, the POP3 server maintains some state information; in particular, it keeps track of which user messages have been marked deleted. However, the POP3 server does not carry state information across POP3 sessions. This lack of state information across sessions greatly simplifies the implementation of a POP3 server.

IMAP

With POP3 access, once Bob has downloaded his messages to the local machine, he can create mail folders and move the downloaded messages into the folders. Bob can then delete messages, move messages across folders, and search for messages (by sender name or subject). But this paradigm—namely, folders and messages in the local machine—poses a problem for the nomadic user, who would prefer to maintain a folder hierarchy on a remote server that can be accessed from any computer. This is not possible with POP3—the POP3 protocol does not provide any means for a user to create remote folders and assign messages to folders.

To solve this and other problems, the IMAP protocol, defined in RFC 2060, was invented. Like POP3, IMAP is a mail access protocol. It has many more features than POP3, but it is also significantly more complex. (And thus the client and server side implementations are significantly more complex.)

An IMAP server will associate each message with a folder; when a message first arrives at the server, it is associated with the recipient's INBOX folder. The recipient can then move the message into a new, user-created folder, read the message, delete the message, and so on. The IMAP protocol provides commands to allow users to create folders and move messages from one folder to another. IMAP also provides commands that allow users to search remote folders for messages matching specific criteria. Note that, unlike POP3, an IMAP server maintains user state information across IMAP sessions—for example, the names of the folders and which messages are associated with which folders.

Another important feature of IMAP is that it has commands that permit a user agent to obtain components of messages. For example, a user agent can obtain just the message header of a message or just one part of a multipart MIME message. This feature is useful when there is a low-bandwidth connection (for example, a wireless or slow-speed modem link) between the user agent and its mail server. With a low-bandwidth connection, the user may not want to download all of the messages in its mailbox, particularly avoiding long messages that might contain, for example, an audio or video clip. You can read all about IMAP at the official IMAP site [IMAP 2004].

Web-Based E-mail

More and more users today are sending and accessing their e-mail through their Web browsers. Hotmail introduced Web-based access in the mid 1990s; now Web-based e-mail is provided by just about every ISP site as well as every major university and corporation. With this service, the user agent is an ordinary Web browser, and the user communicates with its remote mailbox via HTTP. When a recipient, such as Bob, wants to access a message in his mailbox, the e-mail message is sent from Bob's mail server to Bob's browser using the HTTP protocol rather than the POP3 or IMAP protocol. When a sender, such as Alice, wants to send an e-mail message, the e-mail message is sent from her browser to her mail server over HTTP rather than over SMTP. Alice's mail server, however, still sends messages to, and receives messages from, other mail servers using SMTP.

This solution to mail access is enormously convenient for the user on the go. The user need only be able to access a browser in order to send and receive messages. The browser can be in an Internet cafe, in a friend's house, on a PDA, in a hotel room with a Web TV, and so on. As with IMAP, users can organize their messages in a hierarchy of folders on the remote server. In fact, many implementations of Web-based e-mail use an IMAP server to provide the folder functionality. In this case, access to the folders and messages is provided with scripts that run in an HTTP server; the scripts use the IMAP protocol to communicate with an IMAP server.

2.5 DNS—The Internet's Directory Service

We human beings can be identified in many ways. For example, we can be identified by the names that appear on our birth certificates. We can be identified by our Social Security numbers. We can be identified by our driver's license numbers. Although each of these identifiers can be used to identify people, within a given context one identifier may be more appropriate than another. For example, the computers at the IRS (the infamous tax-collecting agency in the United States) prefer to use fixed-length Social Security numbers rather than birth certificate names. On the other hand, ordinary people prefer the more mnemonic birth certificate names rather than Social Security numbers. (Indeed, can you imagine saying, "Hi. My name is 132-67-9875. Please meet my husband, 178-87-1146.")

Just as humans can be identified in many ways, so too can Internet hosts. One identifier for a host is its **hostname**. Hostnames—such as `cnn.com`, `www.yahoo.com`, `gaia.cs.umass.edu`, and `cis.poly.edu`—are mnemonic and are therefore appreciated by humans. However, hostnames provide little, if any, information about the location within the Internet of the host. (A hostname such as `www.eurecom.fr`, which ends with the country code `.fr`, tells us that the host is probably in France, but doesn't say much more.) Furthermore, because hostnames can consist of variable-length alphanumeric characters, they would be difficult to process by routers. For these reasons, hosts are also identified by so-called **IP addresses**.

We discuss IP addresses in some detail in Chapter 4, but it is useful to say a few brief words about them now. An IP address consists of four bytes and has a rigid hierarchical structure. An IP address looks like `121.7.106.83`, where each period separates one of the bytes expressed in decimal notation from 0 to 255. An IP address is hierarchical because as we scan the address from left to right, we obtain more and more specific information about where the host is located in the Internet (that is, within which network, in the network of networks). Similarly, when we scan a postal address from bottom to top, we obtain more and more specific information about where the addressee is located.

2.5.1 Services Provided by DNS

We have just seen that there are two ways to identify a host—by a hostname and by an IP address. People prefer the more mnemonic hostname identifier, while routers prefer fixed-length, hierarchically structured IP addresses. In order to reconcile these preferences, we need a directory service that translates hostnames to IP addresses. This is the main task of the Internet's **domain name system (DNS)**. The DNS is (1) a distributed database implemented in a hierarchy of **DNS servers** and (2) an application-layer protocol that allows hosts to query the distributed database. The DNS servers are often UNIX machines running the Berkeley Internet Name Domain (BIND) software [BIND 2004]. The DNS protocol runs over UDP and uses port 53.

DNS is commonly employed by other application-layer protocols—including HTTP, SMTP, and FTP—to translate user-supplied host names to IP addresses. As an example, consider what happens when a browser (that is, an HTTP client), running on some user's host, requests the URL `www.someschool.edu/index.html`. In order for the user's host to be able to send an HTTP request message to the Web server `www.someschool.edu`, the user's host must first obtain the IP address of `www.someschool.edu`. This is done as follows.

1. The same user machine runs the client side of the DNS application.
2. The browser extracts the hostname, `www.someschool.edu`, from the URL and passes the hostname to the client side of the DNS application.
3. The DNS client sends a query containing the hostname to a DNS server.
4. The DNS client eventually receives a reply, which includes the IP address for the hostname.
5. Once the browser receives the IP address from DNS, it can initiate a TCP connection to the HTTP server process located at that IP address.

We see from this example that DNS adds an additional delay—sometimes substantial—to the Internet applications that use it. Fortunately, as we discuss below, the desired IP address is often cached in a "nearby" DNS server, which helps to reduce DNS network traffic as well as the average DNS delay.

DNS provides a few other important services in addition to translating hostnames to IP addresses:

♦ **Host aliasing.** A host with a complicated hostname can have one or more alias names. For example, a hostname such as `relay1.west-coast.enterprise.com` could have, say, two aliases such as `enterprise.com` and `www.enterprise.com`. In this case, the hostname `relay1.west-coast.enterprise.com` is said to be a **canonical hostname**. Alias hostnames, when present, are typically more mnemonic than canonical hostnames. DNS can be invoked by an application to obtain the canonical hostname for a supplied alias hostname as well as the IP address of the host.

♦ **Mail server aliasing.** For obvious reasons, it is highly desirable that e-mail addresses be mnemonic. For example, if Bob has an account with Hotmail, Bob's e-mail address might be as simple as `bob@hotmail.com`. However, the hostname of the Hotmail mail server is more complicated and much less mnemonic

PRINCIPLES IN PRACTICE

DNS: CRITICAL NETWORK FUNCTIONS VIA THE CLIENT-SERVER PARADIGM

Like HTTP, FTP, and SMTP, the DNS protocol is an application-layer protocol since it (1) runs between communicating end systems using the client-server paradigm, and (2) relies on an underlying end-to-end transport protocol to transfer DNS messages between communicating end systems. In another sense, however, the role of the DNS is quite different from Web, file transfer, and e-mail applications. Unlike these applications, the DNS is not an application with which a user directly interacts. Instead, the DNS provides a core Internet function—namely, translating hostnames to their underlying IP addresses, for user applications and other software in the Internet. We noted in Section 1.2 that much of the complexity in the Internet architecture is located at the "edges" of the network. The DNS, which implements the critical name-to-address translation process using clients and servers located at the edge of the network, is yet another example of that design philosophy.

than simply `hotmail.com` (for example, the canonical hostname might be something like `relay1.west-coast.hotmail.com`). DNS can be invoked by a mail application to obtain the canonical hostname for a supplied alias hostname as well as the IP address of the host. In fact, the MX record (see below) permits a company's mail server and Web server to have identical (aliased) hostnames; for example, a company's Web server and mail server can both be called `enterprise.com`.

♦ **Load distribution.** DNS is also used to perform load distribution among replicated servers, such as replicated Web servers. Busy sites, such as `cnn.com`, are replicated over multiple servers, with each server running on a different end system and each having a different IP address. For replicated Web servers, a *set* of IP addresses is thus associated with one canonical hostname. The DNS database contains this set of IP addresses. When clients make a DNS query for a name mapped to a set of addresses, the server responds with the entire set of IP addresses, but rotates the ordering of the addresses within each reply. Because a client typically sends its HTTP request message to the IP address that is listed first in the set, DNS rotation distributes the traffic among the replicated servers. DNS rotation is also used for e-mail so that multiple mail servers can have the same alias name. Recently, content distribution companies such as Akamai [Akamai 2004] have used DNS in more sophisticated ways to provide Web content distribution (see Chapter 7).

The DNS is specified in RFC 1034 and RFC 1035, and updated in several additional RFCs. It is a complex system, and we only touch upon key aspects of its operation here. The interested reader is referred to these RFCs and the book by Abitz and Liu [Abitz 1993]; see also the retrospective paper [Mockapetris 1988], which provides a nice description of the what and why of DNS.

2.5.2 Overview of How DNS Works

We now present a high-level overview of how DNS works. Our discussion will focus on the hostname-to-IP-address translation service.

Suppose that some application (such as a Web browser or a mail reader) running in a user's host needs to translate a hostname to an IP address. The application will invoke the client side of DNS, specifying the hostname that needs to be translated. (On many UNIX-based machines, `gethostbyname()` is the function call that an application calls in order to perform the translation. In Section 2.7, we will show how a Java application can invoke DNS.) DNS in the user's host then takes over, sending a query message into the network. All DNS query and reply messages are sent within UDP datagrams to port 53. After a delay, ranging from milliseconds to seconds, DNS in the user's host receives a DNS reply message that provides the desired mapping. This mapping is then passed to the invoking application. Thus, from the perspective of the invoking application in the user's host, DNS is a black box providing a simple, straightforward translation service. But in fact, the black box that implements the service is complex, consisting of a large number of DNS servers distributed around the globe, as well as an application-layer protocol that specifies how the DNS servers and querying hosts communicate.

A simple design for DNS would have one DNS server that contains all the mappings. In this centralized design, clients simply direct all queries to the single DNS server, and the DNS server responds directly to the querying clients. Although the simplicity of this design is attractive, it is inappropriate for today's Internet, with its vast (and growing) number of hosts. The problems with a centralized design include:

♦ **A single point of failure.** If the DNS server crashes, so does the entire Internet!

♦ **Traffic volume.** A single DNS server would have to handle all DNS queries (for all the HTTP requests and e-mail messages generated from hundreds of millions of hosts).

♦ **Distant centralized database.** A single DNS server cannot be "close to" all the querying clients. If we put the single DNS server in New York City, then all queries from Australia must travel to the other side of the globe, perhaps over slow and congested links. This can lead to significant delays

♦ **Maintenance.** The single DNS server would have to keep records for all Internet hosts. Not only would this centralized database be huge, but it would have to be updated frequently to account for every new host.

In summary, a centralized database in a single DNS server simply *doesn't scale.* Consequently, the DNS is distributed by design. In fact, the DNS is a wonderful example of how a distributed database can be implemented in the Internet.

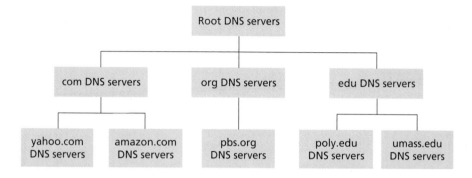

Figure 2.18 ♦ Portion of the hierarchy of DNS servers

A Distributed, Hierarchical Database

In order to deal with the issue of scale, the DNS uses a large number of servers, organized in a hierarchical fashion and distributed around the world. No single DNS server has all of the mappings for all of the hosts in the Internet. Instead, the mappings are distributed across the DNS servers. To a first approximation, there are three classes of DNS servers—root DNS servers, top-level domain (TLD) DNS servers, and authoritative DNS servers—organized in a hierarchy as shown in Figure 2.18. To understand how these three classes of servers interact, suppose a DNS client wants to determine the IP address for the hostname www.amazon.com. To a first approximation, the following events will take place. The client first contacts one of the root servers, which returns IP addresses for TLD servers for the top-level domain com. The client then contacts one of these TLD servers, which returns the IP address of an authoritative server for amazon.com. Finally, the client contacts one of the authoritative servers for amazon.com, which returns the IP address for the hostname www.amazon.com. We'll soon examine this DNS lookup process in more detail. But let's first take a closer look at these three classes of DNS servers:

♦ **Root DNS servers.** In the Internet there are 13 root DNS servers (labeled A through M), most of which are located in North America. A February 2004 map of the root DNS servers is shown in Figure 2.19; a list of the current root DNS servers is available via [Root-servers 2004]. Although we have referred to each of the 13 root DNS servers as if it were a single server, each "server" is actually a cluster of replicated servers, for both security and reliability purposes.

♦ **Top-Level Domain (TLD) servers.** These servers are responsible for top-level domains such as com, org, net, edu, and gov, and all of the country top-level domains such as uk, fr, ca, and jp. As of this writing (spring, 2004), the company Network Solutions maintains the TLD servers for the com top-level domain, and the company Educause maintains the TLD servers for the edu top-level domain.

♦ **Authoritative DNS servers.** Every organization with publicly accessible hosts (such as Web servers and mail servers) on the Internet must provide publicly accessible DNS records that map the names of those hosts to IP addresses. An organization's authoritative DNS server houses these DNS records. An organization can choose to implement its own authoritative DNS server to hold these records; alternatively, the organization can pay to have these records stored in an authoritative DNS server of some service provider. Most universities and large companies implement and maintain their own primary and secondary (backup) authoritative DNS server.

The root, TLD, and authoritative DNS servers all belong to the hierarchy of DNS servers, as shown in Figure 2.18. There is another important type of DNS, called the **local DNS server**. A local DNS server does not strictly belong to the hierarchy of servers but is nevertheless central to the DNS architecture. Each ISP—such as a university, an academic department, an employee's company, or a residential ISP—has a local DNS server (also called a default name server). When a host connects to an ISP, the ISP provides the host with the IP addresses of one or more of its local DNS servers (typically through DHCP, which is discussed in Section 5.4.3). You can easily determine the IP address of your local DNS server by accessing network status windows in Windows or UNIX. A host's local DNS server is typically "close to" the host. For an institutional ISP, the local DNS server may be on the same LAN as the host; for a residential ISP, it is typically separated from the host by

Figure 2.19 ♦ DNS root servers in 2004 (name, organization, location)

no more than a few routers. When a host makes a DNS query, the query is sent to the local DNS server, which acts a proxy, forwarding the query into the DNS server hierarchy as we'll discuss in more detail below.

Let's take a look at a simple example. Suppose the host `cis.poly.edu` desires the IP address of `gaia.cs.umass.edu`. Also suppose that Polytechnic's local DNS server is called `dns.poly.edu` and that an authoritative DNS server for `gaia.cs.umass.edu` is called `dns.umass.edu`. As shown in Figure 2.20, the host `cis.poly.edu` first sends a DNS query message to its local DNS server, `dns.poly.edu`. The query message contains the hostname to be translated, namely, `gaia.cs.umass.edu`. The local DNS server forwards the query message to a root DNS server. The root DNS server takes note of the edu suffix and returns to the local DNS server a list of IP addresses for TLD servers responsible for `edu`. The local DNS server then resends the query message to one of these TLD servers. The TLD server takes note of the `umass.edu` suffix and responds with the

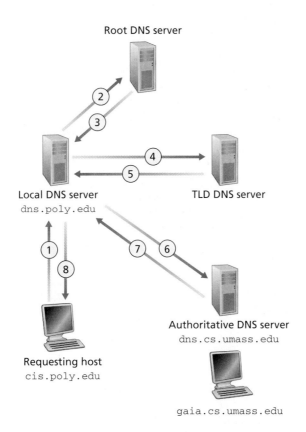

Figure 2.20 ♦ Interaction of the various DNS servers

IP address of the authoritative DNS server for the University of Massachusetts, namely, `dns.umass.edu`. Finally, the local DNS server resends the query message directly to `dns.umass.edu`, which responds with the IP address of `gaia.cs.umass.edu`. Note that in this example, in order to obtain the mapping for one hostname, eight DNS messages were sent: four query messages and four reply messages! We'll soon see how DNS caching reduces this query traffic.

Our previous example assumed that the TLD server knows the authoritative DNS server for the hostname. In general this not always true. Instead, the TLD server may know only of an intermediate DNS server, which in turn knows the authoritative DNS server for the hostname. For example, suppose again that the University of Massachusetts has a DNS server for the university, called `dns.umass.edu`. Also suppose that each of the departments at the University of Massachusetts has its own DNS server, and that each departmental DNS server is authoritative for all hosts in the department. In this case, when the intermediate DNS server, dns.umass.edu, receives a query for a host with hostname ending with `cs.umass.edu`, it returns to dns.poly.edu the IP address of `dns.cs.umass.edu`, which is authoritative for all hostnames ending with `cs.umass.edu`. The local DNS server dns.poly.edu then sends the query to the authoritative DNS server, which returns the desired mapping to local DNS server, which in turn returns the mapping to the requesting host. In this case, a total of 10 DNS messages are sent!

The example shown in Figure 2.20 makes use of both **recursive queries** and **iterative queries**. The query sent from `cis.poly.edu` to `dns.poly.edu` is a recursive query, since the query asks `dns.poly.edu` to obtain the mapping on its behalf. But the subsequent three queries are iterative since all of the replies are directly returned to `dns.poly.edu`. In theory, any DNS query can be iterative or recursive. For example, Figure 2.21 shows a DNS query chain for which all of the queries are recursive. In practice, the queries typically follow the pattern in Figure 2.20: The query from the requesting host to the local DNS server is recursive, and the remaining queries are iterative.

DNS Caching

Our discussion thus far has ignored **DNS caching**, a critically important feature of the DNS system. In truth, DNS extensively exploits DNS caching in order to improve the delay performance and to reduce the number of DNS messages ricocheting around the Internet. The idea behind DNS caching is very simple. In a query chain, when a DNS server receives a DNS reply (containing, for example a mapping from a hostname to an IP address), it can cache the information in the reply in its local memory. For example, in Figure 2.20, each time the local DNS server `dns.poly.edu` receives a reply from some DNS server, it can cache any of the information contained in the reply. If a hostname/IP address pair is cached in a DNS server and another query arrives to the DNS server for the same hostname, the DNS server can provide the desired IP address, even

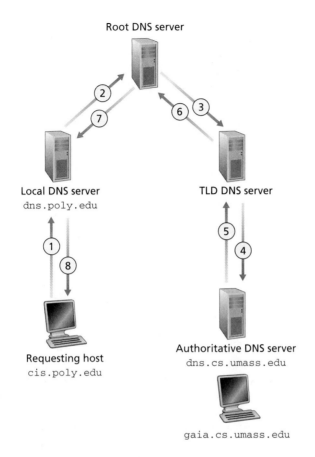

Figure 2.21 ♦ Recursive queries in DNS

if it is not authoritative for the hostname. Because hosts and mappings between host-names and IP addresses are by no means permanent, DNS servers discard cached infor-mation after a period of time (often set to two days).

As an example, suppose that a host `apricot.poly.edu` queries `dns.poly.edu` for the IP address for the hostname `cnn.com`. Furthermore, sup-pose that a few hours later, another Polytechnic University host, say, `kiwi.poly.fr`, also queries `dns.poly.edu` with the same hostname. Because of caching, the local DNS server will be able to immediately return the IP address of `cnn.com` to this sec-ond requesting host without having to query any other DNS servers. A local DNS server can also cache the IP addresses of TLD servers, thereby allowing the local DNS to bypass the root DNS servers in a query chain (this often happens).

2.5.3 DNS Records and Messages

The DNS servers that together implement the DNS distributed database store **resource records (RR)**, including RRs that provide hostname-to-IP address mappings. Each DNS reply message carries one or more resource records. In this and the following subsection, we provide a brief overview of DNS resource records and messages; more details can be found in [Abitz 1993] or in the DNS RFCs [RFC 1034; RFC 1035].

A resource record is a four-tuple that contains the following fields:

```
(Name, Value, Type, TTL)
```

TTL is the time to live of the resource record; it determines when a resource should be removed from a cache. In the example records given below, we ignore the `TTL` field. The meaning of `Name` and `Value` depend on `Type`:

♦ If `Type=A`, then `Name` is a hostname and `Value` is the IP address for the hostname. Thus, a Type A record provides the standard hostname to IP address mapping. As an example, (`relay1.bar.foo.com, 145.37.93.126, A`) is a Type A record.

♦ If `Type=NS`, then `Name` is a domain (such as `foo.com`) and `Value` is the hostname of an authoritative DNS server that knows how to obtain the IP addresses for hosts in the domain. This record is used to route DNS queries further along in the query chain. As an example, (`foo.com, dns.foo.com, NS`) is a Type NS record.

♦ If `Type=CNAME`, then `Value` is a canonical hostname for the alias hostname `Name`. This record can provide querying hosts the canonical name for a hostname. As an example, (`foo.com, relay1.bar.foo.com, CNAME`) is a CNAME record.

♦ If `Type=MX`, then `Value` is the canonical name of a mail server that has an alias hostname `Name`. As an example, (`foo.com. mail.bar.foo.com, MX`) is an MX record. MX records allow the hostnames of mail servers to have simple aliases. Note that by using the MX record, a company can have the same aliased name for its mail server and for one of its other servers (such as its Web server). To obtain the canonical name for the mail server, a DNS client would query for an MX record; to obtain the canonical name for the other server, the DNS client would query for the CNAME record.

If a DNS server is authoritative for a particular hostname, then the DNS server will contain a Type A record for the hostname. (Even if the DNS server is not authoritative, it may contain a Type A record in its cache.) If a server is not authoritative for a hostname, then the server will contain a Type NS record for the domain that includes the hostname; it will also contain a Type A record that provides the IP address of the DNS server in the `Value` field of the NS record. As an example, suppose an edu TLD server is not authoritative for the host `gaia.cs.umass.edu`. Then this server will contain a record for a domain that includes the host `cs.umass.edu`, for example, (`umass.edu, dns.umass.edu, NS`). The edu TLD server would also contain a Type A record, which maps the DNS server `dns.umass.edu` to an IP address, for example, (`dns.umass.edu, 128.119.40.111,A`).

DNS Messages

Earlier in this section we referred to DNS query and reply messages. These are the only two kinds of DNS messages. Furthermore, both query and reply messages have the same format, as shown in Figure 2.22. The semantics of the various fields in a DNS message are as follows:

◆ The first 12 bytes is the *header section,* which has a number of fields. The first field is a 16-bit number that identifies the query. This identifier is copied into the reply message to a query, allowing the client to match received replies with sent queries. There are a number of flags in the flag field. A 1-bit query/reply flag indicates whether the message is a query (0) or a reply (1). A 1-bit authoritative flag is set in a reply message when a DNS server is an authoritative server for a queried name. A 1-bit recursion-desired flag is set when a client (host or DNS server) desires that the DNS server perform recursion when it doesn't have the record. A 1-bit recursion-available field is set in a reply if the DNS server supports recursion. In the header, there are also four number-of fields. These fields indicate the number of occurrences of the four types of data sections that follow the header.

◆ The *question section* contains information about the query that is being made. This section includes (1) a name field that contains the name that is being queried, and (2) a type field that indicates the type of question being asked about the name—for example, a host address associated with a name (type A) or the mail server for a name (type MX).

◆ In a reply from a DNS server, the *answer section* contains the resource records for the name that was originally queried. Recall that in each resource record there is the `Type` (for example, A, NS, CNAME, and MX), the `Value`, and the `TTL`. A reply can return multiple RRs in the answer, since a hostname can have multiple IP addresses (for example, for replicated Web servers, as discussed earlier in this section).

◆ The *authority section* contains records of other authoritative servers.

◆ The *additional section* contains other helpful records. For example, the answer field in a reply to an MX query contains a resource record providing the canonical hostname of a mail server. The additional section contains a Type A record providing the IP address for the canonical hostname of the mail server.

How would you like to send a DNS query message directly from the host you're working on to some DNS server? This can easily be with the **nslookup program**, which is available from most Windows and UNIX platforms. For example, from a Windows host, open the Command Prompt and invoke the nslookup program by simply typing "nslookup". After invoking nslookup, you can send a DNS query to any DNS server (root, TLD, or authoritative). After receiving the reply message from the DNS server, nslookup will display the records included in the reply (in a human readable format). As an alternative to running nslookup from your own host, you can visit one of many Web sites that allow you to remotely employ nslookup. (Just type "nslookup" into a search engine and you'll be brought to one of these sites.)

Inserting Records into the DNS Database

The discussion above focused on how records are retrieved from the DNS database. You might be wondering how records get into the database in the first place. Let's look at how this is done in the context of a specific example. Suppose you have just created an exciting new startup company called Network Utopia. The first thing you'll surely want to do is register the domain name `networkutopia.com` at a registrar. A **registrar** is a commercial entity that verifies the uniqueness of the domain name, enters the domain name into the DNS database (as discussed below), and collects a small fee from you for its services. Prior to 1999, a single registrar,

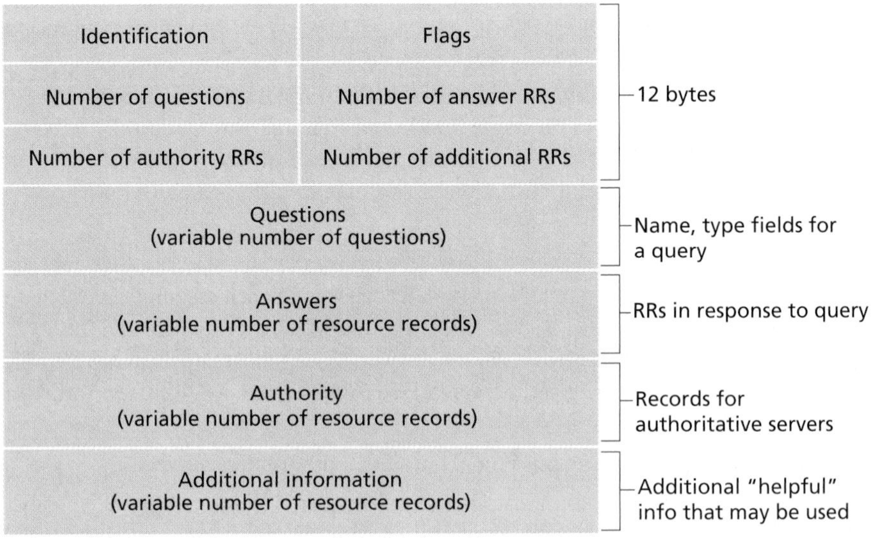

Identification	Flags	
Number of questions	Number of answer RRs	— 12 bytes
Number of authority RRs	Number of additional RRs	
Questions (variable number of questions)		— Name, type fields for a query
Answers (variable number of resource records)		— RRs in response to query
Authority (variable number of resource records)		— Records for authoritative servers
Additional information (variable number of resource records)		— Additional "helpful" info that may be used

Figure 2.22 ♦ DNS message format

Network Solutions, had a monopoly on domain name registration for com, net, and org domains. But now there are many registrars competing for customers, and the Internet Corporation for Assigned Names and Numbers (ICANN) accredits the various registrars. A complete list of accredited registrars is available at http://www.intenic.net.

When you register the domain name networkutopia.com with some registrar, you also need to provide the registrar with the names and IP addresses of your primary and secondary authoritative DNS servers. Suppose the names and IP addresses are dns1.networkutopia.com, dns2.networkutopia.com, 212.212.212.1 and 212.212.212.2. For each of these two authoritative DNS servers, the registrar would then make sure that a type NS and a type A record are entered into the TLD com servers. Specifically, for the primary authoritative server for networkutopia.com, the registrar would insert into the DNS system the following two resource records:

(networkutopia.com, dns1.networkutopia.com, NS)

(dns1.networkutopia.com, 212.212.212.1, A)

You'll also have to make sure that the Type A resource record for your Web server www.networkutopia.com and the Type MX resource record for your mail server mail.networkutopia.com are entered into your authoritative DNS servers. (Until recently, the contents of each DNS server were configured statically, for example, from a configuration file created by a system manager. More recently, an UPDATE option has been added to the DNS protocol to allow data to be dynamically added or deleted from the database via DNS messages. RFC 2136 specifies DNS dynamic updates.)

Once all of these steps are completed, people will be able to visit your Web site and send e-mail to the employees at your company. Let's conclude our discussion of DNS by verifying that this statement is true. This verification also helps to solidify what we have learned about DNS. Suppose Alice in Australia wants to view the Web page www.networkutopia.com. As discussed earlier, her host will first send a DNS query to her local DNS server. The local DNS server will then contact a TLD com server. (The local DNS server will also have to contact a root DNS server if the address of a TLD com server is not cached.) This TLD server contains the type NS and Type A resource records listed above, because the registrar had these resource records inserted into all of the TLD com servers. The TLD com server sends a reply to Alice's local DNS server, with the reply containing the two resource records. The local DNS server then sends a DNS query to 212.212.212.1, asking for the Type A record corresponding to www.networkutopia.com. This record provides the IP address of the desired Web server, say, 212.212.71.4, which the local DNS server passes back to Alice's host. Alice's browser can now initiate a TCP connection to the host 212.212.71.4 and send an HTTP request over the connection. Whew! There's a lot more going on than what meets the eye when one surfs the Web!

2.6 P2P File Sharing

As of this writing (early 2004), P2P file-sharing accounts for more traffic than any other application—including the Web—on the Internet. Thus, in terms of sheer traffic, P2P file sharing can be considered the most important Internet application. Modern P2P file-sharing systems not only share MP3s (typically 3 to 8 Mbytes), but also videos (typically 10 to 1,000 Mbytes), software, documents, and images. Our discussion in this section focuses on the protocol and networking issues in P2P file sharing. There are also many important issues relating to security, privacy, anonymity, copyright infringement, and intellectual property; we direct you to [von Lohmann 2003; Clarke 2002] for a discussion of these and other issues.

Before describing the internals of P2P file-sharing systems, let's walk through a typical example of how Alice, say, might use such a system. Suppose Alice uses the P2P file-sharing application for downloading MP3s. She runs the P2P file-sharing software on her home PC (a peer), and she accesses the Internet through an ADSL connection. She shuts down her PC every night. Her PC does not have a hostname, and every time she reconnects to the Internet her ISP assigns her PC a new IP address.

Suppose that Alice is now connected to the Internet and she has launched her P2P file-sharing application. Using the application, she searches for the MP3 for a song called "Network Love." Soon after she gives the search command, the application displays a list of peers, all of which are currently connected to the Internet and have a copy of "Network Love" for sharing. Each of these peers is typically an ordinary PC, owned by an ordinary Internet user such as Alice. For each peer on the list, the application may display some auxiliary information such as the peer's access bandwidth and estimate of the download time. Alice then requests the MP3 file from one of the peers, say, Bob's PC. A direct TCP connection is established between Alice's PC and Bob's PC, and the MP3 file is sent from Bob's PC to Alice's PC. If Bob inadvertently disconnects his PC from the Internet during the download, then Alice's P2P file-sharing software may attempt to obtain the remainder of the file from another peer that has the file. Also, while Alice is downloading "Network Love" from Bob, some other peer, say Claire's PC, may simultaneously download another MP3, say "Network 'n Roll," directly from Alice's PC. Thus every participating peer is both a consumer and distributor of content.

P2P file sharing is a compelling content distribution paradigm because all content is transferred directly between ordinary peers without passing through third-party servers. Thus, P2P file sharing takes advantage of the resources (bandwidth, storage, and CPU) in a large collection of peers—sometimes millions! In other words, P2P file sharing is highly scalable.

Although no centralized, third-party server gets involved in the file transfer, it is important to keep in mind that P2P file sharing still relies on the client-server paradigm (see Section 2.1.2). Indeed, the requesting peer is the client and the chosen peer is the server. The file is sent from server peer to the client peer with a file-transfer protocol. Since any peer can request or can be chosen, all peers must be capable of running both the client and server sides of the file transfer protocol.

Now suppose that the P2P file-transfer protocol is HTTP, which is typically the case. Elaborating on our example above, when Alice selects Bob for downloading "Network Love," Alice's PC sends Bob an HTTP request for "Network Love," and Bob sends an HTTP response containing "Network Love." Note that while Alice is running the P2P file-sharing application, her peer is both a Web client and a **transient Web server.** Her peer is a Web server because it is serving content within HTTP responses; it is transient because it is only intermittently connected to the Internet and may get a new IP address each time it reconnects to the Internet.

Up to this point we have explained the easy part of the P2P file sharing, namely, how a file is directly transferred from one peer to another. But we have not explained how a peer determines which peers have the objects (i.e., files) it desires. In a P2P file-sharing system, there is typically a large number of connected peers, with each peer having objects to share, including MP3s, videos, images, and software. If peer X is interested in obtaining a particular object, then peer X must have a way of determining the IP addresses of the connected peers that have copies of the desired object. Because peers connect and disconnect, this is a nontrivial problem. Below we discuss three architectures for locating content, each of which has been widely deployed by different P2P file-sharing systems. The interested reader is also encouraged to see the research papers [Stoica 2001; Rowstron 2001; Ratnasamy 2001; Zhao 2004; Maymounkov 2002; Garces-Erce 2003], which provide innovative solutions to the content-location problem.

Centralized Directory

One of the more straightforward approaches to locating content is to provide a **centralized directory**, as was done by Napster, which was the first commercial company to deploy a widescale, successful, P2P application for MP3 distribution. In this design, the P2P file-sharing service uses a large server (or server farm) to provide the directory service. As shown in Figure 2.23, when a user launches the P2P file-sharing application, the application contacts the directory server. Specifically, the application running in the peer informs the directory server of its IP address and of the names of the objects in its local disk that it is making available for sharing (for example, the titles of all of its stored MP3s). In this manner, the directory server knows which objects the peer has available to share. The directory server collects this information from each peer that becomes active, thereby creating a centralized, dynamic database that maps each object name to a set of IP addresses. When an active peer obtains a new object, or removes an object, it informs the directory server, so that the directory server can update its database.

In order to keep its database current, the directory server must be able to determine when a peer becomes disconnected. A peer can become disconnected by closing its P2P client application or simply by disconnecting from the Internet. One way to keep track

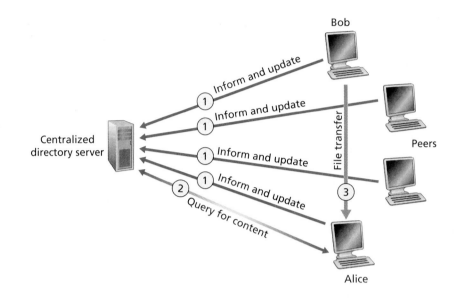

Figure 2.23 ♦ The P2P paradigm with a centralized directory

of which peers remain connected is to send messages periodically to the peers to see if they respond. If the directory server determines that a peer is no longer connected, the directory server removes the peer's IP addresses from the database.

P2P file sharing with a centralized directory uses the hybrid client-server, P2P architecture as discussed in Section 2.1.1. Using a centralized directory for locating content is conceptually straightforward, but it does have a number of drawbacks:

♦ *Single point of failure.* If the directory server crashes, then the entire P2P application crashes. Even if a server farm with redundant servers is used, Internet connections to the server farm can fail, causing the entire application to crash.

♦ *Performance bottleneck.* In a large P2P system, with hundreds of thousands of connected users, a centralized server must maintain a huge database and must respond to thousands of queries per second. In fact, in 2000, when Napster was the most popular P2P application, Napster was plagued by traffic problems at its centralized server.

♦ *Copyright infringement.* Although this topic is beyond the scope of this book, we briefly mention that the recording industry has been concerned (to say the least!) that P2P file-sharing systems allow users to easily obtain copyrighted content for free. (For an excellent discussion of how copyright laws bear on P2P, see [von Lohmann 2003].) When a P2P company has a centralized directory server, legal proceedings may result in the company having to shut down the directory server. It is more difficult to shut down the more decentralized architectures.

In summary, the salient drawback of using a centralized directory server is that the P2P application is only partially decentralized. The file transfer between peers is decentralized, but the process of locating content is highly centralized—a reliability and performance concern.

Query Flooding

Gnutella [Gnutella 2004], a public-domain file-sharing application, locates content using a fully distributed approach. Unlike Napster, Gnutella does not use a centralized server for tracking content in the peers. In fact, Gnutella's approach to locating content is diametrically opposite of that taken by Napster.

The Gnutella client (which includes a user interface) implements the Gnutella protocol and runs on an ordinary peer. The protocol specification is minimal, leaving significant flexibility in how the Gnutella client is designed. Just as there are many Web browsers that implement HTTP, there are many Gnutella clients that implement the Gnutella protocol.

In Gnutella, the peers form an abstract, logical network called an **overlay network**, which is defined in graph-theoretic terms as follows. If peer X maintains a TCP connection with another peer Y, then we say there is an **edge** between X and Y. The graph consisting of all active peers and the connecting edges (ongoing TCP connections) defines the current Gnutella overlay network. Note that an edge is not a physical communication link; instead, an edge is an abstract link which may consist of tens of underlying physical links. An edge may represent the TCP connection between a peer in Lithuania with a peer in Brazil, for example.

Although a Gnutella network may have hundreds of thousands of participating peers, a given peer will typically be connected to fewer than 10 other nodes in the overlay network; see Figure 2.24. Later we'll explain how a Gnutella network is built and maintained as peers join and leave the network. For now let's assume that the overlay network is in place and focus on how a peer locates and retrieves content.

In Gnutella, peers send messages to neighboring peers in the overlay network over the pre-existing TCP connections. When Alice wants to locate "Network Love," her Gnutella client sends a Gnutella Query message, which includes the keywords "Network Love," to all of her neighbors. All of Alice's neighbors forward the Query message to all of their neighbors, which in turn forward the message to all of their neighbors, and so on. This process, shown in Figure 2.24, is referred to as **query flooding**. When a peer receives a Query message, it checks to see whether the keyword matches any of the files it is making available for sharing. If there is a match, it sends back to Alice a QueryHit message, which contains the file name and file size of the match. The QueryHit message follows the reverse path of the Query message, thereby using preexisting TCP connections.

Alice's Gnutella process may receive QueryHit messages from more than one peer. Alice selects one peer from the set of responding peers, say Bob's peer, for downloading "Network Love." Her Gnutella process sets up a direct TCP connection with Bob's Gnutella process and sends into the connection an HTTP GET message that includes the specific file name. Bob then sends to Alice the file within an HTTP response message. Although the Query and QueryHit messages travel in the overlay network, the HTTP GET and response messages are sent outside of the overlay network, directly between the two peers, as shown in Figure 2.24. Once Alice receives the entire file, the Alice-to-Bob TCP connection is terminated.

Although the decentralized Gnutella design is simple and elegant, it is often criticized for being nonscalable. In particular, with query flooding, whenever a peer initiates a query, the query propagates to every other peer in the overlay network, dumping a significant amount of traffic into the Internet. The Gnutella designers responded to this problem by using **limited scope query flooding**. Specifically, when Alice sends out her initial query message, a peer-count field in the message is set to a specific limit (say, 7). Each time the query message reaches a new peer, the peer decrements the peer-count field before forwarding the query to its overlay neighbors. When a peer receives a query with the peer-count field equal to zero, it stops forwarding the query. In this manner, when a peer initiates a query, the flooding is localized to a region of the overlay network. Clearly, this limited scope query flooding reduces the query traffic that is dumped into the Internet. However, it also reduces the number of peers that are queried. In Gnutella, there can be a high

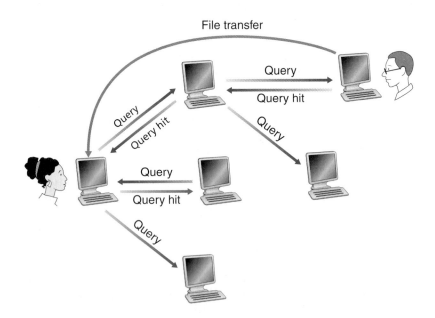

Figure 2.24 ♦ Search and file transfer in Gnutella

probability that you don't locate your desired content even though it is present in some outside-of-scope peer.

A fundamental issue in distributed P2P applications is that of handling peer joins and departures. We now describe what happens when a peer X wants to join the Gnutella network. We explore what actions Gnutella takes for peer departures in the homework problems.

1. The peer X must first find some other peer that is already in the overlay network. One approach to solve this **bootstrap problem** is for X's Gnutella client to maintain a list of peers (IP addresses) that are often up in the Gnutella network; alternatively, X can contact a Gnutella site that maintains such a list.

2. Once X has access to such a list, X sequentially attempts to set up a TCP connection with peers on the list until one connection is created with some peer Y.

3. After the TCP connection is established between X and Y, peer X sends a Gnutella Ping message to Y. The Ping message also includes a peer-count field. On receiving the Ping message, Y forwards it to all its neighbors in the overlay network. The peers continue to forward the Ping message until the peer-count field is zero.

4. Whenever a peer Z receives a Ping message, it responds by sending a Gnutella Pong message through the overlay network back to X. The Pong message includes Z's IP address, the number of files it is sharing, and the total number of Kbytes taken by the files it is sharing.

5. When X receives the Pong messages, it knows the IP addresses of many peers in the Gnutella network in addition to Y. It can then set up TCP connections with some of these other peers, thereby creating multiple edges from itself into the overlay network. Peer X can also attempt to set up TCP connections with other bootstrap nodes. The Gnutella specification does not specify how many peers X should connect to, so it is up to the designer of the Gnutella client.

We have now covered the essential features of the Gnutella protocol. We'll go into a little more detail in the homework problems. In summary, Gnutella is a simple, distributed P2P system that allows a user to query for files that are located at nearby peers (where "nearby" means within a small number of hops in the overlay network).

Exploiting Heterogeneity

We have learned that Napster and Gnutella use two diametrically opposite approaches for locating content. Napster uses a centralized directory server and always locates content when it is present in some participating peer. Gnutella uses a fully distributed architecture, but only locates content in nearby peers in the overlay network. KaZaA [KaZaA 2004] borrows ideas from both Napster and Gnutella, resulting in a powerful P2P file-sharing system, which, as of this writing, contributes more traffic to the Internet than any other application [Gummadi 2003] [Saroiu 2002].

The KaZaA technology is proprietary. Furthermore, KaZaA encrypts all the control traffic (but not the data files). However, from basic descriptions on KaZaA's Web page along with some KaZaA measurement work [Liang 2004], we can explain how the protocol generally works. KaZaA exploits heterogeneity in an intuitive and natural manner.

KaZaA resembles Gnutella in the sense that it does not use a dedicated server (or server farm) for tracking and locating content. However, unlike Gnutella, in KaZaA not all peers are equal. The more powerful peers—that is, the peers with high bandwidth connections and high Internet connectivity—are designated as group leaders and have greater responsibilities. As shown in Figure 2.25, if a peer is not a group leader, then it is is an ordinary peer and is assigned to a group leader. Typically a group leader will have up to a few hundred children peers.

When a peer launches the KaZaA application, the peer establishes a TCP connection with one of the group leaders. The peer then informs its group leader of all the files it is making available for sharing. This allows the group leader to maintain a database that includes the identifiers of all the files its children are sharing, meta data about the files, and the corresponding IP addresses of the children holding the files. In this way, each group leader becomes a mini Napster-like hub. But in contrast with Napster, a group leader is not a dedicated server; instead, it is an ordinary peer.

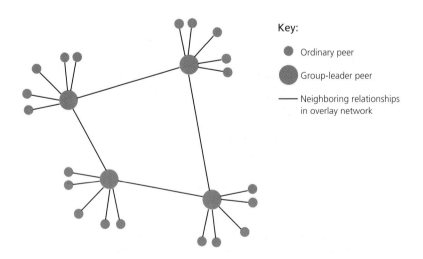

Figure 2.25 ♦ Hierarchical overlay network for P2P file sharing

If each of the mini hubs, along with their children, were isolated entities in KaZaA, then KaZaA would essentially consist of thousands of isolated mini Napsters, with each hub running on a peer rather than on a dedicated application server. This isolated approach would severely limit the amount of content that is available to any one peer. To address this limitation, the group leaders interconnect themselves with TCP connections, creating an overlay network among the group leaders. Thus the group leaders create a network that resembles a Gnutella network. KaZaA shares content information among the various groups. This sharing across groups can be done in many ways. For example, a hub in one group could contact the hubs in some other groups, obtaining copies of the other hubs' databases, merging these databases with its own database, and thereby tracking the content of a larger number of peers. Alternatively, each hub could only track the content of its children, but when it receives a query, it forwards the query to the hubs to which it is connected. (This last approach is similar to query flooding in Gnutella, but with the limited-scope flooding taking place in the overlay network of group leaders).

In KaZaA, each file is identified by a hash of the file. We'll see how this identifier is used shortly. Also in KaZaA, each object has a descriptor, which includes the file name and an unstructured text description of the object. Peers query with keywords, similar to how users query search engines. When a peer seeks a match for keywords, it sends a query with the keywords to its group leader. The group leader responds with a list of peers (either in or out of its group) that have files whose descriptors match the keywords, along with the identifiers of those files. The group leader may then forward the query to one or more other group leaders to which it is connected. Responses from the group leaders follow the reverse path in the overlay network.

In summary, the KaZaA architecture exploits the *heterogeneity of the peers* by designating a small fraction of the more powerful peers as group leaders, which form the top tier of a hierarchical overlay network, as shown in Figure 2.25. As compared to the Gnutella design, with a flat overlay and limited-scope flooding, the hierarchical design allows for significantly more peers to be checked for a match, without creating an excessive quantity of query traffic. (The vast majority of today's KaZaA traffic is file transfer traffic.)

KaZaA also employs a number of techniques that improve its performance. These techniques, which can be employed in most any P2P file-sharing systems, include:

1. **Request queuing.** The user can configure its peer to limit the number of simultaneous uploads to any value. (The default value is in the three to seven range.) If Alice limits her peer to three uploads, and her peer is already uploading three files when she receives a new upload request from Bob, she puts Bob's and all subsequent requests in a local queue. These local limitations ensure that each file being transferred receives a non-negligible amount of bandwidth from the uploading node.

2. **Incentive priorities.** Alice will give queuing priority to users who have in the past uploaded more files than they have downloaded. For example, if both Bob and Claire are in Alice's queue, Bob has downloaded much more than he has uploaded, and Claire has uploaded much more than she has downloaded, than Alice will service Claire's request before Bob's. This mechanism provides an incentive to users to upload files, enhancing the overall scalability of the KaZaA system.

3. **Parallel downloading.** When Claire queries for "Network Love," KaZaA will often return with a list of several peers that have keyword matches. Some of these keyword matches will correspond to the same file, which is verified with the file identifiers. Claire's client can use the byte-range header of HTTP to request different portions of the file from the different peers, thereby down-loading portions of the file from different peers in parallel. For example, if both Alice and Bob have the desired file, Claire's KaZaA client may ask Alice for the first half the file and ask Bob for the second half of the file. This feature allows users to retrieve a file faster in many circumstances.

We briefly mention that there have been numerous reverse engineering efforts for KaZaA; in fact some projects have developed modified KaZaA clients that allow users to access the KaZaA network without fully following the KaZaA protocol. Currently, one remarkably popular modified client is kazaa-lite, which not only eliminates KaZaA's imbedded advertising and gives all users highest priority, but also performs supernode hopping, that is, hopping from one group-leader to another for a single keyword query.

KaZaA, like Napster before it, has been a wildly successful Internet application, spreading to literally millions of users in the space of a few months. The breathtak-ingly fast and widespread adoption of P2P file-sharing applications, and the Web and instant messaging before them, is a telling testament to the wisdom of the over-all architectural design of the Internet, a design that could not have foreseen the rich and ever-expanding set of Internet applications that would be developed over the next 25 years. The network services offered to Internet applications—connection-less datagram transport, connection-oriented reliable datagram transfer, the socket interface, addressing, and naming (DNS), among others—have proven sufficient to allow thousands of applications to be developed. Since these applications have all been layered on top of the existing four lower layers of the Internet protocol stack, they involve only the development of new client-server software for use in end sys-tems. This, in turn, has allowed these applications to be rapidly deployed and adopted as well.

But not all the new Internet applications have been as wildly successful as the Web, instant messaging, and P2P file sharing. Multimedia conferencing and stream-ing multimedia are two applications that have yet to succeed on a grand scale. This may be due to an insufficient set of services being provided by today's Internet architecture (we cover proposed extensions to the Internet architecture to support

CASE HISTORY

KaZaA

As of this writing (April 2004), on a typical day the KaZaA network has more than 3 million users sharing over 5,000 terabytes of content. Because much of this content is copyrighted songs and movies, KaZaA is the nemesis of the both the music and film industries. KaZaA also places severe traffic loads on ISPs. For example, approximately 37 percent of all TCP traffic was consumed by KaZaA on the University of Washington campus network in June 2002—this was more than twice the Web traffic on the same campus at the same time [Saroiu 2002]. So where did this killer application come from and where is it headed?

FastTrack, a privately held Dutch company, first released the free KaZaA program in April 2000. The first release included the hierarchical supernode architecture that remains a distinctive feature today. Over the years, several companies licensed the FastTrack software, including Music City (Morpheus), Grokster, and iMesh. FastTrack, being pursued for copyright infringement by the Recording Industry Association of America (RIAA) and the Dutch courts, sold a major portion of the company to Sharman Networks in February 2002. The resulting corporate structure is complex and confusing. Sharman Networks is incorporated in Vanuatu, a tiny island country in the pacific. The headquarters of Sharman Networks is in Australia. And many of the software developers are in Estonia! This complex and confusing corporate structure is not making things easy for US organizations that would like to pursue KaZaA in court.

One interesting question is whether the KaZaA network would continue to thrive, even if the companies responsible for KaZaA were to shut down (e.g., for legal or financial reasons). As we have just learned, KaZaA employs a highly decentralized architecture without reliance on any central servers. It is very likely that KaZaA, in some form or another, can continue on its own. The recording industry has been actively pursuing alternative means to diminish file sharing over KaZaA, including suing individual KaZaA users and commissioning companies to dump bogus files into the network [Overpeer 2004].

Finally, we (the authors of this book) envision the eventual emergence of wireless P2P file-sharing systems in which individuals—such as high school students—have PDAs endowed with Gigabytes of storage and Wi-Fi (wireless) communication capabilities. These Wi-Fi devices, often tucked away in school backpacks, will operate in so-called *ad hoc* mode, allowing nearby devices to query each other and inconspicuously exchange content over the air! Clearly, it will be difficult for the RIAA or similar organizations to monitor or interfere with such wireless P2P systems.

these applications in Chapter 7), or it may be due to social and/or economic factors; time will tell.

2.7 Socket Programming with TCP

Now that we have looked at a number of important network applications, let's explore how network application programs are actually written. In this section we'll write application programs that use TCP; in the following section we'll write programs that use UDP.

Recall from Section 2.1 that many network applications consist of a pair of programs—a client program and a server program—residing in two different end systems. When these two programs are executed, a client and a server process are created, and these processes communicate with each other by reading from and writing to sockets. When creating a network application, the developer's main task is to write the code for both the client and server programs.

There are two sorts of network applications. One sort is a network application that is an implementation of a protocol standard defined in, for example, an RFC. For such an implementation, the client and server programs must conform to the rules dictated by the RFC. For example, the client program could be an implementation of the client side of the FTP protocol, described in Section 2.3 and explicitly defined in RFC 959; similarly, the server program could be an implementation of the FTP server protocol, also explicitly defined in RFC 959. If one developer writes code for the client program and an independent developer writes code for the server program, and both developers carefully follow the rules of the RFC, then the two programs will be able to interoperate. Indeed, many of today's network applications involve communication between client and server programs that have been created by independent developers—for example, a Netscape browser communicating with an Apache Web server, or an FTP client on a PC uploading a file to a UNIX FTP server. When a client or server program implements a protocol defined in an RFC, it should use the port number associated with the protocol. (Port numbers were briefly discussed in Section 2.1. They are covered in more detail in Chapter 3.)

The other sort of network application is a proprietary network application. In this case the application-layer protocol used by the client and server programs do not necessarily conform to any existing RFC. A single developer (or development team) creates both the client and server programs, and the developer has complete control over what goes in the code. But because the code does not implement a public-domain protocol, other independent developers will not be able to develop code that interoperates with the application. When developing a proprietary application, the developer must be careful not to use one of the well-known port numbers defined in the RFCs.

In this and the next section, we examine the key issues in developing a proprietary client-server application. During the development phase, one of the first decisions the developer must make is whether the application is to run over TCP or over UDP. Recall that TCP is connection oriented and provides a reliable byte-stream channel through which data flows between two end systems. UDP is connectionless and sends independent packets of data from one end system to the other, without any guarantees about delivery.

In this section we develop a simple client application that runs over TCP; in the next section, we develop a simple client application that runs over UDP. We present these simple TCP and UDP applications in Java. We could have written the code in C or C++, but we opted for Java for several reasons. First, the applications are more neatly and cleanly written in Java; with Java there are fewer lines of code, and each line can be explained to the novice programmer without much difficulty. Second, client/server programming in Java is becoming increasingly popular, and may even become the norm in upcoming years. But there is no need to be frightened if you are not familiar with Java. You should be able to follow the code if you have experience programming in another language.

For readers who are interested in client/server programming in C, there are several good references available [Donahoo 2000; Stevens 1997; Frost 1994; Kurose 1996].

2.7.1 Socket Programming with TCP

Recall from Section 2.1 that processes running on different machines communicate with each other by sending messages into sockets. We said that each process was analogous to a house and the process's socket is analogous to a door. As shown in Figure 2.26, the socket is the door between the application process and TCP. The application developer has control of everything on the application-layer side of the socket; however, it has little control of the transport-layer side. (At the very most, the application developer has the ability to fix a few TCP parameters, such as maximum buffer size and maximum segment size.)

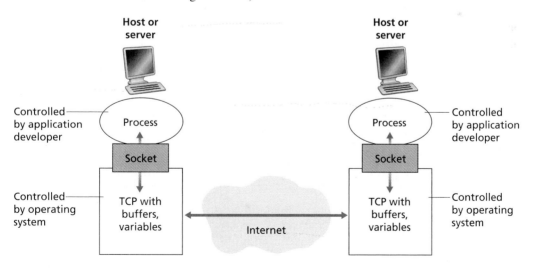

Figure 2.26 ♦ Processes communicating through TCP sockets

Now let's take a closer look at the interaction of the client and server programs. The client has the job of initiating contact with the server. In order for the server to be able to react to the client's initial contact, the server has to be ready. This implies two things. First, the server program cannot be dormant—that is, it must be running as a process before the client attempts to initiate contact. Second, the server program must have some sort of door—more precisely, a socket—that welcomes some initial contact from a client process running on an arbitrary host. Using our house/door analogy for a process/socket, we will sometimes refer to the client's initial contact as "knocking on the welcoming door."

With the server process running, the client process can initiate a TCP connection to the server. This is done in the client program by creating a socket. When the client creates its socket, it specifies the address of the server process, namely, the IP address of the server host and the port number of the server process. Once the socket has been created in the client program, TCP in the client initiates a three-way handshake and establishes a TCP connection with the server. The three-way handshake, which takes place at the transport layer, is completely transparent to the client and server programs.

During the three-way handshake, the client process knocks on the welcoming door of the server process. When the server "hears" the knocking, it creates a new door—more precisely, a new socket—that is dedicated to that particular client. In our example below, the welcoming door is a `ServerSocket` object that we call the `welcomeSocket`. When a client knocks on this door, the program invokes `welcomeSocket's accept()` method, which creates a new door for the client. At the end of the handshaking phase, a TCP connection exists between the client's socket and the server's new socket. Henceforth, we refer to the server's new, dedicated socket as the server's **connection socket**.

From the application's perspective, the TCP connection is a direct virtual pipe between the client's socket and the server's connection socket. The client process can send arbitrary bytes into its socket, and TCP guarantees that the server process will receive (through the connection socket) each byte in the order sent. TCP thus provides a **reliable byte-stream service** between the client and server processes. Furthermore, just as people can go in and out the same door, the client process not only sends bytes into but also receives bytes from its socket; similarly, the server process not only receives bytes from but also sends bytes into its connection socket. This is illustrated in Figure 2.27. Because sockets play a central role in client/server applications, client/server application development is also referred to as socket programming.

Before providing our example client/server application, it is useful to discuss the notion of a stream. A **stream** is a sequence of characters that flow into or out of a process. Each stream is either an **input stream** for the process or an **output stream** for the process. If the stream is an input stream, then it is attached to some input source for the process, such as standard input (the keyboard) or a socket into which data flow from the Internet. If the stream is an output stream, then it is

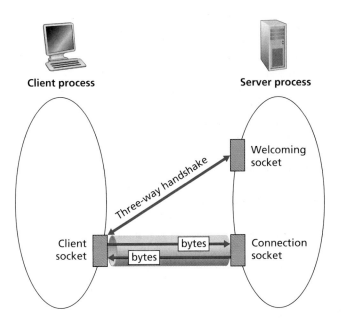

Figure 2.27 ♦ Client socket, welcoming socket, and connection socket

attached to some output source for the process, such as standard output (the monitor) or a socket out of which data flow into the Internet.

2.7.2 An Example Client/Server Application in Java

We use the following simple client/server application to demonstrate socket programming for both TCP and UDP:

1. A client reads a line from its **standard input** (keyboard) and sends the line out its socket to the server.
2. The server reads a line from its connection socket.
3. The server converts the line to uppercase.
4. The server sends the modified line out its connection socket to the client.
5. The client reads the modified line from its socket and prints the line on its **standard output** (monitor).

Figure 2.28 illustrates the main socket-related activity of the client and server.

Next we provide the client/server program pair for a TCP implementation of the application. We provide a detailed, line-by-line analysis after each program. The client program is called `TCPClient.java`, and the server program is called

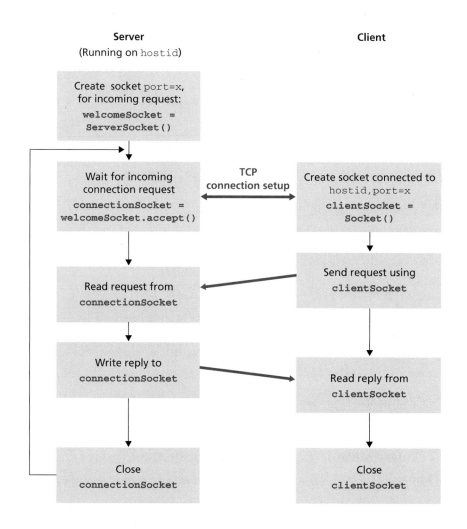

Figure 2.28 ◆ The client-server application, using connection-oriented transport services

TCPServer.java. In order to emphasize the key issues, we intentionally provide code that is to the point but not bulletproof. "Good code" would certainly have a few more auxiliary lines.

Once the two programs are compiled on their respective hosts, the server program is first executed at the server host, which creates a server process at the server host. As discussed above, the server process waits to be contacted by a client process. In this example application, when the client program is executed, a process is created at the client, and this process immediately contacts the server and establishes a TCP connection with it. The user at the client may then use the application to send a line and then receive a capitalized version of the line.

TCPClient.java

Here is the code for the client side of the application:

```
import java.io.*;
import java.net.*;
class TCPClient {
    public static void main(String argv[]) throws Exception
    {
        String sentence;
        String modifiedSentence;
        BufferedReader inFromUser = new BufferedReader(
                new InputStreamReader(System.in));
        Socket clientSocket = new Socket("hostname", 6789);
        DataOutputStream outToServer = new DataOutputStream(
                clientSocket.getOutputStream());
        BufferedReader inFromServer =
            new BufferedReader(new InputStreamReader(
                clientSocket.getInputStream()));
        sentence = inFromUser.readLine();
        outToServer.writeBytes(sentence + '\n');
        modifiedSentence = inFromServer.readLine();
        System.out.println("FROM SERVER: " +
                            modifiedSentence);
        clientSocket.close();
    }
}
```

The program TCPClient creates three streams and one socket, as shown in Figure 2.29. The socket is called clientSocket. The stream inFromUser is an input stream to the program; it is attached to the standard input (that is, the keyboard). When the user types characters on the keyboard, the characters flow into the stream inFromUser. The stream inFromServer is another input stream to the program; it is attached to the socket. Characters that arrive from the network flow into the stream inFromServer. Finally, the stream outToServer is an output stream from the program; it is also attached to the socket. Characters that the client sends to the network flow into the stream outToServer.

Let's now take a look at the various lines in the code.

```
import java.io.*;
import java.net.*;
```

java.io and java.net are java packages. The java.io package contains classes for input and output streams. In particular, the java.io package contains the BufferedReader and DataOutputStream classes, classes that the program uses to create the three streams previously illustrated. The java.net package provides classes for network support. In particular, it contains the Socket and ServerSocket classes. The clientSocket object of this program is derived from the Socket class.

```
class TCPClient {
      public static void main(String argv[]) throws Exception
            {......}
}
```

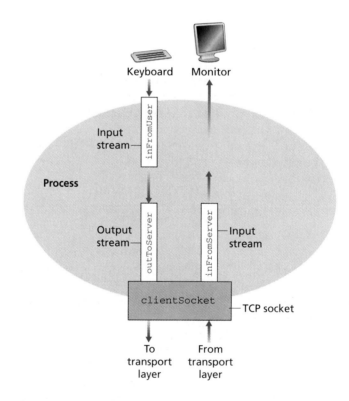

Figure 2.29 ◆ TCPClient has three streams through which characters flow.

So far, what we've seen is standard stuff that you see at the beginning of most Java code. The third line is the beginning of a class definition block. The keyword `class` begins the class definition for the class named `TCPClient`. A class contains variables and methods. The variables and methods of the class are embraced by the curly brackets that begin and end the class definition block. The class `TCPClient` has no class variables and exactly one method, the `main()` method. Methods are similar to the functions or procedures in languages such as C; the main method in the Java language is similar to the main function in C and C++. When the Java interpreter executes an application (by being invoked upon the application's controlling class), it starts by calling the class's main method. The main method then calls all the other methods required to run the application. For this introduction to socket programming in Java, you may ignore the keywords `public`, `static`, `void`, `main`, and `throws Exceptions` (although you must include them in the code).

```
String sentence;
String modifiedSentence;
```

These above two lines declare objects of type `String`. The object `sentence` is the string typed by the user and sent to the server. The object `modifiedSentence` is the string obtained from the server and sent to the user's standard output.

```
BufferedReader inFromUser = new BufferedReader(
     new InputStreamReader(System.in));
```

The above line creates the stream object `inFromUser` of type `BufferedReader`. The input stream is initialized with `System.in`, which attaches the stream to the standard input. The command allows the client to read text from its keyboard.

```
Socket clientSocket = new Socket("hostname", 6789);
```

The above line creates the object `clientSocket` of type `Socket`. It also initiates the TCP connection between client and server. The string `"hostname"` must be replaced with the host name of the server (for example, `"apple.poly.edu"`). Before the TCP connection is actually initiated, the client performs a DNS look-up on the hostname to obtain the host's IP address. The number 6789 is the port number. You can use a different port number; but you must make sure that you use the same port number at the server side of the application. As discussed earlier, the host's IP address along with the application's port number identifies the server process.

```
DataOutputStream outToServer =
   new DataOutputStream(clientSocket.getOutputStream());
BufferedReader inFromServer =
   new BufferedReader(new inputStreamReader(
                        clientSocket.getInputStream()));
```

The above two lines create stream objects that are attached to the socket. The out-ToServer stream provides the process output to the socket. The inFromServer stream provides the process input from the socket (see Figure 2.29).

```
sentence = inFromUser.readLine();
```

This line places a line typed by the user into the string sentence. The string sentence continues to gather characters until the user ends the line by typing a carriage return. The line passes from standard input through the stream inFromUser into the string sentence.

```
outToServer.writeBytes(sentence + '\n');
```

The above line sends the string sentence augmented with a carriage return into the outToServer stream. The augmented sentence flows through the client's socket and into the TCP pipe. The client then waits to receive characters from the server.

```
modifiedSentence = inFromServer.readLine();
```

When characters arrive from the server, they flow through the stream inFrom-Server and get placed into the string modifiedSentence. Characters continue to accumulate in modifiedSentence until the line ends with a carriage return character.

```
System.out.println("FROM SERVER " + modifiedSentence);
```

The above line prints to the monitor the string modifiedSentence returned by the server.

```
clientSocket.close();
```

This last line closes the socket and, hence, closes the TCP connection between the client and the server. It causes TCP in the client to send a TCP message to TCP in the server (see Section 3.5).

TCPServer.java

Now let's take a look at the server program.

```java
import java.io.*;
import java.net.*;
class TCPServer {
   public static void main(String argv[]) throws Exception
      {
         String clientSentence;
         String capitalizedSentence;
         ServerSocket welcomeSocket = new ServerSocket
            (6789);
         while(true) {
            Socket connectionSocket = welcomeSocket.
               accept();
            BufferedReader inFromClient =
               new BufferedReader(new InputStreamReader(
                  connectionSocket.getInputStream()));
            DataOutputStream outToClient =
               new DataOutputStream(
                  connectionSocket.getOutputStream());
            clientSentence = inFromClient.readLine();
            capitalizedSentence =
                  clientSentence.toUpperCase() + '\n';
            outToClient.writeBytes(capitalizedSentence);
         }
      }
}
```

TCPServer has many similarities with TCPClient. Let's now take a look at the lines in TCPServer.java. We will not comment on the lines that are identical or similar to commands in TCPClient.java.

The first line in TCPServer is substantially different from what we saw in TCPClient:

```java
ServerSocket welcomeSocket = new ServerSocket(6789);
```

This line creates the object welcomeSocket, which is of type ServerSocket. The welcomeSocket is a sort of door that listens for a knock from some client. The welcomeSocket listens on port number 6789. The next line is

```java
Socket connectionSocket = welcomeSocket.accept();
```

This line creates a new socket, called `connectionSocket`, when some client knocks on `welcomeSocket`. This socket also has port number 6789. (We'll explain why both sockets have the same port number in Chapter 3.) TCP then establishes a direct virtual pipe between `clientSocket` at the client and `connectionSocket` at the server. The client and server can then send bytes to each other over the pipe, and all bytes sent arrive at the other side in order. With `connectionSocket` established, the server can continue to listen for requests from other clients for the application using `welcomeSocket`. (This version of the program doesn't actually listen for more connection requests, but it can be modified with threads to do so.) The program then creates several stream objects, analogous to the stream objects created in `clientSocket`. Now consider

```
capitalizedSentence = clientSentence.toUpperCase() + '\n';
```

This command is the heart of the application. It takes the line sent by the client, capitalizes it, and adds a carriage return. It uses the method `toUpperCase()`. All the other commands in the program are peripheral; they are used for communication with the client.

To test the program pair, you install and compile `TCPClient.java` in one host and `TCPServer.java` in another host. Be sure to include the proper host name of the server in `TCPClient.java`. You next execute `TCPServer.class`, the compiled server program, in the server. This creates a process in the server that idles until it is contacted by some client. Then you execute `TCPClient.class`, the compiled client program, in the client. This creates a process in the client and establishes a TCP connection between the client and server processes. Finally, to use the application, you type a sentence followed by a carriage return.

To develop your own client/server application, you can begin by slightly modifying the programs. For example, instead of converting all the letters to uppercase, the server can count the number of times the letter *s* appears and return this number.

2.8 Socket Programming with UDP

We learned in the previous section that when two processes communicate over TCP, it is as if there were a pipe between the two processes. This pipe remains in place until one of the two processes closes it. When one of the processes wants to send some bytes to the other process, it simply inserts the bytes into the pipe. The sending process does not have to attach a destination address to the bytes because the pipe is logically connected to the destination. Furthermore, the pipe provides a reliable byte stream channel—the sequence of bytes received by the receiving process is exactly the sequence of bytes that the sender inserted into the pipe.

UDP also allows two (or more) processes running on different hosts to communicate. However, UDP differs from TCP in many fundamental ways. First, UDP is a connectionless service—there isn't an initial handshaking phase during which a pipe is established between the two processes. Because UDP doesn't have a pipe, when a process wants to send a batch of bytes to another process, the sending process must attach the destination process's address to the batch of bytes. And this must be done for each batch of bytes the sending process sends. As an analogy, consider a group of 20 persons who take five taxis to a common destination; as the people enter the taxis, each taxi driver must separately be informed of the destination. Thus, UDP is similar to a taxi service. The destination address is a tuple consisting of the IP address of the destination host and the port number of the destination process. We refer to the batch of information bytes along with the IP destination address and port number as the "packet." UDP provides an unreliable message-oriented service model, in that it makes a best effort to deliver the batch of bytes to the destination but makes no guarantee that the batch of bytes will indeed be delivered. The UDP service contrasts sharply (in several respects) with TCP's reliable byte-stream service model.

After having created a packet, the sending process pushes the packet into the network through a socket. Continuing with our taxi analogy, at the other side of the sending socket, there is a taxi waiting for the packet. The taxi then drives the packet in the direction of the packet's destination address. However, the taxi does not guarantee that it will eventually get the packet to its ultimate destination—the taxi could break down or suffer some other unforeseen problem. In other terms, *UDP provides an unreliable transport service to its communication processes*—it makes no guarantees that a datagram will reach its ultimate destination.

In this section we illustrate socket programming by redeveloping the same application of the previous section, but this time over UDP. We'll see that the code for UDP is different from the TCP code in many important ways. In particular, there is (1) no initial handshaking between the two processes and therefore no need for a welcoming socket, (2) no streams are attached to the sockets, (3) the sending hosts create packets by attaching the IP destination address and port number to each batch of bytes it sends, and (4) the receiving process must unravel each received packet to obtain the packet's information bytes. Recall once again our simple application:

1. A client reads a line from its standard input (keyboard) and sends the line out its socket to the server.
2. The server reads a line from its socket.
3. The server converts the line to uppercase.
4. The server sends the modified line out its socket to the client.
5. The client reads the modified line from its socket and prints the line on its standard output (monitor).

Figure 2.30 highlights the main socket-related activity of the client and server that communicate over a connectionless (UDP) transport service.

UDPClient.java

Here is the code for the client side of the application:

```
import java.io.*;
import java.net.*;
class UDPClient {
   public static void main(String args[]) throws Exception
   {
      BufferedReader inFromUser =
         new BufferedReader(new InputStreamReader
                      (System.in));
      DatagramSocket clientSocket = new DatagramSocket();
      InetAddress IPAddress =
                      InetAddress.getByName("hostname");
      byte[] sendData = new byte[1024];
      byte[] receiveData = new byte[1024];
      String sentence = inFromUser.readLine();
      sendData = sentence.getBytes();
      DatagramPacket sendPacket =
         new DatagramPacket(sendData, sendData.length,
                      IPAddress, 9876);
      clientSocket.send(sendPacket);
      DatagramPacket receivePacket =
         new DatagramPacket(receiveData,
                      receiveData.length);
      clientSocket.receive(receivePacket);
      String modifiedSentence =
         new String(receivePacket.getData());
      System.out.println("FROM SERVER:" +
                      modifiedSentence);
      clientSocket.close();
   }
}
```

The program `UDPClient.java` constructs one stream and one socket, as shown in Figure 2.31. The socket is called `clientSocket`, and it is of type `Datagram-Socket`. Note that UDP uses a different kind of socket than TCP at the client. In particular, with UDP our client uses a `DatagramSocket`, whereas with TCP our client used a `Socket`. The stream `inFromUser` is an input stream to the program;

it is attached to the standard input, that is, to the keyboard. We had an equivalent stream in our TCP version of the program. When the user types characters on the keyboard, the characters flow into the stream `inFromUser`. But in contrast with TCP, there are no streams (input or output) attached to the socket. Instead of feeding bytes to the stream attached to a `Socket` object, UDP will push individual packets through the `DatagramSocket` object.

Let's now take a look at the lines in the code that differ significantly from `TCP-Client.java`.

```
DatagramSocket clientSocket = new DatagramSocket();
```

This line creates the object `clientSocket` of type `DatagramSocket`. In contrast with `TCPClient.java`, this line does not initiate a TCP connection. In particular, the client host does not contact the server host upon execution of this line.

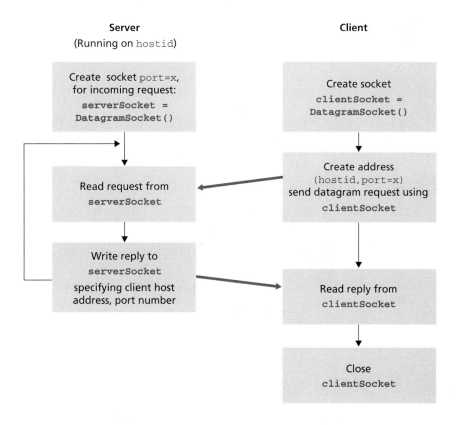

Figure 2.30 ◆ The client-server application, using connectionless transport services

For this reason, the constructor `DatagramSocket()` does not take the server hostname or port number as arguments. Using our door-pipe analogy, the execution of the above line creates a door for the client process but does not create a pipe between the two processes.

```
InetAddress IPAddress = InetAddress.getByName("hostname");
```

In order to send bytes to a destination process, we need the address of the process. Part of this address is the IP address of the destination host. The above line invokes a DNS look-up that translates the hostname (in this example, supplied in the code by the developer) to an IP address. DNS was also invoked by the TCP version of the client, although it was done there implicitly rather than explicitly. The method `getByName()` takes as an argument the hostname of the server and returns the IP

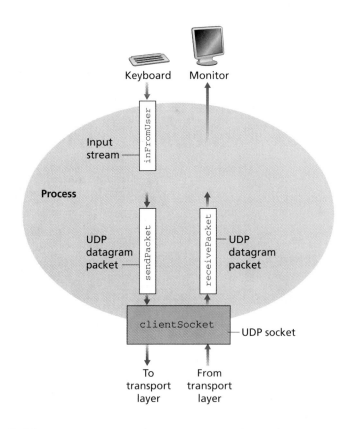

Figure 2.31 ◆ `UDPClient` has one stream; the socket accepts packets from the process and delivers packets to the process.

address of this same server. It places this address in the object `IPAddress` of type `InetAddress`.

```
byte[] sendData = new byte[1024];
byte[] receiveData = new byte[1024];
```

The byte arrays `sendData` and `receiveData` will hold the data the client sends and receives, respectively.

```
sendData = sentence.getBytes();
```

The above line essentially performs a type conversion. It takes the string sentence and renames it as `sendData`, which is an array of bytes.

```
DatagramPacket sendPacket = new DatagramPacket(
    sendData, sendData.length, IPAddress, 9876);
```

This line constructs the packet, `sendPacket`, which the client will pop into the network through its socket. This packet includes that data that is contained in the packet, `sendData`, the length of this data, the IP address of the server, and the port number of the application (which we have set to 9876). Note that `sendPacket` is of type `DatagramPacket`.

```
clientSocket.send(sendPacket);
```

In the above line, the method `send()` of the object `clientSocket` takes the packet just constructed and pops it into the network through `clientSocket`. Once again, note that UDP sends the line of characters in a manner very different from TCP. TCP simply inserted the string of characters into a stream, which had a logical direct connection to the server; UDP creates a packet that includes the address of the server. After sending the packet, the client then waits to receive a packet from the server.

```
DatagramPacket receivePacket =
    new DatagramPacket(receiveData, receiveData.length);
```

In the above line, while waiting for the packet from the server, the client creates a place-holder for the packet, `receivePacket`, an object of type `DatagramPacket`.

```
clientSocket.receive(receivePacket);
```

The client idles until it receives a packet; when it does receive a packet, it puts the packet in `receivePacket`.

```
String modifiedSentence =
    new String(receivePacket.getData());
```

The above line extracts the data from `receivePacket` and performs a type conversion, converting an array of bytes into the string `modifiedSentence`.

```
System.out.println("FROM SERVER:" + modifiedSentence);
```

This line, which is also present in `TCPClient`, prints out the string `modifiedSentence` at the client's monitor.

```
clientSocket.close();
```

This last line closes the socket. Because UDP is connectionless, this line does not cause the client to send a transport-layer message to the server (in contrast with `TCPClient`).

UDPServer.java

Let's now take a look at the server side of the application:

```
import java.io.*;
import java.net.*;
class UDPServer {
    public static void main(String args[]) throws Exception
        {
        DatagramSocket serverSocket = new
                            DatagramSocket(9876);
        byte[] receiveData = new byte[1024];
        byte[] sendData = new byte[1024];
        while(true)
            {
            DatagramPacket receivePacket =
                    new DatagramPacket(receiveData,
                        receiveData.length);
            serverSocket.receive(receivePacket);
            String sentence = new String(
                    receivePacket.getData());
            InetAddress IPAddress =
                        receivePacket.getAddress();
            int port = receivePacket.getPort();
            String capitalizedSentence =
                        sentence.toUpperCase();
```

```
        sendData = capitalizedSentence.getBytes();
        DatagramPacket sendPacket =
        new DatagramPacket(sendData,
                sendData.length, IPAddress, port);
        serverSocket.send(sendPacket);
    }
  }
}
```

The program `UDPServer.java` constructs one socket, as shown in Figure 2.32. The socket is called `serverSocket`. It is an object of type `DatagramSocket`, as was the socket in the client side of the application. Once again, no streams are attached to the socket.

Let's now take a look at the lines in the code that differ from `TCPServer.java`.

```
DatagramSocket serverSocket = new DatagramSocket(9876);
```

The above line constructs the `DatagramSocket serverSocket` at port 9876. All data sent and received will pass through this socket. Because UDP is connectionless, we do not have to create a new socket and continue to listen for new

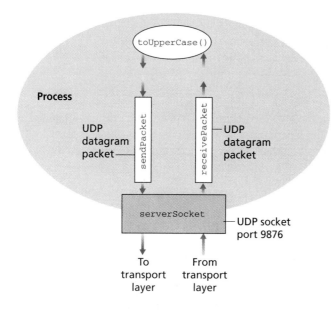

Figure 2.32 ♦ `UDPServer` has no streams; the socket accepts packets from the process and delivers packets to the process.

connection requests, as done in `TCPServer.java`. If multiple clients access this application, they will all send their packets into this single door, `serverSocket`.

```
String sentence = new String(receivePacket.getData());
InetAddress IPAddress = receivePacket.getAddress();
int port = receivePacket.getPort();
```

The above three lines unravel the packet that arrives from the client. The first of the three lines extracts the data from the packet and places the data in the `String` `sentence`; it has an analogous line in `UDPClient`. The second line extracts the IP address; the third line extracts the client port number, which is chosen by the client and is different from the server port number 9876. (We will discuss client port numbers in some detail in the next chapter.) It is necessary for the server to obtain the address (IP address and port number) of the client, so that it can send the capital-ized sentence back to the client.

That completes our analysis of the UDP program pair. To test the application, you install and compile `UDPClient.java` in one host and `UDPServer.java` in another host. (Be sure to include the proper hostname of the server in `UDP Client.java`.) Then execute the two programs on their respective hosts. Unlike with TCP, you can first execute the client side and then the server side. This is because the client process does not attempt to initiate a connection with the server when you execute the client program. Once you have executed the client and server programs, you may use the application by typing a line at the client.

2.9 Building a Simple Web Server

Now that we have studied HTTP in some detail and have learned how to write client/server applications in Java, let us combine this new knowledge and build a simple Web server in Java. We will see that the task is remarkably easy.

2.9.1 Web Server Functions

Our goal is to build a server that does the following:

♦ Handles only one HTTP request
♦ Accepts and parses the HTTP request
♦ Gets the requested file from the server's file system
♦ Creates an HTTP response message consisting of the requested file preceded by header lines
♦ Sends the response directly to the client

Let's try to make the code as simple as possible in order to shed some light on the networking issues. The code that we present will be far from bulletproof! For example, let's not worry about handling exceptions. Let's also assume that the client requests an object that is—for sure—in the server's file system.

WebServer.java

Here is the code for a simple Web server:

```java
import java.io.*;
import java.net.*;
import java.util.*;
class WebServer {
    public static void main(String argv[]) throws Exception {
        String requestMessageLine;
        String fileName;
        ServerSocket listenSocket = new ServerSocket(6789);
        Socket connectionSocket = listenSocket.accept();
        BufferedReader inFromClient =
            new BufferedReader(new InputStreamReader(
                connectionSocket.getInputStream()));
        DataOutputStream outToClient =
            new DataOutputStream(
                connectionSocket.getOutputStream());
        requestMessageLine = inFromClient.readLine();
        StringTokenizer tokenizedLine =
            new StringTokenizer(requestMessageLine);
        if (tokenizedLine.nextToken().equals("GET")){
            fileName = tokenizedLine.nextToken();
            if (fileName.startsWith("/") == true )
                fileName = fileName.substring(1);
            File file = new File(fileName);
            int numOfBytes = (int) file.length();
            FileInputStream inFile = new FileInputStream (
                fileName);
            byte[] fileInBytes = new byte[numOfBytes];
            inFile.read(fileInBytes);
            outToClient.writeBytes(
                "HTTP/1.0 200 Document Follows\r\n");
            if (fileName.endsWith(".jpg"))
                outToClient.writeBytes("Content-Type:
                    image/jpeg\r\n");
            if (fileName.endsWith(".gif"))
```

```
            outToClient.writeBytes("Content-Type:
                    image/gif\r\n");
        outToClient.writeBytes("Content-Length: " +
                numOfBytes + "\r\n");
        outToClient.writeBytes("\r\n");
        outToClient.write(fileInBytes, 0, numOfBytes);
        connectionSocket.close();
        }
    else System.out.println("Bad Request Message");
    }
}
```

Let us now take a look at the code. The first half of the program is almost identical to `TCPServer.java`. As with `TCPServer.java`, we import the `java.io` and `java.net` packages. In addition to these two packages we also import the `java.util` package, which contains the `StringTokenizer` class, which is used for parsing HTTP request messages. Looking now at the lines within the class `WebServer`, we define two string objects:

```
String requestMessageLine;
String fileName;
```

The object `requestMessageLine` is a string that will contain the first line in the HTTP request message. The object `fileName` is a string that will contain the file name of the requested file. The next set of commands is identical to the corresponding set of commands in `TCPServer.java`.

```
ServerSocket listenSocket = new ServerSocket(6789);
Socket connectionSocket = listenSocket.accept();
BufferedReader inFromClient =
    new BufferedReader(new InputStreamReader
            (connectionSocket.getInputStream()));
    DataOutputStream outToClient =
        new DataOutputStream(connectionSocket.
            getOutputStream());
```

Two socket-like objects are created. The first of these objects is `listenSocket`, which is of type `ServerSocket`. The object `listenSocket` is created by the server program before it receives a request for a TCP connection from a client. It listens at port 6789 and waits for a request from some client to establish a TCP connection. When a request for a connection arrives, the `accept()` method of `listenSocket` creates a new object, `connectionSocket`, of type `Socket`.

Next, two streams are created: the `BufferedReader inFromClient` and the `DataOutputStream outToClient`. The HTTP request message comes from the network, through `connectionSocket` and into `inFromClient`; the HTTP response message goes into `outToClient`, through `connectionSocket` and into the network. The remaining portion of the code differs significantly from `TCPServer.java`.

```
requestMessageLine = inFromClient.readLine();
```

The above command reads the first line of the HTTP request message. This line is supposed to be of the form

```
GET file_name HTTP/1.0
```

Our server must now parse the line to extract the file name.

```
StringTokenizer tokenizedLine =
            new StringTokenizer(requestMessageLine);
if (tokenizedLine.nextToken().equals("GET")){
   fileName = tokenizedLine.nextToken();
   if (fileName.startsWith("/") == true )
      fileName = fileName.substring(1);
```

The above commands parse the first line of the request message to obtain the requested file name. The object `tokenizedLine` can be thought of as the original request line with each of the "words" `GET, file_name`, and `HTTP/1.0` placed in a separate placeholder called a token. The server knows from the HTTP RFC that the file name for the requested file is contained in the token that follows the token containing "GET." This file name is put in a string called `fileName`. The purpose of the last `if` statement in the above code is to remove the slash that may precede the file name.

```
FileInputStream inFile = new FileInputStream (fileName);
```

The above command attaches a stream, `inFile`, to the file `fileName`.

```
byte[] fileInBytes = new byte[numOfBytes];
inFile.read(fileInBytes);
```

These commands determine the size of the file and construct an array of bytes of that size. The name of the array is `fileInBytes`. The last command reads from the stream `inFile` to the byte array `fileInBytes`. The program must convert to bytes because the output stream `outToClient` may only be fed with bytes.

Now we are ready to construct the HTTP response message. To this end we must first send the HTTP response header lines into the `DataOutputStream` `outToClient`:

```
outToClient.writeBytes("HTTP/1.0 200 Document
        Follows\r\n");
if (fileName.endsWith(".jpg"))
        outToClient.writeBytes("Content-Type:
        image/jpeg\r\n");
if (fileName.endsWith(".gif"))
        outToClient.writeBytes("Content-Type:
        image/gif\r\n");
outToClient.writeBytes("Content-Length: " + numOfBytes +
        "\r\n");
outToClient.writeBytes("\r\n")
```

The above set of commands is particularly interesting. These commands prepare the header lines for the HTTP response message and send the header lines to the TCP send buffer. The first command sends the mandatory status line `HTTP/1.0 200 Document Follows`, followed by a carriage return and a line feed. The next two command lines prepare a single content-type header line. If the server is to transfer a GIF image, then the server prepares the header line `Content-Type: image/gif`. If, on the other hand, the server is to transfer a JPEG image, then the server prepares the header line `Content-Type: image/jpeg`. (In this simple Web server, no content line is sent if the object is neither a GIF nor a JPEG image.) The server then prepares and sends a content-length header line and a mandatory blank line to precede the object itself that is to be sent. We now must send the file `FileName` into the `DataOutputStream outToClient`.

We can now send the requested file:

```
outToClient.write(fileInBytes, 0, numOfBytes);
```

The above command sends the requested file, `fileInBytes`, to the TCP send buffer. TCP will concatenate the file, `fileInBytes`, to the header lines just created, segment the concatenation if necessary, and send the TCP segments to the client. After serving one request for one file, the server performs some housekeeping by closing the socket `connectionSocket`:

```
connectionSocket.close();
```

To test this Web server, install it on a host. Also put some files in the host. Then use a browser running on any machine to request a file from the server. When you request a file, you will need to use the port number that you include in the server code (for example, 6789). So if your server is located at `somehost.some-where.edu`, the file is `somefile.html`, and the port number is 6789, then the browser should request the following:

`http://somehost.somewhere.edu:6789/somefile.html`

2.10 Summary

In this chapter we've studied the conceptual and the implementation aspects of network applications. We've learned about the ubiquitous client-server architecture adopted by Internet applications and seen its use in the HTTP, FTP, SMTP, POP3, and DNS protocols. We've studied these important application-level protocols, their associated applications (the Web, file transfer, e-mail, and DNS) in some detail. We've also learned about the increasingly prevalent P2P architecture and seen its use in P2P file sharing. We've examined how the socket API can be used to build network applications. We've walked through the use of sockets for connection-oriented (TCP) and connectionless (UDP) end-to-end transport services, and also built a simple Web server using sockets. The first step in our journey down the layered network architecture is complete!

At the very beginning of this book, in Section 1.1, we gave a rather vague, bare-bones definition of a protocol: "the format and the order of messages exchanged between two or more communicating entities, as well as the actions taken on the transmission and/or receipt of a message or other event." The material in this chapter, and in particular our detailed study of the HTTP, FTP, SMTP, POP3, and DNS protocols, has now added considerable substance to this definition. Protocols are a key concept in networking; our study of applications protocols has now given us the opportunity to develop a more intuitive feel for what protocols are all about.

In Section 2.1 we described the service models that TCP and UDP offer to applications that invoke them. We took an even closer look at these service models when we developed simple applications that run over TCP and UDP in Sections 2.7 through 2.9. However, we have said little about how TCP and UDP provide these service models. For example, we have said little about how TCP provides a reliable data transfer service to its applications. In the next chapter we'll take a careful look at not only the *what*, but also the *how* and *why* of transport protocols.

Equipped with knowledge about Internet application structure and application-level protocols, we're now ready to head further down the protocol stack and examine the transport layer in Chapter 3.

Homework Problems and Questions

Chapter 2 Review Questions

SECTION 2.1

1. List five nonproprietary Internet applications and the application-layer protocols that they use.

2. What is the difference between network architecture and application architecture?

3. In what way is instant messaging a hybrid of client-server and P2P architectures?

4. For a communication session between a pair of processes, which process is the client and which is the server?

5. In a P2P file-sharing application, do you agree with the statement, "There is no notion of client and server sides of a communication session"? Why or why not?

6. What information is used by a process running on one host to identify a process running on another host?

7. List the various network-application user agents that you use on a daily basis.

8. Referring to Figure 2.4, we see that none of the applications listed in Figure 2.4 requires both no data loss and timing. Can you conceive of an application that requires no data loss and that is also highly time-sensitive?

SECTIONS 2.2–2.6

9. What is meant by a handshaking protocol?

10. Why do HTTP, FTP, SMTP, POP3, and IMAP run on top of TCP rather than on UDP?

11. Consider an e-commerce site that wants to keep a purchase record for each of its customers. Describe how this can be done with cookies.

12. What is the difference between persistent HTTP with pipelining and persistent HTTP without pipelining? Which of the two is used by HTTP/1.1?

13. Describe how Web caching can reduce the delay in receiving a requested object. Will Web caching reduce the delay for all objects requested by a user or for only some of the objects? Why?

14. Telnet into a Web server and send a multiline request message. Include in the request message the `If-modified-since:` header line to force a response message with the `304 Not Modified` status code.

15. Why is it said that FTP sends control information "out-of-band"?

16. Suppose Alice, with a Web-based e-mail account (such as Hotmail), sends a message to Bob, who accesses his mail from his mail server using POP3. Discuss how the message gets from Alice's host to Bob's host. Be sure to list the series of application-layer protocols that are used to move the message between the two hosts.

17. Print out the header of an e-mail message you have recently received. How many `Received`: header lines are there? Analyze each of the header lines in the message.

18. From a user's perspective, what is the difference between the download-and-delete mode and the download-and-keep mode in POP3?

19. Is it possible for an organization's Web server and mail server to have exactly the same alias for a hostname (for example, `foo.com`)? What would be the type for the RR that contains the hostname of the mail server?

20. What is an overlay network in a P2P file-sharing system? Does it include routers? What are the edges in the overlay network? How is the Gnutella overlay network created and maintained?

21. Find three companies that provide P2P file-sharing services. What type of content is distributed through these companies? How does each of these designs enable users to locate content?

SECTIONS 2.7–2.9

22. The UDP server described in Section 2.8 needed only one socket, whereas the TCP server described in Section 2.7 needed two sockets. Why? If the TCP server were to support n simultaneous connections, each from a different client host, how many sockets would the TCP server need?

23. For the client/server application over TCP described in Section 2.7, why must the server program be executed before the client program? For the client/server application over UDP described in Section 2.8, why may the client program be executed before the server program?

Problems

1. True or false?

   a. When a user requests a Web page that consists of some text and two images. For this page, the client will send one request message and receive three response messages.

   b. Two distinct Web pages (for example, `www.mit.edu/research.html` and `www.mit.edu/students.html`) can be sent over the same persistent connection.

    c. With nonpersistent connections between browser and origin server, it is possible for a single TCP segment to carry two distinct HTTP request messages.

    d. The `Date:` header in the HTTP response message indicates when the object in the response was last modified.

2. Read RFC 959 for FTP. List all of the client commands that are supported by the RFC.

3. Visit `http://www.iana.org`. What are the well-known port numbers for the simple file transfer protocol (SFTP)? For the network news transfer protocol (NNTP)?

4. Consider an HTTP client that wants to retrieve a Web document at a given URL. The IP address of the HTTP server is initially unknown. The Web document at the URL has one embedded GIF image that resides at the same server as the original document. What transport and application-layer protocols besides HTTP are needed in this scenario?

5. Obtain the HTTP/1.1 specification (RFC 2616). Answer the following questions:

    a. Explain the mechanism used for signaling between the client and server to indicate that a persistent connection is being closed. Can the client, the server, or both signal the close of a connection?

    b. What encryption services are provided by HTTP?

6. Suppose within your Web browser you click on a link to obtain a Web page. The IP address for the associated URL is not cached in your local host, so a DNS look-up is necessary to obtain the IP address. Suppose that n DNS servers are visited before your host receives the IP address from DNS; the successive visits incur an RTT of $RTT_1, \ldots, RTT_n$. Further suppose that the Web page associated with the link contains exactly one object, consisting of a small amount of HTML text. Let RTT_0 denote the RTT between the local host and the server containing the object. Assuming zero transmission time of the object, how much time elapses from when the client clicks on the link until the client receives the object?

7. Referring to Problem 6, suppose the HTML file references three very small objects on the same server. Neglecting transmission times, how much time elapses with

    a. Nonpersistent HTTP with no parallel TCP connections?

    b. Nonpersistent HTTP with parallel connections?

    c. Persistent HTTP with pipelining?

8. Two HTTP request methods are GET and POST. Are there any other methods in HTTP/1.0? If so, what are they used for? Are there other methods in HTTP/1.1?

9. Consider Figure 2.11, for which there is an institutional network connected to the Internet. Suppose that the average object size is 900,000 bits and that the average request rate from the institution's browsers to the origin servers is 1.5 requests per second. Also suppose that the amount of time it takes from when the router on the Internet side of the access link forwards an HTTP request until it receives the response in two seconds on average (see Section 2.2.6). Model the total average response time as the sum of the average access delay (that is, the delay from Internet router to institution router) and the average Internet delay. For the average access delay, use $\Delta/(1 - \Delta\beta)$, where Δ is the average time required to send an object over the access link and β is the arrival rate of objects to the access link.

   a. Find the total average response time.

   b. Now suppose a cache is installed in the institutional LAN. Suppose the hit rate is 0.4. Find the total response time.

10. Write a simple TCP program for a server that accepts lines of input from a client and prints the lines onto the server's standard output. (You can do this by modifying the TCPServer.java program in the text.) Compile and execute your program. On any other machine that contains a Web browser, set the proxy server in the browser to the host that is running your server program; also configure the port number appropriately. Your browser should now send its GET request messages to your server, and your server should display the messages on its standard output. Use this platform to determine whether your browser generates conditional GET messages for objects that are locally cached.

11. Read the POP3 RFC, RFC 1939. What is the purpose of the UIDL POP3 command?

12. Consider accessing your e-mail with POP3.

   a. Suppose you have configured your POP mail client to operate in the download-and-delete mode. Complete the following transaction:

   ```
   C: list
   S: 1 498
   S: 2 912
   S: .
   C: retr 1
   S: blah blah ...
   S: .........blah
   S: .
   ?
   ?
   ```

b. Suppose you have configured your POP mail client to operate in the download-and-keep mode. Complete the following transaction:

```
C: list
S: 1 498
S: 2 912
S: .
C: retr 1
S: blah blah ...
S: .........blah
S: .
?
?
```

c. Suppose you have configured your POP mail client to operate in the download-and-keep mode. Using your transcript in part (b), suppose you retrieve messages 1 and 2, exit POP, and then five minutes later you again access POP to retrieve new e-mail. Suppose that in the five-minute interval no new messages have been sent to you. Provide a transcript of this second POP session.

13. a. What is a *whois* database?

b. Use various whois databases on the Internet to obtain the names of two DNS servers. Indicate which whois databases you used.

c. Use nslookup on your local host to send DNS queries to three DNS servers: your local DNS server and the two DNS servers you found in part (b). Try querying for type A, NS, and MX reports. Summarize your findings.

d. Use nslookup to find a Web server that has multiple IP addresses. Does the Web server of your institution (school or company) have multiple IP addresses?

e. Use the ARIN whois database to determine the IP address range used by your university.

f. Describe how an attacker can use whois databases and the nslookup tool to perform reconnaissance on an institution before launching an attack.

g. Discuss why whois databases should be publicly available.

14. Suppose you are downloading MP3s using some P2P file-sharing system. The bottleneck in the Internet is your residential access link, which is a 128 kbps full-duplex link. While you are downloading MP3s, all of a sudden 10 other users start uploading MP3s from your computer. Assuming that your computer is very powerful, and all of these downloads and uploads are not putting any strain on your computer (CPU, disk I/O, and so on), will the simultaneous

uploads—which are also passing through your bottleneck link—slow down your downloads? Why or why not? Also answer the same question for when you have 128 kbps upstream and 512 kbps downstream as part of an ADSL connection

15. Suppose there are N active peers in the Gnutella network, and each pair of peers has an active TCP connection. Additionally, suppose that the TCP connections pass through a total of M routers. How many nodes and edges are there in the corresponding overlay network?

16. In our coverage of Gnutella in Section 2.6, we described in some detail how a new peer joins the Gnutella network. In this problem we want to explore what happens when a peer leaves the Gnutella network. Suppose every participating node maintains TCP connections to at least four distinct peers at all times. Suppose Peer X, which has five TCP connections to other peers, wants to leave.

   a. First consider the case of a graceful departure, that is, Peer X explicitly closes his application, thereby gracefully closing its five TCP connections. What actions would each of the five formerly connected peers take?

   b. Now suppose that X abruptly disconnects from the Internet without notifying its five neighbors that it is closing the TCP connections. What would happen?

17. In this problem we explore the reverse-path routing of the QueryHit messages in Gnutella. Suppose that Alice issues a Query message. Further suppose that Bob receives the Query messages (which may have been forwarded by several intermediate peers) and has a file that matches the query.

   a. Recall that when a peer has a matching file, it sends a QueryHit message along the reverse path of the corresponding Query message. An alternative design would be for Bob to establish a direct TCP connection with Alice and send the QueryHit message over this connection. What are the advantages and disadvantages of such an alternative design?

   b. In the Gnutella protocol, when the peer Alice generates a Query message, it inserts a unique ID in the message's MessageID field. When the peer Bob has a match, it generates QueryHit message using the same MessageID as the Query message. Describe how peers can use the MessageID field and local routing tables to accomplish reverse-path routing.

   c. An alternative approach, which does not use message identifiers, is as follows. When a query message reaches a peer, before forwarding the message, the peer augments the query message with its IP address. Describe how peers can use this mechanism to accomplish reverse-path routing.

18. Repeat problem 17, but now answer the questions as they relate to the Gnutella Ping and Pong messages (rather than the Query and QueryHit messages).

19. In this problem we explore designing a KaZaA-like system that has ordinary nodes, group leaders, and super-group leaders.

    a. Suppose each super-group leader is roughly responsible for 200 group leaders, and each group leader is roughly responsible for 200 ordinary peers. How many super-group leaders would be necessary for a network of four million peers?

    b. What information might each group leader store? What information might each super-group leader store? How might search be performed in such a three-tier design?

20. Consider query flooding in P2P file sharing, as discussed in Section 2.6. Suppose that each peer is connected to at most N neighbors in the overlay network. Also suppose that the node-count field is initially set to K. Suppose Alice makes a query. Find an upper bound on the number of query messages that are sent into the overlay network.

21. Install and compile the Java programs TCPClient and UDPClient on one host and TCPServer and UDPServer on another host.

    a. Suppose you run TCPClient before you run TCPServer. What happens? Why?

    b. Suppose you run UDPClient before you run UDPServer. What happens? Why?

    c. What happens if you use different port numbers for the client and server sides?

22. Rewrite TCPServer.java so that it can accept multiple connections. (*Hint*: You will need to use threads.)

23. Suppose that in UDPClient.java we replace the line

```
DatagramSocket clientSocket = new DatagramSocket( );
```

with

```
DatagramSocket clientSocket = new DatagramSocket(5432);
```

Will it become necessary to change UDPServer.java? What are the port numbers for the sockets in UDPClient and UDPServer? What were they before making this change?

Discussion Questions

1. Why do you think P2P file-sharing applications are so popular? Is it because they (debatably illegally) distribute free music and video? Is it because their massive number of servers efficiently responds to a massive demand for megabytes? Or is it all of these?

2. Are there any efforts underway to build an open source P2P file-sharing system that exploits the heterogeneity of the peers (as does the proprietary KaZaA technology)?

3. Read the paper "The Darknet and the Future of Content Distribution" by Biddle, England, Peinado, and Willman [Biddle 2003]. Do you agree with all of the views of the authors? Why or why not?

4. E-commerce sites and other Web sites often have back-end databases. How do HTTP servers communicate with these back-end databases?

5. What is dynamic HTML? Give examples of Web sites that use dynamic HTML.

6. What are some of the popular server-side scripting languages? What is the purpose of server-side scripting?

7. How can you configure your browser for local caching? What caching options do you have?

8. Can you configure your browser to open multiple simultaneous connections to a Web site? What are the advantages and disadvantages of having a large number of simultaneous TCP connections?

9. In Section 2.4.4 we said that a Web-based e-mail service is often implemented by using both a Web server and an IMAP server. How does the HTTP server communicate with the IMAP server?

10. We have seen that Internet TCP sockets treat the data being sent as a byte stream but UDP sockets recognize message boundaries. What are one advantage and one disadvantage of byte-oriented API versus having the API explicitly recognize and preserve application-defined message boundaries?

11. Suppose you have a database containing astrology data, and you want to make the data available to Web browsers running on PCs, PDAs, and ordinary telephones (using text-to-speech). How might you do this?

12. Discuss the relationship between instant messaging and the protocol SIP.

13. How do buddy lists in instant messaging servers work?

14. What is the Apache Web server? How much does it cost? What functionality does it currently have?

15. Suppose that the Web standards organizations decide to change the naming convention so that each object is named and referenced by a unique name that is location-independent (a so-called URN). Discuss some of the issues surrounding such a change.

16. Consider the incentive schemes currently used by KaZaA to encourage users to be active uploaders. How else may a P2P file-sharing system provide incentives to its users?

Socket Programming Assignments

Assignment 1: Multi-Threaded Web Server

By the end of this programming assignment, you will have developed, in Java, a multithreaded Web server that is capable of serving multiple requests in parallel. You are going to implement version 1.0 of HTTP, as defined in RFC 1945.

Recall that HTTP/1.0 creates a separate TCP connection for each request/response pair. A separate thread handles each of these connections. There will also be a main thread, in which the server listens for clients that want to establish connections. To simplify the programming task, we will develop the code in two stages. In the first stage, you will write a multithreaded server that simply displays the contents of the HTTP request message that it receives. After this program is running properly, you will add the code required to generate an appropriate response.

As you develop the code, you can test your server with a Web browser. But remember that you are not serving through the standard port 80, so you need to specify the port number within the URL that you give your browser. For example, if your host's name is `host.someschool.edu`, your server is listening to port 6789, and you want to retrieve the file `index.html`, then you would specify the following URL within the browser:

```
http://host.someschool.edu:6789/index.html
```

When your server encounters an error, it should send a response message with an appropriate HTML source so that the error information is displayed in the browser window. You can find full details of this assignment, as well as important snippets of Java code, at the Web site http://www.awl.com/kurose-ross.

Assignment 2: Mail Client

In this assignment, you will develop in Java a mail user agent with the following characteristics:

♦ Provides a graphical interface for the sender, with fields for the local mail server, sender's e-mail address, recipient's e-mail address, subject of the message, and the message itself.

♦ Establishes a TCP connection between the mail client and the local mail server. Sends SMTP commands to local mail server. Receives and processes SMTP commands from local mail server.

Here is what your interface will look like:

You will develop the user agent so it sends an e-mail message to at most one recipient at a time. Furthermore, the user agent will assume that the domain part of the recipient's e-mail address is the canonical name of the recipient's SMTP server. (The user agent will not perform a DNS lookup for an MX record, so the sender must supply the actual name of the mail server.) You can find full details of the assignment, as well important snippets of Java code, at the Web site http://www.awl.com/kurose-ross.

Assignment 3: UDP Pinger Lab

In this lab, you will implement a simple UDP-based Ping client and server. The functionality provided by these programs is similar to the standard Ping program available in modern operating systems. Standard Ping works by sending Internet Control Message Protocol (ICMP) ECHO message, which the remote machine echoes back to the sender. The sender can then determine the round-trip time between itself and the computer it pinged.

Java does not provide any functionality to send or receive ICMP messages, which is why in this lab you will implement the pinging in the application layer with standard

UDP sockets and messages. You can find full details of the assignment, as well important snippets of Java code, at the Web site http://www.awl.com/kurose-ross.

Assignment 4: Web Proxy Server

In this lab you'll develop a simple Web proxy server, which is also able to cache Web pages. This server will accept a GET message from a browser, forward the GET message to the destination Web server, receive the HTTP response message from the destination server, and forward the HTTP response message to the browser. This is a very simple proxy server; it only understands simple GET requests. However, the server is able to handle all kinds of objects, not just HTML pages, but also images. You can find full details of the assignment, as well important snippets of Java code, at the Web site http://www.awl.com/kurose-ross.

 # Ethereal Labs

Ethereal Lab: HTTP

Having gotten our feet wet with the Ethereal packet sniffer in Lab 1, we're now ready to use Ethereal to investigate protocols in operation. In this lab, we'll explore several aspects of the HTTP protocol: the basic GET/reply interaction, HTTP message formats, retrieving large HTML files, retrieving HTML files with embedded URLs, persistent and nonpersistent connections, and HTTP authentication and security.

As is the case with all Ethereal labs, the full description of this lab is available at this book's Web site, http://www.awl.com/kurose-ross.

Ethereal Lab: DNS

In this lab, we take a closer look at the client side of the DNS, the protocol that translates Internet hostnames to IP addresses. Recall from Section 2.5 that the client's role in the DNS is relatively simple—a client sends a query to its local DNS server and receives a response back. Much can go on under the covers, invisible to the DNS clients, as the hierarchical DNS servers communicate with each other to either recursively or iteratively resolve the client's DNS query. From the DNS client's standpoint, however, the protocol is quite simple—a query is formulated to the local DNS server and a response is received from that server. We observe DNS in action in this lab.

The full description of this lab is available at this book's Web site, http://www.awl.com/kurose-ross.

AN INTERVIEW WITH...

Tim Berners-Lee

Tim Berners-Lee is the director of the World Wide Web Consortium (W3C) and principal research scientist at MIT's Laboratory for Computer Science. In 1989, while working at the European Particle Physics Laboratory CERN, Tim invented an Internet-based hyper-media initiative for global information sharing, commonly known as the World Wide Web. A year later, he wrote the first Web client and server. Tim received his degree in physics from Oxford University in England in 1976.

You originally studied physics. How is networking similar to physics?

When you study physics, you imagine what rules of behavior on the very small scale could possibly give rise to the large-scale world as we see it. When you design a global system like the Web, you try to invent rules of behavior of Web pages and links and things that could in the large create a large-scale world as we would like it. One is analysis and the other synthesis, but they are very similar.

What influenced you to specialize in networking?

After my physics degree, the telecommunications research companies seemed to be the most interesting places. The microprocessor had just come out, and telecommunications was switching very fast from hardwired logic to microprocessor-based systems. It was very exciting.

What is the most challenging part of your job?

When two groups disagree strongly about something, but want in the end to achieve a common goal, finding exactly what they each mean and where the misunderstandings are can be very demanding. The chair of any working group knows that. However, this is what it takes to make progress toward consensus on a large scale.

What do you envision for the future of networking/the Internet?

As I said in my book, I have a dream for the Web . . . and it has two parts.

In the first part, the Web becomes a much more powerful means for collaboration between people. I have always imagined the information space as something to which everyone has immediate and intuitive access, and not just to browse, but to create. . . . Furthermore, the dream of people-to-people communication through shared knowledge must be possible for groups of all sizes, interacting electronically with as much ease as they do now in person.

181

In the second part of the dream, collaborations extend to computers. Machines become capable of analyzing all the data on the Web—the content, links, and transactions between people and computers. A "Semantic Web," which should make this possible, has yet to emerge, but when it does, the day-to-day mechanisms of trade, bureaucracy, and our daily lives will be handled by machines talking to machines, leaving humans to provide inspiration and intuition. . . . This machine-understandable Web will come about through the implementation of a series of technical advances and social agreements that are now beginning.

Once the two-part dream is reached, the Web will be a place where the whim of a human being and the reasoning of a machine coexist in an ideal, powerful mixture.

What people have inspired you professionally?

My parents, who were involved in the early days of computing, gave me a fascination with the whole subject. Mike Sendall and Peggie Rimmer, for whom I worked at various times at CERN, are among the people who taught me and encouraged me. I later learned to admire the people, including Vanevar Bush, Doug Englebart, and Ted Nelson, who had had similar dreams in their time but had not had the benefit of the existence of PCs and the Internet to be able to realize it.

The mission of the World Wide Web Consortium is to "lead the Web to its full potential." In your view, what is the full potential of the Web? In what ways can this potential be actualized?

We are trying to lead it in the two directions I mentioned, toward collaboration and toward the Semantic Web. All the time we are trying to enhance the universality of the Web to one in which there is just one Web, whatever your browser, it's always available, and anyone can access it no matter what hardware device, software vendor, geographical position, disability, language, or culture.

Transport Layer

Residing between the application and network layers, the transport layer is a central piece of the layered network architecture. It has the critical role of providing communication services directly to the application processes running on different hosts. The pedagogic approach we take in this chapter is to alternate between discussions of transport-layer principles and discussions of how these principles are implemented in existing protocols; as usual, particular emphasis will be given to Internet protocols, in particular the TCP and UDP transport-layer protocols.

We'll begin by discussing the relationship between the transport and network layers. This sets the stage for examining the first critical function of the transport layer—extending the network layer's delivery service between two end systems to a delivery service between two application-layer processes running on the end systems. We'll illustrate this function in our coverage of the Internet's connectionless transport protocol, UDP.

We'll then return to principles and confront one of the most fundamental problems in computer networking—how two entities can communicate reliably over a medium that may lose and corrupt data. Through a series of increasingly complicated (and realistic!) scenarios, we'll build up an array of techniques that transport protocols use to solve this problem. We'll then show how these principles are embodied in TCP, the Internet's connection-oriented transport protocol.

We'll next move on to a second fundamentally important problem in networking—controlling the transmission rate of transport-layer entities in order to avoid, or recover from, congestion within the network. We'll consider the causes and consequences of congestion, as well as commonly used congestion-control techniques. After obtaining a solid understanding of the issues behind congestion control, we'll study TCP's approach to congestion control.

3.1 Introduction and Transport-Layer Services

In the previous two chapters we touched on the role of the transport layer and the services that it provides. Let's quickly review what we have already learned about the transport layer.

A transport-layer protocol provides for **logical communication** between application processes running on different hosts. By *logical communication*, we mean that from an application's perspective, it is as if the hosts running the processes were directly connected; in reality, the hosts may be on opposite sides of the planet, connected via numerous routers and a wide range of link types. Application processes use the logical communication provided by the transport layer to send messages to each other, free from the worry of the details of the physical infrastructure used to carry these messages. Figure 3.1 illustrates the notion of logical communication.

As shown in Figure 3.1, transport-layer protocols are implemented in the end systems but not in network routers. On the sending side, the transport layer converts the messages it receives from a sending application process into transport-layer packets, known as transport-layer segments in Internet terminology. This is done by (possibly) breaking the application messages into smaller chunks and adding a transport-layer header to each chunk to create the transport-layer segment. The transport layer then passes the segment to the network layer at the sending end system, where the segment is encapsulated within a network-layer packet (a datagram) and sent to the destination. It's important to note that network routers act only on the network-layer fields of the datagram; that is, they do not examine the fields of the transport-layer segment encapsulated with the datagram. On the receiving side, the network layer extracts the transport-layer segment from the datagram and passes the segment up to the transport layer. The transport layer then processes the received segment, making available the data in the segment to the receiving application.

More than one transport-layer protocol may be available to network applications. For example, the Internet has two protocols—TCP and UDP. Each of these protocols provides a different set of transport-layer services to the invoking application.

3.1.1 Relationship Between Transport and Network Layers

Recall that the transport layer lies just above the network layer in the protocol stack. Whereas a transport-layer protocol provides logical communication between *processes* running on different hosts, a network-layer protocol provides logical communication between *hosts*. This distinction is subtle but important. Let's examine this distinction with the aid of a household analogy.

Consider two houses, one on the East Coast and the other on the West Coast, with each house being home to a dozen kids. The kids in the East Coast household are cousins of the kids in the West Coast household. The kids in the two households love to

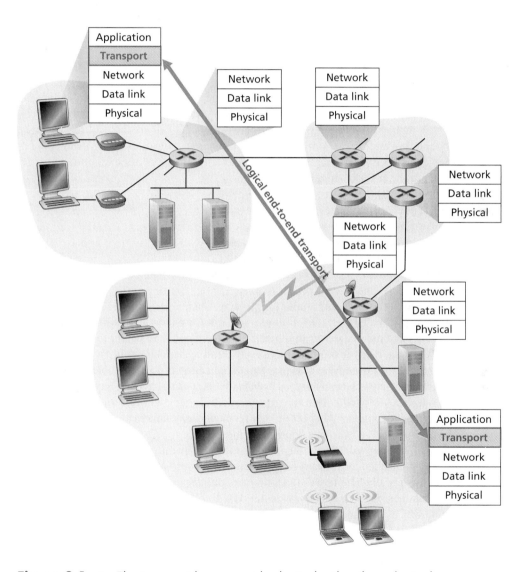

Figure 3.1 ♦ The transport layer provides logical rather than physical communication between application processes.

write to each other—each kid writes each cousin every week, with each letter delivered by the traditional postal service in a separate envelope. Thus, each household sends 144 letters to the other household every week. (These kids would save a lot of money if they had e-mail!) In each of the households there is one kid—Ann in the West Coast house and Bill in the East Coast house—responsible for mail collection and mail distribution. Each week Ann visits all her brothers and sisters, collects the mail, and gives the mail to a postal-service mail carrier, who makes daily visits to the house. When letters arrive at the West Coast house, Ann also has the job of distributing the mail to her brothers and sisters. Bill has a similar job on the East Coast.

In this example, the postal service provides logical communication between the two houses—the postal service moves mail from house to house, not from person to person. On the other hand, Ann and Bill provide logical communication among the cousins—Ann and Bill pick up mail from, and deliver mail to, their brothers and sisters. Note that from the cousins' perspective, Ann and Bill *are* the mail service, even though Ann and Bill are only a part (the end-system part) of the end-to-end delivery process. This household example serves as a nice analogy for explaining how the transport layer relates to the network layer:

> application messages = letters in envelopes
> processes = cousins
> hosts (also called end systems) = houses
> transport-layer protocol = Ann and Bill
> network-layer protocol = postal service (including mail carriers)

Continuing with this analogy, note that Ann and Bill do all their work within their respective homes; they are not involved, for example, in sorting mail in any intermediate mail center or in moving mail from one mail center to another. Similarly, transport-layer protocols live in the end systems. Within an end system, a transport protocol moves messages from application processes to the network edge (that is, the network layer) and vice versa, but it doesn't have any say about how the messages are moved within the network core. In fact, as illustrated in Figure 3.1, intermediate routers neither act on, nor recognize, any information that the transport layer may have added to the application messages.

Continuing with our family saga, suppose now that when Ann and Bill go on vacation, another cousin pair—say, Susan and Harvey—substitute for them and provide the household-internal collection and delivery of mail. Unfortunately for the two families, Susan and Harvey do not do the collection and delivery in exactly the same way as Ann and Bill. Being younger kids, Susan and Harvey pick up and drop off the mail less frequently and occasionally lose letters (which are sometimes chewed up by the family dog). Thus, the cousin-pair Susan and Harvey do not provide the same set of services (that is, the same service model) as Ann and Bill. In an analogous manner, a computer network may make available multiple transport protocols, with each protocol offering a different service model to applications.

The possible services that Ann and Bill can provide are clearly constrained by the possible services that the postal service provides. For example, if the postal service doesn't provide a maximum bound on how long it can take to deliver mail between the two houses (for example, three days), then there is no way that Ann and Bill can guarantee a maximum delay for mail delivery between any of the cousin pairs. In a similar manner, the services that a transport protocol can provide are often constrained by the service model of the underlying network-layer protocol. If the network-layer protocol cannot provide delay or bandwidth guarantees for transport-layer segments sent between hosts, then the transport-layer protocol cannot provide delay or bandwidth guarantees for application messages sent between processes.

Nevertheless, certain services *can* be offered by a transport protocol even when the underlying network protocol doesn't offer the corresponding service at the network layer. For example, as we'll see in this chapter, a transport protocol can offer reliable data transfer service to an application even when the underlying network protocol is unreliable, that is, even when the network protocol loses, garbles, or duplicates packets. As another example (which we'll explore in Chapter 8 when we discuss network security), a transport protocol can use encryption to guarantee that application messages are not read by intruders, even when the network layer cannot guarantee the confidentiality of transport-layer segments.

3.1.2 Overview of the Transport Layer in the Internet

Recall that the Internet, and more generally a TCP/IP network, makes available two distinct transport-layer protocols to the application layer. One of these protocols is **UDP** (User Datagram Protocol), which provides an unreliable, connectionless service to the invoking application. The second of these protocols is **TCP** (Transmission Control Protocol), which provides a reliable, connection-oriented service to the invoking application. When designing a network application, the application developer must specify one of these two transport protocols. As we saw in Sections 2.7 and 2.8, the application developer selects between UDP and TCP when creating sockets.

To simplify terminology, when in an Internet context, we refer to the transport-layer packet as a *segment*. We mention, however, that the Internet literature (for example, the RFCs) also refers to the transport-layer packet for TCP as a segment but often refers to the packet for UDP as a datagram. But this same Internet literature also uses the term *datagram* for the network-layer packet! For an introductory book on computer networking such as this, we believe that it is less confusing to refer to both TCP and UDP packets as segments, and reserve the term *datagram* for the network-layer packet.

Before proceeding with our brief introduction of UDP and TCP, it will be useful to say a few words about the Internet's network layer. (The network layer is examined in detail in Chapter 4.) The Internet's network-layer protocol has a name—IP, for Internet Protocol. IP provides logical communication between hosts.

The IP service model is a **best-effort delivery service**. This means that IP makes its "best effort" to deliver segments between communicating hosts, *but it makes no guarantees.* In particular, it does not guarantee segment delivery, it does not guarantee orderly delivery of segments, and it does not guarantee the integrity of the data in the segments. For these reasons, IP is said to be an **unreliable service**. We also mention here that every host has at least one network-layer address, a so-called IP address. We'll examine IP addressing in detail in Chapter 4; for this chapter we need only keep in mind that *each host has an IP address.*

Having taken a glimpse at the IP service model, let's now summarize the service models provided by UDP and TCP. The most fundamental responsibility of UDP and TCP is to extend IP's delivery service between two end systems to a delivery service between two processes running on the end systems. Extending host-to-host delivery to process-to-process delivery is called **transport-layer multiplexing and demultiplexing**. We'll discuss transport-layer multiplexing and demultiplexing in the next section. UDP and TCP also provide integrity checking by including error-detection fields in their segments' headers. These two minimal transport-layer services—process-to-process data delivery and error checking—are the only two services that UDP provides! In particular, like IP, UDP is an unreliable service—it does not guarantee that data sent by one process will arrive intact (or at all!) to the destination process. UDP is discussed in detail in Section 3.3.

TCP, on the other hand, offers several additional services to applications. First and foremost, it provides **reliable data transfer**. Using flow control, sequence numbers, acknowledgments, and timers (techniques we'll explore in detail in this chapter), TCP ensures that data is delivered from sending process to receiving process, correctly and in order. TCP thus converts IP's unreliable service between end systems into a reliable data transport service between processes. TCP also provides **congestion control**. Congestion control is not so much a service provided to the invoking application as it is a service for the Internet as a whole, a service for the general good. Loosely speaking, TCP congestion control prevents any one TCP connection from swamping the links and switches between communicating hosts with an excessive amount of traffic. In principle, TCP permits TCP connections traversing a congested network link to equally share that link's bandwidth. This is done by regulating the rate at which the sending-side TCPs can send traffic into the network. UDP traffic, on the other hand, is unregulated. An application using UDP transport can send at any rate it pleases, for as long as it pleases.

A protocol that provides reliable data transfer and congestion control is necessarily complex. We'll need several sections to cover the principles of reliable data transfer and congestion control, and additional sections to cover the TCP protocol itself. These topics are investigated in Sections 3.4 through 3.8. The approach taken in this chapter is to alternate between basic principles and the TCP protocol. For example, we'll first discuss reliable data transfer in a general setting and then discuss how TCP specifically provides reliable data transfer. Similarly, we'll first discuss congestion control in a general setting and then discuss how TCP performs congestion control. But before getting into all this good stuff, let's first look at transport-layer multiplexing and demultiplexing.

3.2 Multiplexing and Demultiplexing

In this section we discuss transport-layer multiplexing and demultiplexing, that is, extending the host-to-host delivery service provided by the network layer to a process-to-process delivery service for applications running on the hosts. In order to keep the discussion concrete, we'll discuss this basic transport-layer service in the context of the Internet. We emphasize, however, that a multiplexing/demultiplexing service is needed for all computer networks.

At the destination host, the transport layer receives segments from the network layer just below. The transport layer has the responsibility of delivering the data in these segments to the appropriate application process running in the host. Let's take a look at an example. Suppose you are sitting in front of your computer, and you are downloading Web pages while running one FTP session and two Telnet sessions. You therefore have four network application processes running—two Telnet processes, one FTP process, and one HTTP process. When the transport layer in your computer receives data from the network layer below, it needs to direct the received data to one of these four processes. Let's now examine how this is done.

First recall from Sections 2.7 and 2.8 that a process (as part of a network application) can have one or more **sockets**, doors through which data passes from the network to the process and through which data passes from the process to the network. Thus, as shown in Figure 3.2, the transport layer in the receiving host does not actually deliver data directly to a process, but instead to an intermediary socket. Because at any given time there can be more than one socket in the receiving host, each socket has a unique identifier. The format of the identifier depends on whether the socket is a UDP or a TCP socket, as we'll discuss shortly.

Now let's consider how a receiving host directs an incoming transport-layer segment to the appropriate socket. Each transport-layer segment has a set of fields in the segment for this purpose. At the receiving end, the transport layer examines these fields to identify the receiving socket and then directs the segment to that socket. This job of delivering the data in a transport-layer segment to the correct socket is called **demultiplexing**. The job of gathering data chunks at the source host from different sockets, encapsulating each data chunk with header information (that will later be used in demultiplexing) to create segments, and passing the segments to the network layer is called **multiplexing**. Note that the transport layer in the middle host in Figure 3.2 must demultiplex segments arriving from the network layer below to either process P_1 or P_2 above; this is done by directing the arriving segment's data to the corresponding process's socket. The transport layer in the middle host must also gather outgoing data from these sockets, form transport-layer

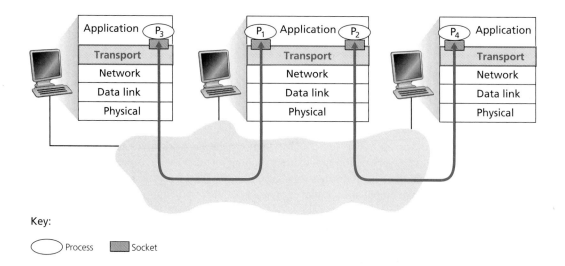

Key:

⬭ Process   ▨ Socket

Figure 3.2 ◆ Transport-layer multiplexing and demultiplexing

segments, and pass these segments down to the network layer. Although we have introduced multiplexing and demultiplexing in the context of the Internet transport protocols, it's important to realize that they are concerns whenever a single protocol at one layer (at the transport layer or elsewhere) is used by multiple protocols at the next higher layer.

To illustrate the demultiplexing job, recall the household metaphor in the previous section. Each of the kids is identified by his or her name. When Bill receives a batch of mail from the mail carrier, he performs a demultiplexing operation by observing to whom the letters are addressed and then hand delivering the mail to his brothers and sisters. Ann performs a multiplexing operation when she collects letters from her brothers and sisters and gives the collected mail to the mail person.

Now that we understand the roles of transport-layer multiplexing and demultiplexing, let us examine how it is actually done in a host. From the discussion above, we know that transport-layer multiplexing requires (1) that sockets have unique identifiers and (2) that each segment have special fields that indicate the socket to which the segment is to be delivered. These special fields, illustrated in Figure 3.3, are the **source port number field** and the **destination port number field**. (The UDP and TCP segments have other fields as well, as discussed in the subsequent sections of this chapter.) Each port number is a 16-bit number, ranging from 0 to 65535. The port numbers ranging from 0 to 1023 are called **well-known port numbers** and are restricted, which means that they are reserved for use by well-known application protocols such as HTTP (which uses port number 80) and FTP (which uses port number 21). The list of well-known port numbers is given in RFC 1700 and is updated at http://www.iana.org [RFC 3232]. When we develop a new application (such as one of the applications developed in Sections 2.7 through 2.9), we must assign the application a port number.

It should now be clear how the transport layer *could* implement the demultiplexing service: Each socket in the host can be assigned a port number, and when a segment arrives to the host, the transport layer examines the destination port number in the segment and directs the segment to the corresponding socket. The segment's data then passes through the socket into the attached process. As we'll see, this is basically how UDP does it. However, we'll also see that multiplexing/demultiplexing in TCP is yet more subtle.

Connectionless Multiplexing and Demultiplexing

Recall from Section 2.8 that a Java program running in a host can create a UDP socket with the line

```
DatagramSocket mySocket = new DatagramSocket();
```

When a UDP socket is created in this manner, the transport layer automatically assigns a port number to the socket. In particular, the transport layer assigns a port number in the range 1024 to 65535 that is currently not being used by any other UDP port in the host. Alternatively, a Java program could create a socket with the line

```
DatagramSocket mySocket = new DatagramSocket(19157);
```

In this case, the application assigns a specific port number—namely, 19157—to the UDP socket. If the application developer writing the code were implementing the

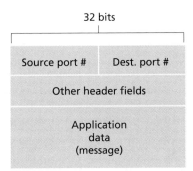

32 bits

Source port #	Dest. port #
Other header fields	
Application data (message)	

Figure 3.3 ♦ Source and destination port-number fields in a transport-layer segment

server side of a "well-known protocol," then the developer would have to assign the corresponding well-known port number. Typically, the client side of the application lets the transport layer automatically (and transparently) assign the port number, whereas the server side of the application assigns a specific port number.

With port numbers assigned to UDP sockets, we can now precisely describe UDP multiplexing/demultiplexing. Suppose a process in Host A, with UDP port 19157, wants to send a chunk of application data to a process with UDP port 46428 in Host B. The transport layer in Host A creates a transport-layer segment that includes the application data, the source port number (19157), the destination port number (46428), and two other values (which will be discussed later, but are unimportant for the current discussion). The transport layer then passes the resulting segment to the network layer. The network layer encapsulates the segment in an IP datagram and makes a best-effort attempt to deliver the segment to the receiving host. If the segment arrives at the receiving Host B, the receiving host examines the destination port number in the segment (46428) and delivers the segment to its socket identified by port 46428. Note that Host B could be running multiple processes, each with its own UDP socket and associated port number. As UDP segments arrive from the network, Host B directs (demultiplexes) each segment to the appropriate socket by examining the segment's destination port number.

It is important to note that a UDP socket is fully identified by a two-tuple consisting of a destination IP address and a destination port number. As a consequence, if two UDP segments have different source IP addresses and/or source port numbers, but have the same *destination* IP address and *destination* port number, then the two segments will be directed to the same destination process via the same destination socket.

You may be wondering now, what is the purpose of the source port number? As shown in Figure 3.4, in the A-to-B segment the source port number serves as part of a "return address"—when B wants to send a segment back to A, the destination port in the B-to-A segment will take its value from the source port value of the A-to-B segment. (The complete return address is A's IP address and the source port number.) As an example, recall the UDP server program studied in Section 2.8. In `UDPServer.java`, the server uses a method to extract the source port number from the segment it receives from the client; it then sends a new segment to the client, with the extracted source port number serving as the destination port number in this new segment.

Connection-Oriented Multiplexing and Demultiplexing

In order to understand TCP demultiplexing, we have to take a close look at TCP sockets and TCP connection establishment. One subtle difference between a TCP socket and a UDP socket is that a TCP socket is identified by a four-tuple: (source IP address, source port number, destination IP address, destination port number). Thus, when a TCP segment arrives from the network to a host, the host uses all four values to direct (demultiplex) the segment to the appropriate socket. In particular,

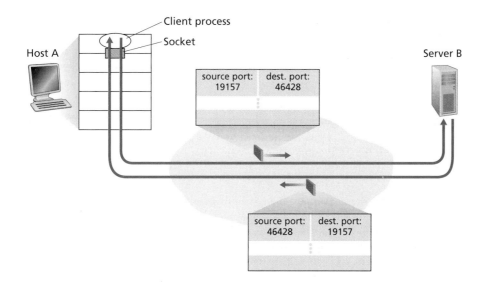

Figure 3.4 ♦ The inversion of source and destination port numbers

and in contrast with UDP, two arriving TCP segments with different source IP addresses or source port numbers will (with the exception of a TCP carrying the original connection-establishment request) be directed to two different sockets. To gain further insight, let's reconsider the TCP client/server programming example in Section 2.7:

♦ The TCP server application has a "welcoming socket," which waits for connection-establishment requests from TCP clients (see Figure 2.27) on port number 6789.

♦ The TCP client generates a connection-establishment segment with the line

```
Socket clientSocket = new Socket("serverHostName", 6789);
```

♦ A connection-establishment request is nothing more than a TCP segment with desti-nation port number 6789 and a special connection-establishment bit set in the TCP header (discussed in Section 3.5). The segment also includes a source port number, which was chosen by the client. The line above also creates a TCP socket for the client process, through which data can enter and leave the client process.

♦ When the host operating system of the computer running the server process receives the incoming connection-request segment with destination port 6789, it locates the server process that is waiting to accept a connection on port number 6789. The server process then creates a new connection:

```
Socket connectionSocket = welcomeSocket.accept();
```

♦ Also, the server notes the following four values in the connection-request segment: (1) the source port number in the segment, (2) the IP address of the source
host, (3) the destination port number in the segment, and (4) its own IP address.
The newly created connection socket is identified by these four values; all subsequently arriving segments whose source port, source IP address, destination port,
and destination IP address match these four values will be demultiplexed to this
socket. With the TCP connection now in place, the client and server can now
send data to each other.

The server host may support many simultaneous TCP sockets, with each socket
attached to a process, and with each socket identified by its own four-tuple. When a
TCP segment arrives to the host, all four fields (source IP address, source port, destination IP address, destination port) are used to direct (demultiplex) the segment to
the appropriate socket.

The situation is illustrated in Figure 3.5, in which Host C initiates two HTTP sessions to server B, and Host A initiates one HTTP session to B. Hosts A and C and server
B each have their own unique IP address—A, C, and B, respectively. Host C assigns
two different source port numbers (26145 and 7532) to its two HTTP connections.
Because Host A is choosing source port numbers independently of C, it might also
assign a source port of 26145 to its HTTP connection. Nevertheless, server B will still
be able to correctly demultiplex the two connections having the same source port number, since the two connections have different source IP addresses.

Web Servers and TCP

Before closing this discussion, it's instructive to say a few additional words about
Web servers and how they use port numbers. Consider a host running a Web server,
such as an Apache Web server, on port 80. When clients (for example, browsers)
send segments to the server, *all* segments will have destination port 80. In particular, both the initial connection-establishment segments and the segments carrying
HTTP request messages will have destination port 80. As we have just described,
the server distinguishes the segments from the different clients by the source IP
addresses and source port numbers.

Web servers typically spawn a new process or create a new thread for each new
client connection. Figure 3.5 shows a Web server that spawns a new process for each
connection. As shown in Figure 3.5, each of these processes has its own connection
socket through which HTTP requests arrive and HTTP responses are sent. We mention, however, that there is not always a one-to-one correspondence between connection sockets and processes. In fact, today's high-performing Web servers often
use only one process, but create a new thread with a new connection socket for each

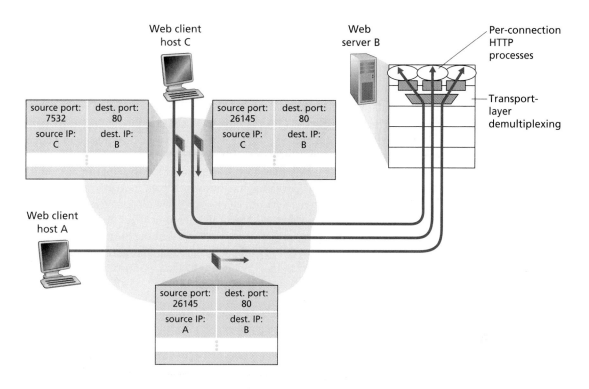

Figure 3.5 ♦ Two clients, using the same destination port number (80) to communicate with the same Web server application

new client connection. (A thread can be viewed as a lightweight subprocess.) If you did the first programming assignment in Chapter 2, you built a Web server that does just this. For such a server, at any given time there may be many connection sockets (with different identifiers) attached to the same process.

If the client and server are using persistent HTTP, then throughout the duration of the persistent connection the client and server exchange HTTP messages via the same server socket. However, if the client and server use nonpersistent HTTP, then a new TCP connection is created and closed for every request/response, and hence a new socket is created and later closed for every request/response. This frequent creating and closing of sockets can severely impact the performance of a busy Web server (although a number of operating system tricks can be used to mitigate the problem). Readers interested in the operating system issues surrounding persistent and nonpersistent HTTP are encouraged to see [Nielsen 1997; Nahum 2002].

Now that we've discussed transport-layer multiplexing and demultiplexing, let's move on and discuss one of the Internet's transport protocols, UDP. In the next section we'll see that UDP adds little more to the network-layer protocol than a multiplexing/demultiplexing service.

3.3   Connectionless Transport: UDP

In this section, we'll take a close look at UDP, how it works, and what it does. We encourage you to refer back to Section 2.1, which includes an overview of the UDP service model, and to Section 2.8, which discusses socket programming over UDP.

To motivate our discussion about UDP, suppose you were interested in designing a no-frills, bare-bones transport protocol. How might you go about doing this? You might first consider using a vacuous transport protocol. In particular, on the sending side, you might consider taking the messages from the application process and passing them directly to the network layer; and on the receiving side, you might consider taking the messages arriving from the network layer and passing them directly to the application process. But as we learned in the previous section, we have to do a little more than nothing! At the very least, the transport layer has to provide a multiplexing/demultiplexing service in order to pass data between the network layer and the correct application-level process.

UDP, defined in RFC 768, does just about as little as a transport protocol can do. Aside from the multiplexing/demultiplexing function and some light error checking, it adds nothing to IP. In fact, if the application developer chooses UDP instead of TCP, then the application is almost directly talking with IP. UDP takes messages from the application process, attaches source and destination port number fields for the multiplexing/demultiplexing service, adds two other small fields, and passes the resulting segment to the network layer. The network layer encapsulates the segment into an IP datagram and then makes a best-effort attempt to deliver the segment to the receiving host. If the segment arrives at the receiving host, UDP uses the destination port number to deliver the segment's data to the correct application process. Note that with UDP there is no handshaking between sending and receiving transport-layer entities before sending a segment. For this reason, UDP is said to be *connectionless*.

DNS is an example of an application-layer protocol that typically uses UDP. When the DNS application in a host wants to make a query, it constructs a DNS query message and passes the message to UDP. Without performing any handshaking with the UDP entity running on the destination end system, the host-side UDP adds header fields to the message and passes the resulting segment to the network layer. The network layer encapsulates the UDP segment into a datagram and sends the datagram to a name server. The DNS application at the querying host then waits for a reply to its query. If it doesn't receive a reply (possibly because the underlying network lost the query or the reply), either it tries sending the query to another name server, or it informs the invoking application that it can't get a reply.

Now you might be wondering why an application developer would ever choose to build an application over UDP rather than over TCP. Isn't TCP always preferable, since TCP provides a reliable data transfer service, while UDP does not? The answer is no, as many applications are better suited for UDP for the following reasons:

♦ *Finer application-level control over what data is sent, and when.* Under UDP, as soon as an application process passes data to UDP, UDP will package the data inside a UDP segment and immediately pass the segment to the network layer. TCP, on the other hand, has a congestion-control mechanism that throttles the transport-layer TCP sender when one or more links between the source and destination hosts become excessively congested. TCP will also continue to resend a segment until the receipt of the segment has been acknowledged by the destination, regardless of how long reliable delivery takes. Since real-time applications often require a minimum sending rate, do not want to overly delay segment transmission, and can tolerate some data loss, TCP's service model is not particularly well matched to these applications' needs. As discussed below, these applications can use UDP and implement, as part of the application, any additional functionality that is needed beyond UDP's no-frills segment-delivery service.

♦ *No connection establishment.* As we'll discuss later, TCP uses a three-way handshake before it starts to transfer data. UDP just blasts away without any formal preliminaries. Thus UDP does not introduce any delay to establish a connection. This is probably the principal reason why DNS runs over UDP rather than TCP—DNS would be much slower if it ran over TCP. HTTP uses TCP rather than UDP, since reliability is critical for Web pages with text. But, as we briefly discussed in Section 2.2, the TCP connection-establishment delay in HTTP is an important contributor to the delays associated with downloading Web documents.

♦ *No connection state.* TCP maintains connection state in the end systems. This connection state includes receive and send buffers, congestion-control parameters, and sequence and acknowledgment number parameters. We will see in Section 3.5 that this state information is needed to implement TCP's reliable data transfer service and to provide congestion control. UDP, on the other hand, does not maintain connection state and does not track any of these parameters. For this reason, a server devoted to a particular application can typically support many more active clients when the application runs over UDP rather than TCP.

♦ *Small packet header overhead.* The TCP segment has 20 bytes of header overhead in every segment, whereas UDP has only 8 bytes of overhead.

Figure 3.6 lists popular Internet applications and the transport protocols that they use. As we expect, e-mail, remote terminal access, the Web, and file transfer run over TCP—all these applications need the reliable data transfer service of TCP. Nevertheless, many important applications run over UDP rather than TCP. UDP is used for RIP routing table updates (see Section 4.6.1). Since RIP updates are sent periodically (typically every five minutes), lost updates will be replaced by more recent updates, thus making the lost, out-of-date update useless. UDP is also used to carry network management (SNMP; see Chapter 9) data. UDP is preferred to TCP in this case, since network management applications must often run when the network is in a stressed state—precisely when reliable, congestion-controlled data transfer is difficult to achieve. Also, as we mentioned earlier, DNS runs over UDP, thereby avoiding TCP's connection-establishment delays.

As shown in Figure 3.6, UDP is also commonly used today with multimedia applications, such as Internet phone, real-time video conferencing, and streaming of stored audio and video. We'll take a close look at these applications in Chapter 7. We just mention now that all of these applications can tolerate a small amount of packet loss, so that reliable data transfer is not absolutely critical for the application's success. Furthermore, real-time applications, like Internet phone and video conferencing, react very poorly to TCP's congestion control. For these reasons, developers of multimedia applications often choose to run their applications over UDP instead of TCP.

Although commonly done today, running multimedia applications over UDP is controversial to say the least. As we mentioned above, UDP has no congestion control. But congestion control is needed to prevent the network from entering a congested state in which very little useful work is done. If everyone were to start streaming high-bit-rate video without using any congestion control, there would be so much packet overflow at routers that very few UDP packets would successfully traverse the source-to-destination path. Moreover, the high loss rates induced by the uncontrolled UDP senders would cause the TCP senders (which, as we'll see, *do* decrease their sending rates in the face of congestion), to dramatically decrease their

Application	Application-Layer Protocol	Underlying Transport Protocol
Electronic mail	SMTP	TCP
Remote terminal access	Telnet	TCP
Web	HTTP	TCP
File transfer	FTP	TCP
Remote file server	NFS	Typically UDP
Streaming multimedia	typically proprietary	Typically UDP
Internet telephony	typically proprietary	Typically UDP
Network management	SNMP	Typically UDP
Routing protocol	RIP	Typically UDP
Name translation	DNS	Typically UDP

Figure 3.6 ♦ Popular Internet applications and their underlying transport protocols

rates. Thus, the lack of congestion control in UDP can result in high loss rates between a UDP sender and receiver, and the crowding out of TCP sessions—a potentially serious problem [Floyd 1999]. Many researchers have proposed new mechanisms to force all sources, including UDP sources, to perform adaptive congestion control [Mahdavi 1997; Floyd 2000; Kohler 2004].

Before discussing the UDP segment structure, we mention that it *is* possible for an application to have reliable data transfer when using UDP. This can be done if reliability is built into the application itself (for example, by adding acknowledgment and retransmission mechanisms, such as those we'll study in the next section). But this is a nontrivial task that would keep an application developer busy debugging for a long time. Nevertheless, building reliability directly into the application allows the application to "have its cake and eat it too." That is, application processes can communicate reliably without being subjected to the transmission-rate constraints imposed by TCP's congestion-control mechanism. Many of today's proprietary streaming applications do just this—they run over UDP, but they have built acknowledgments and retransmissions into the application in order to reduce packet loss; see, for example, [Rhee 1998] and our discussion of multimedia transport in Chapter 7.

3.3.1 UDP Segment Structure

The UDP segment structure, shown in Figure 3.7, is defined in RFC 768. The application data occupies the data field of the UDP segment. For example, for DNS, the data field contains either a query message or a response message. For a streaming audio application, audio samples fill the data field. The UDP header has only four fields, each consisting of two bytes. As discussed in the previous section, the port numbers allow the destination host to pass the application data to the correct process running on the destination end system (that is, to perform the demultiplexing function). The checksum is used by the receiving host to check whether errors have been

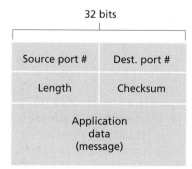

Figure 3.7 ♦ UDP segment structure

introduced into the segment. In truth, the checksum is also calculated over a few of the fields in the IP header in addition to the UDP segment. But we ignore this detail in order to see the forest through the trees. We'll discuss the checksum calculation below. Basic principles of error detection are described in Section 5.2. The length field specifies the length of the UDP segment, including the header, in bytes.

3.3.2 UDP Checksum

The UDP checksum provides for error detection. That is, the checksum is used to determine whether bits within the UDP segment have been altered (for example, by noise in the links or while stored in a router) as it moved from source to destination. UDP at the sender side performs the 1s complement of the sum of all the 16-bit words in the segment, with any overflow encountered during the sum being wrapped around. This result is put in the checksum field of the UDP segment. Here we give a simple example of the checksum calculation. You can find details about efficient implementation of the calculation in the RFC 1071 and performance over real data in [Stone 1998; Stone 2000]. As an example, suppose that we have the following three 16-bit words:

      0110011001100000
      0101010101010101
      1000111100001100

The sum of first two of these 16-bit words is

      0110011001100000
      <u>0101010101010101</u>
      1011101110110101

Adding the third word to the above sum gives

      1011101110110101
      <u>1000111100001100</u>
      0100101011000010

Note that this last addition had overflow, which was wrapped around. The 1s complement is obtained by converting all the 0s to 1s and converting all the 1s to 0s. Thus the 1s complement of the sum 0100101011000010 is 1011010100111101, which becomes the checksum. At the receiver, all four 16-bit words are added, including the checksum. If no errors are introduced into the packet, then clearly the sum at the receiver will be 1111111111111111. If one of the bits is a zero, then we know that errors have been introduced into the packet.

You may wonder why UDP provides a checksum in the first place, as many link-layer protocols (including the popular Ethernet protocol) also provide error checking. The reason is that there is no guarantee that all the links between source and destination provide error checking; that is, one of the links may use a link-layer protocol that does not provide error checking. Furthermore, even if segments are correctly transferred across a link, it's possible that bit errors could be introduced when a segment is stored in a router's memory. Given that neither link-by-link reliability nor in-memory error detection is guaranteed, UDP must provide error detection at the transport layer, *on an end-end basis*, if the end-end data transfer service is to provide error detection. This is an example of the celebrated **end-end principle** in system design [Saltzer 1984], which states that since certainly functionality (error detection, in this case) must be implemented on an end-end basis, "functions placed at the lower levels may be redundant or of little value when compared to the cost of providing them at the higher level."

Because IP is supposed to run over just about any layer-2 protocol, it is useful for the transport layer to provide error checking as a safety measure. Although UDP provides error checking, it does not do anything to recover from an error. Some implementations of UDP simply discard the damaged segment; others pass the damaged segment to the application with a warning.

That wraps up our discussion of UDP. We will soon see that TCP offers reliable data transfer to its applications as well as other services that UDP doesn't offer. Naturally, TCP is also more complex than UDP. Before discussing TCP, however, it will be useful to step back and first discuss the underlying principles of reliable data transfer.

3.4 Principles of Reliable Data Transfer

In this section, we consider the problem of reliable data transfer in a general context. This is appropriate since the problem of implementing reliable data transfer occurs not only at the transport layer, but also at the link layer and the application layer as well. The general problem is thus of central importance to networking. Indeed, if one had to identify a "top-ten" list of fundamentally important problems in all of networking, this would be a candidate to lead the list. In the next section we'll examine TCP and show, in particular, that TCP exploits many of the principles that we are about to describe.

Figure 3.8 illustrates the framework for our study of reliable data transfer. The service abstraction provided to the upper-layer entities is that of a reliable channel through which data can be transferred. With a reliable channel, no transferred data bits are corrupted (flipped from 0 to 1, or vice versa) or lost, and all are delivered in the order in which they were sent. This is precisely the service model offered by TCP to the Internet applications that invoke it.

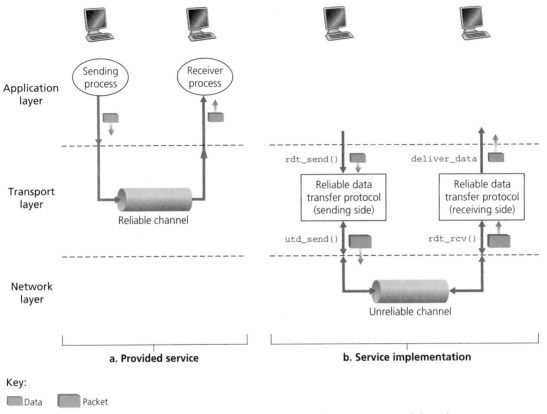

Key:

▢ Data ▢ Packet

Figure 3.8 ♦ Reliable data transfer: Service model and service implementation

It is the responsibility of a **reliable data transfer protocol** to implement this service abstraction. This task is made difficult by the fact that the layer *below* the reliable data transfer protocol may be unreliable. For example, TCP is a reliable data transfer protocol that is implemented on top of an unreliable (IP) end-to-end network layer. More generally, the layer beneath the two reliably communicating endpoints might consist of a single physical link (as in the case of a link-level data transfer protocol) or a global internetwork (as in the case of a transport-level protocol). For our purposes, however, we can view this lower layer simply as an unreliable point-to-point channel.

In this section, we will incrementally develop the sender and receiver sides of a reliable data transfer protocol, considering increasingly complex models of the underlying channel. Figure 3.8(b) illustrates the interfaces for our data transfer protocol. The sending side of the data transfer protocol will be invoked from above by a call to `rdt_send()`. It will pass the data to be delivered to the upper layer at the receiving side. (Here `rdt` stands for *reliable data transfer* protocol and `_send` indicates that the sending side of `rdt` is being called. The first step in developing any protocol is to choose a good name!) On the receiving side, `rdt_rcv()` will be called when a packet arrives from the receiving side of the channel. When the `rdt` protocol wants to deliver data to the upper layer, it will do so by calling `deliver_data()`. In the following we use the terminology "*packet*" rather than transport-layer "*segment*". Because the theory developed in this section applies to computer networks in general and not just to the Internet transport layer, the generic term "*packet*" is perhaps more appropriate here.

In this section we consider only the case of **unidirectional data transfer**, that is, data transfer from the sending to the receiving side. The case of reliable **bidirectional** (that is, full-duplex) **data transfer** is conceptually no more difficult but considerably more tedious to explain. Although we consider only unidirectional data transfer, it is important to note that the sending and receiving sides of our protocol will nonetheless need to transmit packets in *both* directions, as indicated in Figure 3.8. We will see shortly that, in addition to exchanging packets containing the data to be transferred, the sending and receiving sides of `rdt` will also need to exchange control packets back and forth. Both the send and receive sides of `rdt` send packets to the other side by a call to `udt_send()` (where `udt` stands for *unreliable data transfer*).

3.4.1 Building a Reliable Data Transfer Protocol

We now step through a series of protocols, each one becoming more complex, arriving at a flawless, reliable data transfer protocol.

Reliable Data Transfer over a Perfectly Reliable Channel: rdt1.0

We first consider the simplest case, in which the underlying channel is completely reliable. The protocol itself, which we'll call `rdt1.0`, is trivial. The **finite-state machine (FSM)** definitions for the `rdt1.0` sender and receiver are shown in Figure 3.9. The FSM in Figure 3.9(a) defines the operation of the sender, while the FSM in Figure 3.9(b) defines the operation of the receiver. It is important to note that there are *separate* FSMs for the sender and for the receiver. The sender and receiver FSMs in Figure 3.9 each have just one state. The arrows in the FSM description indicate the transition of the protocol from one state to another. (Since each FSM in Figure 3.9 has just one state, a transition is necessarily from the one state back to itself; we'll see more complicated state diagrams shortly.) The event causing the transition is shown above the horizontal line labeling the transition, and the actions taken when the event occurs are shown below the horizontal line. When no action is taken on an event, or no event occurs and an action is taken, we'll use the symbol Λ below or above the horizontal respectively to explicitly denote the lack of an action or event. The initial state of the FSM is indicated by the dashed arrow. Although the FSMs in Figure 3.9 have but one state, the FSMs we will see shortly have multiple states, so it will be important to identify the initial state of each FSM.

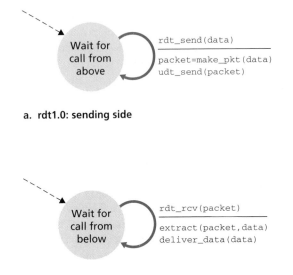

a. rdt1.0: sending side

b. rdt1.0: receiving side

Figure 3.9 ♦ `rdt1.0` – A protocol for a completely reliable channel

The sending side of `rdt` simply accepts data from the upper layer via the `rdt_send(data)` event, creates a packet containing the data (via the action `make_pkt(data)`) and sends the packet into the channel. In practice, the `rdt_send(data)` event would result from a procedure call (for example, to `rdt_send()`) by the upper-layer application.

On the receiving side, `rdt` receives a packet from the underlying channel via the `rdt_rcv(packet)` event, removes the data from the packet (via the action `extract(packet,data)`) and passes the data up to the upper layer (via the action `deliver_data(data)`). In practice, the `rdt_rcv(packet)` event would result from a procedure call (for example, to `rdt_rcv()`) from the lower-layer protocol.

In this simple protocol, there is no difference between a unit of data and a packet. Also, all packet flow is from the sender to receiver; with a perfectly reliable channel there is no need for the receiver side to provide any feedback to the sender since nothing can go wrong! Note that we have also assumed that the receiver is able to receive data as fast as the sender happens to send data. Thus, there is no need for the receiver to ask the sender to slow down!

Reliable Data Transfer over a Channel with Bit Errors: `rdt2.0`

A more realistic model of the underlying channel is one in which bits in a packet may be corrupted. Such bit errors typically occur in the physical components of a network as a packet is transmitted, propagates, or is buffered. We'll continue to assume for the moment that all transmitted packets are received (although their bits may be corrupted) in the order in which they were sent.

Before developing a protocol for reliably communicating over such a channel, first consider how people might deal with such a situation. Consider how you yourself might dictate a long message over the phone. In a typical scenario, the message taker might say "OK" after each sentence has been heard, understood, and recorded. If the message taker hears a garbled sentence, you're asked to repeat the garbled sentence. This message-dictation protocol uses both **positive acknowledgments** ("OK") and **negative acknowledgments** ("Please repeat that."). These control messages allow the receiver to let the sender know what has been received correctly, and what has been received in error and thus requires repeating. In a computer network setting, reliable data transfer protocols based on such retransmission are known as **ARQ (Automatic Repeat reQuest) protocols**.

Fundamentally, three additional protocol capabilities are required in ARQ protocols to handle the presence of bit errors:

♦ *Error detection.* First, a mechanism is needed to allow the receiver to detect when bit errors have occurred. Recall from the previous section that UDP uses the Internet checksum field for exactly this purpose. In Chapter 5 we'll examine error-detection and -correction techniques in greater detail; these techniques allow the receiver to detect and possibly correct packet bit errors. For now, we need only know that these techniques require that extra bits (beyond the bits of original data to be transferred) be sent from the sender to the receiver; these bits will be gathered into the packet checksum field of the `rdt2.0` data packet.

♦ *Receiver feedback.* Since the sender and receiver are typically executing on different end systems, possibly separated by thousands of miles, the only way for the sender to learn of the receiver's view of the world (in this case, whether or not a packet was received correctly) is for the receiver to provide explicit feedback to the sender. The positive (ACK) and negative (NAK) acknowledgment replies in the message-dictation scenario are examples of such feedback. Our `rdt2.0` protocol will similarly send ACK and NAK packets back from the receiver to the sender. In principle, these packets need only be one bit long; for example, a 0 value could indicate a NAK and a value of 1 could indicate an ACK.

♦ *Retransmission.* A packet that is received in error at the receiver will be retransmitted by the sender.

Figure 3.10 shows the FSM representation of `rdt2.0`, a data transfer protocol employing error detection, positive acknowledgments, and negative acknowledgments.

The send side of `rdt2.0` has two states. In the leftmost state, the send-side protocol is waiting for data to be passed down from the upper layer. When the `rdt_send(data)` event occurs, the sender will create a packet (`sndpkt`) containing the data to be sent, along with a packet checksum (for example, as discussed in section 3.3.2 for the case of a UDP segment), and then send the packet via the `udt_send(sndpkt)` operation. In the rightmost state, the sender protocol is waiting for an ACK or a NAK packet from the receiver. If an ACK packet is received (the notation `rdt_rcv(rcvpkt) && isACK (rcvpkt)` in Figure 3.10 corresponds to this event), the sender knows that the most recently transmitted packet has been received correctly and thus the protocol returns to the state of waiting for data from the upper layer. If a NAK is received, the protocol retransmits the last packet and waits for an ACK or NAK to be returned by the receiver in response to the retransmitted data packet. It is important to note that when the sender is in the wait-for-ACK-or-NAK

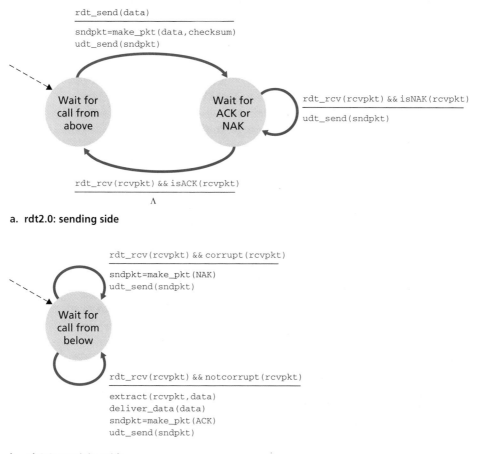

a. **rdt2.0: sending side**

b. **rdt2.0: receiving side**

Figure 3.10 ♦ `rdt2.0`–A protocol for a channel with bit errors

state, it *cannot* get more data from the upper layer; that is, the `rdt_send()` event can not occur; that will happen only after the sender receives an ACK and leaves this state. Thus, the sender will not send a new piece of data until it is sure that the receiver has correctly received the current packet. Because of this behavior, protocols such as `rdt2.0` are known as **stop-and-wait** protocols.

The receiver-side FSM for `rdt2.0` still has a single state. On packet arrival, the receiver replies with either an ACK or a NAK, depending on whether or not the received packet is corrupted. In Figure 3.10, the notation `rdt_rcv(rcvpkt) && corrupt(rcvpkt)` corresponds to the event in which a packet is received and is found to be in error.

Protocol `rdt2.0` may look as if it works but, unfortunately, it has a fatal flaw. In particular, we haven't accounted for the possibility that the ACK or NAK packet could be corrupted! (Before proceeding on, you should think about how this problem may be fixed.) Unfortunately, our slight oversight is not as innocuous as it may seem. Minimally, we will need to add checksum bits to ACK/NAK packets in order to detect such errors. The more difficult question is how the protocol should recover from errors in ACK or NAK packets. The difficulty here is that if an ACK or NAK is corrupted, the sender has no way of knowing whether or not the receiver has correctly received the last piece of transmitted data.

Consider three possibilities for handling corrupted ACKs or NAKs:

◆ For the first possibility, consider what a human might do in the message-dictation scenario. If the speaker didn't understand the "OK" or "Please repeat that" reply from the receiver, the speaker would probably ask, "What did you say?" (thus introducing a new type of sender-to-receiver packet to our protocol). The speaker would then repeat the reply. But what if the speaker's "What did you say?" is corrupted? The receiver, having no idea whether the garbled sentence was part of the dictation or a request to repeat the last reply, would probably then respond with "What did *you* say?" And then, of course, that response might be garbled. Clearly, we're heading down a difficult path.

◆ A second alternative is to add enough checksum bits to allow the sender not only to detect, but also to recover from, bit errors. This solves the immediate problem for a channel that can corrupt packets but not lose them.

◆ A third approach is for the sender simply to resend the current data packet when it receives a garbled ACK or NAK packet. This approach, however, introduces **duplicate packets** into the sender-to-receiver channel. The fundamental difficulty with duplicate packets is that the receiver doesn't know whether the ACK or NAK it last sent was received correctly at the sender. Thus, it cannot know *a priori* whether an arriving packet contains new data or is a retransmission!

A simple solution to this new problem (and one adopted in almost all existing data transfer protocols, including TCP) is to add a new field to the data packet and have the sender number its data packets by putting a **sequence number** into this field. The receiver then need only check this sequence number to determine whether or not the received packet is a retransmission. For this simple case of a stop-and-wait protocol, a 1-bit sequence number will suffice, since it will allow the receiver to know whether the sender is resending the previously transmitted packet (the sequence number of the received packet has the same sequence number as the most recently received packet) or a new packet (the sequence number changes, moving "forward" in modulo-2 arithmetic). Since we are currently assuming a channel that does not lose packets, ACK and NAK packets do not themselves need to indicate the sequence number of the packet they are acknowledging. The sender knows that a received ACK or NAK packet (whether garbled or not) was generated in response to its most recently transmitted data packet.

Figures 3.11 and 3.12 show the FSM description for `rdt2.1`, our fixed version of `rdt2.0`. The `rdt2.1` sender and receiver FSMs each now have twice as many states as before. This is because the protocol state must now reflect whether the packet currently being sent (by the sender) or expected (at the receiver) should have a

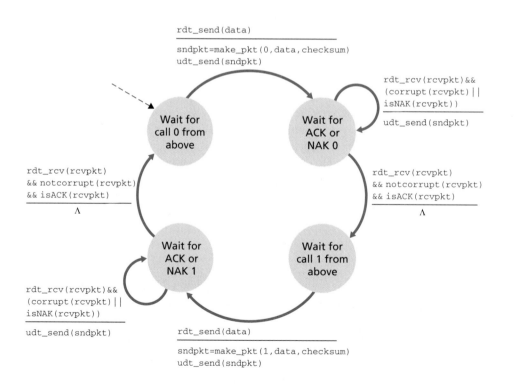

Figure 3.11 ♦ `rdt2.1` sender

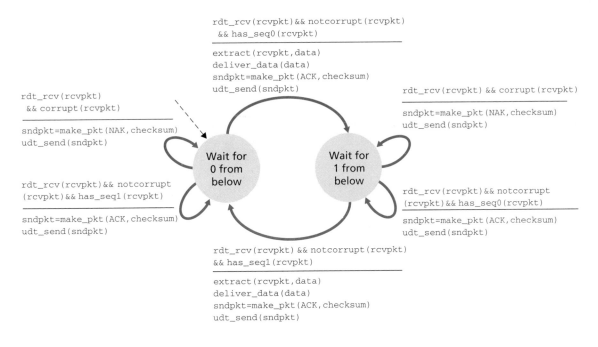

```
rdt_rcv(rcvpkt)&& notcorrupt(rcvpkt)
 && has_seq0(rcvpkt)
```

```
extract(rcvpkt,data)
deliver_data(data)
sndpkt=make_pkt(ACK,checksum)
udt_send(sndpkt)
```

```
rdt_rcv(rcvpkt)
 && corrupt(rcvpkt)
```

```
sndpkt=make_pkt(NAK,checksum)
udt_send(sndpkt)
```

```
rdt_rcv(rcvpkt)&& notcorrupt
(rcvpkt)&& has_seq1(rcvpkt)
```

```
sndpkt=make_pkt(ACK,checksum)
udt_send(sndpkt)
```

```
rdt_rcv(rcvpkt) && corrupt(rcvpkt)
```

```
sndpkt=make_pkt(NAK,checksum)
udt_send(sndpkt)
```

```
rdt_rcv(rcvpkt)&& notcorrupt
(rcvpkt)&& has_seq0(rcvpkt)
```

```
sndpkt=make_pkt(ACK,checksum)
udt_send(sndpkt)
```

Wait for 0 from below   **Wait for 1 from below**

```
rdt_rcv(rcvpkt) && notcorrupt(rcvpkt)
 && has_seq1(rcvpkt)
```

```
extract(rcvpkt,data)
deliver_data(data)
sndpkt=make_pkt(ACK,checksum)
udt_send(sndpkt)
```

Figure 3.12 ♦ `rdt2.1` receiver

sequence number of 0 or 1. Note that the actions in those states where a 0-numbered packet is being sent or expected are mirror images of those where a 1-numbered packet is being sent or expected; the only differences have to do with the handling of the sequence number.

Protocol `rdt2.1` uses both positive and negative acknowledgments from the receiver to the sender. When an out-of-order packet is received, the receiver sends a positive acknowledgment for the packet it has received. When a corrupted packet is received, the receiver sends a negative acknowledgment. We can accomplish the same effect as a NAK if, instead of sending a NAK, we instead send an ACK for the last correctly received packet. A sender that receives two ACKs for the same packet (that is, receives **duplicate ACKs**) knows that the receiver did not correctly receive the packet following the packet that is being ACKed twice. Our NAK-free reliable data transfer protocol for a channel with bit errors is `rdt2.2`, shown in Figures 3.13 and 3.14. One subtle change between `rtdt2.1` and `rdt2.2` is that the receiver must now include the sequence number of the packet being acknowledged by an ACK message (this is done by including the ACK,0 or ACK,1 argument in `make_pkt()` in the receiver FSM), and the sender must now check the sequence number of the packet being acknowledged by a received ACK message (this is done by including the 0 or 1 argument in `isACK()` in the sender FSM).

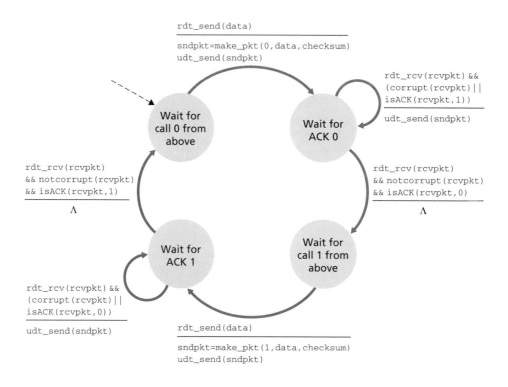

Figure 3.13 ◆ `rdt2.2` sender

Reliable Data Transfer over a Lossy Channel with Bit Errors: `rdt3.0`

Suppose now that in addition to corrupting bits, the underlying channel can *lose* packets as well, a not-uncommon event in today's computer networks (including the Internet). Two additional concerns must now be addressed by the protocol: how to detect packet loss and what to do when packet loss occurs. The use of checksumming, sequence numbers, ACK packets, and retransmissions—the techniques already developed in `rdt2.2`—will allow us to answer the latter concern. Handling the first concern will require adding a new protocol mechanism.

There are many possible approaches toward dealing with packet loss (several more of which are explored in the exercises at the end of the chapter). Here, we'll put the burden of detecting and recovering from lost packets on the sender. Suppose that the sender transmits a data packet and either that packet, or the receiver's ACK of that packet, gets lost. In either case, no reply is forthcoming at the sender from the receiver. If the sender is willing to wait long enough so that it is *certain* that a packet has been lost, it can simply retransmit the data packet. You should convince yourself that this protocol does indeed work.

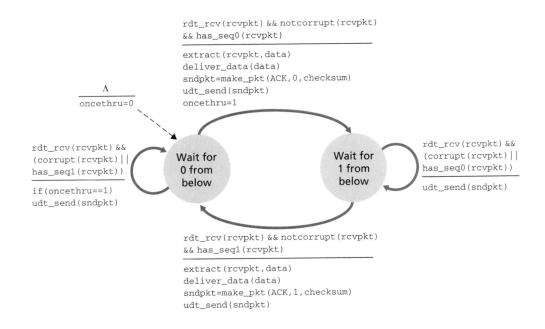

Figure 3.14 ◆ rdt2.2 receiver

But how long must the sender wait to be certain that something has been lost? The sender must clearly wait at least as long as a round-trip delay between the sender and receiver (which may include buffering at intermediate routers) plus whatever amount of time is needed to process a packet at the receiver. In many networks, this worst-case maximum delay is very difficult even to estimate, much less know with certainty. Moreover, the protocol should ideally recover from packet loss as soon as possible; waiting for a worst-case delay could mean a long wait until error recovery is initiated. The approach thus adopted in practice is for the sender to judiciously choose a time value such that packet loss is likely, although not guaranteed, to have happened. If an ACK is not received within this time, the packet is retransmitted. Note that if a packet experiences a particularly large delay, the sender may retransmit the packet even though neither the data packet nor its ACK have been lost. This introduces the possibility of **duplicate data packets** in the sender-to-receiver channel. Happily, protocol rdt2.2 already has enough functionality (that is, sequence numbers) to handle the case of duplicate packets.

From the sender's viewpoint, retransmission is a panacea. The sender does not know whether a data packet was lost, an ACK was lost, or if the packet or ACK was simply overly delayed. In all cases, the action is the same: retransmit. Implementing a time-based retransmission mechanism requires a **countdown timer** that can interrupt the sender after a given amount of time has expired. The sender will thus need to be able to (1) start the timer each time a packet (either a first-time packet, or a retransmission) is sent, (2) respond to a timer interrupt (taking appropriate actions), and (3) stop the timer.

Figure 3.15 shows the sender FSM for `rdt3.0`, a protocol that reliably transfers data over a channel that can corrupt or lose packets; in the homework problems you'll be asked to provide the receiver FSM for `rdt3.0`. Figure 3.16 shows how the protocol operates with no lost or delayed packets and how it handles lost data packets. In Figure 3.16, time moves forward from the top of the diagram toward the bottom of the diagram; note that a receive time for a packet is necessarily later than the send time for a packet as a result of transmission and propagation delays. In Figures 3.16(b)–(d), the send-side brackets indicate the times at which a timer is set and later times out. Several of the more subtle aspects of this protocol are explored in the exercises at the end of this chapter. Because packet sequence numbers alternate between 0 and 1, protocol `rdt3.0` is sometimes known as the **alternating-bit protocol**.

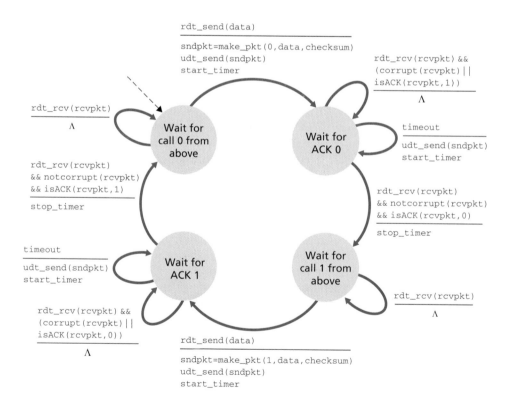

Figure 3.15 ♦ `rdt3.0` sender

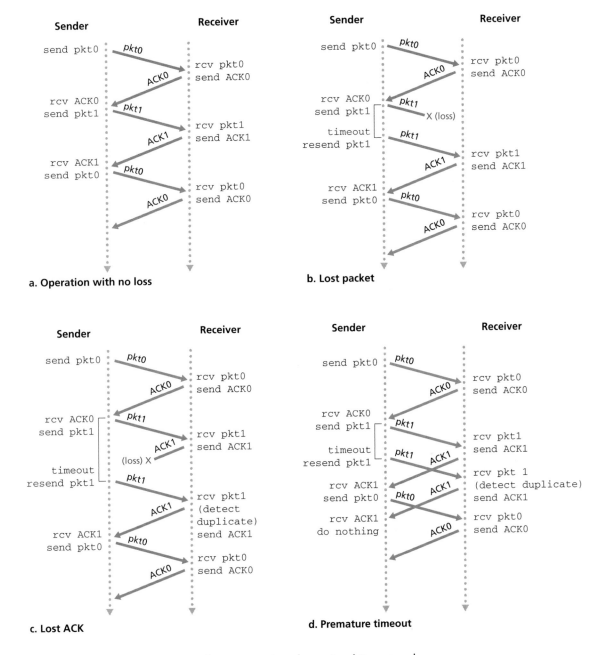

Figure 3.16 ♦ Operation of rdt3.0, the alternating-bit protocol

We have now assembled the key elements of a data transfer protocol. Check-sums, sequence numbers, timers, and positive and negative acknowledgment pack-ets each play a crucial and necessary role in the operation of the protocol. We now have a working reliable data transfer protocol!

3.4.2 Pipelined Reliable Data Transfer Protocols

Protocol `rdt3.0` is a functionally correct protocol, but it is unlikely that anyone would be happy with its performance, particularly in today's high-speed networks. At the heart of `rdt3.0`'s performance problem is the fact that it is a stop-and-wait protocol.

To appreciate the performance impact of this stop-and-wait behavior, consider an idealized case of two hosts, one located on the West Coast of the United States and the other located on the East Coast, as shown in Figure 3.17. The speed-of-light round-trip propagation delay between these two end systems, RTT, is approximately 30 milliseconds. Suppose that they are connected by a channel with a transmission rate, R, of 1Gbps (10^9 bits per second). With a packet size, L, of 1,000 bytes (8,000 bits) per packet, including both header fields and data, the time needed to actually transmit the packet into the 1 Gbps link is

$$t_{trans} = \frac{L}{R} = \frac{8000 \text{ bits/packet}}{10^9 \text{ bits/sec}} = 8 \text{ microseconds}$$

Figure 3.18(a) shows that with our stop-and-wait protocol, if the sender begins sending the packet at $t = 0$, then at $t = L/R = 8$ microseconds, the last bit enters the channel at the sender side. The packet then makes its 15-msec cross-country jour-ney, with the last bit of the packet emerging at the receiver at $t = \text{RTT}/2 + L/R = 15.008$ msec. Assuming for simplicity that ACK packets are extremely small (so that

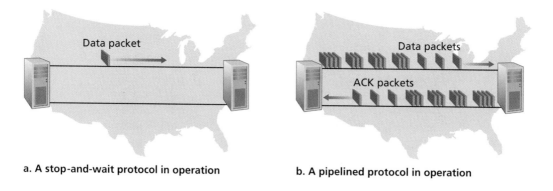

a. A stop-and-wait protocol in operation   b. A pipelined protocol in operation

Figure 3.17 ◆ Stop-and-wait versus pipelined protocol

we can ignore their transmission time) and that the receiver can send an ACK as soon as the last bit of a data packet is received, the ACK emerges back at the sender at $t = $ RTT $+ L/R = 30.008$ msec. At this point, the sender can now transmit the next message. Thus, in 30.008 msec, the sender was sending for only 0.008 msec. If we define the **utilization** of the sender (or the channel) as the fraction of time the sender is actually busy sending bits into the channel, the analysis in Figure 3.18(a) shows that the stop-and-wait protocol has a rather dismal sender utilization, U_{sender}, of

$$ U_{sender} = \frac{L/R}{RTT + L/R} = \frac{.008}{30.008} = 0.00027 $$

That is, the sender was busy only 2.7 hundredths of one percent of the time! Viewed another way, the sender was able to send only 1,000 bytes in 30.008 milliseconds, an effective throughput of only 267 kbps—even though a 1 Gbps link was available! Imagine the unhappy network manager who just paid a fortune for a gigabit capacity link but manages to get a throughput of only 267 kilobits per second! This is a graphic example of how network protocols can limit the capabilities provided by the underlying network hardware. Also, we have neglected lower-layer protocol-processing times at the sender and receiver, as well as the processing and queuing delays that would occur at any intermediate routers between the sender and receiver. Including these effects would serve only to further increase the delay and further accentuate the poor performance.

The solution to this particular performance problem is simple: Rather than operate in a stop-and-wait manner, the sender is allowed to send multiple packets without waiting for acknowledgments, as illustrated in Figure 3.17(b). Figure 3.18(b) shows that if the sender is allowed to transmit three packets before having to wait for acknowledgments, the utilization of the sender is essentially tripled. Since the many in-transit sender-to-receiver packets can be visualized as filling a pipeline, this technique is known as **pipelining**. Pipelining has the following consequences for reliable data transfer protocols:

♦ The range of sequence numbers must be increased, since each in-transit packet (not counting retransmissions) must have a unique sequence number and there may be multiple, in-transit, unacknowledged packets.

♦ The sender and receiver sides of the protocols may have to buffer more than one packet. Minimally, the sender will have to buffer packets that have been transmitted but not yet acknowledged. Buffering of correctly received packets may also be needed at the receiver, as discussed below.

♦ The range of sequence numbers needed and the buffering requirements will depend on the manner in which a data transfer protocol responds to lost, corrupted, and overly delayed packets. Two basic approaches toward pipelined error recovery can be identified: **Go-Back-N** and **selective repeat**.

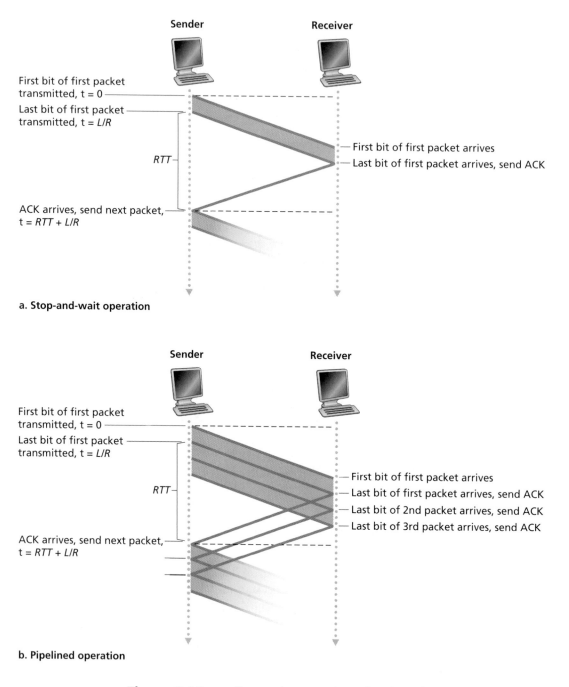

Sender   **Receiver**

First bit of first packet
transmitted, t = 0

Last bit of first packet
transmitted, t = L/R

RTT

First bit of first packet arrives
Last bit of first packet arrives, send ACK

ACK arrives, send next packet,
t = RTT + L/R

a. Stop-and-wait operation

Sender   **Receiver**

First bit of first packet
transmitted, t = 0

Last bit of first packet
transmitted, t = L/R

RTT

First bit of first packet arrives
Last bit of first packet arrives, send ACK
Last bit of 2nd packet arrives, send ACK
Last bit of 3rd packet arrives, send ACK

ACK arrives, send next packet,
t = RTT + L/R

b. Pipelined operation

Figure 3.18 ◆ Stop-and-wait and pipelined sending

3.4.3 Go-Back-N (GBN)

In a **Go-Back-N (GBN) protocol**, the sender is allowed to transmit multiple packets (when available) without waiting for an acknowledgment, but is constrained to have no more than some maximum allowable number, N, of unacknowledged packets in the pipeline. Figure 3.19 shows the sender's view of the range of sequence numbers in a GBN protocol. If we define `base` to be the sequence number of the oldest unacknowledged packet and `nextseqnum` to be the smallest unused sequence number (that is, the sequence number of the next packet to be sent), then four intervals in the range of sequence numbers can be identified. Sequence numbers in the interval `[0,base-1]` correspond to packets that have already been transmitted and acknowledged. The interval `[base,nextseqnum-1]` corresponds to packets that have been sent but not yet acknowledged. Sequence numbers in the interval `[nextseqnum,base+N-1]` can be used for packets that can be sent immediately, should data arrive from the upper layer. Finally, sequence numbers greater than or equal to `base+N` cannot be used until an unacknowledged packet currently in the pipeline (specifically, the packet with sequence number `base`) has been acknowledged.

As suggested by Figure 3.19, the range of permissible sequence numbers for transmitted but not yet acknowledged packets can be viewed as a window of size N over the range of sequence numbers. As the protocol operates, this window slides forward over the sequence number space. For this reason, N is often referred to as the **window size** and the GBN protocol itself as a **sliding-window protocol**. You might be wondering why we would even limit the number of outstanding, unacknowledged packets to a value of N in the first place. Why not allow an unlimited number of such packets? We'll see in Section 3.5 that flow control is one reason to impose a limit on the sender. We'll examine another reason to do so in Section 3.7, when we study TCP congestion control.

In practice, a packet's sequence number is carried in a fixed-length field in the packet header. If k is the number of bits in the packet sequence number field, the range of sequence numbers is thus $[0, 2^k - 1]$. With a finite range of sequence numbers, all arithmetic involving sequence numbers must then be done using modulo 2^k arithmetic. (That is, the sequence number space can be thought of as a ring of size 2^k, where sequence number $2^k - 1$ is immediately followed by sequence number 0.) Recall that

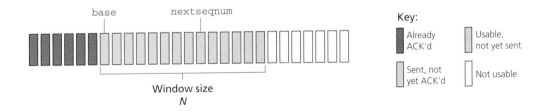

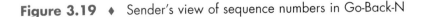

Figure 3.19 ♦ Sender's view of sequence numbers in Go-Back-N

`rdt3.0` had a 1-bit sequence number and a range of sequence numbers of [0,1]. Several of the problems at the end of this chapter explore the consequences of a finite range of sequence numbers. We will see in Section 3.5 that TCP has a 32-bit sequence number field, where TCP sequence numbers count bytes in the byte stream rather than packets.

Figures 3.20 and 3.21 give an extended FSM description of the sender and receiver sides of an ACK-based, NAK-free, GBN protocol. We refer to this FSM description as an *extended FSM* because we have added variables (similar to programming-language variables) for `base` and `nextseqnum,` and added operations on these variables and conditional actions involving these variables. Note that the extended FSM specification is now beginning to look somewhat like a programming-language specification. [Bochman 1984] provides an excellent survey of additional extensions to FSM techniques as well as other programming-language-based techniques for specifying protocols.

The GBN sender must respond to three types of events:

♦ *Invocation from above.* When `rdt_send()` is called from above, the sender first checks to see if the window is full, that is, whether there are *N* outstanding, unacknowledged packets. If the window is not full, a packet is created and sent,

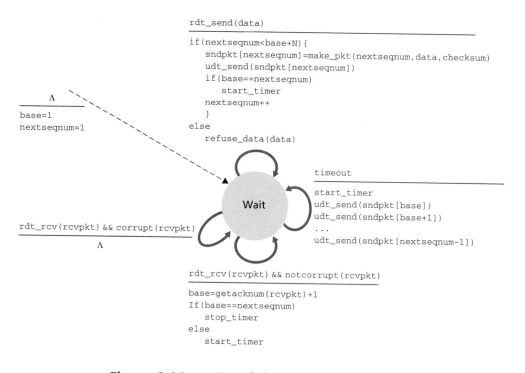

Figure 3.20 ♦ Extended FSM description of GBN sender

and variables are appropriately updated. If the window is full, the sender simply returns the data back to the upper layer, an implicit indication that the window is full. The upper layer would presumably then have to try again later. In a real implementation, the sender would more likely have either buffered (but not immediately sent) this data, or would have a synchronization mechanism (for example, a semaphore or a flag) that would allow the upper layer to call `rdt_send()` only when the window is not full.

♦ *Receipt of an ACK.* In our GBN protocol, an acknowledgment for packet with sequence number n will be taken to be a **cumulative acknowledgment**, indicating that all packets with a sequence number up to and including n have been correctly received at the receiver. We'll come back to this issue shortly when we examine the receiver side of GBN.

♦ *A timeout event.* The protocol's name, "Go-Back-N," is derived from the sender's behavior in the presence of lost or overly delayed packets. As in the stop-and-wait protocol, a timer will again be used to recover from lost data or acknowledgment packets. If a timeout occurs, the sender resends *all* packets that have been previously sent but that have not yet been acknowledged. Our sender in Figure 3.20 uses only a single timer, which can be thought of as a timer for the oldest transmitted but not yet acknowledged packet. If an ACK is received but there are still additional transmitted but not yet acknowledged packets, the timer is restarted. If there are no outstanding unacknowledged packets, the timer is stopped.

The receiver's actions in GBN are also simple. If a packet with sequence number n is received correctly and is in order (that is, the data last delivered to the upper layer came from a packet with sequence number $n - 1$), the receiver sends an ACK

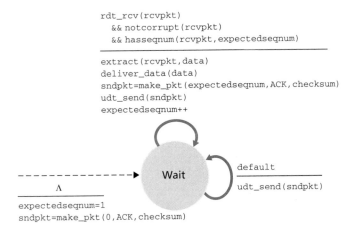

```
rdt_rcv(rcvpkt)
  && notcorrupt(rcvpkt)
  && hasseqnum(rcvpkt,expectedseqnum)
─────────────────────────────────────────────
extract(rcvpkt,data)
deliver_data(data)
sndpkt=make_pkt(expectedseqnum,ACK,checksum)
udt_send(sndpkt)
expectedseqnum++
```

```
                                        default
                                ─────────────────────
                    Wait        udt_send(sndpkt)
```

```
Λ
─────────────────────────
expectedseqnum=1
sndpkt=make_pkt(0,ACK,checksum)
```

Figure 3.21 ♦ Extended FSM description of GBN receiver

for packet n and delivers the data portion of the packet to the upper layer. In all other cases, the receiver discards the packet and resends an ACK for the most recently received in-order packet. Note that since packets are delivered one at a time to the upper layer, if packet k has been received and delivered, then all packets with a sequence number lower than k have also been delivered. Thus, the use of cumulative acknowledgments is a natural choice for GBN.

In our GBN protocol, the receiver discards out-of-order packets. Although it may seem silly and wasteful to discard a correctly received (but out-of-order) packet, there is some justification for doing so. Recall that the receiver must deliver data in order to the upper layer. Suppose now that packet n is expected, but packet n + 1 arrives. Because data must be delivered in order, the receiver *could* buffer (save) packet n + 1 and then deliver this packet to the upper layer after it had later received and delivered packet n. However, if packet n is lost, both it and packet n + 1 will eventually be retransmitted as a result of the GBN retransmission rule at the sender. Thus, the receiver can simply discard packet n + 1. The advantage of this approach is the simplicity of receiver buffering—the receiver need not buffer *any* out-of-order packets. Thus, while the sender must maintain the upper and lower bounds of its window and the position of `nextseqnum` within this window, the only piece of information the receiver need maintain is the sequence number of the next in-order packet. This value is held in the variable `expectedseqnum`, shown in the receiver FSM in Figure 3.21. Of course, the disadvantage of throwing away a correctly received packet is that the subsequent retransmission of that packet might be lost or garbled and thus even more retransmissions would be required.

Figure 3.22 shows the operation of the GBN protocol for the case of a window size of four packets. Because of this window size limitation, the sender sends packets 0 through 3 but then must wait for one or more of these packets to be acknowledged before proceeding. As each successive ACK (for example, ACK0 and ACK1) is received, the window slides forward and the sender can transmit one new packet (pkt4 and pkt5, respectively). On the receiver side, packet 2 is lost and thus packets 3, 4, and 5 are found to be out of order and are discarded.

Before closing our discussion of GBN, it is worth noting that an implementation of this protocol in a protocol stack would likely have a structure similar to that of the extended FSM in Figure 3.20. The implementation would also likely be in the form of various procedures that implement the actions to be taken in response to the various events that can occur. In such **event-based programming**, the various procedures are called (invoked) either by other procedures in the protocol stack, or as the result of an interrupt. In the sender, these events would be (1) a call from the upper-layer entity to invoke `rdt_send()`, (2) a timer interrupt, and (3) a call from the lower layer to invoke `rdt_rcv()` when a packet arrives. The programming exercises at the end of this chapter will give you a chance to actually implement these routines in a simulated, but realistic, network setting.

We note here that the GBN protocol incorporates almost all of the techniques that we will encounter when we study the reliable data transfer components of TCP

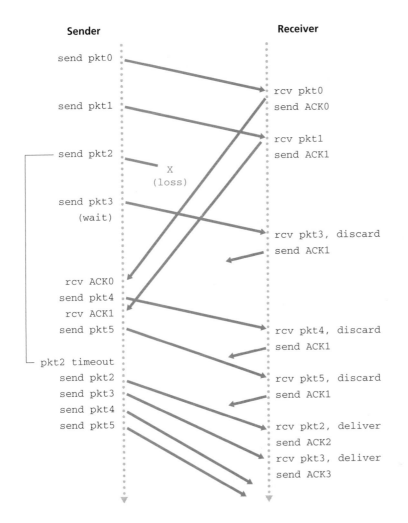

Figure 3.22 ♦ Go-Back-N in operation

in Section 3.5. These techniques include the use of sequence numbers, cumulative acknowledgments, checksums, and a timeout/retransmit operation.

3.4.4 Selective Repeat (SR)

The GBN protocol allows the sender to potentially "fill the pipeline" in Figure 3.17 with packets, thus avoiding the channel utilization problems we noted with stop-and-wait protocols. There are, however, scenarios in which GBN itself suffers from performance problems. In particular, when the window size and bandwidth-delay

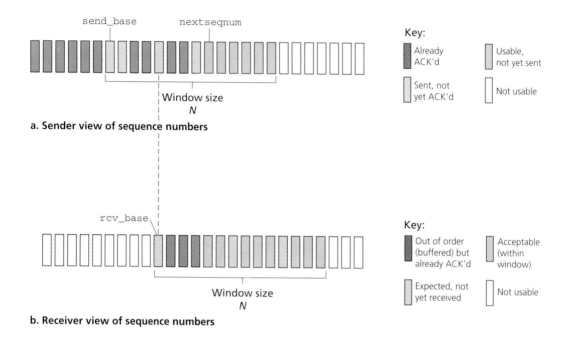

send_base   nextseqnum

Key:

■ Already ACK'd   ▨ Usable, not yet sent

▨ Sent, not yet ACK'd   □ Not usable

Window size
N

a. Sender view of sequence numbers

rcv_base

Key:

■ Out of order (buffered) but already ACK'd   ▨ Acceptable (within window)

▨ Expected, not yet received   □ Not usable

Window size
N

b. Receiver view of sequence numbers

Figure 3.23 ♦ Selective-repeat (SR) sender and receiver views of sequence-number space

product are both large, many packets can be in the pipeline. A single packet error can thus cause GBN to retransmit a large number of packets, many unnecessarily. As the probability of channel errors increases, the pipeline can become filled with these unnecessary retransmissions. Imagine, in our message-dictation scenario, that if every time a word was garbled, the surrounding 1,000 words (for example, a window size of 1,000 words) had to be repeated. The dictation would be slowed by all of the reiterated words.

As the name suggests, selective-repeat protocols avoid unnecessary retransmissions by having the sender retransmit only those packets that it suspects were received in error (that is, were lost or corrupted) at the receiver. This individual, as-needed, retransmission will require that the receiver *individually* acknowledge correctly received packets. A window size of *N* will again be used to limit the number of outstanding, unacknowledged packets in the pipeline. However, unlike GBN, the sender will have already received ACKs for some of the packets in the window. Figure 3.23 shows the SR sender's view of the sequence number space. Figure 3.24 details the various actions taken by the SR sender.

The SR receiver will acknowledge a correctly received packet whether or not it is in order. Out-of-order packets are buffered until any missing packets (that is,

1. *Data received from above.* When data is received from above, the SR sender checks the next available sequence number for the packet. If the sequence number is within the sender's window, the data is packetized and sent; otherwise it is either buffered or returned to the upper layer for later transmission, as in GBN.
2. *Timeout.* Timers are again used to protect against lost packets. However, each packet must now have its own logical timer, since only a single packet will be transmitted on timeout. A single hardware timer can be used to mimic the operation of multiple logical timers [Varghese 1997].
3. *ACK received.* If an ACK is received, the SR sender marks that packet as having been received, provided it is in the window. If the packet's sequence number is equal to send_base, the window base is moved forward to the unacknowledged packet with the smallest sequence number. If the window moves and there are untransmitted packets with sequence numbers that now fall within the window, these packets are transmitted.

Figure 3.24 ♦ SR sender events and actions

packets with lower sequence numbers) are received, at which point a batch of packets can be delivered in order to the upper layer. Figure 3.25 itemizes the various actions taken by the SR receiver. Figure 3.26 shows an example of SR operation in the presence of lost packets. Note that in Figure 3.26, the receiver initially buffers packets 3, 4, and 5, and delivers them together with packet 2 to the upper layer when packet 2 is finally received.

It is important to note that in Step 2 in Figure 3.25, the receiver reacknowledges (rather than ignores) already received packets with certain sequence numbers *below* the current window base. You should convince yourself that this reacknowledgment is indeed needed. Given the sender and receiver sequence number spaces in Figure 3.23, for example, if there is no ACK for packet send_base propagating from the receiver to the sender, the sender will eventually retransmit packet send_base, even though it is clear (to us, not the sender!) that the receiver has already received that packet. If the receiver were not to acknowledge this packet, the sender's window would never move forward! This example illustrates an important aspect of SR protocols (and many other protocols as well). The sender and receiver will not always have an identical view of what has been received correctly and what has not. For SR protocols, this means that the sender and receiver windows will not always coincide.

The lack of synchronization between sender and receiver windows has important consequences when we are faced with the reality of a finite range of sequence numbers. Consider what could happen, for example, with a finite range of four packet sequence numbers, 0, 1, 2, 3, and a window size of three. Suppose packets 0 through 2 are transmitted and correctly received and acknowledged at the receiver. At this point, the receiver's window is over the fourth, fifth, and sixth packets, which have

1. *Packet with sequence number in* [rcv_base, rcv_base+N-1] *is correctly received.* In this case, the received packet falls within the receiver's window and a selective ACK packet is returned to the sender. If the packet was not previously received, it is buffered. If this packet has a sequence number equal to the base of the receive window (rcv_base in Figure 3.22), then this packet, and any previously buffered and consecutively numbered (beginning with rcv_base) packets are delivered to the upper layer. The receive window is then moved forward by the number of packets delivered to the upper layer. As an example, consider Figure 3.26. When a packet with a sequence number of rcv_base=2 is received, it and packets 3, 4, and 5 can be delivered to the upper layer.

2. *Packet with sequence number in* [rcv_base-N, rcv_base-1] *is received.* In this case, an ACK must be generated, even though this is a packet that the receiver has previously acknowledged.

3. *Otherwise.* Ignore the packet.

Figure 3.25 ◆   SR receiver events and actions

sequence numbers 3, 0, and 1, respectively. Now consider two scenarios. In the first scenario, shown in Figure 3.27(a), the ACKs for the first three packets are lost and the sender retransmits these packets. The receiver thus next receives a packet with sequence number 0—a copy of the first packet sent.

In the second scenario, shown in Figure 3.27(b), the ACKs for the first three packets are all delivered correctly. The sender thus moves its window forward and sends the fourth, fifth, and sixth packets, with sequence numbers 3, 0, and 1, respectively. The packet with sequence number 3 is lost, but the packet with sequence number 0 arrives—a packet containing *new* data.

Now consider the receiver's viewpoint in Figure 3.27, which has a figurative curtain between the sender and the receiver, since the receiver cannot "see" the actions taken by the sender. All the receiver observes is the sequence of messages it receives from the channel and sends into the channel. As far as it is concerned, the two scenarios in Figure 3.27 are *identical*. There is no way of distinguishing the retransmission of the first packet from an original transmission of the fifth packet. Clearly, a window size that is 1 less than the size of the sequence number space won't work. But how small must the window size be? A problem at the end of the chapter asks you to show that the window size must be less than or equal to half the size of the sequence number space for SR protocols.

This completes our discussion of reliable data transfer protocols. We've covered a *lot* of ground and introduced numerous mechanisms that together provide for reliable data transfer. Table 3.1 summarizes these mechanisms. Now that we have seen all of these mechanisms in operation and can see the "big picture," we encourage you to review this section again to see how these mechanisms were incrementally added to

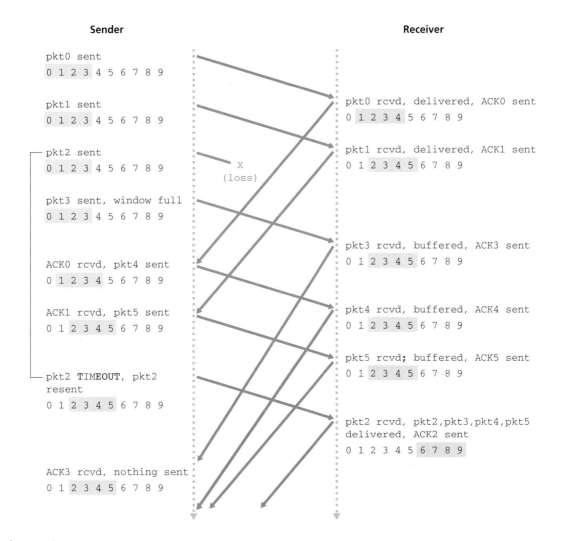

Figure 3.26 ♦ SR operation

cover increasingly complex (and realistic) models of the channel connecting the sender and receiver, or to improve the performance of the protocols.

Let's conclude our discussion of reliable data transfer protocols by considering one remaining assumption in our underlying channel model. Recall that we have assumed that packets cannot be reordered within the channel between the sender and receiver. This is generally a reasonable assumption when the sender and receiver are connected by a single physical wire. However, when the "channel" connecting the two is a network, packet reordering can occur. One manifestation of packet reordering is

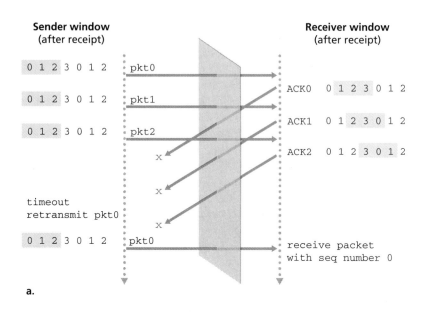

a.

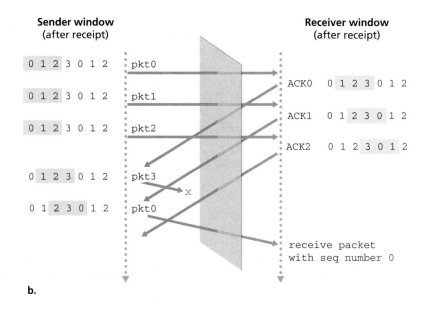

b.

Figure 3.27 ◆ SR receiver dilemma with too-large windows: A new packet or a retransmission?

Mechanism	Use, Comments
Checksum	Used to detect bit errors in a transmitted packet.
Timer	Used to timeout/retransmit a packet, possibly because the packet (or its ACK) was lost within the channel. Because timeouts can occur when a packet is delayed but not lost (premature timeout), or when a packet has been received by the receiver but the receiver-to-sender ACK has been lost, duplicate copies of a packet may received by a receiver.
Sequence number	Used for sequential numbering of packets of data flowing from sender to receiver. Gaps in the sequence numbers of received packets allow the receiver to detect a lost packet. Packets with duplicate sequence numbers allow the receiver to detect duplicate copies of a packet.
Acknowledgment	Used by the receiver to tell the sender that a packet or set of packets has been received correctly. Acknowledgments will typically carry the sequence number of the packet or packets being acknowledged. Acknowledgments may be individual or cumulative, depending on the protocol.
Negative acknowledgment	Used by the receiver to tell the sender that a packet has not been received correctly. Negative acknowledgments will typically carry the sequence number of the packet that was not received correctly.
Window, pipelining	The sender may be restricted to sending only packets with sequence numbers that fall within a given range. By allowing multiple packets to be transmitted but not yet acknowledged, sender utilization can be increased over a stop-and-wait mode of operation. We'll see shortly that the window size may be set on the basis of the receiver's ability to receive and buffer messages, or the level of congestion in the network, or both.

Table 3.1 ♦ Summary of reliable data transfer mechanisms and their use

that old copies of a packet with a sequence or acknowledgment number of x can appear, even though neither the sender's nor the receiver's window contains x. With packet reordering, the channel can be thought of as essentially buffering packets and spontaneously emitting these packets at *any* point in the future. Because sequence numbers may be reused, some care must be taken to guard against such duplicate packets. The approach taken in practice is to ensure that a sequence number is not reused until the sender is "sure" that any previously sent packets with sequence number x are no longer in the network. This is done by assuming that a packet cannot "live" in the network for longer than some fixed maximum amount of time. A maximum packet lifetime of approximately three minutes is assumed in the TCP extensions for high-speed networks [RFC 1323]. [Sunshine 1978] describes a method for using sequence numbers such that reordering problems can be completely avoided.

3.5 Connection-Oriented Transport: TCP

Now that we have covered the underlying principles of reliable data transfer, let's turn to TCP—the Internet's transport-layer, connection-oriented, reliable transport protocol. In this section, we'll see that in order to provide reliable data transfer, TCP relies on many of the underlying principles discussed in the previous section, including error detection, retransmissions, cumulative acknowledgments, timers, and header fields for sequence and acknowledgment numbers. TCP is defined in RFC 793, RFC 1122, RFC 1323, RFC 2018, and RFC 2581.

3.5.1 The TCP Connection

TCP is said to be **connection-oriented** because before one application process can begin to send data to another, the two processes must first "handshake" with each other—that is, they must send some preliminary segments to each other to establish the parameters of the ensuing data transfer. As part of TCP connection establishment, both sides of the connection will initialize many TCP state variables (many of which will be discussed in this section and in Section 3.7) associated with the TCP connection.

The TCP "connection" is not an end-to-end TDM or FDM circuit as in a circuit-switched network. Nor is it a virtual circuit (see Chapter 1), as the connection state resides entirely in the two end systems. Because the TCP protocol runs only in the end systems and not in the intermediate network elements (routers and link-layer switches), the intermediate network elements do not maintain TCP connection state. In fact, the intermediate routers are completely oblivious to TCP connections; they see datagrams, not connections.

A TCP connection provides a **full-duplex service**: If there is a TCP connection between Process A on one host and Process B on another host, then application-layer data can flow from Process A to Process B at the same time as application-layer data flows from Process B to Process A. A TCP connection is also always **point-to-point**, that is, between a single sender and a single receiver. So-called "multicasting" (see Section 4.7)—the transfer of data from one sender to many receivers in a single send operation—is not possible with TCP. With TCP, two hosts are company and three are a crowd!

Let's now take a look at how a TCP connection is established. Suppose a process running in one host wants to initiate a connection with another process in another host. Recall that the process that is initiating the connection is called the *client process*, while the other process is called the *server process*. The client application process first informs the client transport layer that it wants to establish a connection to a process in the server. Recall from Section 2.7, a Java client program does this by issuing the command

```
Socket clientSocket = new Socket("hostname", portNumber);
```

where `hostname` is the name of the server and `portNumber` identifies the process on the server. The transport layer in the client then proceeds to establish a TCP connection with the TCP in the server. At the end of this section we discuss in some detail the connection-establishment procedure. For now it suffices to know that the client first sends a special TCP segment; the server responds with a second special TCP segment; and finally the client responds again with a third special segment. The first two segments carry no payload, that is, no application-layer data; the third of these segments may carry a payload. Because three segments are sent between the two hosts, this connection-establishment procedure is often referred to as a **three-way handshake**.

Once a TCP connection is established, the two application processes can send data to each other. Let us consider the sending of data from the client process to the server process. The client process passes a stream of data through the socket (the door of the process), as described in Section 2.7. Once the data passes through the door, the data is now in the hands of TCP running in the client. As shown in Figure 3.28, TCP directs this data to the connection's **send buffer**, which is one of the buffers that is set aside during the initial three-way handshake. From time to time,

---

CASE HISTORY

VINTON CERF, ROBERT KAHN, AND TCP/IP

In the early 1970s, packet-switched networks began to proliferate, with the ARPAnet—the precursor of the Internet—being just one of many networks. Each of these networks had its own protocol. Two researchers, Vinton Cerf and Robert Kahn, recognized the importance of interconnecting these networks and invented a cross-network protocol called TCP/IP, which stands for Transmission Control Protocol/Internet Protocol. Although Cerf and Kahn began by seeing the protocol as a single entity, it was later split into its two parts, TCP and IP, which operated separately. Cerf and Kahn published a paper on TCP/IP in May 1974 in *IEEE Transactions on Communications Technology* [Cerf 1974].

The TCP/IP protocol, which is the bread and butter of today's Internet, was devised before PCs and workstations, before the proliferation of Ethernets and other local area network technologies, before the Web, streaming audio, and chat. Cerf and Kahn saw the need for a networking protocol that, on the one hand, provides broad support for yet-to-be-defined applications and, on the other hand, allows arbitrary hosts and link-layer protocols to interoperate.

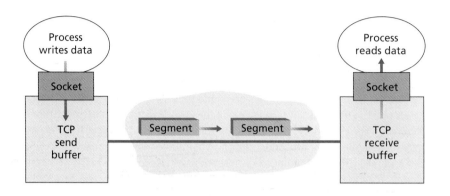

Figure 3.28 ◆ TCP send and receive buffers

TCP will grab chunks of data from the send buffer. Interestingly, the TCP specification [RFC 793] is very laid back about specifying when TCP should actually send buffered data, stating that TCP should "send that data in segments at its own convenience." The maximum amount of data that can be grabbed and placed in a segment is limited by the **maximum segment size (MSS)**. The MSS is typically set by first determining the length of the largest link-layer frame that can be sent by the local sending host (the so-called **maximum transmission unit**, **MTU**), and then setting the MSS to ensure that a TCP segment (when encapsulated in an IP datagram) will fit into a single link-layer frame. Common values for the MTU are 1,460 bytes, 536 bytes, and 512 bytes. Approaches have also been proposed for discovering the Path MTU—the largest link layer frame that can be sent on all links from source to destination [RFC 1191]—and setting the MSS based on the path MTU value. Note that the MSS is the maximum amount of application-layer data in the segment, not the maximum size of the TCP segment including headers. (This terminology is confusing, but we have to live with it, as it is well entrenched.)

TCP pairs each chunk of client data with a TCP header, thereby forming **TCP segments**. The segments are passed down to the network layer, where they are separately encapsulated within network-layer IP datagrams. The IP datagrams are then sent into the network. When TCP receives a segment at the other end, the segment's data is placed in the TCP connection's receive buffer, as shown in Figure 3.28. The application reads the stream of data from this buffer. Each side of the connection has its own send buffer and its own receive buffer. (You can see the online flow-control applet at http://www.awl.com/kurose-ross, which provides an animation of the send and receive buffers.)

We see from this discussion that a TCP connection consists of buffers, variables, and a socket connection to a process in one host, and another set of buffers, variables, and a socket connection to a process in another host. As mentioned earlier, no buffers or variables are allocated to the connection in the network elements (routers, switches, and repeaters) between the hosts.

3.5.2 TCP Segment Structure

Having taken a brief look at the TCP connection, let's examine the TCP segment structure. The TCP segment consists of header fields and a data field. The data field contains a chunk of application data. As mentioned above, the MSS limits the maximum size of a segment's data field. When TCP sends a large file, such as an image as part of a Web page, it typically breaks the file into chunks of size MSS (except for the last chunk, which will often be less than the MSS). Interactive applications, however, often transmit data chunks that are smaller than the MSS; for example, with remote login applications like Telnet, the data field in the TCP segment is often only one byte. Because the TCP header is typically 20 bytes (12 bytes more than the UDP header), segments sent by Telnet may be only 21 bytes in length.

Figure 3.29 shows the structure of the TCP segment. As with UDP, the header includes **source and destination port numbers**, which are used for multiplexing/demultiplexing data from/to upper-layer applications. Also, as with UDP, the header includes a **checksum field**. A TCP segment header also contains the following fields:

♦ The 32-bit **sequence number field** and the 32-bit **acknowledgment number field** are used by the TCP sender and receiver in implementing a reliable data transfer service, as discussed below.

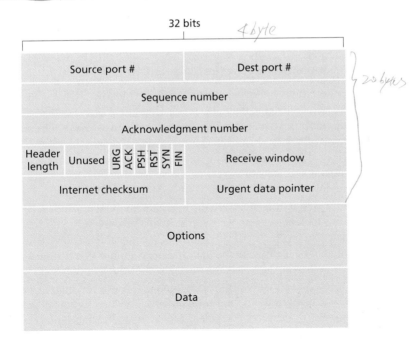

Figure 3.29 ♦ TCP segment structure

♦ The 16-bit **receive window** field is used for flow control. We will see shortly that it is used to indicate the number of bytes that a receiver is willing to accept.

♦ The 4-bit **header length field** specifies the length of the TCP header in 32-bit words. The TCP header can be of variable length due to the TCP options field. (Typically, the options field is empty, so that the length of the typical TCP header is 20 bytes.)

♦ The optional and variable-length **options field** is used when a sender and receiver negotiate the maximum segment size (MSS) or as a window scaling factor for use in high-speed networks. A time-stamping option is also defined. See RFC 854 and RFC 1323 for additional details.

♦ The **flag field** contains 6 bits. The **ACK bit** is used to indicate that the value carried in the acknowledgment field is valid; that is, the segment contains an acknowledgement for a segment that has been successfully received. The **RST**, **SYN**, and **FIN** bits are used for connection setup and teardown, as we will discuss at the end of this section. Setting the **PSH** bit indicates that the receiver should pass the data to the upper layer immediately. Finally, the **URG** bit is used to indicate that there is data in this segment that the sending-side upper-layer entity has marked as "urgent." The location of the last byte of this urgent data is indicated by the 16-bit **urgent data pointer field**. TCP must inform the receiving-side upper-layer entity when urgent data exists and pass it a pointer to the end of the urgent data. (In practice, the PSH, URG, and the urgent data pointer are not used. However, we mention these fields for completeness.)

Sequence Numbers and Acknowledgment Numbers

Two of the most important fields in the TCP segment header are the sequence number field and the acknowledgment number field. These fields are a critical part of TCP's reliable data transfer service. But before discussing how these fields are used to provide reliable data transfer, let us first explain what exactly TCP puts in these fields.

TCP views data as an unstructured, but ordered, stream of bytes. TCP's use of sequence numbers reflects this view in that sequence numbers are over the stream of transmitted bytes and *not* over the series of transmitted segments. The **sequence number for a segment** is therefore the byte-stream number of the first byte in the segment. Let's look at an example. Suppose that a process in Host A wants to send a stream of data to a process in Host B over a TCP connection. The TCP in Host A will implicitly number each byte in the data stream. Suppose that the data stream consists of a file consisting of 500,000 bytes, that the MSS is 1,000 bytes, and that the first byte of the data stream is numbered zero. As shown in Figure 3.30, TCP constructs 500 segments out of the data stream. The first segment gets assigned sequence number 0, the second segment gets assigned sequence number 1,000, the third segment gets assigned sequence number 2,000, and so on. Each sequence number is inserted in the sequence number field in the header of the appropriate TCP segment.

Now let's consider acknowledgment numbers. These are a little trickier than sequence numbers. Recall that TCP is full-duplex, so that Host A may be receiving data from Host B while it sends data to Host B (as part of the same TCP connection). Each of the segments that arrive from Host B has a sequence number for the data flowing from B to A. *The acknowledgment number that Host A puts in its segment is the sequence number of the next byte Host A is expecting from Host B.* It is good to look at a few examples to understand what is going on here. Suppose that Host A has received all bytes numbered 0 through 535 from B and suppose that it is about to send a segment to Host B. Host A is waiting for byte 536 and all the subsequent bytes in Host B's data stream. So Host A puts 536 in the acknowledgment number field of the segment it sends to B.

As another example, suppose that Host A has received one segment from Host B containing bytes 0 through 535 and another segment containing bytes 900 through 1,000. For some reason Host A has not yet received bytes 536 through 899. In this example, Host A is still waiting for byte 536 (and beyond) in order to recreate B's data stream. Thus, A's next segment to B will contain 536 in the acknowledgment number field. Because TCP only acknowledges bytes up to the first missing byte in the stream, TCP is said to provide **cumulative acknowledgments**.

This last example also brings up an important but subtle issue. Host A received the third segment (bytes 900 through 1,000) before receiving the second segment (bytes 536 through 899). Thus, the third segment arrived out of order. The subtle issue is: What does a host do when it receives out-of-order segments in a TCP connection? Interestingly, the TCP RFCs do not impose any rules here and leave the decision up to the people programming a TCP implementation. There are basically two choices: either (1) the receiver immediately discards out-of-order segments (which, as we discussed earlier, can simplify receiver design), or (2) the receiver keeps the out-of-order bytes and waits for the missing bytes to fill in the gaps. Clearly, the latter choice is more efficient in terms of network bandwidth, and is the approach taken in practice.

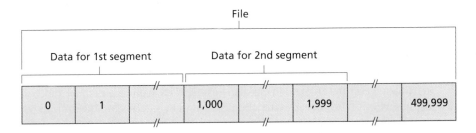

Figure 3.30 ◆ Dividing file data into TCP segments

In Figure 3.30 we assumed that the initial sequence number was zero. In truth, both sides of a TCP connection randomly choose an initial sequence number. This is done to minimize the possibility that a segment that is still present in the network from an earlier, already-terminated connection between two hosts is mistaken for a valid segment in a later connection between these same two hosts (which also happen to be using the same port numbers as the old connection) [Sunshine 1978].

Telnet: A Case Study for Sequence and Acknowledgment Numbers

Telnet, defined in RFC 854, is a popular application-layer protocol used for remote login. It runs over TCP and is designed to work between any pair of hosts. Unlike the bulk data transfer applications discussed in Chapter 2, Telnet is an interactive application. We discuss a Telnet example here, as it nicely illustrates TCP sequence and acknowledgment numbers. We note that many users now prefer to use the ssh protocol rather than Telnet, since data sent in a Telnet connection (including passwords!) are not encrypted, making Telnet vulnerable to eavesdropping attacks (as discussed in Section 8.7).

Suppose Host A initiates a Telnet session with Host B. Because Host A initiates the session, it is labeled the client, and Host B is labeled the server. Each character typed by the user (at the client) will be sent to the remote host; the remote host will send back a copy of each character, which will be displayed on the Telnet user's screen. This "echo back" is used to ensure that characters seen by the Telnet user have already been received and processed at the remote site. Each character thus traverses the network twice between the time the user hits the key and the time the character is displayed on the user's monitor.

Now suppose the user types a single letter, 'C,' and then grabs a coffee. Let's examine the TCP segments that are sent between the client and server. As shown in Figure 3.31, we suppose the starting sequence numbers are 42 and 79 for the client and server, respectively. Recall that the sequence number of a segment is the sequence number of the first byte in the data field. Thus, the first segment sent from the client will have sequence number 42; the first segment sent from the server will have sequence number 79. Recall that the acknowledgment number is the sequence number of the next byte of data that the host is waiting for. After the TCP connection is established but before any data is sent, the client is waiting for byte 79 and the server is waiting for byte 42.

As shown in Figure 3.31, three segments are sent. The first segment is sent from the client to the server, containing the one-byte ASCII representation of the letter 'C' in its data field. This first segment also has 42 in its sequence number field, as we just described. Also, because the client has not yet received any data from the server, this first segment will have 79 in its acknowledgment number field.

The second segment is sent from the server to the client. It serves a dual purpose. First it provides an acknowledgment of the data the server has received. By putting 43 in the acknowledgment field, the server is telling the client that it has

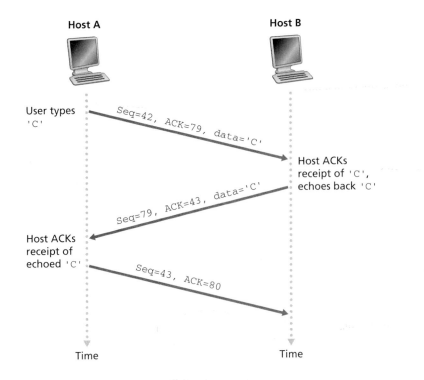

Host A

Host B

User types
'C'

Seq=42, ACK=79, data='C'

Host ACKs
receipt of 'C',
echoes back 'C'

Seq=79, ACK=43, data='C'

Host ACKs
receipt of
echoed 'C'

Seq=43, ACK=80

Time

Time

Figure 3.31 ♦ Sequence and acknowledgement numbers for a simple Telnet application over TCP

successfully received everything up through byte 42 and is now waiting for bytes 43 onward. The second purpose of this segment is to echo back the letter 'C.' Thus, the second segment has the ASCII representation of 'C' in its data field. This second segment has the sequence number 79, the initial sequence number of the server-to-client data flow of this TCP connection, as this is the very first byte of data that the server is sending. Note that the acknowledgment for client-to-server data is carried in a segment carrying server-to-client data; this acknowledgment is said to be **pig-gybacked** on the server-to-client data segment.

The third segment is sent from the client to the server. Its sole purpose is to acknowledge the data it has received from the server. (Recall that the second segment contained data—the letter 'C'—from the server to the client.) This segment has an empty data field (that is, the acknowledgment is not being piggybacked with any client-to-server data). The segment has 80 in the acknowledgment number field because the client has received the stream of bytes up through byte sequence number 79 and it is now waiting for bytes 80 onward. You might think it odd that this segment also has a sequence number since the segment contains no data. But because TCP has a sequence number field, the segment needs to have some sequence number.

3.5.3 Round-Trip Time Estimation and Timeout

TCP, like our `rdt` protocol in Section 3.4, uses a timeout/retransmit mechanism to recover from lost segments. Although this is conceptually simple, many subtle issues arise when we implement a timeout/retransmit mechanism in an actual protocol such as TCP. Perhaps the most obvious question is the length of the timeout intervals. Clearly, the timeout should be larger than the connection's round-trip time (RTT), that is, the time from when a segment is sent until it is acknowledged. Otherwise, unnecessary retransmissions would be sent. But how much larger? How should the RTT be estimated in the first place? Should a timer be associated with each and every unacknowledged segment? So many questions! Our discussion in this section is based on the TCP work in [Jacobson 1988] and the current IETF recommendations for managing TCP timers [RFC 2988].

Estimating the Round-Trip Time

Let's begin our study of TCP timer management by considering how TCP estimates the round-trip time between sender and receiver. This is accomplished as follows. The sample RTT, denoted `SampleRTT`, for a segment is the amount of time between when the segment is sent (that is, passed to IP) and when an acknowledgment for the segment is received. Instead of measuring a `SampleRTT` for every transmitted segment, most TCP implementations take only one `SampleRTT` measurement at a time. That is, at any point in time, the `SampleRTT` is being estimated for only one of the transmitted but currently unacknowledged segments, leading to a new value of `SampleRTT` approximately once every RTT. Also, TCP never computes a `SampleRTT` for a segment that has been retransmitted; it only measures `SampleRTT` for segments that have been transmitted once. (A problem at the end of the chapter asks you to consider why.)

Obviously, the `SampleRTT` values will fluctuate from segment to segment due to congestion in the routers and to the varying load on the end systems. Because of this fluctuation, any given `SampleRTT` value may be atypical. In order to estimate a typical RTT, it is therefore natural to take some sort of average of the `SampleRTT` values. TCP maintains an average, called `EstimatedRTT`, of the `SampleRTT` values. Upon obtaining a new `SampleRTT`, TCP updates `EstimatedRTT` according to the following formula:

$$\text{EstimatedRTT} = (1 - \alpha) \cdot \text{EstimatedRTT} + \alpha \cdot \text{SampleRTT}$$

The formula above is written in the form of a programming-language statement—the new value of `EstimatedRTT` is a weighted combination of the previous value of `EstimatedRTT` and the new value for `SampleRTT`. The recommended value of a is $\alpha = 0.125$ (that is, 1/8) [RFC 2988], in which case the formula above becomes:

```
EstimatedRTT = 0.875 · EstimatedRTT + 0.125 · SampleRTT
```

Note that `EstimatedRTT` is a weighted average of the `SampleRTT` values. As discussed in a homework problem at the end of this chapter, this weighted average puts more weight on recent samples than on old samples. This is natural, as the more recent samples better reflect the current congestion in the network. In statistics, such an average is called an **exponential weighted moving average (EWMA)**. The word "*exponential*" appears in EWMA because the weight of a given `SampleRTT` decays exponentially fast as the updates proceed. In the homework problems you will be asked to derive the exponential term in `EstimatedRTT`.

Figure 3.32 shows the `SampleRTT` values and `EstimatedRTT` for a value of $\alpha = 1/8$ for a TCP connection between gaia.cs.umass.edu (in Amherst, Massachusetts) to fantasia.eurecom.fr (in the south of France). Clearly, the variations in the `SampleRTT` are smoothed out in the computation of the `EstimatedRTT`.

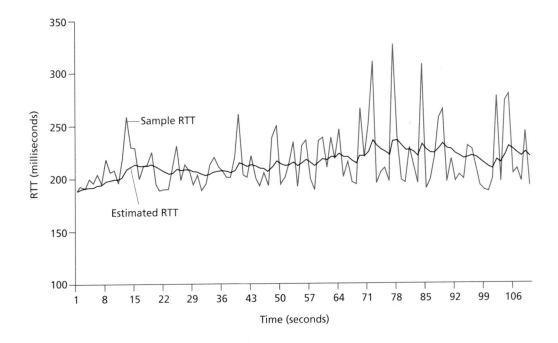

Figure 3.32 ♦ RTT samples and RTT estimates

In addition to having an estimate of the RTT, it is also valuable to have a measure of the variability of the RTT. [RFC 2988] defines the RTT variation, `DevRTT`, as an estimate of how much `SampleRTT` typically deviates from `EstimatedRTT`:

$$\text{DevRTT} = (1 - \beta) \cdot \text{DevRTT} + \beta \cdot | \text{ SampleRTT} - \text{EstimatedRTT } |$$

Note that `DevRTT` is an EWMA of the difference between `SampleRTT` and `EstimatedRTT`. If the `SampleRTT` values have little fluctuation, then `DevRTT` will be small; on the other hand, if there is a lot of fluctuation, `DevRTT` will be large. The recommended value of β is 0.25.

Setting and Managing the Retransmission Timeout Interval

Given values of `EstimatedRTT` and `DevRTT`, what value should be used for TCP's timeout interval? Clearly, the interval should be greater than or equal to `EstimatedRTT`, or unnecessary retransmissions would be sent. But the timeout interval should not be too much larger than `EstimatedRTT`; otherwise,

PRINCIPLES IN PRACTICE

TCP provides reliable data transfer by using positive acknowledgments and timers in much the same way that we studied in Section 3.4. TCP acknowledges data that has been received correctly, and it then retransmits segments when segments or their corresponding acknowledgments are thought to be lost or corrupted. Certain versions of TCP also have an implicit NAK mechanism—with TCP's fast retransmit mechanism, the receipt of three duplicate ACKs for a given segment serves as an implicit NAK for the following segment, triggering retransmission of that segment before timeout. TCP uses sequences of numbers to allow the receiver to identify lost or duplicate segments. Just as in the case of our reliable data transfer protocol, `rdt3.0`, TCP cannot itself tell for certain if a segment, or its ACK, is lost, corrupted, or overly delayed. At the sender, TCP's response will be the same: retransmit the segment in question.

TCP also uses pipelining, allowing the sender to have multiple transmitted but yet-to-be-acknowledged segments outstanding at any given time. We saw earlier that pipelining can greatly improve a session's throughput when the ratio of the segment size to round-trip delay is small. The specific number of outstanding unacknowledged segments that a sender can have is determined by TCP's flow-control and congestion-control mechanisms. TCP flow control is discussed at the end of this section; TCP congestion control is discussed in Section 3.7. For the time being, we must simply be aware that the TCP sender uses pipelining.

when a segment is lost, TCP would not quickly retransmit the segment, leading to large data transfer delays. It is therefore desirable to set the timeout equal to the `EstimatedRTT` plus some margin. The margin should be large when there is a lot of fluctuation in the `SampleRTT` values; it should be small when there is little fluctuation. The value of `DevRTT` should thus come into play here. All of these considerations are taken into account in TCP's method for determining the retransmission timeout interval:

```
TimeoutInterval = EstimatedRTT + 4 · DevRTT
```

3.5.4 Reliable Data Transfer

Recall that the Internet's network-layer service (IP service) is unreliable. IP does not guarantee datagram delivery, does not guarantee in-order delivery of datagrams, and does not guarantee the integrity of the data in the datagrams. With IP service, datagrams can overflow router buffers and never reach their destination, datagrams can arrive out of order, and bits in the datagram can get corrupted (flipped from 0 to 1 and vice versa). Because transport-layer segments are carried across the network by IP datagrams, transport-layer segments can suffer from these problems as well.

TCP creates a **reliable data transfer service** on top of IP's unreliable best-effort service. TCP's reliable data transfer service ensures that the data stream that a process reads out of its TCP receive buffer is uncorrupted, without gaps, without duplication, and in sequence; that is, the byte stream is exactly the same byte stream that was sent by the end system on the other side of the connection. How TCP provides a reliable data transfer involves many of the principles that we studied in Section 3.4.

In our earlier development of reliable data transfer techniques, it was conceptually easiest to assume that an individual timer is associated with each transmitted but not yet acknowledged segment. While this is great in theory, timer management can require considerable overhead. Thus, the recommended TCP timer management procedures [RFC 2988] use only a *single* retransmission timer, even if there are multiple transmitted but not yet acknowledged segments. The TCP protocol provided in this section follows this single-timer recommendation.

We will discuss how TCP provides reliable data transfer in two incremental steps. We first present a highly simplified description of a TCP sender that uses only timeouts to recover from lost segments; we then present a more complete description that uses duplicate acknowledgments in addition to timeouts. In the ensuing discussion, we suppose that data is being sent in only one direction, from Host A to Host B, and that Host A is sending a large file.

Figure 3.33 presents a highly simplified description of a TCP sender. We see that there are three major events related to data transmission and retransmission in the TCP sender: data received from application above; timer timeout; and ACK receipt. Upon the occurrence of the first major event, TCP receives data from the application, encapsulates the data in a segment, and passes the segment to IP. Note that each segment includes a sequence number that is the byte-stream number of the first data byte in the segment, as described in Section 3.5.2. Also note that if the timer is already not running for some other segment, TCP starts the timer when the segment is passed to IP. (It is helpful to think of the timer as being associated with the oldest unacknowledged segment.) The expiration interval for this timer is the

```
/* Assume sender is not constrained by TCP flow or congestion con-
trol, that data from above is less than MSS in size, and that data
transfer is in one direction only. */

NextSeqNum=InitialSeqNumber
SendBase=InitialSeqNumber

loop (forever) {
   switch(event)

      event: data received from application above
         create TCP segment with sequence number NextSeqNum
         if (timer currently not running)
            start timer
         pass segment to IP
         NextSeqNum=NextSeqNum+length(data)
         break;

      event: timer timeout
         retransmit not-yet-acknowledged segment with
            smallest sequence number
         start timer
         break;

      event: ACK received, with ACK field value of y
         if (y > SendBase) {
            SendBase=y
            if (there are currently any not-yet-acknowledged segments)
               start timer
         }
         break;

   } /* end of loop forever */
```

Figure 3.33 ♦ Simplified TCP sender

`TimeoutInterval`, which is calculated from `EstimatedRTT` and `DevRTT`, as described in Section 3.5.3.

The second major event is the timeout. TCP responds to the timeout event by retransmitting the segment that caused the timeout. TCP then restarts the timer.

The third major event that must be handled by the TCP sender is the arrival of an acknowledgment segment (ACK) from the receiver (more specifically, a segment containing a valid ACK field value). On the occurrence of this event, TCP compares the ACK value `y` with its variable `SendBase`. The TCP state variable `SendBase` is the sequence number of the oldest unacknowledged byte. (Thus `SendBase−1` is the sequence number of the last byte that is known to have been received correctly and in order at the receiver.) As indicated earlier, TCP uses cumulative acknowledgments, so that `y` acknowledges the receipt of all bytes before byte number `y`. If `y >` `SendBase`, then the ACK is acknowledging one or more previously unacknowledged segments. Thus the sender updates its `SendBase` variable; it also restarts the timer if there currently are any not-yet-acknowledged segments.

A Few Interesting Scenarios

We have just described a highly simplified version of how TCP provides reliable data transfer. But even this highly simplified version has many subtleties. To get a good feeling for how this protocol works, let's now walk through a few simple scenarios. Figure 3.34 depicts the first scenario, in which Host A sends one segment to Host B. Suppose that this segment has sequence number 92 and contains 8 bytes of data. After sending this segment, Host A waits for a segment from B with acknowledgment number 100. Although the segment from A is received at B, the acknowledgment from B to A gets lost. In this case, the timeout event occurs, and Host A retransmits the same segment. Of course, when Host B receives the retransmission, it observes from the sequence number that the segment contains data that has already been received. Thus, TCP in Host B will discard the bytes in the retransmitted segment.

In a second scenario, shown in Figure 3.35, Host A sends two segments back to back. The first segment has sequence number 92 and 8 bytes of data, and the second segment has sequence number 100 and 20 bytes of data. Suppose that both segments arrive intact at B, and B sends two separate acknowledgments for each of these segments. The first of these acknowledgments has acknowledgment number 100; the second has acknowledgment number 120. Suppose now that neither of the acknowledgments arrives at Host A before the timeout. When the timeout event occurs, Host A resends the first segment with sequence number 92 and restarts the timer. As long as the ACK for the second segment arrives before the new timeout, the second segment will not be retransmitted.

In a third and final scenario, suppose Host A sends the two segments, exactly as in the second example. The acknowledgment of the first segment is lost in the

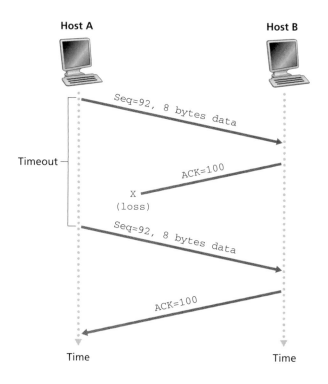

Figure 3.34 ◆ Retransmission due to a lost acknowledgment

network, but just before the timeout event, Host A receives an acknowledgment with acknowledgment number 120. Host A therefore knows that Host B has received *everything* up through byte 119; so Host A does not resend either of the two segments. This scenario is illustrated in Figure 3.36.

Doubling the Timeout Interval

We now discuss a few modifications that most TCP implementations employ. The first concerns the length of the timeout interval after a timer expiration. In this modification, whenever the timeout event occurs, TCP retransmits the not yet acknowledged segment with the smallest sequence number, as described above. But each time TCP retransmits, it sets the next timeout interval to twice the previous value, rather than deriving it from the last `EstimatedRTT` and `DevRTT` (as described in Section 3.5.3). For example, suppose `TimeoutInterval` associated with the oldest not yet acknowledged segment is .75 sec when the timer first expires. TCP will then retransmit this segment and set the new expiration time to 1.5 sec. If the timer expires again 1.5 sec later, TCP will again retransmit this segment, now setting

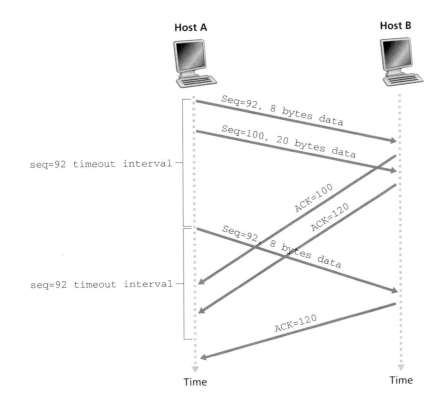

Figure 3.35 ◆ Segment 100 not retransmitted

the expiration time to 3.0 sec. Thus the intervals grow exponentially after each retransmission. However, whenever the timer is started after either of the two other events (that is, data received from application above, and ACK received), the `TimeoutInterval` is derived from the most recent values of `EstimatedRTT` and `DevRTT`.

This modification provides a limited form of congestion control. (More comprehensive forms of TCP congestion control will be studied in Section 3.7.) The timer expiration is most likely caused by congestion in the network, that is, too many packets arriving at one (or more) router queues in the path between the source and destination, causing packets to be dropped and/or long queuing delays. In times of congestion, if the sources continue to retransmit packets persistently, the congestion may get worse. Instead, TCP acts more politely, with each sender retransmitting after longer and longer intervals. We will see that a similar idea is used by Ethernet when we study CSMA/CD in Chapter 5.

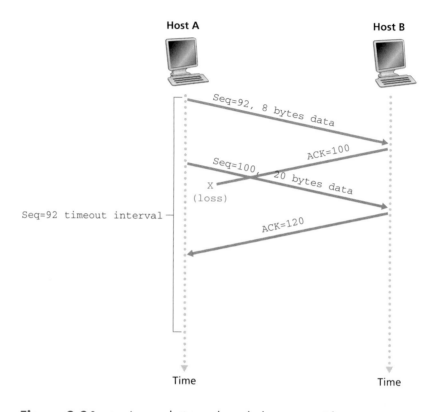

Figure 3.36 ♦ A cumulative acknowledgment avoids retransmission of the first segment.

Fast Retransmit

One of the problems with timeout-triggered retransmissions is that the timeout period can be relatively long. When a segment is lost, this long timeout period forces the sender to delay resending the lost packet, thereby increasing the end-to-end delay. Fortunately, the sender can often detect packet loss well before the timeout event occurs by noting so-called duplicate ACKs. A **duplicate ACK** is an ACK that reacknowledges a segment for which the sender has already received an earlier acknowledgment. To understand the sender's response to a duplicate ACK, we must look at why the receiver sends a duplicate ACK in the first place. Table 3.2 summarizes the TCP receiver's ACK generation policy [RFC 1122, RFC 2581]. When a TCP receiver receives a segment with a sequence number that is larger than the next, expected, in-order sequence number, it detects a gap in the data stream—that is, a missing segment. This gap could be the result of lost or reordered segments within the network. Since TCP does not use negative acknowledgments, the receiver

Event	TCP Receiver Action
Arrival of in-order segment with expected sequence number. All data up to expected sequence number already acknowledged.	Delayed ACK. Wait up to 500 msec for arrival of another in-order segment. If next in-order segment does not arrive in this interval, send an ACK.
Arrival of in-order segment with expected sequence number. One other in-order segment waiting for ACK transmission.	Immediately send single cumulative ACK, ACKing both in-order segments.
Arrival of out-of-order segment with higher-than-expected sequence number. Gap detected.	Immediately send duplicate ACK, indicating sequence number of next expected byte (which is the lower end of the gap).
Arrival of segment that partially or completely fills in gap in received data.	Immediately send ACK, provided that segment starts at the lower end of gap.

Table 3.2 ◆ TCP ACK Generation Recommendation [RFC 1122, RFC 2581]

cannot send an explicit negative acknowledgment back to the sender. Instead, it simply reacknowledges (that is, generates a duplicate ACK for) the last in-order byte of data it has received. (Note that Table 3.2 allows for the case that the receiver does not discard out-of-order segments.)

Because a sender often sends a large number of segments back to back, if one segment is lost, there will likely be many back-to-back duplicate ACKs. If the TCP sender receives three duplicate ACKs for the same data, it takes this as an indication that the segment following the segment that has been ACKed three times has been lost. (In the homework problems, we consider the question of why the sender waits for three duplicate ACKs, rather than just a single duplicate ACK.) In the case that three duplicate ACKs are received, the TCP sender performs a **fast retransmit** [RFC 2581], retransmitting the missing segment *before* that segment's timer expires. For TCP with fast retransmit, the following code snippet replaces the ACK received event in Figure 3.33:

```
event: ACK received, with ACK field value of y
        if (y > SendBase) {
             SendBase=y
             if (there are currently any not yet
                   acknowledged segments)
               start timer
             }
        else { /* a duplicate ACK for already ACKed
              segment */
             increment number of duplicate ACKs
                received for y
             if (number of duplicate ACKS received
               for y==3) {
```

```
            /* TCP fast retransmit */
            resend segment with sequence number y
            }
        break;
```

We noted earlier that many subtle issues arise when a timeout/retransmit mechanism is implemented in an actual protocol such as TCP. The procedures above, which have evolved as a result of more than 15 years of experience with TCP timers, should convince you that this is indeed the case!

Go-Back-N or Selective Repeat?

Let us close our study of TCP's error-recovery mechanism by considering the following question: Is TCP a GBN or an SR protocol? Recall that TCP acknowledgments are cumulative and correctly received but out-of-order segments are not individually ACKed by the receiver. Consequently, as shown in Figure 3.33 (see also Figure 3.19), the TCP sender need only maintain the smallest sequence number of a transmitted but unacknowledged byte (`SendBase`) and the sequence number of the next byte to be sent (`NextSeqNum`). In this sense, TCP looks a lot like a GBN-style protocol. But there are some striking differences between TCP and Go-Back-N. Many TCP implementations will buffer correctly received but out-of-order segments [Stevens 1994]. Consider also what happens when the sender sends a sequence of segments $1, 2, \ldots, N$, and all of the segments arrive in order without error at the receiver. Further suppose that the acknowledgment for packet $n < N$ gets lost, but the remaining $N - 1$ acknowledgments arrive at the sender before their respective timeouts. In this example GBN would retransmit not only packet n, but also all of the subsequent packets $n + 1, n + 2, \ldots, N$. TCP, on the other hand, would retransmit at most, one segment, namely, segment n. Moreover, TCP would not even retransmit segment n if the acknowledgment for segment $n + 1$ arrived before the timeout for segment n.

A proposed modification to TCP, the so-called **selective acknowledgment** [RFC 2018], allows a TCP receiver to acknowledge out-of-order segments selectively rather than just cumulatively acknowledging the last correctly received, in-order segment. When combined with selective retransmission—skipping the retransmission of segments that have already been selectively acknowledged by the receiver—TCP looks a lot like our generic SR protocol. Thus, TCP's error-recovery mechanism is probably best categorized as a hybrid of GBN and SR protocols.

3.5.5 Flow Control

Recall that the hosts on each side of a TCP connection set aside a receive buffer for the connection. When the TCP connection receives bytes that are correct and in sequence, it places the data in the receive buffer. The associated application process will read data from this buffer, but not necessarily at the instant the data arrives. Indeed, the receiving application may be busy with some other task and may not even attempt to read the data until long after it has arrived. If the application is relatively slow at reading the data, the sender can very easily overflow the connection's receive buffer by sending too much data too quickly.

TCP provides a **flow-control service** to its applications to eliminate the possibility of the sender overflowing the receiver's buffer. Flow control is thus a speed-matching service—matching the rate at which the sender is sending against the rate at which the receiving application is reading. As noted earlier, a TCP sender can also be throttled due to congestion within the IP network; this form of sender control is referred to as **congestion control**, a topic we will explore in detail in Sections 3.6 and 3.7. Even though the actions taken by flow and congestion control are similar (the throttling of the sender), they are obviously taken for very different reasons. Unfortunately, many authors use the terms interchangeably, and the savvy reader would be wise to distinguish between them. Let's now discuss how TCP provides its flow-control service. In order to see the forest for the trees, we suppose throughout this section that the TCP implementation is such that the TCP receiver discards out-of-order segments.

TCP provides flow control by having the *sender* maintain a variable called the **receive window**. Informally, the receive window is used to give the sender an idea of how much free buffer space is available at the receiver. Because TCP is full-duplex, the sender at each side of the connection maintains a distinct receive window. Let's investigate the receive window in the context of a file transfer. Suppose that Host A is sending a large file to Host B over a TCP connection. Host B allocates a receive buffer to this connection; denote its size by `RcvBuffer`. From time to time, the application process in Host B reads from the buffer. Define the following variables:

♦ `LastByteRead`: the number of the last byte in the data stream read from the buffer by the application process in B

♦ `LastByteRcvd`: the number of the last byte in the data stream that has arrived from the network and has been placed in the receive buffer at B

Because TCP is not permitted to overflow the allocated buffer, we must have

`LastByteRcvd` − `LastByteRead` ≤ `RcvBuffer`

The receive window, denoted `RcvWindow`, is set to the amount of spare room in the buffer:

`RcvWindow = RcvBuffer` − `[LastByteRcvd` − `LastByteRead]`

Because the spare room changes with time, `RcvWindow` is dynamic. The variable `RcvWindow` is illustrated in Figure 3.37.

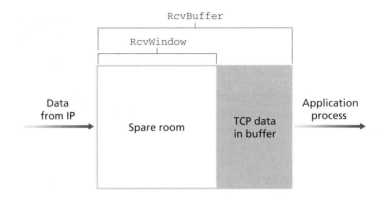

Figure 3.37 ◆ The receive window (`RcvWindow`) and the receive buffer (`RcvBuffer`).

How does the connection use the variable `RcvWindow` to provide the flow-control service? Host B tells Host A how much spare room it has in the connection buffer by placing its current value of `RcvWindow` in the receive window field of every segment it sends to A. Initially, Host B sets `RcvWindow = RcvBuffer`. Note that to pull this off, Host B must keep track of several connection-specific variables.

Host A in turn keeps track of two variables, `LastByteSent` and `LastByteAcked`, which have obvious meanings. Note that the difference between these two variables, `LastByteSent – LastByteAcked`, is the amount of unacknowledged data that A has sent into the connection. By keeping the amount of unacknowledged data less than the value of `RcvWindow`, Host A is assured that it is not overflowing the receive buffer at Host B. Thus, Host A makes sure throughout the connection's life that

`LastByteSent – LastByteAcked ≤ RcvWindow`

There is one minor technical problem with this scheme. To see this, suppose Host B's receive buffer becomes full so that `RcvWindow = 0`. After advertising `RcvWindow = 0` to Host A, also suppose that B has *nothing* to send to A. Now consider what happens. As the application process at B empties the buffer, TCP does not send new segments with new `RcvWindow` values to Host A; indeed, TCP sends a segment to Host A only if it has data to send or if it has an acknowledgment to send. Therefore, Host A is never informed that some space has opened up in Host B's receive buffer—Host A is blocked and can transmit no more data! To solve this problem, the TCP specification requires Host A to continue to send segments with one data byte when B's receive window is zero. These segments will be acknowledged by the receiver. Eventually the buffer will begin to empty and the acknowledgments will contain a nonzero `RcvWindow` value.

The online site at http://www.awl.com/kurose-ross for the text provides an interactive Java applet that illustrates the operation of the TCP receive window.

Having described TCP's flow-control service, we briefly mention here that UDP does not provide flow control. To understand the issue, consider sending a series of UDP segments from a process on Host A to a process on Host B. For a typical UDP implementation, UDP will append the segments in a finite-sized buffer that "precedes" the corresponding socket (that is, the door to the process). The process reads one entire segment at a time from the buffer. If the process does not read the segments fast enough from the buffer, the buffer will overflow and segments will get dropped.

3.5.6 TCP Connection Management

In this subsection we take a closer look at how a TCP connection is established and torn down. Although this topic may not seem particularly thrilling, it is important because TCP connection establishment can significantly add to perceived delays (for example, when surfing the Web). Furthermore, many of the most common network attacks—including the incredibly popular SYN flood attack—exploit vulnerabilities in TCP connection management. Let's first take a look at how a TCP connection is established. Suppose a process running in one host (client) wants to initiate a connection with another process in another host (server). The client application process first informs the client TCP that it wants to establish a connection to a process in the server. The TCP in the client then proceeds to establish a TCP connection with the TCP in the server in the following manner:

♦ **Step 1.** The client-side TCP first sends a special TCP segment to the server-side TCP. This special segment contains no application-layer data. But one of the flag bits in the segment's header (see Figure 3.29), the SYN bit, is set to 1. For this reason, this special segment is referred to as a SYN segment. In addition, the client randomly chooses an initial sequence number (`client_isn`) and puts this number in the sequence number field of the initial TCP SYN segment. This segment is encapsulated within an IP datagram and sent to the server. There has been considerable interest in properly randomizing the choice of the `client_isn` in order to avoid certain security attacks [CERT 2001-09].

♦ **Step 2.** Once the IP datagram containing the TCP SYN segment arrives at the server host (assuming it does arrive!), the server extracts the TCP SYN segment from the datagram, allocates the TCP buffers and variables to the connection, and sends a connection-granted segment to the client TCP. (We'll see in Chapter 8 that the allocation of these buffers and variables before completing the third step of the three-way handshake makes TCP vulnerable to a denial-of-service attack known as SYN flooding.) This connection-granted segment also contains no application-layer data. However, it does contain three important pieces of information in the segment header. First, the SYN bit is set to 1. Second, the acknowledgment field of the TCP segment header is set to `client_isn+1`. Finally, the server chooses its own initial sequence number (`server_isn`) and puts this value in the sequence number field of the TCP segment header. This connection-granted segment is saying, in effect, "I received your SYN packet to start a connection with your initial sequence number, `client_isn`. I agree to establish this connection. My own initial sequence number is `server_isn`." The connection-granted segment is sometimes referred to as a **SYNACK segment**.

♦ **Step 3.** Upon receiving the SYNACK segment, the client also allocates buffers and variables to the connection. The client host then sends the server yet another segment; this last segment acknowledges the server's connection-granted segment (the client does so by putting the value `server_isn+1` in the acknowledgment field of the TCP segment header). The SYN bit is set to zero, since the connection is established.

Once these three steps have been completed, the client and server hosts can send segments containing data to each other. In each of these future segments, the SYN bit will be set to zero. Note that in order to establish the connection, three packets are sent between the two hosts, as illustrated in Figure 3.38. For this reason, this connection-establishment procedure is often referred to as a **three-way handshake**. Several aspects of the TCP three-way handshake are explored in the homework problems (Why are initial sequence numbers needed? Why is a three-way handshake, as opposed to a two-way handshake, needed?). It's interesting to note that a rock climber and a belayer (who is stationed below the rock climber and whose job it is to handle the climber's safety rope) use a three-way-handshake communication protocol that is identical to TCP's to ensure that both sides are ready before the climber begins ascent.

All good things must come to an end, and the same is true with a TCP connection. Either of the two processes participating in a TCP connection can end the connection. When a connection ends, the "resources" (that is, the buffers and variables) in the hosts are deallocated. As an example, suppose the client decides to close the connection, as shown in Figure 3.39. The client application process issues a close command. This causes the client TCP to send a special TCP segment to the server process. This special segment has a flag bit in the segment's header, the FIN bit (see Figure 3.29), set to 1. When the server receives this segment, it sends the client an acknowledgment segment in return. The server then sends its own shutdown segment, which has the FIN bit set to 1. Finally, the client acknowledges the server's shutdown segment. At this point, all the resources in the two hosts are now deallocated.

During the life of a TCP connection, the TCP protocol running in each host makes transitions through various **TCP states**. Figure 3.40 illustrates a typical sequence of TCP states that are visited by the *client* TCP. The client TCP begins in the CLOSED state. The application on the client side initiates a new TCP connection (by creating a Socket object in our Java examples from Chapter 2). This causes

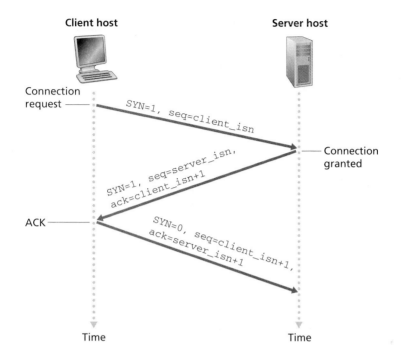

Client host

Server host

Connection
request

SYN=1, seq=client_isn

Connection
granted

SYN=1, seq=server_isn,
ack=client_isn+1

ACK

SYN=0, seq=client_isn+1,
ack=server_isn+1

Time

Time

Figure 3.38 ♦ TCP three-way handshake: segment exchange

TCP in the client to send a SYN segment to TCP in the server. After having sent the SYN segment, the client TCP enters the SYN_SENT state. While in the SYN_SENT state, the client TCP waits for a segment from the server TCP that includes an acknowledgment for the client's previous segment and has the SYN bit set to 1. Having received such a segment, the client TCP enters the ESTABLISHED state. While in the ESTABLISHED state, the TCP client can send and receive TCP segments containing payload (that is, application-generated) data.

Suppose that the client application decides it wants to close the connection. (Note that the server could also choose to close the connection.) This causes the client TCP to send a TCP segment with the FIN bit set to 1 and to enter the FIN_WAIT_1 state. While in the FIN_WAIT_1 state, the client TCP waits for a TCP segment from the server with an acknowledgment. When it receives this segment, the client TCP enters the FIN_WAIT_2 state. While in the FIN_WAIT_2 state, the client waits for another segment from the server with the FIN bit set to 1; after receiving this segment, the client TCP acknowledges the server's segment and enters the TIME_WAIT state. The TIME_WAIT state lets the TCP client resend the final acknowledgment in case the ACK is lost. The time spent in the TIME_WAIT

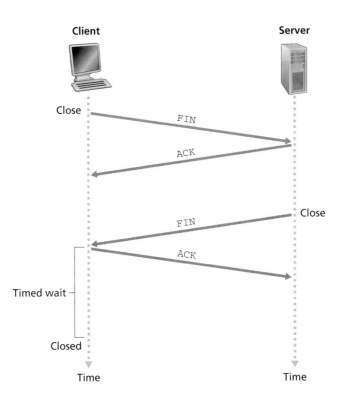

Figure 3.39 ◆ Closing a TCP connection

state is implementation-dependent, but typical values are 30 seconds, 1 minute, and 2 minutes. After the wait, the connection formally closes and all resources on the client side (including port numbers) are released.

Figure 3.41 illustrates the series of states typically visited by the server-side TCP, assuming the client begins connection teardown. The transitions are self-explanatory. In these two state-transition diagrams, we have only shown how a TCP connection is normally established and shut down. We have not described what happens in certain pathological scenarios, for example, when both sides of a connection want to initiate or shut down at the same time. If you are interested in learning about this and other advanced issues concerning TCP, you are encouraged to see Stevens' comprehensive book [Stevens 1994].

Before we bring an end to this section, let's consider what happens when a host receives a TCP segment whose port numbers or source IP address do not jive with any the ongoing sockets in the host. For example, suppose a host receives a TCP SYN packet with destination port 80, but the host is not accepting connections on port 80 (that is, it is not running a Web server on port 80). Then the host will send a special reset

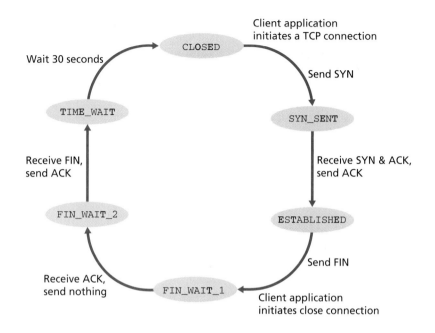

Figure 3.40 ♦ A typical sequence of TCP states visited by a client TCP

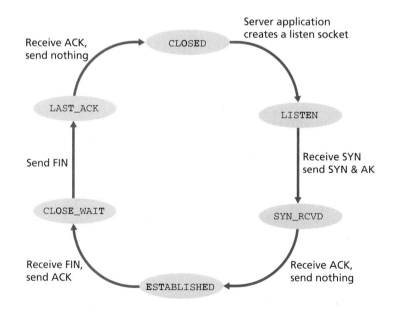

Figure 3.41 ♦ A typical sequence of TCP states visited by a server-side TCP

segment to the source. This TCP segment has the RST flag bit (see Section 3.5.2) set to 1. Thus, when a host sends a reset segment, it is telling the source "I don't have a socket for that segment. Please do not resend the segment." When a host receives a UDP packet whose destination port number doesn't jive with an ongoing UDP sockets, the host sends a special ICMP datagram, as discussed in Chapter 4.

This completes our introduction to error control and flow control in TCP. In Section 3.7 we'll return to TCP and look at TCP congestion control in some depth. Before doing so, however, we first step back and examine congestion-control issues in a broader context.

3.6 Principles of Congestion Control

In the previous sections, we examined both the general principles and specific TCP mechanisms used to provide for a reliable data transfer service in the face of packet loss. We mentioned earlier that, in practice, such loss typically results from the overflowing of router buffers as the network becomes congested. Packet retransmission thus treats a symptom of network congestion (the loss of a specific transport-layer segment) but does not treat the cause of network congestion—too many sources attempting to send data at too high a rate. To treat the cause of network congestion, mechanisms are needed to throttle senders in the face of network congestion.

In this section, we consider the problem of congestion control in a general context, seeking to understand why congestion is a bad thing, how network congestion is manifested in the performance received by upper-layer applications, and various approaches that can be taken to avoid, or react to, network congestion. This more general study of congestion control is appropriate since, as with reliable data transfer, it is high on our "top-ten" list of fundamentally important problems in networking. We conclude this section with a discussion of congestion control in the **available bit-rate (ABR)** service in **asynchronous transfer mode (ATM)** networks. The following section contains a detailed study of TCP's congestion-control algorithm.

3.6.1 The Causes and the Costs of Congestion

Let's begin our general study of congestion control by examining three increasingly complex scenarios in which congestion occurs. In each case, we'll look at why congestion occurs in the first place and at the cost of congestion (in terms of resources not fully utilized and poor performance received by the end systems). We'll not (yet) focus on how to react to, or avoid, congestion but rather focus on the simpler issue of understanding what happens as hosts increase their transmission rate and the network becomes congested.

Scenario 1: Two Senders, a Router with Infinite Buffers

We begin by considering perhaps the simplest congestion scenario possible: Two hosts (A and B) each have a connection that shares a single hop between source and destination, as shown in Figure 3.42.

Let's assume that the application in Host A is sending data into the connection (for example, passing data to the transport-level protocol via a socket) at an average rate of λ_{in} bytes/sec. These data are original in the sense that each unit of data is sent into the socket only once. The underlying transport-level protocol is a simple one. Data is encapsulated and sent; no error recovery (for example, retransmission), flow control, or congestion control is performed. Ignoring the additional overhead due to adding transport- and lower-layer header information, the rate at which Host A offers traffic to the router in this first scenario is thus λ_{in} bytes/sec. Host B operates in a similar manner, and we assume for simplicity that it too is sending at a rate of λ_{in} bytes/sec. Packets from Hosts A and B pass through a router and over a shared outgoing link of capacity R. The router has buffers that allow it to store incoming packets when the packet arrival rate exceeds the outgoing link's capacity. In this first scenario, we assume that the router has an infinite amount of buffer space.

Figure 3.43 plots the performance of Host A's connection under this first scenario. The left graph plots the **per-connection throughput** (number of bytes per second at the receiver) as a function of the connection-sending rate. For a sending rate between 0 and $R/2$, the throughput at the receiver equals the sender's sending rate—everything sent by the sender is received at the receiver with a finite delay. When the sending rate is above $R/2$, however, the throughput is only $R/2$. This upper

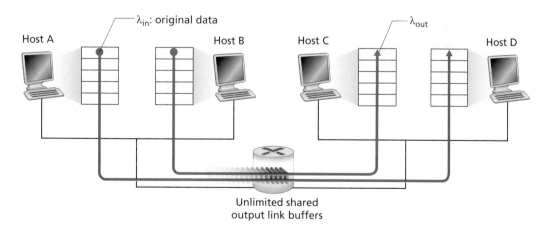

Figure 3.42 ♦ Congestion scenario 1: Two connections sharing a single hop with infinite buffers

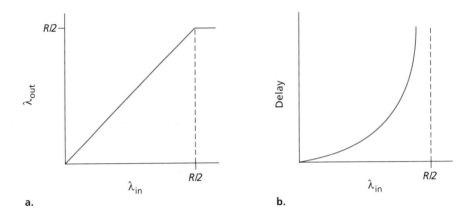

Figure 3.43 ♦ Congestion scenario 1: Throughput and delay as a function of host sending rate

limit on throughput is a consequence of the sharing of link capacity between two connections. The link simply cannot deliver packets to a receiver at a steady-state rate that exceeds $R/2$. No matter how high Hosts A and B set their sending rates, they will each never see a throughput higher than $R/2$.

Achieving a per-connection throughput of $R/2$ might actually appear to be a good thing, because the link is fully utilized in delivering packets to their destinations. The right-hand graph in Figure 3.43, however, shows the consequences of operating near link capacity. As the sending rate approaches $R/2$ (from the left), the average delay becomes larger and larger. When the sending rate exceeds $R/2$, the average number of queued packets in the router is unbounded, and the average delay between source and destination becomes infinite (assuming that the connections operate at these sending rates for an infinite period of time and there is an infinite amount of buffering available). Thus, while operating at an aggregate throughput of near R may be ideal from a throughput standpoint, it is far from ideal from a delay standpoint. *Even in this (extremely) idealized scenario, we've already found one cost of a congested network—large queuing delays are experienced as the packet-arrival rate nears the link capacity.*

Scenario 2: Two Senders and a Router with Finite Buffers

Let us now slightly modify scenario 1 in the following two ways (see Figure 3.44). First, the amount of router buffering is assumed to be finite. A consequence of this real-world assumption is that packets will be dropped when arriving to an already-full buffer. Second, we assume that each connection is reliable. If a packet containing a transport-level segment is dropped at the router, the sender will eventually

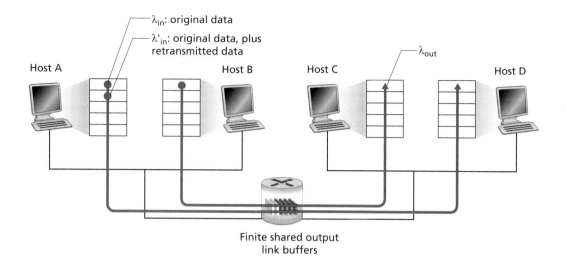

Figure 3.44 ◆ Scenario 2: Two hosts (with retransmissions) and a router with finite buffers

retransmit it. Because packets can be retransmitted, we must now be more careful with our use of the term *sending rate*. Specifically, let us again denote the rate at which the application sends original data into the socket by λ_{in} bytes/sec. The rate at which the transport layer sends segments (containing original data *and* retransmitted data) into the network will be denoted λ'_{in} bytes/sec. λ'_{in} is sometimes referred to as the **offered load** to the network.

The performance realized under scenario 2 will now depend strongly on how retransmission is performed. First, consider the unrealistic case that Host A is able to somehow (magically!) determine whether or not a buffer is free in the router and thus sends a packet only when a buffer is free. In this case, no loss would occur, λ_{in} would be equal to λ'_{in}, and the throughput of the connection would be equal to λ_{in}. This case is shown in Figure 3.45(a). From a throughput standpoint, performance is ideal—everything that is sent is received. Note that the average host sending rate cannot exceed $R/2$ under this scenario, since packet loss is assumed never to occur.

Consider next the slightly more realistic case that the sender retransmits only when a packet is known for certain to be lost. (Again, this assumption is a bit of a stretch. However, it is possible that the sending host might set its timeout large enough to be virtually assured that a packet that has not been acknowledged has been lost.) In this case, the performance might look something like that shown in Figure 3.45(b). To appreciate what is happening here, consider the case that the offered load, λ'_{in} (the rate of original data transmission plus retransmissions), equals $R/2$. According to Figure 3.45(b), at this value of the offered load, the rate at which data are delivered to the receiver application is $R/3$. Thus, out of the 0.5R units of

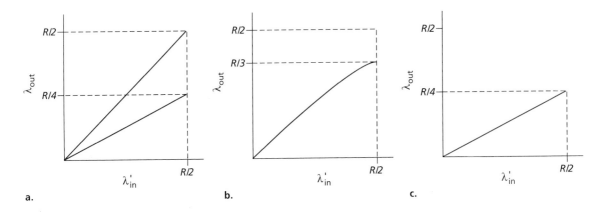

Figure 3.45 ◆ Scenario 2 performance with finite buffers

data transmitted, $0.333R$ bytes/sec (on average) are original data and $0.166R$ bytes/sec (on average) are retransmitted data. *We see here another cost of a congested network—the sender must perform retransmissions in order to compensate for dropped (lost) packets due to buffer overflow.*

Finally, let us consider the case that the sender may time out prematurely and retransmit a packet that has been delayed in the queue but not yet lost. In this case, both the original data packet and the retransmission may both reach the receiver. Of course, the receiver needs but one copy of this packet and will discard the retransmission. In this case, the work done by the router in forwarding the retransmitted copy of the original packet was wasted, as the receiver will have already received the original copy of this packet. The router would have better used the link transmission capacity to send a different packet instead. *Here then is yet another cost of a congested network—unneeded retransmissions by the sender in the face of large delays may cause a router to use its link bandwidth to forward unneeded copies of a packet.* Figure 3.45 (c) shows the throughput versus offered load when each packet is assumed to be forwarded (on average) twice by the router. Since each packet is forwarded twice, the throughput will have an asymptotic value of $R/4$ as the offered load approach $R/2$.

Scenario 3: Four Senders, Routers with Finite Buffers, and Multihop Paths

In our final congestion scenario, four hosts transmit packets, each over overlapping two-hop paths, as shown in Figure 3.46. We again assume that each host uses a time-out/retransmission mechanism to implement a reliable data transfer service, that all hosts have the same value of λ_{in}, and that all router links have capacity R bytes/sec.

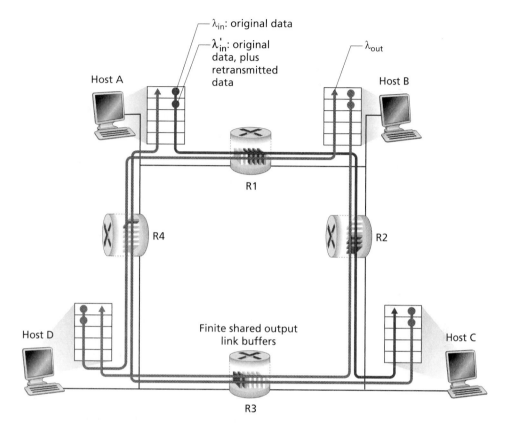

Figure 3.46 ♦ Four senders, routers with finite buffers, and multihop paths

Let's consider the connection from Host A to Host C, passing through routers R1 and R2. The A–C connection shares router R1 with the D–B connection and shares router R2 with the B–D connection. For extremely small values of λ_{in}, buffer overflows are rare (as in congestion scenarios 1 and 2), and the throughput approximately equals the offered load. For slightly larger values of λ_{in}, the corresponding throughput is also larger, since more original data is being transmitted into the network and delivered to the destination, and overflows are still rare. Thus, for small values of λ_{in}, an increase in λ_{in} results in an increase in λ_{out}.

Having considered the case of extremely low traffic, let's next examine the case that λ_{in} (and hence λ'_{in}) is extremely large. Consider router R2. The A–C traffic arriving to router R2 (which arrives at R2 after being forwarded from R1) can have an arrival rate at R2 that is at most R, the capacity of the link from R1 to R2, regardless of the value of λ_{in}. If λ'_{in} is extremely large for all connections (including the B–D connection), then the arrival rate of B–D traffic at R2 can be much larger than that of the A–C traffic. Because the A–C and B–D traffic must compete at router R2 for the limited amount of buffer space, the amount of A–C traffic that successfully gets through R2 (that is, is not lost due to buffer overflow) becomes smaller and smaller as the offered load from B–D gets larger and larger. In the limit, as the offered load approaches infinity, an empty buffer at R2 is immediately filled by a B–D packet, and the throughput of the A–C connection at R2 goes to zero. This, in turn, *implies that the A–C end-to-end throughput goes to zero* in the limit of heavy traffic. These considerations give rise to the offered load versus throughput tradeoff shown in Figure 3.47.

The reason for the eventual decrease in throughput with increasing offered load is evident when one considers the amount of wasted work done by the network. In the high-traffic scenario outlined above, whenever a packet is dropped at a second-hop router, the work done by the first-hop router in forwarding a packet to the second-hop router ends up being "wasted." The network would have been equally well off (more accurately, equally bad off) if the first router had simply discarded that packet and remained idle. More to the point, the transmission capacity used at the first router to forward the packet to the second router could have been much more profitably used to transmit a different packet. (For example, when selecting a packet for transmission, it might be better for a router to give priority to packets that have already traversed some number of upstream routers.) *So here we see yet another cost of dropping a packet due to congestion—when a packet is dropped along a path, the transmission capacity that was used at each of the upstream links to forward that packet to the point at which it is dropped ends up having been wasted.*

3.6.2 Approaches to Congestion Control

In Section 3.7, we'll examine TCP's specific approach to congestion control in great detail. Here, we identify the two broad approaches to congestion control that are taken in practice and discuss specific network architectures and congestion-control protocols embodying these approaches.

At the broadest level, we can distinguish among congestion-control approaches by whether the network layer provides any explicit assistance to the transport layer for congestion-control purposes:

♦ *End-to-end congestion control.* In an end-to-end approach to congestion control, the network layer provides *no explicit support* to the transport layer for congestion-control purposes. Even the presence of congestion in the network must be inferred by the end systems based only on observed network behavior (for example, packet loss and delay). We will see in Section 3.7 that TCP must necessarily take this end-to-end approach toward congestion control, since the IP layer provides no feedback to the end systems regarding network congestion. TCP segment loss (as indicated by a timeout or a triple duplicate acknowledgment) is taken as an indication of network congestion and TCP decreases its window size accordingly. We will also see that new proposals for TCP use increasing round-trip delay values as indicators of increased network congestion.

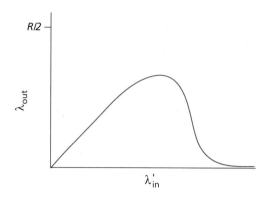

Figure 3.47 ♦ Scenario 3 performance with finite buffers and multihop paths

♦ *Network-assisted congestion control.* With network-assisted congestion control, network-layer components (that is, routers) provide explicit feedback to the sender regarding the congestion state in the network. This feedback may be as simple as a single bit indicating congestion at a link. This approach was taken in the early IBM SNA [Schwartz 1982] and DEC DECnet [Jain 1989; Ramakrishnan 1990] architectures, was recently proposed for TCP/IP networks [Floyd TCP 1994; RFC 2481], and is used in ATM available bit-rate (ABR) congestion control as well, as discussed below. More sophisticated network feedback is also possible. For example, one form of ATM ABR congestion control that we will study shortly allows a router to inform the sender explicitly of the transmission rate it (the router) can support on an outgoing link.

For network-assisted congestion control, congestion information is typically fed back from the network to the sender in one of two ways, as shown in Figure 3.48. Direct feedback may be sent from a network router to the sender. This form of notification typically takes the form of a **choke packet** (essentially saying, "I'm congested!"). The second form of notification occurs when a router marks/updates a field in a packet flowing from sender to receiver to indicate congestion. Upon receipt of a marked packet, the receiver then notifies the sender of the congestion indication. Note that this latter form of notification takes at least a full round-trip time.

3.6.3 Network-Assisted Congestion-Control Example: ATM ABR Congestion Control

We conclude this section with a brief case study of the congestion control algorithm in ATM ABR—a protocol that takes a network-assisted approach toward congestion control. We stress that our goal here is *not* to describe aspects of the ATM architecture in any detail, but rather to illustrate a protocol takes a markedly different

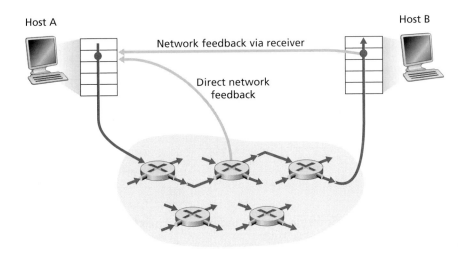

Figure 3.48 ◆ Two feedback pathways for network-indicated congestion information

approach towards congestion control from that of the Internet's TCP protocol. Indeed, we only present below those few aspects of the ATM architecture that are needed to understand ABR congestion control.

Fundamentally ATM takes a virtual-circuit (VC) oriented approach toward packet switching. Recall from our discussion in Chapter 1, this means that each switch on the source-to-destination path will maintain state about the source-to-destination VC. This per-VC state allows a switch to track the behavior of individual senders (e.g., tracking their average transmission rate) and to take source-specific congestion control actions (such as explicitly signaling to the sender to reduce its rate when the switch becomes congested). This per-VC state at network switches makes ATM ideally suited to perform network-assisted congestion control.

ABR has been designed as an elastic data transfer service in a manner reminiscent of TCP. When the network is underloaded, ABR service should be able to take advantage of the spare available bandwidth; when the network is congested, ABR service should throttle its transmission rate to some predetermined minimum transmission rate. A detailed tutorial on ATM ABR congestion control and traffic management is provided in [Jain 1996].

Figure 3.49 shows the framework for ATM ABR congestion control. In our discussion we adopt ATM terminology (for example, using the term *switch* rather than *router*, and the term *cell* rather than *packet*). With ATM ABR service, data cells are transmitted from a source to a destination through a series of intermediate switches. Interspersed with the data cells are **resource-management cells (RM cells)**; these RM cells can be used to convey congestion-related information among the hosts and

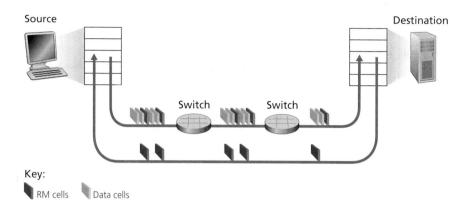

Source

Destination

Key:

RM cells   Data cells

Figure 3.49 ♦ Congestion-control framework for ATM ABR service

switches. When an RM cell is at a destination, it will be turned around and sent back to the sender (possibly after the destination has modified the contents of the RM cell). It is also possible for a switch to generate an RM cell itself and send this RM cell directly to a source. RM cells can thus be used to provide both direct network feedback and network-feedback-via-the-receiver, as shown in Figure 3.49.

ATM ABR congestion control is a rate-based approach. That is, the sender explicitly computes a maximum rate at which it can send and regulates itself accordingly. ABR provides three mechanisms for signaling congestion-related information from the switches to the receiver:

♦ *EFCI bit.* Each *data cell* contains an **explicit forward congestion indication (EFCI) bit**. A congested network switch can set the EFCI bit in a data cell to 1 to signal congestion to the destination host. The destination must check the EFCI bit in all received data cells. When an RM cell arrives at the destination, if the most recently received data cell had the EFCI bit set to 1, then the destination sets the congestion indication bit (the CI bit) of the RM cell to 1 and sends the RM cell back to the sender. Using the EFCI in data cells and the CI bit in RM cells, a sender can thus be notified about congestion at a network switch.

♦ *CI and NI bits.* As noted above, sender-to-receiver RM cells are interspersed with data cells. The rate of RM cell interspersion is a tunable parameter, with the default value being one RM cell every 32 data cells. These RM cells have a **c** and a **no increase (NI) bit** that can be set by a congested network switch. Specifically, a switch can set the NI bit in a passing RM cell to 1 under mild congestion and can set the CI bit to 1 under severe congestion conditions. When a destination host receives an RM cell, it will send the RM cell back to the sender with its CI and NI bits intact (except that CI may be set to 1 by the destination as a result of the EFCI mechanism described above).

♦ *ER setting*. Each RM cell also contains a two-byte **explicit rate (ER) field**. A congested switch may lower the value contained in the ER field in a passing RM cell. In this manner, the ER field will be set to the minimum supportable rate of all switches on the source-to-destination path.

An ATM ABR source adjusts the rate at which it can send cells as a function of the CI, NI, and ER values in a returned RM cell. The rules for making this rate adjustment are rather complicated and a bit tedious. The interested reader is referred to [Jain 1996] for details.

3.7 TCP Congestion Control

In this section we return to our study of TCP. As we learned in Section 3.5, TCP provides a reliable transport service between two processes running on different hosts. Another key component of TCP is its congestion-control mechanism. As indicated in the previous section, TCP must use end-to-end congestion control rather than network-assisted congestion control, since the IP layer provides no explicit feedback to the end systems regarding network congestion.

The approach taken by TCP is to have each sender limit the rate at which it sends traffic into its connection as a function of perceived network congestion. If a TCP sender perceives that there is little congestion on the path between itself and the destination, then the TCP sender increases its send rate; if the sender perceives that there is congestion along the path, then the sender reduces its send rate. But this approach raises three questions. First, how does a TCP sender limit the rate at which it sends traffic into its connection? Second, how does a TCP sender perceive that there is congestion on the path between itself and the destination? And third, what algorithm should the sender use to change its send rate as a function of perceived end-to-end congestion? We will examine these three issues in the context of the TCP Reno congestion control algorithm, which is used in most modern operating systems [Padhye 2001]. To keep the discussion concrete, we'll suppose that the TCP sender is sending a large file.

Let's first examine how a TCP sender limits the rate at which it sends traffic into its connection. In Section 3.5 we saw that each side of a TCP connection consists of a receive buffer, a send buffer, and several variables (`LastByteRead,` `RcvWindow`, and so on). The TCP congestion-control mechanism has each side of a connection keep track of an additional variable, the **congestion window**. The congestion window, denoted `CongWin`, imposes a constraint on the rate at which a TCP sender can send traffic into the network. Specifically, the amount of unacknowledged data at a sender may not exceed the minimum of `CongWin` and `RcvWindow`, that is:

```
LastByteSent − LastByteAcked ≤ min{CongWin, RcvWindow}
```

In order to focus on congestion control (as opposed to flow control), let us henceforth assume that the TCP receive buffer is so large that the receive-window constraint can be ignored; thus, the amount of unacknowledged data at the sender is solely limited by `CongWin`.

The constraint above limits the amount of unacknowledged data at the sender and therefore indirectly limits the sender's send rate. To see this, consider a connection for which loss and packet transmission delays are negligible. Then, roughly, at the beginning of every RTT, the constraint permits the sender to send `CongWin` bytes of data into the connection; at the end of the RTT the sender receives acknowledgments for the data. *Thus the sender's send rate is roughly CongWin/RTT bytes/sec. By adjusting the value of* `CongWin`, *the sender can therefore adjust the rate at which it sends data into its connection.*

Let's next consider how a TCP sender perceives that there is congestion on the path between itself and the destination. Let us define a "loss event" at a TCP sender as the occurrence of either a timeout or the receipt of three duplicate ACKs from the receiver (recall our discussion in Section 3.5.4 of the timeout event in Figure 3.33 and the subsequent modification to include fast retransmit on receipt of three duplicate ACKs). When there is excessive congestion, then one (or more) router buffers along the path overflows, causing a datagram (containing a TCP segment) to be dropped. The dropped datagram, in turn, results in a loss event at the sender—either a timeout or the receipt of three duplicate ACKS—which is taken by the sender to be an indication of congestion on the sender-to-receiver path.

Having considered how congestion in detected, let's next consider the more optimistic case when the network is congestion-free, that is, when a loss event doesn't occur. In this case, acknowledgements for previously unacknowledged segments will be received at the TCP sender. As we'll see, TCP will take the arrival of these acknowledgements as an indication that all is well—that segments being transmitted into the network are being successfully delivered to the destination—and will use acknowledgements to increase its congestion window size (and hence its transmission rate). Note that if acknowledgements arrive at relatively slow rate (e.g., if the end-end path has high delay or contains a low bandwidth link), then the congestion window will be increased at a relatively slow rate. On the other hand, if acknowledgements arrive at a high rate, then the congestion window will be increased more quickly. Because TCP uses acknowledgements to trigger (or clock) its increase in congestion window size, TCP is said to be **self-clocking**.

We're now in a position to consider the details of the algorithm that a TCP sender uses to regulate its sending rate as a function of perceived congestion. This algorithm is the celebrated **TCP congestion control algorithm**. The algorithm has three major components: (1) additive-increase, multiplicative-decrease, (2) slow start, and (3) reaction to timeout events.

Additive-Increase, Multiplicative-Decrease

The basic idea behind TCP congestion control is for the sender to reduce its sending rate (by decreasing its congestion window size, `CongWin`) when a loss event occurs. Since other TCP connections that are passing through the same congested routers are also likely to be experiencing loss events, they, too, are likely to reduce their sending rates by decreasing their own values of `CongWin`. The overall effect, then, is for sources with paths through congested routers to reduce the rate at which they send traffic into the network, which in turn should relieve congestion at the congested routers. But by how much should a TCP sender reduce its congestion window when a loss event occurs? TCP uses a so-called "multiplicative decrease" approach, halving the current value of `CongWin` after a loss event. Thus, if the value of a TCP sender's `CongWin` is currently 20 Kbytes and a loss is detected, `CongWin` is cut in half to 10 Kbytes. If another loss event occurs, `CongWin` is further reduced to 5 Kbytes. The value of `CongWin` may continue to drop, but it is not allowed to drop below 1 MSS. (This is a big-picture description of how the congestion window changes after a loss event. In truth, things are a bit more complicated. As we'll soon see, the value of `CongWin` actually drops to 1 MSS after the timeout event, and then quickly ramps back up to half its previous value.)

Having described how a TCP sender decreases its sending rate in the face of detected congestion, it is natural to consider next how TCP should *increase* its sending rate when it perceives no congestion, that is, when ACKs arrive for previously yet-to-be-acknowledged data. The rationale for an increase in rate is that if there is no detected congestion, then there is likely to be available (unused) bandwidth that could additionally be used by the TCP connection. In such circumstances, TCP increases its congestion window slowly, cautiously probing for additional available bandwidth in the end-to-end path. The TCP sender does this by incrementing `CongWin` a little each time it receives an acknowledgement, with the goal of increasing CongWin by 1 MSS every round trip time [RFC 2581]. This can be accomplished in several ways; a common approach is for the TCP sender to increase its `CongWin` by MSS·(MSS/`CongWin`) bytes whenever a new acknowledgement arrives. For example, if MSS is 1,460 bytes and `CongWin` is 14,600 bytes, then 10 segments are being sent within an RTT. Each arriving ACK (assuming one ACK per segment) increases the congestion window size by 1/10 MSS, and thus after acknowledgments for all 10 segments have been received, the value of the congestion window will have increased by MSS, as desired.

In summary, a TCP sender additively increases its rate when it perceives that the end-end path is congestion-free, and multiplicatively decreases its rate when it detects (via a loss event) that the path is congested. For this reason, TCP congestion control is often referred to as an **additive-increase, multiplicative-decrease (AIMD) algorithm**. The linear increase phase of TCP's congestion control protocol is known as **congestion avoidance**. The value of `CongWin` repeatedly goes through cycles during which it increases linearly and then suddenly drops to half its current value (when a loss event occurs), giving rise to a saw-toothed pattern in long-lived TCP connections, as shown in Figure 3.50.

Slow Start

When a TCP connection begins, the value of `CongWin` is typically initialized to 1 MSS [RFC3390], resulting an initial sending rate of roughly MSS/RTT. As an example, if MSS = 500 bytes and RTT = 200 msecs, then the resulting initial sending rate is only about 20 kbps. Because the available bandwidth to the connection may be much larger than MSS/RTT, it would be a shame to increase the rate only linearly and to have to wait an inordinately long time before the sending rate ramps up to some respectable level. So instead of increasing its rate linearly during this initial phase, a TCP sender increases its rate exponentially by doubling its value of `CongWin` every RTT. The TCP sender continues to increase its sending rate exponentially until there is a loss event, at which time `CongWin` is cut in half and then grows linearly, as described above. Thus, during this initial phase, which is called **slow start (SS)**, the TCP sender begins by transmitting at a slow rate (hence the term *slow start*) but increases its sending rate exponentially. The sender generates the exponential growth by increasing the value of `CongWin` by 1 MSS every time a transmitted segment is acknowledged. Specifically, TCP sends the first segment into the network and waits for an acknowledgment. If this segment is acknowledged before a loss event, the TCP sender increases the congestion window by one MSS and sends out two maximum-sized segments. If these segments are acknowledged before loss events, the sender increases the congestion window by 1 MSS for each of the acknowledged segments, giving a congestion window of 4 MSS, and sends out four maximum-sized segments. This procedure continues as acknowledgments

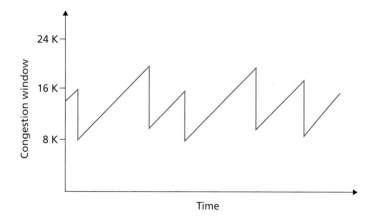

Figure 3.50 ♦ Additive-increase, multiplicative-decrease congestion control

arrive, until eventually a loss event occurs. Thus, the value of `CongWin` effectively doubles every RTT during the slow-start phase.

Reaction to Timeout Events

The picture we have painted so far of TCP's congestion window is that of an exponential ramp-up from 1 MSS (during slow start) until a loss event occurs, at which point the AIMD saw-toothed pattern begins. Although this picture is close to accurate, we would be remiss if we did not mention that in truth TCP congestion control reacts differently to a loss event that is detected via a timeout event than it does to a loss event detected via receipt of triple duplicate ACKs. After a triple duplicate ACK, TCP behaves as we have just described—the congestion window is cut in half and then increases linearly. But after a timeout event, a TCP sender enters a slow-start phase—that is, it sets the congestion window to 1 MSS and then grows the window exponentially. The window continues to grow exponentially until `CongWin` reaches one half of the value it had before the timeout event. At that point, `Cong-Win` grows linearly, just as it would have after a triple duplicate ACK.

TCP manages these more complex dynamics by maintaining a variable called **Threshold**, which determines the window size at which slow start will end and congestion avoidance will begin. The variable `Threshold` is initially set to a large value (65 Kbytes in practice [Stevens 1994]) so that it has no initial effect. Whenever a loss event occurs, the value of `Threshold` is set to one half of the current value of `CongWin`. For example, if the congestion window is 20 Kbytes just before a loss event, then the value of `Threshold` is set to 10 Kbytes and will maintain this value until the next loss event.

Having described the `Threshold` variable, we can now precisely describe how `CongWin` behaves after a timeout event. As indicated above, a TCP sender enters the slow-start phase after a timeout event. While in slow start, it increases the value of `CongWin` exponentially fast until `CongWin` reaches `Threshold`. When `CongWin` reaches `Threshold`, TCP enters the congestion avoidance phase, during which `CongWin` ramps up linearly as described earlier.

Our discussion of TCP's congestion control algorithm is summarized in Table 3.3. At this point it is natural to consider why TCP congestion control behaves differently after a timeout event than after the receipt of a triple duplicate ACK. Specifically, why does a TCP sender behave conservatively after a timeout event, reducing its congestion window to 1 MSS, whereas after receiving a triple duplicate ACK it only cuts its congestion window by half? It is interesting that an early version of TCP, known as **TCP Tahoe**, unconditionally cuts its congestion window to 1 MSS and enters the slow-start phase after either type of loss event. The newer version of TCP, **TCP Reno**, cancels the slow-start phase after a triple duplicate ACK. The philosophy behind canceling slow start in this case is that even though a packet has been lost, the arrival of three duplicate ACKs indicates that some segments (specifically, three additional segments beyond the lost segment) have been received at the

State	Event	TCP Sender Congestion-control Action	Commentary
Slow Start (SS)	ACK receipt for previously unacknowledged data	CongWin = CongWin + MSS, If (CongWin > Threshold) set state to "Congestion Avoidance"	Resulting in a doubling of CongWin every RTT
Congestion Avoidance (CA)	ACK receipt for previously unacknowledged data	CongWin = CongWin + MSS · (MSS/CongWin)	Additive increase, resulting in increasing of CongWin by 1 MSS every RTT
SS or CA	Loss event detected by triple duplicate ACK	Threshold = CongWin/2, CongWin = Threshold, set state to "Congestion Avoidance"	Fast recovery, implementing multiplicative decrease. CongWin will not drop below 1 MSS.
SS or CA	Timeout	Threshold = CongWin/2, CongWin = 1 MSS, set state to "Slow Start"	Enter slow start.
SS or CA	Duplicate ACK	Increment duplicate ACK count for segment being acknowledged	CongWin and Threshold not changed

Table 3.3 ♦ TCP sender congestion control [RFC 2581], assuming initial value of CongWin equals MSS, initial value of Threshold is large (e.g., 65 Kbytes [Stevens 1994]), and TCP sender begins in slow-start state. State value shown is TCP sender state just before event occurs. See [RFC 2581] for additional details.

sender. Thus, unlike the case of a timeout, the network is showing itself to be capable of delivering at least some segments, even if other segments are being lost to congestion. This canceling of the slow-start phase after a triple duplicate ACK is called **fast recovery**.

Figure 3.51 illustrates the evolution of TCP's congestion window for both Reno and Tahoe. In this figure, the threshold is initially equal to 8 MSS. The congestion window climbs exponentially fast during slow start and hits the threshold at the fourth round of transmission. The congestion window then climbs linearly until a triple duplicate ACK occurs, just after transmission round 8. Note that the congestion window is $12 \cdot MSS$ when this loss event occurs. The threshold is then set to $0.5 \cdot$ Cong-Win $= 6 \cdot$ MSS. Under TCP Reno, the congestion window is set to CongWin $= 6 \cdot$ MSS and then grows linearly. Under TCP Tahoe, the congestion window is set to 1 MSS and grows exponentially until the threshold is reached. This congestion-control algorithm is due to V. Jacobson [Jacobson 1988]; a number of modifications to Jacobson's initial algorithm are described in [Stevens 1994] and in [RFC 2581].

As noted above, most TCP implementations currently use the Reno algorithm. Many variations of the Reno algorithm have been proposed [RFC 2582; RFC 2018]. The proposed TCP Vegas algorithm [Brakmo 1995; Ahn 1995] attempts to avoid congestion while maintaining good throughput. The basic idea of Vegas is to

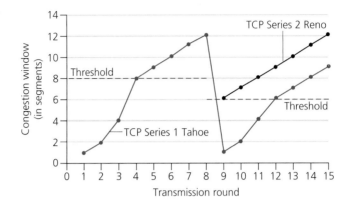

Figure 3.51 ◆ Evolution of TCP's congestion window (Tahoe and Reno)

(1) detect congestion in the routers between source and destination *before* packet loss occurs and (2) lower the rate linearly when this imminent packet loss is detected. Imminent packet loss is predicted by observing the RTT. The longer the RTT of the packets, the greater the congestion in the routers.

Macroscopic Description of TCP Throughput

Given the saw-toothed behavior of TCP, it's natural to consider what the average throughput (that is, the average rate) of a long-lived TCP connection might be. In this analysis we'll ignore the slow-start phases that occur after timeout events. (These phases are typically very short, since the sender grows out of the phase exponentially fast.) During a particular round-trip interval, the rate at which TCP sends data is a function of the congestion window and the current *RTT*. When the window size is *w* bytes and the current round-trip time is *RTT* second*s,* then TCP's transmission rate is roughly *w/RTT*. TCP then probes for additional bandwidth by increasing *w* by 1 MSS each *RTT* until a loss event occurs. Denote by *W* the value of *w* when a loss event occurs. Assuming that *RTT* and *W* are approximately constant over the duration of the connection, the TCP transmission rate ranges from $W/(2 \cdot RTT)$ to *W/RTT*.

These assumptions lead to a highly simplified macroscopic model for the steady-state behavior of TCP. The network drops a packet from the connection when the rate increases to *W/RTT;* the rate is then cut in half and then increases by MSS/*RTT* every *RTT* until it again reaches *W/RTT*. This process repeats itself over and over again. Because TCP's throughput (that is, rate) increases linearly between the two extreme values, we have

$$\text{average throughput of a connection} = \frac{0.75 \cdot W}{RTT}$$

Using this highly idealized model for the steady-state dynamics of TCP, we can also derive an interesting expression that relates a connection's loss rate to its available bandwidth [Mahdavi 1997]. This derivation is outlined in the homework problems. A more sophisticated model that has been found empirically to agree with measured data is [Padhye 2000].

TCP Futures

It is important to realize that TCP congestion control has evolved over the years and indeed continues to evolve. A summary of TCP congestion control as of the late 1990s can be found in [RFC 2581]; for a discussion of recent developments in TCP congestion control, see [Floyd 2001]. What was good for the Internet when the bulk of the TCP connections carried SMTP, FTP, and Telnet traffic is not necessarily good for today's HTTP-dominated Internet or for a future Internet with services that are still undreamed of.

The need for continued evolution of TCP can be illustrated by considering the high-speed TCP connections that are needed for grid-computing applications [Foster 2002]. For example, consider a TCP connection with 1,500-byte segments and a 100 ms *RTT*, and suppose we want to send data through this connection at 10 Gbps. Following [RFC 3649], we note that using the TCP throughput formula above, in order to achieve a 10 Gbps throughput, the average congestion window size would need to be 83,333 segments. That's a *lot* of segments, leading us to be rather concerned that one of these 83,333 in-flight segments might be lost. What would happen in the case of a loss? Or, put another way, what fraction of the transmitted segments could be lost that would allow the TCP congestion control algorithm outlined in Table 3.3 still to achieve the desired 10 Gbps rate? In the homework questions for this chapter, you are led through the derivation of a formula relating the throughput of a TCP connection as a function of the loss rate (L), the roundtrip time (RTT), and the maximum segment size (MSS):

$$\text{average throughput of a connection} = \frac{1.22 \cdot MSS}{RTT \sqrt{L}}$$

Using this formula, we can see that in order to achieve a throughput of 10 Gbps, today's TCP congestion control algorithm can only tolerate a segment loss probability of $2 \cdot 10^{-10}$ (or equivalently, one loss event for every 5,000,000,000 segments)—a very low rate. This observation has led a number of researchers to investigate new versions of TCP that are specifically designed for such high-speed environments; see [Jin 2004, RFC 3649, Kelly 2003] for discussions of these efforts.

3.7.1 Fairness

Consider K TCP connections, each with a different end-to-end path, but all passing through a bottleneck link with transmission rate R bps. (By *bottleneck link*, we mean that for each connection, all the other links along the connection's path are not congested and have abundant transmission capacity as compared with the transmission capacity of the bottleneck link.) Suppose each connection is transferring a large file and there is no UDP traffic passing through the bottleneck link. A congestion-control mechanism is said to be *fair* if the average transmission rate of each connection is approximately R/K; that is, each connection gets an equal share of the link bandwidth.

Is TCP's AIMD algorithm fair, particularly given that different TCP connections may start at different times and thus may have different window sizes at a given point in time? [Chiu 1989] provides an elegant and intuitive explanation of why TCP congestion control converges to provide an equal share of a bottleneck link's bandwidth among competing TCP connections.

Let's consider the simple case of two TCP connections sharing a single link with transmission rate R, as shown in Figure 3.52. Assume that the two connections have the same MSS and RTT (so that if they have the same congestion-window size, then they have the same throughput), that they have a large amount of data to send, and that no other TCP connections or UDP datagrams traverse this shared link. Also, ignore the slow-start phase of TCP and assume the TCP connections are operating in CA mode (AIMD) at all times.

Figure 3.53 plots the throughput realized by the two TCP connections. If TCP is to share the link bandwidth equally between the two connections, then the realized throughput should fall along the 45-degree arrow (equal bandwidth share) emanating from the origin. Ideally, the sum of the two throughputs should equal R. (Certainly, each connection receiving an equal, but zero, share of the link capacity is not a desirable situation!) So the goal should be to have the achieved throughputs fall somewhere near the intersection of the equal bandwidth share line and the full bandwidth utilization line in Figure 3.53.

Suppose that the TCP window sizes are such that at a given point in time, connections 1 and 2 realize throughputs indicated by point A in Figure 3.53. Because

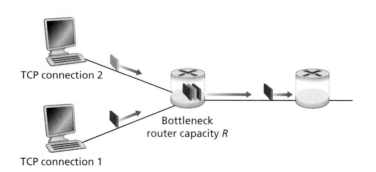

Figure 3.52 ◆ Two TCP connections sharing a single bottleneck link

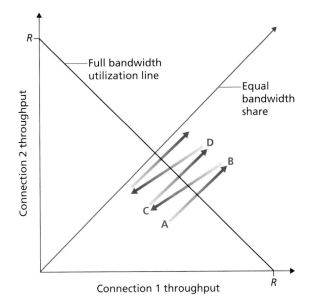

Figure 3.53 ◆ Throughput realized by TCP connections 1 and 2

the amount of link bandwidth jointly consumed by the two connections is less than
R, no loss will occur, and both connections will increase their window by 1 MSS per
RTT as a result of TCP's congestion-avoidance algorithm. Thus, the joint throughput of the two connections proceeds along a 45-degree line (equal increase for both
connections) starting from point A. Eventually, the link bandwidth jointly consumed
by the two connections will be greater than R, and eventually packet loss will occur.
Suppose that connections 1 and 2 experience packet loss when they realize throughputs indicated by point B. Connections 1 and 2 then decrease their windows by a
factor of two. The resulting throughputs realized are thus at point C, halfway along
a vector starting at B and ending at the origin. Because the joint bandwidth use is
less than R at point C, the two connections again increase their throughputs along a
45-degree line starting from C. Eventually, loss will again occur, for example, at
point D, and the two connections again decrease their window sizes by a factor of
two, and so on. You should convince yourself that the bandwidth realized by the two
connections eventually fluctuates along the equal bandwidth share line. You should
also convince yourself that the two connections will converge to this behavior
regardless of where they are in the two-dimensional space! Although a number of
idealized assumptions lie behind this scenario, it still provides an intuitive feel for
why TCP results in an equal sharing of bandwidth among connections.

   In our idealized scenario, we assumed that only TCP connections traverse the
bottleneck link, that the connections have the same RTT value, and that only a single

TCP connection is associated with a host-destination pair. In practice, these conditions are typically not met, and client/server applications can thus obtain very unequal portions of link bandwidth. In particular, it has been shown that when multiple connections share a common bottleneck, those sessions with a smaller RTT are able to grab the available bandwidth at that link more quickly as it becomes free (that is, open their congestion windows faster) and thus will enjoy higher throughput than those connections with larger RTTs [Lakshman 1997].

Fairness and UDP

We have just seen how TCP congestion control regulates an application's transmission rate via the congestion-window mechanism. Many multimedia applications, such as Internet phone and video conferencing, do not run over TCP for this very reason—they do not want their transmission rate throttled, even if the network is very congested. Instead, these applications prefer to run over UDP, which does not have built-in congestion control. When running over UDP, applications can pump their audio and video into the network at a constant rate and occasionally lose packets, rather than reduce their rates to "fair" levels at times of congestion and not lose any packets. From the perspective of TCP, the multimedia applications running over UDP are not being fair—they do not cooperate with the other connections nor adjust their transmission rates appropriately. Because TCP congestion control will decrease its transmission rate in the face of increasing congestion (loss), while UDP sources need not, it is possible for UDP sources to crowd out TCP traffic. A major area of research today is the development of congestion-control mechanisms for the Internet that prevent UDP traffic from bringing the Internet's throughput to a grinding halt [Floyd 1999; Floyd 2000, Kohler 2004].

Fairness and Parallel TCP Connections

But even if we could force UDP traffic to behave fairly, the fairness problem would still not be completely solved. This is because there is nothing to stop a TCP-based application from using multiple parallel connections. For example, Web browsers often use multiple parallel TCP connections to transfer the multiple objects within a Web page. (The exact number of multiple connections is configurable in most browsers.) When an application uses multiple parallel connections, it gets a larger fraction of the bandwidth in a congested link. As an example, consider a link of rate R supporting nine ongoing client/server applications, with each of the applications using one TCP connection. If a new application comes along and also uses one TCP connection, then each application gets approximately the same transmission rate of $R/10$. But if this new application instead uses 11 parallel TCP connections, then the new application gets an unfair allocation of more than $R/2$. Because Web traffic is so pervasive in the Internet, multiple parallel connections are not uncommon.

3.7.2 TCP Delay Modeling

We end this chapter with some simple models for calculating the time it takes TCP to send an object (such as an image, a text file, or an MP3). For a given object, we define the **latency** as the time from when the client initiates a TCP connection until the time at which the client receives the requested object in its entirety. The models presented here give important insight into the key components of latency, including initial TCP handshaking, TCP slow start, and the transmission time of the object.

This simple analysis supposes that the network is uncongested—that is, that the TCP connection transporting the object does not have to share link bandwidth with other TCP or UDP traffic. Also, in order not to obscure the central issues, we carry out the analysis in the context of the simple one-link network as shown in Figure 3.54. (This link might model a single bottleneck on an end-to-end path. See also the homework problems for an explicit extension to the case of multiple links.)

We also make the following simplifying assumptions:

♦ The amount of data that the sender can transmit is limited solely by the sender's congestion window. (Thus, the TCP receive buffers are large.)

♦ Packets are neither lost nor corrupted, so that there are no retransmissions.

♦ All protocol header overheads—including TCP, IP, and link-layer headers—are negligible and ignored.

♦ The object (that is, file) to be transferred consists of an integer number of segments of size MSS (maximum segment size).

♦ The only packets that have non-negligible transmission times are packets that carry maximum-sized TCP segments. Request messages, acknowledgments, and TCP connection-establishment segments are small and have negligible transmission times.

♦ The initial threshold in the TCP congestion-control mechanism is a large value that is never attained by the congestion window.

Client   Server

R bps

Figure 3.54 ♦ A simple one-link network connecting a client and a server

We also introduce the following notation:

♦ The size of the object to be transferred is O bits.

♦ The MSS is S bits (for example, 536 bytes).

♦ The transmission rate of the link from the server to the client is R bps.

Before beginning the formal analysis, let us try to gain some intuition. What would be the latency if there were no congestion-window constraint, that is, if the server were permitted to send segments back to back until the entire object was sent. To answer this question, first note that one RTT is required to initiate the TCP connection. After one RTT, the client sends a request for the object (which is piggybacked onto the third segment in the three-way TCP handshake). After a total of two RTTs, the client begins to receive data from the server. The client receives data from the server for a period of time O/R, the time for the server to transmit the entire object. Thus, in the case of no congestion-window constraint, the total latency is 2 $RTT + O/R$. This represents a lower bound; the slow-start procedure, with its dynamic congestion window, will of course increase this latency.

Static Congestion Window

Although TCP uses a dynamic congestion window, it is instructive to analyze first the case of a static congestion window. Let W, a positive integer, denote a fixed-size static congestion window. For the static congestion window, the server is not permitted to have more than W unacknowledged outstanding segments. When the server receives the request from the client, the server immediately sends W segments back to back to the client. The server then sends one segment into the network for each acknowledgment it receives from the client. The server continues to send one segment for each acknowledgment until all of the segments of the object have been sent. There are two cases to consider:

1. $WS/R > RTT + S/R$. In this case, the server receives an acknowledgment for the first segment in the first window before the server completes the transmission of the first window.

2. $WS/R < RTT + S/R$. In this case, the server transmits the first window's worth of segments before the server receives an acknowledgment for the first segment in the window.

Let us first consider the first case, which is illustrated in Figure 3.55. In this figure the window size is $W = 4$ segments. One RTT is required to initiate the TCP connection. After one RTT, the client sends a request for the object (which is piggybacked onto the third segment in the three-way TCP handshake). After a total of two RTTs, the client begins to receive data from the server. Segments arrive

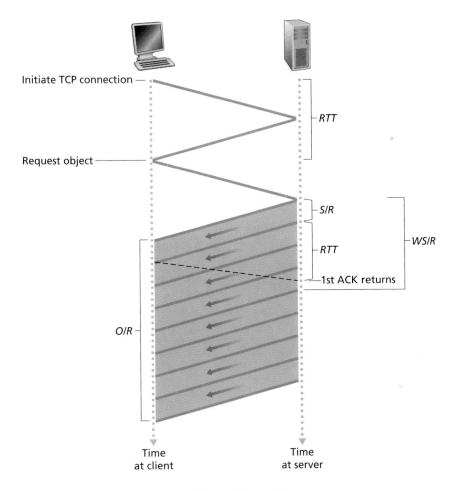

Time
at client

Time
at server

Figure 3.55 ♦ The case $WS/R > RTT + S/R$

periodically from the server every S/R seconds, and the client acknowledges every segment it receives from the server. Because the server receives the first acknowledgment before it completes sending a window's worth of segments, the server continues to transmit segments after having transmitted the first window's worth of segments. And because the acknowledgments arrive periodically at the server every S/R seconds from the time when the first acknowledgment arrives, the server transmits segments continuously until it has transmitted the entire object. Thus, once the server starts to transmit the object at rate R, it continues to transmit the object at rate R until the entire object is transmitted. The latency therefore is $2\,RTT + O/R$.

Now let us consider the second case, which is illustrated in Figure 3.56. In this figure, the window size is $W = 2$ segments. Once again, after a total of two RTTs, the client begins to receive segments from the server. These segments arrive periodically every S/R seconds, and the client acknowledges every segment it receives from the server. But now the server completes the transmission of the first window before the first acknowledgment arrives from the client. Therefore, after sending a window, the server must stall and wait for an acknowledgment before resuming transmission. When an acknowledgment finally arrives, the server sends a new segment to the client. With the first acknowledgment, a window's worth of acknowledgments arrives, and each successive acknowledgment is spaced by S/R seconds. For each of these acknowledgments, the server sends exactly one segment. Thus, the server alternates between two states: a transmitting state, during which it transmits

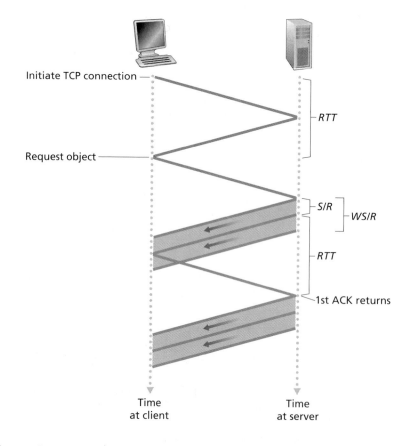

Figure 3.56 ◆ The case $WS/R < RTT + S/R$

W segments, and a stalled state, during which it transmits nothing and waits for an acknowledgment. The latency is equal to 2 RTT plus the time required for the server to transmit the object, O/R, plus the amount of time that the server is in the stalled state. To determine the amount of time the server is in the stalled state, let K be the number of windows of data that cover the object; that is, $K = O/WS$ (if O/WS is not an integer, then round K up to the nearest integer). The server is in the stalled state between the transmission of each of the windows, that is, for $K - 1$ periods of time, with each period lasting RTT $- (W - 1)S/R$ (see Figure 3.56). Thus, for case 2,

$$\text{latency} = 2\ \text{RTT} + O/R + (K - 1)\ [S/R + \text{RTT} - WS/R]$$

Combining the two cases, we obtain

$$\text{latency} = 2\ \text{RTT} + O/R + (K - 1)\ [S/R + \text{RTT} - WS/R]^+$$

where $[x]^+ = \max(x,0)$. Notice that the delay has three components: 2 RTT to set up the TCP connection and to request and begin to receive the object; O/R, the time for the server to transmit the object; and a final term $(K - 1)\ [S/R + \text{RTT} - WS/R]^+$ for the amount of time the server stalls.

This completes our analysis of static windows. The following analysis for dynamic windows is more complicated but parallels that for static windows.

Dynamic Congestion Window

We now take TCP's dynamic congestion window into account in the latency model. Recall that the server starts with a congestion window of one segment and sends one segment to the client. When it receives an acknowledgment for the segment, it increases its congestion window to two segments and sends two segments to the client (spaced apart by S/R seconds). As it receives the acknowledgments for the two segments, it increases the congestion window to four segments and sends four segments to the client (again spaced apart by S/R seconds). The process continues, with the congestion window doubling every RTT. A timing diagram for TCP is illustrated in Figure 3.57.

Note that O/S is the number of segments in the object; in Figure 3.57, $O/S = 15$. Consider the number of segments that are in each of the windows. The first window contains one segment, the second window contains two segments, and the third window contains four segments. More generally, the kth window contains 2^{k-1} segments. Let K be the number of windows that cover the object; in the preceding diagram, $K = 4$. In general, we can express K in terms of O/S as follows:

$$K = \min\left\{k : 2^0 + 2^1 + \ldots + 2^{k-1} \geq \frac{O}{S}\right\}$$

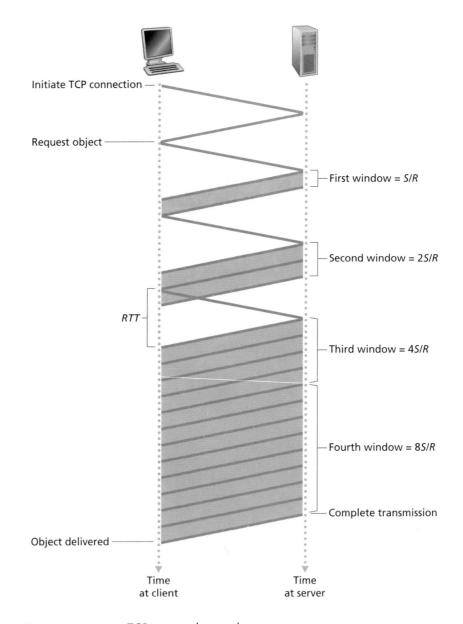

Initiate TCP connection

Request object

First window = S/R

Second window = $2S/R$

RTT

Third window = $4S/R$

Fourth window = $8S/R$

Complete transmission

Object delivered

Time at client

Time at server

Figure 3.57 ♦ TCP timing during slow start

$$= \min\left\{ k : 2^k - 1 \geq \frac{O}{S} \right\}$$

$$= \min\left\{ k : k \geq \log_2\left(\frac{O}{S} + 1\right) \right\}$$

$$= \left\lceil \log_2\left(\frac{O}{S} + 1\right) \right\rceil$$

After transmitting a window's worth of data, the server may stall (that is, stop transmitting) while it waits for an acknowledgment. In Figure 3.55, the server stalls after transmitting the first and second windows but not after transmitting the third. Let us now calculate the amount of stall time after transmitting the kth window. From the time the server begins to transmit the kth window until the time when the server receives an acknowledgment for the first segment in the window is $S/R +$ RTT. The transmission time of the kth window is $(S/R)2^{k-1}$. The stall time is the difference of these two quantities, that is,

$$[S/R + \text{RTT} - 2^{k-1}(S/R)]^+$$

The server can potentially stall after the transmission of each of the first $K - 1$ windows. (The server is done after the transmission of the Kth window.) We can now calculate the latency for transferring the file. The latency has three components: 2 RTT for setting up the TCP connection and requesting the file; O/R, the transmission time of the object; and the sum of all the stalled times. Thus,

$$\text{Latency} = 2RTT + \frac{O}{R} + \sum_{k=1}^{K-1}\left[\frac{S}{R} + RTT - 2^{k-1}\frac{S}{R}\right]^+$$

Compare this equation with the latency equation for static congestion windows; all the terms are exactly the same except that the term WS/R for static windows has been replaced by $2^{k-1}(S/R)$ for dynamic windows. To obtain a more compact expression for the latency, let Q be the number of times the server would stall if the object contained an infinite number of segments. Paralleling a derivation similar to that for K (see homework problems), we obtain:

$$Q = \left\lfloor \log_2(1 + \frac{RTT}{S/R}) \right\rfloor + 1$$

The actual number of times that the server stalls is $P = \min\{Q, K - 1\}$. In Figure 3.55, $P = Q = 2$. Combining the equations (see homework problems) gives the following closed-form expression for the latency:

$$\text{Latency} = 2RTT + \frac{O}{R} + P\left[RTT + \frac{S}{R}\right] - (2^P - 1)\frac{S}{R}$$

Thus, to calculate the latency, we simply must calculate K and Q, set $P = \min \{Q, K{-}1\}$ and plug P into the formula above.

It is interesting to compare the TCP latency with the latency that would occur if there were no congestion control (that is, no congestion-window constraint). With-out congestion control, the latency is $2\,RTT + O/R$, which we define to be the *mini-mum latency*. It is a simple exercise to show that

$$\frac{\text{Latency}}{\text{MinimumLatency}} \leq 1 + \frac{P}{[(O/R)/RTT] + 2}$$

We see from the formula above that TCP slow start will not significantly increase latency if $RTT \ll O/R$, that is, if the round-trip time is much less than the transmis-sion time of the object.

Let us now take a look at some example scenarios. In all the scenarios we set $S = 536$ bytes, a common default value for TCP. We use an RTT of 100 msec, which is a typical value for a continental or intercontinental delay over moderately congested links. First consider sending a rather large object of size $O = 100$ kbytes. The num-ber of windows that cover this object is $K = 8$. For a number of transmission rates, the following table displays the effect of the slow-start mechanism on the latency.

R	O/R	P	Minimum Latency: O/R + 2 RTT	Latency with Slow Start
28 kbps	28.6 sec	1	28.8 sec	28.9 sec
100 kbps	8 sec	2	8.2 sec	8.4 sec
1 Mbps	800 msec	5	1 sec	1.5 sec
10 Mbps	80 msec	7	0.28 sec	0.98 sec

We see from the table that for a large object, slow start adds appreciable delay only when the transmission rate is high. If the transmission rate is low, then acknowledg-ments come back relatively quickly, and TCP quickly ramps up to its maximum rate. For example, when $R = 100$ kbps, the number of stall periods is $P = 2$, whereas the number of windows to transmit is $K = 8$; thus the server stalls only after the first two of eight windows. On the other hand, when $R = 10$ Mbps, the server stalls after each window, which causes a significant increase in the delay.

Now consider sending a small object of size $O = 5$ kbytes. The number of win-dows that cover this object is $K = 4$. For a number of transmission rates, the follow-ing table examines the effect of the slow-start mechanism.

R	O/R	P	Minimum Latency: O/R + 2 RTT	Latency with Slow Start
28 kbps	1.43 sec	1	1.63 sec	1.73 sec
100 kbps	0.4 sec	2	0.6 sec	0.76 sec
1 Mbps	40 msec	3	0.24 sec	0.52 sec
10 Mbps	4 msec	3	0.20 sec	0.50 sec

Once again, slow start adds an appreciable delay when the transmission rate is high. For example, when $R = 1$ Mbps, the server stalls after each window, which causes the latency to be more than twice that of the minimum latency.

For a larger RTT, the effect of slow start becomes significant for small objects for smaller transmission rates. The following table examines the effect of slow start for RTT = 1 second and $O = 5$ kbytes ($K = 4$).

R	O/R	P	Minimum Latency: O/R + 2 RTT	Latency with Slow Start
28 kbps	1.43 sec	3	3.4 sec	5.8 sec
100 kbps	0.4 sec	3	2.4 sec	5.2 sec
1 Mbps	40 msec	3	2.0 sec	5.0 sec
10 Mbps	4 msec	3	2.0 sec	5.0 sec

In summary, slow start can significantly increase latency when the object size is relatively small and the RTT is relatively large. Unfortunately, this is often the case with the Web.

An Example: HTTP

As an application of the latency analysis, let's now calculate the response time for a Web page sent over nonpersistent HTTP. Suppose that the page consists of one base HTML page and M referenced images. To keep things simple, let us assume that each of the $M + 1$ objects contains exactly O bits.

With nonpersistent HTTP, each object is transferred independently, one after the other. The response time of the Web page is therefore the sum of the latencies for the individual objects. Thus

$$\mathrm{Response\ time} = (M+1)\left\{ 2RTT + \frac{O}{R} + P\left[RTT + \frac{S}{R}\right] - (2^{P} - 1)\frac{S}{R}\right\}$$

Note that the response time for nonpersistent HTTP takes the form

Response time = $(M + 1)O/R + 2(M + 1)$RTT + latency due to TCP slow start
for each of the $M + 1$ objects.

Clearly, if there are many objects in the Web page and if RTT is large, then nonpersistent HTTP will have poor response-time performance. In the homework problems, we will investigate the response time for other HTTP transport schemes. The reader is also encouraged to see [Heidemann 1997; Cardwell 2000] for a related analysis.

3.8 Summary

We began this chapter by studying the services that a transport-layer protocol can provide to network applications. At one extreme, the transport-layer protocol can be very simple and offer a no-frills service to applications, providing only a multiplexing/demultiplexing function for communicating processes. The Internet's UDP protocol is an example of such a no-frills transport-layer protocol. At the other extreme, a transport-layer protocol can provide a variety of guarantees to applications, such as reliable delivery of data, delay guarantees, and bandwidth guarantees. Nevertheless, the services that a transport protocol can provide are often constrained by the service model of the underlying network-layer protocol. If the network-layer protocol cannot provide delay or bandwidth guarantees to transport-layer segments, then the transport-layer protocol cannot provide delay or bandwidth guarantees for the messages sent between processes.

We learned in Section 3.4 that a transport-layer protocol can provide reliable data transfer even if the underlying network layer is unreliable. We saw that providing reliable data transfer has many subtle points, but that the task can be accomplished by carefully combining acknowledgments, timers, retransmissions, and sequence numbers.

Although we covered reliable data transfer in this chapter, we should keep in mind that reliable data transfer can be provided by link-, network-, transport-, or application-layer protocols. Any of the upper four layers of the protocol stack can implement acknowledgments, timers, retransmissions, and sequence numbers and provide reliable data transfer to the layer above. In fact, over the years, engineers and computer scientists have independently designed and implemented link-, network-, transport-, and application-layer protocols that provide reliable data transfer (although many of these protocols have quietly disappeared).

In Section 3.5 we took a close look at TCP, the Internet's connection-oriented and reliable transport-layer protocol. We learned that TCP is complex, involving connection management, flow control, and round-trip time estimation, as well as reliable data transfer. In fact, TCP is actually more complex than our description—we intentionally did not discuss a variety of TCP patches, fixes, and improvements that are widely implemented in various versions of TCP. All of this complexity, however, is hidden from the network application. If a client on one host wants to send data reliably to a server on another host, it simply opens a TCP socket to the server and pumps data into that socket. The client/server application is blissfully unaware of TCP's complexity.

In Section 3.6 we examined congestion control from a broad perspective, and in Section 3.7 we showed how TCP implements congestion control. We learned that congestion control is imperative for the well-being of the network. Without congestion control, a network can easily become gridlocked, with little or no data being transported end-to-end. In Section 3.7 we learned that TCP implements an end-to-end congestion-control mechanism that additively increases its transmission rate when the TCP connection's path is judged to be congestion-free, and multiplicatively decreases its transmission rate when loss occurs. This mechanism also strives to give each TCP connection passing through a congested link an equal share of the link bandwidth. We also examined in some depth the impact of TCP connection establishment and slow start on latency. We observed that in many important scenarios, connection establishment and slow start significantly contribute to end-to-end delay. We emphasize once more that while TCP congestion control has evolved over the years, it remains an area of intensive research and will likely continue to evolve in the upcoming years.

In Chapter 1 we said that a computer network can be partitioned into the "network edge" and the "network core." The network edge covers everything that happens in the end systems. Having now covered the application layer and the transport layer, our discussion of the network edge is complete. It is time to explore the network core! This journey begins in the next chapter, where we'll study the network layer, and continues into Chapter 5, where we'll study the link layer.

Homework Problems and Questions

Chapter 3 Review Questions

SECTIONS 3.1–3.3

1. Consider a TCP connection between Host A and Host B. Suppose that the TCP segments traveling from Host A to Host B have source port number x and destination port number y. What are the source and destination port numbers for the segments traveling from Host B to Host A?

2. Describe why an application developer might choose to run an application over UDP rather than TCP.

3. Is it possible for an application to enjoy reliable data transfer even when the application runs over UDP? If so, how?

SECTION 3.5

4. True or false?

a. Host A is sending Host B a large file over a TCP connection. Assume Host B has no data to send Host A. Host B will not send acknowledgments to Host A because Host B cannot piggyback the acknowledgments on data.

b. The size of the TCP `RcvWindow` never changes throughout the duration of the connection.

c. Suppose Host A is sending Host B a large file over a TCP connection. The number of unacknowledged bytes that A sends cannot exceed the size of the receive buffer.

d. Suppose Host A is sending a large file to Host B over a TCP connection. If the sequence number for a segment of this connection is m, then the sequence number for the subsequent segment will necessarily be $m + 1$.

e. The TCP segment has a field in its header for `RcvWindow`.

f. Suppose that the last `SampleRTT` in a TCP connection is equal to 1 sec. Then the current value of `TimeoutInterval` for the connection will necessarily be ≥ 1 sec.

g. Suppose Host A sends over a TCP connection to Host B one segment with sequence number 38 and 4 bytes of data. In this same segment the acknowledgment number is necessarily 42.

5. Suppose Host A sends two TCP segments back to back to Host B over a TCP connection. The first segment has sequence number 90; the second has sequence number 110.

a. How much data is in the first segment?

b. Suppose that the first segment is lost but the second segment arrives at B. In the acknowledgment that Host B sends to Host A, what will be the acknowledgment number?

6. Consider the Telnet example discussed in Section 3.5. A few seconds after the user types the letter 'C,' the user types the letter 'R.' After typing the letter 'R,' how many segments are sent, and what is put in the sequence number and acknowledgment fields of the segments?

SECTION 3.7

7. Suppose two TCP connections are present over some bottleneck link of rate R bps. Both connections have a huge file to send (in the same direction over the bottleneck link). The transmissions of the files start at the same time. What is the transmission rate that TCP would like to give to each of the connections?

8. True or false? Consider congestion control in TCP. When the timer expires at the sender, the threshold is set to one half of its previous value.

Problems

1. Suppose Client A initiates a Telnet session with Server S. At about the same time, Client B also initiates a Telnet session with Server S. Provide possible source and destination port numbers for

   a. The segments sent from A to S.

   b. The segments sent from B to S.

   c. The segments sent from S to A.

   d. The segments sent from S to B.

   e. If A and B are different hosts, is it possible that the source port number in the segments from A to S is the same as that from B to S?

   f. How about if they are the same host?

2. Consider Figure 3.5. What are the source and destination port values in the segments flowing from the server back to the clients' processes? What are the IP addresses in the network-layer datagrams carrying the transport-layer segments?

3. UDP and TCP use 1s complement for their checksums. Suppose you have the following three 8-bit bytes: 01010101, 01110000, 01001100. What is the 1s complement of the sum of these 8-bit bytes? (Note that although UDP and TCP use 16-bit words in computing the checksum, for this problem you are being asked to consider 8-bit summands.) Show all work. Why is it that UDP takes the 1s complement of the sum; that is, why not just use the sum? With the 1s complement scheme, how does the receiver detect errors? Is it possible that a 1-bit error will go undetected? How about a two-bit error?

4. Consider our motivation for correcting protocol `rtd2.1`. Show that the receiver, shown in the figure on the follwing page, when operating with the sender shown in Figure 3.11, can lead the sender and receiver to enter into a deadlock state, where each is waiting for an event that will never occur.

5. In protocol `rdt3.0`, the ACK packets flowing from the receiver to the sender do not have sequence numbers (although they do have an ACK field that contains the sequence number of the packet they are acknowledging). Why is it that our ACK packets do not require sequence numbers?

6. Draw the FSM for the receiver side of protocol `rdt3.0`.

7. Give a trace of the operation of protocol `rdt3.0` when data packets and acknowledgment packets are garbled. Your trace should be similar to that used in Figure 3.16.

8. Consider a channel that can lose packets but has a maximum delay that is known. Modify protocol `rdt2.1` to include sender timeout and retransmit. Informally argue why your protocol can communicate correctly over this channel.

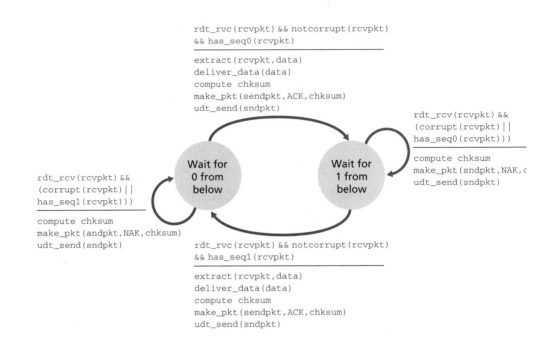

9. The sender side of `rdt3.0` simply ignores (that is, takes no action on) all received packets that are either in error, or have the wrong value in the `acknum` field of an acknowledgment packet. Suppose that in such circumstances, `rdt3.0` were simply to retransmit the current data packet. Would the protocol still work? (*Hint*: Consider what would happen if there were only bit errors; there are no packet losses but premature timeouts can occur. Consider how many times the *n*th packet is sent, in the limit as *n* approaches infinity.)

10. Consider the alternating-bit (also known as stop-and-wait) protocol. Draw a diagram showing that if the network connection between the sender and receiver can reorder messages (that is, that two messages propagating in the medium between the sender and receiver can be reordered), then the alternating-bit protocol will not work correctly (make sure you clearly identify the sense in which it will not work correctly). Your diagram should have the sender on the left and the receiver on the right, with the time axis running down the page, showing data (D) and acknowledgment (A) message exchange. Make sure you indicate the sequence number associated with any data or acknowledgment segment.

11. Consider a reliable data transfer protocol that uses only negative acknowledgments. Suppose the sender sends data only infrequently. Would a NAK-only protocol be preferable to a protocol that uses ACKs? Why? Now suppose the sender has a lot of data to send and the end-to-end connection experiences few

losses. In this second case, would a NAK-only protocol be preferable to a protocol that uses ACKs? Why?

12. Consider the cross-country example shown in Figure 3.17. How big would the window size have to be for the channel utilization to be greater than 90 percent?

13. Design a reliable, pipelined, data transfer protocol that uses only negative acknowledgments. How quickly will your protocol respond to lost packets when the arrival rate of data to the sender is low? When it is high?

14. In the generic SR protocol that we studied in Section 3.4.4, the sender transmits a message as soon as it is available (if it is in the window) without waiting for an acknowledgment. Suppose now that we want an SR protocol that sends messages two at a time. That is, the sender will send a pair of messages and will send the next pair of messages only when it knows that both messages in the first pair have been received correctly.

Suppose that the channel may lose messages but will not corrupt or reorder messages. Design an error-control protocol for the unidirectional reliable transfer of messages. Give an FSM description of the sender and receiver. Describe the format of the packets sent between sender and receiver, and vice versa. If you use any procedure calls other than those in Section 3.4 (for example, udt_send(), start_timer(), rdt_rcv(), and so on), clearly state their actions. Give an example (a timeline trace of sender and receiver) showing how your protocol recovers from a lost packet.

15. Consider a scenario in which a Host, A, wants to simultaneously send messages to Hosts B and C. A is connected to B and C via a broadcast channel—a packet sent by A is carried by the channel to both B and C. Suppose that the broadcast channel connecting A, B, and C can independently lose and corrupt messages (and so, for example, a message sent from A might be correctly received by B, but not by C). Design a stop-and-wait-like error-control protocol for reliably transferring a packet from A to B and C, such that A will not get new data from the upper layer until it knows that both B and C have correctly received the current packet. Give FMS descriptions of A and C. (*Hint*: The FSM for B should be essentially the same as for C.) Also, give a description of the packet format(s) used.

16. Consider the GBN protocol with a sender window size of 3 and a sequence number range of 1,024. Suppose that at time t, the next in-order packet that the receiver is expecting has a sequence number of k. Assume that the medium does not reorder messages. Answer the following questions:

   a. What are the possible sets of sequence numbers inside the sender's window at time t? Justify your answer.

   b. What are all possible values of the ACK field in all possible messages currently propagating back to the sender at time t? Justify your answer.

17. Suppose we have two network entities, A and B. B has a supply of data messages that will be sent to A according to the following conventions. When A gets a request from the layer above to get the next data (D) message from B, A must send a request (R) message to B on the A-to-B channel. Only when B receives an R message can it send a data (D) message back to A on the B-to-A channel. A should deliver exactly one copy of each D message to the layer above. R messages can be lost (but not corrupted) in the A-to-B channel; D messages, once sent, are always delivered correctly. The delay along both channels is unknown and variable.

    Design (give an FSM description of) a protocol that incorporates the appropriate mechanisms to compensate for the loss-prone A-to-B channel and implements message passing to the layer above at entity A, as discussed above. Use only those mechanisms that are absolutely necessary.

18. Consider the GBN and SR protocols. Suppose the sequence number space is of size k. What is the largest allowable sender window that will avoid the occurrence of problems such as that in Figure 3.27 for each of these protocols?

19. Answer true or false to the following questions and briefly justify your answer:

    a. With the SR protocol, it is possible for the sender to receive an ACK for a packet that falls outside of its current window.

    b. With GBN, it is possible for the sender to receive an ACK for a packet that falls outside of its current window.

    c. The alternating-bit protocol is the same as the SR protocol with a sender and receiver window size of 1.

    d. The alternating-bit protocol is the same as the GBN protocol with a sender and receiver window size of 1.

20. Consider transferring an enormous file of L bytes from Host A to Host B. Assume an MSS of 1,460 bytes.

    a. What is the maximum value of L such that TCP sequence numbers are not exhausted? Recall that the TCP sequence number field has 4 bytes.

    b. For the L you obtain in (a), find how long it takes to transmit the file. Assume that a total of 66 bytes of transport, network, and data-link header are added to each segment before the resulting packet is sent out over a 10 Mbps link. Ignore flow control and congestion control so A can pump out the segments back to back and continuously.

21. Consider the TCP procedure for estimating RTT. Suppose that $\alpha = 0.1$. Let $\texttt{SampleRTT}_1$ be the most recent sample RTT, let $\texttt{SampleRTT}_2$ be the next most recent sample RTT, and so on.

    a. For a given TCP connection, suppose four acknowledgments have been returned with corresponding sample RTTs $\texttt{SampleRTT}_4$, $\texttt{SampleRTT}_3$,

$\texttt{SampleRTT}_2$, and $\texttt{SampleRTT}_1$. Express $\texttt{EstimatedRTT}$ in terms of the four sample RTTs.

b. Generalize your formula for n sample RTTs.

c. For the formula in part (b) let n approach infinity. Comment on why this averaging procedure is called an exponential moving average.

22. In Section 3.5.3 we discussed TCP's estimation of RTT. Why do you think TCP avoids measuring the $\texttt{SampleRTT}$ for retransmitted segments?

23. What is the relationship between the variable $\texttt{SendBase}$ in Section 3.5.4 and the variable $\texttt{LastByteRcvd}$ in Section 3.5.5?

24. What is the relationship between the variable $\texttt{LastByteRcvd}$ in Section 3.5.5 and the variable $\texttt{y}$ in Section 3.5.4?

25. In Section 3.5.4, we saw that TCP waits until it has received three duplicate ACKs before performing a fast retransmit. Why do you think the TCP designers chose not to perform a fast retransmit after the first duplicate ACK for a segment is received?

26. Consider Figure 3.45(b). If λ'_{in} increases beyond $R/2$, can λ_{out} increase beyond $R/3$? Explain. Now consider Figure 3.45. If λ'_{in} increases beyond $R/2$, can λ_{out} increase beyond $R/4$ under the assumption that a packet will be forwarded twice on average from the router to the receiver? Explain.

27. Consider the following plot of TCP window size as a function of time.

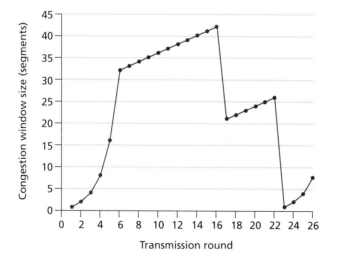

Assuming TCP Reno is the protocol experiencing the behavior shown above, answer the following questions. In all cases, you should provide a short discussion justifying your answer.

    a. Identify the intervals of time when TCP slow start is operating.

    b. Identify the intervals of time when TCP congestion avoidance is operating.

    c. After the 16th transmission round, is segment loss detected by a triple duplicate ACK or by a timeout?

    d. After the 22nd transmission round, is segment loss detected by a triple duplicate ACK or by a timeout?

    e. What is the initial value of `Threshold` at the first transmission round?

    f. What is the value of `Threshold` at the 18th transmission round?

    g. What is the value of `Threshold` at the 24th transmission round?

    h. During what transmission round is the 70th segment sent?

    i. Assuming a packet loss is detected after the 26th round by the receipt of a triple duplicate ACK, what will be the values of the congestion-window size and of `Threshold`?

28. Refer to Figure 3.53, which illustrates the convergence of TCP's AIMD algorithm. Suppose that instead of a multiplicative decrease, TCP decreased the window size by a constant amount. Would the resulting AIAD converge to an equal share algorithm? Justify your answer using a diagram similar to Figure 3.53.

29. In Section 3.5.4 we discussed the doubling of the timeout interval after a timeout event. This mechanism is a form of congestion control. Why does TCP need a window-based congestion-control mechanism (as studied in Section 3.7) in addition to this doubling-timeout-interval mechanism?

30. Host A is sending an enormous file to Host B over a TCP connection. Over this connection there is never any packet loss and the timers never expire. Denote the transmission rate of the link connecting Host A to the Internet by R bps. Suppose that the process in Host A is capable of sending data into its TCP socket at a rate S bps, where $S = 10 \cdot R$. Further suppose that the TCP receive buffer is large enough to hold the entire file, and the send buffer can hold only one percent of the file. What would prevent the process in Host A from continuously passing data to its TCP socket at rate S bps? TCP flow control? TCP congestion control? Or something else? Elaborate.

31. Recall the idealized model for the steady-state dynamics of TCP. In the period of time from when the connection's window size varies from $W/(2 \cdot RTT)$ to W/RTT, only one packet is lost (at the very end of the period).

    a. Show that the loss rate is equal to

$$L = \text{loss rate} = \frac{1}{\frac{3}{8}w^2 + \frac{3}{4}w}$$

b. Use the result above to show that if a connection has loss rate L, then its average bandwidth is approximately given by

$$\approx \frac{1.22 \cdot MSS}{RTT\sqrt{L}}$$

32. In our discussion of TCP Futures in Section 3.7, we noted that to achieve a throughput of 10 Gbps, TCP could only tolerate a segment loss probability of $2 \cdot 10^{-10}$ (or equivalently, one loss event for every 5,000,000,000 segments). Show the derivation for the values of $2 \cdot 10^{-10}$ 1-out-of-5,000,000 for the RTT and MSS values given in Section 3.7 If TCP needed to support a 100 Gbps connection, what would the tolerable loss be?

33. In our discussion of TCP congestion control in Section 3.7, we implicitly assumed that the TCP sender always had data to send. Consider now the case that the TCP sender sends a large amount of data and then goes idle (since it has no more data to send) at t_1. TCP remains idle for a relatively long period of time and then wants to send more data at t_2. What are the advantages and disadvantages of having TCP use the CongWin and Threshold values from t_1 when starting to send data at t$_2$? What alternative would you recommend? Why?

34. Consider sending an object of size $O = 100$ Kbytes from server to client. Let $S = 536$ bytes and $RTT = 100$ msec. Suppose the transport protocol uses static windows with window size W. (See Section 3.7.2.)

    a. For a transmission rate of 28 kbps, determine the minimum possible latency. Determine the minimum window size that achieves this latency.

    b. Repeat (a) for 100 kbps.

    c. Repeat (a) for 1 Mbps.

    d. Repeat (a) for 10 Mbps.

35. Suppose TCP increased its congestion window by two rather than by one for each received acknowledgment during slow start. Thus, the first window consists of one segment, the second of three segments, the third of nine segments, and so on. Using the techniques in Section 3.7.2:

    a. Express K in terms of O and S.

    b. Express Q in terms of RTT, S, and R.

    c. Express latency in terms of $P = \min(K - 1, Q)$, O, R, and RTT.

36. Consider the case $RTT = 1$ sec and $O = 100$ kbytes. Prepare a chart (similar to the charts in Section 3.7.2) that compares the minimum latency ($O/R + 2\,RTT$) with the latency with slow start for $R = 28$ kbps, 100 kbps, 1 Mbps, and 10 Mbps.

37. True or false?

    a. If a Web page consists of exactly one object, then nonpersistent and persistent connections have exactly the same response-time performance.

   b. Consider sending one object of size O from server to browser over TCP. If $O > S$, where S is the maximum segment size, then the server will stall at least once.

   c. Suppose a Web page consists of 10 objects, each of size O bits. For persistent HTTP, the RTT portion of the response time is $20\ RTT$.

   d. Suppose a Web page consists of 10 objects, each of size O bits. For nonpersistent HTTP with five parallel connections, the RTT portion of the response time is 12 RTT.

38. In this problem we fill in some of the details in the derivation of latency in Section 3.7.2.

   a. Derive the formula

   $$Q = \left\lfloor \log_2 (1 + \frac{RTT}{S/R}) \right\rfloor + 1$$

   b. Use the identity

   $$\sum_{k=1}^{P} 2^{k-1} = 2^P - 1$$

   to derive the formula

   $$\text{Latency} = 2RTT + \frac{O}{R} + P\left[RTT + \frac{S}{R} \right] - (2^P - 1)\frac{S}{R}$$

39. The analysis of dynamic windows in Section 3.7.2 assumes that there is one link between server and client. Redo the analysis for T links between server and client. Assume the network has no congestion so the packets experience no queuing delays. The packets do experience a store-and-forward delay, however. The definition of RTT is the same as that given in the section on TCP congestion control. (*Hint*: The time for the server to send out the first segment until it receives the acknowledgment is $TS/R + RTT$.)

40. Recall the discussion at the end of Section 3.7.2 on the response time for a Web page. For the case of nonpersistent connections, determine a general expression for the *fraction* of the response time that is due to TCP slow start.

Discussion Questions

1. Consider streaming stored audio. Does it make sense to run the application over UDP or TCP? Which transport protocol does RealNetworks use? Why?

2. Repeat the question above for the Microsoft streaming products.

3. In Section 3.7 we remarked that a client/server can "unfairly" create many parallel simultaneous connections. What can be done to make the Internet truly fair?

4. Read the research literature to learn what is meant by *TCP friendly*. Also read the Sally Floyd interview at the end of this chapter. Write a one-page description of TCP friendliness.

5. At the end of Section 3.7.1 we discussed the fact that an application can open multiple TCP connections and obtain a higher throughput (or equivalently a faster data transfer time). Why do you think that more applications have not tried to improve their performance by using multiple connections? What would happen if all applications tried to improve their performance by using multiple connections? What are some of the difficulties involved in having a network element determine whether an application is using multiple TCP connections?

Programming Assignments

Implementing a Reliable Transport Protocol

In this laboratory programming assignment, you will be writing the sending and receiving transport-level code for implementing a simple reliable data transfer protocol. There are two versions of this lab, the alternating-bit-protocol version and the GBN version. This lab should be fun—your implementation will differ very little from what would be required in a real-world situation.

Since you probably don't have standalone machines (with an OS that you can modify), your code will have to execute in a simulated hardware/software environment. However, the programming interface provided to your routines—the code that would call your entities from above and from below—is very close to what is done in an actual UNIX environment. (Indeed, the software interfaces described in this programming assignment are much more realistic that the infinite loop senders and receivers that many texts describe.) Stopping and starting timers are also simulated, and timer interrupts will cause your timer handling routine to be activated.

Ethereal Lab: Exploring TCP

In this lab, you'll use your Web browser to access a file from a Web server. As in earlier Ethereal labs, you'll use Ethereal to capture the packets arriving at your computer. Unlike earlier labs, you'll *also* be able to download a Ethereal-readable packet trace from the Web server from which you downloaded the file. In this server trace, you'll find the packets that were generated by your own access of the Web server. You'll analyze the client- and server-side traces to explore aspects of TCP. In particular, you'll evaluate the performance of the TCP connection between your computer and the Web server. You'll trace TCP's window behavior, and infer packet loss, retransmission, flow control and congestion control behavior, and estimated round-trip time.

As is the case with all Ethereal labs, the full description of this lab is available at this book's Web site, http://www.awl.com/kurose-ross.

Sally Floyd

Sally Floyd is a research scientist at AT&T Center for Internet Research at ICSI (ACIRI), an institute dedicated to Internet and networking issues. She is known in the industry for her work in Internet protocol design, in particular reliable multicast, congestion control (TCP), packet scheduling (RED), and protocol analysis. Sally received her BA in Sociology at the University of California, Berkeley, and her MS and PhD in computer science at the same university.

How did you decide to study computer science?

After getting my BA in sociology, I had to figure out how to support myself; I ended up getting a two-year certificate in electronics from the local community college, and then spent ten years working in electronics and computer science. This included eight years as a computer systems engineer for the computers that run the Bay Area Rapid Transit trains. I later decided to learn some more formal computer science and applied to graduate school in UC Berkeley's Computer Science Department.

Why did you decide to specialize in networking?

In graduate school I became interested in theoretical computer science. I first worked on the probabilistic analysis of algorithms and later on computational learning theory. I was also working at LBL [Lawrence Berkeley Laboratory] one day a month and my office was across the hall from Van Jacobson, who was working on TCP congestion-control algorithms at the time. Van asked me if I would like to work over the summer doing some analysis of algorithms for a network-related problem involving the unwanted synchronization of periodic routing messages. It sounded interesting to me, so I did this for the summer.

　　After I finished my thesis, Van offered me a full-time job continuing the work in networking. I hadn't necessarily planned to stay in networking for ten years, but for me, network research is more satisfying than theoretical computer science. I find I am happier in the applied world, where the consequences of my work are more tangible.

What was your first job in the computer industry? What did it entail?

My first computer job was at BART (Bay Area Rapid Transit), from 1975 to 1982, working on the computers that run the BART trains. I started off as a technician, maintaining and repairing the various distributed computer systems involved in running the BART system.

　　These included a central computer system and distributed minicomputer system for controlling train movement; a system of DEC computers for displaying ads and train destinations on the destination signs; and a system of Modcomp computers for collecting information from the fare gates. My last few years at BART were spent on a joint BART/LBL project to design the replacement for BART's aging train-control computer system.

297

What is the most challenging part of your job?

The actual research is the most challenging part. Right now, that means designing and exploring a new mechanism for end-to-end congestion control, based on equation-based congestion control. This is intended not to replace TCP, but instead for unicast traffic such as some rateadaptive real-time traffic that would prefer to avoid the dramatic rate change of reducing its sending rate in half in response to a single packet drop. Equation-based congestion control is also of interest as a potential foundation for multicast congestion control. [More information is on the Web page at http://www.psc.edu/networking/tcp_friendly.html.]

What do you see for the future of networking and the Internet?

One possibility is that the typical congestion encountered by Internet traffic will become less severe as pricing mechanisms come into play and the available bandwidth increases faster than the demand. I view the trend as toward less severe congestion, though a medium-term future of increasing congestion punctuated by occasional congestion collapse does not seem impossible.

   The future of the Internet itself, or of the Internet architecture, is not at all clear to me. There are many factors contributing to rapid change, so that it is hard to predict how the Internet or the Internet architecture will evolve, or even to predict how successfully this evolution will be able to avoid the many potential pitfalls along the way.

What people have inspired you professionally?

Richard Karp, my thesis advisor in graduate school, essentially showed me how to do research, and Van Jacobson, my "group-leader" at LBL, was responsible for my interest in networking and for much of my understanding of the Internet infrastructure. Dave Clark has inspired me through his clear view of the Internet architecture and his role in the development of that architecture through research, writing, and participation in the IETF and other public forums. Deborah Estrin has inspired me through her focus and effectiveness, and her ability to make conscious decisions of what she will work on and why.

   One of the reasons that I have enjoyed working in network research for the last ten years is that there are so many people working in the field whom I like, respect, and am inspired by. They are smart, work hard, and have a strong commitment to the development of the Internet, do impressive work, and can be good companions for a beer and a friendly disagreement (or agreement) after a day of meetings.

4

The Network Layer

We learned in the previous chapter that the transport layer provides various forms of process-to-process communication by relying on the network layer's host-to-host communication service. We also learned that the transport layer does so without any knowledge about how the network layer actually implements this service. So perhaps you're now wondering, what's under the hood of the host-to-host communication service, what makes it tick?

In this chapter we'll learn exactly how the network layer implements the host-to-host communication service. We'll see that unlike the transport layer, there is a piece of the network layer in each and every host and router in the network. Because of this, network-layer protocols are among the most challenging (and therefore among the most interesting!) in the protocol stack.

The network layer is also one of the most complex layers in the protocol stack, and so we'll have a lot of ground to cover here. We'll begin our study with an overview of the network layer and the services it can provide. We'll then revisit the two broad approaches towards structuring network-layer packet delivery—the datagram and the virtual-circuit model—that we first encountered back in Chapter 1, and see the fundamental role that addressing plays in delivering a packet to its destination host.

In this chapter, we'll make an important distinction between the **forwarding** and **routing** functions of the network layer. Forwarding involves the transfer of a packet from an incoming link to an outgoing link within a *single* router. Routing involves *all* of a network's routers, whose collective interactions via routing protocols determine the paths (or routes) that packets take on their trips from source to destination node. Keeping this distinction in mind as you progress through this chapter will help you place many of the topics covered in an appropriate context.

In order to deepen our understanding of packet forwarding, we'll look "inside" a router—at its hardware architecture and organization. We'll then look at packet forwarding in the Internet, along with the celebrated Internet Protocol (IP). We'll investigate network-layer addressing and the IPv4 datagram format. We'll then explore network address translation (NAT), datagram fragmentation, the Internet Control Message Protocol (ICMP) and IPv6.

We'll then turn our attention to the network layer's routing function. We'll see that the job of a routing algorithm is to determine good paths (equivalently, routes), from senders to receivers. We'll first study the theory of routing algorithms, concentrating on the two most prevalent classes of algorithms: link-state and distance-vector algorithms. Since the complexity of routing algorithms grows considerably as the number of network routers increases, hierarchical routing approaches will are also be of interest. We'll then see how theory is put into practice when we cover the Internet's intra-autonomous system routing protocols (RIP, OSPF, and IS-IS) and its inter-autonomous system routing protocol, BGP. We'll close this chapter with a discussion of broadcast and multicast routing.

In summary, this chapter has three major parts. The first part, Sections 4.1 and 4.2, covers network-layer functions and services. The second part, Sections 4.3 and 4.4, covers forwarding. Finally, the third part, Sections 4.5 through 4.7, covers routing.

4.1   Introduction

Figure 4.1 shows a simple network with two hosts, H1 and H2, and several routers on the path between H1 and H2. Suppose that H1 is sending information to H2, and consider the role of the network layer in these hosts and in the intervening routers. The network layer in H1 takes segments from the transport layer in H1, encapsulates each segment into a datagram (that is, a network-layer packet), and then starts the datagrams on their journey to their destination; that is, it sends the datagrams to its nearby router, R1. At the receiving host, H2, the network layer receives the datagrams from its nearby router R2, extracts the transport-layer segments, and delivers the segments up to the transport layer at H2. The primary role of the routers is to forward datagrams from input links to output links. Note that the routers in Figure 4.1 are shown with a truncated protocol stack, that is, with no upper layers above the network layer, because (except for control purposes) routers do not run application- and transport-layer protocols such as those we examined in Chapters 2 and 3.

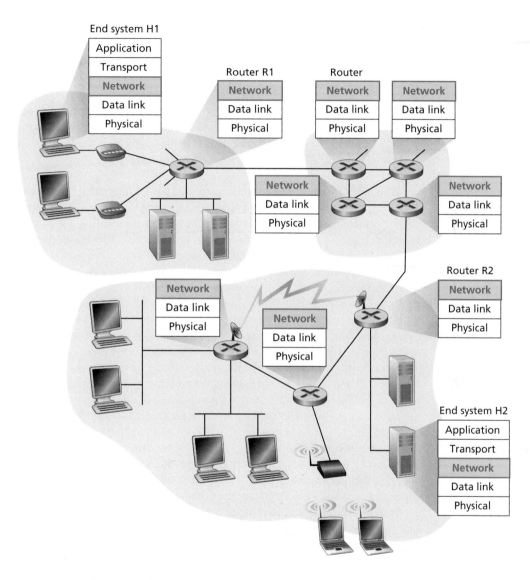

Figure 4.1 ♦ The network layer

4.1.1 Forwarding and Routing

The role of the network layer is thus deceptively simple—to move packets from a sending host to a receiving host. To do so, two important network-layer functions can be identified:

♦ *Forwarding.* When a packet arrives at a router's input link, the router must move the packet to the appropriate output link. For example, a packet arriving from Host H1 to Router R1 must be forwarded to the next router on a path to H2. In Section 4.3, we'll look inside a router and examine how a packet is actually forwarded from an input link at a router to an output link.

♦ *Routing.* The network layer must determine the route or path taken by packets as they flow from a sender to a receiver. The algorithms that calculate these paths are referred to as **routing algorithms**. A routing algorithm would determine, for example, the path along which packets flow from H1 to H2.

The terms *forwarding* and *routing* are often used interchangeably by authors discussing the network layer. We'll use these terms much more precisely in this book. *Forwarding* refers to the router-local action of transferring a packet from an input link interface to the appropriate output link interface. *Routing* refers to the network-wide process that determines the end-to-end paths that packets take from source to destination. Using a driving analogy, consider the trip from Pennsylvania from Florida undertaken by our traveler back in Section 1.3.2. During this trip, our driver passes through many interchanges en route to Florida. We can think of forwarding as the process of getting through a single interchange: A car enters the interchange, gets directions to the next interchange on its journey, and takes the outgoing road to that next interchange. We can think of routing as the process of planning the trip from Pennsylvania to Florida: Before embarking on the trip, the driver has consulted a map and chosen one of many paths possible, with each path consisting of a series of road segments connected at interchanges. In this first part of this chapter, we focus on network-layer topics related to forwarding; we'll then turn our attention to routing.

Every router has a **forwarding table**. A router forwards a packet by examining the value of a field in the arriving packet's header, and then using this value to index into the router's forwarding table. The result from the forwarding table indicates to which of the router's link interfaces the packet is to be forwarded. Depending on the network-layer protocol, this value in the packet's header could be the destination address of the packet or an indication of the connection to which the packet belongs. Figure 4.2 provides an example. In Figure 4.2, a packet with a header field value of 0111 arrives to a router. The router indexes into its forwarding table and determines that the output link interface for this packet is interface 2. The router then internally forwards the packet to interface 2. In Section 4.3 we'll look inside a router and examine the forwarding function in much greater detail.

You might now be wondering how the forwarding tables in the routers are configured. This is a crucial issue, one that exposes the important interplay between routing and forwarding. As shown in Figure 4.2, the routing algorithm determines the values that are inserted into the routers' forwarding tables. The routing algorithm may be centralized (e.g., with an algorithm executing on a central site and downloading routing information to each of the routers) or decentralized (i.e., with a

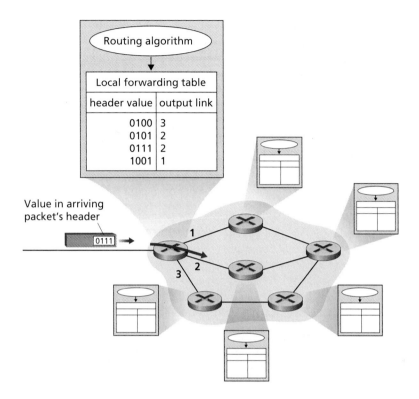

Value in arriving
packet's header

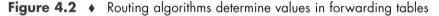

Figure 4.2 ♦ Routing algorithms determine values in forwarding tables

piece of the distributed routing algorithm running in each router). In either case, a router receives routing protocol messages, which are used to configure its forwarding table. The distinct and different purposes of the forwarding and routing functions can be further illustrated by considering the hypothetical (and unrealistic, but technically feasible) case of a network in which all forwarding tables are configured directly by human network operators physically present at the routers. In this case, no routing protocols would be required! Of course, the human operators would need to interact with each other to ensure that the forwarding tables were configured in such a way that packets reached their intended destinations. It's also likely that human configuration would be more error-prone and much slower to respond to changes in the network topology than a routing protocol. We're thus fortunate that all networks have both a forwarding *and* a routing function!

While we're on the topic of terminology, it's worth mentioning two other terms that are often used interchangeably, but that we will use more carefully. We'll reserve the term *packet switch* to mean a general packet-switching device that transfers a packet from input link interface to output link interface, according to the value in a field in the header of the packet. Some packet switches, called **link-layer switches** (examined in Chapter 5), base the forwarding decision on the value in the link-layer field. Other packet switches, called **routers**, base their forwarding decision on the value in the network-layer field. (To fully appreciate this important distinction, you might want to review Section 1.7.2, where we discuss network-layer datagrams and link-layer frames and their relationship.) Since our focus in this chapter is on the network layer, we use the term *router* in place of *packet switch*. We'll even use the term *router* when talking about packet switches in virtual-circuit networks (soon to be discussed).

Connection Setup

We just said that the network layer has two important functions, forwarding and routing. But we'll soon see that in some computer networks there is actually a third important network-layer function, namely, **connection setup**. Recall from our study of TCP that a three-way handshake is required before data can flow from sender to receiver. This allows the sender and receiver to set up the needed state information (for example, sequence number and initial flow-control window size). In an analogous manner, some network-layer architectures—for example, ATM, frame-relay, X.25, but not the Internet—require the routers along the chosen path from source to destination to handshake with each other in order to set up state before network-layer data packets within a given source-to-destination connection can begin to flow. In the network layer, this process is referred to as *connection setup*. We'll examine connection setup in Section 4.2.

4.1.2 Network Service Models

Before delving into the network layer, let's take the broader view and consider the different types of service that might be offered by the network layer. When the transport layer at a sending host transmits a packet into the network (that is, passes it down to the network layer at the sending host), can the transport layer count on the network layer to deliver the packet to the destination? When multiple packets are sent, will they be delivered to the transport layer in the receiving host in the order in which they were sent? Will the amount of time between the sending of two sequential packet transmissions be the same as the amount of time between their reception? Will the network provide any feedback about congestion in the network? What is the abstract view (properties) of the channel connecting the transport layer in the sending and receiving hosts? The answers to these questions and others are determined by the service model provided by the network layer. The **network service model** defines the characteristics of end-to-end transport of data between one edge of the network and the other, that is, between sending and receiving end systems.

Let's now consider some possible services that the network layer could provide. In the sending host, when the transport layer passes a packet to the network layer, specific services that could be provided by the network layer include:

♦ *Guaranteed delivery*. This service guarantees that the packet will eventually arrive at its destination.

♦ *Guaranteed delivery with bounded delay*. This service not only guarantees delivery of the packet, but delivery within a specified host-to-host delay bound (for example, within 100 msec).

Furthermore, the following services could be provided to a *flow of packets* between a given source and destination:

♦ *In-order packet delivery*. This service guarantees that packets arrive at the destination in the order that they were sent.

♦ *Guaranteed minimal bandwidth*. This network-layer service emulates the behavior of a transmission link of a specified bit rate (for example, 1 Mbps) between sending and receiving hosts (even though the actual end-to-end path may traverse several physical links). As long as the sending host transmits bits (as part of packets) at a rate below the specified bit rate, then no packet is lost and each packet arrives within a prespecified host-to-host delay (for example, within 40 msec).

♦ *Guaranteed maximum jitter*. This service guarantees that the amount of time between the transmission of two successive packets at the sender is equal to the amount of time between their receipt at the destination (or that this spacing changes by no more than some specified value).

This is only a partial list of services that a network layer could provide—there are countless variations possible.

The Internet's network layer provides a single service, known as **best-effort service**. From Table 4.1, it might appear that *best-effort service* is a euphemism for *no service at all*. With best-effort service, timing between packets is not guaranteed to be preserved, packets are not guaranteed to be received in the order in which they were sent, nor is the eventual delivery of transmitted packets guaranteed. Given this definition, a network that delivered *no* packets to the destination would satisfy the definition of best-effort delivery service. (Indeed, the public Internet might sometimes appear to be an example of a network that does so!) As we'll discuss shortly, however, there are sound reasons for such a minimalist network-layer service model. We'll cover additional, still-evolving, Internet service models in Chapter 7.

Other network architectures have defined and implemented service models that go beyond the Internet's best-effort service. For example, the ATM network architecture [ATM Forum 2004, Black 1995] provides for multiple service models, meaning that different connections can be provided with different classes of service

Network Architecture	Service Model	Bandwidth Guarantee	No-Loss Guarantee	Ordering	Timing	Congestion Indication
Internet	Best Effort	None	None	Any order possible	Not maintained	None
ATM	CBR	Guaranteed constant rate	Yes	In order	Maintained	Congestion will not occur
ATM	ABR	Guaranteed minimum	None	In order	Not maintained	Congestion indication provided

Table 4.1 ♦ Internet, ATM CBR, and ATM ABR service models

within the same network. A discussion of how an ATM network provides such services is well beyond the scope of this book; our aim here is only to note that alternatives do exist to the Internet's best effort model. Two of the more important ATM service models are constant bit rate and available bit rate service:

♦ *Constant bit rate (CBR) ATM network service.* This was the first ATM service model to be standardized, reflecting early interest by the telephone companies in ATM and the suitability of CBR service for carrying real-time, constant bit rate audio and video traffic. The goal of CBR service is conceptually simple—to provide a flow of packets (known as cells in ATM terminology) with a virtual pipe whose properties are the same as if a dedicated fixed-bandwidth transmission link existed between sending and receiving hosts. With CBR service, a flow of ATM cells is carried across the network in such a way that a cell's end-to-end delay, the variability in a cell's end-end delay (that is, the jitter), and the fraction of cells that are lost or delivered late are all guaranteed to be less than specified values. These values are agreed upon by the sending host and the ATM network when the CBR connection is first established.

♦ *Available bit rate (ABR) ATM network service.* With the Internet offering so-called best-effort service, ATM's ABR might best be characterized as being a slightly-better-than-best-effort service. As with the Internet service model, cells may be lost under ABR service. Unlike in the Internet, however, cells cannot be reordered (although they may be lost), and a minimum cell transmission rate (MCR) is guaranteed to a connection using ABR service. If the network has enough free resources at a given time, a sender may also be able to send cells successfully at a higher rate than the MCR. Additionally, as we saw in Section 3.6, ATM ABR service can provide feedback to the sender (in terms of a congestion notification bit, or an explicit rate at which to send) that controls how the sender adjusts its rate between the MCR and an allowable peak cell rate.

4.2 Virtual Circuit and Datagram Networks

Recall from Chapter 3 that a transport layer can offer applications connectionless service or connection-oriented service. For example, the Internet's transport layer provides each application a choice between two services: UDP, a connectionless service; or TCP, a connection-oriented service. In a similar manner, a network layer can also provide connectionless service or connection service. Network-layer connection and connectionless services in many ways parallel transport-layer connection-oriented and connectionless services. For example, a network-layer connection service begins with handshaking between the source and destination hosts; and a network-layer connectionless service does not have any handshaking preliminaries.

Although the network-layer connection and connectionless services have some parallels with transport-layer connection-oriented and connectionless services, there are crucial differences:

♦ In the network layer these services are host-to-host services provided by the network layer to the transport layer. In the transport layer these services are process-to-process services provided by the transport layer to the application layer.

♦ In all major computer network architectures to date (Internet, ATM, frame relay and so on), the network layer provides either a host-to-host connectionless service or a host-to-host connection service, but not both. Computer networks that provide only a connection service at the network layer are called **virtual-circuit (VC) networks**; computer networks that provide only a connectionless service at the network layer are called **datagram networks**.

♦ The implementations of connection-oriented service in the transport layer and the connection service in the network layer are fundamentally different. We saw in the previous chapter that the transport-layer connection-oriented service is implemented at the edge of the network in the end systems; we'll see shortly that the network-layer connection service is implemented in the routers in the network core as well as in the end systems.

Virtual-circuit and datagram networks are two fundamental classes of computer networks. They use very different information in making their forwarding decisions. Let's now take a closer look at their implementations.

4.2.1 Virtual-Circuit Networks

We've learned that the Internet is a datagram network. However, many alternative network architectures—including those of ATM, frame relay and X.25—are virtual-circuit networks and, therefore, use connections at the network layer. These network-layer connections are called **virtual circuits (VCs)**. Let's now consider how a VC service can be implemented in a computer network.

A VC consists of (1) a path (that is, a series of links and routers) between the source and destination hosts, (2) VC numbers, one number for each link along the path, and (3) entries in the forwarding table in each router along the path. A packet belonging to a virtual circuit will carry a VC number in its header. Because a virtual circuit may have a different VC number on each link, each intervening router must replace the VC number of each traversing packet with a new one. The new VC number is obtained from the forwarding table.

To illustrate the concept, consider the network shown in Figure 4.3. The numbers next to the links of R1 in Figure 4.3 are the link interface numbers. Suppose now that Host A requests that the network establish a VC between itself and Host B. Suppose also that the network chooses the path A-R1-R2-B and assigns VC numbers 12, 22, 32 to the three links in this path for this virtual circuit. In this case, when a packet in this VC leaves Host A, the value in the VC number field in the packet header is 12; when it leaves R1, the value is 22; and when it leaves R2, the value is 32.

How does the router determine the replacement VC number for a packet traversing the router? For a VC network, each router's forwarding table includes VC number translation; for example, the forwarding table in R1 might look something like this:

Incoming Interface	Incoming VC #	Outgoing Interface	Outgoing VC #
1	12	2	22
2	63	1	18
3	7	2	17
1	97	3	87
...	...	...	...

Whenever a new VC is established across a router, an entry is added to the forwarding table. Similarly, whenever a VC terminates, the appropriate entries in each table along its path are removed.

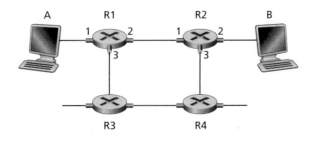

Figure 4.3 ◆ A simple virtual circuit network

You might be wondering why a packet doesn't just keep the same VC number on each of the links along its route. The answer is twofold. First, replacing the number from link to link reduces the length of the VC field in the packet header. Second, and more importantly, VC setup is considerably simplified by permitting a different VC number at each link along the path of the VC. Specifically, with multiple VC numbers, each link in the path can choose a VC number independently of the VC number chosen at other links along the path. If a common VC number were required for all links along the path, the routers would have to exchange and process a substantial number of messages to agree on a common VC number (e.g., one that is not being used by any other existing VC at these routers) to be used for a connection.

In a VC network, the network's routers must maintain **connection state information** for the ongoing connections. Specifically, each time a new connection is established across a router, a new connection entry must be added to the router's forwarding table; and each time a connection is released, an entry must be removed from the table. Note that even if there is no VC-number translation, it is still necessary to maintain connection state information that associates VC numbers with output interface numbers. The issue of whether or not a router maintains connection state information for each ongoing connection is a crucial one—one that we'll return to repeatedly in this book.

There are three identifiable phases in a virtual circuit:

◆ *VC setup.* During the setup phase, the sending transport layer contacts the network layer, specifies the receiver's address, and waits for the network to set up the VC. The network layer determines the path between sender and receiver, that is, the series of links and routers through which all packets of the VC will travel. The network layer also determines the VC number for each link along the path. Finally, the network layer adds an entry in the forwarding table in each router along the path. During VC setup, the network layer may also reserve resources (for example, bandwidth) along the path of the VC.

◆ *Data transfer.* As shown in Figure 4.4, once the VC has been established, packets can begin to flow along the VC.

◆ *VC teardown.* This is initiated when the sender (or receiver) informs the network layer of its desire to terminate the VC. The network layer will then typically inform the end system on the other side of the network of the call termination and update the forwarding tables in each of the packet routers on the path to indicate that the VC no longer exists.

There is a subtle but important distinction between VC setup at the network layer and connection setup at the transport layer (for example, the TCP three-way handshake we studied in Chapter 3). Connection setup at the transport layer involves only the two end systems. During transport-layer connection setup, the two end systems alone determine the parameters (for example, initial sequence number and flow-control window size) of their transport-layer connection. Although the two end systems are aware of the transport-layer connection, the routers within the network are completely oblivious to it. On the other hand, with a VC network layer, *routers along the path between the two end systems are involved in VC setup, and each router is fully aware of all the VCs passing through it.*

The messages that the end systems send into the network to initiate or terminate a VC, and the messages passed between the routers to set up the VC (that is, to modify connection state in router tables) are known as **signaling messages**, and the protocols used to exchange these messages are often referred to as **signaling protocols**. VC setup is shown pictorially in Figure 4.4. We'll not cover VC signaling protocols in this book; see [Black 1997] for a general discussion of signaling in connection-oriented networks and [ITU-T Q.2931 1994] for the specification of ATM's Q.2931 signaling protocol.

4.2.2 Datagram Networks

In a **datagram network**, each time an end system wants to send a packet, it stamps the packet with the address of the destination end system and then pops the packet into the network. As shown in Figure 4.5, this is done without any VC setup. Routers in a datagram network do not maintain any state information about VCs (because there are no VCs!).

As a packet is transmitted from source to destination, it passes through a series of routers. Each of these routers uses the packet's destination address to forward the packet. Specifically, each router has a forwarding table that maps destination addresses to link interfaces; when a packet arrives at the router, the router uses the

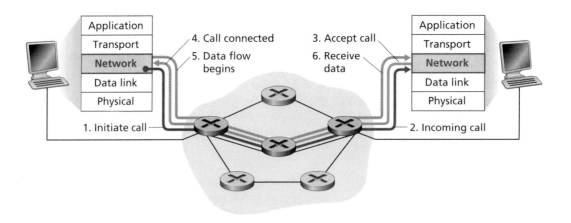

Figure 4.4 ◆ Virtual-circuit setup

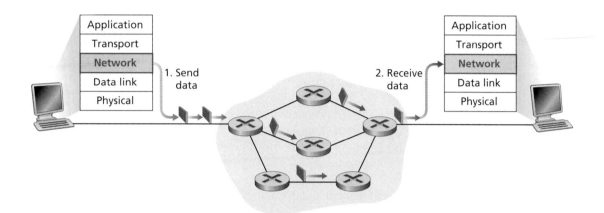

Figure 4.5 ◆ Datagram network

packet's destination address to lookup the appropriate output link interface in the forwarding table. The router then forwards the packet to that output link interface.

To get some further insight into the lookup operation, let's look at a specific example. Suppose that all destination addresses are 32 bits (which just happens to be the length of the destination address in an IP datagram). A brute-force implementation of the forwarding table would have one entry for every possible destination address. Since there are more than 4 billion possible addresses, this option is totally out the question—it would require a humongous forwarding table.

Now let's further suppose that our router has four links, numbered 0 through 3, and that packets are to be forwarded to the link interfaces as follows:

Destination Address Range	Link Interface
11001000 00010111 00010000 00000000 through 11001000 00010111 00010111 11111111	0
11001000 00010111 00011000 00000000 through 11001000 00010111 00011000 11111111	1
11001000 00010111 00011001 00000000 through 11001000 00010111 00011111 11111111	2
otherwise	3

Clearly, for this example, it is not necessary to have 4 billion entries in the router's forwarding table. We could, for example, have the following forwarding table with just four entries:

Prefix Match	Link Interface
11001000 00010111 00010	0
11001000 00010111 00011000	1
11001000 00010111 00011	2
otherwise	3

With this style of forwarding table, the router matches a **prefix** of the packet's destination address with the entries in the table; if there's a match, the router forwards the packet to link associated with the match. For example, suppose the packet's destination address is 11001000 00010111 00010110 10100001; because the 21-bit prefix of this address matches the first entry in the table, the router forwards the packet to link interface 0. If a prefix doesn't match any of the first three entries, then the router forwards the packet to interface 3. Although this sounds simple enough, there's an important subtlety here. You may have noticed that it is possible for a destination address to match more than one entry. For example, the first 24 bits of the address 11001000 00010111 00011000 10101010 match the second entry in the table, and the first 21 bits of the address match the third entry in the table. When there are multiple matches, the router uses the **longest prefix matching rule**; that is, it finds the longest matching entry in the table and forwards the packet to the link interface associated with the longest prefix match.

Of course, for longest prefix matching to be effective, each output link interface should be responsible for forwarding large blocks of contiguous destination addresses. We'll see in Section 4.4 that Internet addresses are typically assigned in a hierarchical fashion so that this contiguous property is prevalent in the forwarding tables of most routers. Nevertheless, there is some concern within the Internet research community that more and more holes are being punctured into the address space, causing the contiguous blocks to get smaller and smaller and the forwarding tables to get larger and larger. (See [Maennel 2002], [RFC 3221], and the Principles in Practice discussion in Section 4.4.)

Although routers in datagram networks maintain no connection state information, they nevertheless maintain forwarding state information in their forwarding tables. However, the time scale at which this forwarding state information changes is relatively slow. Indeed, in a datagram network the forwarding tables are modified by the routing algorithms, which typically update a forwarding table every one-to-five minutes or so. In a VC network, a forwarding table in a router is modified whenever a new connection is setup through the router or whenever an existing connection through the router is torn down. This could easily happen at a microsecond timescale in a backbone, tier-1 router.

Because forwarding tables in datagram networks can be modified at any time, a series of packets sent from one end system to another may follow different paths through the network and may arrive out of order. [Paxson 1997] and [Jaiswal 2003] present interesting measurement studies of packet reordering and other phenomena in the public Internet.

4.2.3 Origins of VC and Datagram Networks

The evolution of datagram and VC networks reflects their origins. The notion of a virtual circuit as a central organizing principle has its roots in the telephony world, which uses real circuits. With call setup and per-call state being maintained at the routers within the network, a VC network is arguably more complex than a datagram network (although see [Molinero 2002] for an interesting comparison of the complexity of circuit- versus packet-switched networks). This, too, is in keeping with its telephony heritage. Telephone networks, by necessity, had their complexity within the network, since they were connecting dumb end-system devices such as rotary telephones. (For those too young to know, a rotary phone is an analog telephone with no buttons—only a dial.)

The Internet as a datagram network, on the other hand, grew out of the need to connect computers together. Given more sophisticated end-system devices, the Internet architects chose to make the network-layer service model as simple as possible. As we have already seen in Chapters 2 and 3, additional functionality (for example, in-order delivery, reliable data transfer, congestion control, and DNS name resolution) is then implemented at a higher layer, in the end systems. This inverts the model of the telephone network, with some interesting consequences.

♦ The resulting Internet network-layer service model, which makes minimal (no!) service guarantees (and hence imposes minimal requirements on the network layer), also makes it easier to interconnect networks that use very different link-layer technologies (for example, satellite, Ethernet, fiber, or radio) and have very different transmission rates and loss characteristics. We will address the interconnection of IP networks in detail in Section 4.4.

♦ As we saw in Chapter 2, applications such as e-mail, the Web, and even a network layer–centric service such as the DNS, are implemented in hosts (servers) at the edge of the network. The ability to add a new service simply by attaching a host to the network and defining a new application-layer protocol (such as HTTP) has allowed new applications such as the Web to be deployed in the Internet in a remarkably short period of time.

As we'll see in Chapter 7, there is considerable debate in the Internet community about how the Internet's network-layer architecture should evolve in order to support real-time services such as multimedia. An interesting comparison of the VC-oriented ATM network architecture and a proposed next generation Internet architecture is given in [Crowcroft 1995].

4.3   What's Inside a Router?

Now that we've seen an overview of the functions and services of the network layer, let's turn our attention to the network layer's **forwarding function**—the actual transfer of packets from a router's incoming links to the appropriate outgoing links. We already took a brief look at a few forwarding issues in Section 4.2, namely, addressing and longest prefix matching. In this section we'll look at specific router architectures for transferring packets from incoming links to outgoing links. Our coverage here is necessarily brief, as an entire course would be needed to cover router design in depth. Consequently, we'll make a special effort in this section to provide pointers to material that covers this topic in more depth. We mention here in passing that the words *forwarding* and *switching* are often used interchangeably by computer-networking researchers and practitioners; we'll use both terms in this textbook.

A high-level view of a generic router architecture is shown in Figure 4.6. Four components of a router can be identified.

♦ *Input ports.* The input port performs several functions. It performs the physical layer functions (the leftmost box of the input port and the rightmost box of the output port in Figure 4.6) of terminating an incoming physical link to a router. It performs the data link layer functions (represented by the middle boxes in the input and output ports) needed to interoperate with the data link layer functions at the remote side of

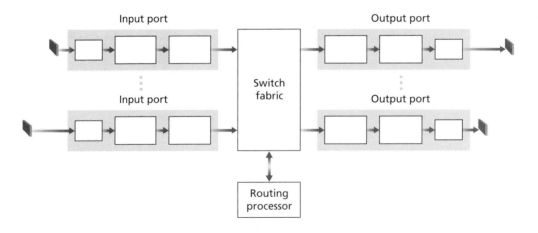

Figure 4.6 ♦ Router architecture

the incoming link. It also performs a lookup and forwarding function (the rightmost box of the input port and the leftmost box of the output port) so that a packet forwarded into the switching fabric of the router emerges at the appropriate output port. Control packets (for example, packets carrying routing protocol information) are forwarded from an input port to the routing processor. In practice, multiple ports are often gathered together on a single **line card** within a router.

♦ *Switching fabric.* The switching fabric connects the router's input ports to its output ports. This switching fabric is completely contained within the router—a network inside of a network router!

♦ *Output ports.* An output port stores the packets that have been forwarded to it through the switching fabric and then transmits the packets on the outgoing link. The output port thus performs the reverse data link and physical layer functionality of the input port. When a link is bidirectional (that is, carries traffic in both directions), an output port to the link will typically be paired with the input port for that link, on the same line card.

♦ *Routing processor.* The routing processor executes the routing protocols (for example, the protocols we study in Section 4.6), maintains the routing information and forwarding tables, and performs network management functions (see Chapter 9) within the router.

In the following subsections, we'll look at input ports, the switching fabric, and output ports in more detail. [Chao 2001; Turner 1988; Giacopelli 1990; McKeown 1997a; Partridge 1998] provide a discussion of some specific router architectures. [McKeown 1997b] provides a particularly readable overview of modern router architectures, using the Cisco 12000 router as an example. For concreteness, the ensuing discussion assumes that the computer network is a packet network, and that forwarding decisions are based on the packet's destination address (rather than a VC number in a virtual-circuit network). However, the concepts and techniques are similar for a virtual-circuit network.

4.3.1 Input Ports

A more detailed view of input port functionality is given in Figure 4.7. As discussed above, the input port's line termination function and data link processing implement the physical and data link layers associated with an individual input link to the router. The lookup/forwarding module in the input port is central to the forwarding function of the router. In many routers, it is here that the router determines the output port to which an arriving packet will be forwarded via the switching fabric. The choice of the output port is made using the information contained in the forwarding table. Although the forwarding table is computed by the routing processor, a shadow copy of the forwarding table is typically stored at each input port and updated, as

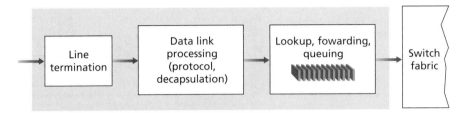

Figure 4.7 ♦ Input port processing

needed, by the routing processor. With local copies of the forwarding table, the forwarding decision can be made locally, at each input port, without invoking the centralized routing processor. Such *decentralized* forwarding avoids creating a forwarding processing bottleneck at a single point within the router.

In routers with limited processing capabilities at the input port, the input port may simply forward the packet to the centralized routing processor, which will then perform the forwarding table lookup and forward the packet to the appropriate output port. This is the approach taken when a workstation or a server serves as a

---

CASE HISTORY

CISCO SYSTEMS: DOMINATING THE NETWORK CORE

As of this writing (March 2004), Cisco employs more than 30,000 people and has a market capitalization of about $150 billion. Cisco currently dominates the Internet router market and in recent years has moved into the Internet telephony market, where it competes head-to-head with the telephone equipment companies, such as Lucent, Alcatel, Nortel, and Siemens. How did this gorilla of a networking company come to be? It all started in 1984 (only 20 years ago) in the living room of a Silicon Valley apartment.

Len Bosak and his wife Sandy Lerner were working at Stanford University when they had the idea to build and sell Internet routers to research and academic institutions. Sandy Lerner came up with the name Cisco (an abbreviation for San Francisco), and she also designed the company's bridge logo. Corporate headquarters was their living room, and they financed the project with credit cards and moonlighting consulting jobs. At the end of 1986, Cisco's revenues reached $250,000 a month. At the end of 1987, Cisco succeeded in attracting venture capital—$2 million dollars from Sequoia Capital in exchange for one third of the company. Over the next few years, Cisco continued to grow and grab more and more market share. At the same time, relations between Bosak/Lerner and Cisco management became strained. Cisco went public in 1990; in the same year Lerner and Bosak left the company.

router; here, the routing processor is really just the workstation's CPU, and the input port is really just a network interface card (for example, an Ethernet card).

Given the existence of a forwarding table, table lookup is conceptually simple—we just search through the forwarding table looking for the longest prefix match, as described in Section 4.2.2. In practice, however, life is not so simple. Perhaps the most important complicating factor is that backbone routers must operate at high speeds, performing millions of lookups per second. Indeed, it is desirable for the input port processing to be able to proceed at **line speed**, that is, for a lookup to be performed in less than the amount of time needed to receive a packet at the input port. In this case, input processing of a received packet can be completed before the next receive operation is complete. To get an idea of the performance requirements for a lookup, consider that a OC48 link runs at 2.5 Gbps. With packets 256 bytes long, this implies a lookup speed of approximately 1 million lookups per second.

Given the need to operate at today's high link speeds, a linear search through a large forwarding table is impossible. A more reasonable technique is to store the forwarding table entries in a tree data structure. Each level in the tree can be thought of as corresponding to a bit in the destination address. To look up an address, one simply starts at the root node of the tree. If the first address bit is a zero, then the left subtree will contain the forwarding table entry for the destination address; otherwise it will be in the right subtree. The appropriate subtree is then traversed using the remaining address bits—if the next address bit is a zero, the left subtree of the initial subtree is chosen; otherwise, the right subtree of the initial subtree is chosen. In this manner, one can look up the forwarding table entry in N steps, where N is the number of bits in the address. (Note that this is essentially a binary search through an address space of size 2^N.) An improvement over binary search techniques is described in [Srinivasan 1999], and a general survey of packet classification algorithms can be found in [Gupta 2001].

But even with $N = 32$ (for example, a 32-bit IP address) steps, the lookup speed via binary search is not fast enough for today's backbone routing requirements. For example, assuming a memory access at each step, fewer than a million address lookups per second could be performed with 40 ns memory access times. Several techniques have thus been explored to increase lookup speeds. **Content addressable memories (CAMs)** allow a 32-bit IP address to be presented to the CAM, which returns the content of the forwarding table entry for that address in essentially constant time. The Cisco 8500 series router [Cisco 8500 1999] has a 64K CAM for each input port.

Another technique for speeding up lookup is to keep recently accessed forwarding table entries in a cache [Feldmeier 1988]. Here, the concern is the potential size of the cache. Most recently, even faster data structures, which allow forwarding table entries to be located in $\log(N)$ steps [Waldvogel 1997], or which compress forwarding tables in novel ways [Brodnik 1997], have been proposed. A hardware-based approach to lookup that is optimized for the common case that the address being looked up has 24 or fewer significant bits is discussed in [Gupta 1998].

Once the output port for a packet has been determined via the lookup, the packet can be forwarded into the switching fabric. However, a packet may be temporarily blocked from entering the switching fabric (due to the fact that packets from other input ports are currently using the fabric). A blocked packet must thus be queued at the input port and then scheduled to cross the switching fabric at a later point in time. We'll take a closer look at the blocking, queuing, and scheduling of packets (at both input ports and output ports) within a router in Section 4.3.4.

4.3.2 Switching Fabric

The switching fabric is at the very heart of a router. It is through the switching fabric that the packets are actually switched (that is, forwarded) from an input port to an output port. Switching can be accomplished in a number of ways, as indicated in Figure 4.8.

♦ *Switching via memory.* The simplest, earliest routers were often traditional computers, with switching between input and output ports being done under direct

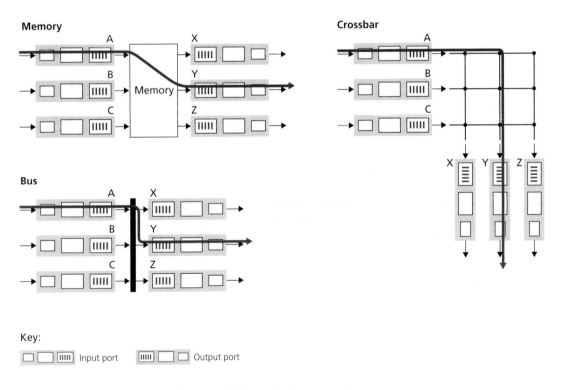

Key:

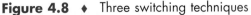

Figure 4.8 ♦ Three switching techniques

control of the CPU (routing processor). Input and output ports functioned as traditional I/O devices in a traditional operating system. An input port with an arriving packet first signaled the routing processor via an interrupt. The packet was then copied from the input port into processor memory. The routing processor then extracted the destination address from the header, looked up the appropriate output port in the forwarding table, and copied the packet to the output port's buffers. Note that if the memory bandwidth is such that B packets per second can be written into, or read from, memory, then the overall forwarding throughput (the total rate at which packets are transferred from input ports to output ports) must be less than $B/2$.

Many modern routers also switch via memory. A major difference from early routers, however, is that the lookup of the destination address and the storing of the packet into the appropriate memory location is performed by processors on the input line cards. In some ways, routers that switch via memory look very much like shared memory multiprocessors, with the processors on a line card switching packets into the memory of the appropriate output port. Cisco's Catalyst 8500 series switches [Cisco 8500 1999] and Bay Networks Accelar 1200 series routers forward packets via a shared memory. An abstract model for studying the properties of memory-based switching and a comparison with other forms of switching can be found in [Iyer 2002].

♦ *Switching via a bus.* In this approach, the input ports transfer a packet directly to the output port over a shared bus, without intervention by the routing processor (note that when switching via memory, the packet must also cross the system bus going to/from memory). Although the routing processor is not involved in the bus transfer, because the bus is shared only one packet at a time can be transferred over the bus. A packet arriving at an input port and finding the bus busy with the transfer of another packet is blocked from passing through the switching fabric and is queued at the input port. Because every packet must cross the single bus, the switching bandwidth of the router is limited to the bus speed.

Given that bus bandwidths of over 1 Gbps are possible in today's technology, switching via a bus is often sufficient for routers that operate in access and enterprise networks (for example, local area and corporate networks). Bus-based switching has been adopted in a number of current router products, including the Cisco 1900 [Cisco Switches 1999], which switches packets over a 1 Gbps Packet Exchange Bus. 3Com's CoreBuilder 5000 system [Kapoor 1997] interconnects ports that reside on different switch modules over its PacketChannel data bus, with a bandwidth of 2 Gbps.

♦ *Switching via an interconnection network.* One way to overcome the bandwidth limitation of a single, shared bus is to use a more sophisticated interconnection network, such as those that have been used in the past to interconnect processors in a multiprocessor computer architecture. A crossbar switch is an interconnection network consisting of $2n$ buses that connect n input ports to n output ports, as shown in Figure 4.8. A packet arriving at an input port travels along the horizontal bus attached to the input port until it intersects with the vertical bus leading to the desired output port. If the vertical bus leading to the output port is free, the packet is transferred to the output port. If the vertical bus is being used to transfer a packet from another input port to this same output port, the arriving packet is blocked and must be queued at the input port.

Delta and Omega switching fabrics have also been proposed as an interconnection network between input and output ports. See [Tobagi 1990] for a survey of switch architectures. Cisco 12000 Family switches [Cisco 12000 1998] use an interconnection network, providing up to 60 Gbps through the switching fabric. One current trend in interconnection network design [Keshav 1998] is to fragment a variable-length IP packet into fixed-length cells, then tag and switch the fixed-length cells through the interconnection network. The cells are then reassembled into the original packet at the output port. The fixed-length cell and internal tag can considerably simplify and speed up the switching of the packet through the interconnection network.

4.3.3 Output Ports

Output port processing, shown in Figure 4.9, takes the packets that have been stored in the output port's memory and transmits them over the outgoing link. The data link protocol processing and line termination are the send-side link- and physical-layer functionality that interact with the input port on the other end of the outgoing link, as discussed above in Section 4.3.1. The queuing and buffer management functionality are needed when the switch fabric delivers packets to the output port at a rate that exceeds the output link rate; we'll cover output port queuing below.

4.3.4 Where Does Queuing Occur?

If we look at the input and output port functionality and the configurations shown in Figure 4.8, it is evident that packet queues can form at both the input ports and the output ports. It is important to consider these queues in a bit more detail, since as

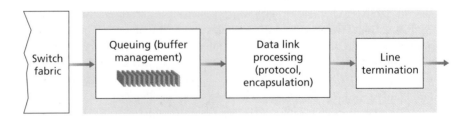

Figure 4.9 ◆ Output port processing

these queues grow large, the router's buffer space will eventually be exhausted and **packet loss** will occur. Recall that in our earlier discussions, we said that packets were lost within the network or dropped at a router. It is here, at these queues within a router, where such packets are actually dropped and lost. The actual location of packet loss (either at the input port queues or the output port queues) will depend on the traffic load, the relative speed of the switching fabric, and the line speed, as discussed below.

Suppose that the input line speeds and output line speeds are all identical, and that there are n input ports and n output ports. Define the **switching fabric speed** as the rate at which the switching fabric can move packets from input ports to output ports. If the switching fabric speed is at least n times as fast as the input line speed, then no queuing can occur at the input ports. This is because even in the worst case, where all n input lines are receiving packets, the switch will be able to transfer n packets from input port to output port in the time it takes each of the n input ports to (simultaneously) receive a *single* packet. But what can happen at the output ports? Let us suppose still that the switching fabric is at least n times as fast as the line speeds. In the worst case, the packets arriving at each of the n input ports will be destined to the *same* output port. In this case, in the time it takes to receive (or send) a single packet, n packets will arrive at this output port. Since the output port can transmit only a single packet in a unit of time (the packet transmission time), the n arriving packets will have to queue (wait) for transmission over the outgoing link. Then n more packets can possibly arrive in the time it takes to transmit just one of the n packets that had previously been queued. And so on. Eventually, the number of queued packets can grow large enough to exhaust the memory space at the output port, in which case packets are dropped.

Output port queuing is illustrated in Figure 4.10. At time t, a packet has arrived at each of the incoming input ports, each destined for the uppermost outgoing port. Assuming identical line speeds and a switch operating at three times the line speed, one time unit later (that is, in the time needed to receive or send a packet), all three original packets have been transferred to the outgoing port and are queued awaiting transmission. In the next time unit, one of these three packets will have been transmitted over the outgoing link. In our example, two *new* packets have arrived at the incoming side of the switch; one of these packets is destined for this uppermost output port.

A consequence of output port queuing is that a **packet scheduler** at the output port must choose one packet among those queued for transmission. This selection might be done on a simple basis, such as first-come-first-served (FCFS) scheduling, or a more sophisticated scheduling discipline such as weighted fair queuing (WFQ), which shares the outgoing link fairly among the different end-to-end connections that have packets queued for transmission. Packet scheduling plays a crucial role in providing **quality-of-service guarantees**. We'll thus cover packet scheduling extensively in Chapter 7. A discussion of output port packet scheduling disciplines is [Cisco Queue 1995].

Output port contention at time t

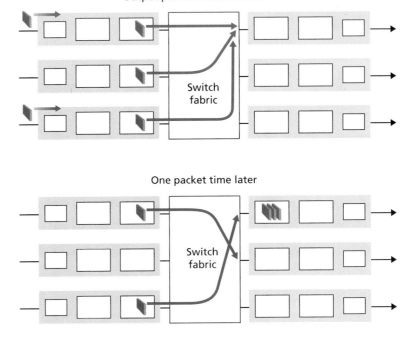

One packet time later

Figure 4.10 ♦ Output port queuing

Similarly, if there is not enough memory to buffer an incoming packet, a decision must be made to either drop the arriving packet (a policy known as **drop-tail**) or remove one or more already-queued packets to make room for the newly arrived packet. In some cases, it may be advantageous to drop (or mark the header of) a packet *before* the buffer is full in order to provide a congestion signal to the sender. A number of packet-dropping and -marking policies (which collectively have become known as **active queue management (AQM)** algorithms) have been proposed and analyzed [Labrador 1999, Hollot 2002]. One of the most widely studied and implemented AQM algorithms is the **Random Early Detection (RED)** algorithm. Under RED, a weighted average is maintained for the length of the output queue. If the average queue length is less than a minimum threshold, min_{th}, when a packet arrives, the packet is admitted to the queue. Conversely, if the queue is full or the average queue length is greater than a maximum threshold, max_{th}, when a packet arrives, the packet is marked or dropped. Finally, if the packet arrives to find an average queue length in the interval $[min_{th}, max_{th}]$, the packet is marked or dropped with a probability that is typically some function of the average queue length, min_{th}, and max_{th}. A number of probabilistic marking/dropping functions have been proposed, and various versions of RED have been analytically modeled, simulated, and/or implemented. [Christiansen 2001] and [Floyd 2004] provide overviews and pointers to additional reading.

If the switch fabric is not fast enough (relative to the input line speeds) to transfer *all* arriving packets through the fabric without delay, then packet queuing can also occur at the input ports, as packets must join input port queues to wait their turn to be transferred through the switching fabric to the output port. To illustrate an important consequence of this queuing, consider a crossbar switching fabric and suppose that (1) all link speeds are identical, (2) that one packet can be transferred from any one input port to a given output port in the same amount of time it takes for a packet to be received on an input link, and (3) packets are moved from a given input queue to their desired output queue in an FCFS manner. Multiple packets can be transferred in parallel, as long as their output ports are different. However, if two packets at the front of two input queues are destined for the same output queue, then one of the packets will be blocked and must wait at the input queue—the switching fabric can transfer only one packet to a given output port at a time.

Figure 4.11 shows an example in which two packets (shaded dark blue) at the front of their input queues are destined for the same upper-right output port. Suppose that the switch fabric chooses to transfer the packet from the front of the upper-left queue. In this case, the dark blue packet in the lower-left queue must wait. But not only must this dark blue packet wait, so too must the light blue packet that is queued behind that packet in the lower-left queue, even though there is *no* contention for the middle-right output port (the destination for the light blue packet). This phenomenon is known as **head-of-the-line (HOL) blocking** in an input-queued switch— a queued packet in an input queue must wait for transfer through the fabric (even though its output port is free) because it is blocked by another packet at the head of the line. [Karol 1987] shows that due to HOL blocking, the input queue will grow to unbounded length (informally, this is equivalent to saying that significant packet loss will occur) under certain assumptions as soon as the packet arrival rate on the input links reaches only 58 percent of their capacity. A number of solutions to HOL blocking are discussed in [McKeown 1997b].

4.4 The Internet Protocol (IP): Forwarding and Addressing in the Internet

Our discussion of network-layer addressing and forwarding thus far has been without reference to any specific computer network. In this section, we'll turn our attention to how addressing and forwarding are done in the Internet. We'll see that Internet addressing and forwarding are important components of the Internet Protocol (IP). There are two versions of IP in use today. We'll first examine the widely

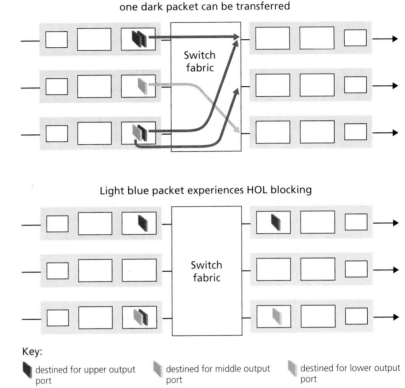

Figure 4.11 ◆ HOL blocking at an input queued switch

deployed IP protocol version 4, which is usually referred to simply as IPv4 [RFC 791]. We'll examine IP version 6 [RFC 2373; RFC 2460], which has been proposed to replace IPv4, at the end of this section.

But before beginning our foray into IP, let's take a step back and consider the components that make up the Internet's network layer. As shown in Figure 4.12, the Internet's network layer has three major components. The first component is the IP protocol, the topic of this section. The second major component is the routing component, which determines the path a datagram follows from source to destination. We mentioned earlier that routing protocols compute the forwarding tables that are used to forward packets through the network. We'll study the Internet's routing protocols in Section 4.6. The final component of the network layer is a facility to report errors in datagrams and respond to requests for certain network-layer information. We'll cover the Internet's network-layer error- and information-reporting protocol, the Internet Control Message Protocol (ICMP), in Section 4.4.3.

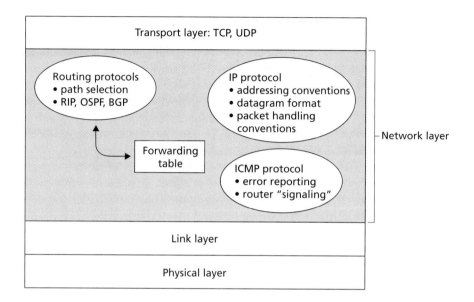

Figure 4.12 ♦ A look inside the Internet's network layer

4.4.1 Datagram Format

Recall that a network-layer packet is referred to as a *datagram*. We begin our study of IP with an overview of the syntax and semantics of the IPv4 datagram. You might be thinking that nothing could be drier than the syntax and semantics of a packet's bits. Nevertheless, the datagram plays a central role in the Internet—every networking student and professional needs to see it, absorb it, and master it. The IPv4 datagram format is shown in Figure 4.13. The key fields in the IPv4 datagram are the following:

♦ *Version number.* These 4 bits specify the IP protocol version of the datagram. By looking at the version number, the router can determine how to interpret the remainder of the IP datagram. Different versions of IP use different datagram formats. The datagram format for the current version of IP, IPv4, is shown in Figure 4.13. The datagram format for the new version of IP (IPv6) is discussed in at the end of this section.

♦ *Header length.* Because an IPv4 datagram can contain a variable number of options (which are included in the IPv4 datagram header) these 4 bits are needed to determine where in the IP datagram the data actually begins. Most IP datagrams do not contain options so the typical IP datagram has a 20-byte header.

♦ *Type of service.* The type of service (TOS) bits were included in the IPv4 header to allow different types of IP datagrams (for example, datagrams particularly requiring

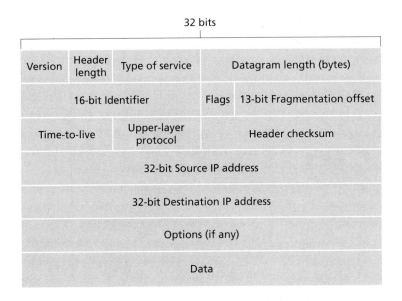

32 bits

Version	Header length	Type of service	Datagram length (bytes)	
16-bit Identifier			Flags	13-bit Fragmentation offset
Time-to-live		Upper-layer protocol	Header checksum	
32-bit Source IP address				
32-bit Destination IP address				
Options (if any)				
Data				

Figure 4.13 ♦ IPv4 datagram format

low delay, high throughput, or reliability) to be distinguished from each other. For example, it might be useful to distinguish real-time datagrams (such as those used by an IP telephony application) from non-real-time traffic (for example, FTP). One major routing vendor (Cisco) interprets the first three TOS bits as defining differential levels of service that can be provided by the router. The specific level of service to be provided is a policy issue determined by the router's administrator. We'll explore the topic of differentiated service in detail in Chapter 7.

♦ *Datagram length.* This is the total length of the IP datagram (header plus data), measured in bytes. Since this field is 16 bits long, the theoretical maximum size of the IP datagram is 65,535 bytes. However, datagrams are rarely larger than 1,500 bytes.

♦ *Identifier, flags, fragmentation offset.* These three fields have to do with so-called IP fragmentation, a topic we will consider in depth shortly. Interestingly, the new version of IP, IPv6, does not allow for fragmentation at routers.

♦ *Time-to-live.* The time-to-live (TTL) field is included to ensure that datagrams do not circulate forever (due to, for example, a long-lived routing loop) in the network. This field is decremented by one each time the datagram is processed by a router. If the TTL field reaches 0, the datagram must be dropped.

♦ *Protocol.* This field is used only when an IP datagram reaches its final destination. The value of this field indicates the specific transport-layer protocol to which the data portion of this IP datagram should be passed. For example, a value of 6 indicates that the data portion is passed to TCP, while a value of 17 indicates that the data is passed to UDP. For a list of all possible values, see [RFC 1700; RFC 3232]. Note that the protocol number in the IP datagram has a role that is analogous to the role of the port number field in the transport-layer segment. The protocol number is the glue that binds the network and transport layers together, whereas the port number is the glue that binds the transport and application layers together. We'll see in Chapter 5 that the link-layer frame also has a special field that binds the link layer to the network layer.

♦ *Header checksum.* The header checksum aids a router in detecting bit errors in a received IP datagram. The header checksum is computed by treating each 2 bytes in the header as a number and summing these numbers using 1s complement arithmetic. As discussed in Section 3.3, the 1s complement of this sum, known as the Internet checksum, is stored in the checksum field. A router computes the header checksum for each received IP datagram and detects an error condition if the checksum carried in the datagram header does not equal the computed checksum. Routers typically discard datagrams for which an error has been detected. Note that the checksum must be recomputed and stored again at each router, as the TTL field, and possibly options fields as well, may change. An interesting discussion of fast algorithms for computing the Internet checksum is [RFC 1071]. A question often asked at this point is, why does TCP/IP perform error checking at both the transport and network layers? There are several reasons for this repetition. First, note that only the IP header is checksummed at the IP layer, while the TCP/UDP checksum is computed over the entire TCP/UDP segment. Second, TCP/UDP and IP do not necessarily both have to belong to the same protocol stack. TCP can, in principle, run over a different protocol (for example, ATM) and IP can carry data that will not be passed to TCP/UDP.

♦ *Source and destination IP addresses.* When a source creates a datagram, it inserts its IP address into the source IP address field and inserts the address of the ultimate destination into the destination IP address field. Often the source host determines the destination address via a DNS lookup, as discussed in Chapter 2. We'll discuss IP addressing in detail in Section 4.4.2.

♦ *Options.* The options fields allow an IP header to be extended. Header options were meant to be used rarely—hence the decision to save overhead by not including the information in options fields in every datagram header. However, the mere existence of options does complicate matters—since datagram headers can be of variable length, one cannot determine a priori where the data field will start. Also, since some datagrams may require options processing and others may not, the amount of time needed to process an IP datagram at a router can vary greatly. These considerations become particularly important for IP processing in high-performance routers and hosts. For these reasons and others, IP options were dropped in the IPv6 header, as discussed in Section 4.4.4.

♦ *Data (payload).* Finally, we come to the last and most important field—the *raison d'être* for the datagram in the first place! In most circumstances, the data field of the IP datagram contains the transport-layer segment (TCP or UDP) to be delivered to the destination. However, the data field can carry other types of data, such as ICMP messages (discussed in Section 4.4.3).

Note that an IP datagram has a total of 20 bytes of header (assuming no options). If the datagram carries a TCP segment, then each (nonfragmented) datagram carries a total of 40 bytes of header (20 bytes of IP header plus 20 bytes of TCP header) along with the application-layer message.

IP Datagram Fragmentation

We'll see in Chapter 5 that not all link-layer protocols can carry network-layer packets of the same size. Some protocols can carry big datagrams, whereas other protocols can carry only little packets. For example, Ethernet frames can carry up to 1,500 bytes of data, whereas frames for some wide-area links can carry no more than 576 bytes. The maximum amount of data that a link-layer frame can carry is called the maximum transmission unit (MTU). Because each IP datagram is encapsulated within the link-layer frame for transport from one router to the next router, the MTU of the link-layer protocol places a hard limit on the length of an IP datagram. Having a hard limit on the size of an IP datagram is not much of a problem. What is a problem is that each of the links along the route between sender and destination can use different link-layer protocols, and each of these protocols can have different MTUs.

To understand the forwarding issue better, imagine that *you* are a router that interconnects several links, each running different link-layer protocols with different MTUs. Suppose you receive an IP datagram from one link. You check your forwarding table to determine the outgoing link, and this outgoing link has an MTU that is smaller than the length of the IP datagram. Time to panic—how are you going to squeeze this oversized IP datagram into the payload field of the link-layer frame? The solution is to fragment the data in the IP datagram into two or more smaller IP datagrams, then send these smaller datagrams over the outgoing link. Each of these smaller datagrams is referred to as a **fragment.**

Fragments need to be reassembled before they reach the transport layer at the destination. Indeed, both TCP and UDP are expecting to receive complete, unfragmented segments from the network layer. The designers of IPv4 felt that reassembling datagrams in the routers would introduce significant complication into the protocol and put a damper on router performance. (If you were a router, would you want to be reassembling fragments on top of everything else you had to do?) Sticking to the principle of keeping the network core simple, the designers of IPv4 decided to put the job of datagram reassembly in the end systems rather than in network routers.

When a destination host receives a series of datagrams from the same source, it needs to determine whether any of these datagrams are fragments of some original, larger datagram. If some datagrams are fragments, it must further determine when it has received the last fragment and how the fragments it has received should be pieced back together to form the original datagram. To allow the destination host to perform these reassembly tasks, the designers of IP (version 4) put *identification, flag,* and *fragmentation offset* fields in the IP datagram. When a datagram is created, the sending host stamps the datagram with an identification number as well as source and destination addresses. Typically, the sending host increments the identification number for each datagram it sends. When a router needs to fragment a datagram, each resulting datagram (that is, fragment) is stamped with the source address, destination address, and identification number of the original datagram. When the destination receives a series of datagrams from the same sending host, it can examine the identification numbers of the datagrams to determine which of the datagrams are actually fragments of the same larger datagram. Because IP is an unreliable service, one or more of the fragments may never arrive at the destination. For this reason, in order for the destination host to be absolutely sure it has received the last fragment of the original datagram, the last fragment has a flag bit set to 0, whereas all the other fragments have this flag bit set to 1. Also, in order for the destination host to determine whether a fragment is missing (and also to be able to reassemble the fragments in their proper order), the offset field is used to specify where the fragment fits within the original IP datagram.

Figure 4.14 illustrates an example. A datagram of 4,000 bytes (20 bytes of IP header plus 3,980 bytes of IP payload) arrives at a router and must be forwarded to a link with an MTU of 1,500 bytes. This implies that the 3,980 data bytes in the original datagram must be allocated to three separate fragments (each of which is also an IP datagram). Suppose that the original datagram is stamped with an identification number of 777. The characteristics of the three fragments are shown in Table 4.2. The values in Table 4.2 reflect the requirement that the amount of original payload data in all but the last fragment be a multiple of 8 bytes, and that the offset value be specified in units of 8-byte chunks.

The payload of the datagram is passed to the transport layer at the destination only after the IP layer has fully reconstructed the original IP datagram. If one or more of the fragments does not arrive at the destination, the incomplete datagram is discarded and not passed to the transport layer. But, as we learned in the previous chapter, if TCP is being used at the transport layer, then TCP will recover from this loss by having the source retransmit the data in the original datagram.

At this book's Web site, we provide a Java applet that generates fragments. You provide the incoming datagram size, the MTU, and the incoming datagram identification. It automatically generates the fragments for you. See http://www.awl .com/kurose-ross.

Fragment	Bytes	ID	Offset	Flag
1st fragment	1,480 bytes in the data field of the IP datagram	identification = 777	offset = 0 (meaning the data should be inserted beginning at byte 0)	flag = 1 (meaning there is more)
2nd fragment	1,480 bytes of data	identification = 777	offset = 185 (meaning the data should be inserted beginning at byte 1,480. Note that 185 · 8 = 1,480)	flag = 1 (meaning there is more)
3rd fragment	1,020 bytes (= 3,980−1,480−1,480) of data	identification = 777	offset = 370 (meaning the data should be inserted beginning at byte 2,960. Note that 370 · 8 = 2960)	flag = 0 (meaning this is the last fragment)

Table 4.2 ◆ IP fragments

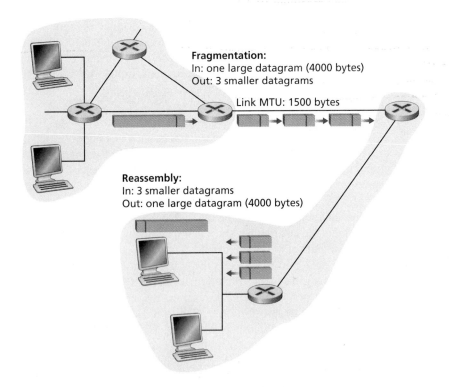

Fragmentation:
In: one large datagram (4000 bytes)
Out: 3 smaller datagrams

Link MTU: 1500 bytes

Reassembly:
In: 3 smaller datagrams
Out: one large datagram (4000 bytes)

Figure 4.14 ◆ IP fragmentation and reassembly

4.4.2 IPv4 Addressing

We now turn our attention to IPv4 addressing. Although you may be thinking that addressing must be a straightforward topic, hopefully by the end of this chapter you'll be convinced that Internet addressing is not only a juicy, subtle, and interesting topic but also one that is of central importance to the Internet. Excellent treatments of IPv4 addressing are [Semeria 1996] and the first chapter in [Stewart 1999].

Before discussing IP addressing, however, we'll need to say a few words about how hosts and routers are connected into the network. A host typically has only a single link into the network; when IP in the host wants to send a datagram, it does so over this link. The boundary between the host and the physical link is called an **interface**. Now consider a router and its interfaces. Because a router's job is to receive a datagram on one link and forward the datagram on some other link, a router necessarily has two or more links to which it is connected. The boundary between the router and any one of its links is also called an interface. A router thus has multiple interfaces, one for each of its links. Because every host and router is capable of sending and receiving IP datagrams, IP requires each host and router interface to have its own IP address. Thus, an IP address is technically associated with an interface, rather than with the host or router containing that interface.

Each IP address is 32 bits long (equivalently, 4 bytes), and there are thus a total of 2^{32} possible IP addresses. By approximating 2^{10} by 10^3, it is easy to see that there are about 4 billion possible IP addresses. These addresses are typically written in so-called **dotted-decimal notation**, in which each byte of the address is written in its decimal form and is separated by a period (dot) from other bytes in the address. For example, consider the IP address 193.32.216.9. The 193 is the decimal equivalent of the first 8 bits of the address; the 32 is the decimal equivalent of the second 8 bits of the address, and so on. Thus, the address 193.32.216.9 in binary notation is

$$11000001\ 00100000\ 11011000\ 00001001$$

Each interface on every host and router in the global Internet must have an IP address that is globally unique (except for interfaces behind NATs, as discussed at the end of this section). These addresses cannot be chosen in a willy-nilly manner, however. A portion of an interface's IP address will be determined by the subnet to which it is connected.

Figure 4.15 provides an example of IP addressing and interfaces. In this figure, one router (with three interfaces) is used to interconnect seven hosts. Take a close look at the IP addresses assigned to the host and router interfaces; there are several things to notice. The three hosts in the upper-left portion of Figure 4.15, and the router interface to which they are connected, all have an IP address of the form 223.1.1.xxx. That is, they all have the same leftmost 24 bits in their IP address. The four interfaces are also interconnected to each other by a network *that contains no routers*. (This network could be, for example, an Ethernet LAN, in which case the interfaces would be interconnected by an Ethernet hub or an Ethernet switch; see Chapter 5.) In IP terms, this network interconnecting three host interfaces and one router interface forms a **subnet** [RFC 950]. (A subnet also called an *IP network* or simply a *network* in the Internet literature.) IP addressing assigns an address to this subnet: 223.1.1.0/24, where the /24 notation, sometimes known as a **subnet mask**, indicates that the leftmost 24 bits of the 32-bit quantity define the subnet address. The subnet 223.1.1.0/24 thus consists of the three host interfaces (223.1.1.1, 223.1.1.2, and 223.1.1.3) and one router interface (223.1.1.4). Any additional hosts attached to the 223.1.1.0/24 subnet would be *required* to have an address of the form 223.1.1.xxx. There are two additional subnets shown in Figure 4.15: the 223.1.2.0/24 network and the 223.1.3.0/24 subnet. Figure 4.16 illustrates the three IP subnets present in Figure 4.15.

The IP definition of a subnet is not restricted to Ethernet segments that connect multiple hosts to a router interface. To get some insight here, consider Figure 4.17, which shows three routers that are interconnected with each other by point-to-point links. Each router has three interfaces, one for each point-to-point link and one for the broadcast link that directly connects the router to a pair of hosts. What subnets are present here? Three subnets, 223.1.1.0/24, 223.1.2.0/24, and 223.1.3.0/24 are similar to the subnets we encountered in Figure 4.15. But note that there are three additional subnets in this example as well: one subnet, 223.1.9.0/24, for the interfaces that connect routers R1 and R2; another subnet, 223.1.8.0/24, for the interfaces that

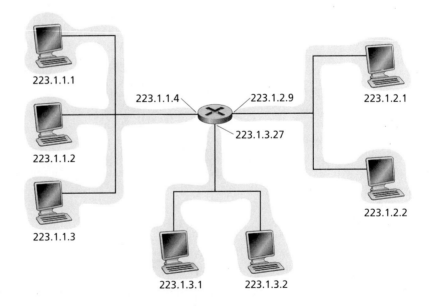

Figure 4.15 ♦ Interface addresses and subnets

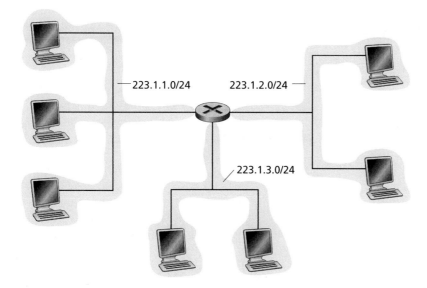

Figure 4.16 ♦ Subnet addresses

connect routers R2 and R3; and a third subnet, 223.1.7.0/24, for the interfaces that connect routers R3 and R1. For a general interconnected system of routers and hosts, we can use the following recipe to define the subnets in the system.

> *To determine the subnets, detach each interface from its host or router, creating islands of isolated networks, with interfaces terminating the endpoints of the isolated networks. Each of these isolated networks is called a* **subnet***.*

If we apply this procedure to the interconnected system in Figure 4.17, we get six islands or subnets.

From the discussion above, it's clear that an organization (such as a company or academic institution) with multiple Ethernet segments and point-to-point links will have multiple subnets, with all of the devices on a given subnet having the same subnet address. In principle, the different subnets could have quite different subnet addresses. In practice, however, their subnet addresses often have much in common. To understand why, let's next turn our attention to how addressing is handled in the global Internet.

The Internet's address assignment strategy is known as **Classless Interdomain Routing (CIDR**—pronounced *cider*) [RFC 1519]. CIDR generalizes the notion of subnet addressing. As with subnet addressing, the 32-bit IP address is divided into two parts and again has the dotted-decimal form *a.b.c.d/x*, where *x* indicates the number of bits in the first part of the address.

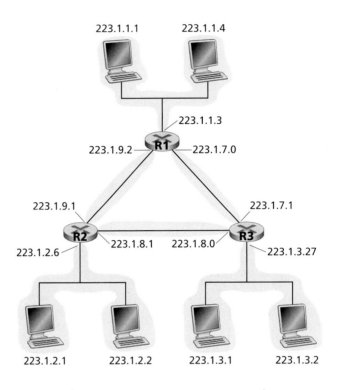

Figure 4.17 ◆ Three routers interconnecting six subnets

The *x* most significant bits of an address of the form *a.b.c.d/x* constitute the network portion of the IP address, and are often referred to as the **prefix** (or *network prefix*) of the address. An organization is typically assigned a block of contiguous addresses, that is, a range of addresses with a common prefix (see Principles in Practice sidebar). In this case, the IP addresses of devices within the organization will share the common prefix. When we cover the Internet's BGP routing protocol in Section 4.6, we'll see that only these *x* leading prefix bits are considered by routers outside the organization's network. That is, when a router outside the organization forwards a datagram whose destination address is inside the organization, only the leading *x* bits of the address need be considered. This considerably reduces the size of the forwarding table in these routers, since a *single* entry of the form *a.b.c.d/x* will be sufficient to forward packets to *any* destination within the organization.

The remaining 32-*x* bits of an address can be thought of as distinguishing among the devices *within* the organization, all of which have the same network prefix. These are the bits that will be considered when forwarding packets at routers *within* the organization. These lower-order bits may (or may not) have an additional subnetting structure, such as that discussed above. For example, suppose the first 21 bits of the CIDRized address *a.b.c.d/21* specify the organization's network prefix and are common to the IP addresses of all devices in that organization. The remaining 11 bits then identify the specific hosts in the organization. The organization's internal structure might be such that these 11 rightmost bits are used for subnetting within the organization, as discussed above. For example, *a.b.c.d/24* might refer to a specific subnet within the organization.

Before CIDR was adopted, the network portions of an IP address were constrained to be 8, 16, or 24 bits in length, an addressing scheme known as **classful addressing**, since subnets with an 8-, 16-, and 24-bit subnet addresses were known as class A, B, and C networks, respectively. The requirement that the subnet portion of an IP address be exactly 1, 2, or 3 bytes long turned out to be problematic for supporting the rapidly growing number of organizations with small and medium-sized subnets. A class C (/24) subnet could accommodate only up to $2^8 - 2 = 254$ hosts (two of the $2^8 = 256$ addresses are reserved for special use)—too small for many organizations. However, a class B (/16) subnet, which supports up 65,634 hosts, was too large. Under classful addressing, an organization with, say, 2,000 hosts was typically allocated a class B (/16) subnet address. This led to a rapid depletion of the class B address space and poor utilization of the assigned address space. For example, the organization that used a class B address for its 2,000 hosts was allocated enough of the address space for up to 65,534 interfaces—leaving more than 63,000 addresses that could not be used by other organizations.

We would be remiss if we did not mention yet another type of IP address, the IP broadcast address 255.255.255.255. When a host emits a datagram with destination address 255.255.255.255, the message is delivered to all hosts on the same subnet. Routers optionally forward the message into neighboring subnets as well (although they usually don't). In Chapter 5 we'll look at an example of how IP broadcast is used when discussing the DHCP protocol.

Having now studied IP addressing in detail, we need to know how hosts and subnets get their addresses in the first place. Let's begin by looking at how an organization gets a block of addresses for its devices, and then look at how a device (such as a host) is assigned an address from with the organization's block of addresses.

Obtaining a Block of Addresses

In order to obtain a block of IP addresses for use within an organization's subnet, a network administrator might first contact its ISP, which would provide addresses from a larger block of addresses that had already been allocated to the ISP. For example, the ISP may itself have been allocated the address block 200.23.16.0/20. The ISP, in turn, could divide its address block into eight equal-sized contiguous address blocks and give one of these address blocks out to each of up to eight organizations that are supported by this ISP, as shown below. (We have underlined the subnet part of these addresses for your convenience.)

ISP's block	200.23.16.0/20	<u>11001000 00010111 0001</u>0000 00000000
Organization 0	200.23.16.0/23	<u>11001000 00010111 0001000</u>0 00000000
Organization 1	200.23.18.0/23	<u>11001000 00010111 0001001</u>0 00000000
Organization 2	200.23.20.0/23	<u>11001000 00010111 0001010</u>0 00000000
. . . . . .		. . .
Organization 7	200.23.30.0/23	<u>11001000 00010111 0001111</u>0 00000000

PRINCIPLES IN PRACTICE

This example of an ISP that connects eight organizations to the Internet nicely illustrates how carefully allocated CIDRized addresses facilitate routing. Suppose, as shown in Figure 4.18, that the ISP (which we'll call Fly-By-Night-ISP) advertises to the outside world that it should be sent any datagrams whose first 20 address bits match 200.23.16.0/20. The rest of the world need not know that within the address block 200.23.16.0/20 there are in fact eight other organizations, each with their own subnets. This ability to use a single prefix to advertise multiple networks is often referred to as **address aggregation** (also **route aggregation** or **route summarization**).

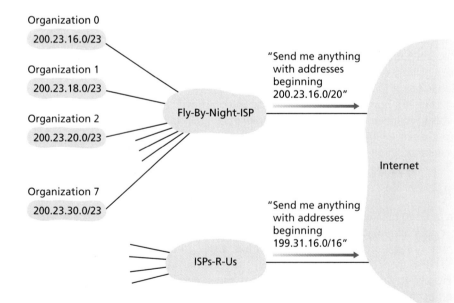

Figure 4.18 ♦ Hierarchical addressing and route aggregation

Address aggregation works extremely well when addresses are allocated in blocks to ISPs and then from ISPs to client organizations. But what happens when addresses are not allocated in such a hierarchical manner? What would happen, for example, if Fly-by-Night-ISP acquires ISPs-R-Us and then has Organization 1 connect to the Internet through its subsidiary ISPs-R-Us? As shown in Figure 4.18, the subsidiary ISPs-R-Us owns the address block 199.31.0.0/16, but Organization 1's IP addresses are unfortunately outside of this address block. What should be done here? Certainly, Organization 1 could renumber all of its routers and hosts to have addresses within the ISPs-R-Us address block. But this is a costly solution, and Organization 1 might well be re-assigned to another subsidiary in the future. The solution typically adopted is for Organization 1 to keep its IP addresses in 200.23.18.0/23. In this case, as shown in Figure 4.19, Fly-By-Night-ISP continues to advertise the address block 200.23.16.0/20 and ISPs-R-Us continues to advertise 199.31.0.0/16. However, ISPs-R-Us now *also* advertises the block of addresses for Organization 1, 200.23.18.0/23. When other routers in the larger Internet see the address blocks 200.23.16.0/20 (from Fly-By-Night-ISP) and 200.23.18.0/23 (from ISPs-R-Us) and want to route to an address in the block 200.23.18.0/23, they will use longest prefix matching (see Section 4.2.2), and route toward ISPs-R-Us, as it advertises the longest (most specific) address prefix that matches the destination address.

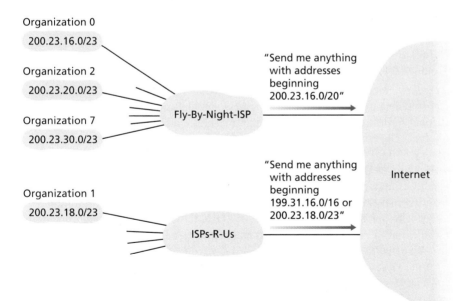

Figure 4.19 ♦ ISPs-R-Us has a more specific route to Organization 1

While obtaining a set of addresses from an ISP is one way to get a block of addresses, it is not the only way. Clearly, there must also be a way for the ISP itself to get a block of addresses. Is there a global authority that has ultimate responsibility for managing the IP address space and allocating address blocks to ISPs and other organizations? Indeed there is! IP addresses are managed under the authority of the Internet Corporation for Assigned Names and Numbers (ICANN) [ICANN 2004], based on guidelines set forth in RFC 2050. The role of the nonprofit ICANN organization [NTIA 1998] is not only to allocate IP addresses, but also to manage the DNS root servers. It also has the very contentious job of assigning domain names and resolving domain name disputes. The ICANN allocates addresses to regional Internet registries (for example, ARIN, RIPE, APNIC, and LACNIC, which together form the Address Supporting Organization of ICANN [ASO-ICANN 2004]), which handle the allocation/management of addresses within their regions.

Obtaining a Host Address

Once an organization has obtained a block of addresses, it can assign individual IP addresses to the host and router interfaces in its organization. For the router interface addresses, the system administrator manually configures the IP addresses into the router (often remotely, with a network management tool). There are two ways in which a host can be assigned an IP address:

♦ *Manual configuration.* A system administrator manually configures the IP address into the host (typically in a file).

♦ *Dynamic Host Configuration Protocol (DHCP) [RFC 2131].* DHCP allows a host to obtain (be allocated) an IP address automatically, as well as to learn additional information, such as its subnet mask, the address of its first-hop router (often called the default gateway), and the address of its local DNS server.

Because of DHCP's ability to automate the network-related aspects of connecting a host into a network, it is often referred to as a **plug-and-play protocol**. This capability makes it *very* attractive to the network administrator who would otherwise have to perform these tasks manually! DHCP is also enjoying widespread use in residential Internet access networks and in wireless LANs, where hosts join and leave the network frequently.

A network administrator can configure DHCP so that a given host receives a persistent IP address, so that each time the host joins the network it is assigned the same IP address. But many organizations and residential ISPs do not have enough IP addresses for all of their hosts. When this is the case, DHCP is used to assign each of its connecting hosts a **temporary IP address**. As an example, consider a residential ISP that has 2,000 customers, but no more than 400 of these customers are ever online at the same time. To handle all of its 2,000 customers, the ISP doesn't need a block of 2,000 addresses. Instead, by using a DHCP server to assign addresses dynamically, it only needs a block of 512 addresses (for example, a block of the form a.b.c.d/23). As the hosts join and leave, the DHCP server needs to update its list of available IP addresses. Each time a host joins, the DHCP server allocates an arbitrary address from its current pool of available addresses; each time a host leaves, an address is returned to the pool.

Another important reason why DHCP has found such widespread use is the advent of mobile computing. Consider, for example, the student who carries a laptop from a dormitory room to a library to a classroom. It is likely that in each location, the student will be connecting into a new subnet and hence will need a new IP address at each location. DHCP is ideally suited to this situation, as there are many users coming and going, and addresses are needed for only a limited amount of time.

The DHCP protocol actually straddles the boundary between the network and link layers in the five-layer Internet protocol stack. We'll therefore delay a detailed discussion of how the DHCP service is implemented until Chapter 5, which covers the link layer.

Network Address Translation (NAT)

Given our discussion about Internet addresses and the IPv4 datagram format, we're now well aware that every IP-capable device needs an IP address. With the proliferation of small office, home office (SOHO) subnets, this would seem to imply that whenever a SOHO wants to install a LAN to connect multiple machines, a range of addresses would need to be allocated by the ISP to cover all of the SOHO's machines. If the subnet grew bigger (for example, the kids at home have not only their own computers, but have bought handheld PDAs, IP-capable phones, and networked Game Boys as well), a larger block of addresses would have to be allocated. But what if the ISP had already allocated the contiguous portions of the SOHO network's current address range? And what typical homeowner wants (or should need) to know how to manage IP addresses in the first place? Fortunately, there is a simpler approach to address allocation that has found increasingly widespread use in such scenarios: **network address translation** (**NAT**) [RFC 2663; RFC 3022].

Figure 4.20 shows the operation of a NAT-enabled router. The NAT-enabled router, residing in the home, has an interface that is part of the home network on the right of Figure 4.20. Addressing within the home network is exactly as we have seen above—all four interfaces in the home network have the same subnet address of 10.0.0/24. The address space 10.0.0.0/8 is one of three portions of the IP address space that is reserved in [RFC 1918] for a private network or a **realm** with private addresses, such as the home network in Figure 4.20. A *realm with private addresses* refers to a network whose addresses only have meaning to devices within that network. To see why this is important, consider the fact that there are hundreds of thousands of home networks, many using the same address space, 10.0.0.0/24. Devices within a given home network can send packets to each other using 10.0.0.0/24 addressing. However, packets forwarded *beyond* the home network into the larger global Internet clearly cannot use these addresses (as either a source or a destination address) because there are hundreds of thousands of networks using this block of addresses. That is, the 10.0.0.0/24 addresses can only have meaning within the given home network. But if private addresses only have meaning within a given network, how is addressing handled when packets are sent to or received from the global Internet, where addresses are necessarily unique? The answer lies in understanding NAT.

The NAT-enabled router does not *look* like a router to the outside world. Instead the NAT router behaves to the outside world as a *single* device with a *single* IP address. In Figure 4.20, all traffic leaving the home router for the larger Internet has a source IP address of 138.76.29.7, and all traffic entering the home must have a destination address of 138.76.29.7. In essence, the NAT-enabled router is hiding the details of the home network from the outside world. (As an aside, you might wonder where the home network computers get their addresses and where the router gets its single IP address. Often, the answer is the same—DHCP! The router gets its address from the ISP's DHCP server, and the router runs a DHCP server to provide addresses to computers within the NAT-DHCP-router-controlled home network's address space.)

If all datagrams arriving at the NAT router from the WAN have the same destination IP address (specifically, that of the WAN-side interface of the NAT router), then how does the router know the internal host to which it should forward a given datagram? The trick is to use a **NAT translation table** at the NAT router, and to include port numbers as well as IP addresses in the table entries.

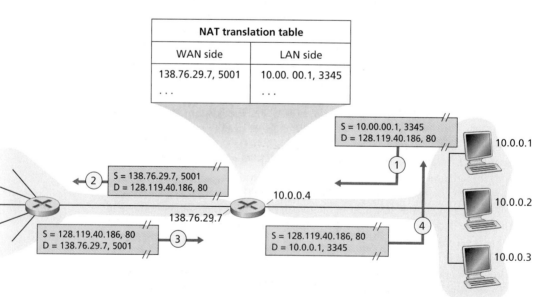

NAT translation table	
WAN side	LAN side
138.76.29.7, 5001	10.00. 00.1, 3345
. . .	. . .

Figure 4.20 ♦ Network address translation

Consider the example in Figure 4.20. Suppose a user sitting in a home network behind host 10.0.0.1 requests a Web page on some Web server (port 80) with IP address 128.119.40.186. The host 10.0.0.1 assigns the (arbitrary) source port number 3345 and sends the datagram into the LAN. The NAT router receives the datagram, generates a new source port number 5001 for the datagram, replaces the source IP address with its WAN-side IP address 138.76.29.7, and replaces the original source port number 3345 with the new source port number 5001. When generating a new source port number, the NAT router can select any source port number that is not currently in the NAT translation table. (Note that because a port number field is 16 bits long, the NAT protocol can support over 60,000 simultaneous connections with a single WAN-side IP address for the router!) NAT in the router also adds an entry to its NAT translation table. The Web server, blissfully unaware that the arriving datagram containing the HTTP request has been manipulated by the NAT router, responds with a datagram whose destination address is the IP address of the NAT router, and whose destination port number is 5001. When this datagram arrives at the NAT router, the router indexes the NAT translation table using the destination IP address and destination port number to obtain the appropriate IP address (10.0.0.1) and destination port number (3345) for the browser in the home network. The router then rewrites the datagram's destination address and destination port number, and forwards the datagram into the home network.

NAT has enjoyed widespread deployment in recent years. But we should mention that many purists in the IETF community loudly object to NAT. First, they argue, port numbers are meant to be used for addressing processes, not for addressing hosts. (This violation can indeed cause problems for servers running on the home network, since, as we have seen in Chapter 2, server processes wait for incoming requests at well-known port numbers.) Second, they argue, routers are supposed to process packets only up to layer 3. Third, they argue, the NAT protocol violates the so-called end-to-end argument; that is, hosts should be talking directly with each other, without interfering nodes modifying IP addresses and port numbers. And fourth, they argue, we should use IPv6 (see Section 4.4.4) to solve the shortage of IP addresses, rather than recklessly patching up the problem with a stopgap solution like NAT. But like it or not, NAT has become an important component of the Internet.

Yet another major problem with NAT is that it interferes with P2P applications, including P2P file sharing applications and P2P voice-over-IP applications. Recall from Chapter 2 that in a P2P application, any participating Peer A should be able to initiate a TCP connection to any other participating Peer B. The essence of the problem is that if Peer B is behind a NAT, it cannot act as a server and accept TCP connections (unless the NAT is specifically configured for the P2P application). As we'll see in the homework problems, this NAT problem can be circumvented if Peer A first contacts Peer B through an intermediate Peer C which is not behind a NAT and to which B has established an on-going TCP connection. Peer A can then ask Peer B, via Peer C, to initiate a TCP connection directly back to Peer A. Once the direct P2P TCP connection is established between Peers A and B, the two peers can exchange messages or files. This hack, called **connection reversal**, is actually used by many P2P applications. But if both Peer A and Peer B are behind their own NATs, then, for all practical purposes, it is impossible to establish a TCP connection between the two peers without application-specific NAT configuration.

Our discussion of NAT here has been necessarily brief. There are many other important aspects of NAT, including static versus dynamic NAT, and the effects of NAT on higher-layer protocols and on security. For more details, and a discussion of the pros and cons of NAT, see [Cisco NAT 2004; Phifer 2000].

4.4.3 Internet Control Message Protocol (ICMP)

Recall that the network layer of the Internet has three main components: the IP protocol, discussed in the previous section; the Internet routing protocols (including RIP, OSPF, and BGP), which are covered in Section 4.6; and ICMP, which is the subject of this section.

ICMP, specified in RFC 792, is used by hosts and routers to communicate network-layer information to each other. The most typical use of ICMP is for error reporting. For example, when running a Telnet, FTP, or HTTP session, you may have encountered an error message such as "Destination network unreachable." This message had its origins in ICMP. At some point, an IP router was unable to find a path to the host specified in your Telnet, FTP, or HTTP application. That router created and sent a type-3 ICMP message to your host indicating the error.

ICMP is often considered part of IP but architecturally lies just above IP, as ICMP messages are carried inside IP datagrams. That is, ICMP messages are carried as IP payload, just as TCP or UDP segments are carried as IP payload. Similarly, when a host receives an IP datagram with ICMP specified as the upper-layer protocol, it demultiplexes the datagram's contents to ICMP, just as it would demultiplex a datagram's content to TCP or UDP.

ICMP messages have a type and a code field, and contain the header and the first 8 bytes of the IP datagram that caused the ICMP message to be generated in the first place (so that the sender can determine the datagram that caused the error). Selected ICMP message types are shown in Figure 4.21. Note that ICMP messages are used not only for signaling error conditions.

The well-known ping program sends an ICMP type 8 code 0 message to the specified host. The destination host, seeing the echo request, sends back a type 0 code 0 ICMP echo reply. Most TCP/IP implementations support the ping server directly in the operating system; that is, the server is not a process. Chapter 11 of [Stevens 1990] provides the source code for the ping client program. Note that the client program needs to be able to instruct the operating system to generate an ICMP message of type 8 code 0.

Another interesting ICMP message is the source quench message. This message is seldom used in practice. Its original purpose was to perform congestion control—to allow a congested router to send an ICMP source quench message to a host to force that host to reduce its transmission rate. We have seen in Chapter 3 that TCP has its own congestion-control mechanism that operates at the transport layer, without the use of network-layer feedback such as the ICMP source quench message.

In Chapter 1 we introduced the Traceroute program, which allows us to trace a route from a host to any host in the world. Interestingly, Traceroute is implemented with ICMP messages. To determine the names and addresses of the routers between source and destination, Traceroute in the source sends a series of ordinary IP datagrams to the destination. Each of these datagrams carries a UDP segment with an unlikely UDP port number. The first of these datagrams has a TTL of 1, the second of 2, the third of 3, and so on. The source also starts timers for each of the datagrams. When the nth datagram arrives at the nth router, the nth router observes that the TTL of the datagram has just expired. According to the rules of the IP protocol, the router discards the datagram and sends an ICMP warning message to the source (type 11 code 0). This warning message includes the name of the router and its IP

ICMP Type	Code	Description
0	0	echo reply (to ping)
3	0	destination network unreachable
3	1	destination host unreachable
3	2	destination protocol unreachable
3	3	destination port unreachable
3	6	destination network unknown
3	7	destination host unknown
4	0	source quench (congestion control)
8	0	echo request
9	0	router advertisement
10	0	router discovery
11	0	TTL expired
12	0	IP header bad

Figure 4.21 ◆ ICMP message types

address. When this ICMP message arrives back at the source, the source obtains the round-trip time from the timer and the name and IP address of the *n*th router from the ICMP message.

How does a Traceroute source know when to stop sending UDP segments? Recall that the source increments the TTL field for each datagram it sends. Thus, one of the datagrams will eventually make it all the way to the destination host. Because this datagram contains a UDP segment with an unlikely port number, the destination host sends a port unreachable ICMP message (type 3 code 3) back to the source. When the source host receives this particular ICMP message, it knows it does not need to send additional probe packets. (The standard Traceroute program actually sends sets of three packets with the same TTL; thus the Traceroute output provides three results for each TTL.)

In this manner, the source host learns the number and the identities of routers that lie between it and the destination host and the round-trip time between the two hosts. Note that the Traceroute client program must be able to instruct the operating system to generate UDP datagrams with specific TTL values and must also be able to be notified by its operating system when ICMP messages arrive. Now that you understand how Traceroute works, you may want to go back and play with it some more.

4.4.4 IPv6

In the early 1990s, the Internet Engineering Task Force began an effort to develop a successor to the IPv4 protocol. A prime motivation for this effort was the realization that the 32-bit IP address space was beginning to be used up, with new subnets and IP nodes being attached to the Internet (and being allocated unique IP addresses) at a breathtaking rate. To respond to this need for a large IP address space, a new IP protocol, IPv6, was developed. The designers of IPv6 also took this opportunity to tweak and augment other aspects of IPv4, based on the accumulated operational experience with IPv4.

The point in time when IPv4 addresses would be completely allocated (and hence no new subnets could attach to the Internet) was the subject of considerable debate. Based on current trends in address allocation at the time, the estimates of the two leaders of the IETF's Address Lifetime Expectations working group were that addresses would become exhausted in 2008 and 2018, respectively [Solensky 1996]. In 1996, the American Registry for Internet Numbers (ARIN) reported that all of the IPv4 class A addresses had been assigned, 62 percent of the class B addresses had been assigned, and 37 percent of the class C addresses had been assigned [ARIN 1996]. Although these estimates and numbers suggested that a considerable amount of time might be left until the IPv4 address space was exhausted, it was realized that considerable time would be needed to deploy a new technology on such an extensive scale, and so the Next Generation IP (IPng) effort [Bradner 1996; RFC 1752] was begun. The result of this effort was the specification of IP version 6 (IPv6) [RFC 2460]. (An often-asked question is what happened to IPv5. It was initially envisioned that the ST-2 protocol would become IPv5, but ST-2 was later dropped in favor of the RSVP protocol, that we'll discuss in Chapter 7.)

Excellent sources of information about IPv6 are The IP Next Generation Homepage [Hinden 2004] and a book on the subject by Huitema [Huitema 1998].

IPv6 Datagram Format

The format of the IPv6 datagram is shown in Figure 4.22. The most important changes introduced in IPv6 are evident in the datagram format:

♦ *Expanded addressing capabilities.* IPv6 increases the size of the IP address from 32 to 128 bits. This ensures that the world won't run out of IP addresses. Now, every grain of sand on the planet can be IP-addressable. In addition to unicast and multicast addresses, IPv6 has introduced a new type of address, called an **anycast address**, which allows a datagram to be delivered to any one of a group of hosts. (This feature could be used, for example, to send an HTTP GET to the nearest of a number of mirror sites that contain a given document.)

♦ *A streamlined 40-byte header.* As discussed below, a number of IPv4 fields have been dropped or made optional. The resulting 40-byte fixed-length header allows for faster processing of the IP datagram. A new encoding of options allows for more flexible options processing.

♦ *Flow labeling and priority.* IPv6 has an elusive definition of a **flow**. RFC 1752 and RFC 2460 state that this allows "labeling of packets belonging to particular

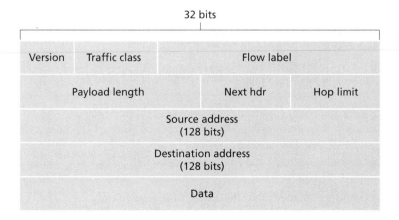

Figure 4.22 ♦ IPv6 datagram format

flows for which the sender requests special handling, such as a nondefault quality of service or real-time service." For example, audio and video transmission might likely be treated as a flow. On the other hand, the more traditional applications, such as file transfer and e-mail, might not be treated as flows. It is possible that the traffic carried by a high-priority user (for example, someone paying for better service for their traffic) might also be treated as a flow. What is clear, however, is that the designers of IPv6 foresee the eventual need to be able to differentiate among the flows, even if the exact meaning of a flow has not yet been determined. The IPv6 header also has an 8-bit traffic class field. This field, like the TOS field in IPv4, can be used to give priority to certain datagrams within a flow, or it can be used to give priority to datagrams from certain applications (for example, ICMP) over datagrams from other applications (for example, network news).

As noted above, a comparison of Figure 4.22 with Figure 4.13 reveals the simpler, more streamlined structure of the IPv6 datagram. The following fields are defined in IPv6:

♦ *Version.* This 4-bit field identifies the IP version number. Not surprisingly, IPv6 carries a value of 6 in this field. Note that putting a 4 in this field does not create a valid IPv4 datagram. (If it did, life would be a lot simpler—see the discussion below regarding the transition from IPv4 to IPv6.)

♦ *Traffic class.* This 8-bit field is similar in spirit to the TOS field we saw in IPv4.

♦ *Flow label.* As discussed above, this 20-bit field is used to identify a flow of datagrams.

♦ *Payload length.* This 16-bit value is treated as an unsigned integer giving the number of bytes in the IPv6 datagram following the fixed-length, 40-byte datagram header.

♦ *Next header.* This field identifies the protocol to which the contents (data field) of this datagram will be delivered (for example, to TCP or UDP). The field uses the same values as the protocol field in the IPv4 header.

♦ *Hop limit.* The contents of this field are decremented by one by each router that forwards the datagram. If the hop limit count reaches zero, the datagram is discarded.

♦ *Source and destination addresses.* The various formats of the IPv6 128-bit address are described in RFC 2373.

♦ *Data.* This is the payload portion of the IPv6 datagram. When the datagram reaches its destination, the payload will be removed from the IP datagram and passed on to the protocol specified in the next header field.

The discussion above identified the purpose of the fields that are included in the IPv6 datagram. Comparing the IPv6 datagram format in Figure 4.22 with the IPv4 datagram format that we saw in Figure 4.13, we notice that several fields appearing in the IPv4 datagram are no longer present in the IPv6 datagram:

♦ *Fragmentation/Reassembly.* IPv6 does not allow for fragmentation and reassembly at intermediate routers; these operations can be performed only by the source and destination. If an IPv6 datagram received by a router is too large to be forwarded over the outgoing link, the router simply drops the datagram and sends a "Packet Too Big" ICMP error message (see below) back to the sender. The sender can then resend the data, using a smaller IP datagram size. Fragmentation and reassembly is a time-consuming operation; removing this functionality from the routers and placing it squarely in the end systems considerably speeds up IP forwarding within the network.

♦ *Header checksum.* Because the transport layer (for example, TCP and UDP) and data link (for example, Ethernet) protocols in the Internet layers perform check-summing, the designers of IP probably felt that this functionality was sufficiently redundant in the network layer that it could be removed. Once again, fast processing of IP packets was a central concern. Recall from our discussion of IPv4 in Section 4.4.1, that since the IPv4 header contains a TTL field (similar to the hop limit field in IPv6), the IPv4 header checksum needed to be recomputed at every router. As with fragmentation and reassembly, this too was a costly operation in IPv4.

♦ *Options.* An options field is no longer a part of the standard IP header. However, it has not gone away. Instead, the options field is one of the possible next headers pointed to from within the IPv6 header. That is, just as TCP or UDP protocol headers can be the next header within an IP packet, so too can an options field. The removal of the options field results in a fixed-length, 40-byte IP header.

Recall from our discussion in Section 4.4.3 that the ICMP protocol is used by IP nodes to report error conditions and provide limited information (for example, the echo reply to a ping message) to an end system. A new version of ICMP has been defined for IPv6 in RFC 2463. In addition to reorganizing the existing ICMP type and code definitions, ICMPv6 also added new types and codes required by the new IPv6 functionality. These include the "Packet Too Big" type, and an "unrecognized IPv6 options" error code. In addition, ICMPv6 subsumes the functionality of the Internet Group Management Protocol (IGMP) that we'll study in Section 4.7. IGMP, which is used to manage a host's joining and leaving of multicast groups, was previously a separate protocol from ICMP in IPv4.

Transitioning from IPv4 to IPv6

Now that we have seen the technical details of IPv6, let us consider a very practical matter: How will the public Internet, which is based on IPv4, be transitioned to

IPv6? The problem is that while new IPv6-capable systems can be made backward-compatible, that is, can send, route, and receive IPv4 datagrams, already deployed IPv4-capable systems are not capable of handling IPv6 datagrams. Several options are possible.

One option would be to declare a flag day—a given time and date when all Internet machines would be turned off and upgraded from IPv4 to IPv6. The last major technology transition (from using NCP to using TCP for reliable transport service) occurred almost 20 years ago. Even back then [RFC 801], when the Internet was tiny and still being administered by a small number of "wizards," it was realized that such a flag day was not possible. A flag day involving hundreds of millions of machines and millions of network administrators and users is even more unthinkable today. RFC 2893 describes two approaches (which can be used either alone or together) for gradually integrating IPv6 hosts and routers into an IPv4 world (with the long-term goal, of course, of having all IPv4 nodes eventually transition to IPv6).

Probably the most straightforward way to introduce IPv6-capable nodes is a **dual-stack** approach, where IPv6 nodes also have a complete IPv4 implementation as well. Such a node, referred to as an IPv6/IPv4 node in RFC 2893, has the ability to send and receive both IPv4 and IPv6 datagrams. When interoperating with an IPv4 node, an IPv6/IPv4 node can use IPv4 datagrams; when interoperating with an IPv6 node, it can speak IPv6. IPv6/IPv4 nodes must have both IPv6 and IPv4 addresses. They must furthermore be able to determine whether another node is IPv6-capable or IPv4-only. This problem can be solved using the DNS (see Chapter 2), which can return an IPv6 address if the node name being resolved is IPv6-capable, or otherwise return an IPv4 address. Of course, if the node issuing the DNS request is only IPv4-capable, the DNS returns only an IPv4 address.

In the dual-stack approach, if either the sender or the receiver is only IPv4-capable, an IPv4 datagram must be used. As a result, it is possible that two IPv6-capable nodes can end up, in essence, sending IPv4 datagrams to each other. This is illustrated in Figure 4.23. Suppose Node A is IPv6-capable and wants to send an IP datagram to Node F, which is also IPv6-capable. Nodes A and B can exchange an IPv6 datagram. However, Node B must create an IPv4 datagram to send to C. Certainly, the data field of the IPv6 datagram can be copied into the data field of the IPv4 datagram and appropriate address mapping can be done. However, in performing the conversion from IPv6 to IPv4, there will be IPv6-specific fields in the IPv6 datagram (for example, the flow identifier field) that have no counterpart in IPv4. The information in these fields will be lost. Thus, even though E and F can exchange IPv6 datagrams, the arriving IPv4 datagrams at E from D do not contain all of the fields that were in the original IPv6 datagram sent from A.

An alternative to the dual-stack approach, also discussed in RFC 2893, is known as **tunneling**. Tunneling can solve the problem noted above, allowing, for example, E to receive the IPv6 datagram originated by A. The basic idea behind tunneling is the following. Suppose two IPv6 nodes (for example, B and E in Figure

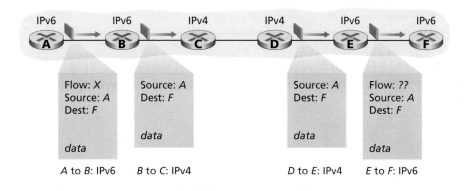

Figure 4.23 ♦ A dual-stack approach

4.23) want to interoperate using IPv6 datagrams but are connected to each other by intervening IPv4 routers. We refer to the intervening set of IPv4 routers between two IPv6 routers as a **tunnel**, as illustrated in Figure 4.24. With tunneling, the IPv6 node on the sending side of the tunnel (for example, B) takes the *entire* IPv6 datagram and puts it in the data (payload) field of an IPv4 datagram. This IPv4 datagram is then addressed to the IPv6 node on the receiving side of the tunnel (for example, E) and sent to the first node in the tunnel (for example, C). The intervening IPv4 routers in the tunnel route this IPv4 datagram among themselves, just as they would any other datagram, blissfully unaware that the IPv4 datagram itself contains a complete IPv6 datagram. The IPv6 node on the receiving side of the tunnel eventually receives the IPv4 datagram (it is the destination of the IPv4 datagram!), determines that the IPv4 datagram contains an IPv6 datagram, extracts the IPv6 datagram, and then routes the IPv6 datagram exactly as it would if it had received the IPv6 datagram from a directly connected IPv6 neighbor.

We end this section by noting that the adoption of IPv6 has been slow to take off [Lawton 2001]. Recall that one of the main motivations for IPv6 was the depletion of available IPv4 addresses. We saw in Section 4.4.2 that advances such as CIDRized IPv4 addresses, DHCP, and NAT have all contributed toward solving this problem, at least in the short term. It is possible, however, that the proliferation of devices such as IP-enabled phones and other portable devices may provide the needed push for more widespread deployment of IPv6. Europe's Third Generation Partnership Program [3GPP 2004] has specified IPv6 as the standard addressing scheme for mobile multimedia. Even if IPv6 hasn't been widely deployed in the first nine years of its young life, a long-term view is clearly called for. Today's phone number system took several decades to take hold, but it has been in place now for nearly half a century with no sign of going away. Similarly, it may take some time for IPv6 to take hold, but it too may then be around for a long time thereafter. Brian Carpenter, former chair of the Internet Architecture Board [IAB 2004] and author of

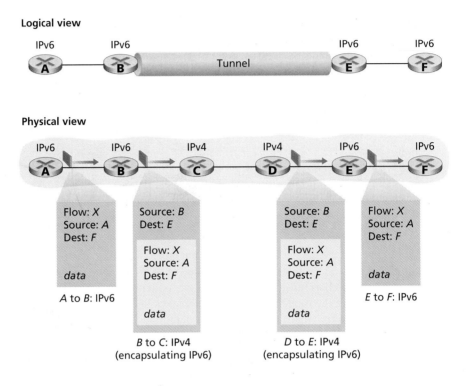

Figure 4.24 ♦ Tunneling

several IPv6-related RFCs, says, "I have always looked at this as a 15-year process starting in 1995." [Lawton 2001]. By Carpenter's dates, we're nearing the two-thirds point!

One important lesson that we can learn from the IPv6 experience is that it is enormously difficult to change network-layer protocols. Since the early 1990s, numerous new network-layer protocols have been trumpeted as the next major revolution for the Internet, but most of these protocols have had limited penetration to date. These protocols include IPv6, multicast protocols (Section 4.7), and resource reservation protocols (Chapter 7). Indeed, introducing new protocols into the network layer is like replacing the foundation of a house—it is difficult to do without tearing the whole house down or at least temporarily relocating the house's residents. On the other hand, the Internet has witnessed rapid deployment of new protocols at the application layer. The classic examples, of course, are the Web, instant messaging, and P2P file sharing. Other examples include audio and video streaming and distributed games. Introducing new application-layer protocols is like adding a new layer of paint to a house—it is relatively easy to do, and if you choose an attractive color, others in the neighborhood will copy you. In summary, in the future we can expect to see changes in the Internet's network layer, but these changes will likely occur on a time scale that is much slower than the changes that will occur at the application layer.

4.5 Routing Algorithms

So far in this chapter, we've mostly explored the network layer's forwarding function. We learned that when a packet arrives to a router, the router indexes a forwarding table and determines the link interface to which the packet is to be directed. We also learned that routing algorithms, operating in network routers, exchange and compute the information that is used to configure these forwarding tables. The interplay between routing algorithms and forwarding tables was shown in Figure 4.2. Having explored forwarding in some depth we now turn our attention to the other major topic of this chapter, namely, the network layer's critical routing function. Whether the network layer provides a datagram service (in which case different packets between a given source-destination pair may take different routes) or a VC service (in which case all packets between a given source and destination will take the same path), the network layer must nonetheless determine the path that packets take from senders to receivers. We'll see that the job of routing is to determine good paths (equivalently, routes), from senders to receivers, through the network of routers.

Typically a host is attached directly to one router, the **default router** for the host (also called the **first-hop router** for the host). Whenever a host emits a packet, the packet is transferred to its default router. We refer to the default router of the source host as the **source router** and the default router of the destination host as the **destination router**. The problem of routing a packet from source host to destination host clearly boils down to the problem of routing the packet from source router to destination router, which is the focus of this section.

The purpose of a routing algorithm is then simple: given a set of routers, with links connecting the routers, a routing algorithm finds a "good" path from source router to destination router. Typically, a good path is one that has the least cost. We'll see, however, that in practice, real-world concerns such as policy issues (for example, a rule such as "router x, belonging to organization Y, should not forward any packets originating from the network owned by organization Z") also come into play to complicate the conceptually simple and elegant algorithms whose theory underlies the practice of routing in today's networks.

A graph is used to formulate routing problems. Recall that a **graph** $G = (N,E)$ is a set N of nodes and a collection E of edges, where each edge is a pair of nodes from N. In the context of network-layer routing, the nodes in the graph represent routers—the points at which packet-forwarding decisions are made—and the edges connecting these nodes represent the physical links between these routers. Such a graph abstraction of a computer network is shown in Figure 4.25. To view some graphs representing real network maps, see [Dodge 2004, Cheswick 2000]; for a discussion of how well different graph-based models model the Internet, see [Zegura 1997, Faloutsos 1999].

As shown in Figure 4.25, an edge also has a value representing its cost. Typically, an edge's cost may reflect the physical length of the corresponding link (for example, a transoceanic link might have a higher cost than a short-haul terrestrial link), the link speed, or the monetary cost associated with a link. For our purposes, we'll simply take the edge costs as a given and won't worry about how they are determined. For any edge (x,y) in E, we denote $c(x,y)$ for the cost of the edge between nodes x and y. If the pair (x,y) does not belong to E, we set $c(x,y) = \infty$. Also, throughout we consider only undirected graphs (i.e., graphs whose edges do not have a direction), so that edge (x,y) is the same as edge (y,x) and that $c(x,y) = c(y,x)$. Also, a node y is said to be a **neighbor** of node x if (x,y) belongs to E.

Given that costs are assigned to the various edges in the graph abstraction, a natural goal of a routing algorithm is to identify the least costly paths between sources and destinations. To make this problem more precise, recall that a **path** in a graph $G = (N,E)$ is a sequence of nodes $(x_1, x_2,..., x_p)$ such that each of the pairs (x_1, x_2), (x_1, x_3),...,(x_{p-1}, x_p) are edges in E. The cost of a path $(x_1, x_2,..., x_p)$ is simply the sum of all the edge costs along the path, that is, $c(x_1, x_2) + c(x_2,x_3) + ...+ c(x_{p-1},x_p)$. Given any two nodes x and y, there are typically many paths between the two nodes, with each path having a cost. One or more of these paths is a **least-cost path**. The least-cost problem is therefore clear: Find a path between the source and destination that has least cost. In Figure 4.25, for example, the least-cost path between source node u and destination node w is (u, x, y, w) with a path cost of 3. Note that if all edges in the graph have the same cost, the least-cost path is also the **shortest path** (that is, the path with the smallest number of links between the source and the destination).

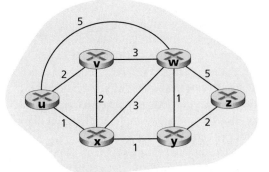

Figure 4.25 ♦ Abstract graph model of a computer network

As a simple exercise, try finding the least-cost path from nodes u to z in Figure 4.25 and reflect for a moment on how you calculated that path. If you are like most people, you found the path from u to z by examining Figure 4.25, tracing a few routes from u to z, and somehow convincing yourself that the path you had chosen had the least cost among all possible paths. (Did you check all of the 17 possible paths between u and z? Probably not!) Such a calculation is an example of a centralized routing algorithm—the routing algorithm was run in one location, your brain, with complete information about the network. Broadly, one way in which we can classify routing algorithms is according to whether they are global or decentralized.

♦ A **global routing algorithm** computes the least-cost path between a source and destination using complete, global knowledge about the network. That is, the algorithm takes the connectivity between all nodes and all link costs as inputs. This then requires that the algorithm somehow obtain this information before actually performing the calculation. The calculation itself can be run at one site (a centralized global routing algorithm) or replicated at multiple sites. The key distinguishing feature here, however, is that a global algorithm has complete information about connectivity and link costs. In practice, algorithms with global state information are often referred to as **link-state (LS) algorithms**, since the algorithm must be aware of the cost of each link in the network. We'll study LS algorithms in Section 4.5.1.

♦ In a **decentralized routing algorithm**, the calculation of the least-cost path is carried out in an iterative, distributed manner. No node has complete information about the costs of all network links. Instead, each node begins with only the knowledge of the costs of its own directly attached links. Then, through an iterative process of calculation and exchange of information with its neighboring nodes (that is, nodes that are at the other end of links to which it itself is attached), a node gradually calculates the least-cost path to a destination or set of destinations. The decentralized routing algorithm we'll study below in Section 4.5.2 is called a distance-vector (DV) algorithm, because each node maintains a vector of estimates of the costs (distances) to all other nodes in the network.

A second broad way to classify routing algorithms is according to whether they are static or dynamic. In **static routing algorithms**, routes change very slowly over time, often as a result of human intervention (for example, a human manually editing a router's forwarding table). **Dynamic routing algorithms** change the routing paths as the network traffic loads or topology change. A dynamic algorithm can be run either periodically or in direct response to topology or link cost changes. While dynamic algorithms are more responsive to network changes, they are also more susceptible to problems such as routing loops and oscillation in routes.

A third way to classify routing algorithms is according to whether they are load-sensitive or load-insensitive. In a **load-sensitive algorithm**, link costs vary dynamically to reflect the current level of congestion in the underlying link. If a high cost is associated with a link that is currently congested, a routing algorithm will tend to choose routes around such a congested link. While early ARPAnet routing algorithms were load-sensitive [McQuillan 1980], a number of difficulties were encountered [Huitema 1998]. Today's Internet routing algorithms (such RIP, OSPF, and BGP) are **load-insensitive**, as a link's cost does not explicitly reflect its current (or recent past) level of congestion.

4.5.1 The Link-State (LS) Routing Algorithm

Recall that in a link-state algorithm, the network topology and all link costs are known, that is, available as input to the LS algorithm. In practice this is accomplished by having each node broadcast link-state packets to *all* other nodes in the network, with each link-state packet containing the identities and costs of its attached links. In practice (for example, with the Internet's OSPF routing protocol, discussed in Section 4.6.1) this is often accomplished by a **link-state broadcast** algorithm [Perlman 1999]. We'll cover broadcast algorithms in Section 4.7. The result of the nodes' broadcast is that all nodes have an identical and complete view of the network. Each node can then run the LS algorithm and compute the same set of least-cost paths as every other node.

The link-state routing algorithm we present below is known as *Dijkstra's algorithm*, named after its inventor. A closely related algorithm is Prim's algorithm; see [Cormen 2001] for a general discussion of graph algorithms. Dijkstra's algorithm computes the least-cost path from one node (the source, which we will refer to as u) to all other nodes in the network. Dijkstra's algorithm is iterative and has the property that after the kth iteration of the algorithm, the least-cost paths are known to k destination nodes, and among the least-cost paths to all destination nodes, these k paths will have the k smallest costs. Let us define the following notation:

- $D(v)$: cost of the least-cost path from the source node to destination v as of this iteration of the algorithm.
- $p(v)$: previous node (neighbor of v) along the current least-cost path from the source to v.
- N': subset of nodes; v is in N' if the least cost from path the source to v is definitively known.

The global routing algorithm consists of an initialization step followed by a loop. The number of times the loop is executed is equal to the number of nodes in the network. Upon termination, the algorithm will have calculated the shortest paths from the source node u to every other node in the network.

Link-state (LS) Algorithm for Source Node *u*

```
1   Initialization:
2      N' = {u}
3      for all nodes v
4         if v is a neighbor of u
5            then D(v) = c(u,v)
6            else D(v) = ∞
7
8   Loop
9      find w not in N' such that D(w) is a minimum
10     add w to N'
11     update D(v) for each neighbor v of w and not in N':
12           D(v) = min( D(v), D(w) + c(w,v) )
13     /* new cost to v is either old cost to v or known
14      least path cost to w plus cost from w to v */
15  until N'= N
```

As an example, let's consider the network in Figure 4.25 and compute the least-cost paths from *u* to all possible destinations. A tabular summary of the algorithm's computation is shown in Table 4.3, where each line in the table gives the values of the algorithm's variables at the end of the iteration. Let's consider the few first steps in detail.

♦ In the initialization step, the currently known least-cost paths from *u* to its directly attached neighbors, *v, x,* and *w,* are initialized to 2, 1, and 5, respectively. Note in particular that the cost to *w* is set to 5 (even though we will soon see that a lesser-cost path does indeed exist) since this is the cost of the direct (one hop) link from *u* to *w.* The costs to *y* and *z* are set to infinity because they are not directly connected to *u.*

♦ In the first iteration, we look among those nodes not yet added to the set *N'* and find that node with the least cost as of the end of the previous iteration. That node is *x,* with a cost of 1, and thus *x* is added to the set *N'.* Line 12 of the LS algorithm is then performed to update *D(v)* for all nodes *v,* yielding the results shown in the second line (Step 1) in Table 4.3. The cost of the path to *v* is unchanged. The cost of the path to *w* (which was 5 at the end of the initialization) through node *x* is found to have a cost of 4. Hence this lower-cost path is selected and *w*'s predecessor along the shortest path from *u* is set to *x.* Similarly, the cost to *y* (through *x*) is computed to be 2, and the table is updated accordingly.

♦ In the second iteration, nodes *v* and *y* are found to have the least-cost paths (2), and we break the tie arbitrarily and add *y* to the set *N'* so that *N'* now contains *u, x,* and *y.* The cost to the remaining nodes not yet in *N',* that is, nodes *v, w,* and *z,* are updated via line 12 of the LS algorithm, yielding the results shown in the third row in the Table 4.3.

♦ And so on. . . .

When the LS algorithm terminates, we have, for each node, its predecessor along the least-cost path from the source node. For each predecessor, we also have *its* predecessor, and so in this manner we can construct the entire path from the source to all destinations. The forwarding table in a node, say node u, can then be constructed from this information by storing, for each destination, the next-hop node on the least-cost path from u to the destination.

What is the computational complexity of this algorithm? That is, given n nodes (not counting the source), how much computation must be done in the worst case to find the least-cost paths from the source to all destinations? In the first iteration, we need to search through all n nodes to determine the node, w, not in N' that has the minimum cost. In the second iteration, we need to check $n - 1$ nodes to determine the minimum cost; in the third iteration $n - 2$ nodes, and so on. Overall, the total number of nodes we need to search through over all the iterations is $n(n + 1)/2$, and thus we say that the preceding implementation of the LS algorithm has worst-case complexity of order n squared: $O(n^2)$. (A more sophisticated implementation of this algorithm, using a data structure known as a heap, can find the minimum in line 9 in logarithmic rather than linear time, thus reducing the complexity.)

Before completing our discussion of the LS algorithm, let us consider a pathology that can arise. Figure 4.26 shows a simple network topology where link costs are equal to the load carried on the link, for example, reflecting the delay that would be experienced. In this example, link costs are not symmetric; that is, $c(u,v)$ equals $c(v,u)$ only if the load carried on both directions on the link (u,v) is the same. In this example, node z originates a unit of traffic destined for w, node x also originates a unit of traffic destined for w, and node y injects an amount of traffic equal to e, also destined for w. The initial routing is shown in Figure 4.26(a) with the link costs corresponding to the amount of traffic carried.

step	N'	D(v),p(v)	D(w),p(w)	D(x),p(x)	D(y),p(y)	D(z),p(z)
0	u	2,u	5,u	1,u	∞	∞
1	ux	2,u	4,x		2,x	∞
2	uxy	2,u	3,y			4,y
3	uxyv		3,y			4,y
4	uxyvw					4,y
5	uxyvwz					

Table 4.3 ♦ Running the link-state algorithm on the network in Figure 4.25

When the LS algorithm is next run, node y determines (based on the link costs shown in Figure 4.26(a)) that the clockwise path to w has a cost of 1, while the counterclockwise path to w (which it had been using) has a cost of $1 + e$. Hence y's least-cost path to w is now clockwise. Similarly, x determines that its new least-cost path to w is also clockwise, resulting in costs shown in Figure 4.26(b). When the LS algorithm is run next, nodes x, y, and z all detect a zero-cost path to w in the counterclockwise direction, and all route their traffic to the counterclockwise routes. The next time the LS algorithm is run, x, y, and z all then route their traffic to the clockwise routes.

What can be done to prevent such oscillations (which can occur in any algorithm, not just an LS algorithm, that uses a congestion or delay-based link metric)?

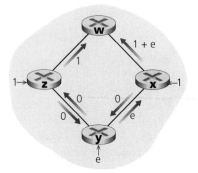

a. Initial routing

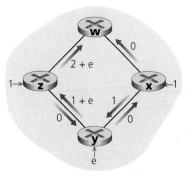

b. *x, y* detect better path to *w*, clockwise

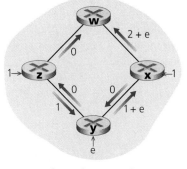

c. *x, y, z* detect better path to *w*, counterclockwise

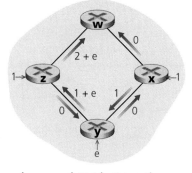

d. *x, y, z,* detect better path to *w*, clockwise

Figure 4.26 ♦ Oscillations with link-state routing

One solution would be to mandate that link costs not depend on the amount of traffic carried—an unacceptable solution since one goal of routing is to avoid highly congested (for example, high-delay) links. Another solution is to ensure that not all routers run the LS algorithm at the same time. This seems a more reasonable solution, since we would hope that even if routers ran the LS algorithm with the same periodicity, the execution instance of the algorithm would not be the same at each node. Interestingly, researchers have found that routers in the Internet can self-synchronize among themselves [Floyd Synchronization 1994]. That is, even though they initially execute the algorithm with the same period but at different instants of time, the algorithm execution instance can eventually become, and remain, synchronized at the routers. One way to avoid such self-synchronization is for each router to randomize the time it sends out a link advertisement.

Having studied the LS algorithm, let's consider the other major routing algorithm that is used in practice today—the distance-vector routing algorithm.

4.5.2 The Distance-Vector (DV) Routing Algorithm

Whereas the LS algorithm is an algorithm using global information, the **distance-vector (DV)** algorithm is iterative, asynchronous, and distributed. It is *distributed* in that each node receives some information from one or more of its *directly attached* neighbors, performs a calculation, and then distributes the results of its calculation back to its neighbors. It is *iterative* in that this process continues on until no more information is exchanged between neighbors. (Interestingly, the algorithm is also self-terminating—there is no signal that the computation should stop; it just stops.) The algorithm is *asynchronous* in that it does not require all of the nodes to operate in lockstep with each other. We'll see that an asynchronous, iterative, self-terminating, distributed algorithm is much more interesting and fun than a centralized algorithm!

Before we present the DV algorithm, it will prove beneficial to discuss an important relationship that exists among the costs of the least-cost paths. Let $d_x(y)$ be the cost of the least-cost path from node x to node y. Then the least costs are related by the celebrated Bellman-Ford equation, namely,

$$d_x(y) = min_v\{c(x,v) + d_v(y)\}, \tag{4.1}$$

where the min_v in the equation is taken over all of x's neighbors. The Bellman-Ford equation is rather intuitive. Indeed, after traveling from x to v, if we then take the least-cost path from v to y, the path cost will be $c(x,v) + d_v(y)$. Since we must begin by traveling to some neighbor v, the least cost from x to y is the minimum of $c(x,v) + d_v(y)$ taken over all neighbors v.

But for those who might be skeptical about the validity of the equation, let's check it for source node u and destination node z in Figure 4.25. The source node u has three neighbors: nodes v, x and w. By walking along various paths in the graph, it is easy to see that $d_v(z) = 5$, $d_x(z) = 3$ and $d_w(z) = 3$. Plugging these values into Equation 4.1, along with the costs $c(u,v) = 2$, $c(u,x) = 5$ and $c(u,w) = 1$, gives $d_u(z) = \min\{2 + 5, 5 + 3, 1 + 3\} = 4$, which is obviously true and which is exactly what the Dijskstra algorithm gave us for the same network. This quick verification should help relieve any skepticism you may have.

The Bellman-Ford equation is not just an intellectual curiosity. It actually has significant practical importance. In particular, the solution to the Bellman-Ford equation provides the entries in node x's forwarding table. To see this, let v^* be any neighboring node that achieves the minimum in Equation 4.1. Then, if node x wants to send a packet to node y along a least-cost path, it should first forward the packet to node v^*. Thus, node x's forwarding table would specify node v^* as the next-hop router for the ultimate destination y. Another important practical contribution of the Bellman-Ford equation is that it suggests the form of the neighbor-to-neighbor communication that will take place in the DV algorithm.

The basic idea is as follows. Each node x begins with $D_x(y)$, an estimate of the cost of the least-cost path from itself to node y, for all nodes in N. Let $\mathbf{D}_x = [D_x(y): y$ in $N]$ be node x's distance vector, which is the vector of cost estimates from x to all other nodes, y, in N. With the DV algorithm, each node x maintains the following routing data:

♦ For each neighbor v, the cost $c(x,v)$ from x to directly attached neighbor, v

♦ Node x's distance vector, that is, $\mathbf{D}_x = [D_x(y): y$ in $N]$, containing x's estimate of its cost to all destinations, y, in N

♦ The distance vectors of each of its neighbors, that is, $\mathbf{D}_v = [D_v(y): y$ in $N]$ for each neighbor v of x

In the distributed, asynchronous algorithm, from time to time, each node sends a copy of its distance vector to each of its neighbors. When a node x receives a new distance vector from any of its neighbors v, it saves v's distance vector, and then uses the Bellman-Ford equation to update its own distance vector as follows:

$$D_x(y) = \min_v\{c(x,v) + D_v(y)\} \quad \text{for each node } y \text{ in } N$$

If node x's distance vector has changed as a result of this update step, node x will then send its updated distance vector to each of its neighbors, which can in turn update their own distance vectors. Miraculously enough, as long as all the nodes continue to exchange their distance vectors in an asynchronous fashion, each cost estimate $D_x(y)$ converges to $d_x(y)$, the actual cost of least-cost path from node x to node y [Bersekas 1992]!

Distance Vector (DV) Algorithm

At each node, *x*:

```
1   Initialization:
2       for all destinations y in N:
3           Dx(y) = c(x,y)    /* if y is not a neighbor than c(x,y) = ∞ /*
4       for each neighbor w
5           Dw(y) = ∞ for all destinations y in N
6       for each neighbor w
7           send distance vector Dx =  [Dx(y): y in N] to w
8
9   loop
10      wait (until I see a link cost change to some neighbor w or
11              until I receive a distance vector from some neighbor w)
12
13      for each y in N:
14          Dx(y) = minv{c(x,v) + Dv(y)}
15
16      if Dx(y) changed for any destination y
17          send distance vector Dx =  [Dx(y): y in N] to all neighbors
18
19  forever
```

The DV algorithm shows how a node *x* updates its distance vector estimate when it either sees a cost change in one of its directly attached links or receives a distance vector update from some neighbor. But to update its own forwarding table for a given destination *y*, what node *x* really needs to know is not the shortest-path distance to *y* but instead the neighboring node $v^*(y)$ that is the next-hop router along the shortest path to *y*. As you might expect, the next-hop router $v^*(y)$ is the neighbor *v* that achieves the minimum in Line 14 of the DV algorithm. (If there are multiple neighbors *v* that achieve the minimum, then $v^*(y)$ can be any of the minimizing neighbors.) Thus, in Lines 13-14, for each destination *y*, node *x* also determines $v^*(y)$ and updates its forwarding table for destination *y*.

Recall that the LS algorithm is a global algorithm in the sense that it requires each node to first obtain a complete map of the network before running the Dijkstra algorithm. The DV algorithm is *decentralized* and does not use such global information. Indeed, the only information a node will have is the costs of the links to its directly attached neighbors and information it receives from these neighbors. Each node waits for an update from any neighbor (Lines 10–11), calculates its new distance vector when receiving an update (Line 14) and distributes its new distance vector to its neighbors (Lines 16–17). The DV algorithm is used in many routing protocols in practice, including the Internet's RIP and BGP, ISO IDRP, Novell IPX, and the original ARPAnet.

Figure 4.27 illustrates the operation of the DV algorithm for the simple three-node network shown at the top of the figure. The operation of the algorithm is illustrated in a synchronous manner, where all nodes simultaneously receive distance vectors from their neighbors, compute their new distance vectors, and inform their neighbors if their distance vectors have changed. After studying this example, you should convince yourself that the algorithm operates correctly in an asynchronous manner as well, with node computations and update generation/reception occurring at any time.

The leftmost column of the figure displays three initial **routing tables** for each of the three nodes. For example, the table in the upper-left corner is node x's initial routing table. Within a specific routing table, each row is a distance vector—specifically, each node's routing table includes its own distance vector and that of each of its neighbors. Thus, the first row in node x's initial routing table is $D_x = [D_x(x), D_x(y), D_x(z)] = [0, 2, 7]$. The second and third rows in this table are the most recently received distance vectors from nodes y and z, respectively. Because at initialization, node x has not received anything from node y or z, the entries in the second and third rows are initialized to infinity.

After initialization, each node sends its distance vector to each of its two neighbors. This is illustrated in Figure 4.27 by the arrows from the first column of tables to the second column of tables. For example, node x sends its distance vector $D_x = [0, 2, 7]$ to both nodes y and z. After receiving the updates, each node recomputes its own distance vector. For example, node x computes

$$D_x(x) = 0$$

$$D_x(y) = \min\{c(x,y) + D_y(y), c(x,z) + D_z(y)\} = \min\{2 + 0, 7 + 1\} = 2$$

$$D_x(z) = \min\{c(x,y) + D_y(z), c(x,z) + D_z(z)\} = \min\{2 + 1, 7 + 0\} = 3$$

The second column therefore displays, for each node, the node's new distance vector along with distance vectors just received from its neighbors. Note, for example, that node x's estimate for the least cost to node z, $D_x(z)$, has changed from 7 to 3. Also note that for both nodes y and z, node y achieves the corresponding minimums. Thus, at this stage of the algorithm, the next-hop routers are $v*(y) = y$ and $v*(z) = y$.

After the nodes recompute their distance vectors, they again send their updated distance vectors to their neighbors (if there has been a change). This is illustrated in Figure 4.27 by the arrows from the second column of tables to the third column of tables. Note that only nodes x and z send updates: node y's distance vector didn't change so node y doesn't send an update. After receiving the updates, the nodes then recompute their distance vectors and update their routing tables, which are shown in the third column.

The process of receiving updated distance vectors from neighbors, recomputing routing table entries, and informing neighbors of changed costs of the least-cost path

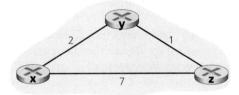

Node x table

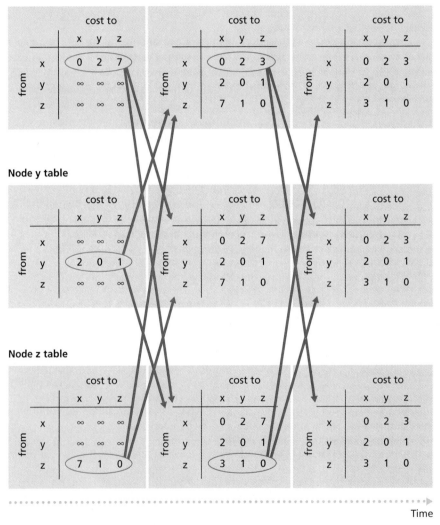

Figure 4.27 ♦ Distance vector (DV) algorithm

to a destination continues until no update messages are sent. At this point, since no update messages are sent, no further routing table calculations will occur and the algorithm will enter a quiescent state; that is, all nodes will be performing the wait in Lines 10–11 of the DV algorithm. The algorithm remains in the quiescent state until a link cost changes, as discussed next.

Distance-Vector Algorithm: Link-Cost Changes and Link Failure

When a node running the DV algorithm detects a change in the link cost from itself to a neighbor (Lines 10–11), it updates its distance vector (Lines 13–14) and, if there's a change in the cost of the least-cost path, informs its neighbors (Lines 16–17) of its new distance vector. Figure 4.28(a) illustrates a scenario where the link cost from y to x changes from 4 to 1. We focus here only on y and z's distance table entries to destination x. The DV algorithm causes the following sequence of events to occur:

♦ At time t_0, y detects the link-cost change (the cost has changed from 4 to 1), updates its distance vector, and informs its neighbors of this change since its distance vector has changed.

♦ At time t_1, z receives the update from y and updates its table. It computes a new least cost to x (it has decreased from a cost of 5 to a cost of 2) and sends its new distance vector to its neighbors.

♦ At time t_2, y receives z's update and updates its distance table. y's least costs do not change and hence y does not send any message to z. The algorithm comes to a quiescent state.

Thus, only two iterations are required for the DV algorithm to reach a quiescent state. The good news about the decreased cost between x and y has propagated quickly through the network.

Let's now consider what can happen when a link cost *increases*. Suppose that the link cost between x and y increases from 4 to 60, as shown in Figure 4.28(b).

1. Before the link cost changes, $D_y(x) = 4$, $D_y(z) = 1$, $D_z(y) = 1$, and $D_z(x) = 5$. At time t_0, y detects the link-cost change (the cost has changed from 4 to 60). y computes its new minimum-cost path to x to have a cost of

$$D_y(x) = \min\{c(y,x) + D_x(x), c(y,z) + D_z(x)\} = \{60 + 0, 1 + 5\} = 6$$

Of course, with our global view of the network, we can see that this new cost via z is *wrong*. But the only information node y has is that its direct cost to x is 60 and that z has last told y that z could get to x with a cost of 5. So in order to get to x, y would now route through z, fully expecting that z will be able to get to x with a cost of 5. As of t_1 we have a **routing loop**—in order to get to x, y

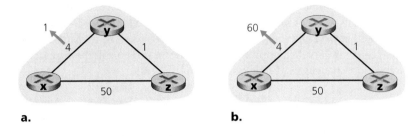

Figure 4.28 ◆ Changes in link cost

routes through z, and z routes through y. A routing loop is like a black hole—a packet destined for x arriving at y or z as of t_1 will bounce back and forth between these two nodes forever (or until the forwarding tables are changed).

2. Since node y has computed a new minimum cost to x, it informs z of its new distance vector at time t_1.

3. Sometime after t_1, z receives y's new distance vector, which indicates that y's minimum cost to x is 6. z knows it can get to y with a cost of 1 and hence computes a new least cost to x of $D_z(x) = \min\{50 + 0, 1 + 6\} = 7$. Since z's least cost to x has increased, it then informs y of its new distance vector at t_2.

4. In a similar manner, after receiving z's new distance vector, y determines $D_y(x) = 8$ and sends z its distance vector. z then determines $D_z(x) = 9$ and sends y its distance vector, and so on.

How long will the process continue? You should convince yourself that the loop will persist for 44 iterations (message exchanges between y and z)—until z eventually computes the cost of its path via y to be greater than 50. At this point, z will (finally!) determine that its least-cost path to x is via its direct connection to x. y will then route to x via z. The result of the bad news about the increase in link cost has indeed traveled slowly! What would have happened if the link cost $c(y,x)$ had changed from 4 to 10,000 and the cost $c(z,x)$ had been 9,999? Because of such scenarios, the problem we have seen is sometimes referred to as the count-to-infinity problem.

Distance-Vector Algorithm: Adding Poisoned Reverse

The specific looping scenario just described can be avoided using a technique known as *poisoned reverse*. The idea is simple—if z routes through y to get to destination x, then z will advertise to y that its distance to x is infinity, that is, z will advertise to y that $D_z(x) = \infty$ (even though z knows $D_z(x) = 5$ in truth). z will continue telling this little white lie to y as long as it routes to x via y. Since y believes that z has no path to x, y will never attempt to route to x via z, as long as z continues to route to x via y (and lies about doing so).

Let's now see how poisoned reverse solves the particular looping problem we encountered before in Figure 4.28(b). As a result of the poisoned reverse, y's distance table indicates $D_z(x) = \infty$. When the cost of the (x,y) link changes from 4 to 60 at time t_0, y updates its table and continues to route directly to x, albeit at a higher cost of 60, and informs z of its new cost to x, that is, $D_y(x) = 60$. After receiving the update at t_1, z immediately shifts its route to x to be via the direct (x,y) link at a cost of 50. Since this is a new least-cost path to x, and since the path no longer passes through y, z now informs y that $D_z(x) = 50$ at t_2. After receiving the update from z, y updates its distance table with $D_y(x) = 51$. Also, since z is now on y's least-cost path to x, y poisons the reverse path from z to x by informing z at time t_3 that $D_y(x) = \infty$ (even though y knows that $D_y(x) = 51$ in truth).

Does poisoned reverse solve the general count-to-infinity problem? It does not. You should convince yourself that loops involving three or more nodes (rather than simply two immediately neighboring nodes will not be detected by the poisoned reverse technique.

A Comparison of LS and DV Routing Algorithms

The DV and LS algorithms take complementary approaches towards computing routing. In the DV algorithm, each node talks to *only* its directly connected neighbors, but it provides its neighbors with least-cost estimates from itself to *all* the nodes (that it knows about) in the network. In the LS algorithm, each node talks with *all* other nodes (via broadcast), but it tells them *only* the costs of its directly connected links. Let's conclude our study of LS and DV algorithms with a quick comparison of some of their attributes. Recall that N is the set of nodes (routers) and E is the set of edges (links).

♦ *Message complexity.* We have seen that LS requires each node to know the cost of each link in the network. This requires $O(|N|\,|E|)$ messages to be sent. Also, whenever a link cost changes, the new link cost must be sent to all nodes. The DV algorithm requires message exchanges between directly connected neighbors at each iteration. We have seen that the time needed for the algorithm to converge can depend on many factors. When link costs change, the DV algorithm will propagate the results of the changed link cost only if the new link cost results in a changed least-cost path for one of the nodes attached to that link.

♦ *Speed of convergence.* We have seen that our implementation of LS is an $O(|N|^2)$ algorithm requiring $O(N\,|E|))$ messages. The DV algorithm can converge slowly and can have routing loops while the algorithm is converging. DV also suffers from the count-to-infinity problem.

♦ *Robustness.* What can happen if a router fails, misbehaves, or is sabotaged? Under LS, a router could broadcast an incorrect cost for one of its attached links (but no others). A node could also corrupt or drop any packets it received as part of an LS broadcast. But an LS node is computing only its own forwarding tables; other nodes are performing the similar calculations for themselves. This means route calculations are somewhat separated under LS, providing a degree of robustness. Under DV, a node can advertise incorrect least-cost paths to any or all destinations. (Indeed, in 1997, a malfunctioning router in a small ISP provided national backbone routers with erroneous routing information. This caused other routers to flood the malfunctioning router with traffic and caused large portions of the Internet to become disconnected for up to several hours [Neumann 1997].) More generally, we note that, at each iteration, a node's calculation in DV is passed on to its neighbor and then indirectly to its neighbor's neighbor on the next iteration. In this sense, an incorrect node calculation can be diffused through the entire network under DV.

In the end, neither algorithm is an obvious winner over the other; indeed, both algorithms are used in the Internet.

Other Routing Algorithms

The LS and DV algorithms we have studied are not only widely used in practice, they are essentially the *only* routing algorithms used in practice today in the Internet. Nonetheless, many routing algorithms have been proposed by researchers over the past 30 years, ranging from the extremely simple to the very sophisticated and complex. A broad class of routing algorithms is based on viewing packet traffic as flows between sources and destinations in a network. In this approach, the routing problem can be formulated mathematically as a constrained optimization problem known as a network flow problem [Bertsekas 1991]. Yet another set of routing algorithms we mention here are those derived from the telephony world. These **circuit-switched routing algorithms** are of interest to packet-switched data networking in cases where per-link resources (for example, buffers, or a fraction of the link bandwidth) are to be reserved for each connection that is routed over the link. While the formulation of the routing problem might appear quite different from the least-cost routing formulation we have seen in this chapter, there are a number of similarities, at least as far as the path-finding algorithm (routing algorithm) is concerned. See [Ash 1998; Ross 1995; Girard 1990] for a detailed discussion of this research area.

4.5.3 Hierarchical Routing

In our study of LS and DV algorithms, we've viewed the network simply as a collection of interconnected routers. One router was indistinguishable from another in the sense that all routers executed the same routing algorithm to compute routing paths through the entire network. In practice, this model and its view of a homogenous set of routers all executing the same routing algorithm is a bit simplistic for at least two important reasons:

♦ *Scale.* As the number of routers becomes large, the overhead involved in computing, storing, and communicating routing information (for example, LS updates or least-cost path changes) becomes prohibitive. Today's public Internet consists of hundreds of millions of hosts. Storing routing information to each of these hosts would clearly require enormous amounts of memory. The overhead required to broadcast LS updates among all of the routers in the public Internet would leave no bandwidth left for sending data packets! A distance vector algorithm that iterated among such a large number of routers would surely never converge. Clearly, something must be done to reduce the complexity of route computation in networks as large as the public Internet.

♦ *Administrative autonomy.* Although researchers tend to ignore issues such as a company's desire to run its routers as it pleases (for example, to run whatever routing algorithm it chooses) or to hide aspects of its networks' internal organization from the outside, these are important considerations. Ideally, an organization should be able to run and administer its network as it wishes, while still being able to connect its network to other outside networks.

Both of these problems can be solved by organizing routers into **autonomous systems (ASs)**, with each AS consisting of a group of routers that are typically under the same administrative control (e.g., operated by the same ISP or belonging to the same company network). Routers within the same AS all run the same routing algorithm (for example, an LS or DV algorithm) and have information about each other—exactly as was the case in our idealized model in the preceding section. The routing algorithm running within an autonomous system is called an **intra-autonomous system routing protocol**. It will be necessary, of course, to connect ASs to each other, and thus one or more of the routers in an AS will have the added task of being responsible for forwarding packets to destinations outside the AS; these routers are called **gateway routers**.

Figure 4.29 provides a simple example with three ASs: AS1, AS2, and AS3. In this figure, the heavy lines represent direct link connections between pairs of routers. The thinner lines hanging from the routers represent subnets that are directly connected to the routers. AS1 has four routers—1a, 1b, 1c, and 1d—which run the intra-AS routing protocol used within AS1. Thus, each of these four routers knows how to forward packets along the optimal path to any destination within AS1. Similarly, autonomous systems AS2 and AS3 each have three routers. Note that the intra-AS routing protocols running in AS1, AS2, and AS3 need not be the same. Also note that the routers 1b, 1c, 2a, and 3a are all gateway routers.

It should now be clear how the routers in an AS determine routing paths for source-destination pairs that are internal to the AS. But there is still a big missing piece to the end-to-end routing puzzle. How does a router, within some AS, know how to route a packet to a destination that is outside the AS? It's easy to answer this question if the AS has only one gateway router that connects to only one other AS.

In this case, because the AS's intra-AS routing algorithm has determined the least-cost path from each internal router to the gateway router, each internal router knows how it should forward the packet. The gateway router, upon receiving the packet, forwards the packet on the one link that leads outside the AS. The AS on the other side of the link then takes over the responsibility of routing the packet to its ultimate destination. As an example, suppose router 2b in Figure 4.29 receives a packet whose destination is outside of AS2. Router 2b will then either forward the packet to router 2a or 2c, as specified by router 2b's forwarding table, which was configured by AS2's intra-AS routing protocol. The packet will eventually arrive to the gateway router 2a, which will forward the packet to 1b. Once the packet has left 2a, AS2's job is done with this one packet.

So the problem is easy when the source AS has only one link that leads outside the AS. But what if the source AS has two or more links (through one or more gateway routers) that lead outside the AS? Then the problem of knowing where to forward the packet becomes significantly more challenging. For example, consider a router in AS1 and suppose it receives a packet whose destination is outside the AS. The router should clearly forward the packet to one of its two gateway routers, 1b or 1c, but which one? To solve this problem, AS1 needs (1) to learn which destinations are reachable via AS2 and which destinations are reachable via AS3 and (2) to propagate this reachability information to all the routers within AS1, so that each router can configure its forwarding table to handle external-AS destinations. These two

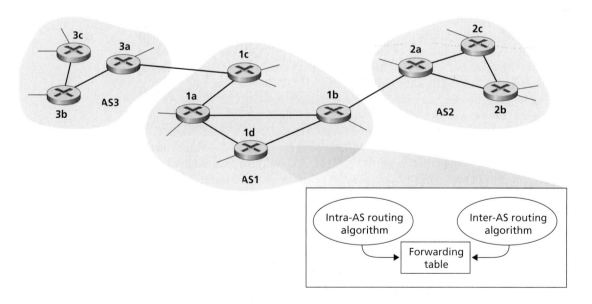

Figure 4.29 ◆ An example of interconnected autonomous systems

tasks—obtaining reachability information from neighboring ASs and propagating the reachability information to all routers internal to the AS—are handled by the **inter-AS routing protocol.** Since the inter-AS routing protocol involves communication between two ASs, the two communicating ASs must run the same inter-AS routing protocol. In fact, in the Internet all ASs run the same inter-AS routing protocol, called BGP4, which is discussed in the next section. As shown in Figure 4.29, each router receives information from an intra-AS routing protocol and an inter-AS routing protocol, and uses the information from both protocols to configure its forwarding table.

As an example, consider a subnet x (identified by its CDIRized address), and suppose that AS1 learns from the inter-AS routing protocol that subnet x is reachable from AS3 but is *not* reachable from AS2. AS1 then propagates this information to all of its routers. When router 1d learns that subnet x is reachable from AS3, and hence from gateway 1c, it then determines, from the information provided by the intra-AS routing protocol, the router interface that is on the least-cost path from router 1d to gateway router 1c. Say this is interface I. The router 1d can then put the entry (x, I) into its forwarding table. (This example, and others presented in this section, get the general ideas across but are simplifications of what really happens in the Internet. In the next section we'll provide a more detailed description, albeit more complicated, when we discuss BGP.)

Following up on the previous example, now suppose that AS2 and AS3 connect to other ASs, which are not shown in the diagram. Also suppose that AS1 learns from the inter-AS routing protocol that subnet x is reachable both from AS2, via gateway 1b, and from AS3, via gateway 1c. AS1 would then propagate this information to all its routers, including router 1d. In order to configure its forwarding table, router 1d would have to determine to which gateway router, 1b or 1c, it should direct packets that are destined for subnet x. One approach, which is often employed in practice, is to use **hot-potato routing**. In hot-potato routing, the AS gets rid of the packet (the hot potato) as quickly as possible (more precisely, as inexpensively as possible). This is done by having a router send the packet to the gateway router that has the smallest router-to-gateway cost among all gateways with a path to the destination. In the context of the current example, hot-potato routing, running in 1d, would use information from the intra-AS routing protocol to determine the path costs to 1b and 1c, and then choose the path with the least cost. Once this path is chosen, router 1d adds an entry for subnet x in its forwarding table. Figure 4.30 summarizes the actions taken at router 1d for adding the new entry for x to the forwarding table.

When an AS learns about a destination from a neighboring AS, the AS can advertise this routing information to some of its other neighboring ASs. For example, suppose AS1 learns from AS2 that subnet x is reachable via AS2. AS1 could then tell AS3 that x is reachable via AS1. In this manner, if AS3 needs to route a packet destined to x, AS3 would forward the packet to AS1, which would in turn forward the packet to AS2. As we'll see in our discussion of BGP, an AS has quite a bit of flexibility in deciding which destinations it advertises to its neighboring ASs.

| Learn from inter-AS protocol that subnet x is reachable via multiple gateways. | → | Use routing info from intra-AS protocol to determine costs of least-cost paths to each of the gateways. | → | Hot potato routing: Choose the gateway that has the smallest least cost. | → | Determine from forwarding table the interface I that leads to least-cost gateway. Enter (x,I) in forwarding table. |

Figure 4.30 ♦ Steps in adding an outside-AS destination in a router's forwarding table

This is a *policy* decision, typically depending more on economic issues than on technical issues.

Recall from Section 1.5 that the Internet consists of a hierarchy of interconnected ISPs. So what is the relationship between ISPs and ASs? You might think that the routers in an ISP, and the links that interconnect them, constitute a single AS. Although this is often the case, many ISPs partition their network into multiple ASs. For example, some tier-1 ISPs use one AS for their entire network; others break up their ISP into tens of interconnected ASs.

In summary, the problems of scale and administrative authority are solved by defining autonomous systems. Within an AS, all routers run the same intra-autonomous system routing protocol. Among themselves, the ASs run the same inter-AS routing protocol. The problem of scale is solved because an intra-AS router need only know about routers within its AS. The problem of administrative authority is solved since an organization can run whatever intra-AS routing protocol it chooses; however, each pair of connected ASs needs to run the same inter-AS routing protocol to exchange reachability information.

In the following section, we'll examine two intra-AS routing protocols (RIP and OSPF) and the inter-AS routing protocol (BGP) that are used in today's Internet. These case studies will nicely round out our study of hierarchical routing.

4.6 Routing in the Internet

Having studied Internet addressing and the IP protocol, we now turn our attention to the Internet's routing protocols; their job is to determine the path taken by a datagram between source and destination. We'll see that the Internet's routing protocols embody many of the principles we learned earlier in this chapter. The link-state and distance-vector approaches studied in Sections 4.5.1 and 4.5.2, and the notion of an autonomous system considered in Section 4.5.3 are all central to how routing is done in today's Internet.

Recall from Section 4.5.3 that an autonomous system (AS) is a collection of routers under the same administrative and technical control, and that all run the same routing protocol among themselves. Each AS, in turn, typically contains multiple subnets (where we use the term subnet in the precise, addressing sense in Section 4.4.2).

4.6.1 Intra-AS Routing in the Internet: RIP

An intra-AS routing protocol is used to determine how routing is performed within an autonomous system (AS). Intra-AS routing protocols are also known as **interior gateway protocols**. Historically, two routing protocols have been used extensively for routing within an autonomous system in the Internet: the **Routing Information Protocol (RIP)** and **Open Shortest Path First (OSPF)**. A routing protocol closely related to OSPF is the **IS-IS** protocol [RFC 1142, Perlman 1999]. We first discuss RIP and then consider OSPF.

RIP was one of the earliest intra-AS Internet routing protocols and is still in widespread use today. It traces its origins and its name to the Xerox Network Systems (XNS) architecture. The widespread deployment of RIP was due in great part to its inclusion in 1982 of the Berkeley Software Distribution (BSD) version of UNIX supporting TCP/IP. RIP version 1 is defined in RFC 1058, with a backward-compatible version 2 defined in RFC 2453.

RIP is a distance-vector protocol that operates in a manner very close to the idealized DV protocol we examined in Section 4.5.2. The version of RIP specified in RFC 1058 uses hop count as a cost metric; that is, each link has a cost of 1. In the DV algorithm in Section 4.5.2, for simplicity, costs were defined between pairs of routers. In RIP (and also in OSPF), costs are actually from source router to a destination subnet. RIP uses the term *hop*, which is the number of subnets traversed along the shortest path from source router to destination subnet, including the destination subnet. Figure 4.31 illustrates an AS with six leaf subnets. The table in the figure indicates the number of hops from the source A to all the leaf subnets.

The maximum cost of a path is limited to 15, thus limiting the use of RIP to autonomous systems that are fewer than 15 hops in diameter. Recall that in DV protocols, neighboring routers exchange distance vectors with each other. The distance vector for any one router is the current estimate of the shortest path distances from that router to the subnets in the AS. In RIP, routing updates are exchanged between neighbors approximately every 30 seconds using a **RIP response message**. The response message sent by a router or host contains a list of up to 25 destination subnets within the AS, as well as the sender's distance to each of those subnets. Response messages are also known as **RIP advertisements**.

Let's take a look at a simple example of how RIP advertisements work. Consider the portion of an AS shown in Figure 4.32. In this figure, lines connecting the routers denote subnets. Only selected routers (*A, B, C,* and *D*) and subnets (*w, x, y,*

Destination	Hops
u	1
v	2
w	2
x	3
y	3
z	2

Figure 4.31 ♦ Number of hops from source router A to various subnets

and *z*) are labeled. Dotted lines indicate that the AS continues on; thus this autonomous system has many more routers and links than are shown.

Each router maintains a RIP table known as a **routing table**. A router's routing table includes both the router's distance vector and the router's forwarding table. Figure 4.33 shows the routing table for router *D*. Note that the routing table has three columns. The first column is for the destination subnet, the second column indicates the identity of the next router along the shortest path to the destination subnet, and the third column indicates the number of hops (that is, the number of subnets that have to be traversed, including the destination subnet) to get to the destination subnet along the shortest path. For this example, the table indicates that to send a datagram from router *D* to destination subnet *w*, the datagram should first be forwarded to neighboring router *A;* the table also indicates that destination subnet *w* is two hops away along the shortest path. Similarly, the table indicates that subnet *z* is seven hops away via router *B*. In principle, a routing table will have one row for each subnet in the AS, although RIP version 2 allows subnet entries to be aggregated using route aggregation techniques similar to those we examined in Section 4.4. The table in Figure 4.33, and the subsequent tables to come, are only partially complete.

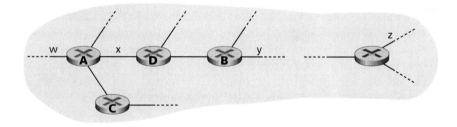

Figure 4.32 ♦ A portion of an autonomous system

Destination Subnet	Next Router	Number of Hops to Destination
w	A	2
y	B	2
z	B	7
x	—	1
. . . .	. . . .	. . . .

Figure 4.33 ◆ Routing table in router *D* before receiving advertisement from router *A*

Now suppose that 30 seconds later, router *D* receives from router *A* the advertisement shown in Figure 4.34. Note that this advertisement is nothing other than the routing table information from router *A*! This information indicates, in particular, that subnet *z* is only four hops away from router *A*. Router *D*, upon receiving this advertisement, merges the advertisement (Figure 4.34) with the old routing table (Figure 4.33). In particular, router *D* learns that there is now a path through router *A* to subnet *z* that is shorter than the path through router *B*. Thus, router *D* updates its routing table to account for the shorter shortest path, as shown in Figure 4.35. How is it, you might ask, that the shortest path to subnet *z* has become shorter? Possibly, the decentralized distance vector algorithm is still in the process of converging (see Section 4.5.2), or perhaps new links and/or routers were added to the AS, thus changing the shortest paths in the AS.

Let's next consider a few of the implementation aspects of RIP. Recall that RIP routers exchange advertisements approximately every 30 seconds. If a router does not hear from its neighbor at least once every 180 seconds, that neighbor is considered to be no longer reachable; that is, either the neighbor has died or the connecting link has gone down. When this happens, RIP modifies the local routing table and

Destination Subnet	Next Router	Number of Hops to Destination
z	C	4
w	—	1
x	—	1
. . . .	. . . .	. . . .

Figure 4.34 ◆ Advertisement from router *A*

Destination Subnet	Next Router	Number of Hops to Destination
w	A	2
y	B	2
z	A	5
. . . .	. . . .	. . . .

Figure 4.35   ◆   Routing table in router *D* after receiving advertisement from router *A*

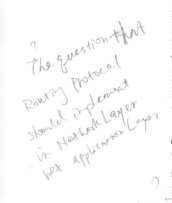

then propagates this information by sending advertisements to its neighboring routers (the ones that are still reachable). A router can also request information about its neighbor's cost to a given destination using RIP's request message. Routers send RIP request and response messages to each other over UDP using port number 520. The UDP segment is carried between routers in a standard IP datagram. The fact that RIP uses a transport-layer protocol (UDP) on top of a network-layer protocol (IP) to implement network-layer functionality (a routing algorithm) may seem rather convoluted (it is!). Looking a little deeper at how RIP is implemented will clear this up.

Figure 4.36 sketches how RIP is typically implemented in a UNIX system, for example, a UNIX workstation serving as a router. A process called routed (pronounced "route dee") executes RIP, that is, maintains routing information and exchanges messages with routed processes running in neighboring routers. Because RIP is implemented as an application-layer process (albeit a very special one that is able to manipulate the routing tables within the UNIX kernel), it can send and receive messages over a standard socket and use a standard transport protocol. As shown, RIP is implemented as an application-layer protocol (see Chapter 2) running over UDP.

4.6.2 Intra-AS Routing in the Internet: OSPF

Like RIP, OSPF routing is widely used for intra-AS routing in the Internet. OSPF and its closely related cousin, IS-IS, are typically deployed in upper-tier ISPs whereas RIP is deployed in lower-tier ISPs and enterprise networks. The Open in OSPF indicates that the routing protocol specification is publicly available (for example, as opposed to Cisco's EIGRP protocol). The most recent version of OSPF, version 2, is defined in RFC 2328, a public document.

OSPF was conceived as the successor to RIP and as such has a number of advanced features. At its heart, however, OSPF is a link-state protocol that uses flooding of link-state information and a Dijkstra least-cost path algorithm. With

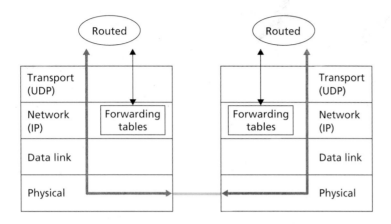

Figure 4.36 ♦ Implementation of RIP as the *routed* daemon

OSPF, a router constructs a complete topological map (that is, a graph) of the entire autonomous system. The router then locally runs Dijkstra's shortest-path algorithm to determine a shortest-path tree to all subnets, with itself as the root node. Individual link costs are configured by the network administrator (see Principles and Practice: Setting OSPF Weights). The administrator might choose to set all link costs to 1, thus achieving minimum-hop routing, or might choose to set the link weights to be inversely proportional to link capacity in order to discourage traffic from using low-bandwidth links. OSPF does not mandate a policy for how link weights are set (that is the job of the network administrator), but instead provides the mechanisms (protocol) for determining least-cost path routing for the given set of link weights.

With OSPF, a router broadcasts routing information to *all* other routers in the autonomous system, not just to its neighboring routers. A router broadcasts link-state information whenever there is a change in a link's state (for example, a change in cost or a change in up/down status). It also broadcasts a link's state periodically (at least once every 30 minutes), even if the link's state has not changed. RFC 2328 notes that "this periodic updating of link state advertisements adds robustness to the link state algorithm." OSPF advertisements are contained in OSPF messages that are carried directly by IP, with an upper-layer protocol of 89 for OSPF. Thus, the OSPF protocol must itself implement functionality such as reliable message transfer and link-state broadcast. The OSPF protocol also checks that links are operational (via a HELLO message that is sent to an attached neighbor) and allows an OSPF router to obtain a neighboring router's database of network-wide link state.

Some of the advances embodied in OSPF include the following:

♦ *Security.* Exchanges between OSPF routers (for example, link-state updates) are authenticated. With authentication, only trusted routers can participate in the OSPF protocol within a an AS, thus preventing malicious intruders (or networking students taking their newfound knowledge out for a joyride) from injecting incorrect information into router tables. By default, OSPF packets between routers are not authenticated and could be forged. Two types of authentication can be configured—simple and MD5 (see Chapter 8 for a discussion on MD5 and authentication in general). With simple authentication, the same password is configured on each router. When a router sends an OSPF packet, it includes the password in plaintext. Clearly, simple authentication is not secure. MD5 authentication is based on shared secret keys that are configured in all the routers. Each router computes an MD5 hash for each OSPF packet based on the content of the packet and the configured secret key. Then it includes the resulting hash value in the OSPF packet. The receiving router, using the preconfigured secret key, will compute an MD5 hash of the packet and compare it with the hash value that the packet carries, thus verifying the packet's authenticity. Sequence numbers are also used with MD5 authentication to protect against replay attacks.

♦ *Multiple same-cost paths.* When multiple paths to a destination have the same cost, OSPF allows multiple paths to be used (that is, a single path need not be chosen for carrying all traffic when multiple equal-cost paths exist).

♦ *Integrated support for unicast and multicast routing.* Multicast OSPF (MOSPF) [RFC 1584] provides simple extensions to OSPF to provide for multicast routing (a topic we cover in more depth in Section 4.7.2). MOSPF uses the existing OSPF link database and adds a new type of link-state advertisement to the existing OSPF link-state broadcast mechanism.

♦ *Support for hierarchy within a single routing domain.* Perhaps the most significant advance in OSPF is the ability to structure an autonomous system hierarchically. Section 4.5.3 has already looked at the many advantages of hierarchical routing structures. We cover the implementation of OSPF hierarchical routing in the remainder of this section.

An OSPF autonomous system can be configured into areas. Each area runs its own OSPF link-state routing algorithm, with each router in an area broadcasting its link state to all other routers in that area. The internal details of an area thus remain invisible to all routers outside the area. Intra-area routing involves only those routers within the same area.

Within each area, one or more **area border routers** are responsible for routing packets outside the area. Exactly one OSPF area in the AS is configured to be the **backbone** area. The primary role of the backbone area is to route traffic between the other areas in the AS. The backbone always contains all area border routers in the AS and may contain nonborder routers as well. Inter-area routing within the AS requires that the packet be first routed to an area border router (intra-area routing), then routed through the backbone to the area border router that is in the destination area, and then routed to the final destination.

A diagram of a hierarchically structured OSPF network is shown in Figure 4.37. We can identify four types of OSPF routers in Figure 4.37:

♦ *Internal routers.* These routers are in nonbackbone areas and perform only intra-AS routing.

♦ *Area border routers.* These routers belong to both an area and the backbone.

♦ *Backbone routers (nonborder routers).* These routers perform routing within the backbone but themselves are not area border routers. Within a nonbackbone area, internal routers learn of the existence of routes to other areas from information (essentially a link-state advertisement, but advertising the cost of a route to another area, rather than a link cost) broadcast within the area by its backbone routers.

♦ *Boundary routers.* A boundary router exchanges routing information with routers belonging to other autonomous systems. This router might, for example, use BGP to perform inter-AS routing. It is through such a boundary router that other routers learn about paths to external networks.

OSPF is a relatively complex protocol, and our coverage here has been necessarily brief; [Huitema 1998; Moy 1998; RFC 2328] provide additional details.

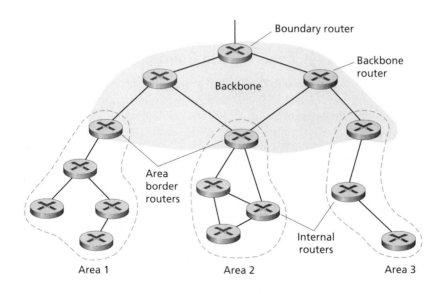

Figure 4.37 ♦ Hierarchically structured OSPF AS with four areas

PRINCIPLES IN PRACTICE

SETTING OSPF LINK WEIGHTS

Our discussion of link-state routing has implicitly assumed that link weights are set, a routing algorithm such as OSPF is run, and traffic flows according to the routing tables computed by the LS algorithm. In terms of cause and effect, the link weights are given (i.e., they come first) and result (via Dijkstra's algorithm) in routing paths that minimize overall cost. In this viewpoint, link weights reflect the cost of using a link (e.g., if link weights are inversely proportional to capacity, then the use of high capacity links would have smaller weights and thus be more attractive from a routing standpoint) and Disjkstra's algorithm serves to minimize overall cost.

In practice, the cause and effect relationship between link weights and routing paths may be reversed, with network operators configuring link weights in order to obtain routing paths that achieve certain traffic engineering goals [Fortz 2000, Fortz 2002]. For example, suppose a network operator has an estimate of traffic flow entering the network at each ingress point and destined for each egress point. The operator may then want to put in place a specific routing of ingress-to-egress flows that minimizes the maximum utilization over all of the network's links. But with a routing algorithm such as OSPF, the operator's main "knobs" for tuning the routing of flows through the network are the links weights. Thus, in order to achieve the goal of minimizing the maximum link utilization, the operator must find the set of link weights that achieve this goal. This is a reversal of the cause and effect relationship—the desired routing of flows is known, and the OSPF link weights must be found such that the OSPF routing algorithm results in this desired routing of flows.

4.6.3 Inter–Autonomous System Routing: BGP

We just learned how ISPs use RIP and OSPF to determine optimal paths for source-destination pairs that are internal to the same AS. Let's now examine how paths are determined for source-destination pairs that span multiple ASs. The **Border Gateway Protocol** version 4, specified in RFC 1771 (see also [RFC 1772; RFC 1773]), is the *de facto* standard inter-AS routing protocol in today's Internet. It is commonly referred to as BGP4 or simply as **BGP**. As an inter-AS routing protocol (see Section 4.5.3), BGP provides each AS a means to

1. Obtain subnet reachability information from neighboring ASs.
2. Propagate the reachability information to all routers internal to the AS.
3. Determine "good" routes to subnets based on the reachability information and on AS policy.

In particular, BGP allows each subnet to advertise its existence to the rest of the Internet. A subnet screams "I exist and I am here," and BGP makes sure that all the

ASs in the Internet know about the subnet and how to get there. If it weren't for BGP, each subnet would be isolated—alone and unknown by the rest of the Internet.

BGP Basics

BGP is extremely complex; entire books have been devoted to the subject. Furthermore, even after having read the books and RFCs, you may find it difficult to fully master BGP without having practiced BGP for many months (if not years) as a designer or administrator of an upper-tier ISP. Nevertheless, because BGP is an absolutely critical protocol for the Internet—in essence, it is the protocol that glues the whole thing together—we need to acquire at least a rudimentary understanding of how it works. We begin by describing how BGP might work in the context of the simple example network we studied earlier in Figure 4.29. In this description, we build on our discussion of hierarchical routing in Section 4.5.3; we encourage you to review that material.

In BGP, pairs of routers exchange routing information over semi-permanent TCP connections using port 179. The semi-permanent TCP connections for the network in Figure 4.29 are shown in Figure 4.38. There is typically one such BGP TCP connection for each link that directly connects two routers in two different ASs; thus, in Figure 4.38, there is a TCP connection between gateway routers 3a and 1c and another TCP connection between gateway routers 1b and 2a. There are also semipermanent BGP TCP connections between routers within an AS. In particular, Figure 4.38 displays a common configuration of one TCP connection for each pair of routers internal to an AS, creating a mesh of TCP connections within each AS. For each TCP connection, the two routers at the end the connection are called **BGP peers**, and the TCP connection along with all the BGP messages sent over the connection is called a **BGP session**. Furthermore, a BGP session that spans two ASs is called an **external BGP (eBGP) session**, and a BGP session between routers in the same AS is called an **internal BGP (iBGP) session**. In Figure 4.38, the eBGP sessions are shown with the long dashes; the iBGP sessions are shown with the short dashes. Note that BGP session lines in Figure 4.38 do not always correspond to the physical links in Figure 4.29.

BGP allows each AS to learn which destinations are reachable via its neighboring ASs. In BGP, destinations are not hosts but instead are CDIRized **prefixes**, with each prefix representing a subnet or a collection of subnets. Thus, for example, suppose there are four subnets attached to AS2: 138.16.64/24, 138.16.65/24, 138.16.66/24, and 138.16.67/24. Then AS2 could aggregate the prefixes for these four subnets and use BGP to advertise the single prefix to 138.16.64/22 to AS1. As another example, suppose that only the first three of those four subnets are in AS2 and the fourth subnet, 138.16.67/24, is in AS3. Then, as described in the Principles and Practice in Section 4.4.2, because routers use longest-prefix matching for forwarding datagrams, AS3 could advertise to AS1 the more specific prefix 138.16.67/24 and AS2 could *still* advertise to AS1 the aggregated prefix

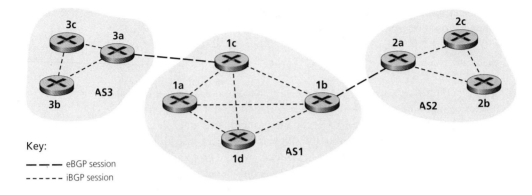

Figure 4.38 ♦ eBGP and iBGP sessions

138.16.64/22. We can think of each prefix advertisement as a promise. When one AS advertises a prefix to another AS, the advertising AS is promising that it will forward any datagram destined for the prefix along a path toward the prefix.

Let's now examine how BGP would distribute prefix reachability information over the BGP sessions shown in Figure 4.38. As you might expect, using the eBGP session between the gateway routers 3a and 1c, AS3 sends AS1 the list of prefixes that are reachable from AS3; and AS1 sends AS3 the list of prefixes that are reachable from AS1. Similarly, AS1 and AS2 exchange prefix reachability information through their gateway routers 1b and 2a. Also as you may expect, when a gateway router (in any AS) receives eBGP-learned prefixes, the gateway router uses its iBGP sessions to distribute the prefixes to the other routers in the AS. Thus, not only will non-eBGP routers in AS1 learn about AS3's prefixes, but so will the gateway router 1b learn about them. The gateway router 1b (in AS1) can therefore re-advertise AS3's prefixes to AS2. When a router (gateway or not) learns about a new prefix, it creates an entry for the prefix in its forwarding table, as described in Section 4.5.3.

Path Attributes and BGP Routes

Having now a preliminary understanding of BGP, let's get a little deeper into it (while still brushing some of less important details under the rug!). In BGP, an autonomous system is identified by its globally unique **autonomous system number (ASN)** [RFC 1930]. (Technically, not every AS has an ASN. In particular, a so-called stub AS that carries only traffic for which it is a source or destination will not typically have an ASN; we ignore this technicality in our discussion in order to better see the forest for the trees.) AS numbers, like IP addresses, are assigned by ICANN regional registries [ICANN 2004].

When a router advertises a prefix across a BGP session, it includes with the prefix a number of **BGP attributes**. In BGP jargon, a prefix along with its attributes is called a **route**. Thus, BGP peers advertise routes to each other. Two of the more important attributes are AS-PATH and NEXT-HOP:

♦ *AS-PATH*. This attribute contains the ASs through which the advertisement for the prefix has passed. When a prefix is passed into an AS, the AS adds its ASN to the AS-PATH attribute. For example, consider Figure 4.38 and suppose that prefix 138.16.64/24 is first advertised from AS2 to AS1; if AS1 then advertises the prefix to AS3, the AS-PATH would be AS2 AS1. Routers use the AS-PATH attribute to detect and prevent looping advertisements; specifically, if a router sees that its AS is contained in the path list, it will reject the advertisement. As we'll soon discuss, routers also use the AS-PATH attribute in choosing among multiple paths to the same prefix.

♦ *NEXT-HOP*. A pair of ASs, say AS A and AS B, may have multiple physical links that directly connect them. Thus, when a packet is forwarded from AS A to AS B, it could be sent over any one of the links that directly connect the ASs. When a gateway router in AS B sends a router advertisement to a gateway router in AS A, it includes in the advertisement its IP address (more specifically, the IP address of the interface that leads to the gateway router in AS A). A router in AS A may receive from eBGP and iBGP multiple routes to the same prefix, each passing through a different next-hop router. When configuring its forwarding table, this router would have to select among the multiple routes.

BGP also includes attributes that allow routers to assign preference metrics to the routes, and an attribute that indicates how the prefix was inserted into BGP at the origin AS. For a full discussion of route attributes, see [Griffin 2002; Stewart 1999; Halabi 2000; Feamster 2004].

When a gateway router receives a router advertisement, it uses its **import policy** to decide whether to accept or filter the route and whether to set certain attributes such as the router preference metrics. The import policy may filter a route because the AS may not want to send traffic over one of the ASs in the route's AS-PATH. The gateway router may also filter a route because it already knows of a preferable route to the same prefix.

BGP Route Selection

As described earlier in this section, BGP uses eBGP and iBGP to distribute routes to all the routers within ASs. From this distribution, a router may learn about more than one route to any one prefix, in which case the router must select one of the possible routes. The inputs into this route selection process is the set of all routes that have been learned and accepted by the router. If there are two or more routes to the same prefix, then BGP sequentially invokes the following elimination rules until one route remains.

♦ Routes are assigned a local preference value as one of their attritbutes. The local preference of a route could have been set by the router or could have been learned by another router in the same AS. This is a policy decision that is left up to the AS's network administrator. (We will shortly discuss BGP policy isses in some detail.) The routes with the highest local preference values are selected.

♦ From the remaining routes (all with the same local preference value), the route with the shortest AS-PATH is selected. If this rule were the only rule for route selection, then BGP would be using a DV algorithm for path determination, where the distance metric uses the number of AS hops rather than the number of router hops.

♦ From the remaining routes (all with the same local preference value and the same AS-PATH length), the route with the closest NEXT-HOP router is selected. Here, closest means the router for which the cost of the least-cost path, determined by the intra-AS algorithm, is the smallest. This process is often referred to as hot-potato routing.

♦ If more than one route still remains, the router uses BGP identifiers to select the route; see [Stewart 1999].

The elimination rules are even more complicated than described above. To avoid nightmares about BGP, it's best to learn about BGP selection rules in small doses!

Routing Policy

Let's illustrate some of the basic concepts of BGP routing with a simple example. Figure 4.39 shows six interconnected autonomous systems: A, B, C, W, X, and Y. It is important to note that A, B, C, W, X, and Y are ASs, not routers. Let's assume that autonomous systems W, X, and Y are stub networks and that A, B, and C are back-bone provider networks. All traffic entering a **stub network** must be destined for that network, and all traffic leaving a stub network must have originated in that network. W and Y are clearly stub networks. X is a **multi-homed stub network,** since it is connected to the rest of the network via two different providers (a scenario that is becoming increasingly common in practice). However, like W and Y, X itself must be the source/destination of all traffic leaving/entering X. But how will this stub network behavior be implemented and enforced? How will X be prevented from forwarding traffic between B and C? This can easily be accomplished by controlling the manner in which BGP routes are advertised. In particular, X will function as a stub network if it advertises (to its neighbors B and C) that it has no paths to any other destinations except itself. That is, even though X may know of a path,

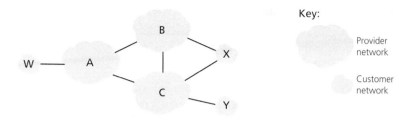

Figure 4.39 ♦ A simple BGP scenario

say XCY, that reaches network Y, it will *not* advertise this path to B. Since B is unaware that X has a path to Y, B would never forward traffic destined to Y (or C) via X. This simple example illustrates how a selective route advertisement policy can be used to implement customer/provider routing relationships.

Let's next focus on a provider network, say AS B. Suppose that B has learned (from A) that A has a path AW to W. B can thus install the route BAW into its routing information base. Clearly, B also wants to advertise the path BAW to its customer, X, so that X knows that it can route to W via B. But should B advertise the path BAW to C? If it does so, then C could route traffic to W via CBAW. If A, B, and C are all backbone providers, than B might rightly feel that it should not have to shoulder the burden (and cost!) of carrying transit traffic between A and C. B might rightly feel that it is A and C's job (and cost!) to make sure that C can route to/from A's customers via a direct connection between A and C. There are currently no official standards that govern how backbone ISPs route among themselves. However, a rule of thumb followed by commercial ISPs is that any traffic flowing across an ISP's backbone network must have either a source or a destination (or both) in a network that is a customer of that ISP; otherwise the traffic would be getting a free ride on the ISP's network. Individual peering agreements (that would govern questions such as those raised above) are typically negotiated between pairs of ISPs and are often confidential; [Huston 1999a] provides an interesting discussion of peering agreements. For a detailed description of how routing policy reflects commercial relationships among ISPs see [Gao 2001].

As noted above, BGP is the *de facto* standard for inter-AS routing for the public Internet. To see the contents of various BGP routing tables (large!) extracting from routers in tier-1 ISPs, see http://www.routeviews.org. BGP routing tables often contain tens of thousands of prefixes and corresponding attributes. Statistics about the size and characteristics of BGP routing tables are presented in [Huston 2001].

This completes our brief introduction to BGP. Understanding BGP is important because it plays a central role in the Internet. We encourage you to see the references [Griffin 2002; Stewart 1999; Labovitz 1997; Halabi 2000; Huitema 1998; Gao 2001; Feamster 2004] to learn more about BGP.

PRINCIPLES IN PRACTICE

WHY ARE THERE DIFFERENT INTER-AS AND INTRA-AS ROUTING PROTOCOLS?

Having now studied the details of specific inter-AS and intra-AS routing protocols deployed in today's Internet, let's conclude by considering perhaps the most fundamental question we could ask about these protocols in the first place (hopefully, you have been wondering this all along, and have not lost the forest for the trees!): Why are different inter-AS and intra-AS routing protocols used?

The answer to this question gets at the heart of the differences between the goals of routing within an AS and among ASs:

♦ *Policy.* Among ASs, policy issues dominate. It may well be important that traffic originating in a given AS not be able to pass through another specific AS. Similarly, a given AS may well want to control what transit traffic it carries between other ASs. We have seen that BGP carries path attributes and provides for controlled distribution of routing information so that such policy-based routing decisions can be made. Within an AS, everything is nominally under the same administrative control, and thus policy issues play a much less important role in choosing routes within the AS.

♦ *Scale.* The ability of a routing algorithm and its data structures to scale to handle routing to/among large numbers of networks is a critical issue in inter-AS routing. Within an AS, scalability is less of a concern. For one thing, if a single administrative domain becomes too large, it is always possible to divide it into two ASs and perform inter-AS routing between the two new ASs. (Recall that OSPF allows such a hierarchy to be built by splitting an AS into areas.)

♦ *Performance.* Because inter-AS routing is so policy oriented, the quality (for example, performance) of the routes used is often of secondary concern (that is, a longer or more costly route that satisfies certain policy criteria may well be taken over a route that is shorter but does not meet that criteria). Indeed, we saw that among ASs, there is not even the notion of cost (other than AS hop count) associated with routes. Within a single AS, however, such policy concerns are of less importance, allowing routing to focus more on the level of performance realized on a route.

4.7 Broadcast and Multicast Routing

Thus far in this chapter, our focus has been on routing protocols that support unicast (i.e., point-to-point) communication, in which a single source node sends a packet to a single destination node. In this section, we turn our attention to broadcast and multicast routing protocols. In **broadcast routing**, the network layer provides a service of delivering a packet sent from a source node to all other nodes in the network; **multicast routing** enables a single source node to send a copy of a packet to a subset of the other network nodes. In Section 4.7.1 we'll consider broadcast routing algorithms and their embodiment in routing protocols. We'll examine multicast routing in Section 4.7.2.

4.7.1 Broadcast Routing Algorithms

Perhaps the most straightforward way to accomplish broadcast communication is for the sending node to send a separate copy of the packet to each destination, as shown in Figure 4.40(a). Given N destination nodes, the source node simply makes N copies of the packet, addresses each copy to a different destination, and then transmits the N copies to the N destinations using unicast routing. This **N-way-unicast** approach to broadcasting is simple—no new network-layer routing protocol, packet-duplication, or forwarding functionality is needed. There are, however, several drawbacks to this approach. The first drawback is its inefficiency. If the source node is connected to the rest of the network via a single link, then N separate copies of the (same) packet will traverse this single link. It would clearly be more efficient to send only a single copy of a packet over this first hop and then have the node at the other end of the first hop make and forward any additional needed copies. That is, it would be more efficient for the network nodes themselves (rather than just the source node) to create duplicate copies of a packet. For example, in Figure 4.40(b), only a single copy of a packet traverses the R1-R2 link. That packet is then duplicated at R2, with a single copy being sent over links R2-R3 and R2-R4.

The additional drawbacks of N-way-unicast are perhaps more subtle, but no less important. An implicit assumption of N-way-unicast is that broadcast recipients, and their addresses, are known to the sender. But how is this information obtained? Most likely, additional protocol mechanisms (such as a broadcast membership or

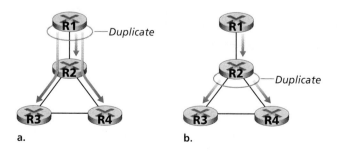

Duplicate creation/transmission

a.

b.

Figure 4.40 ◆ Source-duplication versus in-network duplication.

destination-registration protocol) would be required. This would add more overhead and, importantly, additional complexity to a protocol that had initially seemed quite simple. A final drawback of *N*-way-unicast relates to the purposes for which broadcast is to be used. In Section 4.5, we learned that link-state routing protocols use broadcast to disseminate the link-state information that is used to compute unicast routes. Clearly, in situations where broadcast is used to create and update unicast routes, it would be unwise (at best!) to rely on the unicast routing infrastructure to achieve broadcast.

Given the several drawbacks of *N*-way-unicast broadcast, approaches in which the network nodes themselves play an active role in packet duplication, packet forwarding, and computation of the broadcast routes are clearly of interest. We'll examine several such approaches below and again adopt the graph notation introduced in Section 4.5. We again model the network as a graph, $G = (N,E)$, where N is a set of nodes and a collection E of edges, where each edge is a pair of nodes from N. We'll be a bit sloppy with our notation and use N to refer to both the set of nodes, as well as the cardinality ($|N|$) or size of that set when there is no confusion.

Uncontrolled Flooding

The most obvious technique for achieving broadcast is a **flooding** approach in which the source node sends a copy of the packet to all of its neighbors. When a node receives a broadcast packet, it duplicates the packet and forwards it to all of its neighbors (except the neighbor from which it received the packet). Clearly, if the graph is connected, this scheme will eventually deliver a copy of the broadcast packet to all nodes in the graph. Although this scheme is simple and elegant, it has a fatal flaw (before you read on, see if you can figure out this fatal flaw): If the graph has cycles, then one or more copies of each broadcast packet will cycle indefinitely. For example, in Figure 4.40, R2 will flood to R3, R3 will flood to R4, R4 will flood to R2, and R2 will flood (again!) to R3, and so on. This simple scenario results in the endless cycling of two broadcast packets, one clockwise, and one counterclockwise. But there can be an even more calamitous fatal flaw: When a node is connected to more than two other nodes, it will create and forward multiple copies of the broadcast packet, each of which will create multiple copies of themselves (at other nodes with more then two neighbors), and so on. This **broadcast storm**, resulting from the endless multiplication of broadcast packets, would eventually result in so many broadcast packets being created that the network would be rendered useless. (See the homework questions at the end of the chapter for a problem analyzing the rate at which such a broadcast storm grows.)

Controlled Flooding

The key to avoiding a broadcast storm is for a node to judiciously choose when to flood a packet and (e.g., if it has already received and flooded an earlier copy of a packet) when not to flood a packet. In practice, this can be done in one of several ways.

In **sequence-number-controlled flooding**, a source node puts its address (or other unique identifier) as well as a **broadcast sequence number** into a broadcast packet, then sends the packet to all of its neighbors. Each node maintains a list of the source address and sequence number of each broadcast packet it has already received, duplicated, and forwarded. When a node receives a broadcast packet, it first checks whether the packet is in this list. If so, the packet is dropped; if not, the packet is duplicated and forwarded to all the node's neighbors (except the node from which the packet has just been received). The Gnutella protocol, discussed in Chapter 2, uses sequence-number-controlled flooding to broadcast queries in its overlay network. (In Gnutella, message duplication and forwarding is performed at the application layer, rather than at the network layer.)

A second approach to controlled flooding is known as **reverse path forwarding (RPF)** [Dalal 1978], also sometimes referred to as reverse path broadcast (RPB). The idea behind RPF is simple, yet elegant. When a router receives a broadcast packet with a given source address, it transmits the packet on all of its outgoing links (except the one on which it was received) only if the packet arrived on the link that is on its own shortest unicast path back to the source. Otherwise, the router simply discards the incoming packet without forwarding it on any of its outgoing links. Such a packet can be dropped because the router knows it either will receive, or has already received, a copy of this packet on the link that is on its own shortest path back to the sender. (You might want to convince yourself that this will, in fact, happen and that looping and broadcast storms will not occur.) Note that RPF does not use unicast routing to actually deliver a packet to a destination, nor does it require that a router know the complete shortest path from itself to the source. RPF need only know the next neighbor on its unicast shortest path to the sender; it uses this neighbor's identity only to determine whether or not to flood a received broadcast packet.

Figure 4.41 illustrates RPF. Suppose that the links drawn with thick lines represent the least-cost paths from the receivers to the source (A). Node A initially broadcasts a source-A packet to nodes C and B. Node B will forward the source-A packet it has received from A (since A is on its least-cost path to A) to both C and D. B will ignore (drop, without forwarding) any source-A packets it receives from any other nodes (for example, from routers C or D). Let us now consider node C, which will receive a source-A packet directly from A as well as from B. Since B is not on C's own shortest path back to A, C will ignore any source-A packets it receives from B. On the other hand, when C receives a source-A packet directly from A, it will forward the packet to nodes B, E, and F.

Spanning-Tree Broadcast

While sequence-number controlled flooding and RPF avoid broadcast storms, they do not completely avoid the transmission of redundant broadcast packets. For example, in Figure 4.42, nodes B, C, D, E, and F receive either one or two redundant packets. Ideally, every node should receive only one copy of the broadcast packet.

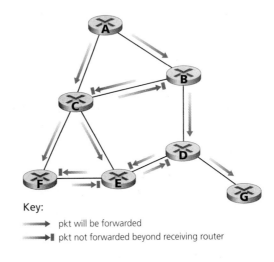

Key:

➡ pkt will be forwarded

➡▌ pkt not forwarded beyond receiving router

Figure 4.41 ◆ Reverse path forwarding

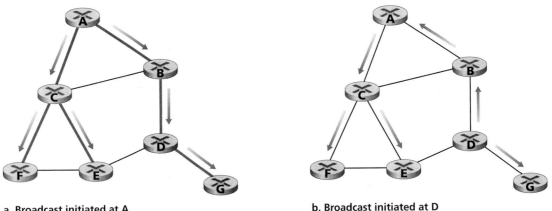

a. Broadcast initiated at A

b. Broadcast initiated at D

Figure 4.42 ◆ Broadcast along a spanning tree

Examining the tree consisting of the nodes connected by thick lines in Figure 4.42(a), you can see that if broadcast packets were forwarded only along links within this tree, each and every network node would receive exactly one copy of the broadcast packet—exactly the solution we were looking for! This tree is an example of a **spanning tree**—a tree that contains each and every node in a graph. More formally, a spanning tree of a graph $G = (N,E)$ is a graph $G' = (N,E')$ such that E' is a subset of E, G' is connected, G' contains no cycles, and G' contains all the original nodes in *G*. If each link has an associated cost and the cost of a tree is the sum of the link costs, then a spanning tree whose cost is the minimum of all of the graph's spanning trees is called (not surprisingly) a **minimum spanning tree**.

Thus, another approach to providing broadcast is for the network nodes to first construct a spanning tree. When a source node wants to send a broadcast packet, it sends the packet out on all of the incident links that belong to the spanning tree. A node receiving a broadcast packet then forwards the packet to all its neighbors in the spanning tree (except the neighbor from which it received the packet). Not only does spanning tree eliminate redundant broadcast packets, but once in place, the spanning tree can be used by any node to begin a broadcast, as shown in Figures 4.42(a) and 4.42(b). Note that a node need not be aware of the entire tree; it simply needs to know which of its neighbors in *G* are spanning-tree neighbors.

The main complexity associated with the spanning-tree approach is the creation and maintenance of the spanning tree. Numerous distributed spanning-tree algorithms have been developed [Gallager 1983, Gartner 2003]. We consider only one simple algorithm here. In the **center-based approach** to building a spanning tree, a center node (also known as a **rendezvous point** or a **core**) is defined. Nodes then unicast tree-join messages addressed to the center node. A tree-join message is forwarded using unicast routing toward the center until it either arrives at a node that already belongs to the spanning tree or arrives at the center. In either case, the path that the tree-join message has followed defines the branch of the spanning tree between the edge node that initiated the tree-join message and the center. One can think of this new path as being grafted onto the existing spanning tree.

Figure 4.43 illustrates the construction of a center-based spanning tree. Suppose that node *E* is selected as the center of the tree. Suppose that node *F* first joins the tree

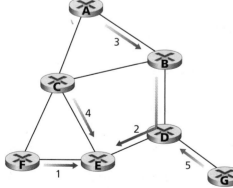

a. Stepwise construction of spanning tree

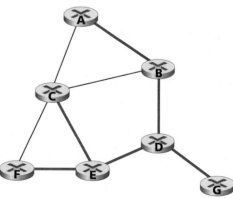

b. Constructed spanning tree

Figure 4.43 ♦ Center-based construction of a spanning tree

and forwards a tree-join message to E. The single link EF becomes the initial spanning tree. Node B then joins the spanning tree by sending its tree-join message to E. Suppose that the unicast path route to E from B is via D. In this case, the tree-join message results in the path BDE being grafted onto the spanning tree. Node A next joins the spanning group by forwarding its tree-join message towards E. If A's unicast path to E is through B, then since B has already joined the spanning tree, the arrival of A's tree-join message at B will result in the AB link being immediately grafted onto the spanning tree. Node C joins the spanning tree next by forwarding its tree-join message directly to E. Finally, because the unicast routing from G to E must be via node D, when G sends its tree-join message to E, the GD link is grafted onto the spanning tree at node D.

Broadcast Algorithms in Practice

Broadcast protocols are used in practice at both the application and network layers. As discussed in Section 2.6, Gnutella [Gnutella 2004] uses application-level broadcast in order to broadcast queries for content among Gnutella peers. Here, a link between two distributed application-level peer processes in the Gnutella network is actually a TCP connection. Gnutella uses a form of sequence-number-controlled flooding in which a 16-bit identifier and a 16-bit payload descriptor (which identifies the Gnutella message type) are used to detect whether a received broadcast query has been previously received, duplicated, and forwarded. As also discussed in Section 2.6, Gnutella also uses a time-to-live (TTL) field to limit the number of hops over which a flooded query will be forwarded. When a Gnutella process receives and duplicates a query, it decrements the TTL field before forwarding the query. Thus, a flooded Gnutella query will only reach peers that are within a given number (the initial value of TTL) of application-level hops from the query initiator. Gnutella's flooding mechanism is thus sometimes referred to as *limited-scope flooding*.

A form of sequence-number controlled flooding is also used to broadcast link-state advertisements (LSAs) in the OSPF [RFC 2328, Perlman 1999] routing algorithm, and in the Intermediate-System-to-Intermediate-System (IS-IS) routing algorithm [RFC 1142, Perlman 1999]. OSPF uses a 32-bit sequence number, as well as a 16-bit age field to identify link-state advertisements (LSAs). Recall that an OSPF node broadcasts LSAs for its attached links periodically, when a link cost to a neighbor changes, or when a link goes up/down. LSA sequence numbers are used to detect duplicate LSAs, but also serve a second important function in OSPF. With flooding, it is possible for an LSA generated by the source at time t to arrive *after* a newer LSA that was generated by the same source at time $t + \delta$. The sequence numbers used by the source node allow an older LSA to be distinguished from a newer LSA. The age field serves a purpose similar to that of a TTL value. The initial age field value is set to zero and is incremented at each hop as it flooded, and is also incremented as it sits in a router's memory waiting to be flooded. Although we have only briefly described the LSA flooding algorithm here, we note that designing LSA broadcast protocols can be very tricky business indeed. [RFC 789; Perlman 1999, Section 12.2.3.3] describe an incident in which incorrectly transmitted LSAs by two malfunctioning routers caused an early version of an LSA flooding algorithm to take down the entire ARPAnet!

4.7.2 Multicast

We've seen in the previous section that with broadcast service, packets are delivered to each and every node in the network. In this section we turn our attention to **multicast** service, in which a multicast packet is delivered to only a *subset* of network nodes. A number of emerging network applications require the delivery of packets from one or more senders to a group of receivers. These applications include bulk data transfer (for example, the transfer of a software upgrade from the software developer to users needing the upgrade), streaming continuous media (for example, the transfer of the audio, video, and text of a live lecture to a set of distributed lecture participants), shared data applications (for example, a whiteboard or teleconferencing application that is shared among many distributed participants), data feeds (for example, stock quotes), Web cache updating, and interactive gaming (for example, distributed interactive virtual environments or multiplayer games such as Quake).

In multicast communication, we are immediately faced with two problems—how to identify the receivers of a multicast packet and how to address a packet sent to these receivers. In the case of unicast communication, the IP address of the receiver (destination) is carried in each IP unicast datagram and identifies the single recipient; in the case of broadcast, *all* nodes need to receive the broadcast packet, so no destination addresses are needed. But in the case of multicast, we now have multiple receivers. Does it make sense for each multicast packet to carry the IP addresses of all of the multiple recipients? While this approach might be workable with a small number of recipients, it would not scale well to the case of hundreds or thousands of receivers; the amount of addressing information in the datagram would swamp the amount of data actually carried in the packet's payload field. Explicit identification of the receivers by the sender also requires that the sender know the identities and addresses of all of the receivers. We will see shortly that there are cases where this requirement might be undesirable.

For these reasons, in the Internet architecture (and other network architectures such as ATM [Black 1995]), a multicast packet is addressed using **address indirection**. That is, a single identifier is used for the group of receivers, and a copy of the packet that is addressed to the group using this single identifier is delivered to all of the multicast receivers associated with that group. In the Internet, the single identifier that represents a group of receivers is a class D multicast address. The group of receivers associated with a class D address is referred to as a **multicast group**. The multicast group abstraction is illustrated in Figure 4.44. Here, four hosts (shown in shaded blue) are associated with the multicast group address of 226.17.30.197 and will receive all datagrams addressed to that multicast address. The difficulty that we must

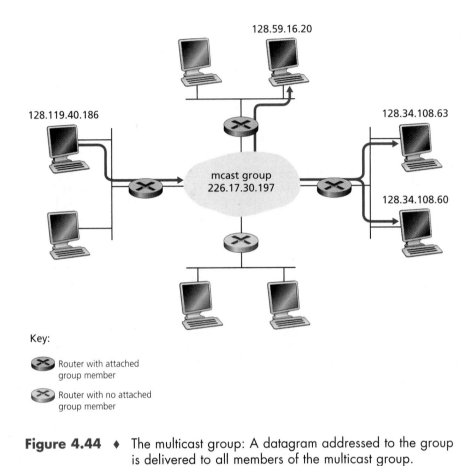

Figure 4.44 ♦ The multicast group: A datagram addressed to the group is delivered to all members of the multicast group.

still address is the fact that each host has a unique IP unicast address that is completely independent of the address of the multicast group in which it is participating.

While the multicast group abstraction is simple, it raises a host (pun intended) of questions. How does a group get started and how does it terminate? How is the group address chosen? How are new hosts added to the group (either as senders or receivers)? Can anyone join a group (and send to, or receive from, that group) or is group membership restricted and, if so, by whom? Do group members know the identities of the other group members as part of the network-layer protocol? How do the network nodes interoperate with each other to deliver a multicast datagram to all group members? For the Internet, the answers to all of these questions involve the Internet Group Management Protocol [RFC 3376]. So, let us next consider the IGMP and then return to these broader questions.

Internet Group Management Protocol

The IGMP protocol version 3 [RFC 3376] operates between a host and its directly attached router (informally, we can think of the directly attached router as the first-hop router that a host would see on a path to any other host outside its own local network, or the last-hop router on any path to that host), as shown in Figure 4.45. Figure 4.45 shows three first-hop multicast routers, each connected to its attached hosts via one outgoing local interface. This local interface is attached to a LAN in this example, and while each LAN has multiple attached hosts, at most a few of these hosts will typically belong to a given multicast group at any given time.

IGMP provides the means for a host to inform its attached router that an application running on the host wants to join a specific multicast group. Given that the scope of IGMP interaction is limited to a host and its attached router, another protocol is clearly required to coordinate the multicast routers (including the attached routers) throughout the Internet, so that multicast datagrams are routed to their final destinations. This latter functionality is accomplished by network-layer multicast routing algorithms, such as PIM, DVMRP, and MOSPF. Network-layer multicast in the Internet thus consists of two complementary components: IGMP and multicast routing protocols.

Although IGMP's name suggests it manages the group of hosts joined to a multicast group, the name is a bit misleading since IGMP operates *locally*, between a host and an attached router. Despite its name, IGMP is *not* a protocol that operates

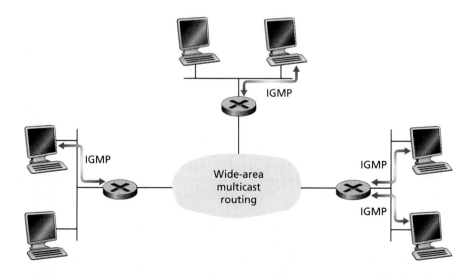

Figure 4.45 ◆ The two components of network-layer multicast: IGMP and multicast routing protocols

among all the hosts that have joined a multicast group. Indeed, there is no network-layer multicast group membership protocol that operates among all the Internet hosts in a group. There is no network-layer protocol, for example, that allows a host to determine the identities of all of the other hosts, network-wide, that have joined the multicast group. (See the homework problems for a further exploration of the consequences of this design choice.)

IGMP has only three message types. The IGMP message format is summarized in Figure 4.46. Like ICMP, IGMP messages are carried (encapsulated) within an IP datagram, with an IP protocol number of 2. A general `membership_query` message is sent by a router to all hosts on an attached interface (for example, to all hosts on a local area network) to determine the set of all multicast groups that have been joined by the hosts on that interface. A router can also determine whether a specific multicast group has been joined by hosts on an attached interface using a specific `membership_query`. The specific query includes the multicast address of the group being queried in the multicast group address field of the IGMP `membership_query` message, as shown in Figure 4.46. Hosts respond to a membership_query message with an IGMP `membership_report` message, as illustrated in Figure 4.47. `Membership_report` messages can also be generated by a host when an application first joins a multicast group without waiting for a `membership_query` message from the router.

The final type of IGMP message is the `leave_group` message. Interestingly, this message is optional. But if it is optional, how does a router detect that there are no longer any hosts on an attached interface that are joined to a given multicast group? The answer to this question lies in the use of the IGMP `membership_query` message. The router *infers* that no hosts are joined to a given multicast group when no host responds to a `membership_query` message with the given group address. This is an example of what is sometimes called **soft state** in an Internet protocol. In a soft-state protocol, the state (in this case of IGMP, the fact that there are hosts joined to a given multicast group) is removed via a time-out event (in this case, via a periodic `membership_query` message from the router) if it is not explicitly refreshed (in this case, by a `membership_report` message from an attached host). It has been argued that soft-state protocols result in simpler control than hard-state protocols, which not only require state to be explicitly added and removed, but also require mechanisms to recover from the situation

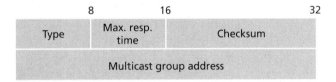

Figure 4.46 ✦ IGMP message format

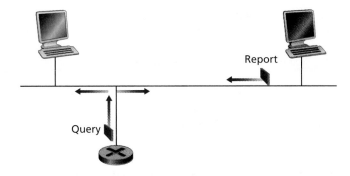

Figure 4.47 ♦ IGMP member query and membership report

where the entity responsible for removing state has terminated prematurely or failed [Sharma 1997]. Interesting discussions of soft state can be found in [Raman 1999; Ji 2003]; see also the sidebar in Section 7.9.

Having examined the protocol for joining and leaving multicast groups, we are now in a better position to reflect on the current Internet multicast service model, which is based on the work of Steve Deering [RFC 1112; Deering 1990]. In this multicast service model, any host can join a multicast group at the network layer. A host simply issues a `membership_report` IGMP message to its attached router. That router, working in concert with other Internet routers, will soon begin delivering multicast datagrams to the host. Joining a multicast group is thus receiver-driven. A sender need not be concerned with explicitly adding receivers to the multicast group, but neither can it control who joins the group and therefore who receives datagrams sent to that group. Similarly, in early versions of IGMP, a receiver could not specify a set of specific sources from which it wanted to receive (or avoid receiving) multicast packets; IGMPv3 provides for this specification.

In many ways, the current Internet multicast service model reflects the same philosophy as the Internet unicast service model—an extremely simple network layer with additional functionality (such as group membership) being provided in the upper-layer protocols in the hosts at the edges of the network. This philosophy has been unquestionably successful for the unicast case; whether the minimalist network-layer philosophy will be equally successful for the multicast service model remains an open question. A number of alternate multicast service models have recently been proposed presented in [Holbrook 1999, RFC 3569]. An interesting discussion of the current Internet multicast service model and deployment issues is [Diot 2000].

Multicast Routing Algorithms

Figure 4.48 illustrates the setting for the **multicast routing problem**. We consider a single multicast group and assume that any router that has an attached host that has joined this group may either send or receive traffic addressed to this group. In Figure 4.48, hosts joined to the multicast group are shaded in color; their immediately attached router is also shaded in color. As shown in Figure 4.48, among the population of multicast routers, only a subset of these routers (those with attached hosts that are joined to the multicast group) actually need to receive the multicast traffic. In Figure 4.48, only routers A, B, E, and F need to receive the multicast traffic. Since none of the hosts attached to router D are joined to the multicast group and since router C has no attached hosts, neither C nor D needs to receive the multicast group traffic.

The goal of multicast routing then is to find a tree of links that connects all of the routers that have attached hosts belonging to the multicast group. Multicast packets will then be routed along this tree from the sender to all of the hosts belonging to the multicast tree. Of course, the tree may contain routers that do not have attached hosts belonging to the multicast group (for example, in Figure 4.48, it is impossible to connect routers A, B, E, and F in a tree without involving either router C and/or D).

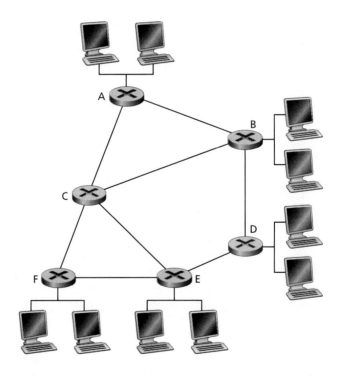

Figure 4.48 ♦ Multicast hosts, their attached routers, and other routers

In practice, two approaches have been adopted for determining the multicast routing tree, both of which we have already studied in the context of broadcast routring. The two approaches differ according to whether a single group-shared tree is used to distribute the traffic for *all* senders in the group, or whether a source-specific routing tree is constructed for each individual sender.

♦ *Multicast routing using a group-shared tree.* As in the case of spanning-tree broadcast, multicast routing over a group-shared tree is based on building a tree that includes all edge routers with attached hosts belonging to the multicast group. In practice, a center-based approach is used to construct the multicast routing tree, with edge routers with attached hosts belonging to the multicast group sending (via unicast) join messages addressed to the center node. As in the broadcast case, a join message is forwarded using unicast routing toward the center until it either arrives at a router that already belongs to the multicast tree or arrives at the center. All routers along the path that the join message follows will then forward received multicast packets to the edge router that initiated the multicast join. A critical question for center-based tree multicast routing is the process used to select the center. Center-selection algorithms are discussed in [Wall 1980; Thaler 1997; Estrin 1997].

♦ *Multicast routing using a source-based tree.* While group-shared tree multicast routing constructs a single, shared routing tree to route packets from *all* senders, the second approach constructs a multicast routing tree for *each* source in the multicast group. In practice, an RPF algorithm (with source node x) is used to construct a multicast forwarding tree for multicast datagrams originating at source x. The RPF algorithm we have studied requires a bit of tweaking for use in multicast. To see why, consider router D in Figure 4.49. Under broadcast RPF, it would forward packets to router G, even though router G has no attached hosts that are joined to the multicast group. While this is not so bad for this case where D has only a single downstream router, G, imagine what would happen if there were thousands of routers downstream from D! Each of these thousands of routers would receive unwanted multicast packets. (This scenario is not as far-fetched as it might seem. The initial MBone [Casner 1992; Macedonia 1994], the first global multicast network, suffered from precisely this problem at first.). The solution to the problem of receiving unwanted multicast packets under RPF is known as **pruning**. A multicast router that receives multicast packets and has no attached hosts joined to that group will send a prune message to its upstream router. If a router receives prune messages from each of its downstream routers, then it can forward a prune message upstream.

Multicast Routing in the Internet

The first multicast routing protocol used in the Internet and the most widely supported multicast routing algorithm is the **Distance-Vector Multicast Routing**

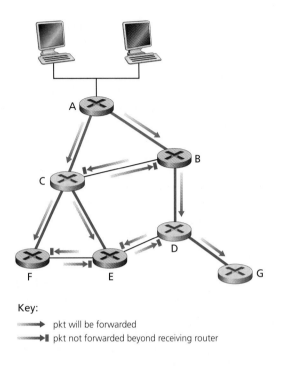

Key:

⟶ pkt will be forwarded

⟶▌ pkt not forwarded beyond receiving router

Figure 4.49 ♦ Reverse path forwarding, the multicast case

Protocol (DVMRP) [RFC 1075]. DVMRP implements source-based trees with reverse path forwarding and pruning. DVMRP uses a distance vector algorithm that allows each router to compute the outgoing link (next hop) that is on its shortest path back to each possible source. This information is then used in the RPF algorithm, as discussed above. A public copy of DVMRP software is available at [mrouted 1996].

In addition to computing next-hop information, DVMRP also computes a list of dependent downstream routers for pruning purposes. When a router has received a prune message from all of its dependent downstream routers for a given group, it will propagate a prune message upstream to the router from which it receives its multicast traffic for that group. A DVMRP prune message contains a prune lifetime (with a default value of two hours) that indicates how long a pruned branch will remain pruned before being automatically restored. DVMRP graft messages are sent by a router to its upstream neighbor to force a previously pruned branch to be added back on to the multicast tree.

The second widely used Internet multicast routing protocol is the **Protocol-Independent Multicast (PIM) routing protocol** [Deering 1996; RFC 2362; Estrin 1998b], which explicitly envisions two multicast distribution scenarios. In **dense mode**, multicast group members are densely located; that is, many or most of the routers in the area need to be involved in routing multicast datagrams. In **sparse mode**, the number of routers with attached group members is small with respect to the total number of routers; group members are widely dispersed. PIM accommodates this dense versus sparse dichotomy by offering two explicit modes of operation: dense mode and sparse mode. PIM dense mode is a flood-and-prune reverse path forwarding technique similar in spirit to DVMRP. PIM sparse mode is a center-based approach, similar to the core-based tree (CBT) multicast routing protocol [RFC 2201; RFC 2189]. One novel feature of PIM is that it gives us the ability to switch from a group-shared tree to a source-specific tree after joining the rendezvous point. A source-specific tree may be preferred due to the decreased traffic concentration that occurs when multiple source-specific trees are used (see homework problems). In PIM sparse mode, the router that receives a datagram to send from one of its attached hosts will unicast the datagram to the rendezvous point. The rendezvous point (RP) then multicasts the datagram via the group-shared tree. The RP notifies the sender that it must stop sending to the RP whenever there are no routers joined to the tree (that is, no one is listening).

In our discussion above, we have assumed that all routers are running the same multicast routing protocol. As we saw with unicasting, this will typically be the case within a single autonomous system (AS). However, different ASs may choose to run different multicast routing protocols. Interoperability rules have been defined for the major Internet multicast routing protocols [RFC 2715]. (The rules are particularly messy due to the very different approaches taken to multicast routing by sparse- and dense-mode protocols.) What is still missing, however, is an inter-AS multicast routing protocol to route multicast datagrams among different ASs. To date, DVMRP has served as the *de facto* inter-AS multicast routing protocol.

Finally we mention that to date IP multicast has not yet taken off in a big way. Many video streaming companies and content distribution companies instead use overlays to create application-layer multicast distribution networks. As with IPv6, IP multicast has struggled—and continues to struggle—to make significant inroads in the Internet.

4.8 Summary

In this chapter, we began our journey into the network core. We learned that the network layer involves each and every host and router in the network. Because of this, network-layer protocols are among the most challenging in the protocol stack.

We learned that a router may need to process millions of flows of packets between different source-destination pairs at the same time. To permit a router to process such a large number of flows, network designers have learned over the years that the router's tasks should be as simple as possible. Many measures can be taken to make the router's job easier, including using a datagram network layer rather than a virtual circuit network layer, using a streamlined and fixed-sized header (as in

IPv6), eliminating fragmentation (also done in IPv6), and providing the one and only best-effort service. Perhaps the most important trick here is *not* to keep track of individual flows, but instead base routing decisions solely on hierarchically structured destination addresses in the packets. It is interesting to note that the postal service has been using this approach for many years.

In this chapter, we also looked at the underlying principles of routing algorithms. We learned how routing algorithms abstract the computer network to a graph with nodes and links. With this abstraction, we can exploit the rich theory of shortest-path routing in graphs, which has been developed over the past 40 years in the operations research and algorithms communities. We saw that there are two broad approaches, a centralized (global) approach, in which each node obtains a complete map of the network and independently applies a shortest-path routing algorithm; and a decentralized approach, in which individual nodes have only a partial picture of the entire network, yet the nodes work together to deliver packets along the shortest routes. We also studied how hierarchy is used to deal with the problem of scale by partitioning large networks into independent administrative domains called autonomous systems (ASs). Each AS independently routes its datagrams through the AS, just as each country independently routes its postal mail through the country. We learned how centralized, decentralized, and hierarchical approaches are embodied in the principal routing protocols in the Internet: RIP, OSPF, and BGP. We concluded our study of routing algorithms by considering broadcast and multicast routing.

Having completed our study of the network layer, our journey now takes us one step further down the protocol stack, namely, to the link layer. Like the network layer, the link layer is also part of the network core. But we will see in the next chapter that the link layer has the much more localized task of moving packets between nodes on the same link or LAN. Although this task may appear on the surface to be trivial compared with that of the network layer's tasks, we will see that the link layer involves a number of important and fascinating issues that can keep us busy for a long time.

Homework Problems and Questions

Chapter 4 Review Questions

SECTIONS 4.1–4.2

1. Let's review some of the terminology used in this textbook. Recall that the name of a transport-layer packet is *segment* and that the name of a link-layer packet is *frame*. What is the name of a network-layer packet? Recall that both routers and link-layer switches are called *packet switches*. What is the fundamental difference between a router and link-layer switch? Recall that we use the term *routers* for both datagram networks and VC networks.

2. What are the two most important network-layer functions in a datagram network? What are three most important network-layer functions in a circuit-switched network?

3. What is the difference between routing and forwarding?

4. Do the routers in both datagram networks and virtual-circuit networks use forwarding tables? If so, describe the forwarding tables for both classes of networks.

5. Describe some hypothetical services that the network layer can provide to a single packet. Do the same for a flow of packets. Are any of your hypothetical services provided by the Internet's network layer? Are any provided by ATM's CBR service model? Are any provided by ATM's ABR service model?

6. List some applications that would benefit from ATM's CBR service model.

SECTION 4.3

7. Discuss why each input port in a high-speed router stores a shadow copy of the forwarding table.

8. Three types of switching fabrics are discussed in Section 4.3. List and briefly describe each type.

9. Describe how packet loss can occur at input ports. Describe how packet loss at input ports can be eliminated (without using infinite buffers).

10. Describe how packet loss can occur at output ports.

11. What is HOL blocking? Does it occur in input ports or output ports?

SECTION 4.4

12. Do routers have IP addresses? If so, how many?

13. What is the 32-bit binary equivalent of the IP address 223.1.3.27?

14. Visit a host that uses DHCP to obtain its IP address, network mask, default router, and IP address of its local DNS server. List these values.

15. Suppose there are three routers between a source host and a destination host. Ignoring fragmentation, an IP datagram sent from the source host to the destination host will travel over how many interfaces? How many forwarding tables will be indexed to move the datagram from the source to the destination?

16. Suppose an application generates chunks of 40 bytes of data every 20 msec, and each chunk gets encapsulated in a TCP segment and then an IP datagram. What percentage of each datagram will be overhead, and what percentage will be application data?

17. Suppose Host A sends Host B a TCP segment encapsulated in an IP datagram. When Host B receives the datagram, how does the network layer in Host B know it should pass the segment (that is, the payload of the datagram) to TCP rather than to UDP or to something else?

18. Suppose you purchase a wireless router and connect it to your cable modem. Also suppose that your ISP dynamically assigns your connected device (that is, your wireless router) one IP address. Also suppose that you have five PCs at home that use 802.11 to wirelessly connect to your wireless router. How are IP addresses assigned to the five PCs? Does the wireless router use NAT? Why or why not?

19. Compare and contrast the IPv4 and the IPv6 header fields. Do they have any fields in common?

20. It has been said that when IPv6 tunnels through IPv4 routers, IPv6 treats the IPv4 tunnels as link-layer protocols. Do you agree with this statement? Why or why not?

SECTION 4.5

21. Compare and contrast link state and distance vector routing algorithms.

22. Discuss how a hierarchical organization of the Internet has made it possible to scale to millions of users.

23. Is it necessary that every autonomous system use the same intra-AS routing algorithm? Why or why not?

SECTION 4.6

24. Consider Figure 4.31. Starting with the original table in *D,* suppose that *D* receives from *A* the following advertisement:

Destination Subnet	Next Router	Number of Hops to Destination
z	C	10
w	—	1
x	—	1
. . . .	. . . .	. . . .

Will the table in *D* change? If so how?

25. Compare and contrast the advertisements used by RIP and OSPF.

26. Fill in the blank: RIP advertisements typically announce the number of hops to various destinations. BGP updates, on the other hand, announce the _____ to the various destinations.

27. Why are different inter-AS and intra-AS protocols used in the Internet?

28. Why are policy considerations as important for intra-AS protocols, such as OSPF and RIP, as they are for an inter-AS routing protocol like BGP?

29. Define and contrast the following terms: *subnet, prefix,* and *BGP route.*

30. How does BGP use the NEXT-HOP attribute? How does it use the AS-PATH attribute?

31. Describe how a network administrator of an upper-tier ISP can implement policy when configuring BGP.

SECTION 4.7

32. What is an important difference between implementing the broadacst abstraction via multiple unicasts, and a single network- (router-) supported broadcast?

33. For each of the three general approaches we studied for broadcast communication (uncontrolled flooding, controlled flooding, and spanning-tree broadcast), are the following statements true or false? You may assume that no packets are lost due to buffer overflow and all packets are delivered on a link in the order in which they were sent.

   a. A node may receive multiple copies of the same packet.

   b. A node may forward multiple copies of a packet over the same outgoing link.

34. When a host joins a multicast group, must it change its IP address to that of the multicast group it is joining?

35. What are the roles played by the IGMP protocol and a wide-area multicast routing protocol?

36. What is the difference between a group-shared tree and a source-based tree in the context of multicast routing?

Problems

1. Consider some of the pros and cons of virtual-circuit and datagram networks.

   a. Suppose that in the network layer, routers were subjected to stressful conditions that might cause them to fail fairly often. At a high level, what actions would need to be taken on such router failure? Does this argue in favor of VC or datagram architecture?

   b. Suppose that in order to provide a guarantee regarding the level of performance (for example, delay) that would be seen along a source-to-destination path, the network requires a sender to declare its peak traffic rate. If the declared peak traffic rate and the existing declared traffic rates are such that there is no way to get traffic from the source to the destination that meets the required delay requirements, the source is not allowed access to the network. Would such an approach be more easily accomplished within a VC or a datagram architecture?

2. Consider a virtual-circuit network. Suppose the VC number is a 16-bit field.

   a. What is the maximum number of virtual circuits that can be carried over the link?

   b. Suppose a central node determines paths and VC numbers at connection setup. Suppose the same VC number is used on each link along the VC's path. Describe how the central node might determine the VC number at connection setup. Is it possible that there are fewer VCs in progress than the maximum as determined in part (a) yet there is no common free VC number?

   c. Suppose that different VC numbers are permitted in each link along a VC's path. During connection setup, after an end-to-end path is determined, describe how the links can choose their VC numbers and configure their forwarding tables in a decentralized manner, without reliance on a central node.

3. A bare-bones forwarding table in a VC network has four columns. What is the meaning of the values in each of these columns? A bare-bones forwarding table in a datagram network has two columns. What is the meaning of the values in each of these columns?

4. Consider a VC network with a 2-bit field for the VC number. Suppose that the network wants to set up a virtual circuit over four links: link A, link B, link C, and link D. Suppose that each of these links is currently carrying two other virtual circuits, and the VC numbers of these other VCs are as follows:

Link A	Link B	Link C	Link D
00	01	10	11
01	10	11	00

   In answering the following questions, keep in mind that each of the existing VCs may only traverse one of the four links.

   a. If each VC is required to use the same VC number on all links along its path, what VC number could be assigned to the new VC?

   b. If each VC is permitted to have a different VC numbers in the different links along its path (so that forwarding table must perform VC number translation), how many different combinations of four VC numbers (one for each of the four links) could be used?

5. In the text we have used the term *connection-oriented service* to describe the transport layer and *connection service* for the network layer. Why the subtle shades in terminology?

6. In Section 4.3, we noted that there can be no input queuing if the switching fabric is *n* times faster than the input line rates, assuming *n* input lines all have the same line rate. Explain (in words) why this should be so.

7. Consider a datagram network using 32-bit host addresses. Suppose a router has four links, numbered 0 through 3, and packets are to be forwarded to the link interfaces as follows:

Destination Address Range	Link Interface
11100000 00000000 00000000 00000000 through 11100000 11111111 11111111 11111111	0
11100001 00000000 00000000 00000000 through 11100001 00000000 11111111 11111111	1
11100001 00000001 00000000 00000000 through 11100001 11111111 11111111 11111111	2
otherwise	3

   a. Provide a forwarding table that has four entries, uses longest-prefix matching, and forwards packets to the correct link interfaces.

   b. Describe how your forwarding table determines the appropriate link interface for datagrams with destination addresses:

   11001000 10010001 01010001 01010101
   11100001 00000000 11000011 00111100
   11100001 10000000 00010001 01110111

8. Consider a datagram network using 8-bit host addresses. Suppose a router uses longest prefix matching and has the following forwarding table:

Prefix Match	Interface
00	0
01	1
10	2
11	3

   For each of the four interfaces, give the associated range of destination host addresses and the number of addresses in the range.

9. Consider a datagram network using 8-bit host addresses. Suppose a router uses longest prefix matching and has the following forwarding table:

Prefix Match	Interface
1	0
11	1
111	2
otherwise	3

For each of the four interfaces, give the associated range of destination host addresses and the number of addresses in the range.

10. Consider a router that interconnects three subnets: Subnet 1, Subnet 2, and Subnet 3. Suppose all of the interfaces in each of these three subnets are required to have the prefix 223.1.17/24. Also suppose that Subnet 1 is required to support up to 125 interfaces, and Subnets 2 and 3 are each required to support up to 60 interfaces. Provide three network addresses (of the form a.b.c.d/x) that satisfy these constraints.

11. In Section 4.2.2 an example forwarding table (using longest prefix matching) is given. Rewrite this forwarding table using the a.b.c.d/x notation instead of the binary string notation.

12. In Problem 7 you are asked to provide a forwarding table (using longest prefix matching). Rewrite this forwarding table using the a.b.c.d/x notation instead of the binary string notation.

13. Consider a subnet with prefix 101.101.101.64/26. Give an example of one IP address (of form xxx.xxx.xxx.xxx) that can be assigned to this network. Suppose an ISP owns the block of addresses of the form 101.101.128/17. Suppose it wants to create four subnets from this block, with each block having the same number of IP addresses. What are the prefixes (of form a.b.c.d/x) for the four subnets?

14. Consider the topology shown in Figure 4.17. Denote the three subnets with hosts (starting clockwise at 12:00) as Networks A, B, and C. Denote the subnets without hosts as Networks D, E, and F.

    a. Assign network addresses to each of these six subnets, with the following constraints: All addresses must be allocated from 214.97.254/17; Subnet A should have enough addresses to support 250 interfaces; Subnet B should have enough addresses to support 120 interfaces; and Subnet C should have enough addresses to support 120 interfaces. Of course, subnets D, E and F should each be able to support two interfaces. For each subnet, the assignment should take the form a.b.c.d/x or a.b.c.d/x – e.f.g.h/y.

    b. Using your answer to part (a), provide the forwarding tables (using longest prefix matching) for each of the three routers.

15. Consider sending a 3,000-byte datagram into a link that has an MTU of 500 bytes. Suppose the original datagram is stamped with the identification number 422. How many fragments are generated? What are their characteristics?

16. Suppose datagrams are limited to 1,500 bytes (including header) between source Host A and destination Host B. Assuming a 20-byte IP header, how many datagrams would be required to send an MP3 consisting of 4 million bytes?

17. Consider the network setup in Figure 4.20. Suppose that the ISP instead assigns the router the address 126.13.89.67 and that network address of the home network is 192.168/16.

    a. Assign addresses to all interfaces in the home network.

    b. Suppose each host has two ongoing TCP connections, all to port 80 at host 128.119.40.86. Provide the six corresponding entries in the NAT translation table.

18. In this problem we'll explore the impact of NATs on P2P applications. Suppose a peer with user name Arnold discovers through querying that a peer with user name Bernard has a file it wants to download. Also suppose that Bernard is behind a NAT whereas Arnold isn't. Let 138.76.29.7 be the WAN-side address of the NAT and let 10.0.0.1 be the internal IP address for Bernard. Assume that the NAT is not specifically configured for the P2P application.

    a. Discuss why Arnold's peer cannot initiate a TCP connection to Bernard's peer, even if Arnold knows the WAN-side address of the NAT, 138.76.29.7.

    b. Now suppose that Bernard has established an ongoing TCP connection to another peer, Cindy, which is not behind a NAT. Also suppose that Arnold learned from Cindy that Bernard has the desired file and that Arnold can establish (or already has established) a TCP connection with Cindy. Describe how Arnold can use these two TCP connections (one from Bernard to Cindy and the other from Arnold to Cindy) to instruct Bernard to initiate a direct TCP connection (that is, not passing through Cindy) back to Arnold. This technique is sometimes called *connection reversal*. Note that even though Bernard is behind a NAT, Arnold can use this direct TCP connection to request the file, and Bernard can use the connection to deliver the file.

19. Following up on the previous problem, now suppose that both Arnold and Bernard are behind NATs. Try to devise a technique that will allow Arnold to establish a TCP connection with Bernard without application-specific NAT configuration. If you have difficulty devising such a technique, discuss why.

20. Looking at Figure 4.25, enumerate the paths from *u* to *z* that do not contain any loops.

21. Consider the following network. With the indicated link costs, use Dijkstra's shortest-path algorithm to compute the shortest path from x to all network nodes. Show how the algorithm works by computing a table similar to Table 4.3.

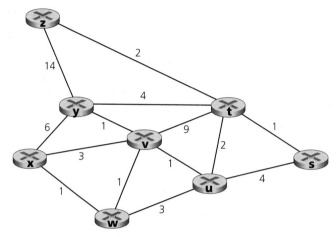

22. Consider the network shown in Problem 21. Using Dijkstra's algorithm, and showing your work using a table similar to Table 4.3, do the following.

    a. Compute the shortest path from s to all network nodes.

    b. Compute the shortest path from t to all network nodes.

    c. Compute the shortest path from u to all network nodes.

    d. Compute the shortest path from v to all network nodes.

    e. Compute the shortest path from w to all network nodes.

    f. Compute the shortest path from y to all network nodes.

    g. Compute the shortest path from z to all network nodes.

23. Consider the network shown below, and assume that each node initially knows the costs to each of its neighbors. Consider the distance vector algorithm and show the distance table entries at node z.

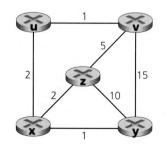

24. Consider a general topology (that is, not the specific network shown above) and a synchronous version of the distance vector algorithm. Suppose that at each iteration, a node exchanges its distance vectors with its neighbors and receives their distance vectors. Assuming that the algorithm begins with each node knowing only the costs to its immediate neighbors, what is the maximum number of iterations required before the distributed algorithm converges? Justify your answer.

25. Consider the network fragment shown below. x has only two attached neighbors, w and y. w has a minimum-cost path to destination u (not shown) of 5, and y has a minimum-cost path to u of 6. The complete paths from w and y to u (and between w and y) are not shown. All link costs in the network have strictly positive integer values.

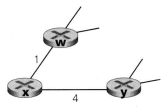

a. Give x's distance vector for destinations w, y, and u.

b. Give a link-cost change for either $c(x,w)$ or $c(x,y)$ such that x will inform its neighbors of a new minimum-cost path to u as a result of executing the distance vector algorithm.

c. Give a link-cost change for either $c(x,w)$ or $c(x,y)$ such that x will *not* inform its neighbors of a new minimum-cost path to u as a result of executing the distance vector algorithm.

26. Consider the three-node topology shown in Figure 4.27. Rather than having the link costs shown in Figure 4.27, the link costs are $c(x,y) = 5$, $c(y,z) = 6$, $c(z,x) = 2$. Compute the distance tables after the initialization step and after each iteration of a synchronous version of the distance vector algorithm (as we did in our earlier discussion of Figure 4.27).

27. Describe how loops in paths can be detected in BGP.

28. Consider the following network. ISP B provides national backbone service to regional ISP A. ISP C provides national backbone service to regional ISP D. B and C peer with each other in two places using BGP. Consider traffic going from A to D. B would prefer to hand that traffic over to C on the West Coast (so that C would have to absorb the cost of carrying the traffic cross-country), while C would prefer to get the traffic via its East Coast peering point with B (so that B would have carried the traffic across the country). What BGP

mechanism might C use, so that B would hand over A-to-D traffic at their East Coast peering point? To answer this question, you will need to dig into the BGP specification.

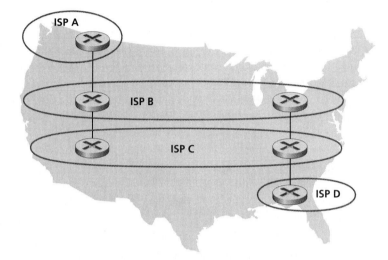

29. In Figure 4.39, consider the path information that reaches stub networks W, X, and Y. Based on the information available at W and X, what are their respective views of the network topology? Justify your answer. The topology view at Y is shown below.

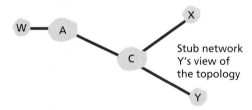

Stub network Y's view of the topology

30. Consider the eight-node network (with nodes labeled s to z) in Problem 21. Show the minimal-cost tree rooted at s that includes (as end hosts) nodes u, v, w, and y. Informally argue why your tree is a minimal-cost tree.

31. Consider the two basic approaches identified for achieving broadcast: unicast emulation and network-layer (i.e., router-assisted) broadcast, and suppose spanning-tree broadcast is used to achive network-layer broadcast. Consider a single sender and 32 receivers. Suppose the sender is connected to the receivers by a binary tree of routers. What is the cost of sending a broadcast packet, in the cases of unicast emulation and network-layer broadcast, for this topology? Here, each

time a packet (or copy of a packet) is sent over a single link, it incurs a unit of cost. What topology for interconnecting the sender, receivers, and routers will bring the cost of unicast emulation and true network-layer broadcast as far apart as possible? You can choose as many routers as you'd like.

32. Consider the operation of the reverse path forwarding (RPF) algorithm in Figure 4.41. Using the same topology, find a set of paths from all nodes to the source node *A* (and indicate these paths in a graph using thicker-shaded lines as in Figure 4.41 such that if these paths were the least-cost paths, then node *B* would receive a copy of *A*'s broadcast message from nodes *A*, *C*, and *D* under RPF.

33. Consider the topology shown in Figure 4.41. Suppose that all links have unit coast and that node *E* is the broadcast source. Using arrows like those shown in Figure 4.41, indicate links over which packets will be forwarded using RPF, and links over which packets will not be forwarded, given that node *E* is the source.

34. Consider the topology shown in Figure 4.43, and suppose that each link has unit cost. Suppose node *C* is chosen as the center in a center-based multicast routing algorithm. Assuming that each attached router uses its least-cost path to node *C* to send join messages to *C,* draw the resulting center-based routing tree. Is the resulting tree a minimum-cost tree? Justify your answer.

35. In Section 4.5.1 we studied Dijkstra's link-state routing algorithm for computing the unicast paths that are individually the least-cost paths from the source to all destinations. The union of these paths might be thought of as forming a **least-unicast-cost path tree** (or a shortest unicast path tree, if all link costs are identical). By constructing a counterexample, show that the least-cost path tree is *not* always the same as a minimum spanning tree.

36. Consider a network in which all nodes are connected to three other nodes. In a single time step, a node can receive all transmitted broadcast packets from its neighbors, duplicate the packets, and send them to all of its neighbors (except to the node that sent a given packet). At the next time step, neighboring nodes can receive, duplicate, and forward these packets, and so on. Suppose that uncontrolled flooding is used to provide broadcast in such a network. At time step *t*, how many copies of the broadcast packet will be transmitted, assuming that during time step 1, a single broadcast packet is transmitted by the source node to its three neighbors.

37. We saw in Section 4.7 that there is no network-layer protocol that can be used to identify the hosts participating in a multicast group. Given this, how can multicast applications learn the identities of the hosts that are participating in a multicast group?

38. Design (give a pseudocode description of) an application-level protocol that maintains the host addresses of all hosts participating in a multicast group. Specifically identify the network service (unicast or multicast) that is used by your protocol, and indicate whether your protocol is sending messages in-band

or out-of-band (with respect to the application data flow among the multicast group participants) and why.

39. What is the size of the multicast address space? Suppose now that two multicast groups randomly choose a multicast address. What is the probability that they choose the same address? Suppose now that 1,000 multicast groups are ongoing at the same time and choose their multicast group addresses at random. What is the probability that they interfere with each other?

Discussion Questions

1. Find three companies that are currently selling high-speed router products. Compare the products.

2. Use the whois service at the American Registry for Internet Numbers (http://www.arin.net/whois) to determine the IP address blocks for three universities. Can the whois services be used to determine with certainty the location of a specific IP address?

3. Is it possible to write the ping client program (using ICMP messages) in Java? Why or why not?

4. In Section 4.4, we indicated that deployment of IPv6 has been slow. Why has it been slow? What is needed to accelerate its deployment?

5. Discuss some of the problems NATs create for IPsec security (see [Phifer 2000]).

6. Suppose ASs X and Z are not directly connected but instead are connected by AS Y. Further suppose that X has a peering agreement with Y, and that Y has a peering agreement with Z. Finally, suppose that Z wants to transit all of Y's traffic but does not want to transit X's traffic. Does BGP allow Z to implement this policy?

7. In Section 4.7 we identified a number of multicast applications. Which of these applications are well suited for the minimalist Internet multicast service model? Why? Which applications are not particularly well suited for this service model?

Programming Assignment

In this programming assignment, you will be writing a "distributed" set of procedures that implement a distributed asynchronous distance vector routing for the network shown below.

You are to write the following routines that will "execute" asynchronously within the emulated environment provided for this assignment. For node 0, you will write the routines:

- *rtinit0( )*. This routine will be called once at the beginning of the emulation. *rtinit0( )* has no arguments. It should initialize your distance table in node 0 to reflect the direct costs of 1, 3, and 7 to nodes 1, 2, and 3, respectively. In the figure above, all links are bidirectional and the costs in both directions are identical. After initializing the distance table and any other data structures needed by your node 0 routines, it should then send its directly connected neighbors (in this case, 1, 2, and 3) the cost of its minimum-cost paths to all other network nodes. This minimum-cost information is sent to neighboring nodes in a routing update packet by calling the routine *tolayer2( )*, as described in the full assignment. The format of the routing update packet is also described in the full assignment.

- *rtupdate0(struct rtpkt *rcvdpkt)*. This routine will be called when node 0 receives a routing packet that was sent to it by one of its directly connected neighbors. The parameter **rcvdpkt* is a pointer to the packet that was received. *rtupdate0( )* is the "heart" of the distance vector algorithm. The values it receives in a routing update packet from some other node *i* contain *i*'s current shortest-path costs to all other network nodes. *rtupdate0( )* uses these received values to update its own distance table (as specified by the distance vector algorithm). If its own minimum cost to another node changes as a result of the update, node 0 informs its directly connected neighbors of this change in minimum cost by sending them a routing packet. Recall that in the distance vector algorithm, only directly connected nodes will exchange routing packets. Thus, nodes 1 and 2 will communicate with each other, but nodes 1 and 3 will not communicate with each other.

Similar routines are defined for nodes 1, 2, and 3. Thus, you will write eight procedures in all: *rtinit0( )*, *rtinit1( )*, *rtinit2( )*, *rtinit3( )*, *rtupdate0( )*, *rtupdate1( )*, *rtupdate2( )*, and *rtupdate3( )*. These routines will together implement a distributed, asynchronous computation of the distance tables for the topology and costs shown in the figure on the preceding page.

You can find the full details of the programming assignment, as well as C code that you will need to create the simulated hardware/software environment at http://www.awl.com/kurose-ross. A Java version of the assignment is also available.

Ethereal Lab

In the companion Web site for this textbook, http://www.awl.com/kurose-ross, you'll find two Ethereal lab assignments. The first lab examines the operation of IP protocol, and the IP datagram format in particular. The second lab explores the use of the ICMP protocol in the ping and traceroute commands.

Vinton G. Cerf

Vinton G. Cerf is senior vice president of Architecture and Technology for WorldCom. He is widely known as the co-designer of the TCP/IP protocols and the architecture of the Internet. As vice president of MCI Digital Information Services from 1982 to 1986, he led the engineering of MCI Mail, the first commercial e-mail service to be connected to the Internet. During his tenure from 1976 to 1982 with the US Department of Defense's Advanced Research Projects Agency (DARPA), he played a key role leading the development of Internet and Internet-related data packet and security technologies. Vinton holds a BS in Mathematics from Stanford University and a PhD in computer science from UCLA.

What brought you to specialize in networking?

I was working as a programmer at UCLA in the late 1960s. My job was supported by the US Defense Advanced Research Projects Agency (called ARPA then, called DARPA now). I was working in the laboratory of Professor Leonard Kleinrock on the Network Measurement Center of the newly-created ARPANET. The first node of the ARPANET was installed at UCLA on September 1, 1969. I was responsible for programming a computer that was used to capture performance information about the ARPANET and to report this information back for comparison with mathematical models and predictions of the performance of the network.

Several of the other graduate students and I were made responsible for working on the so-called host-level protocols of the ARPANET—the procedures and formats that would allow many different kinds of computers on the network to interact with each other. It was a fascinating exploration into a new world (for me) of distributed computing and communication.

Did you imagine that IP would become as pervasive as it is today when you first designed the protocol?

When Bob Kahn and I first worked on this in 1973, I think we were mostly very focused on the central question: how can we make heterogeneous packet networks interoperate with one another, assuming we cannot actually change the networks themselves. We hoped that we could find a way to permit an arbitrary collection of packet-switched networks to be interconnected in a transparent fashion, so that host computers could communicate end-to-end without having to do any translations in between. I think we knew that we were dealing with powerful and expandable technology but I doubt we had a clear image of what the world would be like with hundreds of millions of computers all interlinked on the Internet.

What do you now envision for the future of networking and the Internet? What major challenges/obstacles do you think lie ahead in their development?

I believe the Internet itself and networks in general will continue to proliferate. Already there is convincing evidence that there will be billions of Internet-enabled devices on the Internet, including appliances like cell phones, refrigerators, personal digital assistants, home servers, televisions, as well as the usual array of laptops, servers, and so on. Big challenges include support for mobility, battery life, capacity of the access links to the network, and ability to scale the optical core of the network up in an unlimited fashion. Designing an interplanetary extension of the Internet is a project in which I am deeply engaged at the Jet Propulsion Laboratory. We will need to cut over from IPv4 [32-bit addresses] to IPv6 [128 bits]. The list is long!

Who has inspired you professionally?

My colleague Bob Kahn; my thesis advisor, Gerald Estrin; my best friend, Steve Crocker (we met in high school and he introduced me to computers in 1960!); and the thousands of engineers who continue to evolve the Internet today.

Do you have any advice for students entering the networking/Internet field?

Think outside the limitations of existing systems—imagine what might be possible; but then do the hard work of figuring out how to get there from the current state of affairs. Dare to dream: a half dozen colleagues and I at the Jet Propulsion Laboratory have been working on the design of an interplanetary extension of the terrestrial Internet. It may take decades to implement this, mission by mission, but to paraphrase: "A man's reach should exceed his grasp, or what are the heavens for?"

5

The Link Layer and Local Area Networks

In the previous chapter we learned that the network layer provides a communication service between two hosts. As shown in Figure 5.1, this communication path consists of a series of communication links, starting at the source host, passing through a series of routers, and ending at the destination host. As we continue to proceed down the protocol stack, from the network layer to the link layer, we naturally wonder how packets are sent across the individual links within the end-to-end communication path. How are the network-layer datagrams encapsulated in the link-layer frames for transmission over a single link? Can link-layer protocols provide router-to-router reliable data transfer? Can different link-layer protocols be used in the different links along the communication path? We will answer these and other important questions in this chapter.

In discussing the link layer, we will find that there are two fundamentally different types of link-layer channels. The first type consists of broadcast channels, which are common in local area networks (LANs), wireless LANs, satellite networks, and hybrid fiber coaxial cable (HFC) access networks. For a broadcast channel, many hosts are connected to the same communication channel, and a so-called medium access protocol is needed to coordinate transmissions and avoid collisions. The second type of link-layer channel is the point-to-point communication link, such as between two routers or between a residential dial-up modem and an ISP router. Coordinating access to a point-to-point link is trivial, but there are still

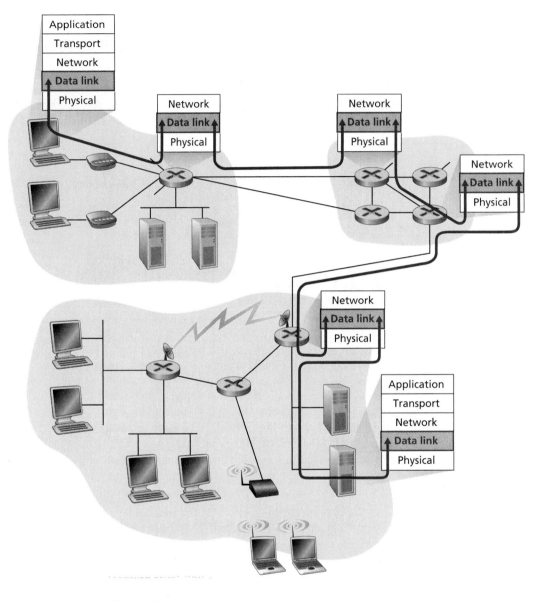

Figure 5.1 ♦ The link layer

important issues surrounding framing, reliable data transfer, error detection, and flow control.

We'll explore several important link-layer technologies in this chapter. We'll take an in-depth look at Ethernet, by far the most prevalent wired LAN technology. We'll also look at point-to-point protocol (PPP), the protocol of choice for dial-up residential hosts.

Although Wi-Fi, and more generally wireless LANs, are certainly link-layer topics, they are not covered in this chapter. This is not because Wi-Fi is an unimportant topic—quite the opposite, as the Wi-Fi revolution is dramatically changing how people access and use the Internet. Wi-Fi is instead covered in depth in Chapter 6, which is devoted to wireless computer networking and mobility.

5.1 Link Layer: Introduction and Services

Let's begin with some useful terminology. We'll find it convenient in this chapter to refer to the hosts and the routers simply as **nodes** since, as we'll see shortly, we will not be particularly concerned whether a node is a router or a host. We will also refer to the communication channels that connect adjacent nodes along the communication path as **links**. In order for a datagram to be transferred from source host to destination host, it must be moved over each of the *individual links* in the end-to-end path. Over a given link, a transmitting node encapsulates the datagram in a link-layer frame and transmits the frame into the link; and a receiving node receives the frame and extracts the datagram.

5.1.1 The Services Provided by the Link Layer

A link-layer protocol is used to move a datagram over an individual link. The **link-layer protocol** defines the format of the packets exchanged between the nodes at the ends of the link, as well as the actions taken by these nodes when the packets are sent and received. Recall from Chapter 1 that the units of data exchanged by a link-layer protocol are called **frames**, and that each link-layer frame typically encapsulates one network-layer datagram. As we'll see shortly, the actions taken by a link-layer protocol when sending and receiving frames include error detection, retransmission, flow control, and random access. Examples of link-layer protocols include Ethernet, 802.11 wireless LANs (also known as Wi-Fi), token ring, and PPP; in many contexts, ATM can be considered a link-layer protocol as well. We'll cover many of these protocols in detail in the latter half of this chapter.

Whereas the network layer has the end-to-end job of moving transport-layer segments from the source host to the destination host, a link-layer protocol has the node-to-node job of moving network-layer datagrams over a *single link* in the path. An important characteristic of the link layer is that a datagram may be handled by different link-layer protocols on the different links in the path. For example, a datagram may be handled by Ethernet on the first link, PPP on the last link, and a link-layer WAN protocol in the intermediate links. It is important to note that the services provided by the link-layer protocols may be different. For example, a link-layer protocol may or may not provide reliable delivery. Thus, the network layer must be able to accomplish its end-to-end job in the presence of a heterogeneous set of individual link-layer services.

In order to gain insight into the link layer and how it relates to the network layer, let's consider a transportation analogy. A travel agent who is planning a trip for a tourist traveling from Princeton, New Jersey, to Lausanne, Switzerland decides that it is most convenient for the tourist to take a limousine from Princeton to JFK airport, then a plane from JFK airport to Geneva's airport, and finally a train from Geneva's airport to Lausanne's train station. Once the travel agent makes the three reservations, it is the responsibility of the Princeton limousine company to get the tourist from Princeton to JFK; it is the responsibility of the airline company to get the tourist from JFK to Geneva; and it is the responsibility of the Swiss train service to get the tourist from Geneva to Lausanne. Each of the three segments of the trip is "direct" between two "adjacent" locations. Note that the three transportation segments are managed by different companies and use entirely different transportation modes (limousine, plane, and train). Although the transportation modes are different, they each provide the basic service of moving passengers from one location to an adjacent location. In this transportation analogy, the tourist is a datagram, each transportation segment is a communication link, the transportation mode is a link-layer protocol, and the travel agent is a routing protocol.

Although the basic service of any link layer is to move a datagram from one node to an adjacent node over a single communication link, the details of the provided service can vary from one link-layer protocol to the next. Possible services that can be offered by a link-layer protocol include:

♦ *Framing.* Almost all link-layer protocols encapsulate each network-layer datagram within a link-layer frame before transmission over the link. A frame consists of a data field, in which the network-layer datagram is inserted, and a number of header fields. (A frame may also include trailer fields; however, we will refer to both header and trailer fields as header fields.) The structure of the frame is specified by the link-layer protocol. We'll see several different frame formats when we examine specific link-layer protocols in the second half of this chapter.

♦ *Link Access.* A medium access control (MAC) protocol specifies the rules by which a frame is transmitted onto the link. For point-to-point links that have a single sender at one end of the link and a single receiver at the other end of the link, the MAC protocol is simple (or nonexistent)—the sender can send a frame whenever the link is idle. The more interesting case is when multiple nodes share a single broadcast link—the so-called multiple access problem. Here, the MAC protocol serves to coordinate the frame transmissions of the many nodes; we cover MAC protocols in detail in Section 5.3.

♦ *Reliable delivery.* When a link-layer protocol provides reliable delivery service, it guarantees to move each network-layer datagram across the link without error. Recall that certain transport-layer protocols (such as TCP) also provide a reliable delivery service. Similar to a transport-layer reliable delivery service, a link-layer reliable delivery service is achieved with acknowledgments and retransmissions (see Section 3.4). A link-layer reliable delivery service is often used for links that are prone to high error rates, such as a wireless link, with the goal of correcting an error locally—on the link where the error occurs—rather than forcing an end-to-end retransmission of the data by a transport- or application-layer protocol. However, link-layer reliable delivery can be considered an unnecessary overhead for low bit-error links, including fiber, coax, and many twisted-pair copper links. For this reason, many wired link-layer protocols do not provide a reliable delivery service.

♦ *Flow control.* The nodes on each side of a link have a limited amount of frame buffering capacity. This is a potential problem, as a receiving node may receive frames at a rate faster than it can process them. Without flow control, the receiver's buffer can overflow and frames can get lost. Similar to the transport layer, a link-layer protocol can provide flow control in order to prevent the sending node on one side of a link from overwhelming the receiving node on the other side of the link.

♦ *Error detection.* A node's receiver can incorrectly decide that a bit in a frame is zero when it was transmitted as a one, and vice versa. Such bit errors are introduced by signal attenuation and electromagnetic noise. Because there is no need to forward a datagram that has an error, many link-layer protocols provide a mechanism to detect the presence of one or more errors. This is done by having the transmitting node set error-detection bits in the frame, and having the receiving node perform an error check. Error detection is a very common service among link-layer protocols. Recall from Chapters 3 and 4 that the Internet's transport layer and network layers also provide a limited form of error detection. Error detection in the link layer is usually more sophisticated and is implemented in hardware.

♦ *Error correction.* Error correction is similar to error detection, except that a receiver not only detects whether errors have been introduced in the frame but also determines exactly where in the frame the errors have occurred (and then corrects these errors). Some protocols (such as ATM) provide link-layer error correction for the packet header rather than for the entire packet. We cover error detection and correction in Section 5.2.

♦ *Half-duplex and full-duplex.* With full-duplex transmission, the nodes at both ends of a link may transmit packets at the same time. With half-duplex transmission, a node cannot both transmit and receive at the same time.

As noted above, many of the services provided by the link layer have strong parallels with services provided at the transport layer. For example, both the link layer and the transport layer can provide reliable delivery. Although the mechanisms used to provide reliable delivery in the two layers are similar (see Section 3.4), the two reliable delivery services are not the same. A transport protocol provides reliable delivery between two processes on an end-to-end basis; a reliable link-layer protocol provides the reliable delivery service between two nodes connected by a single link. Similarly, both link-layer and transport-layer protocols can provide flow control and error detection; again, flow control in a transport-layer protocol is provided on an end-to-end basis, whereas it is provided in a link-layer protocol on a node-to-adjacent-node basis.

5.1.2 Adapters Communicating

For a given communication link, the link-layer protocol is, for the most part, implemented in an **adapter**. An adapter is a board (or a PCMCIA card) that typically contains RAM, DSP chips, a host bus interface, and a link interface. Adapters are also commonly known as **network interface cards (NICs)**. As shown in Figure 5.2, the network layer in the transmitting node (that is, a host or router) passes a network-layer datagram to the adapter that handles the sending side of the communication link. The adapter encapsulates the datagram in a frame and then transmits the frame into the communication link. At the other side, the receiving adapter receives the entire frame, extracts the network-layer datagram, and passes it to the network layer. If the link-layer protocol provides error detection, then it is the sending adapter that sets the error detection bits and it is the receiving adapter that performs error checking. If the link-layer protocol provides reliable delivery, then the mechanisms for reliable delivery (for example, sequence numbers, timers, and acknowledgments) are implemented entirely in the adapters. If the link-layer protocol uses random access (see Section 5.3), then the random access protocol is implemented entirely in the adapters.

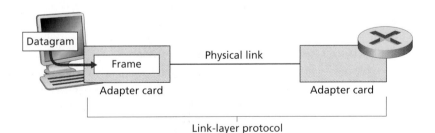

Figure 5.2 ◆ The link-layer protocol for a communication link is implemented in the adapters at the two ends of the link.

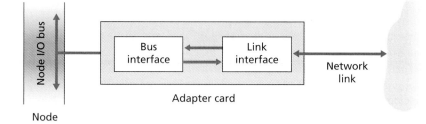

Figure 5.3 ♦ The adapter is a semi-autonomous unit.

An adapter is a semi-autonomous unit. For example, an adapter can receive a frame, determine if the frame is in error, and discard the frame without notifying other components (e.g., a central processing unit) in the node in which it is housed (which we will refer to as the adapter's *parent* node). When receiving a frame, an adapter will interrupt its parent node only if it wants to pass a network-layer datagram up the protocol stack. Similarly, when a node passes a datagram down the protocol stack to an adapter, the node fully delegates to the adapter the task of transmitting the datagram across that link. An adapter is semi-autonomous, not fully autonomous. Although we have shown the adapter as a separate box in Figure 5.3, the adapter is typically housed in the same physical box as the rest of the node, shares power and buses with the rest of the node, and is ultimately under the control of the node.

As shown in Figure 5.3, the main components of an adapter are the bus interface and the link interface. The bus interface is responsible for communicating with the adapter's parent node. It transfers data and control information between the adapter and the parent node. The link interface is responsible for implementing the link-layer protocol. In addition to framing and deframing datagrams, it may provide error detection, random access, and other link-layer functions. It also includes the transmit and receive circuitry. For popular link-layer technologies, such as Ethernet and Wi-Fi, the link interface is implemented by chip sets that can be bought on the commodity market. For this reason, Ethernet and Wi-Fi adapters are incredibly cheap—often less than $20. You can learn more about adapter architecture for 10, 100, and 1,000 Mbps Ethernet and for 155 Mbps ATM by visiting the 3Com adapter page [3Com 2004].

5.2 Error-Detection and -Correction Techniques

In the previous section, we noted that **bit-level error detection and correction**— detecting and correcting the corruption of bits in a link-layer frame sent from one node to another physically connected neighboring node—are two services often provided by the link layer. We saw in Chapter 3 that error-detection and -correction services are also often offered at the transport layer as well. In this section, we'll examine a few of the simplest techniques that can be used to detect and, in some cases, correct such bit errors. A full treatment of the theory and implementation of this topic is itself the topic of many textbooks (for example, [Schwartz 1980] or [Bertsekas 1991]), and our treatment here is necessarily brief. Our goal here is to develop an intuitive feel for the capabilities that error-detection and -correction techniques provide, and to see how a few simple techniques work and are used in practice in the link layer.

Figure 5.4 illustrates the setting for our study. At the sending node, data, D, to be protected against bit errors, is augmented with error-detection and -correction bits (EDC). Typically, the data to be protected includes not only the datagram passed down from the network layer for transmission across the link, but also link-level addressing information, sequence numbers, and other fields in the link frame header. Both D and EDC are sent to the receiving node in a link-level frame. At the receiving node, a sequence of bits, D' and EDC' are received. Note that D' and EDC' may differ from the original D and EDC as a result of in-transit bit flips.

The receiver's challenge is to determine whether or not D' is the same as the original D, given that it has only received D' and EDC'. The exact wording of the

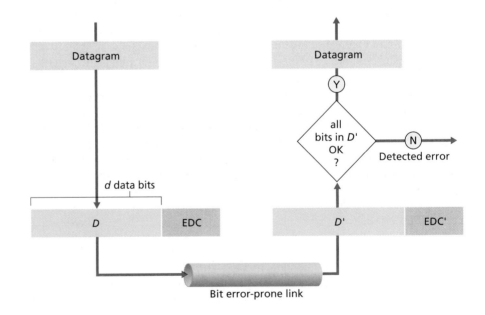

Figure 5.4 ♦ Error-detection and -correction scenario

receiver's decision in Figure 5.4 (we ask whether an error is detected, not whether an error has occurred!) is important. Error-detection and -correction techniques allow the receiver to sometimes, *but not always,* detect that bit errors have occurred. Even with the use of error detection bits there still may be **undetected bit errors**; that is, the receiver may be unaware that the received information contains bit errors. As a consequence, the receiver might deliver a corrupted datagram to the network layer, or be unaware that the contents of a field in the frame's header has been corrupted. We thus want to choose an error-detection scheme that keeps the probability of such occurrences small. Generally, more sophisticated error-detection and -correction techniques (that is, those that have a smaller probability of allowing undetected bit errors) incur a larger overhead—more computation is needed to compute and transmit a larger number of error-detection and -correction bits.

Let's now examine three techniques for detecting errors in the transmitted data—parity checks (to illustrate the basic ideas behind error detection and correction), checksumming methods (which are more typically employed in the transport layer), and cyclic redundancy checks (which are more typically employed in the link layer in the adapters).

5.2.1 Parity Checks

Perhaps the simplest form of error detection is the use of a single **parity bit**. Suppose that the information to be sent, D in Figure 5.4, has d bits. In an even parity scheme, the sender simply includes one additional bit and chooses its value such that the total number of 1s in the $d + 1$ bits (the original information plus a parity bit) is even. For odd parity schemes, the parity bit value is chosen such that there is an odd number of 1s. Figure 5.5 illustrates an even parity scheme, with the single parity bit being stored in a separate field.

Receiver operation is also simple with a single parity bit. The receiver need only count the number of 1s in the received $d + 1$ bits. If an odd number of 1-valued bits are found with an even parity scheme, the receiver knows that at least one bit error has occurred. More precisely, it knows that some *odd* number of bit errors have occurred.

But what happens if an even number of bit errors occurs? You should convince yourself that this would result in an undetected error. If the probability of bit errors

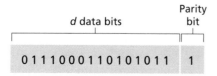

Parity
bit

d data bits

0 1 1 1 0 0 0 1 1 0 1 0 1 0 1 1   1

Figure 5.5 ◆ One-bit even parity

is small and errors can be assumed to occur independently from one bit to the next, the probability of multiple bit errors in a packet would be extremely small. In this case, a single parity bit might suffice. However, measurements have shown that, rather than occurring independently, errors are often clustered together in "bursts." Under burst error conditions, the probability of undetected errors in a frame protected by single-bit parity can approach 50 percent [Spragins 1991]. Clearly, a more robust error-detection scheme is needed (and, fortunately, is used in practice!). But before examining error-detection schemes that are used in practice, let's consider a simple generalization of one-bit parity that will provide us with insight into error-correction techniques.

Figure 5.6 shows a two-dimensional generalization of the single-bit parity scheme. Here, the d bits in D are divided into i rows and j columns. A parity value is computed for each row and for each column. The resulting $i + j + 1$ parity bits comprise the link-layer frame's error-detection bits.

Suppose now that a single bit error occurs in the original d bits of information. With this **two-dimensional parity** scheme, the parity of both the column and the

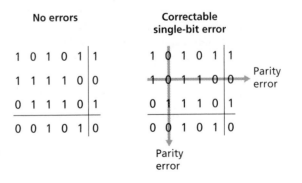

Figure 5.6 ♦ Two-dimensional even parity

row containing the flipped bit will be in error. The receiver can thus not only *detect* the fact that a single bit error has occurred, but can use the column and row indices of the column and row with parity errors to actually identify the bit that was corrupted and *correct* that error! Figure 5.6 shows an example in which the 1-valued bit in position (2,2) is corrupted and switched to a 0—an error that is both detectable and correctable at the receiver. Although our discussion has focused on the original *d* bits of information, a single error in the parity bits themselves is also detectable and correctable. Two-dimensional parity can also detect (but not correct!) any combination of two errors in a packet. Other properties of the two-dimensional parity scheme are explored in the problems at the end of the chapter.

The ability of the receiver to both detect and correct errors is known as **forward error correction (FEC)**. These techniques are commonly used in audio storage and playback devices such as audio CDs. In a network setting, FEC techniques can be used by themselves, or in conjunction with the ARQ techniques we examined in Chapter 3. FEC techniques are valuable because they can decrease the number of sender retransmissions required. Perhaps more important, they allow for immediate correction of errors at the receiver. This avoids having to wait for the round-trip propagation delay needed for the sender to receive a NAK packet and for the retransmitted packet to propagate back to the receiver—a potentially important advantage for real-time network applications [Rubenstein 1998]. Recent work examining the use of FEC in error-control protocols includes [Biersack 1992; Nonnenmacher 1998; Byers 1998; Shacham 1990].

5.2.2 Checksumming Methods

In checksumming techniques, the *d* bits of data in Figure 5.4 are treated as a sequence of *k*-bit integers. One simple checksumming method is to simply sum these *k*-bit integers and use the resulting sum as the error detection bits. The so-called **Internet checksum** is based on this approach—bytes of data are treated as 16-bit integers and summed. The 1s complement of this sum then forms the Internet checksum that is carried in the segment header. As discussed in Section 3.3, the receiver checks the checksum by taking the 1's complement of the sum of the received data (including the checksum) and checking whether the result is all 1 bits. If any of the bits are 0, an error is indicated. RFC 1071 discusses the Internet checksum algorithm and its implementation in detail. In the TCP and UDP protocols, the Internet checksum is computed over all fields (header and data fields included). In other protocols, for example, XTP [Strayer 1992], one checksum is computed over the header and another checksum is computed over the entire packet.

Checksumming methods require relatively little packet overhead. For example, the checksums in TCP and UDP use only 16 bits. However, they provide relatively weak protection against errors as compared with cyclic redundancy check, which is discussed below and which is often used in the link layer. A natural question at this point is, Why is checksumming used at the transport layer and cyclic redundancy check used at the link layer? Recall that the transport layer is typically implemented in software in a host as part of the host's operating system. Because transport-layer error detection is implemented in software, it is important to have a simple and fast error-detection scheme such as checksumming. On the other hand, error detection at the link layer is implemented in dedicated hardware in adapters, which can rapidly perform the more complex CRC operations.

The principal reason checksumming is used at the transport layer and the stronger CRC is used at the link layer is that checksumming is easy to implement in software.

McAuley [McAuley 1994] describes improved weighted checksum codes that are suitable for high-speed software implementation and Feldmeier [Feldmeier 1995] presents fast software implementation techniques for not only weighted checksum codes, but CRC (see below) and other codes as well.

5.2.3 Cyclic Redundancy Check (CRC)

An error-detection technique used widely in today's computer networks is based on **cyclic redundancy check (CRC) codes.** CRC codes are also known as **polynomial codes**, since it is possible to view the bit string to be sent as a polynomial whose coefficients are the 0 and 1 values in the bit string, with operations on the bit string interpreted as polynomial arithmetic.

CRC codes operate as follows. Consider the d-bit piece of data, D, that the sending node wants to send to the receiving node. The sender and receiver must first agree on an $r + 1$ bit pattern, known as a **generator**, which we will denote as G. We will require that the most significant (leftmost) bit of G be a 1. The key idea behind CRC codes is shown in Figure 5.7. For a given piece of data, D, the sender will choose r additional bits, R, and append them to D such that the resulting $d + r$ bit pattern (interpreted as a binary number) is exactly divisible by G using modulo-2 arithmetic. The process of error checking with CRCs is thus simple: The receiver divides the $d + r$ received bits by G. If the remainder is nonzero, the receiver knows that an error has occurred; otherwise the data is accepted as being correct.

All CRC calculations are done in modulo-2 arithmetic without carries in addition or borrows in subtraction. This means that addition and subtraction are identical,

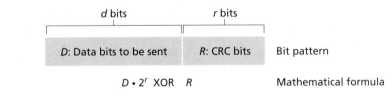

Figure 5.7 ◆ CRC codes

and both are equivalent to the bitwise exclusive-or (XOR) of the operands. Thus, for example,

```
1011 XOR 0101 = 1110
1001 XOR 1101 = 0100
```

Also, we similarly have

```
1011 − 0101 = 1110
1001 − 1101 = 0100
```

Multiplication and division are the same as in base-2 arithmetic, except that any required addition or subtraction is done without carries or borrows. As in regular binary arithmetic, multiplication by 2^k left shifts a bit pattern by k places. Thus, given D and R, the quantity $D \cdot 2^r$ XOR R yields the $d + r$ bit pattern shown in Figure 5.7. We'll use this algebraic characterization of the $d + r$ bit pattern from Figure 5.7 in our discussion below.

Let us now turn to the crucial question of how the sender computes R. Recall that we want to find R such that there is an n such that

$$D \cdot 2^r \text{ XOR } R = nG$$

That is, we want to choose R such that G divides into $D \cdot 2^r$ XOR R without remainder. If we XOR (that is, add modulo-2, without carry) R to both sides of the above equation, we get

$$D \cdot 2^r = nG \text{ XOR } R$$

This equation tells us that if we divide $D \cdot 2^r$ by G, the value of the remainder is precisely R. In other words, we can calculate R as

$$R = \text{remainder} \frac{D \cdot 2^r}{G}$$

Figure 5.8 illustrates this calculation for the case of $D = 101110$, $d = 6$, $G = 1001$, and $r = 3$. The 9 bits transmitted in this case are 101110 011. You should check these calculations for yourself and also check that indeed $D \cdot 2^r = 101011 \cdot G$ XOR R.

International standards have been defined for 8-, 12-, 16-, and 32-bit generators, G. An 8-bit CRC is used to protect the 5-byte header in ATM cells. The CRC-32 32-bit standard, which has been adopted in a number of link-level IEEE protocols, uses a generator of

$$G_{\text{CRC-32}} = 100000100110000010001110110110111$$

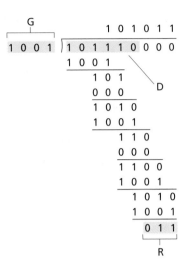

Figure 5.8 ♦ A sample CRC calculation

Each of the CRC standards can detect burst errors of fewer than $r + 1$ bits. (This means that all consecutive bit errors of r bits or fewer will be detected.) Furthermore, under appropriate assumptions, a burst of length greater than $r + 1$ bits is detected with probability $1 - 0.5^r$. Also, each of the CRC standards can detect any odd number of bit errors. The theory behind CRC codes and even more powerful codes is beyond the scope of this text. The text [Schwartz 1980] provides an excellent introduction to this topic.

5.3 Multiple Access Protocols

In the introduction to this chapter, we noted that there are two types of network links: point-to-point links and broadcast links. A **point-to-point link** consists of a single sender at one end of the link and a single receiver at the other end of the link. Many link-layer protocols have been designed for point-to-point links; the point-to-point protocol (PPP) is one such protocol that we'll cover later in this chapter. The second type of link, a **broadcast link**, can have multiple sending and receiving nodes all connected to the same, single, shared broadcast channel. The term *broadcast* is used here because when any one node transmits a frame, the channel broadcasts the frame and each of the other nodes receives a copy. Ethernet and wireless LANs are examples of broadcast link-layer technologies. In this section we'll take a step back from specific link-layer protocols and first examine a problem of central importance to the link layer: how to coordinate the access of multiple sending and receiving nodes to a shared broadcast channel—the **multiple access problem**. Broadcast channels are often used in LANs, networks that are geographically concentrated in a single building (or on a corporate or university campus). Thus, we'll also look at how multiple access channels are used in LANs at the end of this section.

We are all familiar with the notion of broadcasting—television has been using it since its invention. But traditional television is a one-way broadcast (that is, one fixed node transmitting to many receiving nodes), while nodes on a computer network broadcast channel can both send and receive. Perhaps a more apt human analogy for a broadcast channel is a cocktail party, where many people gather in a large room (the air providing the broadcast medium) to talk and listen. A second good analogy is something many readers will be familiar with—a classroom—where teacher(s) and student(s) similarly share the same, single, broadcast medium. A central problem in both scenarios is that of determining who gets to talk (that is, transmit into the channel), and when. As humans, we've evolved an elaborate set of protocols for sharing the broadcast channel:

"Give everyone a chance to speak."

"Don't speak until you are spoken to."

"Don't monopolize the conversation."

"Raise your hand if you have a question."

"Don't interrupt when someone is speaking."

"Don't fall asleep when someone is talking."

Computer networks similarly have protocols—so-called **multiple access protocols**—by which nodes regulate their transmission onto the shared broadcast channel. As shown in Figure 5.9, multiple access protocols are needed in a wide variety of network settings, including both wired and wireless local area networks, and satellite networks. Although technically each node accesses the broadcast channel through its adapter, in this section we will refer to the *node* as the sending and receiving device. In practice, hundreds or even thousands of nodes can directly communicate over a broadcast channel.

Because all nodes are capable of transmitting frames, more than two nodes can transmit frames at the same time. When this happens, all of the nodes receive multiple frames at the same time; that is, the transmitted frames **collide** at all of the receivers. Typically, when there is a collision, none of the receiving nodes can make any sense of any of the frames that were transmitted; in a sense, the signals of the colliding frames become inextricably tangled together. Thus, all the frames involved in the collision are lost, and the broadcast channel is wasted during the collision interval. Clearly, if many nodes want to transmit frames frequently, many transmissions will result in collisions, and much of the bandwidth of the broadcast channel will be wasted.

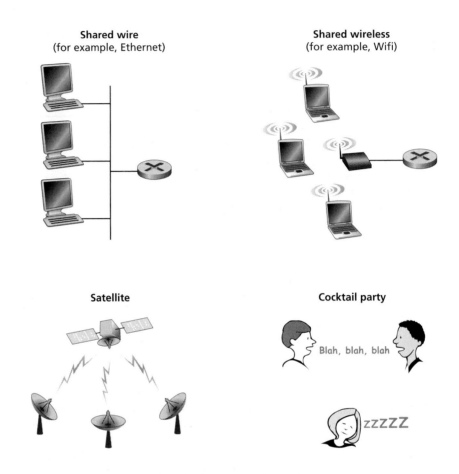

Figure 5.9 ♦ Various multiple access channels

In order to ensure that the broadcast channel performs useful work when multiple nodes are active, it is necessary to somehow coordinate the transmissions of the active nodes. This coordination job is the responsibility of the multiple access protocol. Over the past 30 years, thousands of papers and hundreds of PhD dissertations have been written on multiple access protocols; a comprehensive survey of this body of work is [Rom 1990]. Furthermore, active research in multiple access protocols continues due to the continued emergence of new types of links, particularly new wireless links.

Over the years, dozens of multiple access protocols have been implemented in a variety of link-layer technologies. Nevertheless, we can classify just about any multiple access protocol as belonging to one of three categories: **channel partitioning protocols**, **random access protocols**, and **taking-turns protocols**. We'll cover these categories of multiple access protocols in the following three subsections.

Let us conclude this overview by noting that, ideally, a multiple access protocol for a broadcast channel of rate R bits per second should have the following desirable characteristics:

1. When only one node has data to send, that node has a throughput of R bps.
2. When M nodes have data to send, each of these nodes has a throughput of R/M bps. This need not necessarily imply that each of the M nodes always has an instantaneous rate of R/M, but rather that each node should have an average transmission rate of R/M over some suitably defined interval of time.
3. The protocol is decentralized; that is, there are no master nodes that can fail and bring down the entire system.
4. The protocol is simple, so that it is inexpensive to implement.

5.3.1 Channel Partitioning Protocols

Recall from our early discussion back in Section 1.3 that time-division multiplexing (TDM) and frequency-division multiplexing (FDM) are two techniques that can be used to partition a broadcast channel's bandwidth among all nodes sharing that channel. As an example, suppose the channel supports N nodes and that the transmission rate of the channel is R bps. TDM divides time into **time frames** and further divides each time frame into N **time slots**. (The TDM time frame should not be confused with the link-layer unit of data exchanged between sending and receiving adapters, which is also called a frame. In order to reduce confusion, in this subsection we refer to the link-layer unit of data exchanged as a packet.) Each slot time is then assigned to one of the N nodes. Whenever a node has a packet to send, it transmits the packet's bits during its assigned time slot in the revolving TDM frame. Typically, slot sizes are chosen so that a single packet can be transmitted during a slot time. Figure 5.10 shows a simple four-node TDM example. Returning to our cocktail party analogy, a TDM-regulated cocktail party would allow one partygoer to speak for a fixed period of time, then allow another partygoer to speak for the same amount of time, and so on. Once everyone had had a chance to talk, the pattern would repeat.

TDM is appealing because it eliminates collisions and is perfectly fair: Each node gets a dedicated transmission rate of R/N bps during each frame time. However, it has two major drawbacks. First, a node is limited to an average rate of R/N bps even when it is the only node with packets to send. A second drawback is that a node must always wait for its turn in the transmission sequence—again, even when it is the only node with a frame to send. Imagine the partygoer who is the only one with anything to say (and imagine that this is the even rarer circumstance where everyone at the party wants to hear what that one person has to say). Clearly, TDM would be a poor choice for a multiple access protocol for this particular party.

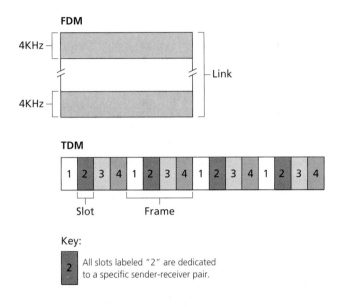

Figure 5.10 ♦ A four-node TDM and FDM example

While TDM shares the broadcast channel in time, FDM divides the R bps channel into different frequencies (each with a bandwidth of R/N) and assigns each frequency to one of the N nodes. FDM thus creates N smaller channels of R/N bps out of the single, larger R bps channel. FDM shares both the advantages and drawbacks of TDM. It avoids collisions and divides the bandwidth fairly among the N nodes. However, FDM also shares a principal disadvantage with TDM—a node is limited to a bandwidth of R/N, even when it is the only node with packets to send.

A third channel-partitioning protocol is **code division multiple access (CDMA)**. While TDM and FDM assign time slots and frequencies, respectively, to the nodes, CDMA assigns a different *code* to each node. Each node then uses its unique code to encode the data bits it sends. If the codes are chosen carefully, CDMA networks have the wonderful property that different nodes can transmit *simultaneously* and yet have their respective receivers correctly receive a sender's encoded data bits (assuming the receiver knows the sender's code) in spite of interfering transmissions by other nodes. CDMA has been used in military systems for some time (due to its anti-jamming properties) and now has widespread civilian use, particularly in wireless multiple access channels. Because CDMA's use is so tightly tied to wireless channels, we'll save our discussion of the technical details of CDMA until Chapter 6. For now, it will suffice to know that CDMA codes, like time slots in TDM and frequencies in FDM, can be allocated to the multiple access channel users.

5.3.2 Random Access Protocols

The second broad class of multiple access protocols are random access protocols. In a random access protocol, a transmitting node always transmits at the full rate of the channel, namely, R bps. When there is a collision, each node involved in the collision repeatedly retransmits its frame (that is, packet) until the frame gets through without a collision. But when a node experiences a collision, it doesn't necessarily retransmit the frame right away. *Instead it waits a random delay before retransmitting the frame.* Each node involved in a collision chooses independent random delays. Because the random delays are independently chosen, it is possible that one of the nodes will pick a delay that is sufficiently less than the delays of the other colliding nodes and will therefore be able to sneak its frame into the channel without a collision.

There are dozens if not hundreds of random access protocols described in the literature [Rom 1990; Bertsekas 1991]. In this section we'll describe a few of the most commonly used random access protocols—the ALOHA protocols [Abramson 1970; Abramson 1985] and the carrier sense multiple access (CSMA) protocols [Kleinrock 1975b]. Later, in Section 5.5, we'll cover the details of Ethernet [Metcalfe 1976], a popular and widely deployed CSMA protocol.

Slotted ALOHA

Let's begin our study of random access protocols with one of the most simple random access protocols, the slotted ALOHA protocol. In our description of slotted ALOHA, we assume the following:

♦ All frames consist of exactly L bits.
♦ Time is divided into slots of size L/R seconds (that is, a slot equals the time to transmit one frame).
♦ Nodes start to transmit frames only at the beginnings of slots.
♦ The nodes are synchronized so that each node knows when the slots begin.
♦ If two or more frames collide in a slot, then all the nodes detect the collision event before the slot ends.

Let p be a probability, that is, a number between 0 and 1. The operation of slotted ALOHA in each node is simple:

♦ When the node has a fresh frame to send, it waits until the beginning of the next slot and transmits the entire frame in the slot.
♦ If there isn't a collision, the node has successfully transmitted its frame and thus need not consider retransmitting the frame. (The node can prepare a new frame for transmission, if it has one.)

♦ If there is a collision, the node detects the collision before the end of the slot. The node retransmits its frame in each subsequent slot with probability p until the frame is transmitted without a collision.

By retransmitting with probability p, we mean that the node effectively tosses a biased coin; the event heads corresponds to "retransmit," which occurs with probability p. The event tails corresponds to "skip the slot and toss the coin again in the next slot"; this occurs with probability $(1 - p)$. All nodes involved in the collision toss their coins independently.

Slotted ALOHA would appear to have many advantages. Unlike channel partitioning, slotted ALOHA allows a node to transmit continuously at the full rate, R, when that node is the only active node. (A node is said to be active if it has frames to send.) Slotted ALOHA is also highly decentralized, because each node detects collisions and independently decides when to retransmit. (Slotted ALOHA does, however, require the slots to be synchronized in the nodes; shortly we'll discuss an unslotted version of the ALOHA protocol, as well as CSMA protocols, none of which require such synchronization and are therefore fully decentralized.) Slotted ALOHA is also an extremely simple protocol.

Slotted ALOHA works well when there is only one active node, but how efficient is it when there are multiple active nodes? There are two possible efficiency concerns here. First, as shown in Figure 5.11, when there are multiple active nodes, a certain fraction of the slots will have collisions and will therefore be "wasted." The second concern is that another fraction of the slots will be *empty* because all active nodes refrain from transmitting as a result of the probabilistic transmission policy. The only "unwasted" slots will be those in which exactly one node transmits. A slot in which exactly one node transmits is said to be a **successful slot**. The **efficiency** of a slotted multiple access protocol is defined to be the long-run fraction of successful slots in the case when there are a large number of active nodes, each always having a large number of frames to send. Note that if no form of access control were used, and each node were to immediately retransmit after each collision, the efficiency would be zero. Slotted ALOHA clearly increases the efficiency beyond zero, but by how much?

We now proceed to outline the derivation of the maximum efficiency of slotted ALOHA. To keep this derivation simple, let's modify the protocol a little and assume that each node attempts to transmit a frame in each slot with probability p. (That is, we assume that each node always has a frame to send and that the node transmits with probability p for a fresh frame as well as for a frame that has already suffered a collision.) Suppose there are N nodes. Then the probability that a given slot is a successful slot is the probability that one of the nodes transmits and that the remaining $N - 1$ nodes do not transmit. The probability that a given node transmits is p; the probability that the remaining nodes do not transmit is $(1 - p)^{N-1}$. Therefore the probability a given node has a success is $p(1 - p)^{N-1}$. Because there are N nodes, the probability that an arbitrary node has a success is $Np(1 - p)^{N-1}$.

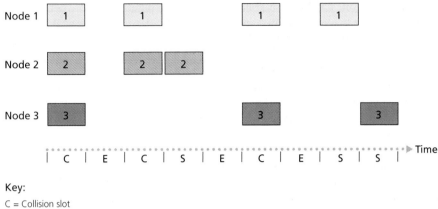

Key:
C = Collision slot
E = Empty slot
S = Successful slot

Figure 5.11 ♦ Nodes 1, 2, and 3 collide in the first slot. Node 2 finally succeeds in the fourth slot, node 1 in the eighth slot, and node 3 in the ninth slot.

Thus, when there are N active nodes, the efficiency of slotted ALOHA is $Np(1 - p)^{N-1}$. To obtain the *maximum* efficiency for N active nodes, we have to find the $p*$ that maximizes this expression. (See the homework problems for a general outline of this derivation.) And to obtain the maximum efficiency for a large number of active nodes, we take the limit of $Np*(1 - p*)^{N-1}$ as N approaches infinity. (Again, see the homework problems.) After performing these calculations, we'll find that the maximum efficiency of the protocol is given by $1/e = 0.37$. That is, when a large number of nodes have many frames to transmit, then (at best) only 37 percent of the slots do useful work. Thus the effective transmission rate of the channel is not R bps but only $0.37\,R$ bps! A similar analysis also shows that 37 percent of the slots go empty and 26 percent of slots have collisions. Imagine the poor network administrator who has purchased a 100-Mbps slotted ALOHA system, expecting to be able to use the network to transmit data among a large number of users at an aggregate rate of, say, 80 Mbps! Although the channel is capable of transmitting a given frame at the full channel rate of 100 Mbps, in the long run, the successful throughput of this channel will be less than 37 Mbps.

ALOHA

The slotted ALOHA protocol required that all nodes synchronize their transmissions to start at the beginning of a slot. The first ALOHA protocol [Abramson 1970] was actually an unslotted, fully decentralized protocol. In pure ALOHA, when a frame first arrives (that is, a network-layer datagram is passed down from the network layer at the sending node), the node immediately transmits the frame in its entirety into the broadcast channel. If a transmitted frame experiences a collision with one or more other transmissions, the node will then immediately (after completely transmitting its collided frame) retransmit the frame with probability p. Otherwise, the node waits for a frame transmission time. After this wait, it then transmits the frame with probability p, or waits (remaining idle) for another frame time with probability $1 - p$.

To determine the maximum efficiency of pure ALOHA, we focus on an individual node. We'll make the same assumptions as in our slotted ALOHA analysis and take the frame transmission time to be the unit of time. At any given time, the probability that a node is transmitting a frame is p. Suppose this frame begins transmission at time t_0. As shown in Figure 5.12, in order for this frame to be successfully transmitted, no other nodes can begin their transmission in the interval of time $[t_0 - 1, t_0]$. Such a transmission would overlap with the beginning of the transmission of node i's frame. The probability that all other nodes do not begin a transmission in this interval is $(1 - p)^{N-1}$. Similarly, no other node can begin a transmission while node i is transmitting, as such a transmission would overlap with the latter part of node i's transmission. The probability that all other nodes do not begin a transmission in this interval is also $(1 - p)^{N-1}$. Thus, the probability that a given node has a successful transmission is $p(1 - p)^{2(N-1)}$. By taking limits as in the slotted ALOHA case, we find that the maximum efficiency of the pure ALOHA protocol is only $1/(2e)$—exactly half that of slotted ALOHA. This then is the price to be paid for a fully decentralized ALOHA protocol.

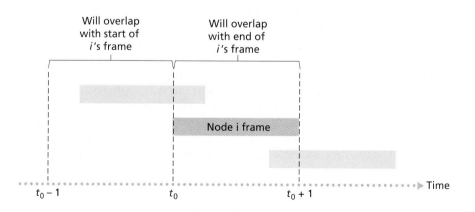

Figure 5.12 ♦ Interfering transmissions in pure ALOHA

CASE HISTORY

NORM ABRAMSON AND ALOHANET

Norm Abramson, a PhD engineer, had a passion for surfing and an interest in packet switching. This combination of interests brought him to the University of Hawaii in 1969. Hawaii consists of many mountainous islands, making it difficult to install and operate land-based networks. When not surfing, Abramson thought about how to design a network that does packet switching over radio. The network he designed had one central host and several secondary nodes scattered over the Hawaiian Islands. The network had two channels, each using a different frequency band. The downlink channel broadcasted packets from the central host to the secondary hosts; and the upstream channel sent packets from the secondary hosts to the central host. In addition to sending informational packets, the central host also sent on the downstream channel an acknowledgment for each packet successfully received from the secondary hosts.

Because the secondary hosts transmitted packets in a decentralized fashion, collisions on the upstream channel inevitably occurred. This observation led Abramson to devise the pure ALOHA protocol, as described in this chapter. In 1970, with continued funding from ARPA, Abramson connected his ALOHAnet to the ARPAnet. Abramson's work is important not only because it was the first example of a radio packet network, but also because it inspired Bob Metcalfe. A few years after Abramson invented it, Metcalfe modified the ALOHA protocol to create the CSMA/CD protocol and the Ethernet LAN.

Carrier Sense Multiple Access (CSMA)

In both slotted and pure ALOHA, a node's decision to transmit is made independently of the activity of the other nodes attached to the broadcast channel. In particular, a node neither pays attention to whether another node happens to be transmitting when it begins to transmit, nor stops transmitting if another node begins to interfere with its transmission. In our cocktail party analogy, ALOHA protocols are quite like a boorish partygoer who continues to chatter away regardless of whether other people are talking. As humans, we have human protocols that allow us not only to behave with more civility, but also to decrease the amount of time spent "colliding" with each other in conversation and, consequently, to increase the amount of data we exchange in our conversations. Specifically, there are two important rules for polite human conversation:

♦ *Listen before speaking.* If someone else is speaking, wait until they are finished. In the networking world, this is called **carrier sensing**—a node listens to the channel before transmitting. If a frame from another node is currently being transmitted into the channel, a node then waits ("backs off") a random amount of time and then again senses the channel. If the channel is sensed to be idle, the node then begins frame transmission. Otherwise, the node waits another random amount of time and repeats this process.

♦ *If someone else begins talking at the same time, stop talking.* In the networking world, this is called **collision detection**—a transmitting node listens to the channel while it is transmitting. If it detects that another node is transmitting an interfering frame, it stops transmitting and uses some protocol to determine when it should next attempt to transmit.

These two rules are embodied in the family of **carrier sense multiple access (CSMA)** and **CSMA with collision detection (CSMA/CD)** protocols [Kleinrock 1975b; Metcalfe 1976; Lam 1980; Rom 1990]. Many variations on CSMA and CSMA/CD have been proposed. You can consult these references for the details of these protocols. We'll study the CSMA/CD scheme used in Ethernet in detail in Section 5.5. Here, we'll consider a few of the most important, and fundamental, characteristics of CSMA and CSMA/CD.

The first question that you might ask about CSMA is why, if all nodes perform carrier sensing, do collisions occur in the first place? After all, a node will refrain from transmitting whenever it senses that another node is transmitting. The answer to the question can best be illustrated using space-time diagrams [Molle 1987]. Figure 5.13 shows a space-time diagram of four nodes (A, B, C, D) attached to a linear broadcast bus. The horizontal axis shows the position of each node in space; the vertical axis represents time.

At time t_0, node B senses the channel is idle, as no other nodes are currently transmitting. Node B thus begins transmitting, with its bits propagating in both directions along the broadcast medium. The downward propagation of B's bits in Figure 5.13 with increasing time indicates that a nonzero amount of time is needed for B's bits actually to propagate (albeit at near the speed of light) along the broadcast medium. At time t_1 ($t_1 > t_0$), node D has a frame to send. Although node B is currently transmitting at time t_1, the bits being transmitted by B have yet to reach D, and thus D senses the channel idle at t_1. In accordance with the CSMA protocol, D thus begins transmitting its frame. A short time later, B's transmission begins to interfere with D's transmission at D. From Figure 5.13, it is evident that the end-to-end **channel propagation delay** of a broadcast channel—the time it takes for a signal to propagate from one of the nodes to another—will play a crucial role in determining its performance. The longer this propagation delay, the larger the chance that a carrier-sensing node is not yet able to sense a transmission that has already begun at another node in the network.

In Figure 5.13, nodes do not perform collision detection; both B and D continue to transmit their frames in their entirety even though a collision has occurred. When a node performs collision detection, it ceases transmission as soon as it detects a

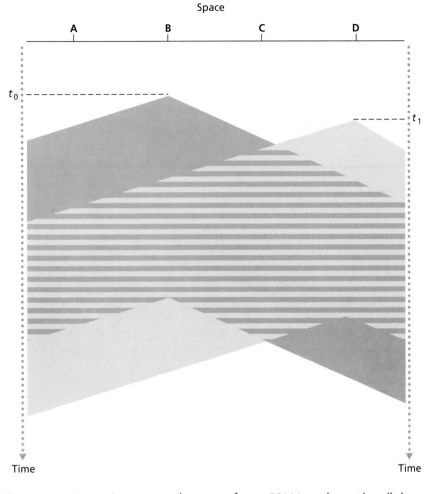

Figure 5.13 ♦ Space-time diagram of two CSMA nodes with colliding transmissions

collision. Figure 5.14 shows the same scenario as in Figure 5.13, except that the two nodes each abort their transmission a short time after detecting a collision. Clearly, adding collision detection to a multiple access protocol will help protocol performance by not transmitting a useless, damaged (by interference with a frame from another node) frame in its entirety. The Ethernet protocol we will study in Section 5.5 is a CSMA protocol that uses collision detection.

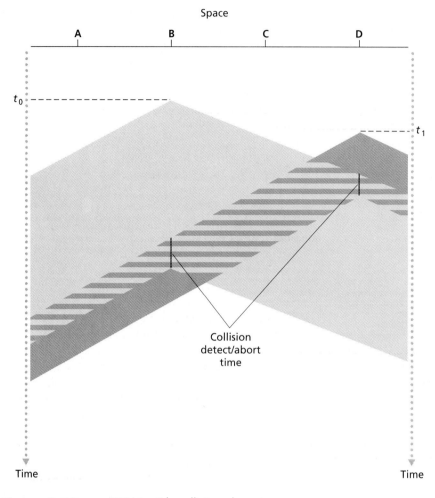

Figure 5.14   ◆   CSMA with collision detection

5.3.3 Taking-Turns Protocols

Recall that two desirable properties of a multiple access protocol are (1) when only one node is active, the active node has a throughput of R bps, and (2) when M nodes are active, then each active node has a throughput of nearly R/M bps. The ALOHA and CSMA protocols have this first property but not the second. This has motivated researchers to create another class of protocols—the **taking-turns protocols**. As with random access protocols, there are dozens of taking-turns protocols, and each one of these protocols has many variations. We'll discuss two of the more important protocols here. The first one is the **polling protocol**. The polling protocol requires one of the nodes to be designated as a master node. The master node **polls** each of the nodes in a round-robin fashion. In particular, the master node first sends a message to node 1, saying that it (node 1) can transmit up to some maximum number of frames. After node 1 transmits some frames, the master node tells node 2 it (node 2) can transmit up to the maximum number of frames. (The master node can determine when a node has finished sending its frames by observing the lack of a signal on the channel.) The procedure continues in this manner, with the master node polling each of the nodes in a cyclic manner.

The polling protocol eliminates the collisions and the empty slots that plague the random access protocols. This allows polling to achieve a much higher efficiency. But it also has a few drawbacks. The first drawback is that the protocol introduces a polling delay—the amount of time required to notify a node that it can transmit. If, for example, only one node is active, then the node will transmit at a rate less than R bps, as the master node must poll each of the inactive nodes in turn each time the active node has sent its maximum number of frames. The second drawback, which is potentially more serious, is that if the master node fails, the entire channel becomes inoperative.

The second taking-turn protocol is the **token-passing protocol**. In this protocol there is no master node. A small, special-purpose frame known as a **token** is exchanged among the nodes in some fixed order. For example, node 1 might always send the token to node 2, node 2 might always send the token to node 3, node N might always send the token to node 1. When a node receives a token, it holds onto the token only if it has some frames to transmit; otherwise, it immediately forwards the token to the next node. If a node does have frames to transmit when it receives the token, it sends up to a maximum number of frames and then forwards the token to the next node. Token passing is decentralized and highly efficient. But it has its problems as well. For example, the failure of one node can crash the entire channel. Or if a node accidentally neglects to release the token, then some recovery procedure must be invoked to get the token back in circulation. Over the years many token-passing protocols have been developed, and each one had to address these as well as other sticky issues; we'll mention two of these protocols, FDDI and IEEE 802.5, in the following section.

5.3.4 Local Area Networks (LANs)

Multiple access protocols are used in conjunction with many different types of broadcast channels. They have been used for satellite and wireless channels, whose nodes transmit over a common frequency spectrum. They are currently used in the upstream channel for cable access to the Internet (see Section 1.5), and they are extensively used in local area networks (LANs).

Recall that a LAN is a computer network concentrated in a geographical area, such as in a building or on a university campus. When a user accesses the Internet from a university or corporate campus, the access is almost always by way of a

LAN—specifically, the access is from host to LAN to router to Internet, as shown in Figure 5.15. The transmission rate, R, of most LANs is very high. Even in the early 1980s, 10 Mbps LANs were common; today, 100 Mbps LANs are common, and 1 Gbps and 10 Gbps LANs are available.

In the 1980s and the early 1990s, two classes of LAN technologies were popular in the workplace. The first class consists of the Ethernet LANs (also known as 802.3 LANs [Spurgeon 2004]), which are random-access based. The second class of LAN technologies consists of token-passing technologies, including **token ring** (also known as IEEE 802.5) and **fiber distributed data interface (FDDI)** (Jain 1994). Because we'll explore the Ethernet technologies in some detail in Section 5.5, we focus our discussion here on the token-passing LANs. Our discussion of token-passing technologies is intentionally brief, because relentless Ethernet competition has made these technologies nearly extinct. Nevertheless, in order to provide examples of token-passing technology and to give a little historical perspective, it is useful to say a few words about token rings.

In a token ring LAN, the N nodes of the LAN (hosts and routers) are connected in a ring by direct links. The topology of the token ring defines the token-passing order. When a node obtains the token and sends a frame, the frame propagates around the entire ring, thereby creating a virtual broadcast channel. The destination node reads the frame from the link-layer medium as the frame propagates by. The

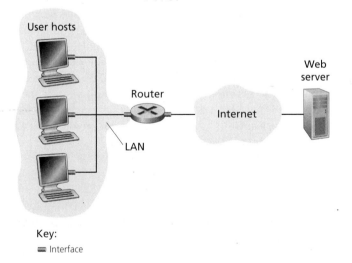

Figure 5.15 ◆ User hosts access an Internet Web server through a LAN. The broadcast channel between a user host and the router consists of one link.

node that sends the frame has the responsibility of removing the frame from the ring. FDDI was designed for geographically larger LANs, including **metropolitan area networks (MANs)**. For geographically large LANs (spread out over several kilometers) it is inefficient to let a frame propagate back to the sending node once the frame has passed the destination node. FDDI has the destination node remove the frame from the ring. (Strictly speaking, FDDI is thus not a pure broadcast channel, as every node does not receive every transmitted frame.)

5.4 Link-Layer Addressing

Nodes—that is hosts and routers—have link-layer addresses. Now you might find this surprising, remembering from Chapter 4 that nodes have network-layer addresses as well. You might be asking, why in the world do we need to have addresses at both the network and link layers? In addition to describing the syntax and function of the link-layer addresses, in this section we hope to shed some light on why the two layers of addresses are useful and, in fact, indispensable.

Additionally, we will cover two critical and address-related topics in this section. The first is the Address Resolution Protocol (ARP), which provides a mechanism for nodes to translate IP addresses to link-layer addresses. The second is Dynamic Host Configuration Protocol (DHCP). We discussed the DHCP service in Chapter 4; here, we'll leverage our knowledge about link-layer addresses to describe how the DHCP service is implemented.

5.4.1 MAC Addresses

In truth, it is not a node (that is, host or router) that has a link-layer address but instead a node's adapter that has a link-layer address. This is illustrated in Figure 5.16. A link-layer address is variously called a **LAN address**, a **physical address,** or a **MAC address**. Because MAC address seems to be the most popular term, we'll henceforth refer to link-layer addresses as MAC addresses. For most LANs (including Ethernet and 802.11 wireless LANs), the MAC address is 6 bytes long, giving 2^{48} possible MAC addresses. As shown in Figure 5.16, these 6-byte addresses are typically expressed in hexadecimal notation, with each byte of the address expressed as a pair of hexadecimal numbers. An important fact about MAC addresses is that they are permanent—when an adapter is manufactured, a MAC address is burned into the adapter's ROM.

One interesting property of MAC addresses is that no two adapters have the same address. This might seem surprising given that adapters are manufactured in many countries by many companies. How does a company manufacturing adapters in Taiwan make sure that it is using different addresses from a company manufacturing adapters in Belgium? The answer is that the IEEE manages the MAC address

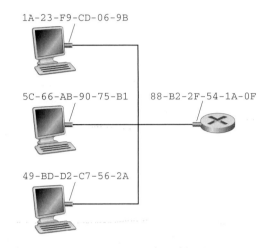

Figure 5.16 ♦ Each adapter connected to a LAN has a unique MAC address.

space. In particular, when a company wants to manufacture adapters, it purchases a chunk of the address space consisting of 2^{24} addresses for a nominal fee. IEEE allocates the chunk of 2^{24} addresses by fixing the first 24 bits of a MAC address and letting the company create unique combinations of the last 24 bits for each adapter.

An adapter's MAC address has a flat structure (as opposed to a hierarchical structure) and doesn't change no matter where the adapter goes. A portable computer with an Ethernet card always has the same MAC address, no matter where the computer goes. A PDA with an 802.11 interface always has the same MAC address, no matter where the PDA goes. Recall that, in contrast, an IP address has a hierarchical structure (that is, a network part and a host part), and a node's IP address needs to be changed when the host moves. An adapter's MAC address is analogous to a person's social security number, which also has a flat addressing structure and which doesn't change no matter where the person goes. An IP address is analogous to a person's postal address, which is hierarchical and which needs to be changed whenever a person moves. Just as a person may find it useful to have both a postal address and a Social Security number, it is useful for a node to have both a network-layer address and a MAC address.

As we described at the beginning of this section, when an adapter wants to send a frame to some destination adapter, the sending adapter inserts the destination adapter's MAC address into the frame and then sends the frame into the LAN. If the LAN is a broadcast LAN (such as 802.11 and many Ethernet LANs), the frame is received and processed by all other adapters on the LAN. In particular, each adapter that receives the frame will check to see whether destination MAC address in the frame matches its own MAC address. If there is a match, the adapter extracts the

PRINCIPLES IN PRACTICE

KEEPING THE LAYERS INDEPENDENT

There are several reasons why nodes have MAC addresses in addition to network-layer addresses. First, LANs are designed for arbitrary network-layer protocols, not just for IP and the Internet. If adapters were assigned IP addresses rather than "neutral" MAC addresses, then adapters would not easily be able to support other network-layer protocols (for example, IPX or DECnet). Second, if adapters were to use network-layer addresses instead of MAC addresses, the network-layer address would have to be stored in the adapter RAM and reconfigured every time the adapter was moved (or powered up). Another option is not to use any addresses in the adapters and have each adapter pass the data (typically, an IP datagram) of each frame it receives up the protocol stack to its parent node. The parent node could then check for a matching network-layer address. One problem with this option is that the parent node would be interrupted by every frame sent on the LAN, including by frames that were destined for other nodes on the same broadcast LAN. In summary, in order for the layers to be largely independent building blocks in a network architecture, many layers need to have their own addressing scheme. We have now seen three types of addresses: host names for the application layer, IP addresses for the network layer, and MAC addresses for the link layer.

enclosed datagram and passes the datagram up the protocol stack to its parent node. If there isn't a match, the adapter discards the frame, without passing the network-layer datagram up the protocol stack. Thus, only the adaptor in the destination node will interrupt its parent node when it receives a frame.

However, sometimes a sending adapter *does* want all the other adapters on the LAN to receive and *process* the frame it is about to send. In this case, the sending adapter inserts a special MAC **broadcast address** into the destination address field of the frame. For LANs that use 6-byte addresses (such as Ethernet and token-passing LANs), the broadcast address is a string of 48 consecutive 1s (that is, FF-FF-FF-FF-FF-FF in hexadecimal notation).

5.4.2 Address Resolution Protocol (ARP)

Because there are both network-layer addresses (for example, Internet IP addresses) and link-layer addresses (that is, MAC addresses), there is a need to translate between them. For the Internet, this is the job of the **address resolution protocol (ARP)** [RFC 826].

To understand the need for a protocol such as ARP, consider the network shown in Figure 5.17. In this simple example, each node has a single IP address, and each node's adapter has a single MAC address. As usual, IP addresses are shown in dotted-decimal notation and MAC addresses are shown in hexadecimal notation. Now suppose that the node with IP address 222.222.222.220 wants to send an IP datagram to node 222.222.222.222. (For example, destination node 222.222.222.222 may be a Web server, and the sending node 222.222.222.220 may have determined the Web server's IP address from DNS.) In this example, both the source and destination nodes are in the same network (LAN), in the addressing sense of Section 4.4.2. To send a datagram, the source node must give its adapter not only the IP datagram but also the MAC address for destination node 222.222.222.222. Given the IP datagram and the MAC address, the sending node's adapter will construct a link-layer frame containing the destination node's MAC address and send the frame into the LAN.

The important question addressed in this section is, How does the sending node determine the MAC address for the destination node with IP address 222.222.222.222? As you might have guessed, it uses ARP. An ARP module in the sending node takes as input any IP address on the same LAN and returns the corresponding MAC address. In the example at hand, the sending node 222.222.222.220 provides its ARP module the IP address 222.222.222.222, and the ARP module returns the corresponding MAC address 49-BD-D2-C7-56-2A.

So we see that ARP resolves an IP address to a MAC address. In many ways it is analogous to DNS (studied in Section 2.5), which resolves hostnames to IP addresses. However, one important difference between the two resolvers is that DNS resolves hostnames for hosts anywhere in the Internet, whereas ARP resolves IP addresses only for nodes on the same subnet. If a node in California were to try

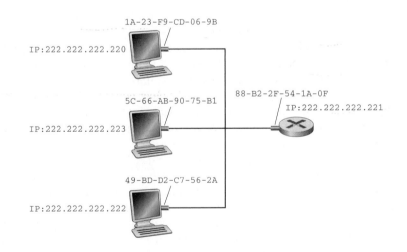

IP:222.222.222.220

1A-23-F9-CD-06-9B

5C-66-AB-90-75-B1

IP:222.222.222.223

88-B2-2F-54-1A-0F
IP:222.222.222.221

49-BD-D2-C7-56-2A

IP:222.222.222.222

Figure 5.17 ◆ Each node on a LAN has an IP address, and each node's adapter has a MAC address.

IP Address	MAC Address	TTL
222.222.222.221	88-B2-2F-54-1A-0F	13:45:00
222.222.222.223	5C-66-AB-90-75-B1	13:52:00

Figure 5.18 ♦ A possible ARP table in node 222.222.222.220

to use ARP to resolve the IP address for a node in Mississippi, ARP would return with an error.

Now that we have explained what ARP does, let's look at how it works. Each node (host or router) has in its RAM an **ARP table,** which contains mappings of IP addresses to MAC addresses. Figure 5.18 shows what an ARP table in node 222.222.222.220 might look like. The ARP table also contains a time-to-live (TTL) value, which indicates when each mapping will be deleted from the table. Note that the table does not necessarily contain an entry for every node on the subnet; some nodes may have had entries that have expired, whereas other nodes may never have been entered into the table. A typical expiration time for an entry is 20 minutes from when an entry is placed in an ARP table.

Now suppose that node 222.222.222.220 wants to send a datagram that is IP-addressed to another node on that subnet. The sending node needs to obtain the MAC address of the destination node, given the IP address of that node. This task is easy if the sending node's ARP table has an entry for the destination node. But what if the ARP table doesn't currently have an entry for the destination node? In particular, suppose node 222.222.222.220 wants to send a datagram to node 222.222.222.222. In this case, the sending node uses the ARP protocol to resolve the address. First, the sending node constructs a special packet called an **ARP packet.** An ARP packet has several fields, including the sending and receiving IP and MAC addresses. Both ARP query and response packets have the same format. The purpose of the ARP query packet is to query all the other nodes on the subnet to determine the MAC address corresponding to the IP address that is being resolved.

Returning to our example, node 222.222.222.220 passes an ARP query packet to the adapter along with an indication that the adapter should send the packet to the MAC broadcast address, namely, FF-FF-FF-FF-FF-FF. The adapter encapsulates the ARP packet in a link-layer frame, uses the broadcast address for the frame's destination address, and transmits the frame into the subnet. Recalling our Social Security number/postal address analogy, note that an ARP query is equivalent to a person shouting out in a crowded room of cubicles in some company (say, AnyCorp): "What is the Social Security number of the person whose postal address is Cubicle 13, Room 112, AnyCorp, Palo Alto, California?" The frame containing the ARP query is received by all the other adapters on the subnet, and (because of the broadcast address) each adapter passes the ARP packet within the frame up to its parent node. Each node checks to see if its IP address matches the destination IP address in the ARP packet. The (at most) one node with a match sends back to the querying node a response ARP packet with the desired mapping. The querying node 222.222.222.220 can then update its ARP table and send its IP datagram.

There are a couple of interesting things to note about the ARP protocol. First, the query ARP message is sent within a broadcast frame, whereas the response ARP message is sent within a standard frame. Before reading on you should think about why this is so. Second, ARP is plug-and-play; that is, a node's ARP table gets built automatically—it doesn't have to be configured by a system administrator. And if a node becomes disconnected from the subnet, its entry is eventually deleted from the tables of the nodes remaining in the subnet.

Sending a Datagram to a Node Off the Subnet

It should now be clear how ARP operates when a node wants to send a datagram to another node *on the same subnet*. (Subnets are precisely defined in Section 4.4.2.) But now let's look at the more complicated situation when a node on a subnet wants to send a network-layer datagram to a node *off the subnet* (that is, across a router onto another subnet). Let us discuss this issue in the context of Figure 5.19, which shows a simple network consisting of two subnets interconnected by a router.

There are several interesting things to note about Figure 5.19. First, there are two types of nodes: hosts and routers. Each host has exactly one IP address and one adapter. But, as discussed in Chapter 4, a router has an IP address for *each* of its interfaces. For each router interface there is also an ARP module (in the router) and an adapter. Because the router in Figure 5.19 has two interfaces, it has two IP addresses, two ARP modules, and two adapters. Of course, each adapter in the network has its own MAC address.

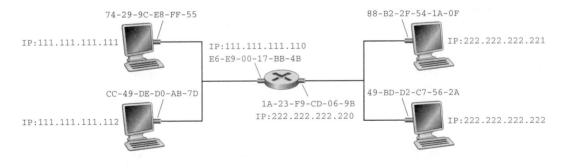

Figure 5.19 ◆ Two subnets interconnected by a router

Also note that Subnet 1 has the network address 111.111.111/24 and that Subnet 2 has the network address 222.222.222/24. Thus all of the interfaces connected to Subnet 1 have addresses of the form 111.111.111.xxx and all of the interfaces connected to Subnet 2 have the form 222.222.222.xxx.

Now let us examine how a host on Subnet 1 would send a datagram to a host on Subnet 2. Specifically, suppose that host 111.111.111.111 wants to send an IP datagram to a host 222.222.222.222. The sending host passes the datagram to its adapter, as usual. But the sending host must also indicate to its adapter an appropriate destination MAC address. What MAC address should the adapter use? One might be tempted to guess that the appropriate MAC address is that of the adapter for host 222.222.222.222, namely, 49-BD-D2-C7-56-2A. This guess, however, would be wrong. If the sending adapter were to use that MAC address, then none of the adapters on Subnet 1 would bother to pass the IP datagram up to its network layer, since the frame's destination address would not match the MAC address of any adapter on Subnet 1. The datagram would just die and go to datagram heaven.

If we look carefully at Figure 5.19, we see that in order for a datagram to go from 111.111.111.111 to a node on Subnet 2, the datagram must first be sent to the router interface 111.111.111.110. Thus, the appropriate MAC address for the frame is the address of the adapter for router interface 111.111.111.110, namely, E6-E9-00-17-BB-4B. How does the sending host acquire the MAC address for 111.111.111.110? By using ARP, of course! Once the sending adapter has this MAC address, it creates a frame and sends the frame into Subnet 1. The router adapter on Subnet 1 sees that the link-layer frame is addressed to it, and therefore passes the frame to the network layer of the router. Hooray! The IP datagram has successfully been moved from source host to the router! But we are not finished. We still have to move the datagram from the router to the destination. The router now has to determine the correct interface on which the datagram is to be forwarded. As discussed in Chapter 4, this is done by consulting a forwarding table in the router. The forwarding table tells the router that the datagram is to be forwarded via router interface 222.222.222.220. This interface then passes the datagram to its adapter, which encapsulates the datagram in a new frame and sends the frame into Subnet 2. This time, the destination MAC address of the frame is indeed the MAC address of the ultimate destination. And how does the router obtain this destination MAC address? From ARP, of course!

ARP for Ethernet is defined in RFC 826. A nice introduction to ARP is given in the TCP/IP tutorial, RFC 1180. We'll explore ARP in more detail in the homework problems.

5.4.3 Dynamic Host Configuration Protocol

In Chapter 4, when discussing IP addresses, we briefly considered the service provided by DHCP, a protocol that is extensively used in corporate, university, and home-network LANs to dynamically assign IP addresses to hosts. Having described the service in Chapter 4, we'll now use our newly acquired knowledge about MAC addresses to describe how DHCP actually works.

DHCP is a client-server protocol. A client is typically a newly arriving host wanting to obtain network configuration information, including an IP address for itself. In the simplest case, each subnet (in the addressing sense described in Section 4.4.2) will have a DHCP server. If no server is present on the subnet, a DHCP relay agent (typically a router) that knows the address of a DHCP server for that network is needed. Figure 5.20 shows a DHCP server attached to subnet 223.1.2/24, with the router serving as the relay agent for arriving clients attached to subnets 223.1.1/24 and 223.1.3/24.

For a newly arriving host, the DHCP protocol is a four-step process:

♦ *DHCP server discovery.* The first task of a newly arriving host is to find a DHCP server with which to interact. This is done using a **DHCP discover message**, which a client sends within a UDP packet to port 67. The UDP packet is encapsulated in an IP datagram. But to whom should this datagram be sent? The host doesn't even know the IP address of the network to which it is attaching, much less the address of a DHCP server for this network. Given this, the DHCP client

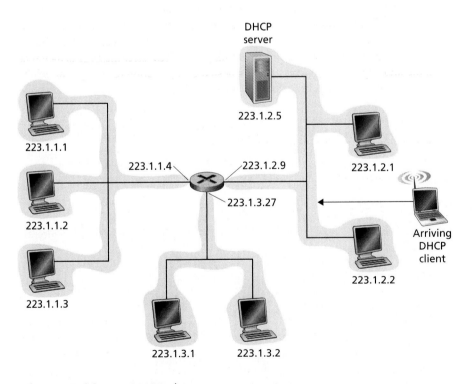

Figure 5.20 ♦ DHCP client-server scenario

creates an IP datagram containing its DHCP discover message along with the broadcast destination IP address of 255.255.255.255 and a "this host" source IP address of 0.0.0.0. The DHCP client passes the IP datagram to its adapter, which encapsulates the datagram in a link-layer frame. This link-layer frame includes the MAC broadcast address (FF-FF-FF-FF-FF-FF) in the destination address field. The DHCP client then sends the broadcast frame, containing the discovery message, into the subnet. This broadcast frame will be received by all adapters on the network. If a DHCP server is attached to the same subnet, it will process the encapsulated discovery message (see below); if a DHCP relay agent is attached to the subnet, it will forward the frame to the network with a DHCP server. (This relayed frame will have a different source MAC address.) The discovery message contains a transaction ID that allows subsequent responses to be matched to the discovery request.

♦ *DHCP server offer(s).* A DHCP server receiving a DHCP discover message responds to the client with a **DHCP offer message**. Since several DHCP servers can be present on the subnet, the client may find itself in the enviable position of being able to choose from among several offers. Each server offer message contains the transaction ID of the received discover message, the proposed IP address for the client, the network mask, and an IP **address lease time**—the amount of time for which the IP address will be valid. It is common for the server to set the lease time to several hours or days [Droms 1999]. The link-layer frame containing the IP datagram containing the UDP segment containing the DHCP offer message is then sent to the arriving client. (If you find this nested encapsulation dizzying, you might want to step back and get your bearings by re-reading Section 1.7.)

♦ *DHCP request.* The newly arriving client will choose from among one or more server offers and respond to its selected offer with a DHCP request message, echoing back the configuration parameters.

♦ *DHCP ACK.* The server responds to the DHCP request message with a DHCP ACK message, confirming the requested parameters.

Once the client receives the DHCP ACK, the interaction is complete and the client can use the DHCP-allocated IP address for the lease duration. Since a client may want to use its address beyond the lease's expiration, DHCP also provides a mechanism that allows a client to renew its lease on an IP address.

A simple DHCP client-server interaction is shown in Figure 5.21 for the network setting shown in Figure 5.20. In this figure, yiaddr (as in "your Internet address") indicates the address being allocated to the newly arriving client.

The value of DHCP's plug-and-play capability is clear. Consider the student who moves from classroom to library to dorm room with a laptop, joins a new subnet, and thus obtains a new IP address at each location. It is unimaginable that a system administrator would have to reconfigure laptops at each location, and few students (except those taking a computer networking class!) would have the expertise to configure

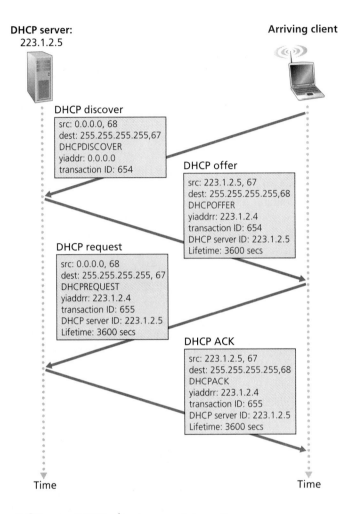

Figure 5.21 ♦ DHCP client-server interaction

their laptops manually. From a mobility aspect, however, DHCP does have short-comings. Since a new IP address is obtained from DHCP each time a node connects to a new subnet, a connection to a remote application cannot be maintained as a mobile node moves between subnets. We will examine mobile IP—a recent extension to the IP infrastructure that allows a mobile node to use its single permanent address as it moves between subnets—in Chapter 6.

Additional details about DHCP can be found in [Droms 1999] and [dhc 2004]. An open source reference implementation of DHCP is available from the Internet Systems Consortium [ISC 2004].

5.5 Ethernet

Ethernet has pretty much taken over the wired LAN market. In the 1980s and the early 1990s, Ethernet faced many challenges from other LAN technologies, including token ring, FDDI, and ATM. Some of these other technologies succeeded in capturing a part of the LAN market for a few years. But since its invention in the mid-1970s, Ethernet has continued to evolve and grow and has held on to its dominant position. Today, Ethernet is by far the most prevalent wired LAN technology, and it is likely to remain so for the foreseeable future. One might say that Ethernet has been to local area networking what the Internet has been to global networking.

There are many reasons for Ethernet's success. First, Ethernet was the first widely deployed high-speed LAN. Because it was deployed early, network administrators became intimately familiar with Ethernet—its wonders and its quirks—and were reluctant to switch over to other LAN technologies when they came on the scene. Second, token ring, FDDI, and ATM were more complex and expensive than Ethernet, which further discouraged network administrators from switching over. Third, the most compelling reason to switch to another LAN technology (such as FDDI or ATM) was usually the higher data rate of the new technology; however, Ethernet always fought back, producing versions that operated at equal data rates or higher. Switched Ethernet was also introduced in the early 1990s, which further increased its effective data rates. Finally, because Ethernet has been so popular, Ethernet hardware (in particular, adapters, hubs, and switches) has become a commodity and is remarkably cheap.

The original Ethernet LAN was invented in the mid-1970s by Bob Metcalfe and David Boggs. Figure 5.22 shows Metcalfe's schematic for Ethernet. In this figure

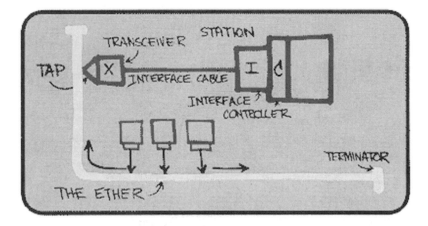

Figure 5.22 ♦ The original Metcalfe design led to the 10Base5 Ethernet standard, which included an interface cable that connected the Ethernet adapter to an external transceiver.

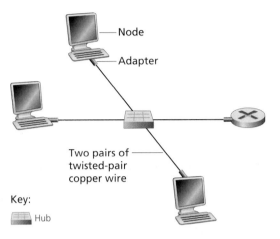

Figure 5.23   ◆   Star topology for Ethernet. Nodes are interconnected with a hub.

you'll notice that the original Ethernet LAN used a bus to interconnect the nodes. This bus topology actually persisted throughout the 1980s and much of the 1990s; in particular, the Ethernet 10Base2 technology, using a thin coaxial cable for the bus, was immensely popular in the 1990s. However, except for an occasional legacy installation, almost all Ethernet installations today use a star topology, as shown in Figure 5.23. At the center of the star topology is a **hub** or a **switch**. We'll discuss hubs and switches in some detail soon. An excellent source of online information about Ethernet is Spurgeon's Ethernet Web site [Spurgeon 2004].

5.5.1 Ethernet Frame Structure

The Ethernet frame is shown in Figure 5.24. We can learn a lot about Ethernet by examining the Ethernet frame. To give this discussion about Ethernet frames a tangible context, let's consider sending an IP datagram from one host to another host, with both hosts on the same Ethernet LAN (for example, the Ethernet LAN in Figure 5.23.) Although the payload of our Ethernet frame is an IP datagram, we note in passing that an Ethernet frame can carry other network-layer packets as well. Let the sending adapter, adapter A, have the MAC address AA-AA-AA-AA-AA-AA and the receiving adapter, adapter B, have the MAC address BB-BB-BB-BB-BB-BB. The sending adapter encapsulates the IP datagram within an Ethernet frame and passes the frame to the physical layer. The receiving adapter receives the frame from the physical layer, extracts the IP datagram, and passes the IP datagram to the network layer. In this context, let us now examine the six fields of the Ethernet frame, as shown in Figure 5.24.

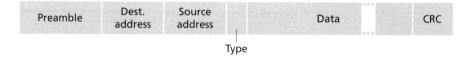

Figure 5.24 ♦ Ethernet frame structure

♦ *Data Field (46 to 1,500 bytes).* This field carries the IP datagram. The maximum transfer unit (MTU) of Ethernet is 1,500 bytes. This means that if the IP datagram exceeds 1,500 bytes, then the host has to fragment the datagram, as discussed in Section 4.4.1. The minimum size of the data field is 46 bytes. This means that if the IP datagram is less than 46 bytes, the data field has to be "stuffed" to fill it out to 46 bytes. When stuffing is used, the data passed to the network layer contains the stuffing as well as an IP datagram. The network layer uses the length field in the IP datagram header to remove the stuffing.

♦ *Destination Address (6 bytes).* This field contains the MAC address of the destination adapter, BB-BB-BB-BB-BB-BB. When adapter B receives an Ethernet frame whose destination address is either BB-BB-BB-BB-BB-BB or the MAC broadcast address, it passes the contents of the frame's data field to the network layer; if it receives a frame with any other MAC address, it discards the frame.

♦ *Source Address (6 bytes).* This field contains the MAC address of the adapter that transmits the frame onto the LAN, in this example, AA-AA-AA-AA-AA-AA.

♦ *Type Field (2 bytes).* The type field permits Ethernet to multiplex network-layer protocols. To understand this, we need to keep in mind that hosts can use other network-layer protocols besides IP. In fact, a given host may support multiple network-layer protocols using different protocols for different applications. For this reason, when the Ethernet frame arrives at adapter B, adapter B needs to know to which network-layer protocol it should pass (that is, demultiplex) the contents of the data field. IP and other network-layer protocols (for example, Novell IPX or AppleTalk) each have their own, standardized type number. Furthermore, the ARP protocol (discussed in the previous section) has its own type number. Note that the type field is analogous to the protocol field in the network-layer datagram and the port-number fields in the transport-layer segment; all of these fields serve to glue a protocol at one layer to a protocol at the layer above.

♦ *Cyclic Redundancy Check (CRC) (4 bytes).* As discussed in Section 5.2.3, the purpose of the CRC field is to allow the receiving adapter, adapter B, to detect whether any errors have been introduced into the frame, that is, if bits in the frame have been toggled. Causes of bit errors include attenuation in signal strength and ambient electromagnetic energy that leaks into the Ethernet cables and interface cards. Error detection is performed as follows. When host A constructs the Ethernet frame, it calculates a CRC field, which is obtained from a mapping of the other bits in the frame (except for the preamble bits). When host B receives the frame, it applies the same mapping to the frame and checks to see if the result of the mapping is equal to what is in the CRC field. This operation at the receiving host is called the **CRC check**. If the CRC check fails (that is, if the result of the mapping does not equal the contents of the CRC field), then host B knows that there is an error in the frame.

♦ *Preamble (8 bytes).* The Ethernet frame begins with an 8-byte preamble field. Each of the first 7 bytes of the preamble has a value of 10101010; the last byte is 10101011. The first 7 bytes of the preamble serve to "wake up" the receiving adapters and to synchronize their clocks to that of the sender's clock. Why should the clocks be out of synchronization? Keep in mind that adapter A aims to transmit the frame at 10 Mbps, 100 Mbps, or 1 Gbps, depending on the type of Ethernet LAN. However, because nothing is absolutely perfect, adapter A will not transmit the frame at exactly the target rate; there will always be some *drift* from the target rate, a drift which is not known *a priori* by the other adapters on the LAN. A receiving adapter can lock onto adapter A's clock simply by locking onto the bits in the first 7 bytes of the preamble. The last 2 bits of the eighth byte of the preamble (the first two consecutive 1s) alert adapter B that the "important stuff" is about to come. When host B sees the two consecutive 1s, it knows that the next 6 bytes are the destination address. An adapter can tell when a frame ends by simply detecting absence of current.

Ethernet uses baseband transmission; that is, the adapter sends a digital signal directly into the broadcast channel. The interface card does not shift the signal into another frequency band, as is done in ADSL and cable modem systems. Many Ethernet technologies (e.g., 10BaseT) also use Manchester encoding, as shown in Figure 5.25. With Manchester encoding, each bit contains a transition; a 1 has a transition from up to down, whereas a 0 has a transition from down to up. The reason for Manchester encoding is that the clocks in the sending and receiving adapters are not perfectly synchronized. By including a transition in the middle of each bit, the receiving host can synchronize its clock to that of the sending host. Once the receiving adapter's clock is synchronized, the receiver can delineate each bit and determine whether it is a 1 or 0. Manchester encoding is a physical-layer operation rather than a link-layer operation; however, we have briefly described it here because it is used extensively in Ethernet.

An Unreliable Connectionless Service

All of the Ethernet technologies provide **connectionless service** to the network layer. That is, when adapter A wants to send a datagram to adapter B, adapter A encapsulates the datagram in an Ethernet frame and sends the frame into the LAN, without first handshaking with adapter B. This layer-2 connectionless service is analogous to IP's layer-3 datagram service and UDP's layer-4 connectionless service.

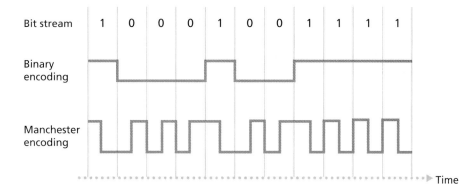

Figure 5.25 ♦ Manchester encoding

CASE HISTORY

BOB METCALFE AND ETHERNET

As a PhD student at Harvard University in the early 1970s, Bob Metcalfe worked on the ARPAnet at MIT. During his studies, he also became exposed to Abramson's work on ALOHA and random access protocols. After completing his PhD and just before beginning a job at Xerox Palo Alto Research Center (Xerox PARC), he visited Abramson and his University of Hawaii colleagues for three months, getting a first-hand look at ALOHAnet. At Xerox PARC, Metcalfe became exposed to Alto computers, which in many ways were the forerunners of the personal computers of the 1980s. Metcalfe saw the need to network these computers in an inexpensive manner. So armed with his knowledge about ARPAnet, ALOHAnet, and random access protocols, Metcalfe—along with colleague David Boggs—invented Ethernet.

Metcalfe and Boggs's original Ethernet ran at 2.94 Mbps and linked up to 256 hosts separated by up to one mile. Metcalfe and Boggs succeeded at getting most of the researchers at Xerox PARC to communicate through their Alto computers. Metcalfe then forged an alliance between Xerox, Digital, and Intel to establish Ethernet as a 10 Mbps Ethernet standard, ratified by the IEEE. Xerox did not show much interest in commercializing Ethernet. In 1979, Metcalfe formed his own company, 3Com, which developed and commercialized networking technology, including Ethernet technology. In particular, 3Com developed and marketed Ethernet cards in the early 1980s for the immensely popular IBM PCs. Metcalfe left 3Com in 1990, when it had 2,000 people and $400 million dollars in revenue. As of November 2003, 3Com employed over 2,900 people worldwide.

All of the Ethernet technologies provide an **unreliable service** to the network layer. Specifically, when adapter B receives a frame from adapter A, it runs the frame through a CRC check, but neither sends an acknowledgment when a frame passes the CRC check nor sends a negative acknowledgment when a frame fails the CRC check. When a frame fails the CRC check, adapter B simply discards the frame. Thus, Adapter A has no idea whether its transmitted frame passed the CRC check. This lack of reliable transport (at the link layer) helps to make Ethernet simple and cheap. But it also means that the stream of datagrams passed to the network layer can have gaps.

If there are gaps due to discarded Ethernet frames, does the application at Host B see gaps as well? As we learned in Chapter 3, this depends solely on whether the application is using UDP or TCP. If the application is using UDP, then the application in Host B will indeed suffer from gaps in the data. On the other hand, if the application is using TCP, then TCP in Host B will not acknowledge the data contained in discarded frames, causing TCP in Host A to retransmit. Note that when TCP retransmits data, the data will eventually return to the Ethernet adapter at which it was discarded. Thus, in this sense, Ethernet does retransmit data, although Ethernet is unaware of whether it is transmitting a brand-new datagram with brand-new data, or a datagram that contains data that has already been transmitted at least once.

5.5.2 CSMA/CD: Ethernet's Multiple Access Protocol

When the nodes are interconnected with a hub (as opposed to a link-layer switch), the Ethernet LAN is a true broadcast LAN – that is, when an adapter transmits a frame, all of the adapters on the LAN receive the frame. Because Ethernet can employ broadcast, it needs a multiple access protocol. Ethernet uses the celebrated CSMA/CD multiple access protocol. Recall from Section 5.3 that CSMA/CD does the following:

1. An adapter may begin to transmit at any time; that is, no slots are used.
2. An adapter never transmits a frame when it senses that some other adapter is transmitting; that is, it uses carrier sensing.
3. A transmitting adapter aborts its transmission as soon as it detects that another adapter is also transmitting; that is, it uses collision detection.
4. Before attempting a retransmission, an adapter waits a random time that is typically small compared with the time to transmit a frame.

These mechanisms give CSMA/CD much better performance than slotted ALOHA in a LAN environment. In fact, if the maximum propagation delay between stations is very small, the efficiency of CSMA/CD can approach 100 percent. But note that the second and third mechanisms listed above require each Ethernet adapter to be able to (1) sense when some other adapter is transmitting and (2) detect a collision while it is transmitting. Ethernet adapters perform these two tasks by measuring voltage levels before and during transmission.

Each adapter runs the CSMA/CD protocol without explicit coordination with the other adapters on the Ethernet. Within a specific adapter, the CSMA/CD protocol works as follows:

1. The adapter obtains a network-layer datagram from its parent node, prepares an Ethernet frame, and puts the frame in an adapter buffer.
2. If the adapter senses that the channel is idle (that is, there is no signal energy entering the adapter from the channel for 96 bit times), it starts to transmit the frame. If the adapter senses that the channel is busy, it waits until it senses no signal energy (plus 96 bit times) and then starts to transmit the frame.
3. While transmitting, the adapter monitors for the presence of signal energy coming from other adapters. If the adapter transmits the entire frame without detecting signal energy from other adapters, the adapter is finished with the frame.
4. If the adapter detects signal energy from other adapters while transmitting, it stops transmitting its frame and instead transmits a 48-bit jam signal.
5. After aborting (that is, transmitting the jam signal), the adapter enters an **exponential backoff** phase. Specifically, when transmitting a given frame, after experiencing the nth collision in a row for this frame, the adapter chooses a value for K at random from $\{0,1,2,\ldots,2^{m-1}\}$ where $m = \min(n,10)$. The adapter then waits $K \cdot 512$ bit times and then returns to Step 2.

A few comments about the CSMA/CD protocol are certainly in order. The purpose of the jam signal is to make sure that all other transmitting adapters become aware of the collision. Let's look at an example. Suppose adapter A begins to transmit a frame, and just before A's signal reaches adapter B, adapter B begins to transmit. So B will have transmitted only a few bits when it aborts its transmission. These few bits will indeed propagate to A, but they may not constitute enough energy for A to detect the collision. To make sure that A detects the collision (so that it too can also abort), B transmits the 48-bit jam signal.

Next consider the exponential backoff algorithm. The first thing to notice here is that a bit time (that is, the time to transmit a single bit) is very short; for a 10 Mbps Ethernet, a bit time is 0.1 microsecond. Now let's look at an example. Suppose that an adapter attempts to transmit a frame for the first time and while transmitting it detects a collision. The adapter then chooses $K = 0$ with probability 0.5 or chooses $K = 1$ with probability 0.5. If the adapter chooses $K = 0$, then it immediately jumps to Step 2 after transmitting the jam signal. If the adapter chooses $K = 1$, it waits 51.2 microseconds before returning to Step 2. After a second collision, K is chosen with equal probability from $\{0,1,2,3\}$. After three collisions, K is chosen with equal probability from $\{0,1,2,3,4,5,6,7\}$. After 10 or more collisions, K is chosen with equal probability from $\{0,1,2,\ldots,1023\}$. Thus the size of the sets from which K is chosen grows exponentially with the number of collisions (until $n = 10$); it is for this reason that Ethernet's backoff algorithm is referred to as *exponential backoff*.

The Ethernet standard imposes limits on the distance between any two nodes. These limits ensure that if adapter A chooses a lower value of K than all the other adapters involved in a collision, then adapter A will be able to transmit its frame without experiencing a new collision. We will explore this property in more detail in the homework problems.

Why use exponential backoff? Why not, for example, select K from $\{0,1,2,3,4,5,6,7\}$ after every collision? The reason is that when an adapter experiences its first collision, it has no idea how many adapters are involved in the collision. If there are only a small number of colliding adapters, it makes sense to choose K from a small set of small values. On the other hand, if many adapters are involved in the collision, it makes sense to choose K from a larger, more dispersed set of values (why?). By increasing the size of the set after each collision, the adapter appropriately adapts to these different scenarios.

We also note here that each time an adapter prepares a new frame for transmission, it runs the CSMA/CD algorithm presented above. In particular, the adapter does not take into account any collisions that may have occurred in the recent past. So it is possible that an adapter with a new frame will immediately be able to sneak in a successful transmission while several other adapters are in the exponential backoff state.

Ethernet Efficiency

When only one node has a frame to send, the node can transmit at the full rate of the Ethernet technology (either 10 Mbps, 100 Mbps, or 1 Gbps). However, if many nodes have frames to transmit, the effective transmission rate of the channel can be much less. We define the **efficiency of Ethernet** to be the long-run fraction of time during which frames are being transmitted on the channel without collisions when there is a large number of active nodes, with each node having a large number of frames to send. In order to present a closed-form approximation of the efficiency of Ethernet, let t_{prop} denote the maximum time it takes signal energy to propagate between any two adapters. Let t_{trans} be the time to transmit a maximum-size Ethernet frame (approximately 1.2 msecs for a 10 Mbps Ethernet). A derivation of the efficiency of Ethernet is beyond the scope of this book (see [Lam 1980] and [Bertsekas 1991]). Here we simply state the following approximation:

$$\text{Efficiency} = \frac{1}{1 + 5t_{prop}/t_{trans}}$$

We see from this formula that as t_{prop} approaches 0, the efficiency approaches 1. This matches our intuition that if the propagation delay is zero, colliding nodes will abort immediately without wasting the channel. Also, as t_{trans} becomes very large, efficiency approaches 1. This is also intuitive because when a frame grabs the channel, it will hold on to the channel for a very long time; thus the channel will be doing productive work most of the time.

5.5.3 Ethernet Technologies

In 2004 the most common Ethernet technologies are 10BaseT and 100BaseT, which uses twisted-pair copper wire in a star topology and have transmission rates of 10 Mbps and 100 Mbps, respectively. These Ethernet technologies are standardized by the IEEE 802.3 working groups. For this reason, an Ethernet LAN is often referred to as an 802.3 LAN.

Figure 5.26 illustrates 10BaseT/100BaseT technology. Each adapter on each node has a direct, point-to-point connection to the hub. This connection consists of two pairs of twisted-pair copper wire, one for transmitting and the other for receiving. At the end of the connection there is an RJ-45 connector, which resembles the RJ-11 connector used for ordinary telephones. The T in 10BaseT and 100BaseT stands for "twisted pair." For both 10BaseT and 100BaseT, the maximum length of the connection between an adapter and the hub is 100 meters; thus, the maximum length between any two nodes is 200 meters. As we will discuss in the next section, this maximum distance can be increased by deploying tiers of hubs or switches and by fiber links.

A **hub** is a physical-layer device that acts on individual bits rather than on frames. It has two or more interfaces. When a bit, representing a zero or a one, arrives from one interface, the hub simply re-creates the bit, boosts its energy

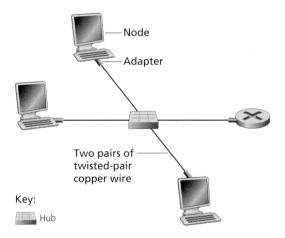

Figure 5.26 ♦ Star topology for 10BaseT and 100BaseT

strength, and transmits the bit onto all the other interfaces. It is important to keep in mind that hubs do not implement carrier sensing or any other part of CSMA/CD; a hub repeats an incoming bit on all outgoing interfaces even if there is signal energy on some of the interfaces. Because hubs broadcast bits, each adapter on a 10/100 BaseT Ethernet can (1) sense the channel to determine whether it is idle and (2) detect a collision while it is transmitting.

Hubs also provide network management features. For example, if an adapter malfunctions and continually sends Ethernet frames (called a *jabbering adapter*), a 10/100 BaseT network will continue to function, because the hub will detect the problem and internally disconnect the malfunctioning adapter. With this feature, the network administrator doesn't have to get out of bed and drive back to work in order to correct the problem. Also, most hubs can gather information and report the information to a host that connects directly to the hub. As discussed in Chapter 9 (Network Management) this monitoring host provides a graphical interface that displays statistics and graphs, such as bandwidth usage, collision rates, average frame sizes, and so on. Network administrators can use this information not only to debug and correct problems, but also to plan how the LAN should evolve in the future.

Many Ethernet adapters today are 10/100 Mbps adapters. This means that they can be used for both 10BaseT and 100BaseT Ethernets. 100BaseT typically uses category-5 twisted pair (a high-quality twisted pair of wires with many twists). Unlike 10BaseT, 100BaseT does not use Manchester encoding but instead uses a more efficient encoding called 4B5B: Every group of five clock periods is used to send 4 bits in order to provide enough transitions to allow clock synchronization.

We briefly mention at this point that both 10 Mbps and 100 Mbps Ethernet technologies can employ fiber links. A fiber link is often used to interconnect to hubs that are in different buildings on the same campus. Fiber is expensive because of the cost of its connectors, but it has excellent noise immunity. The IEEE 802 standards permit a LAN to have a larger geographical reach when fiber is used to connect backbone nodes.

Gigabit Ethernet and 10 Gbps Ethernet

Gigabit Ethernet is an extension to the highly successful 10 Mbps and 100 Mbps Ethernet standards. Offering a raw data rate of 1,000 Mbps, Gigabit Ethernet maintains full compatibility with the huge installed base of Ethernet equipment. The standard for Gigabit Ethernet, referred to as IEEE 802.3z, does the following:

♦ Uses the standard Ethernet frame format (Figure 5.24) and is backward compatible with 10BaseT and 100BaseT technologies. This allows for easy integration of Gigabit Ethernet with the existing installed base of Ethernet equipment.

♦ Allows for point-to-point links as well as shared broadcast channels. Point-to-point links use switches (see Section 5.6), whereas broadcast channels use hubs, as described above for 10BaseT and 100BaseT. In Gigabit Ethernet jargon, hubs are called *buffered distributors*.

♦ Uses CSMA/CD for shared broadcast channels. In order to have acceptable efficiency, the maximum distance between nodes must be severely restricted.

♦ Allows for full-duplex operation at 1,000 Mbps in both directions for point-to-point channels.

Like 10BaseT and 100BaseT, Gigabit Ethernet has a star topology with a hub or switch at its center. (Ethernet switches will be discussed in Section 5.6.) Gigabit Ethernet often serves as a backbone for interconnecting multiple 10 Mbps and 100 Mbps Ethernet LANs. Initially operating over optical fiber, Gigabit Ethernet is now able to run over category 5 UTP cabling.

With products that emerged in 2001, 10 Gigabit Ethernet further extended the popular Ethernet technology. Additionally, the 10 Gigabit Ethernet standard, 802.3ae, extends Ethernet technology to point-to-point wide-area-network (WAN) links. See Spurgeon's Ethernet Web site [Spurgeon 2004] for good information and links about Gigabit and 10 Gigabit Ethernet.

5.6 Interconnections: Hubs and Switches

Institutions—including companies, universities, and high schools—typically consist of many departments, each managing its own Ethernet LAN. Naturally, an institution will want its departments to interconnect their departmental LAN segments. In this section we consider two approaches to connecting LANs: hubs and switches. Both are in widespread use today.

5.6.1 Hubs

The simplest way to interconnect LANs is to use hubs. Figure 5.27 shows how three academic departments in a university might interconnect their LANs. In this figure, each of the three departments has a 10BaseT Ethernet that provides network access to the faculty, staff, and students of the department. Each host in a department has a point-to-point connection to the departmental hub. A fourth hub, called a **backbone hub**, has point-to-point connections to the departmental hubs, interconnecting the LANs of the three departments. The design shown in Figure 5.27 is a **multi-tier hub design** because the hubs are arranged in a hierarchy. It is also possible to create multi-tier designs with more than two tiers—for example, one tier for the departments, one tier for the schools within the university (engineering school, business school, and so on), and one tier at the highest university level.

In a multi-tier design, we refer to the entire interconnected network as a LAN, and we refer to each of the departmental portions of the LAN (that is, the departmental hub

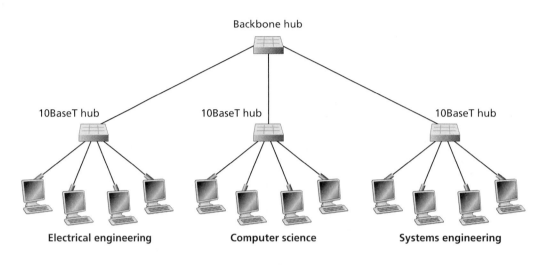

Figure 5.27   ◆   Three departmental Ethernets interconnected with a hub.

and the hosts that connect to the hub) as a **LAN segment**. It is important to note that all of the LAN segments in Figure 5.27 belong to the same collision domain; that is, whenever two or more nodes on the LAN segments transmit at the same time, there will be a collision and all of the transmitting nodes will enter exponential backoff.

Interconnecting departmental LANs with a backbone hub has many benefits. First and foremost, it provides interdepartmental communication among the hosts in the various departments. Second, it extends the maximum distance between any pair of nodes on the LAN. For example, with 10BaseT the maximum distance between a node and its hub is 100 meters; therefore, in a single LAN segment the maximum distance between any pair of nodes is 200 meters. By interconnecting the hubs, this maximum distance can be extended, since the distance between directly connected hubs can also be 100 meters when using twisted pair (and more when using fiber). A third benefit is that the multi-tier design provides a degree of graceful degradation. Specifically, if any one of the departmental hubs starts to malfunction, the backbone hub can detect the problem and disconnect the departmental hub from the LAN; in this manner, the remaining departments can continue to operate and communicate while the faulty departmental hub gets repaired.

Although a backbone hub is a useful interconnection device, it has three serious limitations that hinder its deployment. First, and perhaps most important, when departmental LANs are interconnected with a hub, the (previously independent) collision domains of the departments are transformed into one large, common collision domain. Let us explore this issue in the context of Figure 5.27. Before interconnecting the three departments, each departmental LAN had a maximum throughput of 10 Mbps, so that the maximum aggregate throughput of the three

LANs was 30 Mbps. But once the three LANs are interconnected with a hub, all of the hosts in the three departments belong to the same collision domain, and the maximum aggregate throughput is reduced to 10 Mbps.

A second limitation is that if the various departments use different Ethernet technologies, then it may not be possible to interconnect the departmental hubs with a backbone hub. For example, if some departments use 10BaseT and the remaining departments use 100BaseT, then it is impossible to interconnect all the departments without some frame buffering at the interconnection point; since a hub is essentially a repeater that does not buffer frames, it cannot interconnect LAN segments operating at different rates.

A third limitation is that each of the Ethernet technologies (10Base2, 10BaseT, 100BaseT, and so on) has restrictions on the maximum allowable number of nodes in a collision domain, the maximum distance between two hosts in a collision domain, and the maximum allowable number of tiers in a multi-tier design. These restrictions constrain both the total number of hosts that can connect to a multi-tier LAN as well as the geographical reach of the multi-tier LAN.

5.6.2 Link-Layer Switches

In contrast to hubs, which are physical-layer devices, link-layer switches—simply called **switches**—operate on Ethernet frames and thus are layer-2 devices. In fact, as full-fledged packet switches, switches forward frames based on LAN destination addresses. When a frame comes into a switch interface, the switch examines the layer-2 destination address of the frame and attempts to forward the frame on the interface that leads to the destination.

Figure 5.28 shows how the three academic departments of our previous example might be interconnected with a switch. The three numbers next to the switch are the interface numbers for the three switch interfaces. When the departments are interconnected by a switch, as in Figure 5.28, we again refer to the entire interconnected network as a LAN, and we again refer to each of the departmental portions of the network as LAN segments. But in contrast to the multi-tier hub design in Figure 5.27, each LAN segment is now an isolated collision domain.

Switches can overcome many of the problems that plague hubs. First, switches permit interdepartmental communication while preserving isolated collision domains for each of the departments. Second, switches can interconnect different LAN technologies, including 10BaseT, 100BaseT, and Gigabit Ethernet. Third, there is no limit to how large a LAN can be when switches are used to interconnect LAN segments; in theory, using switches, it is possible to build a LAN that spans the entire globe. Also, as we'll discuss at the end of this section, switches operate in full duplex and provide cut-through switching.

Figure 5.29 shows how an institution with several departments and several critical servers might deploy a combination of hubs, switches, and routers. In Figure 5.29, each of the three departments has its own 10 Mbps Ethernet segment with its

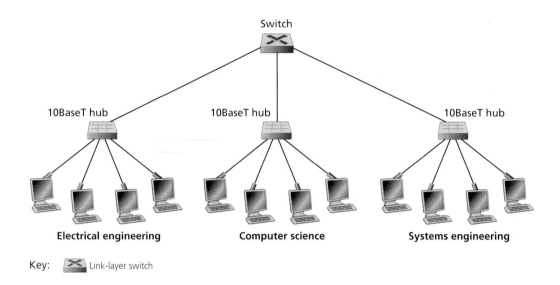

Switch

10BaseT hub   10BaseT hub   10BaseT hub

Electrical engineering   **Computer science**   **Systems engineering**

Key: ✕ Link-layer switch

Figure 5.28 ◆ Three departmental LANs interconnected with a switch.

own hub. Because each departmental hub has a connection to the switch, all intradepartmental traffic is confined to the Ethernet segment of the department. The Web and mail servers each have dedicated 100 Mbps access to the switch. Finally, a router, leading to the Internet, has dedicated 100 Mbps access to the switch. Note that this switch has at least three 10 Mbps interfaces and three 100 Mbps interfaces.

Switch Forwarding and Filtering

Filtering is the ability of a switch to determine whether a frame should be forwarded to some interface or should just be dropped. **Forwarding** is the ability to determine the interfaces to which a frame should be directed, and then directing the frame to those interfaces. Switch filtering and forwarding are done with a **switch table**. The switch table contains entries for some, but not necessarily all, of the nodes on a LAN. An entry in the switch table contains (1) the MAC address of a node, (2) the switch interface that leads toward the node, and (3) the time at which the entry for the node was placed in the table. An example switch table for the LAN in Figure 5.28 is shown in Figure 5.30. Although this description of frame forwarding may sound similar to our discussion of datagram forwarding in Chapter 4, we'll see shortly that there are important differences. We note here that the addresses used by switches are MAC addresses rather than network-layer addresses. We will also see shortly that a switch table is constructed in a very different manner from routing tables.

To understand how switch filtering and forwarding works, suppose a frame with destination address DD-DD-DD-DD-DD-DD arrives at the switch on interface

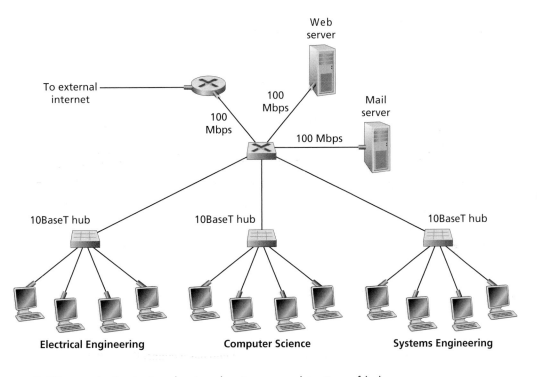

Figure 5.29 ♦ An institutional network using a combination of hubs, Ethernet switches, and a router

x. The switch indexes its table with the MAC address DD-DD-DD-DD-DD-DD and finds its corresponding interface y that is known to lead to destination address DD-DD-DD-DD-DD-DD. (We'll see shortly what happens if the address DD-DD-DD-DD-DD-DD is not in the table.)

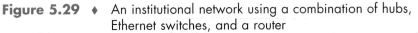

Address	Interface	Time
62-FE-F7-11-89-A3	1	9:32
7C-BA-B2-B4-91-10	3	9:36
....	....	....

Figure 5.30 ♦ Portion of a switch table for the LAN in Figure 5.28

♦ If x equals y, then the frame is coming from a LAN segment that contains adapter DD-DD-DD-DD-DD-DD. There being no need to forward the frame to any of the other interfaces, the switch performs the filtering function by discarding the frame.

♦ If x does not equal y, then the frame needs to be forwarded to the LAN segment attached to interface y. The switch performs its forwarding function by putting the frame in an output buffer that precedes interface y.

These simple rules allow a switch to preserve separate collision domains for each of the different LAN segments connected to its interfaces. The rules also allow two sets of nodes on different LAN segments to communicate simultaneously without interfering with each other.

Let's walk through these rules for the network in Figure 5.28 and its switch table in Figure 5.30. Suppose that a frame with destination address 62-FE-F7-11-89-A3 arrives at the switch from interface 1. The switch examines its table and sees that the destination is on the LAN segment connected to interface 1 (that is, the Electrical Engineering LAN). This means that the frame has already been broadcast on the LAN segment that contains the destination. The switch therefore filters (that is, discards) the frame. Now suppose a frame with the same destination address arrives from interface 2. The switch again examines its table and sees that the destination is in the direction of interface 1; it therefore forwards the frame to the output buffer preceding interface 1. It should be clear from this example that as long as the switch table is complete and accurate, the switch isolates the departmental collision domains while permitting the departments to communicate.

Hubs versus Switches

Recall that when a hub forwards a frame onto a link, it just sends the bits onto the link without bothering to sense whether another transmission is currently taking place on the link. In contrast, when a switch wants to forward a frame onto a link, it runs the CSMA/CD algorithm discussed in Section 5.3. In particular, the switch refrains from transmitting if it senses that some other node on the LAN segment into which it wants to send a frame is transmitting; furthermore, the switch uses exponential backoff when one of its transmissions results in a collision. Thus switch interfaces behave very much like node adapters. But, technically speaking, they are *not* node adapters because neither a switch nor its interfaces have MAC addresses. Recall that a node (that is, a host or router) adapter always inserts its MAC address into the source address of every frame it transmits. A switch, on the other hand, does not change the source address of the frame.

One significant feature of switches is that they can be used to combine Ethernet segments using different Ethernet technologies. For example, if in Figure 5.28 Electrical Engineering has a 10Base2 Ethernet, Computer Science has a 100BaseT

Ethernet, and Systems Engineering has a 10BaseT Ethernet, then a switch can be purchased that can interconnect the three LANs. With Gigabit Ethernet switches, it is possible to have an additional 1 Gbps connection to a router, which in turn connects to a larger university network. As we mentioned earlier, this feature of being able to interconnect different link rates is not available with hubs.

Also, when switches are used as interconnection devices, there is no theoretical limit to the geographical reach of a LAN. In theory, we can build a LAN that spans the globe by interconnecting hubs in a long, linear topology, with each pair of neighboring hubs interconnected by a switch. With this design, each of the hubs has its own collision domain, and there is no limit on how long the LAN can be. We shall see shortly, however, that it is undesirable to build very large networks exclusively using switches as interconnection devices—large networks need routers as well.

Self-Learning

A switch has the wonderful property (particularly for the already-overworked network administrator) that its table is built automatically, dynamically, and autonomously—without any intervention from a network administrator or from a configuration protocol. In other words, switches are **self-learning**. This capability is accomplished as follows:

1. The switch table is initially empty.
2. When a frame arrives on one of the interfaces and the frame's destination address is not in the table, the switch forwards copies of the frame to the output buffers preceding *all* of the other interfaces. (At each of these other interfaces, the frame is transmitted into that LAN segment using CSMA/CD.)
3. For each incoming frame received on an interface, the switch stores in its table (1) the MAC address in the frame's *source address field,* (2) the interface from which the frame arrived, (3) the current time. In this manner the switch records in its table the LAN segment on which the sending node resides. If every node in the LAN eventually sends a frame, then every node will eventually get recorded in the table.
4. When a frame arrives on one of the interfaces and the frame's destination address is in the table, the switch forwards the frame to the appropriate interface.
5. The switch deletes an address in the table if no frames are received with that address as the source address after some period of time (the **aging time**). In this manner, if a PC is replaced by another PC (with a different adapter), the MAC address of the original PC will eventually be purged from the switch table.

Let's walk through the self-learning property for the network in Figure 5.28 and its corresponding switch table in Figure 5.30. Suppose at time 9:39 a frame with

Address	Interface	Time
01-12-23-34-45-56	2	9:39
62-FE-F7-11-89-A3	1	9:32
7C-BA-B2-B4-91-10	3	9:36
....	....	....

Figure 5.31 ♦ Switch learns about the location of an adapter with address 01-12-23-34-45-56

source address 01-12-23-34-45-56 arrives from interface 2. Suppose that this address is not in the switch table. Then the switch adds a new entry to the table, as shown in Figure 5.31.

Continuing with this same example, suppose that the aging time for this switch is 60 minutes, and no frames with source address 62-FE-F7-11-89-A3 arrive to the switch between 9:32 and 10:32. Then at time 10:32, the switch removes this address from its table.

Switches are **plug-and-play devices** because they require no intervention from a network administrator or user. A network administrator wanting to install a switch need do nothing more than connect the LAN segments to the switch interfaces. The administrator need not configure the switch tables at the time of installation or when a host is removed from one of the LAN segments.

Dedicated Access and Full Duplex

A switch with a large number of interfaces facilitates direct connections between hosts and the switch. When a host has a direct connection to a switch (rather than a shared LAN connection), the host is said to have **dedicated access**. In Figure 5.32, a switch provides dedicated access to six hosts.

A switch and the hosts directly connected to the switch operate in the full-duplex mode. Let's see how this done. To make the discussion concrete, suppose that each connection in the network in Figure 5.32 uses two pairs of twisted-pair cooper wire (as in 10BaseT and 100BaseT), one pair for transmitting from host to switch, and the other pair for transmitting from switch to host. Because of the dedicated access, when Host A transmits a frame on its upstream wire pair, there is no possibility that the frame will collide with a transmission from some other host or from the switch. Similarly, because switches "store and forward," the switch will transmit at most one frame at a time onto any one of the downstream wire pairs. Thus with direct upstream and downstream connections, neither collision detection nor carrier sensing are needed. In fact, each link becomes a point-to-point link, obviating the need for a medium-access protocol whatsoever! Thus, by disabling in each adapter the carrier sensing, the collision detection, and the looping back of transmitted data onto the

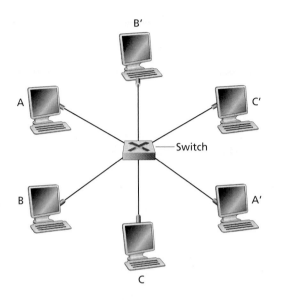

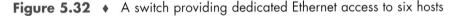

Figure 5.32 ♦ A switch providing dedicated Ethernet access to six hosts

receiver input, a full-duplex channel is created between each host and the switch. For example, in Figure 5.32, host A can send a file to A′ while B is sending a file to B′ and C is sending a file to C′. If each host has a 10 Mbps adapter card, then the aggregate throughput during the three simultaneous file transfers is 30 Mbps. If A and A′ have 100 Mbps adapters and the remaining hosts have 10 Mbps adapters, then the aggregate throughput during the three simultaneous file transfers is 120 Mbps.

Cut-Through Switching

In addition to large numbers of interfaces, support for multitudes of physical media types and transmission rates, and enticing network management features, switch manufacturers often tout that their switches use **cut-through switching** rather than store-and-forward packet switching, used by routers. The difference between store-and-forward and cut-through switching is subtle. To understand this difference, consider a packet that is being forwarded through a packet switch (that is, a router or switch). As discussed in Section 4.4, the packet arrives at the switch on an *input port* and leaves the switch on an *output port*. At the output port, there may or may not be other packets queued in the output port's buffer. When there are packets in the output buffer, there is absolutely no difference between store-and-forward and cut-through switching. The two switching techniques differ only when the output buffer is empty.

Recall from Chapter 1 that when a packet is forwarded through a store-and-forward packet switch, the packet is first gathered and stored in its entirety before the packet switch begins to transmit it on the outbound link. In the case that the output buffer becomes empty before the whole packet has arrived to the switch, this gathering generates a store-and-forward delay at the switch—a delay that contributes to the total end-to-end delay (see Section 1.6). An upper bound on this delay is L/R, where L is the length of the packet and R is transmission rate of the *inbound* link. Note that a packet incurs a store-and-forward delay only if the output buffer becomes empty before the entire packet arrives to the switch.

With cut-through switching, if the buffer becomes empty before the entire packet has arrived, the switch can start to transmit the front of the packet while the back of the packet continues to arrive. Of course, before the packet on the outbound link is transmitted, the portion of the packet that contains the destination address must first arrive. (This small delay is inevitable for all types of switching, as the switch must determine the appropriate outbound link.) In summary, with cut-through switching, a packet need not be fully stored before it is forwarded; instead the packet is forwarded through the switch when the output link is free. If the output link is a multiple access network that is shared with other hosts (for example, the output link connects to a hub), then the switch must also sense the link as idle before it can cut-through a packet.

To shed some insight on the difference between store-and-forward and cut-through switching, let us recall the caravan analogy introduced in Section 1.6. In this analogy, there is a highway with occasional tollbooths, with each tollbooth having a single attendant. On the highway there is a caravan of 10 cars traveling together, each at the same constant speed. The cars in the caravan are the only cars on the highway. Each tollbooth services the cars at a constant rate, so that when the cars leave the tollbooth they are equally spaced apart. As before, we can think of the caravan as being a packet, each car in the caravan as being a bit, and the tollbooth service rate as the link transmission rate. Consider now what the cars in the caravan do when they arrive to a tollbooth. If each car proceeds directly to the tollbooth on arrival, then the tollbooth is a cut-through tollbooth. If, on the other hand, each car waits at the entrance until all the remaining cars in the caravan have arrived, then the tollbooth is a store-and-forward tollbooth. The store-and-forward tollbooth clearly delays the caravan more than the cut-through tollbooth.

A cut-through switch can reduce a packet's end-to-end delay, but by how much? As we mentioned above, the maximum store-and-forward delay is L/R, where L is the packet size and R is the rate of the inbound link. The maximum delay is approximately 1.2 msec for 10 Mbps Ethernet and 0.12 msec for 100 Mbps Ethernet (corresponding to a maximum-size Ethernet packet). Thus, a cut-through switch reduces the delay by only 0.12 to 1.2 msec, and this reduction occurs only when the outbound link is lightly loaded. How significant is this delay? Probably not very much in most practical applications, so you may want to think twice about selling the family house before investing in the cut-through feature.

Switches Versus Routers

As we learned in Chapter 4, routers are store-and-forward packet switches that forward packets using network-layer addresses. Although a switch is also a store-and-forward packet switch, it is fundamentally different from a router in that it forwards packets using MAC addresses. Whereas a router is a layer-3 packet switch, a switch is a layer-2 packet switch.

Even though switches and routers are fundamentally different, network administrators must often choose between them when installing an interconnection device. For example, for the network in Figure 5.28, the network administrator could have just as easily used a router instead of a switch. Indeed, a router would have also kept the three collision domains separate while permitting interdepartmental communication. Given that both switches and routers are candidates for interconnection devices, what are the pros and cons of the two approaches?

First consider the pros and cons of switches. As mentioned above, switches are plug-and-play, a property that is cherished by all the overworked network administrators of the world. Switches can also have relatively high packet filtering and forwarding rates—as shown in Figure 5.33, switches have to process packets only up through layer 2, whereas routers have to process frames up through layer 3. On the other hand, the topology of a switched network is restricted to a spanning tree. Also a large switched network would require large ARP tables in the nodes and would generate substantial ARP traffic and processing. Furthermore, switches do not offer any protection against broadcast storms—if one host goes haywire and transmits an endless stream of Ethernet broadcast frames, the switches will forward all of these frames, causing the entire network to collapse.

Now consider the pros and cons of routers. Because network addressing is often hierarchical (and not flat, as is MAC addressing), packets do not normally cycle through routers even when the network has redundant paths. (However, packets can cycle when router tables are misconfigured; but as we learned in Chapter 4, IP uses a special datagram header field to limit the cycling.) Thus, packets are not restricted to a spanning tree and can use the best path between source and destination. Because routers do not have the spanning tree restriction, they have allowed the Internet to be built with a rich topology that includes, for example, multiple active links between Europe and North America. Another feature of routers is that they provide firewall protection against layer-2 broadcast storms. Perhaps the most significant drawback of routers, though, is that they are not plug-and-play—they and the hosts that connect to them need their IP addresses to be configured. Also, routers often have a larger per-packet processing time than switches, because they have to process up through the layer-3 fields. Finally, there are two different ways to pronounce the word *router*, either as "rootor" or as "rowter," and people waste a lot of time arguing over the proper pronunciation [Perlman 1999].

Given that both switches and routers have their pros and cons, when should an institutional network (for example, university campus network or a corporate

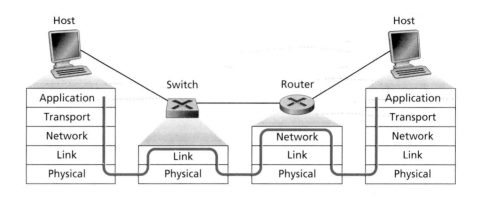

Figure 5.33   ◆   Packet processing in switches, routers, and hosts

campus network) use switches, and when should it use routers? Typically, small networks consisting of a few hundred hosts have a few LAN segments. Switches suffice for these small networks, as they localize traffic and increase aggregate throughput without requiring any configuration of IP addresses. But larger networks consisting of thousands of hosts typically include routers within the network (in addition to switches). The routers provide a more robust isolation of traffic, control broadcast storms, and use more "intelligent" routes among the hosts in the network.

We have learned in this section that hubs, switches, and routers can all be used as interconnection devices for hosts and LAN segments. Table 5.1 provides a summary of the features of each of these interconnection devices. The Cisco Web site provides numerous comparisons of the different interconnection technologies [Cisco Switches 2004].

	Hubs	Routers	Switches
Traffic isolation	No	Yes	Yes
Plug and play	Yes	No	Yes
Optimal routing	No	Yes	No
Cut-through	Yes	No	Yes

Table 5.1   ◆   Comparison of the typical features of popular interconnection devices

5.7 PPP: The Point-to-Point Protocol

Most of our discussion of link-layer protocols thus far has focused on protocols for broadcast channels. In this section we cover a link-layer protocol for point-to-point links—PPP, the point-to-point protocol. Because PPP is typically the protocol of choice for a dial-up link from a residential host, it is undoubtedly one of the most widely deployed link-layer protocols today. The other important link-layer protocol in use today is the high-level data link control (HDLC) protocol; see [Spragins 1991] for a discussion of HDLC. Our discussion here of the simpler PPP protocol will allow us to explore many of the most important features of a point-to-point link-layer protocol.

As its name implies, the point-to-point protocol (PPP) [RFC 1661; RFC 2153] is a link-layer protocol that operates over a **point-to-point link**—a link directly connecting two nodes, one on each end of the link. The point-to-point link over which PPP operates might be a serial dial-up telephone line (for example, a 56K modem connection), a SONET/SDH link, an X.25 connection, or an ISDN circuit. As noted above, PPP has become the protocol of choice for connecting home users to their ISPs over a dial-up connection.

Before diving into the details of PPP, it is instructive to examine the original requirements that the IETF placed on the design of PPP [RFC 1547]:

♦ *Packet framing.* The PPP protocol link-layer sender must be able to take a network-level packet and encapsulate it within the PPP link-layer frame such that the receiver will be able to identify the start and end of both the link-layer frame and the network-layer packet within the frame.

♦ *Transparency.* The PPP protocol must not place any constraints on data appearing on the network-layer packet (headers or data). Thus, for example, PPP cannot forbid the use of certain bit patterns in the network-layer packet. We'll return to this issue shortly in our discussion of byte stuffing.

♦ *Multiple network-layer protocols.* The PPP protocol must be able to support multiple network-layer protocols (for example, IP and DECnet) running over the same physical link at the same time. Just as the IP protocol is required to multiplex different transport-level protocols (for example, TCP and UDP) over a single end-to-end connection, so too must PPP be able to multiplex different network-layer protocols over a single point-to-point connection. This requirement means that at a minimum, PPP will likely require a protocol type field or some similar mechanism so the receiving-side PPP can demultiplex a received frame up to the appropriate network-layer protocol.

♦ *Multiple types of links.* In addition to being able to carry multiple higher-level protocols, PPP must also be able to operate over a wide variety of link types, including links that are either serial (transmitting a bit at a time in a given direction) or parallel (transmitting bits in parallel), synchronous (transmitting a clock signal along with the data bits) or asynchronous, low-speed or high-speed, electrical or optical.

♦ *Error detection.* A PPP receiver must be able to detect bit errors in the received frame.

♦ *Connection liveness.* PPP must be able to detect a failure at the link level (for example, the inability to transfer data from the sending side of the link to the receiving side of the link) and signal this error condition to the network layer.

♦ *Network-layer address negotiation.* PPP must provide a mechanism for the communicating network layers (for example, IP) to learn or configure each other's network-layer address.

♦ *Simplicity.* PPP was required to meet a number of additional requirements beyond those listed above. On top of all of these requirements, first and foremost is simplicity. RFC 1547 states, "The watchword for a point-to-point protocol should be simplicity." A tall order indeed, given all of the other requirements placed on the design of PPP! More than fifty RFCs now define the various aspects of this "simple" protocol.

While it may appear that many requirements were placed on the design of PPP, the situation could actually have been much more difficult! The design specifications for PPP also explicitly note protocol functionality that PPP was *not* required to implement:

♦ *Error correction.* PPP is required to detect bit errors but is *not* required to correct them.

♦ *Flow control.* A PPP receiver is expected to be able to receive frames at the full rate of the underlying physical layer. If a higher layer cannot receive packets at this full rate, it is then up to the higher layer to drop packets or throttle the sender at the higher layer. That is, rather than having the PPP sender throttle its own transmission rate, it is the responsibility of a higher-level protocol to throttle the rate at which packets are delivered to PPP for sending.

♦ *Sequencing.* PPP is *not* required to deliver frames to the link receiver in the same order in which they were sent by the link sender. It is interesting to note that while this flexibility is compatible with the IP service model (which allows IP packets to be delivered end-to-end in any order), other network-layer protocols that operate over PPP do require sequenced end-to-end packet delivery.

♦ *Multipoint links.* PPP need only operate over links that have a single sender and a single receiver. Other link-layer protocols (e.g., HDLC) can accommodate multiple receivers (e.g., an Ethernet-like scenario) on a link.

Having now considered the design goals (and nongoals) for PPP, let us see how the design of PPP met these goals.

5.7.1 PPP Data Framing

Figure 5.34 shows a PPP data frame that uses HDLC-like framing [RFC 1662]. The PPP frame contains the following fields:

♦ *Flag field.* Every PPP frame begins and ends with a 1-byte flag field with a value of 01111110.

♦ *Address field.* The only possible value for this field is 11111111.

♦ *Control field.* The only possible value for this field is 00000011. Because both the address and control fields can take only a fixed value, you might wonder why the fields are defined in the first place. The PPP specification [RFC 1662] states that other values "may be defined at a later time," although none has been defined to date. Because these fields take fixed values, PPP allows the sender to simply not send the address and control bytes, thus saving 2 bytes of overhead in the PPP frame.

♦ *Protocol.* The protocol field tells the PPP receiver the upper-layer protocol to which the received encapsulated data (that is, the contents of the PPP frame's info field) belongs. On receipt of a PPP frame, the PPP receiver will check the frame for correctness and then pass the encapsulated data on to the appropriate protocol. RFC 1700 and RFC 3232 define the 16-bit protocol codes used by PPP. Of interest to us is the IP protocol (that is, the data encapsulated in the PPP frame in an IP datagram), which has a value of 21 hexadecimal; other network-layer protocols such as AppleTalk (29) and DECnet (27); the PPP link control protocol (C021 hexadecimal) that we discuss in detail in the following section; and the IP Control Protocol (IPCP) (8021). This last protocol is called by PPP when a link is first activated in order to configure the IP-level connection between the IP-capable devices on each end of the link (see below).

♦ *Information.* This field contains the encapsulated packet (data) that is being sent by an upper-layer protocol (for example, IP) over the PPP link. The default maximum length of the information field is 1,500 bytes, although this can be changed when the link is first configured, as discussed below.

♦ *Checksum.* The checksum field is used to detect bit errors in a transmitted frame. It uses either a 2- or 4-byte HDLC-standard cyclic redundancy check.

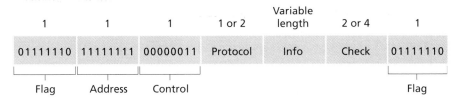

1	1	1	1 or 2	Variable length	2 or 4	1
01111110	11111111	00000011	Protocol	Info	Check	01111110
Flag	Address	Control				Flag

Figure 5.34 ♦ PPP data frame format

Byte Stuffing

Before closing our discussion of PPP framing, let us consider a problem that arises when any protocol uses a specific bit pattern in a flag field to delineate the beginning or end of the frame. What happens if the flag pattern itself occurs elsewhere in the packet? For example, what happens if the flag field value of 01111110 appears in the information field? Will the receiver incorrectly detect the end of the PPP frame?

One way to solve this problem would be for PPP to forbid the upper-layer protocol from sending data containing the flag field bit pattern. The PPP requirement of transparency discussed above obviates this possibility. An alternative solution, and the one taken in PPP and many other protocols, is to use a technique known as **byte stuffing**.

PPP defines a special control escape byte, 01111101. If the flag sequence, 01111110 appears anywhere in the frame, except in the flag field, PPP precedes that instance of the flag pattern with the control escape byte. That is, it "stuffs" (adds) a control escape byte into the transmitted data stream, before the 01111110, to indicate that the following 011111110 is *not* a flag value but is, in fact, actual data. A receiver that sees a 01111110 preceded by a 01111101 will, of course, remove the stuffed control escape to reconstruct the original data. Similarly, if the control escape byte bit pattern itself appears as actual data, it too must be preceded by a stuffed control escape byte. Thus, when the receiver sees a single control escape byte by itself in the data stream, it knows that the byte was stuffed into the data stream. A pair of control escape bytes occurring back to back means that one instance of the control escape byte appears in the original data being sent. Figure 5.35 illustrates PPP byte stuffing. (Actually, PPP also XORs the data byte being escaped with 20 hexadecimal, a detail we omit here for simplicity.)

5.7.2 PPP Link-Control Protocol (LCP) and Network-Control Protocols

Thus far, we have seen how PPP frames the data being sent over the point-to-point link. But how does the link get initialized when a host or router on one end of the PPP link is first turned on? The initialization, maintenance, error reporting, and shutdown of a PPP link is accomplished using PPP's **link-control protocol (LCP)** and family of PPP network-control protocols.

Before any data is exchanged over a PPP link, the two peers (one at each end of the PPP link) must first perform a considerable amount of work to configure the link, in much the same way that a TCP sender and receiver must perform a three-way handshake (see Section 3.5) to set the parameters of the TCP connection before TCP data segments are transmitted. Figure 5.36 illustrates the state transition diagram for the LCP protocol for configuring, maintaining, and terminating the PPP link.

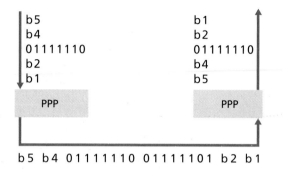

Figure 5.35 ♦ Byte stuffing

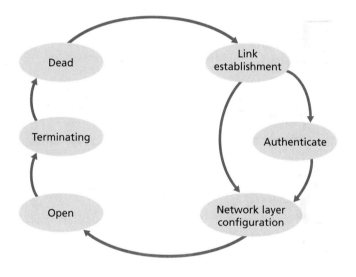

Figure 5.36 ♦ PPP link-control protocol states

The PPP link always begins and ends in the dead state. When an event such as a carrier detection or network administrator intervention indicates that a physical layer is present and ready to be used, PPP enters the link-establishment state. In this state, one end of the link sends its desired link configuration options using an LCP `configure-request` frame (a PPP frame with the protocol field set to LCP and the PPP information field containing the specific configuration request). The other side then responds with a `configure-ack` frame (all options acceptable), a `configure-nak` frame (all options understood but not acceptable), or a `configure-reject` frame (options not recognizable or not acceptable for negotiation). LCP configuration options include a maximum frame size for the link, the specification of an authentication protocol (if any) to be used, and an option to skip the use of the address and control fields in PPP frames.

Once the link has been established, link options negotiated, and the authentication (if any) performed, the two sides of the PPP link then exchange network layer–specific network-control packets with each other. If IP is running over the PPP link, the IP control protocol [RFC 1332] is used to configure the IP protocol modules at each end of the PPP link. IPCP data are carried within a PPP frame (with a protocol field value of 8021), just as LCP data are carried in a PPP frame. IPCP allows the two IP modules to exchange or configure their IP addresses and negotiate whether or not IP datagrams will be sent in compressed form. Similar network-control protocols are defined for other network-layer protocols, such as DECnet [RFC 1762] and AppleTalk [RFC 1378]. Once the network layer has been configured, PPP may then begin sending network-layer datagrams—the link is in the opened state and data has begun to flow across the PPP link. The LCP `echo-request` frame and `echo-reply` frame can be exchanged between the two PPP endpoints in order to check the status of the link.

The PPP link remains configured for communication until an LCP `terminate-request` packet is sent. If a `terminate-request` LCP frame is sent by one end of the PPP link and replied to with a `terminate-ack` LCP frame, the link then enters the dead state.

In summary, PPP is a link-layer protocol by which two communicating link-level peers, one on each end of a point-to-point link, exchange PPP frames containing network-layer datagrams. The principal components of PPP are:

♦ *Framing.* A method for encapsulating data in a PPP frame, identifying the beginning and end of the frame, and detecting errors in the frame.

♦ *Link-control protocol.* A protocol for initializing, maintaining, and taking down the PPP link.

♦ *Network-control protocols.* A family of protocols, one for each upper-layer network protocol, that allows the network-layer modules to configure themselves before network-level datagrams begin flowing across the PPP link.

5.8 Link Virtualization: A Network as a Link Layer

Because this chapter concerns link-layer protocols, and given that we're now nearing the chapter's end, let's reflect on how our understanding of the term *link* has evolved. We began this chapter by viewing the link as a physical wire connecting two communicating hosts, as illustrated in Figure 5.2. In studying multiple access protocols (Figure 5.9), we saw that multiple hosts could be connected by a shared wire and that the "wire" connecting the hosts could be radio spectra or other media. This led us to consider the link a bit more abstractly as a channel, rather than as a wire. In our study of Ethernet LANs (Figures 5.26–5.28) we saw that the interconnecting media could actually be a rather complex switched infrastructure. Throughout this evolution, however, the hosts themselves maintained the view that the interconnecting medium was simply a link-layer channel connecting two or more hosts. We saw, for example, that an Ethernet host can be blissfully unaware of whether it is connected to other LAN hosts by a single short LAN segment (Figure 5.9) or by a geographically dispersed switched LAN (Figure 5.28).

In Section 5.7 we saw that the PPP protocol is often used over a modem connection between two hosts. Here, the link connecting the two hosts is actually the telephone network—a logically separate, global telecommunications network with its own switches, links, and protocol stacks for data transfer and signaling. From the Internet link-layer point of view, however, the dial-up connection through the telephone network is viewed as a simple "wire." In this sense, the Internet virtualizes the telephone network, viewing the telephone network as a link-layer technology providing link-layer connectivity between two Internet hosts. You may recall from our discussion of overlay networks in Chapter 2 that an overlay network similarly views the Internet as a means for providing connectivity between overlay nodes, seeking to overlay the Internet in the same way that the Internet overlays the telephone network.

In this section, we'll consider asynchronous transfer mode (ATM) and Multiprotocol Label Switching (MPLS) networks. Unlike the circuit-switched telephone network, both ATM and MPLS are packet-switched, virtual-circuit networks in their own right. They have their own packet formats and forwarding behaviors. Thus, from a pedagogical viewpoint, a discussion of ATM and MPLS fits well into a study of either the network layer or the link layer. From an Internet viewpoint, however, we can consider ATM and MPLS, like the telephone network and switched-Ethernets, as link-layer technologies that serve to interconnect IP devices. Thus, we'll consider both MPLS and ATM in our discussion of the link layer. Frame-relay networks can also be used to interconnect IP devices, though they represent a slightly older (but still deployed) technology and will not be covered here; see the very readable book [Goralski 1999] for details. Our treatment of ATM and MPLS will be necessarily brief, as entire books could be (and have been) written on these networks. We'll focus here primarily on how these networks serve to interconnect IP devices, although we'll dive a bit deeper into the underlying technologies as well.

5.8.1 Asynchronous Transfer Mode (ATM) Networks

The standards for **asynchronous transfer mode (ATM)** networks were first developed in the mid-1980s, with the goal of designing a single networking technology that would transport real-time audio and video as well as text, e-mail, and image files. Two groups, the ATM Forum [ATM 2004] and the International Telecommunications Union [ITU 2004], were involved in the development of ATM standards. They defined a complete end-to-end standard, ranging from the specification of the application interface to ATM down to the bit-level framing of ATM data over various fiber, copper, and radio physical layers. In practice, ATM has been used primarily within telephone and IP networks, serving, for example, as a link-layer technology to connect IP routers, as discussed above.

Principal Characteristics of ATM

As discussed in Section 4.1, ATM supports several service models, including constant bit rate service, variable bit rate service, available bit rate service, and unspecified bit rate service. ATM is a packet-switched, virtual-circuit (VC) network architecture. Recall that we've considered VCs at some length in Section 4.2.1. ATM's overall architecture is organized into three layers, as shown in Figure 5.37.

The **ATM adaptation layer (AAL)** is roughly analogous to the Internet's transport layer and is present only at the ATM devices at the edge of the ATM network. On the sending side, the AAL is passed data from a higher-level application or protocol (such as IP, if ATM is being used to connected IP devices). On the receiving side it passes data up to the higher layer protocol or application. AALs have been defined for constant bit rate services and circuit emulation (AAL1), for variable-bit-rate services such as variable-bit-rate video (AAL2), and for data services such as IP-datagram transport (AAL5). Among the services performed by the AAL are error detection and segmentation/reassembly. The unit of data handled by the AAL is referred to by the rather generic name of **AAL protocol data unit (PDU)**, which is roughly equivalent to a UDP or TCP segment.

The AAL5 PDU is shown in Figure 5.38. The PDU's fields are relatively straightforward. The PAD ensures that the PDU is an integer multiple of 48 bytes, because the PDU will be segmented to fit into the 48-byte payloads of the underlying ATM packets (known as *ATM cells*). The length field identifies the size of the PDU payload, so that the PAD can be removed at the receiver. The CRC field

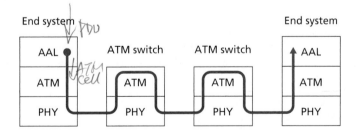

Figure 5.37   ◆   The three ATM layers. The AAL layer is only present at the edges of the ATM network.

0-65535	0-47	2	4
CPCS-PDU payload	PAD	Length	CRC

Figure 5.38 ♦ AAL5 PDU

provides for error detection using the same cyclic redundancy check as Ethernet. The payload field can be up to 65,535 bytes long.

Let's now drop down one layer and consider the **ATM layer**, which lies at the heart of the ATM architecture. The ATM layer defines the structure of the ATM cell and the meaning of the fields within the cell. The ATM cell is as important to an ATM network as the IP datagram is to an IP network. The first 5 bytes of the cell constitute the ATM header; the remaining 48 bytes constitute the ATM payload. Figure 5.39 shows the structure of the ATM cell header.

The fields in the ATM cell have the following functions:

♦ **Virtual-channel identifier (VCI).** Indicates the virtual channel to which the cell belongs. As with most network technologies that use virtual circuits, a cell's VCI is translated from link to link (see Section 4.2.1).

♦ **Payload type (PT).** Indicates the type of payload contained in the cell. There are several data payload types, several maintenance payload types, and an idle cell payload type. The PT field also includes a bit that serves to indicate the last cell in a fragmented AAL PDU.

♦ **Cell-loss priority (CLP) bit.** Can be set by the source to differentiate between high-priority traffic and low-priority traffic. If congestion occurs and an ATM switch must discard cells, the switch can use this bit to first discard low-priority traffic.

♦ **Header error control (HEC) byte.** Error-detection bits that protect the cell header.

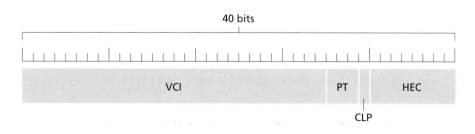

Figure 5.39 ♦ The format of the ATM cell header

Before a source can begin sending cells to a destination, the ATM network must first establish a **virtual channel (VC)** from source to destination. A virtual channel is nothing more than a virtual circuit, as described in Section 4.2.1. Each VC is a path consisting of a sequence of links between source and destination. A **virtual channel identifier (VCI)** is associated with each link on the VC. Whenever a VC is established or torn down, VC translation tables must be updated (see Section 4.3.1.). If permanent VCs are used, there is no need for dynamic VC establishment and teardown. When dynamic VC establishment and teardown are called for, the Q.2931 protocol [Black 1997, ITU-T Q.2931] provides signaling needed among the ATM switches and end systems.

The **ATM physical layer** is at the very bottom of the ATM protocol stack, and deals with voltages, bit timings, and framing on the physical medium. A good deal of the physical layer depends on the link's physical characteristics. There are two broad classes of physical layers: Those that have a transmission frame structure (for example, T1, T3, SONET, or SDH) and those that do not. If the physical layer has a frame structure, then it is responsible for generating and delineating frames. The use of the term *frames* here should not be confused with the link-layer (e.g., Ethernet) frames used in the earlier sections of this chapter. The transmission frame here is a physical-layer TDM-like mechanism for organizing the bits sent on a link. Some possible physical layers include:

♦ SONET/SDH (synchronous optical network/synchronous digital hierarchy) over single-mode fiber. Like T1 and T3, SONET and SDH have frame structures that establish bit synchronization between the transmitter and receiver at the two ends of the link. There are several standardized rates, including:

OC-1: 51.84 Mbps

OC-3: 155.52 Mbps

OC-12: 622.08 Mbps

OC-48: 2.5 Gbps

♦ T1/T3 frames over fiber, microwave, and copper.

♦ Cell-based with no frames. In this case, the clock at receiver is derived from a transmitted signal.

IP over ATM

Now let's consider how an ATM network can be used to provide connectivity between IP devices. Figure 5.40 shows an ATM backbone with four entry/exit points for Internet IP traffic. Note that each entry/exit point is a router. An ATM backbone can span an entire continent and may have tens or even hundreds of ATM switches. Most ATM backbones have a permanent VC between each pair of entry/exit points. By using permanent VCs, ATM cells are routed from entry point to exit point without having to establish and tear down VCs dynamically. Permanent VCs, however, are feasible only

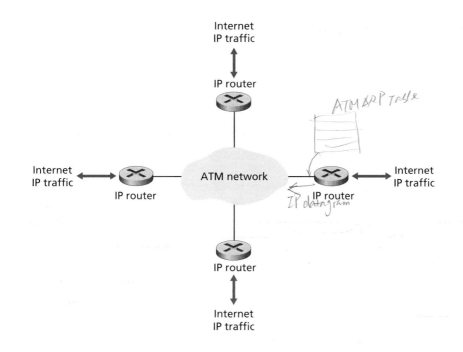

Figure 5.40 ◆ ATM network in the core of an Internet backbone

when the number of entry/exit points is relatively small. For n entry points, $n(n-1)$ permanent VCs are needed to directly connect n entry/exit points.

Each router interface that connects to the ATM network will need two addresses, in much the same way that an IP host has two addresses for an Ethernet interface: an IP address and a MAC address. Similarly, an ATM interface will have an IP address and an ATM address. Consider now an IP datagram crossing the ATM network shown in Figure 5.40. In the simplest case, the ATM network appears as a single logical link—ATM interconnects these four routers just as Ethernet can be used to connect four routers. Let us refer to the router at which the datagram enters the ATM network as the "entry router" and the router at which the datagram leaves the network as the "exit router." The entry router does the following:

1. Examines the destination address of the datagram.
2. Indexes its routing table and determines the IP address of the exit router (that is, the next router in the datagram's route).
3. To get the datagram to the exit router, the entry router views ATM as just another link-layer protocol. To move the datagram to the next router, we must determine the physical address of the next-hop router. Recall from our discussion in Section 5.4.2, that this is done using ARP. In the case of an ATM

interface, the entry router indexes an ATM ARP table with the IP address of the exit router and determines the ATM address of the exit router. The ATMARP protocol is described in [RFC 2225].

4. IP in the entry router then passes the datagram along with the ATM address of the exit router down to the link layer (that is, ATM).

After these four steps have been completed, the job of moving the datagram to the exit router is out of the hands of IP and in the hands of ATM. ATM must now move the datagram to the ATM destination address obtained in Step 3 above. This task has two subtasks:

1. Determine the VCI for the VC that leads to the ATM destination address.
2. Segment the datagram into cells at the sending side of the VC (that is, at the entry router), and reassemble the cells into the original datagram at the receiving side of the VC (that is, at the exit router).

The first subtask is straightforward. The interface at the sending side maintains a table that maps ATM addresses to VCIs. Because we're assuming that the VCs are permanent, this table is static and up-to-date. (If the VCs were not permanent, then the ATM Q.2931 signaling protocol would be needed to establish and tear down the VCs dynamically.) The second task merits more careful consideration. One approach is to use IP fragmentation, as discussed in Section 4.4. With IP fragmentation, the sending router would first break the original datagram into fragments, with each fragment being no more than 48 bytes, so that the fragment could fit into the payload of the ATM cell. But this fragmentation approach has a big problem—each IP fragment typically has 20 bytes of header, so that an ATM cell carrying a fragment would have 25 bytes of "overhead" and only 28 bytes of useful information. ATM thus uses AAL5 to provide more efficient segmentation/reassembly of a datagram.

The ATM network then moves each cell across the network to the ATM destination address. At each ATM switch between the ATM source and the ATM destination, the ATM cell is processed by the ATM physical and ATM layers, but not by the AAL layer. At each switch the VCI is typically translated (see Section 4.2.1) and the HEC is recalculated. When the cells arrive at the ATM destination address, they are directed to an AAL buffer that has been allocated to the particular VC. The AAL5 PDU is then reconstructed and the IP datagram is extracted and passed up the protocol stack to the IP layer.

5.8.2 Multiprotocol Label Switching (MPLS)

Multiprotocol Label Switching (MPLS) evolved from number of industry efforts in the mid-to-late 1990s to improve the forwarding speed of IP routers by adopting a key concept from the world of virtual-circuit networks: a fixed-length label. The goal was not to abandon the destination-based IP datagram-forwarding infrastructure for one based on fixed-length labels and virtual circuits, but to augment it by selectively labeling datagrams and allowing routers to forward datagrams based on fixed-length labels (rather than destination IP addresses) when possible. Importantly, these techniques work hand-in-hand with IP, using IP addressing and routing. The IETF unified these efforts in the MPLS protocol [RFC 3031, RFC 3032], effectively blending VC techniques into a routed datagram network.

Let's begin our study of MPLS by considering the format of a link-layer frame that is handled by an MPLS-capable router. Figure 5.41 shows that a link-layer frame transmitted on a PPP link or LAN (such as Ethernet) has a small MPLS header added between the layer-2 (i.e., PPP or Ethernet) header and layer-3 (i.e., IP) header. RFC 3032 defines the format of MPLS header for such links; headers are defined for ATM and frame-relayed networks as well in other RFCs. Among the fields in the MPLS header are the label (which serves the role of the virtual circuit identifier that we encountered back in Section 4.2.1), 3 bits reserved for experimental use, a single S bit, which is used to indicate the end of a series of "stacked" MPLS headers (an advanced topic that we'll not cover here), and a time-to-live field.

It's immediately evident from Figure 5.41 that an MPLS-enhanced frame can only be sent between routers that are both MPLS capable (since an non-MPLS-capable router would be quite confused when it found an MPLS header where it had expected to find the IP header!). An MPLS-capable router is often referred to as a **label-switched router**, since it forwards an MPLS frame by looking up the MPLS label in its forwarding table and then immediately passing the datagram to the appropriate output interface. Thus, the MPLS-capable router need not extract the destination address and perform a lookup of the longest prefix match in the forwarding table. But how does a router know if its neighbor is indeed MPLS capable, and how does a router know what label to associate with the given IP destination? To answer these questions, we'll need to take a look at the interaction among a group of MPLS-capable routers.

In the example in Figure 5.42, routers R1 through R4 are MPLS-capable. R5 and R6 are standard IP routers. R1 has advertised to R2 and R3 that it (R1) can route to destination A, and that a received frame with MPLS label 6 will be forwarded to

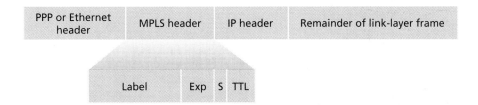

Figure 5.41 ♦ MPLS header: Located between link- and network-layer headers

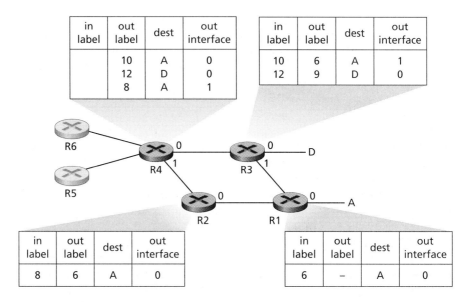

in label	out label	dest	out interface
	10	A	0
	12	D	0
	8	A	1

in label	out label	dest	out interface
10	6	A	1
12	9	D	0

in label	out label	dest	out interface
8	6	A	0

in label	out label	dest	out interface
6	–	A	0

Figure 5.42   ◆   MPLS-enhanced forwarding

destination A. Router R3 has advertised to router R4 that it can route to destinations A and D, and that incoming frames with MPLS labels 10 and 12 respectively will be switched toward those destinations. Router R2 has also advertised to router R4 that it (R2) can reach destination A, and that a received frame with MPLS label 8 with be switched toward A. Note that Router R4 is now in the interesting position having *two* MPLS paths to reach A via interface 0 with outbound MPLS label 10, and via interface 1 with an MPLS label of 8. The broad picture painted in Figure 5.42 is that IP R4, R5, A, and D are connected together via an MPLS infrastructure (MPLS-capable routers R1, R2, R3, and R4) in much the same way that a switched LAN or an ATM network can connect together IP devices. And like a switched LAN or ATM network, the MPLS-capable routers R1 through R4 do so *without ever touching the IP header of a packet.*

In our discussion above, we've not specified the specific protocol used to distribute labels between among the MPLS-capable routers, as the details of this signaling are well beyond the scope of this book. We note, however, that the IETF working group on MPLS has specified in RFC 3468 that an extension of the RSVP protocol (which we'll study in Chapter 7), known as RSVP-TE [RFC 3209] will be the focus of its efforts for MPLS signaling. Thus, the interested reader is encouraged to consult RFC 3209.

Thus far, the emphasis of our discussion of MPLS has been on the fact that MPLS performs switching based on labels, without needing to consider the IP address of a packet. The true advantages of MPLS and the reason for current interest in MPLS, however, lie not in the potential increases in switching speeds, but rather in the new traffic management capabilities that MPLS enables. As noted above, R4 has *two* MPLS paths to A. If forwarding were performed up at the IP layer on the basis of IP address, the IP routing protocols we studied in Chapter 4 would specify only a single, least cost path to A. Thus, MPLS provides the ability to forward packets along routes that would not be possible using standard IP routing protocols. This is one simple form of **traffic engineering** using MPLS [RFC 3346, Xiao 2000], in which a network operator can override normal IP routing and force some of the traffic headed toward a given destination along one path, and other traffic destined toward the same destination along another path (whether for policy, performance, or some other reason).

It is also possible to use MPLS for many other purposes as well. It can be used to perform fast restoration of MPLS forwarding paths, e.g., to reroute traffic over a precomputed failover path in response to link failure [Kar 2000, Huang 2002, RFC 3469]. MPLS can also be used to implement the differentiated service framework ("diff-serv") that we will study in Chapter 7. Finally, we note that MPLS can, and has, been used to implement so-called **virtual private networks** (VPN). In implementing a VPN for a customer, an ISP uses its MPLS-enabled network to connect together the customer's various networks. MPLS can be used to isolate both the resources and addressing used by the customer's VPN from that of other users crossing the ISP's network; see [DeClercq 2002] for details.

Our discussion of MPLS has been necessarily brief, and we encourage you to consult the references we've mentioned. We note that with so many possible uses for MPLS, it appears that it is rapidly becoming the Swiss Army knife of Internet traffic engineering!

5.9 Summary

In this chapter, we've examined the link layer—its services, the principles underlying its operation, and a number of important specific protocols that use these principles in implementing link-layer services.

We saw that the basic service of the link layer is to move a network-layer datagram from one node (router or host) to an adjacent node. We saw that all link-layer protocols operate by encapsulating a network-layer datagram within a link-layer frame before transmitting the frame over the link to the adjacent node. Beyond this common framing function, however, we learned that different link-layer protocols provide very different link access, delivery (reliability, error detection/correction), flow control, and transmission (e.g., full-duplex versus half-duplex) services. These differences are due in part to the wide variety of link types over which link-layer protocols must operate. A simple point-to-point link has a single sender and receiver communicating over a single "wire." A multiple access link is shared among many senders and receivers; consequently, the link-layer protocol for a multiple access channel has a protocol (its multiple access protocol) for coordinating link access. In the cases of ATM and MPLS, the "link" connecting two adjacent nodes (for example, two IP routers that are adjacent in an IP sense—that they are next-hop IP routers toward some destination) may actually be a *network* in and of itself. In one sense, the idea of a network being considered as a link should not seem odd. A telephone link connecting a home modem/computer to a remote modem/router, for example, is actually a path through a sophisticated and complex telephone *network*.

Among the principles underlying link-layer communication, we examined error-detection and correction techniques, multiple access protocols, link-layer addressing, and the construction of extended LANs via hubs, and switches. In the case of error detection/correction, we examined how it is possible to add additional bits to a frame's header in order to detect, and in some cases correct, bit-flip errors that might occur when the frame is transmitted over the link. We covered simple parity and checksumming schemes, as well as the more robust cyclic redundancy check. We then moved on to the topic of multiple access protocols. We identified and studied three broad approaches for coordinating access to a broadcast channel: channel partitioning approaches (TDM, FDM, CDMA), random access approaches (the ALOHA protocols and CSMA protocols), and taking-turns approaches (polling and token passing). We saw that a consequence of having multiple nodes share a single broadcast channel was the need to provide node addresses at the link layer. We learned that physical addresses were quite different from network-layer addresses and that, in the case of the Internet, a special protocol (ARP—the address resolution protocol) is used to translate between these two forms of addressing. We then examined how nodes sharing a broadcast channel form a LAN and how multiple LANs can be connected together to form larger LANs—all *without* the intervention of network-layer routing to interconnect these local nodes.

We also covered a number of specific link-layer protocols in detail—Ethernet and PPP. We ended our study of the link layer by focusing on how ATM and MPLS networks provide link-layer services when they interconnect IP routers. Having covered the link layer, *our journey down the protocol stack is now over*! Certainly, the physical layer lies below the data link layer, but the details of the physical layer are probably best left for another course (for example, in communication theory, rather than computer networking). We have, however, touched upon several aspects of the physical layer in this chapter (for example, our brief discussions of Manchester encoding in Section 5.5) and in Chapter 1 (our discussion of physical media in Section 1.4). We consider the physical layer again when we consider wireless link characteristics in the next chapter.

Although our journey down the protocol stack is over, our study of computer networking is not yet at an end. In the following four chapters we cover wireless networking, multimedia networking, network security, and network management. These four topics do not fit conveniently into any one layer; indeed, each topic crosscuts many layers. Understanding these topics (billed as advanced topics in some networking texts) thus requires a firm foundation in all layers of the protocol stack—a foundation that our study of the data link layer has now completed!

Homework Problems and Questions

Chapter 5 Review Questions

SECTIONS 5.1–5.2

1. If all the links in the Internet were to provide the reliable delivery service, would the TCP reliable delivery service be redundant? Why or why not?

2. What are some of the possible services that a link-layer protocol can offer to the network layer? Which of these link-layer services have corresponding services in IP? In TCP?

SECTION 5.3

3. Suppose two nodes start to transmit at the same time a packet of length L over a broadcast channel of rate R. Denote the propagation delay between the two nodes as t_{prop}. Will there be a collision if $t_{prop} < L/R$? Why or why not?

4. In Section 5.3, we listed four desirable characteristics of a broadcast channel. Which of these characteristics does slotted ALOHA have? Which of these characteristics does token passing have?

5. Describe polling and token-passing protocols using the analogy of cocktail party interactions.

6. Why would the token-ring protocol be inefficient if a LAN had a very large perimeter?

SECTION 5.4

7. How big is the MAC address space? The IPv4 address space? The IPv6 address space?

8. Suppose nodes A, B, and C each attach to the same broadcast LAN (through their adapters). If A sends thousands of IP datagrams to B with each encapsulating frame addressed to the MAC address of B, will C's adapter process these frames? If so, will C's adapter pass the IP datagrams in these frames to C (that is, the adapter's parent node)? How would your answers change if A sent frames with the MAC broadcast address?

9. Why is an ARP query sent within a broadcast frame? Why is an ARP response sent within a frame with a specific destination MAC address?

10. For the network in Figure 5.19, the router has two ARP modules, each with its own ARP table. Is it possible that the same MAC address appears in both tables?

SECTION 5.5

11. Compare the frame structures for 10BaseT, 100BaseT, and Gigabit Ethernet. How do they differ?

12. Suppose a 10 Mbps adapter sends into a channel an infinite stream of 1s using Manchester encoding. The signal emerging from the adapter has how many transitions per second?

13. In CSMA/CD, after the fifth collision, what is the probability that a node chooses $K = 4$? The result $K = 4$ corresponds to a delay of how many seconds on a 10 Mbps Ethernet?

Problems

1. Suppose the information content of a packet is the bit pattern 1010101010101011 and an even parity scheme is being used. What would the value of the checksum field be for the case of a two-dimensional parity scheme? Your answer should be such that a minimum-length checksum field is used.

2. Show (give an example other than the one in Figure 5.6) that two-dimensional parity checks can correct and detect a single bit error. Show (give an example) of a double-bit error that can be detected but not corrected.

3. Suppose the information portion of a packet (D in Figure 5.4) contains 10 bytes consisting of the 8-bit unsigned binary representation of the integers 0 through 9. Compute the Internet checksum for this data.

4. Consider the 4-bit generator, G, shown in Figure 5.8, and suppose that D has the value 10101010. What is the value of R?

5. In Section 5.3, we provided an outline of the derivation of the efficiency of slotted ALOHA. In this problem we'll complete the derivation.

   a. Recall that when there are N active nodes the efficiency of slotted ALOHA is $Np(1 - p)^{N-1}$. Find the value of p that maximizes this expression.

   b. Using the value of p found in (a), find the efficiency of slotted ALOHA by letting N approach infinity. *Hint*: $(1 - 1/N)^N$ approaches $1/e$ as N approaches infinity.

6. Show that the maximum efficiency of pure ALOHA is $1/(2e)$. *Note*: This problem is easy if you have completed the problem above!

7. Graph the efficiency of slotted ALOHA and pure ALOHA as a function of p for $N = 100$.

8. Consider a broadcast channel with N nodes and a transmission rate of R bps. Suppose the broadcast channel uses polling (with an additional polling node)

for multiple access. Suppose the amount of time from when a node completes transmission until the subsequent node is permitted to transmit (that is, the polling delay) is t_{poll}. Suppose that within a polling round, a given node is allowed to transmit at most Q bits. What is the maximum throughput of the broadcast channel?

9. Consider three LANs interconnected by two routers, as shown in the diagram below.

   a. Redraw the diagram to include adapters.

   b. Assign IP addresses to all of the interfaces. For Subnet 1 use addresses of the form 111.111.111.xxx; for Subnet 2 uses addresses of the form 122.222.222.xxx; and for Subnet 3 use addresses of the form 133.133.133.xxx.

   c. Assign MAC addresses to all of the adapters.

   d. Consider sending an IP datagram from Host A to Host F. Suppose all of the ARP tables are up to date. Enumerate all the steps as done for the single-router example in Section 5.4.2.

   e. Repeat (d), now assuming that the ARP table in the sending host is empty (and the other tables are up to date).

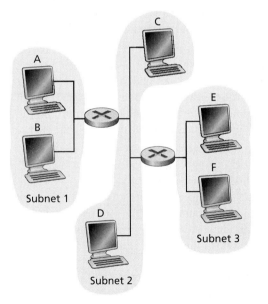

10. Recall that with the CSMA/CD protocol, the adapter waits $K \cdot 512$ bit times after a collision, where K is drawn randomly. For $K = 100$, how long does the adapter wait until returning to Step 2 for a 10 Mbps Ethernet? For a 100 Mbps Ethernet?

11. Suppose nodes A and B are on the same 10 Mbps Ethernet segment, and the propagation delay between the two nodes is 225 bit times. Suppose node A begins transmitting a frame and, before it finishes, node B begins transmitting a frame. Can A finish transmitting before it detects that B has transmitted? Why or why not? If the answer is yes, then A incorrectly believes that its frame was successfully transmitted without a collision. *Hint*: Suppose at time $t = 0$ bit times, A begins transmitting a frame. In the worst case, A transmits a minimum-sized frame of $512 + 64$ bit times. So A would finish transmitting the frame at $t = 512 + 64$ bit times. Thus, the answer is no, if B's signal reaches A before bit time $t = 512 + 64$ bits. In the worst case, when does B's signal reach A?

12. Suppose nodes A and B are on the same 10 Mbps Ethernet segment and the propagation delay between the two nodes is 225 bit times. Suppose A and B send frames at the same time, the frames collide, and then A and B choose different values of K in the CSMA/CD algorithm. Assuming no other nodes are active, can the retransmissions from A and B collide? For our purposes, it suffices to work out the following example. Suppose A and B begin transmission at $t = 0$ bit times. They both detect collisions at $t = 225$ bit times. They finish transmitting a jam signal at $t = 225 + 48 = 273$ bit times. Suppose $K_A = 0$ and $K_B = 1$. At what time does B schedule its retransmission? At what time does A begin transmission? (*Note*: The nodes must wait for an idle channel after returning to Step 2—see protocol.) At what time does A's signal reach B? Does B refrain from transmitting at its scheduled time?

13. Consider a 100 Mbps 100BaseT Ethernet. In order to have an efficiency of 0.50, what should be the maximum distance between a node and the hub? Assume a frame length of 64 bytes and that there are no repeaters. Does this maximum distance also ensure that a transmitting node A will be able to detect whether any other node transmitted while A was transmitting? Why or why not? How does your maximum distance compare with the actual 100 Mbps standard?

14. In this problem you will derive the efficiency of a CSMA/CD-like multiple access protocol. In this protocol, time is slotted and all adapters are synchronized to the slots. Unlike slotted ALOHA, however, the length of a slot (in seconds) is much less than a frame time (the time to transmit a frame). Let S be the length of a slot. Suppose all frames are of constant length $L = kRS$, where R is the transmission rate of the channel and k is a large integer. Suppose there are N nodes, each with an infinite number of frames to send. We also assume that $t_{prop} < S$, so that all nodes can detect a collision before the end of a slot time. The protocol is as follows:

   ♦ If, for a given slot, no node has possession of the channel, all nodes contend for the channel; in particular, each node transmits in the slot with probability p. If exactly one node transmits in the slot, that node takes possession of the channel for the subsequent $k - 1$ slots and transmits its entire frame.

♦ If some node has possession of the channel, all other nodes refrain from transmitting until the node that possesses the channel has finished transmitting its frame. Once this node has transmitted its frame, all nodes contend for the channel.

Note that the channel alternates between two states: the productive state, which lasts exactly k slots, and the nonproductive state, which lasts for a random number of slots. Clearly, the channel efficiency is the ratio of $k/(k + x)$, where x is the expected number of consecutive unproductive slots.

a. For fixed N and p, determine the efficiency of this protocol.

b. For fixed N, determine the p that maximizes the efficiency.

c. Using the p (which is a function of N) found in (b), determine the efficiency as N approaches infinity.

d. Show that this efficiency approaches 1 as the frame length becomes large.

15. Suppose two nodes, A and B, are attached to opposite ends of a 900 m cable, and that they each have one frame of 1,000 bits (including all headers and preambles) to send to each other. Both nodes attempt to transmit at time $t = 0$. Suppose there are four repeaters between A and B, each inserting a 20-bit delay. Assume the transmission rate is 10 Mbps, and CSMA/CD with backoff intervals of multiples of 512 bits is used. After the first collision, A draws $K = 0$ and B draws $K = 1$ in the exponential backoff protocol. Ignore the jam signal and the 96-bit time delay.

a. What is the one-way propagation delay (including repeater delays) between A and B in seconds? Assume that the signal propagation speed is $2 \cdot 10^8$ m/sec.

b. At what time (in seconds) is A's packet completely delivered at B?

c. Now suppose that only A has a packet to send and that the repeaters are replaced with switches. Suppose that each switch has a 20-bit processing delay in addition to a store-and-forward delay. At what time, in seconds, is A's packet delivered at B?

16. Recall that ATM uses 53-byte packets consisting of 5 header bytes and 48 payload bytes. Fifty-three bytes is unusually small for fixed-length packets; most networking protocols (IP, Ethernet, Frame Relay, and so forth) use packets that are, on average, significantly larger. One of the drawbacks of a small packet size is that a large fraction of link bandwidth is consumed by overhead bytes; in the case of ATM, almost 10 percent of the bandwidth is "wasted" by the ATM header. In this problem we investigate why such a small packet size was chosen. To this end, suppose that the ATM cell consists of P bytes (possibly different from 48) and 5 bytes of header.

a. Consider sending a digitally encoded voice source directly over ATM. Suppose the source is encoded at a constant rate of 64 kbps. Assume each cell is entirely filled before the source sends the cell into the network. The time required to fill a cell is the **packetization delay**. In terms of L, determine the packetization delay in milliseconds.

b. Packetization delays greater than 20 msec can cause a noticeable and unpleasant echo. Determine the packetization delay for $L = 1,500$ bytes (roughly corresponding to a maximum-sized Ethernet packet) and for $L = 48$ (corresponding to an ATM cell).

c. Calculate the store-and-forward delay at a single ATM switch for a link rate of $R = 155$ Mbps (a popular link speed for ATM) for $L = 1,500$ bytes, and for $L = 48$ bytes.

d. Comment on the advantages of using a small cell size.

17. Consider the MPLS network shown in Figure 5.42, and suppose that routers R5 and R6 are now MPLS enabled. Suppose that we want to perform traffic engineering so that packets from R6 destined for A are switched to A via R6-R4-R3-R1, and packets from R5 destined for A are switched via R5-R4-R2-R1. Show the MPLS tables in R5 and R6, as well as the modified table in R4, that would make this possible.

Discussion Questions

You are encouraged to surf the Web in seeking answers to the following questions.

1. Roughly, what is the current price range of a 10/100 Mbps adapter? Of a Gigabit Ethernet adapter? How do these prices compare with a 56 kbps dial-up modem or with an ADSL modem?

2. Hubs and switches are often priced by number of interfaces (also called *ports* in LAN jargon). Roughly, what is the current per-interface price range for a 10 Mbps hub? For a 100 Mbps hub? For a switch consisting of only 10 Mbps interfaces? For a switch consisting of only 100 Mbps interfaces?

3. Many of the functions of an adapter can be performed in software that runs on the node's CPU. What are the advantages and disadvantages of moving this functionality from the adapter to the node?

4. Search the Web for the protocol numbers used in an Ethernet frame for an IP datagram and for an ARP packet.

5. Read references [Xiao 2000, Huang 2002, and RFC 3346] on traffic engineering using MPLS. List a set of goals for traffic engineering. Which of these goals can only be met with MPLS, and which of these goals are met by using existing (non-MPLS) protocols? In the latter case, what advantages does MPLS offer?

Ethereal Lab

In the companion Web site for this textbook, http://www.awl.com/kurose-ross, you'll find two Ethereal lab assignments for this chapter The first lab examines the operation of the IEEE 802.3 protocol and the Ethernet frame format. The second lab explores the use of the DHCP protocol that we studied in Section 5.4.3.

Simon S. Lam

Simon S. Lam is Professor and Regents Chair in Computer Sciences at the University of Texas at Austin. From 1971 to 1974, he was with the ARPA Network Measurement Center at UCLA, where he worked on satellite and radio packet switching. He led a research group that invented secure sockets and prototyped the first secure sockets layer (named Secure Network Programming) in 1993. His research interests are in design and analysis of network protocols and security services. He received his BSEE from Washington State University and his MS and PhD from UCLA.

Why did you decide to specialize in networking?

When I arrived at UCLA as a new graduate student in Fall 1969, my intention was to study control theory. Then I took the queueing theory classes of Leonard Kleinrock and was very impressed by him. For a while, I was working on adaptive control of queueing systems as a possible thesis topic. In early 1972, Larry Roberts initiated the ARPANET Satellite System project (later called Packet Satellite). Professor Kleinrock asked me to join the project. The first thing we did was to introduce a simple, yet realistic, backoff algorithm to the slotted Aloha protocol. Shortly thereafter, I found many interesting research problems, such as Aloha's instability problem and need for adaptive backoff, which would form the core of my thesis.

You were active in the early days of the Internet in the 1970s, beginning with your student days at UCLA. What was it like then? Did people have any inkling of what the Internet would become?

The atmosphere was really no different from other system-building projects I have seen in industry and academia. The initially stated goal of the ARPANET was fairly modest, that is., to provide access to expensive computers from remote locations so that many more scientists could use them. However, with the startup of the Packet Satellite project in 1972 and the Packet Radio project in 1973, ARPA's goal had expanded substantially. By 1973, ARPA was building three different packet networks at the same time and it became necessary for Vint Cerf and Bob Kahn to develop an interconnection strategy.

Back then, all of these progressive developments in networking were viewed (I believe) as logical rather than magical. No one could have envisioned the scale of the Internet and power of personal computers today. It was a decade before appearance of the first PCs. To put things in perspective, most students submitted their computer programs as decks of punched cards for batch processing. Only some students had direct access to computers, which were typically housed in a restricted area. Modems were slow and still a rarity. As a graduate student, I had only a phone on my desk, and I used pencil and paper to do most of my work.

Where do you see the field of networking and the Internet, heading in the future?

In the past, the simplicity of Internet's IP protocol was its greatest strength in vanquishing competition and becoming the de facto standard for internetworking. Unlike competitors, such as X.25 in the 1980s and ATM in the 1990s, IP can run on top of any link-layer networking technology because it offers only a best-effort datagram service. Thus any packet network can connect to the Internet.

Unfortunately, IP's greatest strength is now a shortcoming. IP is like a straitjacket that confines the Internet's development to specific directions. The IP layer is too economically important to tinker with to support new functionalities, such as multicast and QoS. In recent years, many researchers have redirected their efforts to the application and transport layers for multicast and QoS support. Most of the other current Internet research topics, such as security and P2P systems, involve the application layer only. There is also a great deal of research on wireless ad hoc networks, sensor networks, and satellite networks. These networks can be viewed either as standalone systems or link-layer systems, which can flourish because they are outside of the IP straitjacket.

Many people are excited about the possibility of P2P systems as a platform for novel Internet applications. However, P2P systems are highly inefficient in their use of Internet resources. A concern of mine is whether the transmission and switching capacity of the Internet core will continue to increase faster than the traffic demand on the Internet as it grows to interconnect all kinds of devices and support future P2P-enabled applications. Without substantial overprovisioning of capacity, ensuring network stability in the presence of malicious attacks and congestion would be a major task.

What is the most challenging part of your job?

The most challenging part of my job as a professor is teaching and motivating *every* student in my class, and *every* doctoral student under my supervision, rather than just the high achievers. The very bright and motivated may require a little guidance but not much else. I often learn more from these students than they learn from me. Educating and motivating the underachievers present a major challenge.

What impacts do you foresee technology having on learning in the future?

Eventually, almost all human knowledge will be accessible through the Internet, which will be the most powerful tool for learning. This vast knowledge base will have the potential of leveling the playing field for students all over the world. For example, motivated students in any country will be able to access the best class Web sites, multimedia lectures, and teaching materials. Already, it was said that the IEEE and ACM digital libraries have accelerated the development of computer science researchers in China. In time, the Internet will transcend all geographic barriers to learning.

6

Wireless and Mobile Networks

In the telephony world, the past 10 years have arguably been the decade of cellular telephony. The number of worldwide mobile cellular subscribers increased from 34 million in 1993 to more than 1 billion in 2003, with the number of cellular subscribers now surpassing the number of main telephone lines [ITU Statistics 2004]. The many advantages of cell phones are evident to all—anywhere, anytime, untethered access to the global telephone network via a highly portable lightweight device. With the advent of laptops, palmtops, PDAs and their promise of anywhere, anytime, untethered access to the global Internet, is a similar explosion in the use of wireless Internet devices just around the corner?

Regardless of the future growth of wireless Internet devices, it's already clear that wireless networks and the mobility-related services they enable are here to stay. From a networking standpoint, the challenges posed by these networks, particularly at the data link and network layers, are so different from traditional wired computer networks that an individual chapter devoted to the study of wireless and mobile networks (i.e., *this* chapter) is appropriate.

We'll begin this chapter with a discussion of mobile users, wireless links and networks, and their relationship to the larger (typically wired) networks to which they connect. We'll draw a distinction between the challenges posed by the *wireless* nature of the communication links in such networks, and by the *mobility* that these wireless links enable. Making this important distinction—between wireless and mobility—will allow us to better isolate, identify, and master the key concepts in each area. Note that there are indeed many networked environments in which the network nodes are wireless but not mobile (e.g., wireless home or office networks with stationary workstations and large displays), and limited forms of mobility that do not require wireless links (e.g., a worker who uses a wired laptop at home, shuts down the laptop, drives to work, and attaches the laptop to the company's wired network). Of course, many of the most exciting networked environments are those in which users are both wireless *and* mobile—for example, a scenario in which a mobile user (say in the back seat of car) maintains a voice-over-IP call and multiple ongoing TCP connections while racing down the autobahn at 160 kilometers per hour. It is here, at the intersection of wireless and mobility, that we'll find the most interesting technical challenges!

We'll begin by first illustrating the setting in which we'll consider wireless communication and mobility—a network in which wireless (and possibly mobile) users are connected into the larger network infrastructure by a wireless link at the network's edge. We'll then consider the characteristics of this wireless link in Section 6.2. We include a brief introduction to Code Division Multiple Access (CDMA), a shared-medium access protocol that is often used in wireless networks, in Section 6.2. In Section 6.3, we'll examine the link-level aspects of the IEEE 802.11 (Wi-Fi) wireless LAN standard in some depth; we'll also say a few words about Bluetooth. In Section 6.4 we provide an overview of cellular Internet access, including the emerging 3G cellular technologies that provide both voice and high-speed Internet access. In Section 6.5, we'll turn our attention to mobility, focusing on the problems of locating a mobile user, routing to the mobile user, and "handing off" the mobile user who dynamically moves from one point of attachment to the network to another. We'll examine how these mobility services are implemented in the mobile IP standard and in GSM, in Sections 6.6 and 6.7, respectively. Finally, we'll consider the impact of wireless links and mobility on transport-layer protocols and networked applications in Section 6.8.

6.1 Introduction

Figure 6.1 shows the setting in which we'll consider the topics of wireless data communication and mobility. We'll begin by keeping our discussion general enough to cover a wide range of networks, including both wireless LANs such as IEEE 802.11 and cellular networks such as a 3G network; we'll dive down into a more detailed discussion of specific wireless architectures in later sections. We can identify the following elements in a wireless network:

♦ *Wireless hosts.* As in the case of wired networks, hosts are the end-system devices that run applications. A **wireless host** might be a laptop, palmtop, PDA, phone, or desktop computer. The hosts themselves may or may not be mobile.

CASE HISTORY

PUBLIC WI-FI ACCESS: COMING SOON TO A CORNER NEAR YOU?

Only five years ago, wireless computer networks were somewhat of an oddity. Although massive investment was pouring into licensing radio spectrum for 3G systems (see Case History: 3G Cellular Mobile Versus Wireless LANS), 3G systems were (and still are) only at early stages of deployment. At the time, a few early adopters were beginning to try out the just-standardized IEEE 802.11 wireless LAN technology. What a difference five years can make! Today many corporations, universities, and homes have their own wireless IEEE 802.11 LANs. Even more remarkably, the number of wireless hot spots—public locations where users can find 802.11 wireless access—is rapidly expanding. The Gartner Group estimates there were 71,000 public hot spots in 2003, a nearly fifty-fold increase since 2001. In the United States, eateries such as Starbucks and McDonalds offer Wi-Fi access in a number of locations. In New York City, Verizon Communications has located Wi-Fi access points at over one thousand of its public phone booths and has connected the phone booths to the Internet [Verizon 2004], providing Wi-Fi access to passersby and nearby businesses. In early 2004, T-Mobile [T-Mobile 2004] provided more that 4,000 public Wi-Fi hotspots in locations such as airports, restaurants, and bookstores. A recent startup, Cometa, announced plans in 2003 to set up 20,000 commercial Wi-Fi hotspots in 50 metropolitan areas by 2005. With this level of activity, the dream of nearly ubiquitous, anytime, untethered access to the global Internet may be closer than we think!

♦ *Wireless links.* A host connects to a base station (defined below) or to another wireless host through a **wireless communication link**. Different wireless link technologies have different transmission rates and can transmit over different distances. Figure 6.2 shows a few of the key characteristics of the more popular wireless link standards. We'll cover these standards later in the first half of this chapter; we'll also consider other wireless link characteristics (such as their bit error rates and their causes) in Section 6.2.

♦ In Figure 6.1, wireless links connect hosts located at the edge of the network into the larger network infrastructure. We hasten to add that wireless links are also sometimes used *within* a network and to connect routers, switches, and other network equipment. However, our focus in this chapter will be on the use of wireless communication around the edges of the network, as it is here that many of the most exciting technical challenges, and most of the growth, are occurring.

♦ *Base station.* The **base station** is a key part of the wireless network infrastructure. Unlike the wireless host and wireless link, a base station has no obvious counterpart in a wired network. A base station is responsible for sending and receiving data (e.g., packets) to and from a wireless host that is associated with

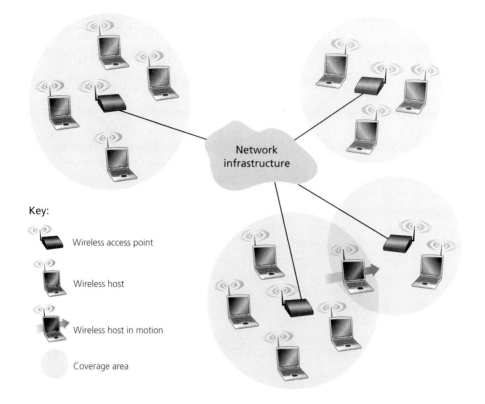

Key:

Wireless access point

Wireless host

Wireless host in motion

Coverage area

Figure 6.1 ♦ Elements of a wireless network

that base station. A base station will often be responsible for coordinating the transmission of multiple wireless hosts with which it is associated. When we say a wireless host is "associated" with a base station, we mean that (1) the host is within wireless communication distance of the base station, and (2) the host uses that base station to relay data between it (the host) and the larger network. **Cell towers** in cellular networks and **access points** in an 802.11 wireless LANs are examples of base stations.

In Figure 6.1, the base station is connected to the larger network (i.e., the Internet, corporate, or home network, or telephone network), thus functioning as a link-layer relay between the wireless host and the rest of the world with which the host communicates.

Hosts associated with a base station are often referred to as operating in **infrastructure mode**, since all traditional network services (e.g., address assignment and routing) are provided by the network to which a host is connected via the base station. In **ad hoc networks**, wireless hosts have no such infrastructure with which to connect. In the absence of such infrastructure, the hosts themselves must provide for services such as routing, address assignment, DNS-like name translation, and more. In this book, we'll focus our attention primarily on infrastructure-mode networks.

When a mobile host moves beyond the range of one base station and into the range of another, it will change its point of attachment into the larger network (i.e., change the base station with which it is associated)—a process referred to as **handoff**. Such mobility raises many challenging questions. If a host can move, how does one find its current location in the network so that data can be forwarded to the mobile host? How is addressing performed, given that a host can be in one of many possible locations? If the host moves *during* a TCP connection or phone call, how is data routed so that the connection continues uninterrupted? These and many (many!) other questions make wireless and mobile networking an area of exciting networking research.

♦ *Network infrastructure.* This is the larger network with which a wireless host may wish to communicate.

Let's now dig deeper into the technical challenges that arise in wireless and mobile networks. We'll begin by first considering the individual wireless link, deferring our discussion of mobility until later in this chapter.

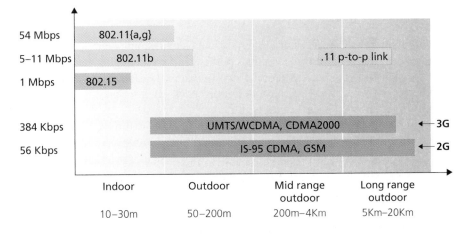

Figure 6.2 ♦ Link characteristics of selected wireless network standards

6.2 Wireless Links and Network Characteristics

Let's begin by considering a simple wired network, say a home network, with a wired Ethernet switch (see Section 5.6) interconnecting the hosts. If we replace the wired Ethernet with a wireless 802.11 network, a wireless NIC card would replace the wired Ethernet cards at the hosts, and an access point would replace the Ethernet switch, but virtually no changes would be needed at the network layer or above. This suggests that we focus our attention on the link layer when looking for important differences between wired and wireless networks. Indeed, we can find a number of important differences between a wired link and a wireless link:

♦ *Decreasing signal strength.* Electromagnetic radiation attenuates as it passes through matter (e.g., a radio signal passing through a wall). Even in free space, the signal will disperse, resulting in decreased signal strength (sometimes referred to as **path loss**) as the distance between sender and receiver increases.

♦ *Interference from other sources.* Radio sources transmitting in the same frequency band will interfere with each other. For example, 2.4 GHz wireless phones and 802.11b wireless LANs transmit in the same frequency band. Thus, the 802.11b wireless LAN user talking on a 2.4GHz wireless phone can expect that neither the network nor the phone will perform particularly well. In addition to interference from transmitting sources, electromagnetic noise within the environment (e.g., a nearby motor, a microwave) can result in interference.

♦ *Multipath propagation.* **Multipath propagation** occurs when portions of the electromagnetic wave reflect off objects and the ground, taking paths of different lengths between a sender and receiver. This results in the blurring of the received signal at the receiver. Moving objects between the sender and receiver can cause multipath propagation to change over time.

The discussion above suggests that bit errors will be more common in wireless links than in wired links. For this reason, it is perhaps not surprising that wireless link protocols (such as the 802.11 protocol we'll examine in the following section) employ not only powerful CRC error detection codes, but also link-level ARQ protocols that retransmit corrupted frames.

A higher and time-varying bit error rate are not the only differences between a wired and wireless link. Recall that in the case of wired broadcast links, all nodes receive the transmissions from all other nodes. In the case of wireless links, the situation is not as simple, as shown in Figure 6.3. Suppose that Station A is transmitting to Station B. Suppose also that Station C is transmitting to Station B. With the so-called **hidden terminal problem**, physical obstructions in the environment (for example, a mountain or a building) may prevent A and C from hearing each other's transmissions, even though A's and C's transmissions are indeed interfering at the destination, B. This is shown in Figure 6.3(a). A second scenario that results in undetectable collisions at the receiver results from the **fading** of a signal's strength as it propagates through the wireless medium. Figure 6.3(b) illustrates the case where A and C are placed such that their signals are not strong enough to detect each other's transmissions, yet their transmissions *are* strong enough to interfere with each other at station B. As we'll see in Section 6.3, the hidden terminal problem and fading make multiple access in a wireless network considerably more complex than in a wired network.

6.2.1 CDMA

Recall from Chapter 5 that when hosts communicate over a shared medium, a protocol is needed so that the signals sent by multiple senders do not interfere at the receivers. In Chapter 5 we described three classes of medium access protocols: channel partitioning, random access, and taking turns. Code division multiple access (CDMA) is yet a fourth type of a shared-medium access protocol, one that is prevalent in wireless LAN and cellular technologies. Because CDMA is so important in the wireless world, we'll take a quick look at CDMA now, before getting into specific wireless access technologies in the subsequent sections.

In a CDMA protocol, each bit being sent is encoded by multiplying the bit by a signal (the code) that changes at a much faster rate (known as the **chipping rate**) than the original sequence of data bits. Figure 6.4 shows a simple, idealized CDMA encoding/decoding scenario. Suppose that the rate at which original data bits reach the CDMA encoder defines the unit of time; that is, each original data bit to be transmitted requires a one-bit slot time. Let d_i be the value of the data bit for the ith

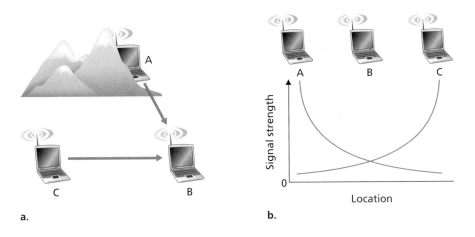

Figure 6.3 ♦ Hidden terminal problem (a) and fading (b)

bit slot. For mathematical convenience, we represent a data bit with a 0 value as −1. Each bit slot is further subdivided into M mini-slots; in Figure 6.4, $M = 8$, although in practice M is much larger. The CDMA code used by the sender consists of a sequence of M values, c_m, $m = 1, \ldots, M$, each taking a +1 or −1 value. In the example in Figure 6.4, the M-bit CDMA code being used by the sender is (1, 1, 1, −1, 1, −1, −1, −1).

To illustrate how CDMA works, let us focus on the ith data bit, d_i. For the mth mini-slot of the bit-transmission time of d_i, the output of the CDMA encoder, $Z_{i,m}$, is the value of d_i multiplied by the mth bit in the assigned CDMA code, c_m:

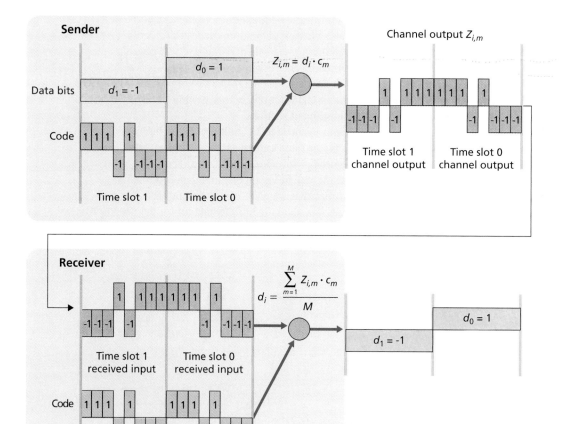

Figure 6.4 ◆ A simple CDMA example: sender encoding, receiver decoding

$$Z_{i,m} = d_i \cdot c_m \tag{6.1}$$

In a simple world, with no interfering senders, the receiver would receive the encoded bits, $Z_{i,m}$, and recover the original data bit, d_i, by computing:

$$d_i = \frac{1}{M} \sum_{m=1}^{M} Z_{i,m} \cdot c_m \tag{6.2}$$

The reader might want to work through the details of the example in Figure 6.4 to see that the original data bits are indeed correctly recovered at the receiver using Equation 6.2.

The world is far from ideal, however, and as noted above, CDMA must work in the presence of interfering senders that are encoding and transmitting their data using a different assigned code. But how can a CDMA receiver recover a sender's original data bits when those data bits are being tangled with bits being transmitted by other senders? CDMA works under the assumption that the interfering transmitted bit signals are additive. This means, for example, that if three senders send a 1 value, and a fourth sender sends a −1 value during the same mini-slot, then the received signal at all receivers during that mini-slot is a 2 (since $1 + 1 + 1 − 1 = 2$). In the presence of multiple senders, sender s computes its encoded transmissions, $Z^s_{i,m}$, in exactly the same manner as in Equation 6.1. The value received at a receiver during the mth mini-slot of the ith bit slot, however, is now the *sum* of the transmitted bits from all N senders during that mini-slot:

$$Z^*_{i,m} = \sum_{s=1}^{N} Z^s_{i,m}$$

Amazingly, if the senders' codes are chosen carefully, each receiver can recover the data sent by a given sender out of the aggregate signal simply by using the sender's code in exactly the same manner as in Equation 6.2:

$$d_i = \frac{1}{M} \sum_{m=1}^{M} Z^*_{i,m} \cdot c \tag{6.3}$$

Figure 6.5 illustrates a two-sender CDMA example. The M-bit CDMA code being used by the upper sender is $(1, 1, 1, −1, 1, −1, −1, −1)$, while the CDMA code being used by the lower sender is $(1, −1, 1, 1, 1, −1, 1, 1)$. Figure 6.5 illustrates a receiver recovering the original data bits from the upper sender. Note that the receiver is able to extract the data from sender 1 in spite of the interfering transmission from sender 2.

Recall our cocktail analogy from Chapter 5. A CDMA protocol is similar to having partygoers speaking in multiple languages; in such circumstances humans are actually quite good at locking into the conversation in the language they understand, while filtering out the remaining conversations. We see here that

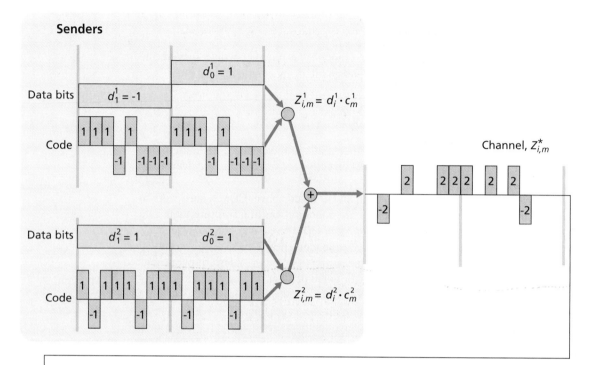

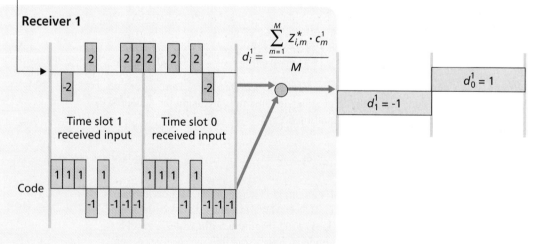

Figure 6.5   ♦   A two-sender CDMA example

CDMA is a partitioning protocol in that it partitions the codespace (as opposed to time or frequency) and assigns each node a dedicated piece of the codespace.

Our discussion here of CDMA is necessarily brief; in practice a number of difficult issues must be addressed. First, in order for the CDMA receivers to be able to extract a particular sender's signal, the CDMA codes must be carefully chosen. Second, our discussion has assumed that the received signal strengths from various senders are the same; in reality this can be difficult to achieve. There is a considerable body of literature addressing these and other issues related to CDMA; see [Pickholtz 1982; Viterbi 1995] for details.

6.3 Wi-Fi: 802.11 Wireless LANs

Pervasive in the workplace, the home, educational institutions, cafés, airports, and street corners, wireless LANs are now one of the most important access network technologies in the Internet today. Although many technologies and standards for wireless LANs were developed in the 1990s, one particular class of standards has clearly emerged as the winner: the **IEEE 802.11 wireless LAN**, also known as **Wi-Fi**. In this section, we'll take a close look at 802.11 wireless LANs, examining the 802.11 frame structure, the 802.11 medium access protocol, and the internetworking of 802.11 LANs with wired Ethernet LANs.

There are several 802.11 standards for wireless LAN technology, including 802.11b, 802.11a, and 802.11g. Table 6.1 summarizes the main characteristics of these standards. As of this writing (spring 2004), the 802.11b wireless LANs are by far the most prevalent. However, 802.11a and 802.11g products are also widely available, and these higher-speed wireless LANs should enjoy significant deployment in the coming years.

The three 802.11 standards share many characteristics. They all use the same medium access protocol, CSMA/CA, which we'll discuss shortly. All three use the same frame structure for their link-layer frames as well. All three standards have the

Standard	Frequency Range	Data Rate
802.11b	2.4-2.485 GHz	up to 11 Mbps
802.11a	5.1-5.8 GHz	up to 54 Mbps
802.11g	2.4-2.485 GHz	up to 54 Mbps

Table 6.1 ♦ Summary of IEEE 802.11 Standards

ability to reduce their transmission rate in order to reach out over greater distances. And all three standards allow for both "infrastructure mode and "ad hoc mode," as we'll also shortly discuss. However, as shown in Table 6.1, the three standards have some major differences at the physical layer.

The 802.11b wireless LAN has a data rate of 11 Mbps, which is more than sufficient for most home networks with broadband cable or DSL Internet access. 802.11b LANs operate in the unlicensed frequency band of 2.4-2.485 GHz, competing for frequency spectrum with 2.4 GHz phones and microwave ovens. 802.11a wireless LANs can run at significantly higher bit rates, but do so at higher frequencies. By operating at a higher frequency, however, 802.11a LANs have a shorter transmission distance for a given power level and suffer more from multipath propagation. 802.11g LANs, operating in the same lower frequency band as 802.11b yet with the higher-speed transmission rates of 802.11a, should allow users to eat their cake and have it too.

6.3.1 The 802.11 Architecture

Figure 6.6 illustrates the principal components of the 802.11 wireless LAN architecture. The fundamental building block of the 802.11 architecture is the **basic service set (BSS)**. A BSS contains one or more wireless stations and a central **base station**, known as an **access point (AP)** in 802.11 parlance. Figure 6.6 shows the AP in each of two BSSs connecting to an interconnection device (such as a hub, switch or router), which in turn leads to the Internet. In a typical home network, there is one AP and one router (often packaged with a cable or ADSL modem, all in the same box) that connects the BSS to the Internet.

As with Ethernet devices, each 802.11 wireless station has a 6-byte MAC address that is stored in the firmware of the station's adaptor (that is, 802.11 network interface card). Each AP also has a MAC address for its wireless interface. As with Ethernet, these MAC addresses are administered by IEEE and are (in theory) globally unique.

As noted in Section 6.1, wireless LANs that deploy APs are often referred to as **infrastructure wireless LANs**, with the "infrastructure" being the APs along with the wired Ethernet infrastructure that interconnect the APs and a router. Figure 6.7 shows that IEEE 802.11 stations can also group themselves together to form an ad hoc network—a network with no central control and with no connections to the "outside world." Here, the network is formed "on the fly," by mobile devices that have found themselves in proximity to each other, that have a need to communicate, and that find no preexisting network infrastructure in their location. An ad hoc network might be formed when people with laptops get together (for example, in a conference room, a train, or a car) and want to exchange data in the absence of a centralized AP. There has been tremendous interest in ad hoc networking, as communicating portable devices continue to proliferate. In this section, though, we'll focus our attention on infrastructure wireless LANs.

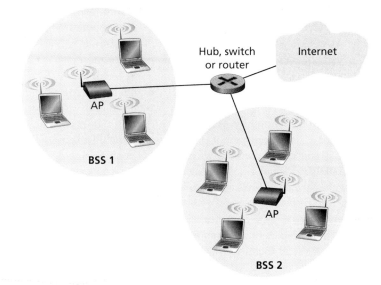

Figure 6.6 ♦ IEEE 802.11 LAN architecture

Channels and Association

In 802.11, each wireless station needs to associate with an AP before it can send or receive 802.11 frames containing network-layer data. Although all of the 802.11 standards use association, we'll discuss this topic specifically in the context of IEEE 802.11b.

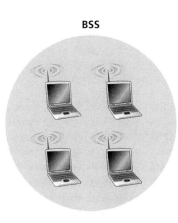

Figure 6.7 ♦ An IEEE 802.11 ad hoc network

When a network administrator installs an AP, the administrator assigns a one- or two-word **Service Set Identifier (SSID)** to the access point. (When you "view available networks" in Microsoft Windows XP, for example, a list is displayed showing the SSID of each AP in range.) The administrator must also assign a channel number to the AP. To understand channel numbers, recall that 802.11b operates in the frequency range of 2.4 GHZ to 2.485 GHz. Within this 85 MHz band, 802.11b defines 11 partially overlapping channels. Any two channels are non-overlapping if and only if they are separated by four or more channels. In particular, the set of channels 1, 6, and 11 is the only set of three non-overlapping channels. This means that an administrator could create a wireless LAN with an aggregate maximum transmission rate of 33 Mbps by installing three 802.11b APs at the same physical location, assigning channels 1, 6, and 11 to the APs, and interconnecting each of the APs with a switch.

Now that we have a basic understanding of 802.11 channels, let's describe an interesting (and not completely uncommon) situation—that of a Wi-Fi jungle. A **Wi-Fi jungle** is any physical location where a wireless station receives a sufficiently strong signal from two or more APs. For example, in many cafés in New York City, a wireless station can pick up a signal from numerous nearby APs. One of the APs might be managed by the café, while the other APs might be in residential apartments near the café. Each of these APs would likely be located in a different subnet and would have been independently assigned a channel.

Now suppose you enter such a Wi-Fi jungle with your portable computer, seeking wireless Internet access and a blueberry muffin. Suppose there are five APs in the jungle. To gain Internet access, your wireless station will need to join exactly one of the subnets and hence need to **associate** with exactly one of the APs. Associating means the wireless station creates a virtual wire between itself and the AP. Specifically, only the associated AP will send data frames (that is, frames containing data, such as a datagram) to your wireless station, and your wireless station will send data frames into the Internet only through the associated AP. But how does your wireless station associate with a particular AP? And more fundamentally, how does your wireless station know which APs, if any, are out there in the jungle?

The 802.11 standard requires that an AP periodically send **beacon frames**, each of which includes the AP's SSID and MAC address. Your wireless station, knowing that APs are sending out beacon frames, scans the 11 channels, seeking beacon frames from any APs that may be out there (some of which may be transmitting on the same channel—it's a jungle out there!). Having learned about available APs from the beacon frames, you (or your wireless host) select one of the APs for association. After selecting the AP, your wireless host and the chosen AP dialogue with each other using the 802.11 association protocol. If all goes well in this dialogue, your wireless station becomes associated with the selected AP. Implicitly, during the association phase, your wireless station is joining the subnet to which the selected AP belongs. Just after the association phase, the wireless station will typically send a DHCP discovery message (see Section 5.4.3) into the subnet via the associated AP in order to obtain an IP address in the AP's subnet. At this point, the rest of the Internet now views your computer simply as a host in the AP's subnet.

In order to create an association with a particular AP, the wireless station may be required to authenticate itself to the AP. 802.11 wireless LANs provide a number of alternatives for authentication and access. One approach, used by many companies, is to permit access to a wireless network based on a station's MAC address. A second approach, used by many Internet cafés, employs user names and passwords. In both cases, the AP typically communicates with an authentication server, relaying information between the wireless endpoint station and the authentication server using a protocol such as RADIUS [RFC 2138] or DIAMETER [RFC 3588]. Separating the authentication server from the AP allows one authentication server to serve many APs, centralizing the (often sensitive) decisions of authentication and access within the single server, and keeping AP costs and complexity low. We'll see in Section 8.8.4 that the new IEEE 802.11i protocol defining security aspects of the 802.11 protocol family takes precisely this approach.

6.3.2 The 802.11 MAC Protocol

Once a wireless station is associated with an AP, it can start sending and receiving data frames to and from the access point. But because multiple stations may want to transmit data frames at the same time over the same channel, a multiple access protocol is needed to coordinate the transmissions. Here, a **station** is either a wireless station or an AP. As discussed in Chapter 5 and Section 6.2.1, broadly speaking there are four classes of multiple access protocols: channel partitioning, random access, taking turns, and CDMA. Inspired by the huge success of Ethernet and its random access protocol, the designers of 802.11 chose a random access protocol for 802.11 wireless LANs. This random access protocol is referred to as **CSMA with collision avoidance**, or more succinctly as **CSMA/CA**. As with Ethernet's CSMA/CD, the "CSMA" in CSMA/CA stands for "carrier sense multiple access," meaning that each station senses the channel before transmitting, and refrains from transmitting when the channel is sensed busy. Although both Ethernet and 802.11 use carrier-sensing random access, the two MAC protocols have important differences. First, instead of using collision detection, 802.11 uses collision avoidance techniques. Second, because of the relatively high bit-error rates of wireless channels, 802.11 (unlike Ethernet) uses a link-layer acknowledgement/retransmission (ARQ) scheme. We'll describe 802.11's collision avoidance and link-layer acknowledgment schemes below.

Recall from Sections 5.3 and 5.5 that with Ethernet's collision-detection algorithm, an Ethernet station listens to the channel as it transmits. If, while transmitting, it detects that another station is also transmitting, it aborts its transmission and tries to transmit again after waiting a small, random amount of time. Unlike the 802.3 Ethernet protocol, the 802.11 MAC protocol does *not* implement collision detection. There are two important reasons for this:

♦ The ability to detect collisions requires the ability to send (the station's own signal) and receive (to determine whether another station is also transmitting) at the same time. Because the strength of the received signal is typically very small compared to the strength of transmitted signal at the 802.11 adapter, it is costly to build hardware that can detect a collision.

♦ More importantly, even if the adapter could transmit and listen at the same time (and presumably abort transmission when it senses a busy channel), the adapter would still not be able to detect all collisions due to the hidden terminal problem and fading, as discussed in Section 6.2.

Because 802.11wireless LANs do not use collision detection, once a station begins to transmit a frame, *it transmits the frame in its entirety*; that is, once a station gets started, there is no turning back. As one might expect, transmitting entire frames (particularly long frames) when collisions are prevalent can significantly degrade a multiple access protocol's performance. In order to reduce the likelihood of collisions, 802.11 employs several collision avoidance techniques, which we'll shortly discuss.

Before considering collision avoidance, however, we'll first need to examine 802.11's **link-layer acknowledgment** scheme. Recall from Section 6.2 that when a station in a wireless LAN sends a frame, the frame may not reach the destination station intact for a variety of reasons. To deal with this non-negligible chance of failure, the 802.11 MAC uses link-layer acknowledgments. As shown in Figure 6.8, when the destination station receives a frame that passes the CRC check, it waits a short period of time known as the **Short Inter-frame Spacing (SIFS)** and then sends back an acknowledgment frame. If the transmitting station does not receive an acknowledgment within a given amount of time, it assumes that an error has occurred and retransmits the frame, again using the CSMA/CA protocol to access the channel. If an acknowledgment is not received after some fixed number of retransmissions, the transmitting station gives up and discards the frame.

Having discussed how 802.11 uses link-layer acknowledgments, we're now in a position to describe the 802.11 CSMA/CA protocol. Suppose that a station (wireless station or an AP) has a frame to transmit.

1. If initially the station senses the channel idle, it transmits its frame after a short period of time known as the **Distributed Inter-frame Space (DIFS)**; see Figure 6.8.
2. Otherwise, the station chooses a random backoff value and counts down this value when the channel is sensed idle. When the channel is sensed busy, the counter value remains frozen.
3. When the counter reaches zero (note that this can only occur when the channel is sensed idle), the station transmits the entire frame and then waits for an acknowledgement.

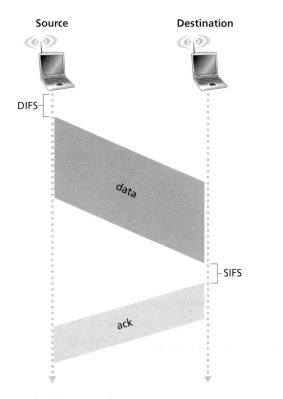

Source   Destination

DIFS

data

SIFS

ack

Figure 6.8 ♦ 802.11 uses link-layer acknowledgments

4. If an acknowledgment is received, the transmitting station knows that its frame has been correctly received at the destination station. If the station has another frame to send, it begins the CSMA/CA protocol at step 2. If the acknowledgment isn't received, the transmitting station reenters the backoff phase in step 2, with the random value chosen from a larger interval.

The observant reader may have noted that in step 2, the station chooses a random backoff value and begins a countdown, effectively delaying its transmission even if the channel is sensed idle. Under Ethernet's CSMA/CD multiple access protocol (Section 5.5.2), however, a station begins transmitting as soon as the channel is sensed idle. Why do CSMA/CD and CDMA/CA take such different approaches here?

To answer this question, let's consider a scenario in which two stations each have a data frame to transmit, but neither station transmits immediately because each senses that a third station is already transmitting. With Ethernet's CSMA/CD, the two stations would each transmit as soon as they detect that the third station has finished transmitting. This would cause a collision, which isn't a serious issue in CSMA/CD, since both stations would abort their transmissions and thus avoid the useless transmission of the remainder of a frame that has suffered a collision. In 802.11, however, the situation is quite different. Because 802.11 does not detect a collision and abort transmission, a frame suffering a collision will be transmitted in its entirety. The goal in 802.11 is thus to avoid collisions whenever possible. In 802.11, if the two stations sense the channel busy, they both immediately enter random backoff, hopefully choosing different backoff values. If these values are indeed different, once the channel becomes idle, one of the two stations will begin transmitting before the other, and (if the two stations are not hidden from each other) the "losing station" will hear the "winning station's" signal, freeze its counter, and refrain from transmitting until the winning station has completed its transmission. In this manner, a costly collision is avoided. Of course, collisions can still occur with 802.11 in this scenario: The two stations could be hidden from each other, or the two stations could choose identical random backoff values.

Dealing with Hidden Terminals: RTS and CTS

The 802.11 MAC protocol also includes a nifty (but optional) reservation scheme that helps avoid collisions even in the presence of hidden terminals. Let's investigate this scheme in the context of Figure 6.9, which shows two wireless stations and one access point. Both of the wireless stations are within range of the AP (whose coverage is shown as a shaded circle) and both have associated with the AP. However, due to fading, the signal ranges of wireless stations are limited to the interiors of the shaded circles shown in Figure 6.9. Thus, each of the wireless stations is hidden from the other, although neither is hidden from the AP.

Let's now consider why hidden terminals can be problematic. Suppose Station H1 is transmitting a frame and halfway through H1's transmission, the network layer at Station H2 passes a frame (which we will refer to as a DATA frame here) to the 802.11 MAC. H2, not hearing the transmission from H1 will first wait a short random amount of time and then transmit the DATA frame, resulting in a collision. The channel will therefore be wasted during the entire period of H1's transmission as well as during H2's transmission.

In order to avoid this problem, the IEEE 802.11 protocol allows a station to use a short **Request to Send (RTS)** control frame and a short **Clear to Send (CTS)** control frame to *reserve* access to the channel. When a sender wants to send a DATA frame, it can first send an RTS frame to the AP, indicating the total time required to transmit the DATA frame and the acknowledgement (ACK) frame. When the AP receives the RTS frame, it responds by broadcasting a CTS frame. This CTS frame serves two purposes: It gives the sender explicit permission to send and also instructs the other stations not to send for the reserved duration.

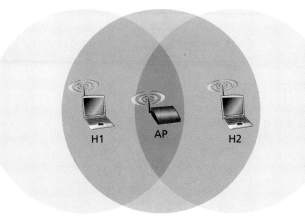

Figure 6.9 ♦ Hidden terminal example: H1 is hidden from H2, and vice versa

Thus, in Figure 6.10, before transmitting a DATA frame, H1 first broadcasts an RTS frame, which is heard by all stations in its circle, including the AP. The AP then responds with a CTS frame, which is heard by all stations within its range, including H1 and H2. Station H2, having heard the CTS, refrains from transmitting for the time specified in the CTS frame. The RTS, CTS, DATA, and ACK frames are shown in Figure 6.10.

The use of the RTS and CTS frames can improve performance in two important ways:

♦ The hidden station problem is mitigated, since a long DATA frame is transmitted only after the channel has been reserved.

♦ Because the RTS and CTS frames are short, a collision involving an RTS or CTS frame will last only for the duration of the short RTS or CTS frame. Once the RTS and CTS frames are correctly transmitted, the following DATA and ACK frames should be transmitted without collisions.

You are encouraged to check out the 802.11 applet in the textbook's companion Web site. This interactive applet illustrates the CSMA/CA protocol, including the RTS/CTS exchange sequence.

Although the RTS/CTS exchange can help reduce collisions, it also introduces delay and consumes channel resources. For this reason, the RTS/CTS exchange is only used (if at all) to reserve the channel for the transmission of a long DATA frame. In practice, each wireless station can set an RTS threshold such that the

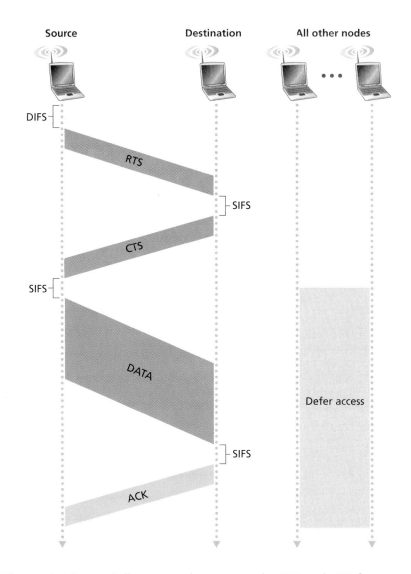

Figure 6.10 ◆ Collision avoidance using the RTS and CTS frames

RTS/CTS sequence is used only when the frame is longer than the threshold. For many wireless stations, the default RTS threshold value is larger than the maximum frame length, so the RTS/CTS sequence is skipped for all DATA frames sent.

Using 802.11 as a Point-to-Point Link

Our discussion so far has focused on the use of 802.11 in a multiple access setting. We should mention that if two nodes each have a directional antenna, they can point their directional antennae at each other and run the 802.11 protocol over what is an essentially a point-to-point link. Given the low cost of commodity 802.11 hardware, the use of directional antennae and an increased transmission power allow 802.11 to be used as an inexpensive means of providing wireless point-to-point connections over tens of kilometers distance. [Bhagwat 2003] describes such a multi-hop wireless network operating in the rural Ganges plains in India that contains point-to-point 802.11 links.

6.3.3 The IEEE 802.11 Frame

Although the 802.11 frame shares many similarities with an Ethernet frame, it also contains a number of fields that are specific to its use for wireless links. The 802.11 frame is shown in Figure 6.11. The numbers above each of the fields in the frame represent the lengths of the fields in *bytes*; the numbers above each of the subfields in the frame control field represent the lengths of the subfields in *bits*. Let's now examine the fields in the frame as well as some of the more important subfields in the frame's control field.

Payload and CRC Fields

At the heart of the frame is the payload, which typically consists of an IP datagram or an ARP packet. Although the field is permitted to be as long as 2,312 bytes, it is typically fewer than 1,500 bytes, holding an IP datagram or an ARP packet. As with an Ethernet frame, an 802.11 frame includes a cyclic redundancy check (CRC) so

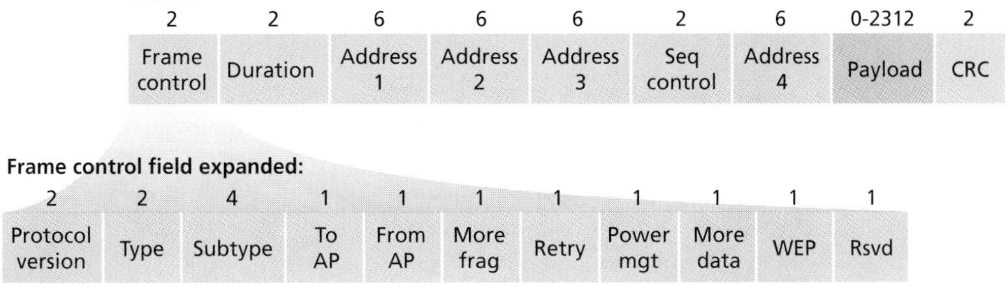

Figure 6.11 ♦ The 802.11 frame

that the receiver can detect bit errors in the received frame. As we've seen, bit errors are much more common in wireless LANs than in wired LANs, so the CRC is even more useful here.

Address Fields

Perhaps the most striking difference in the 802.11 frame is that it has *four* address fields, each of which can hold a 6-byte MAC address. But why four address fields? Doesn't a source MAC field and destination MAC field suffice, as they do for Ethernet? It turns out that three address fields are needed for internetworking purposes—specifically, for moving the network-layer datagram from a wireless station through an AP to a router interface. The fourth address field is used in ad hoc networks, but not in infrastructure networks. Since we are only considering infrastructure networks here, let's focus our attention on the first three address fields. The 802.11 standard defines these fields as follows:

♦ Address 2 is the MAC address of the station that transmits the frame. Thus, if a wireless station transmits the frame, that station's MAC address is inserted in the address 2 field. Similarly, if an AP transmits the frame, the AP's MAC address is inserted in the address 2 field.

♦ Address 1 is the MAC address of the wireless station that is to receive the frame. Thus if a mobile wireless station transmits the frame, address 1 contains the MAC address of the destination AP. Similarly, if an AP transmits the frame, address 1 contains the MAC address of the destination wireless station.

♦ To understand address 3, recall that the BSS (consisting of the AP and wireless stations) is part of a subnet, and that this subnet connects to other subnets via some router interface. Address 3 contains the MAC address of this router interface.

To gain further insight into the purpose of address 3, let's walk through an internetworking example in the context of Figure 6.12. In this figure, there are two APs, each of which is responsible for a number of wireless stations. Each of the APs has a direct connection to a router, which in turn connects to the global Internet. We should keep in mind that an AP is a link-layer device, and thus neither "speaks" IP nor understands IP addresses. Consider now moving a datagram from the router interface R1 to the wireless Station H1. The router is not aware that there is an AP between it and H1; from the router's perspective, H1 is just a host in one of the subnets to which it (the router) is connected.

♦ The router, which knows the IP address of H1 (from the destination address of the datagram), uses ARP to determine the MAC address of H1, just as in an ordinary Ethernet LAN. After obtaining H1's MAC address, router interface R1 encapsulates the datagram within an Ethernet frame. The source address field of

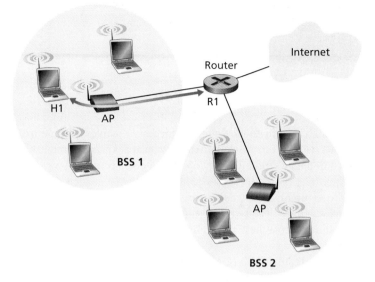

Figure 6.12 ♦ The use of address fields in 802.11 frames: Moving a frame between H1 and R1

this frame contains R1's MAC address and the destination address field contains H1's MAC address.

♦ When the Ethernet frame arrives at the AP, the AP converts the 802.3 Ethernet frame to an 802.11 frame before transmitting the frame into the wireless channel. The AP fills in address 1 and address 2 with H1's MAC address and its own MAC address, respectively, as described above. For address 3, the AP inserts the MAC address of R1. In this manner, H1 can to determine (from address 3) the MAC address of the router interface that sent the datagram into the subnet.

Now consider what happens when the wireless station H1 responds by moving a datagram from H1 to R1.

♦ H1 creates an 802.11 frame, filling the fields for address 1 and address 2 with the AP's MAC address and H1's MAC address, respectively, as described above. For address 3, H1 inserts R1's MAC address.

♦ When the AP receives the 802.11 frame, it converts the frame to an Ethernet frame. The source address field for this frame is H1's MAC address, and the destination address field is R1's MAC address. Thus, address 3 allows the AP to determine the appropriate destination MAC address when constructing the Ethernet frame.

In summary, address 3 plays a crucial role for internetworking the BSS with a wired LAN.

Sequence Number, Duration, and Frame Control Fields

Recall that in 802.11, whenever a station correctly receives a frame from another station, it sends back an acknowledgment. Because acknowledgments can get lost, the sending station may send multiple copies of a given frame. As we saw in our discussion of the rdt2.1 protocol (Section 3.4.1), the use of sequence numbers allows the receiver to distinguish between a newly transmitted frame and the retransmission of a previous frame. The sequence number field in the 802.11 frame thus serves exactly the same purpose here at the link layer as it did in the transport layer in Chapter 3.

Keep in mind that the 802.11 protocol allows a transmitting station to reserve the channel for a period of time that includes the time to transmit its data frame and the time to transmit an acknowledgment. This duration value is included is the frame's duration field (both for data frames and for the RTS and CTS frames).

As shown in Figure 6.11, the frame control field includes many subfields. We'll say just a few words about some of the more important subfields; for a more complete discussion, you are encouraged to consult the 802.11 specification [Held 2001; Crow 1997; IEEE 802.11 1999]. The *type* and *subtype* fields are used to distinguish the association, RTS, CTS, ACK, and data frames. The *to* and *from* fields are used to define the meanings of the different address fields. (These meanings change depending on whether ad hoc or infrastructure modes are used and, in the case of infrastructure mode, whether a wireless station or an AP is sending the frame.) Finally the WEP field indicates whether encryption is being used or not. (WEP is discussed in Chapter 8.)

6.3.4 Mobility in the Same IP Subnet

In order to increase the physical range of a wireless LAN, companies and universities will often deploy multiple BSSs within the same IP subnet. This naturally raises the issue of mobility among the BSSs—how do wireless stations seamlessly move from one BSS to another while maintaining ongoing TCP sessions? As we'll see in this subsection, mobility can be handled in a relatively straightforward manner when the BSSs are part of the subnet. When stations move between subnets, more sophisticated mobility management protocols will be needed, such as those we'll study in Sections 6.5 and 6.6.

Let's now look at a specific example of mobility between BSSs in the same subnet. Figure 6.13 shows two interconnected BSSs with a host, H1, moving from

BSS1 to BSS2. Because in this example the interconnection device that connects the two BSSs is *not* a router, all of the stations in the two BSSs, including the APs, belong to the same IP subnet. Thus, when H1 moves from BSS1 to BSS2, it may keep its IP address and all of its ongoing TCP connections. If the interconnection device were a router, then H1 would either have to change its IP address, and either drop its ongoing TCP connections, or make use of a network-layer mobility protocol, such as mobile IP, as discussed in Section 6.6.

But what specifically happens when H1 moves from BSS1 to BSS2? As H1 wanders away from AP1, H1 detects a weakening signal from AP1 and starts to scan for a stronger signal. H1 receives beacon frames from AP2 (which in many corporate and university settings will have the same SSID as AP1). H1 then disassociates with AP1 and associates with AP2, while keeping its IP address and maintaining its ongoing TCP sessions.

This all works fine if the interconnection device is a hub. But if the device is a switch—as it often is—then special care must be taken. As you may recall from Chapter 5, switches are "self-learning" and automatically build their forwarding tables. This self-learning feature nicely handles occasional moves (for example, when an employee gets transferred from one department to another); however, switches were not designed to support highly mobile users who want to maintain TCP connections while moving between BSSs. To appreciate the problem here, recall that before the move, the switch has an entry in its forwarding table that pairs H1's MAC address and the outgoing switch interface through which H1 can be reached. If H1 is initially in BSS1, then a datagram destined to H1 will be directed to via AP1. Once H1 associates with BSS2, however, its frames should be directed to AP2. One solution (a bit of a hack, really) is for AP2 to send a broadcast Ethernet

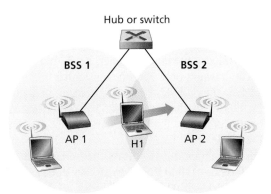

Figure 6.13 ♦ Mobility in the same subnet

frame with H1's source address to the switch just after the new association. When the switch receives the frame, it updates its forwarding table, allowing H1 to be reached via AP2. The 802.11f standards group is developing an inter-AP protocol to handle these and related issues.

6.3.5 802.15 and Bluetooth

As noted in Figure 6.2, the IEEE 801.11 Wi-Fi standard is aimed at communication among devices separated by up to 100 meters, while network access over cellular telephony networks spans the range of tens of kilometers. Before delving into the details of these longer distance cellular wireless networks, let's briefly consider the 802.15 **wireless personal area network (WPAN)** standard, a cousin of 802.11 in the IEEE 802 family that is meant to provide connectivity among personal devices separated by up to 10 meters or so. 802.15 is essentially a low-power, short-range, low-rate "cable replacement" technology for interconnecting notebooks, peripheral devices, cellular phones, and PDAs, whereas 802.11 is a higher-power, medium-range, higher-rate "access" technology.

An IEEE 802.15 network operates over a short range, at low power, and at low cost. The link and physical layers of 802.15 are based on the earlier **Bluetooth** specification for personal area networks [Held 2001, Bisdikian 2001]. 802.15 networks operate in the 2.4 GHz unlicensed radio band in a TDM manner, with time slots of 625 microseconds. During each time slot, a sender transmits on one of 79 channels, with the channel changing in a known but pseudo-random manner from slot to slot. This form of channel hopping, known as **frequency-hopping spread spectrum (FHSS)** spreads transmissions in time over the frequency spectrum. 802.15 can provide data rates up to 721 kbps.

802.15 networks are ad hoc networks: No network infrastructure (e.g., an access point) is needed to interconnect 802.15 devices. Thus, 802.15 devices must organize themselves. 802.15 devices are first organized into a **piconet** of up to eight active devices, as shown in Figure 6.14. One of these devices is designated as the master, with the remaining devices acting as slaves. The master node truly rules the piconet—its clock determines time in the piconet, it can transmit in each odd number slot, and a slave can transmit only after the master has communicated with it in the previous slot and even then the slave can only transmit to the master. In addition to the slave devices, there can also be up to 255 parked devices in the network. These devices cannot communicate until their status has been changed from parked to active by the master node.

For more information about 802.15 WPANs, the interested reader should consult the Bluetooth references [Held 2001, Bisdikian 2001] or the official IEEE 802.15 Web site [IEEE 802.15 2004].

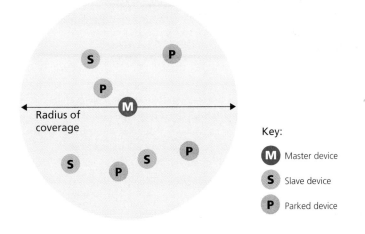

Radius of coverage

Key:

M Master device

S Slave device

P Parked device

Figure 6.14 ♦ An 802.15 piconet

6.4 Cellular Internet Access

In the previous section we examined how an Internet host can access the Internet when inside a Wi-Fi hotspot, that is, when it is within the vicinity of an 802.11 access point. But most Wi-Fi hot spots have a small coverage area of between 10 and 100 meters in diameter. What do we do then when we have a desperate need for wireless Internet access and we cannot access a Wi-Fi hotspot?

Given that cellular telephony is now ubiquitous in many areas throughout the world, a natural strategy is to extend cellular networks so that they support not only voice telephony but wireless Internet access as well. Ideally, this Internet access would be at a reasonably high speed and would provide for seamless mobility, allowing users to maintain their TCP sessions while traveling, for example, on a bus or a train. With sufficiently high upstream and downstream bit rates, the user could even maintain video-conferencing sessions while roaming about. This scenario is not that far-fetched. As of this writing (spring 2004), many cellular telephony providers offer their subscribers a cellular Internet access service for under $100 per month with typical downstream and upstream bit rates in the low hundreds of kilobits per second.

In this section, we provide a brief overview of current and emerging cellular Internet access technologies. Our focus here will again be on the wireless first hop between the cellular phone and the wired telephone network infrastructure; in Section 6.7 we'll consider how calls are routed to a user moving between base stations. Our brief discussion will necessarily provide only a simplified and high-level

CASE HISTORY

3G CELLULAR MOBILE VERSUS WIRELESS LANS

Many cellular mobile phone operators are deploying 3G cellular mobile systems with 2 Mbps indoor and 384 kbps outdoor data rates. The 3G systems are being deployed in licensed radio-frequency bands, with some operators paying as much as $2,000 per subscriber to governments for the licenses. The 3G systems will allow users to access the Internet from remote outdoor locations while on the move, in a manner similar to today's cellular phone access. For example, 3G technology will permit a user to access road map information while driving a car, or movie theater information while sunbathing on a beach. Nevertheless, many experts today are beginning to question whether 3G technology will be successful, given its cost and its competition from wireless LAN technology [Weinstein 2002]. In particular, these experts argue:

♦ The emerging wireless LAN infrastructure will become nearly ubiquitous. IEEE 802.11 wireless LANs, operating at 11 Mbps and higher, are enjoying widespread deployment, as noted in an earlier sidebar (Public Wi-Fi Access). Soon almost all portable computers and PDAs will have factory-equipped 802.11 LAN cards. Furthermore, emerging Internet appliances—such as wireless cameras and picture frames—will also use the small and low-powered wireless LAN cards.

♦ The bulk of the wireless data traffic will originate or terminate in local environments. Assuming that the wireless traffic originating/terminating from shopping malls, office buildings, and so on is carried by the inexpensive wireless LANs, there will be relatively little traffic for the expensive 3G systems.

♦ Wireless LAN base stations could also handle mobile phone appliances. This allows low-cost data access for cellular mobile appliances as well as wireless LAN appliances. Thus, a cell phone without a wireless LAN card, but present in a local environment, will be able to bypass the operators' 3G systems to access the Internet.

Of course, many other experts believe that 3G will not only be a major success, but will also dramatically revolutionize the way we work and live. Of course, both Wi-Fi and 3G may become prevalent wireless technologies, with roaming wireless devices automatically selecting the access technology that provides the best service in their current physical location (see the discussion of 4G wireless access in this section).

description of cellular technologies. Modern cellular communications, of course, has great breadth and depth, with many universities offering several courses on the topic. Readers seeking a deeper understanding are encouraged to see [Goodman 1997; Scourias 1997; Korhonen 2003; Kaaranen 2001; Lin 2001], as well as the particularly excellent and exhaustive reference [Mouly 1992].

6.4.1 An Overview of Cellular Architecture

The term *cellular* refers to the fact that a geographical area is partitioned into a number of geographic coverage areas, known as **cells**, as shown in left side of Figure 6.15. Each cell contains a base station, which transmits signals to, and receives signals from, the mobile stations in its cell. The coverage area of a cell depends on many factors, including the transmitting power of the base station, the transmitting power of the mobile station, obstructing buildings in the cell, and the height of base station antennae. Although Figure 6.15 shows each cell containing one base station residing in the middle of the cell, many systems today place the base stations at corners where three cells intersect, so that a single base station with directional antennas can service three cells.

Basic Network Architecture

As shown in Figure 6.15, each base station is connected to a wide-area network—such as the Public Switched Telephone Network (PSTN) or directly to the Internet—via a

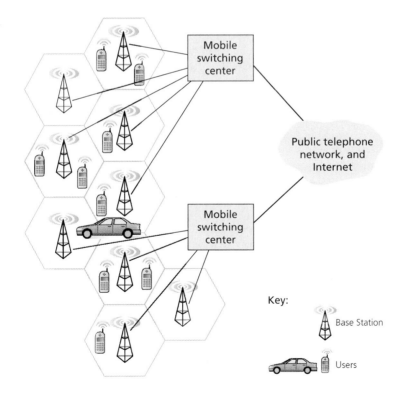

Figure 6.15 ♦ Components of a cellular network architecture

wired infrastructure. Specifically, Figure 6.15 shows that each base station is connected to a **mobile switching center (MSC)**, which manages call establishment and teardown to and from mobile users. An MSC contains much of functionality that is found in an ordinary telephone switching center (such as a PBX or central office), but augmented with the additional functionality required to handle the mobility of its users.

Air Interface Access Techniques

Typically many simultaneous calls take place in a given cell. These calls need to share the portion of the radio spectrum that is allocated to the cellular service provider. Most cellular systems today use one of two broad approaches for sharing radio spectrum:

♦ *A combination of frequency division multiplexing (FDM) and time division multiplexing (TDM).* Recall from Chapter 1 with pure FDM, the channel is partitioned into a number of frequency bands, with each band devoted to a call. Also recall from Chapter 1 that with pure TDM, time is partitioned into frames with each frame is further partitioned into slots, with each call being assigned the use a particular slot in the revolving frame. In combined FDM/TDM systems, the channel is partitioned into a number of frequency sub-bands; within each sub-band, time is partitioned into frames and slots. Thus, for a combined FDM/TDM system, if the channel is partitioned into F sub-bands and time is partitioned into T slots, then the channel will be able to support $F \cdot T$ simultaneous calls.

♦ *Code division multiple access (CDMA).* Recall from Section 6.2.1 that CDMA does not partition in frequency or in time. Instead, all users share the same radio frequency at the same time. Each user in a cell is allocated a distinct sequence of bits, called a chipping sequence. As we saw in Section 6.2.1, when the sender and receiver use the same chipping sequence, the receiver can recover the sender's transmission from among the simultaneous transmissions from other senders. A major advantage of CDMA is that it eliminates the need for frequency allocation. When using an FDM/TDM system, the receivers are sensitive to interference from other signals in the same frequency band. Thus, a given frequency can be reused in an FDM/TDM system only in cells that are located sufficiently far apart to avoid such interference. Such **frequency reuse** is not a major concern when designing CDMA systems.

6.4.2 Cellular Standards and Technologies: A Brief Survey

When people talk about cellular technology, they often classify the technology as belonging to one of several "generations". The earlier generations were designed primarily for voice traffic; the more recent cellular systems support Internet access as well as voice. Because this book is about computer networking and not voice telephony, we are, of course, more interested in recent generations of cellular systems. But because the recent generations directly evolved from the earlier generations, we nevertheless begin our survey with a brief discussion of first- and second-generation wireless systems.

In surveying the generations, we'll be quickly running through an alphabet soup of jargon for the various technologies. As a reader, you shouldn't feel obligated to fully absorb or memorize all the terms and acronyms in this alphabet soup. The purpose of this survey is to put the various wireless generations into perspective as well as to provide a quick reference guide for the various terms and acronyms.

First generation (1G) systems were analog FDMA systems designed for voice-only communication. These 1G systems are almost extinct now, having been replaced by the digital 2G systems.

Second Generation (2G)

Second generation systems, although digital, were also designed for voice communication. But because the current 2.5G and 3G systems, designed to handle data communications, have grown out of the 2G, it's important to say a few words about 2G. A 2G cell phone converts an analog voice signal into digital format before modulating and then transmitting the signal into the air. The digital technology in 2G has many advantages over the analog 1G technology, including increased service capacity within a cell, improved security to reduce fraud, and more advanced services such as caller ID and messaging. Most of today's cellular providers use 2G technology. Various 2G standards and technologies have been widely deployed, including:

◆ *Interim Standard 136 (**IS-136**) TDMA.* This is a combined FDM/TDM system that evolved from 1G FDMA technology. It has been widely deployed in North America.

◆ *Global System for Mobile Communications (**GSM**).* In the 1980s Europeans recognized the need for a pan-European digital system that would replace their incompatible 1G systems, providing seamless mobility between countries as well as features and capabilities not possible with analog systems. This need led to the GSM standard for cellular communications. Europeans deployed GSM technology with great success in the early 1990s. GSM then spread into Asia and North America, and is now the now the most widely deployed cellular communications standard. The GSM standard for 2G cellular systems uses combined FDM/TDM for the air interface. GSM systems consist of 200 kHz frequency bands, with each band supporting 8 TDM calls. GSM encodes speech at 13 kbps and 12.2 kbps.

◆ ***IS-95** CDMA.* Unlike IS-136 and GSM, which use FDM/TDM, IS-95 CDMA uses code division multiple access (see Section 6.2.1). The company Qualcomm demonstrated the viability of CDMA for cellular telephony in the late 1980s;

since then many IS-95 systems have been deployed, particularly in North America and Korea.

Transition from Second Generation to Third Generation (2.5G)

2G systems such as IS-95, GSM, and IS-136 are optimized for voice service and are not particularly well adapted for data communications. In the 1990s, standard organizations recognized the need for a 3G cellular technology that was appropriate for both voice and data communications (including Internet access). However, because broad deployment of 3G technology takes many years, companies developed interim protocols and standards that enable data transmission over the existing 2G infrastructure. Such systems have been collectively dubbed "2.5G cellular systems." These include:

♦ **General Packet Radio Service (GPRS).** GPRS evolved from GSM. For data services, GSM effectively emulates a modem between the user device and the destination data network—that is, GSM uses circuit switching for its data as well as voice traffic. As we learned in Chapter 1, circuit switching is highly inefficient for bursty data. Furthermore, standard GSM supports data rates only up to 9.6 kbps, which is intolerably slow for just about anything besides plain text. GPRS is an interim solution that provides more efficient packet-based data service at higher data rates (typically in the 40 kbps to 60 kbps range). GPRS service is provided by an underlying GSM network. However, unlike vanilla GSM, a mobile GPRS station can use more than one time slot within a given channel in an on-demand basis. With GPRS, a number of slots are set aside for data communications and allocated dynamically to the mobile stations as a function their instantaneous demands.

♦ **Enhanced Data Rates for Global Evolution (EDGE).** The main goal of EDGE is to increase the data rate capabilities of a GSM/GPRS network, that is, to better exploit the 200 KHz GSM channel with its eight-slot TDMA frames. This is done primarily by replacing GSM's modulation scheme with a more powerful scheme. In theory, EDGE can provide users with 384 kbps for data communications. An excellent overview of EDGE is [Ericsson 2004].

♦ **CDMA2000, Phase 1**. This 2.5G technology evolved from IS-95. It can provide packet-data services up to 144.4 kbps and sets the stage for 3G deployment of CDMA2000, Phase 2.

Third Generation (3G)

3G cellular systems are required to provide telephone service as well as data communications at significantly higher speeds than their 2G counterparts. In particular, 3G systems are mandated to provide:

♦ 144 kbps at driving speeds

♦ 384 kbps for outside stationary use or walking speeds

♦ 2 Mbps for indoors

There are two major (and competing) standards in the 3G arena:

♦ ***Universal Mobile Telecommunications Service (UMTS)***. UMTS is an evolution of GSM to support 3G capabilities. The UMTS network architecture borrows heavily from the established GSM network architecture. However, UMTS's radio access is significantly different from the FDMA/TDMA scheme used in GSM. Specifically, UMTS uses a CDMA technique called Direct Sequence Wideband CDMA (DS-WCDMA). Not surprisingly, since UMTS has its roots in GSM, UMTS is being broadly deployed in Europe

♦ ***CDMA-2000***. CDMA-2000 is an evolution of the IS-95 2G system and is backward compatible with IS-95. As you would expect from its name, it also uses CDMA as part of its air interface. CDMA-2000 is being deployed in North America and parts of Asia.

Fourth Generation (4G)

Now that we have examined both wireless LAN technology and the gamut of the cellular access technologies, let's take a step back and reflect on what we, as users, would ideally like for wireless Internet access. Here is a wish list that may come to mind:

♦ We would like ubiquitous wireless Internet access. Whether at home, in the office, in a car, in a café, or on a beach, we'd like to be able to access the Internet.

♦ As a function of our physical location and the speed at which we're moving, we'd like to be able to access the Internet at the highest possible rate. For example, if we're on a street corner where both 11 Mbps 802.11b and 384 kbps 3G access are available, we would like our system to automatically select 802.11b, the system that offers the highest bit rate at that time and place.

♦ As we roam throughout this heterogeneous environment, we are automatically and transparently switched from one access technology to another (for example, from 802.11 to 3G), depending on availability, without any user intervention.

♦ Of course, as we roam about, we want to maintain our ongoing TCP connections. Furthermore, we'd like the system to know where we are, so that new calls can continue to reach us as we move.

♦ We'd like the system to support voice and real-time video over IP, so that we can all wear Dick Tracy watches and video conference with our friends and colleagues, no matter where we are.

And of course we'd like this for free (or more realistically, at least at low cost). Although this may sound like a wireless nirvana, the good news is that most of the critical technology components are already available. It is really now an issue of integrating protocols and technologies to make this wish list a reality. These components include access technologies such as 802.11 and 3G, as well as mobility management protocols (see Sections 6.5, 6.6, and 6.7), encryption and authentication protocols (see Chapter 8), and the multimedia networking protocols (such as SIP for voice-over-IP, discussed in Chapter 7).

6.5   Mobility Management: Principles

Having now covered the *wireless* nature of the communication links in a wireless network, it's now time to turn our attention to the *mobility* that these wireless links enable. In the broadest sense, a mobile node is one that changes its point of attachment into the network over time. Because the term *mobility* has taken on many meanings in both the computer and telephony worlds, it will serve us well first to consider several dimensions of mobility in some detail.

♦ *From the network layer's standpoint, how mobile is a user?* A physically mobile user will present a very different set of challenges to the network layer, depending on how he or she moves between points of attachment to the network. At one end of the spectrum in Figure 6.16, a user may carry a laptop with a wireless network interface card around in a building. As we saw in Section 6.3.4, this user is *not* mobile from a network-layer perspective. Moreover, if the user associates with the same access point regardless of location, the user is not even mobile from the perspective of the link layer.

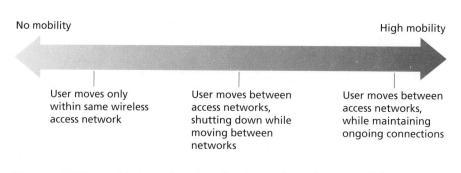

Figure 6.16 ♦ Various degrees of mobility, from the network layer's point of view

At the other end of the spectrum, consider the user zooming along the autobahn in a BMW at 150 kilometers per hour, passing through multiple wireless access networks and wanting to maintain an uninterrupted TCP connection to a remote application throughout the trip. This user is *definitely* mobile! In between these extremes is a user who takes a laptop from one location (e.g., office or dormitory) into another (e.g., coffeeshop, classroom) and wants to connect into the network in the new location. This user is also mobile (although less so than the BMW driver!) but does not need to maintain an ongoing connection while moving between points of attachment to the network. Figure 6.16 illustrates this spectrum of user mobility from the network layer's perspective.

♦ *How important is it for the mobile node's address to always remain the same?* With mobile telephony, your phone number—essentially the network-layer address of your phone—remains the same as you travel from one provider's mobile phone network to another. Must a laptop similarly maintain the same IP address while moving between IP networks?

The answer to this question will depend strongly on the applications being run. For the BMW driver who wants to maintain an uninterrupted TCP connection to a remote application while zipping along the autobahn, it would be convenient to maintain the same IP address. Recall from Chapter 3 that an Internet application needs to know the IP address and port number of the remote entity with which it is communicating. If a mobile entity is able to maintain its IP address as it moves, mobility becomes invisible from the application standpoint. There is great value to this transparency—an application need not be concerned with a potentially changing IP address, and the same application code serves mobile and nonmobile connections alike. We'll see in the following section that mobile IP provides this transparency, allowing a mobile node to maintain its permanent IP address while moving among networks.

On the other hand, a less glamorous mobile user might simply want to turn off an office laptop, bring that laptop home, power up, and work from home. If the laptop functions primarily as a client in client-server applications (e.g., send/read e-mail, browse the Web, Telnet to a remote host) from home, the particular IP address used by the laptop is not that important. In particular, one could get by fine with an address that is temporarily allocated to the laptop by the ISP serving the home. We saw in Section 5.4.3 that DHCP already provides this functionality.

♦ *What supporting wired infrastructure is available?* In all of our scenarios above, we've implicitly assumed that there is a fixed infrastructure to which the mobile user can connect, for example, the home's ISP network, the wireless access network in the office, or the wireless access networks lining the autobahn. What if no such infrastructure exists? If two users are within communication proximity of each other, can they establish a network connection in the absence of any other network-layer infrastructure? Ad hoc networking provides precisely these capabilities. This rapidly developing area is at the cutting edge of mobile networking research and is beyond the scope of this book. [Perkins 2000] and the IETF Mobile Ad Hoc Network (manet) working group Web pages [manet 2004] provide thorough treatments of the subject.

In order to illustrate the issues involved in allowing a mobile user to maintain ongoing connections while moving between networks, let's consider a human analogy. A twenty-something adult moving out of the family home becomes mobile, living in a series of dormitories and/or apartments, and often changing addresses. If an old friend wants to get in touch, how can that friend find the address of her mobile friend? One common way is to contact the family, since a mobile adult will often register his or her current address with the family (if for no other reason than so that the parents can send money to help pay the rent!). The family home, with its permanent address, becomes that one place that others can go as a first step in communicating with the mobile adult. Later communication from the friend may be either indirect (for example, with mail being sent first to the parents' home and then forwarded to the mobile adult) or direct (for example, with the friend using the address obtained from the parents to send mail directly to her mobile friend).

In a network setting, the permanent home of a mobile node (such as a laptop or PDA) is known as the **home network**, and the entity within the home network that performs the mobility management functions discussed below on behalf of the mobile node is known as the **home agent**. The network in which the mobile node is currently residing is known as the **foreign** (or **visited**) **network**, and the entity within the foreign network that helps the mobile node with the mobility management functions discussed below is known as a **foreign agent**. For mobile professionals, their home network might likely be their company network, while the visited network might be the network of a colleague they are visiting. A **correspondent** is the entity wishing to communicate with the mobile node. Figure 6.17 illustrates these concepts, as well as addressing concepts considered below. In Figure 6.17, note that agents are shown as being collocated with routers (e.g., as processes running on routers), but alternatively they could be executing on other hosts or servers in the network.

6.5.1 Addressing

We noted above that in order for user mobility to be transparent to network applications, it is desirable for a mobile node to keep its address as it moves from one network to another. When a mobile node is resident in a foreign network, all traffic addressed to the node's permanent address now needs to be routed to the foreign network. How can this be done? One option is for the foreign network to advertise to all other networks that the mobile node is resident in its network. This could be via the usual exchange of intradomain and interdomain routing information and would require few changes to the existing routing infrastructure. The foreign network could simply advertise to its neighbors that it has a highly specific route to the mobile node's permanent address (that is, essentially inform other networks that it

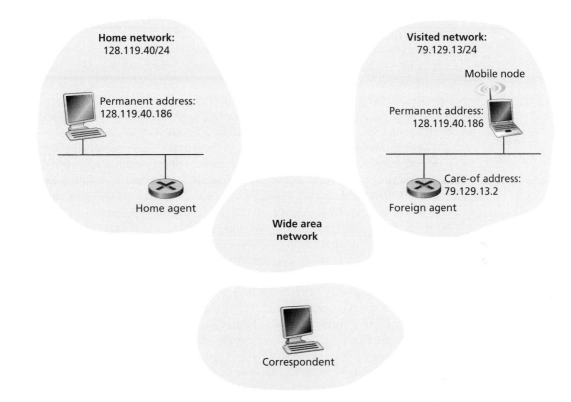

Figure 6.17 ♦ Initial elements of a mobile network architecture

has the correct path for routing datagrams to the mobile node's permanent address; see Section 4.4). These neighbors would then propagate this routing information throughout the network as part of the normal procedure of updating routing information and fowarding tables. When the mobile node leaves one foreign network and joins another, the new foreign network would advertise a new, highly specific route to the mobile node, and the old foreign network would withdraw its routing information regarding the mobile node.

This solves two problems at once, and it does so without making significant changes to the network-layer infrastructure. Other networks know the location of the mobile node, and it is easy to route datagrams to the mobile node, since the forwarding tables will direct datagrams to the foreign network. A significant drawback, however, is that of scalability. If mobility management were to be the responsibility of network routers, the routers would have to maintain forwarding table entries for potentially millions of mobile nodes, and update these entries as nodes move. Some additional drawbacks are explored in the problems at the end of this chapter.

An alternative approach (and one that has been adopted in practice) is to push mobility functionality from the network core to the network edge—a recurring theme in our study of Internet architecture. A natural way to do this is via the mobile node's home network. In much the same way that parents of the mobile twenty-something track their child's location, the home agent in the mobile node's home network can track the foreign network in which the mobile node resides. A protocol between the mobile node (or a foreign agent representing the mobile node) and the home agent will certainly be needed to update the mobile node's location.

Let's now consider the foreign agent in more detail. The conceptually simplest approach, shown in Figure 6.17, is to locate foreign agents at the edge routers in the foreign network. One role of the foreign agent is to create a so-called **care-of address (COA)** for the mobile node, with the network portion of the COA matching that of the foreign network. There are thus two addresses associated with a mobile mode, its **permanent address** (analogous to our mobile youth's family's home address) and its COA, sometimes known as a **foreign address** (analogous to the address of the house in which our mobile youth is currently residing). In the example in Figure 6.17, the permanent address of the mobile node is 128.119.40.186. When visiting network 79.129.13/24, the mobile node has a COA of 79.129.13.2. A second role of the foreign agent is to inform the home agent that the mobile node is resident in its (the foreign agent's) network and has the given COA. We'll see shortly that the COA will be used to "reroute" datagrams to the mobile node via its foreign agent.

Although we have separated the functionality of the mobile node and the foreign agent, it is worth noting that the mobile node can also assume the responsibilities of the foreign agent. For example, the mobile node could obtain a COA in the foreign network (for example, using a protocol such as DHCP) and itself inform the home agent of its COA.

6.5.2 Routing to a Mobile Node

We have now seen how a mobile node obtains a COA and how the home agent can be informed of that address. But having the home agent know the COA solves only part of the problem. How should datagrams be addressed and forwarded to the mobile node? Since only the home agent (and not network-wide routers) knows the location of the mobile node, it will no longer suffice to simply address a datagram to the mobile node's permanent address and send it into the network-layer infrastructure. Something more must be done. Two approaches can be identified, which we will refer to as indirect and direct routing.

Indirect Routing to a Mobile Node

Let's first consider a correspondent that wants to send a datagram to a mobile node. In the **indirect routing** approach, the correspondent simply addresses the datagram to the mobile node's permanent address and sends the datagram into the network, blissfully unaware of whether the mobile node is resident in its home network or is visiting a foreign network; mobility is thus completely transparent to the correspondent. Such datagrams are first routed, as usual, to the mobile node's home network. This is illustrated in step 1 in Figure 6.18.

Let's now turn our attention to the home agent. In addition to being responsible for interacting with a foreign agent to track the mobile node's COA, the home agent has another very important function. Its second job is to be on the lookout for arriving datagrams addressed to nodes whose home network is that of the home agent but that are currently resident in a foreign network. The home agent intercepts these datagrams and then forwards them to a mobile node in a two-step process. The datagram is first forwarded to the foreign agent, using the mobile node's COA (step 2 in Figure 6.18), and then forwarded from the foreign agent to the mobile node (step 3 in Figure 6.18).

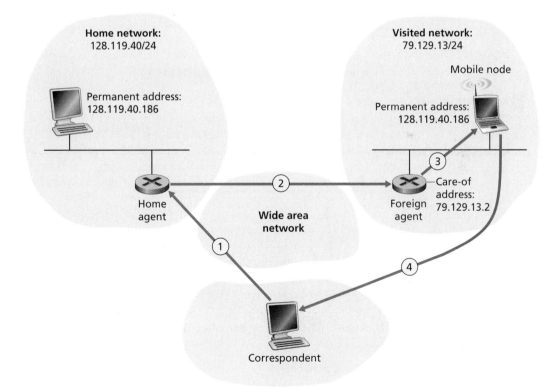

Figure 6.18 ♦ Indirect forwarding to a mobile node

It is instructive to consider this rerouting in more detail. The home agent will need to address the datagram using the mobile node's COA, so that the network layer will route the datagram to the foreign network. On the other hand, it is desirable to leave the correspondent's datagram intact, since the application receiving the datagram should be unaware that the datagram was forwarded via the home agent. Both goals can be satisfied by having the home agent **encapsulate** the correspondent's original complete datagram within a new (larger) datagram. This larger datagram is addressed and delivered to the mobile node's COA. The foreign agent, who "owns" the COA will receive and decapsulate the datagram, that is, remove the correspondent's original datagram from within the larger encapsulating datagram and forward (step 3 in Figure 6.18) the original datagram to the mobile node. Figure 6.19 shows a correspondent's original datagram being sent to the home network, an encapsulated datagram being sent to the foreign agent, and the original datagram being delivered to the mobile node. The sharp reader will note that the encapsulation/decapsulation described here is identical to the notion of tunneling, discussed in Chapter 4 in the context of IP multicast and IPv6.

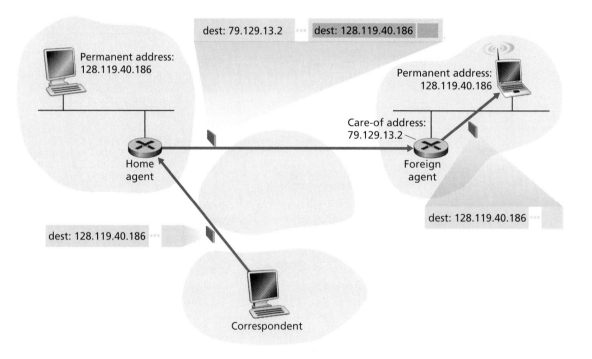

Figure 6.19 ♦ Encapsulation and decapsulation

Let's next consider how a mobile node sends datagrams to a correspondent. This is quite simple, as the mobile node can address its datagram *directly* to the correspondent (using its own permanent address as the source address, and the correspondent's address as the destination address). Since the mobile node knows the correspondent's address, there is no need to route the datagram back through the home agent. This is shown as step 4 in Figure 6.18.

Let's summarize our discussion of indirect routing by listing the new network-layer functionality required to support mobility.

♦ *A mobile-node–to–foreign-agent protocol.* The mobile node will register with the foreign agent when attaching to the foreign network. Similarly, a mobile node will deregister with the foreign agent when it leaves the foreign network.

♦ *A foreign-agent–to–home-agent registration protocol.* The foreign agent will register the mobile node's COA with the home agent. A foreign agent need not explicitly deregister a COA when a mobile node leaves its network, because the subsequent registration of a new COA, when the mobile node moves to a new network, will take care of this.

♦ *A home-agent datagram encapsulation protocol.* Encapsulation and forwarding of the correspondent's original datagram within a datagram addressed to the COA.

♦ *A foreign-agent decapsulation protocol.* Extraction of the correspondent's original datagram from the encapsulating datagram, and the forwarding of the original datagram to the mobile node.

The discussion above provides all the pieces—foreign agents, the home agent, and indirect forwarding—needed for a mobile node to maintain an ongoing connection while moving among networks. As an example of how these pieces fit together, assume the mobile node is attached to foreign network A, has registered a COA in network A with its home agent, and is receiving datagrams that are being indirectly routed through its home agent. The mobile node now moves to foreign network B and registers with the foreign agent in network B, which informs the home agent of the mobile node's new COA. From this point on, the home agent will reroute datagrams to foreign network B. As far as a correspondent is concerned, mobility is transparent—datagrams are routed via the same home agent both before and after the move. As far as the home agent is concerned, there is no disruption in the flow of datagrams—arriving datagrams are first forwarded to foreign network A; after the change in COA, datagrams are forwarded to foreign network B. But will the mobile node see an interrupted flow of datagrams as it moves between networks? As long as the time between the mobile node's disconnection from network A (at which point it can no longer receive datagrams via A) and its attachment to network B (at which point it will register a new COA with its home agent) is small, few datagrams will be lost. Recall from Chapter 3 that end-to-end connections can suffer datagram loss due to network congestion. Hence occasional datagram loss within a connection when a node moves between networks is by no means a catastrophic problem. If loss-free communication is required, upper-layer mechanisms will recover from datagram loss, whether such loss results from network congestion or from user mobility.

An indirect routing approach is used in the mobile IP standard [RFC 3220], as discussed in the Section 6.6.

Direct Routing to a Mobile Node

The indirect routing approach illustrated in Figure 6.18 suffers from an inefficiency known as the **triangle routing problem**—datagrams addressed to the mobile node must be routed first to the home agent and then to the foreign network, even when a much more efficient route exists between the correspondent and the mobile node. In the worst case, imagine a mobile user who is visiting the foreign network of a colleague. The two are sitting side by side and exchanging data over the network. Datagrams from the correspondent (in this case the colleague of the visitor) are routed to the mobile user's home agent and then back again to the foreign network!

Direct routing overcomes the inefficiency of triangle routing, but does so at the cost of additional complexity. In the direct routing approach, a **correspondent agent** in the correspondent's network first learns the COA of the mobile node. This can be done by having the correspondent agent query the home agent, assuming that (as in the case of indirect routing), the mobile node has an up-to-date value for its COA registered with its home agent). It is also possible for the correspondent itself to perform the function of the correspondent agent, just as a mobile node could perform the function of the foreign agent.) This is shown as steps 1 and 2 in Figure 6.20. The correspondent agent then tunnels datagrams directly to the mobile node's COA, in a manner analogous to the tunneling performed by the home agent, steps 3 and 4 in Figure 6.20.

While direct routing overcomes the triangle routing problem, it introduces two important additional challenges:

♦ A *mobile-user location protocol* is needed for the correspondent agent to query the home agent to obtain the mobile node's COA (steps 1 and 2 in Figure 6.20).

♦ When the mobile node moves from one foreign network to another, how will data now be forwarded to the new foreign network? In the case of indirect routing, this problem was easily solved by updating the COA maintained by the home agent. However, with direct routing, the home agent is queried for the COA by the correspondent agent only once, at the beginning of the session. Thus, updating the COA at the home agent, while necessary, will not be enough to solve the problem of routing data to the mobile node's new foreign network.

One solution would be to create a new protocol to notify the correspondent of the changing COA. An alternate solution, and one that we'll see is adopted in

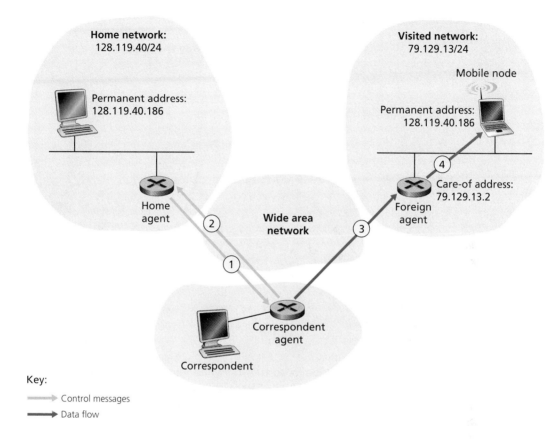

Figure 6.20 ◆ Direct routing to a mobile user

practice in GSM networks, works as follows. Suppose data is currently being for-warded to the mobile node in the foreign network where the mobile node was located when the session first started (step 1 in Figure 6.21). We'll identify the for-eign agent in that foreign network where the mobile node was first found as the **anchor foreign agent**. When the mobile node moves to a new foreign network (step 2 in Figure 6.21), the mobile node registers with the new foreign agent (step 3), and the new foreign agent provides the anchor foreign agent with the mobile node's new COA (step 4). When the anchor foreign agent receives an encapsulated datagram for a departed mobile node it can then re-encapsulate the datagram and forward it to the mobile node (step 5) using the new COA. If the mobile node later moves yet again to a new foreign network, the foreign agent in that new visited network would then contact the anchor foreign agent in order to set up forwarding to this new foreign network.

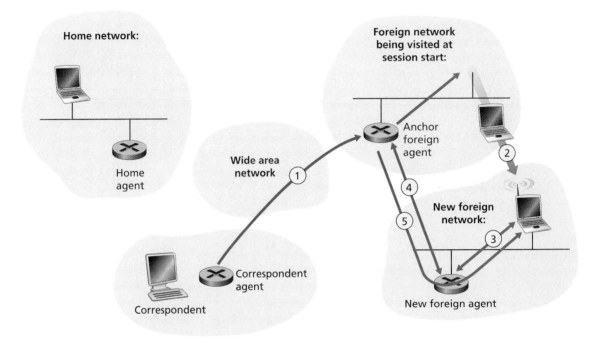

Figure 6.21 ◆ Mobile transfer between networks with direct routing

6.6 Mobile IP

The Internet architecture and protocols for supporting mobility, collectively known as mobile IP, are defined primarily in RFC 3220. Mobile IP is a flexible standard, supporting many different modes of operation, for example, operation with or without a foreign agent, multiple ways for agents and mobile nodes to discover each other, use of single or multiple COAs, and multiple forms of encapsulation. As such, mobile IP is a complex standard, and would require an entire book to describe in detail; indeed one such book is [Perkins 1998b]. Our modest goal here is to provide an overview of the most important aspects of mobile IP and to illustrate its use in a few common-case scenarios.

The mobile IP architecture contains many of the elements we have considered above, including the concepts of home agents, foreign agents, care-of addresses, and encapsulation/decapsulation. The current standard [RFC 3220] specifies the use of indirect routing to the mobile node.

The mobile IP standard consists of three main pieces:

♦ *Agent discovery.* Mobile IP defines the protocols used by a home or foreign agent to advertise its services to mobile nodes, and protocols for mobile nodes to solicit the services of a foreign or home agent.

♦ *Registration with the home agent.* Mobile IP defines the protocols used by the mobile node and/or foreign agent to register and deregister COAs with a mobile node's home agent.

♦ *Indirect routing of datagrams.* The standard also defines the manner in which datagrams are forwarded to mobile nodes by a home agent, including rules for forwarding datagrams, rules for handling error conditions, and several forms of encapsulation [RFC 2003, RFC 2004].

Security considerations are prominent throughout the mobile IP standard. For example, authentication of a mobile node is clearly needed to ensure that a malicious user does not register a bogus care-of address with a home agent, which could cause all datagrams addressed to an IP address to be redirected to the malicious user. Mobile IP achieves security using many of the mechanisms that we will examine in Chapter 8, so we will not address security considerations in our discussion below.

Agent Discovery

A mobile IP node arriving to a new network, whether attaching to a foreign network or returning to its home network, must learn the identity of the corresponding foreign or home agent. Indeed it is the discovery of a new foreign agent, with a new network address, that allows the network layer in a mobile node to learn that it has moved into a new foreign network. This process is known as **agent discovery**. Agent discovery can be accomplished in one of two ways: via agent advertisement or via agent solicitation.

With **agent advertisement**, a foreign or home agent advertises its services using an extension to the existing router discovery protocol [RFC 1256]. The agent periodically broadcasts an ICMP message with a type field of 9 (router discovery) on all links to which it is connected. The router discovery message contains the IP address of the router (that is, the agent), thus allowing a mobile node to learn the agent's IP address. The router discovery message also contains a mobility agent advertisement extension that contains additional information needed by the mobile node. Among the more important fields in the extension are the following:

♦ *Home agent bit (H).* Indicates that the agent is a home agent for the network in which it resides.

♦ *Foreign agent bit (F).* Indicates that the agent is a foreign agent for the network in which it resides.

♦ *Registration required bit (R).* Indicates that a mobile user in this network *must* register with a foreign agent. In particular, a mobile user cannot obtain a care-of address in the foreign network (for example, using DHCP) and assume the functionality of the foreign agent for itself, without registering with the foreign agent.

♦ *M, G encapsulation bits.* Indicate whether a form of encapsulation other than IP-in-IP encapsulation will be used.

♦ *Care-of address (COA) fields.* A list of one or more care-of addresses provided by the foreign agent. In our example below, the COA will be associated with the foreign agent, who will receive datagrams sent to the COA and then forward them to the appropriate mobile node. The mobile user will select one of these addresses as its COA when registering with its home agent.

Figure 6.22 illustrates some of the key fields in the agent advertisement message.

With **agent solicitation**, a mobile node wanting to learn about agents without waiting to receive an agent advertisement can broadcast an agent solicitation message, which is simply an ICMP message with type value 10. An agent receiving the solicitation will unicast an agent advertisement directly to the mobile node, which can then proceed as if it had received an unsolicited advertisement.

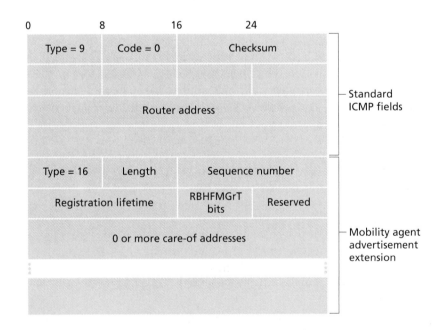

Figure 6.22 ♦ ICMP router discovery message with mobility agent advertisement extension

Registration with the Home Agent

Once a mobile IP node has received a COA, that address must be registered with the home agent. This can be done either via the foreign agent (who then registers the COA with the home agent) or directly by the mobile IP node itself. We consider the former case below. Four steps are involved.

1. Following the receipt of a foreign agent advertisement, a mobile node sends a mobile IP registration message to the foreign agent. The registration message is carried within a UDP datagram and sent to port 434. The registration message carries a COA advertised by the foreign agent, the address of the home agent (HA), the permanent address of the mobile node (MA), the requested lifetime of the registration, and a 64-bit registration identification. The requested registration lifetime is the number of seconds that the registration is to be valid. If the registration is not renewed at the home agent within the specified lifetime, the registration will become invalid. The registration identifier acts like a sequence number and serves to match a received registration reply with a registration request, as discussed below.

2. The foreign agent receives the registration message and records the mobile node's permanent IP address. The foreign agent now knows that it should be looking for datagrams containing an encapsulated datagram whose destination address matches the permanent address of the mobile node. The foreign agent then sends a mobile IP registration message (again, within a UDP datagram) to port 434 of the home agent. The message contains the COA, HA, MA, encapsulation format requested, requested registration lifetime, and registration identification.

3. The home agent receives the registration request and checks for authenticity and correctness. The home agent binds the mobile node's permanent IP address with the COA; in the future, datagrams arriving at the home agent and addressed to the mobile node will now be encapsulated and tunneled to the COA. The home agent sends a mobile IP registration reply containing the HA, MA, actual registration lifetime, and the registration identification of the request that is being satisfied with this reply.

4. The foreign agent receives the registration reply and then forwards it to the mobile node.

At this point registration is complete, and the mobile node can receive datagrams sent to its permanent address. Figure 6.23 illustrates these steps. Note that the home agent specifies a lifetime that is smaller than the lifetime requested by the mobile node.

A foreign agent need not explicitly deregister a COA when a mobile node leaves its network. This will occur automatically, when the mobile node moves to a new network (whether another foreign network or its home network) and registers a new COA.

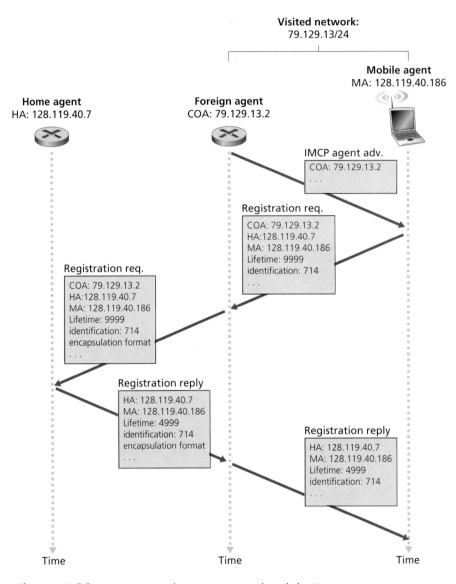

Figure 6.23 ◆ Agent advertisement and mobile IP registration

The mobile IP standard allows many additional scenarios and capabilities in addition to those described above. The interested reader should consult [Perkins 1998b; RFC 3220].

6.7 Managing Mobility in Cellular Networks

Having examined how mobility is managed in IP networks, let's now turn our attention to networks with an even longer history of supporting mobility—cellular telephony networks. Whereas we focused on the first-hop wireless link in cellular networks in Section 6.4, we'll focus here on mobility, using the GSM cellular network architecture [Goodman 1997; Mouly 1992; Scourias 1997; Kaaranen 2001, Korhonen 2002] as our case study, since it is a mature and widely deployed technology. As in the case of mobile IP, we'll see that a number of the fundamental principles we identified in Section 6.5 are embodied in GSM's network architecture.

Like mobile IP, GSM adopts an indirect routing approach (see Section 6.5.2), first routing the correspondent's call to the mobile's home network and from there to the visited network. In GSM terminology, the mobile's home network is referred to as the mobile's **home public land mobile network (home PLMN)**. Since the PLMN acronym is a bit of a mouthful, and mindful of our quest to avoid an alphabet soup of acronyms, we'll refer to the GSM home PLMN simply as the **home network**. The home network is the cellular provider with which the mobile user has a subscription (i.e., the provider that bills the user for monthly cellular service). The visited PLMN, which we'll refer to simply as the **visited network**, is the network in which the mobile is currently residing

As in the case of mobile IP, the responsibilities of the home and visited networks are quite different.

♦ The home network maintains a database known as the **home location register (HLR)**, which contains the permanent cell phone number and subscriber profile information for each of its subscribers. Importantly, the HLR also contains information about the current locations of these subscribers. That is, if a mobile user is currently roaming in another provider's cellular network, the HLR contains enough information to obtain (via a process we'll describe shortly) an address in the visited network to which a call to the mobile user should be routed. As we'll see, a special switch in the home network, known as the **Gateway Mobile services Switching Center (GMSC)** is contacted by a correspondent when a call is placed to a mobile user. Again, in our quest to avoid an alphabet soup of acronyms, we'll refer to the GMSC here by a more descriptive term, **home MSC**.

♦ The visited network maintains a database known as the **visitor location register (VLR)**. The VLR contains an entry for each mobile user that is *currently* in the portion of the network served by the VLR. VLR entries thus come and go as mobile users enter and leave the network. A VLR is usually co-located with the mobile switching center (MSC) that coordinates the setup of a call to and from the visited network.

In practice, a provider's cellular network will serve as a home network for its subscribers and as a visited network for mobile users whose subscription is with a different cellular provider.

6.7.1 Routing Calls to a Mobile User

We're now in a position to describe how a call is placed to a mobile GSM user in a visited network. We'll consider a simple example below; more complex scenarios are described in [Mouly 1992]. The steps, as illustrated in Figure 6.24, are as follows:

1. The correspondent dials the mobile user's phone number. This number itself does not refer to a particular telephone line or location (after all, the phone number is fixed and the user is mobile!). The leading digits in the number are sufficient to globally identify the mobile's home network. The call is routed from the correspondent through the public switched telephone network to the home MSC in the mobile's home network. This is the first leg of the call.
2. The home MSC receives the call and interrogates the HLR to determine the location of the mobile user. In the simplest case, the HLR returns the **mobile**

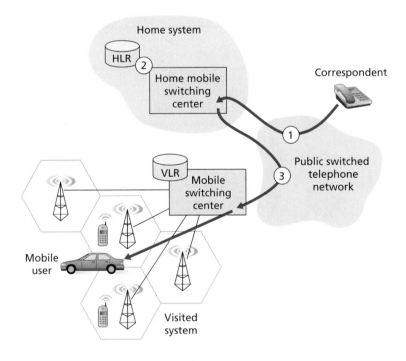

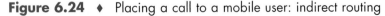

Figure 6.24 ♦ Placing a call to a mobile user: indirect routing

station roaming number (MSRN), which we will refer to as the **roaming number**. Note that this number is different from the mobile's permanent phone number, which is associated with the mobile's home network. The roaming number is ephemeral: It is temporarily assigned to a mobile when it enters a visited network. The roaming number serves a role similar to that of the care-of-address in mobile IP and, like the COA, is invisible to the correspondent and the mobile. If HLR does not have the roaming number, it returns the address of the VLR in the visited network. In this case (not shown in Figure 6.24), the home MSC will need to query the VLR to obtain the roaming number of the mobile node. But how does the HLR get the roaming number or the VLR address in the first place? What happens to these values when the mobile user moves to another visited network? We'll consider these important questions shortly.

3. Given the roaming number, the home MSC sets up the second leg of the call through the network to the MSC in the visited network. The call is completed, being routed from the correspondent to the home MSC, and from there to the visited MSC, and from there to the base station serving the mobile user.

An unresolved question in step 2 is how the HLR obtains information about the location of the mobile user. When a mobile telephone is switched on or enters a part of a visited network that is covered by a new VLR, the mobile must register with the visited network. This is done through the exchange of signaling messages between the mobile and the VLR. The visited VLR, in turn, sends a location update request message to the mobile's HLR. This message informs the HLR of either the roaming number at which the mobile can be contacted, or the address of the VLR (which can then later be queried to obtain the mobile number). As part of this exchange, the VLR also obtains subscriber information from the HLR about the mobile and determines what services (if any) should be accorded the mobile user by the visited network.

6.7.2 Handoffs in GSM

A **handoff** occurs when a mobile station changes its association from one base station to another during a call. As shown in Figure 6.25, a mobile's call is initially (before handoff) routed to the mobile through one base station (which we'll refer to as the old base station), and after handoff is routed to the mobile through another base station (which we'll refer to as the new base station). Note that a handoff between base stations results not only in the mobile transmitting/receiving to/from a new base station, but also in the rerouting of the ongoing call from a switching point within the network to the new base station. Let's initially assume that the old and new base stations share the same MSC, and that the rerouting occurs at this MSC.

There may be several reasons for handoff to occur, including (1) the signal between the current base station and the mobile may have deteriorated to such an extent that the call is in danger of being dropped, and (2) a cell may have become a

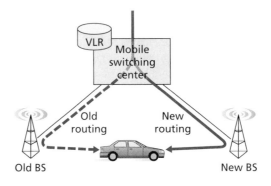

Figure 6.25   ◆   Handoff scenario between base stations with a common MSC

overloaded, handling a large number of calls. This congestion may be alleviated by handing off mobiles to less congested nearby cells.

While it is associated with a base station, a mobile periodically measures the strength of a beacon signal from its current base station as well as beacon signals from nearby base stations that it can "hear." These measurements are reported once or twice a second to the mobile's current base station. Handoff in GSM is initiated by the old base station based on these measurements, the current loads of mobiles in nearby cells, and other factors [Mouly 1992]. The GSM standard does not specify the specific algorithm to be used by a base station to determine whether or not to perform handoff.

Figure 6.26 illustrates the steps involved when a base station does decide to handoff a mobile user:

1. The old base station (BS) informs the visited MSC that a handoff is to be performed and the BS (or possible set of BSs) to which the mobile is to be handed off.
2. The visited MSC initiates path setup to the new BS, allocating the resources need to carry the rerouted call, and signaling the new BS that a handoff is about to occur.
3. The new BS allocates and activates a radio channel for use by the mobile.
4. The new BS signals back to the visited MSC and the old BS that the visited-MSC-to-new-BS path has been established and that the mobile should be informed of the impending handoff. The new BS provides all of the information that the mobile will need to associate with the new BS.
5. The mobile is informed that it should perform a handoff. Note that up until this point, the mobile has been blissfully unaware that the network has been laying the groundwork (e.g., allocating a channel in the new BS and allocating a path from the visited MSC to the new BS) for a handoff.

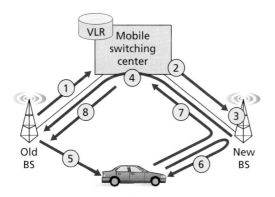

Figure 6.26 ◆ Steps in accomplishing a handoff between base stations with a common MSC

6. The mobile and the new BS exchange one or more messages to fully activate the new channel in the new BS.
7. The mobile sends a handoff complete message to the new BS, which is forwarded up to the visited MSC. The visited MSC then reroutes the on-going call to the mobile via the new BS.
8. The resources allocated along the path to the old BS are then released.

Let's conclude our discussion of handoff by considering what happens when the mobile moves to a BS that is associated with a *different* MSC than the old BS, and what happens when this inter-MSC handoff occurs more than once. As shown in Figure 6.27, GSM defines the notion of an **anchor MSC**. The anchor MSC is the MSC visited by the mobile when a call first begins; the anchor MSC thus remains unchanged during the call. Throughout the call's duration and regardless of the number of inter-MSC transfers performed by the mobile, the call is routed from the home MSC to the anchor MSC, and then from the anchor MSC to the visited MSC where the mobile is currently located. When a mobile moves from the coverage area of one MSC to another, the ongoing call is rerouted from the anchor MSC to the new visited MSC containing the new base station. Thus, at all times there are at most three MSCs (the home MSC, the anchor MSC, and the visited MSC) between the correspondent and the mobile. Figure 6.27 illustrates the routing of a call among the MSCs visited by a mobile user.

Rather than maintaining a single MSC-hop from the anchor MSC to the current MSC, an alternative approach would have been to simply chain the MSCs visited by the mobile, having an old MSC forward the ongoing call to the new MSC each time the mobile moves to a new MSC. Such MSC-chaining can in fact occur in IS-41 cellular networks, with an optional path minimization step to remove MSCs between the anchor MSC and the current visited MSC [Lin 2001].

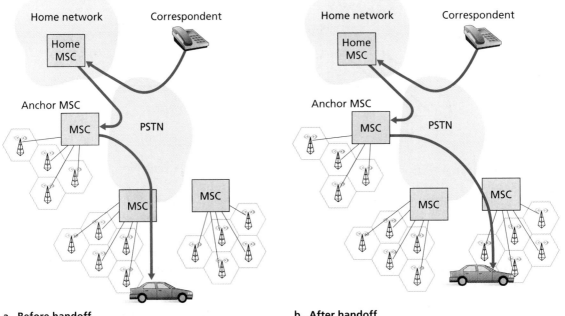

a. Before handoff

b. After handoff

Figure 6.27 ♦ Rerouting via the anchor MSC

Let's wrap up our discussion of GSM mobility management with a comparison of mobility management in GSM and Mobile IP. The comparison in Table 6.2 indicates that although IP and cellular networks are fundamentally different in many ways, they share a surprising a number of common functional elements and overall approaches in handling mobility.

6.8 Wireless and Mobility: Impact on Higher-layer Protocols

In this chapter, we've seen that wireless networks differ significantly from their wired counterparts at both the link layer (as a result wireless channel characteristics such as fading, multipath, and hidden terminals) and at the network layer (as a result of mobile users who change their points of attachment to the network). But are there important differences at the transport and application layers? It's tempting to think that these differences will be minor, since the network layer provides the same best-effort delivery service model to upper layers in both wired and wireless networks.

GSM element	Comment on GSM element	Mobile IP element
Home system	Network to which the mobile user's permanent phone number belongs	Home network
Gateway mobile switching center or simply home MSC, Home location register (HLR)	Home MSC: point of contact to obtain routable address of mobile user. HLR: database in home system containing permanent phone number, profile information, current location of mobile user, subscription information	Home agent
Visited system	Network other than home system where mobile user is currently residing	Visited network
Visited mobile services switching center, Visitor location record (VLR)	Visited MSC: responsible for setting up calls to/from mobile nodes in cells associated with MSC. VLR: temporary database entry in visited system, containing subscription information for each visiting mobile user	Foreign agent
Mobile station roaming number (MSRN) or simply roaming number	Routable address for telephone call segment between home MSC and visited MSC, visible to neither the mobile nor the correspondent.	Care-of-address

Table 6.2 ♦ Commonalities between mobile IP and GSM mobility

Similarly, if protocols such as TCP or UDP are used to provide transport-layer services to applications in both wired and wireless networks, then the application layer should remain unchanged as well. In one sense our intuition is right—TCP and UDP can (and do) operate in networks with wireless links. On the other hand, transport protocols in general, and TCP in particular, can sometimes have very different performance in wired and wireless networks, and it is here, in terms of performance, that differences are manifested. Let's see why.

Recall that TCP retransmits a segment that is either lost or corrupted on the path between sender and receiver. In the case of mobile users, loss can result from either network congestion (router buffer overflow) or from handoff (e.g., from delays in rerouting segments to a mobile's new point-of-attachment to the network). In all cases, TCP's receiver-to-sender ACK indicates only that a segment was not received intact; the sender is unaware of whether the segment was lost due to congestion, during handoff, or due to detected bit errors. In all cases, the sender's response is the same—to retransmit the segment. TCP's congestion control response is *also* the same in all cases—TCP decreases its congestion window, as discussed in Section 3.7. By unconditionally decreasing its congestion window, TCP implicitly assumes that segment loss results from congestion rather than corruption or handoff. We saw in Section 6.2 that bit errors are much more common in wireless networks than in wired networks. When such bit errors occur or when handoff loss occurs, there's really no reason for the TCP sender to decrease its congestion window (and thus decrease its sending rate). Indeed, it may well be the case that router buffers are empty and packets are flowing along the end-end path unimpeded by congestion.

Researchers realized in the early to mid 1990s that given high bit-error rates on wireless links and the possibility of handoff loss, TCP's congestion control response could be problematic in a wireless setting. Two broad classes of approaches are possible for dealing with this problem [Balakrishnan 1995]:

♦ *Local recovery.* The goal of local recovery approaches is to recover from bit errors when and where (e.g., at the wireless link) they occur. This includes (1) protocols that recover from loss or corruption at the link layer (e.g., the 802.11 ARQ protocol we studied in Section 6.3, or more sophisticated approaches that use both ARQ and FEC [Ayanoglu 1995]); (2) transport-layer protocols that split a TCP connection into two segments, one from the source to the wireless link, and one from the wireless link to the destination [Bakre 1995; Brown 1997]; and (3) TCP-aware link-layer protocols [Balakrishnan 1995; Liu 2002].

♦ *TCP sender awareness of wireless links.* In the local recovery approaches, the TCP sender is blissfully unaware that its segments are traversing a wireless link. An alternative approach is for the TCP sender and receiver to be aware of the existence of a wireless link, to distinguish between congestive losses occurring in the wired network and corruption/loss occurring at the wireless link, and to invoke congestion control only in response to congestive wired-network losses. [Balakrishnan 1995] investigates various types of TCP, assuming that end systems can make this distinction. [Wei 2004] investigates techniques for distinguishing between losses on the wired and wireless segments of an end-end path.

Our treatment of TCP over wireless links has been necessarily brief here. We encourage you to consult the references for details of this ongoing area of research.

Having considered transport layer protocols, let us next consider the effect of wireless and mobility on application-layer protocols. Here, an important consideration is that wireless links often have relatively low bandwidths, as we saw in Figure 6.2. As a result, applications that operate over wireless links, particularly over cellular wireless links, must treat bandwidth as a scare commodity. For example, a Web server serving content to a Web browser executing on 3G phone will likely not be able to provide the same image-rich content that it gives to a browser operating over a wired connection. Although wireless links do provide challenges at the application layer, the mobility they enable also makes possible a rich set of location-aware and context-aware applications [Chen 2000]. More generally, wireless and mobile networks will play a key role in realizing the ubiquitous computing environments of the future [Weiser 1991]. It's fair to say that we've only seen the tip of the iceberg when it comes to impact of wireless and mobile networks on networked applications and their protocols!

6.9 Summary

Wireless and mobile networks have revolutionized telephony and are having an increasingly profound impact in the world of computer networks as well. With their anytime, anywhere, untethered access into the global network infrastructure, they are not only making network access more ubiquitous, they are also enabling an exciting new set of location-dependent services. Given the growing importance of wireless and networks, this chapter has focused on the principles, common link technologies, and network architectures for supporting wireless and mobile communication.

We began this chapter with an introduction to wireless and mobile networks, drawing an important distinction between the challenges posed by the *wireless* nature of the communication links in such networks, and by the *mobility* that these wireless links enable. This allowed us to better isolate, identify, and master the key concepts in each area. We focused first on wireless communication, considering the characteristics of a wireless link in Section 6.2. In Sections 6.3 and 6.4, we examined the link-level aspects of the IEEE 802.11 (Wi-Fi) wireless LAN standard, and cellular Internet access. We then turned our attention to the issue of mobility. In Section 6.5 we identified several forms of mobility, with points along this spectrum posing different challenges and admitting different solutions. We considered the problems of locating and routing to a mobile user, as well as approaches for handing off the mobile user who dynamically moves from one point of attachment to the network to another. We examined how these issues were addressed in the mobile IP standard and in GSM, in Sections 6.6 and 6.7, respectively. Finally, we considered the impact of wireless links and mobility on transport-layer protocols and networked applications in Section 6.8.

Although we have devoted an entire chapter to the study of wireless and mobile networks, an entire book (or more) would be required to fully explore this exciting and rapidly expanding field. We encourage you to delve more deeply into this field by consulting the many references provided in this chapter.

Homework Problems and Questions

Chapter 6 • Review Questions

1. Describe the role of the beacon frames in 802.11.

2. Discuss the methods that are available to authenticate users for 802.11 networks.

3. True or false: Before a 802.11 station transmits a data frame, it must first send an RTS frame and receive a corresponding CTS frame.

4. Why are acknowledgments used in 802.11 but not in wired Ethernet?

5. True or false: Ethernet and 802.11 use the same frame structure.

6. Describe how the RTS threshold works.

7. Suppose the IEEE 802.11 RTS and CTS frames were as long as the standard DATA and ACK frames. Would there be any advantage to using the CTS and RTS frames? Why or why not?

8. Section 6.3.4 discusses 802.11 mobility, in which a wireless station moves from one BSS to another within the same subnet. When the APs are interconnected with a switch, an AP may need to send a frame with a spoofed MAC address to get the switch to forward frames properly. Why?

9. We learned in Section 6.3.2 that there two major 3G standards: UMTS and CDMA-2000. These two standards each owe their lineage to which 2G and 2.5G standards?

Problems

1. Consider the single-sender CDMA example in Figure 6.4. What would be the sender's output (for the 2 data bits shown) if the sender's CDMA code were $(1, -1, 1, -1, 1, -1, 1, -1)$?

2. Consider sender 2 in Figure 6.5. What is the sender's output to the channel (before it is added to the signal from sender 1), $Z_{i,m}^2$?

3. Suppose that the receiver in Figure 6.5 wanted to receive the data being sent by sender 2. Show (by calculation) that the receiver is indeed able to recover sender 2's data from the aggregate channel signal by using sender 2's code.

4. Suppose there are two ISPs providing Wi-Fi access in a particular café, with each ISP operating its own AP and having its own IP address block.

   a. Further suppose that by accident, each ISP has configured its AP to operate over channel 11. Will the 802.11 protocol completely break down in this situation? Discuss what happens when two stations, each associated with a different ISP, attempt to transmit at the same time.

   b. Now suppose that one AP operates over channel 1 and the other over channel 11.

5. In step 4 of the CSMA/CA protocol, a station that successfully transmits a frame begins the CSMA/CA protocol for a second frame at step 2, rather than at step 1. What rationale might the designers of CSMA/CA have had in mind by having such a station not transmit the second frame immediately (if the channel is sensed idle)?

6. Suppose an 802.11b station is configured to always reserve the channel with the RTS/CTS sequence. Suppose this station suddenly wants to transmit 1,000

bytes of data, and all other stations are idle at this time. As a function of SIFS and DIFS, and ignoring propagation delay and assuming no bit errors, calculate the time required to transmit the frame and receive the acknowledgment.

7. In Section 6.5, one proposed solution that allowed mobile users to maintain their IP addresses as they moved among foreign networks was to have a foreign network advertise a highly specific route to the mobile user and use the existing routing infrastructure to propagate this information throughout the network. We identified scalability as one concern. Suppose that when a mobile user moves from one network to another, the new foreign network advertises a specific route to the mobile user, and the old foreign network withdraws its route. Consider how routing information propagates in a distance vector algorithm (particularly for the case of interdomain routing among networks that span the globe).

   a. Will other routers be able to route datagrams immediately to the new foreign network as soon as the foreign network begins advertising its route?

   b. Is it possible for different routers to believe that different foreign networks contain the mobile user?

   c. Discuss the timescale over which other routers in the network will eventually learn the path to the mobile users.

8. Suppose the correspondent in Figure 6.17 were mobile. Sketch the additional network-layer infrastructure that would be needed to route the datagram from the original mobile user to the (now mobile) correspondent. Show the structure of the datagram(s) between the original mobile user and the (now mobile) correspondent, as in Figure 6.18.

9. In mobile IP, what effect will mobility have on end-to-end delays of datagrams between the source and destination?

10. Consider the chaining example discussed at the end of Section 6.7.2. Suppose a mobile user visits foreign networks A, B, and C, and that a correspondent begins a connection to the mobile user when it is resident in foreign network A. List the sequence of messages between foreign agents, and between foreign agents and the home agent as the mobile user moves from network A to network B to network C. Next, suppose chaining is not performed, and the correspondent (as well as the home agent) must be explicitly notified of the changes in the mobile user's care-of address. List the sequence of messages that would need to be exchanged in this second scenario.

11. Consider two mobile nodes in a foreign network having a foreign agent. Is it possible for the two mobile nodes to use the same care-of address in mobile IP? Explain your answer.

12. In our discussion of how the VLR updated the HLR with information about the mobiles current location, what are the advantages and disadvantages of providing the MSRN as opposed to the address of the VLR to the HLR?

 Discussion Questions

1. List five products on the market today that provide a Bluetooth or 802.15 interface.

2. Is the 3G wireless service available in your region? How is it priced? What applications are being supported?

3. As a user of IEEE 802.11, what kinds of problems have you observed? How can 802.11 designs evolve to overcome these problems?

Ethereal Lab

In the companion Web site for this textbook, http://www.awl.com/kurose-ross, you'll find an Ethereal lab for this chapter that captures and studies the 802.11 frames exchanged between a wireless laptop and an access point.

AN INTERVIEW WITH...

Charlie Perkins

Charles E. Perkins is a Nokia Fellow in the Communication System Laboratory at Nokia Research Center, investigating mobile wireless networking and dynamic configuration protocols. He is the editor of several ACM and IEEE journals for areas related to wireless networking. He serves as document editor for the mobile-IP working group of the Internet Engineering Task Force (IETF), and has written or cowritten standards-track documents in the mobileip, manet, IPv6, and seamoby (Seamless Mobility) working groups. He is also associate editor for *Mobile Communications and Computing Review*, the official publication of ACM SIGMOBILE, and has served on the editorial staff for *IEEE Internet Computing* magazine. Charles has written and edited books on Mobile IP and Ad Hoc Networking, and has published a number of papers and award-winning articles in the areas of mobile networking, ad hoc networking, route optimization for mobile networking, resource discovery, and automatic configuration for mobile computers.

Why did you decide to specialize in wireless/mobility?

My involvement with wireless networking and mobility was a natural outgrowth of project work at IBM Research in the late 1980s. We had radio links and were trying to build a "ThinkPad" style of device (like, a Palm Pilot) with wireless connectivity and handwriting recognition.

We built a simple solution (later called "Mobile IP") and noticed that it worked. This is, of course, unusual compared to most research solutions. Using our experience with Mobile IP, we engineered a quick and effective modification to RIP that accomplished ad hoc. This also worked pretty well. By "working," I mean that the applications ran just fine without any modifications, and the network didn't bog down from our new designs. These properties go under the names "application transparency" and "scalability."

Of course, working in the lab is amazingly different than commercial success, and both of these technologies still have a lot of unmet commercial potential.

What was your first job in the computer industry?

I worked at TRW Controls, in Houston, Texas. It was a drastic change from university study.

One thing I learned at TRW Controls is how poor the support software is for even the most critical utility control systems. These systems were meant to control the flow of electricity in huge power networks, and the underlying software was built in ways that would raise the hair on your neck. Plus, the schedules were always compressed, and the programmers were deeply cynical about the intentions of management and their working conditions. The whole system needed to be redesigned from the ground up. I don't have much reason to believe that things have changed during the last 30 years, especially given recent events surrounding the blackout of 2003. In fact, given deregulation, it's almost certainly worse. I was very happy to leave TRW Controls and join Tektronix (Tek Labs).

What is the most challenging part of your job?

The most challenging part of my job is to understand what I should be doing to help my company. Also, I take it as part of my job to shape the wireless technologies that I come into contact with, into providing better service and a more enjoyable daily experience for people. My company is in the business of "connecting people," and I hope to help make those connections as harmonious and smooth as possible. Doing this in a way to also maximize the profit potential of the technologies we develop makes every day into a new challenge. Specifically in the area of wireless, I believe that security technology has to be developed to be desirable and appreciated (like a raincoat) instead of burdensome and dreaded (as it mostly is today).

On a more detailed technical level, where in fact I am much more comfortable, I try to solve network protocol problems in a way that places the least burden on the wireless devices (and their batteries!) and presents the users with the least inconvenience. Interconnecting today's wireless telephones with the Internet by way of new high-speed wireless technologies is terrifically interesting technically, and offers unlimited potential for commercial success for those who can find the right paths forward.

What do you see for the future of wireless?

The entire wireless industry is undergoing tremendous changes and there is no end in sight. New high-speed wireless technologies are emerging and may have unforeseen practical effects that could fundamentally change society. Our current expectations of privacy and the limitations on our ability to communicate with each other (voice, image, and data) could be unrecognizable within ten years. As enterprises convert more and more to wireless communications, it is quite possible that new security measures will be taken that would significantly change our workplace experience.

It seems pretty clear that we will get more spectrum allocated to various schemes for radio communications. These can be very high speed. Soon, I expect it will be quite feasible for communities to offer their citizens complete high-speed wireless communications, as if a whole town were a local area network. This could have the effect of reinvigorating the sense of community which has long been lost in our society, at least in the United States. Of course, the community would still demand access to the Internet. Disk storage is getting so inexpensive, that one can imagine high-speed wireless access to untold libraries of humanity's intellectual treasures, as well as the latest news.

Wireless will likely accelerate the growth of the Internet. As wireless devices get cheaper and cheaper, we will see Internet communications everywhere (earrings, multiplayer games, subway fare readers). This will motivate new applications and new security solutions.

These are predictions that have often been made, but only within the last few years has the technology become available. Now the huge barrier will be rights management and access controls. If citizens do not engage in the process of formulating their rights in these matters, the long-held dreams will still remain dreams. Or, worse, they may be replaced by new nightmares. The Internet is everyone's business, and wireless brings it right up front and personal. I'm there to help it be the wonderful tool it should be.

Multimedia Networking

Having completed our journey down the protocol stack in the first part of this book, we now have a strong grounding in the principles and practice of computer networking. This foundation will serve us well as we turn to a topic that cuts across many layers of the protocol stack: multimedia networking.

The last few years have witnessed an explosive growth in the development and deployment of networked applications that transmit and receive audio and video over the Internet. New multimedia networking applications (also referred to as continuous-media applications)—streaming video, IP telephony, Internet radio, teleconferencing, interactive games, virtual worlds, distance learning, and much more—seem to be announced daily. The service requirements of these applications differ significantly from those of the elastic applications (e-mail, Web, remote login, file sharing) studied in Chapter 2. In particular, many multimedia applications are highly sensitive to end-to-end delay and delay variation but can tolerate occasional loss of data. In the first half of this chapter we'll examine how multimedia applications can be designed to make the best of the best-effort Internet, which provides no end-to-end delay guarantees. In the second half of this chapter we'll examine a number of activities that are currently under way to extend the Internet architecture to provide explicit support for the service requirements of multimedia applications.

7.1 Multimedia Networking Applications

In our discussion of application service requirements in Chapter 2, we identified a number of axes along which these requirements can be classified. Two of these axes—timing considerations and tolerance of data loss—are particularly important for networked multimedia applications. Timing considerations are important because many multimedia applications are highly **delay-sensitive**. We will see shortly that in many multimedia applications, packets that incur a sender-to-receiver delay of more than a few hundred milliseconds are essentially useless. On the other hand, networked multimedia applications are for the most part **loss-tolerant**—occasional loss only causes occasional glitches in the audio/video playback, and these losses can often be partially or fully concealed. These delay-sensitive but loss-tolerant characteristics are clearly different from those of elastic applications such as the Web, e-mail, FTP, and Telnet. For elastic applications, long delays are annoying but not particularly harmful, and the completeness and integrity of the transferred data is of paramount importance.

7.1.1 Examples of Multimedia Applications

The Internet carries a large variety of exciting multimedia applications. In this subsection, we consider three broad classes of multimedia applications: streaming stored audio/video, streaming live audio/video, and real-time interactive audio/video.

In this chapter we do *not* cover download-and-then-play applications, such as fully downloading an MP3 over a P2P file-sharing application before playing back the MP3. Indeed, download-and-then-play applications are elastic, file-transfer applications without any special delay requirements. We examined file transfer (HTTP and FTP) and P2P file-sharing systems in Chapter 2.

Streaming Stored Audio and Video

In this class of applications, clients request on-demand compressed audio or video files that are stored on servers. Stored audio files might contain audio from a professor's lecture (you are urged to visit the Web site for this book to try this out), rock songs, symphonies, archives of famous radio broadcasts, or archived historical recordings. Stored video files might contain video of a professor's lecture, full-length movies, prerecorded television shows, documentaries, video archives of historical events, cartoons, or music video clips. This class of applications has three key distinguishing features.

♦ *Stored media.* The multimedia content has been prerecorded and is stored at the server. As a result, a user may pause, rewind, fast-forward, or index through the multimedia content. The time from when a client makes such a request until the action manifests itself at the client should be on the order of one to ten seconds for acceptable responsiveness.

♦ *Streaming.* In a streaming stored audio/video application, a client typically begins playout of the audio/video a few seconds after it begins receiving the file from the server. This means that the client will be playing out audio/video from one location in the file while it is receiving later parts of the file from the server. This technique, known as **streaming**, avoids having to download the entire file (and incurring a potentially long delay) before beginning playout. There are many streaming multimedia products, including RealPlayer from RealNetworks [RealNetworks 2004], Apple's QuickTime [QuickTime 2004], and Microsoft's Windows Media [Microsoft Media Player 2004].

♦ *Continuous playout.* Once playout of the multimedia content begins, it should proceed according to the original timing of the recording. This places critical delay constraints on data delivery. Data must be received from the server in time for its playout at the client. Although stored media applications have continuous playout requirements, their end-to-end delay constraints are nevertheless less stringent than those for live, interactive applications such as Internet telephony and video conferencing (see below).

Streaming Live Audio and Video

This class of applications is similar to traditional broadcast radio and television, except that transmission takes place over the Internet. These applications allow a user to receive a *live* radio or television transmission emitted from any corner of the world. (For example, one of the authors of this book often listens to his favorite Philadelphia radio stations when traveling. The other author regularly listened to live broadcasts of his university's beloved basketball team while he was living in France for a year.)

Since streaming live audio/video is not stored, a client cannot fast-forward through the media. However, with local storage of received data, other interactive operations such as pausing and rewinding through live multimedia transmissions are possible in some applications. Live, broadcast-like applications often have many clients who are receiving the same audio/video program. Distribution of live audio/video to many receivers can be efficiently accomplished using the IP multicasting techniques described in Section 4.7. At the time of this writing, however, live audio/video distribution is more often accomplished through multiple separate unicast streams. As with streaming stored multimedia, continuous playout is required, although the timing constraints are less stringent than for real-time interactive applications. Delays of up to tens of seconds from when the user requests the delivery/playout of a live transmission to when playout begins can be tolerated.

CASE HISTORY

REALNETWORKS: BRINGING AUDIO TO THE INTERNET FOREGROUND

RealNetworks, a pioneer in streaming audio and video products, was the first company to bring audio to the Internet mainstream. The company began under the name Progressive Networks in 1995. Its initial product—the RealAudio system— included an audio encoder, an audio server, and an audio player. The RealAudio system enabled users to browse, select, and play back audio content on demand, as easily as using a standard video cassette player/recorder. It quickly became popular for providers of entertainment, information, and news content to deliver audio-on-demand services that can be accessed and played back immediately. In early 1997, RealNetworks expanded its product line to include video as well as audio. RealNetwork products currently incorporate the RTP and RTSP protocols.

Over the past few years, RealNetworks has seen tough competition from Microsoft, which began to market its own streaming media products in the late 1990's. RealNetworks and Microsoft have diverged on some of the underlying technology choices in their players. Waging the tug of war in the marketplace and in Internet standards groups, both companies are seeking to have their own formats and protocols become the standard for the Internet.

Real-Time Interactive Audio and Video

This class of applications allows people to use audio/video to communicate with each other in real time. Real-time interactive audio over the Internet is often referred to as **Internet phone**, since, from the user's perspective, it is similar to the traditional circuit-switched telephone service. Internet phone can potentially provide private branch exchange (PBX), local, and long-distance telephone service at very low cost. It can also facilitate the deployment of new services that are not easily supported by the traditional circuit-switched networks, including Web-phone integration, group real-time communication, directory services, caller filtering, and more. There are hundreds of Internet telephone products currently available [VON 2004]. For example, users of Microsoft's Instant Messenger can make PC-to-phone and PC-to-PC voice calls. With real-time interactive video, also called video conferencing, individuals communicate visually as well as orally. There are also many real-time interactive video products currently available for the Internet, including Microsoft's NetMeeting. Note that in a real-time interactive audio/video application, a user can speak or move at any time. For a conversation with interaction among multiple speakers, the delay from when a user speaks or moves until the action is manifested at the receiving hosts should be less than a few hundred milliseconds. For voice, delays smaller than 150 milliseconds are not perceived by a human listener, delays between 150 and 400 milliseconds can be acceptable, and delays exceeding 400 milliseconds can result in frustrating, if not completely unintelligible, voice conversations.

7.1.2 Hurdles for Multimedia in Today's Internet

Recall that the IP protocol deployed in the Internet today provides a **best-effort service** to all the datagrams it carries. In other words, the Internet makes its best

---

CASE HISTORY

VOICE OVER THE INTERNET

Given the worldwide popularity of the telephone system, many Internet visionaries have repeatedly predicted since the late 1980s that the next Internet killer application would be some sort of voice application. These predictions were accompanied by Internet telephony research and product development. For example, researchers created Internet phone prototypes in the 1980s, building on research on packetized voice transmission from the 1970's [Cohen 1977, RFC 741], years before the Web was popularized. And numerous startups produced PC-to-PC Internet phone products throughout the 1990s. But none of these prototypes or products really caught on with mainstream Internet users (even though some were bundled with popular browsers). Not until 1999 did voice communication begin to be popularized in the Internet.

The PC-to-phone application began to see significant usage in the late 1990s. This application allows an Internet user with an Internet connection and a microphone to call any ordinary telephone. Net2Phone [Net2Phone 2004] and Dialpad [Dialpad 2004] are two companies that have provided PC-to-phone service. These PC-to-phone services are low-cost and are hence popular with people who love to talk but are on a tight budget. Furthermore, a number of companies offer PC-to-phone-like services to the enterprise. As we'll discuss in this chapter, for a PC-to-phone call, the call is routed over the Internet from a PC to a gateway, and over circuit-switched telephone networks from the gateway to the telephone (fixed or mobile). For communication over the Internet between the PC and gateway, a number of popular protocols are often used, including RTP, SIP, and H.323, all of which are discussed in this chapter. A second class of applications is phone-to-Internet-to-phone, allowing consumers to make long-distance calls at lower cost while using traditional phone handsets on both ends. Many of the prepaid phone cards that can be purchased at newspaper stands and drugstores use the phone-to-Internet-to-phone mode. A third class of applications is asynchronous voice over the Internet [Wimba 2004]. Most major networking equipment companies—including Cisco, Lucent, and Alcatel—offer complete product lines for voice over IP for telephone operators and business customers [VON 2004].

effort to move each datagram from sender to receiver as quickly as possible, but it does not make any promises whatsoever about the end-to-end delay for an individual packet. Nor does the service make any promises about the variation of packet delay within a packet stream. Because TCP and UDP run over IP, it follows that neither of these transport protocols makes any delay guarantees to invoking applications. Due to the lack of any special effort to deliver packets in a timely manner, it is an extremely challenging problem to develop successful multimedia networking applications for the Internet. To date, multimedia over the Internet has achieved significant but limited success. For example, streaming stored audio/video with user-interactivity delays of five to ten seconds is now commonplace in the Internet. But during peak traffic periods, performance may be unsatisfactory, particularly when intervening links are congested (such as congested transoceanic links).

Internet phone and real-time interactive video has, to date, been less successful than streaming stored audio/video. Indeed, real-time interactive voice and video impose rigid constraints on packet delay and packet jitter. **Packet jitter** is the variability of packet delays within the same packet stream. Real-time voice and video can work well in regions where bandwidth is plentiful, and hence delay and jitter are minimal. But quality can deteriorate to unacceptable levels as soon as the real-time voice or video packet stream hits a moderately congested link.

The design of multimedia applications would certainly be more straightforward if there were some sort of first-class and second-class Internet services, whereby first-class packets were limited in number and received priority service in router queues. Such a first-class service could be satisfactory for delay-sensitive applications. But to date, the Internet has mostly taken an egalitarian approach to packet scheduling in router queues. All packets receive equal service; no packets, including delay-sensitive audio and video packets, receive special priority in the router queues. No matter how much money you have or how important you are, you must join the end of the line and wait your turn! In the latter half of this chapter, we'll examine proposed architectures that aim to remove this restriction.

So for the time being we have to live with best-effort service. But given this constraint, we can make several design decisions and employ a few tricks to improve the user-perceived quality of a multimedia networking application. For example, we can send the audio and video over UDP, and thereby circumvent TCP's low throughput when TCP enters its slow-start phase. We can delay playback at the receiver by 100 msecs or more in order to diminish the effects of network-induced jitter. We can timestamp packets at the sender so that the receiver knows when the packets should be played back. For stored audio/video we can prefetch data during playback when client storage and extra bandwidth are available. We can even send redundant information in order to mitigate the effects of network-induced packet loss. We'll investigate many of these techniques in the rest of the first half of this chapter.

7.1.3 How Should the Internet Evolve to Support Multimedia Better?

Today there is a tremendous—and sometimes ferocious—debate about how the Internet should evolve in order to better accommodate multimedia traffic with its rigid timing constraints. At one extreme, some researchers argue that fundamental changes should be made to the Internet so that applications can explicitly reserve end-to-end bandwidth. These researchers believe that if a user wants to make, for example, an Internet phone call from Host A to Host B, then the user's Internet phone application should be able to reserve bandwidth explicitly in each link along a route between the two hosts. But permitting applications to make reservations and requiring the network to honor the reservations requires some big changes. First we need a protocol that, on the behalf of applications, reserves link bandwidth on the path from the senders to their receivers. Second, we must modify scheduling policies in the router queues so that bandwidth reservations can be honored. With these new scheduling policies, not all packets get equal treatment; instead, those that reserve (and pay) more get more. Third, in order to honor reservations, the applications must give the network a description of the traffic that they intend to send into the network. The network must then police each application's traffic to make sure that it abides by the description. Finally, the network must have a means of determining whether it has sufficient available bandwidth to support any new reservation request. These mechanisms, when combined, require new and complex software in the hosts and routers as well as new types of services. We'll look into these mechanisms in more detail, when we examine the Intserv model in Section 7.8.

   At the other extreme, some researchers argue that it isn't necessary to make any fundamental changes to best-effort service and the underlying Internet protocols. Instead they advocate a laissez-faire approach:

♦ As demand increases, the ISPs (both top-tier and lower-tier ISPs) will scale their networks to meet the demand. Specifically, ISPs will add more bandwidth and switching capacity to provide satisfactory delay and packet-loss performance within their networks. The ISPs will thereby provide better service to their customers (users and customer ISPs), translating to higher revenues through more customers and higher service fees. As discussed in Chapter 2, ISPs can also install caches in their networks, which bring stored content (Web pages as well as stored audio and video) closer to the users, thereby reducing traffic in higher-tier ISPs.

♦ Content distribution networks (CDNs), replicate stored content and put the replicated content at the edges of the Internet. Given that a large fraction of the traffic flowing through the Internet is stored content (Web pages, MP3s, video), CDNs can significantly alleviate the traffic loads on the ISPs and the peering interfaces between ISPs. Furthermore, CDNs provide a differentiated service to content providers: content providers that pay for a CDN service can deliver content faster and more effectively. We'll study CDNs later in this chapter in Section 7.5.

♦ To deal with live streaming traffic (such as a sporting event), which is being sent to millions of users simultaneously, **multicast overlay networks** can be deployed. A multicast overlay network consists of servers scattered throughout the ISP network (and potentially throughout the entire Internet). These servers and the logical links between them collectively form an overlay network, which multicasts (see Section 4.7) traffic from the source to the millions of users. Unlike multicast IP, for which the multicast function is handled by routers at the IP layer, overlay networks multicast at the application layer. For example, the source host might send the stream to three overlay servers; each of the overlay servers may forward the stream to three more overlay servers; the process continues, creating a distribution tree on top of the underlying IP network with routers and hosts. By multicasting popular live traffic through overlay networks, overall traffic loads in the Internet can be reduced over the case of unicast distribution.

Between the reservation camp and the laissez-faire camp there is a yet a third camp—the differentiated services (Diffserv) camp. This camp wants to make relatively small changes at the network and transport layers, and introduce simple pricing and policing schemes at the edge of the network (that is, at the interface between the user and the user's ISP). The idea is to introduce a small number of traffic classes (possibly just two classes), assign each datagram to one of the classes, give datagrams different levels of service according to their class in the router queues, and charge users according to the class of packets that they are sending into the network. We'll cover differentiated services in Section 7.8.

7.1.4 Audio and Video Compression

Before audio and video can be transmitted over a computer network, it must be digitized and compressed. The need for digitization is obvious: computer networks transmit bits, so all transmitted information must be represented as a sequence of bits. Compression is important because uncompressed audio and video consume a tremendous amount of storage and bandwidth; removing the inherent redundancies in digitized audio and video signals can reduce the amount of data that needs to be stored and transmitted by orders of magnitude. As an example, a single image consisting of 1024 pixels (1024 pixels, with each pixel encoded into 24 bits (8 bits each for the colors red, green, and blue), requires 3 Mbytes of storage without compression. It would take seven minutes to send this image over a 64 kbps link. If the image is compressed at a modest 10:1 compression ratio, the storage requirement is reduced to 300 Kbytes and the transmission time also drops by a factor of ten.

The fields of audio and video compression are vast. They have been active areas of research for more than fifty years, and there are now literally hundreds of popular techniques and standards for both audio and video compression. Most universities offer entire courses on audio and video compression and often offer separate courses on each. We therefore provide here a brief and high-level introduction to the subject.

Audio Compression in the Internet

A continuously varying analog audio signal (which could emanate from speech or music) is normally converted to a digital signal as follows:

♦ The analog audio signal is first sampled at some fixed rate, for example, at 8,000 samples per second. The value of each sample is an arbitrary real number.

♦ Each of the samples is then rounded to one of a finite number of values. This operation is referred to as **quantization**. The number of finite values—called quantization values—is typically a power of two, for example, 256 quantization values.

♦ Each of the quantization values is represented by a fixed number of bits. For example, if there are 256 quantization values, then each value—and hence each sample—is represented by 1 byte. Each of the samples is converted to its bit representation. The bit representations of all the samples are concatenated together to form the digital representation of the signal.

As an example, if an analog audio signal is sampled at 8,000 samples per second and each sample is quantized and represented by 8 bits, then the resulting digital signal will have a rate of 64,000 bits per second. This digital signal can then be converted back—that is, decoded—to an analog signal for playback. However, the decoded analog signal is typically different from the original audio signal. By increasing the sampling rate and the number of quantization values, the decoded signal can approximate the original analog signal. Thus, there is a clear trade-off between the quality of the decoded signal and the storage and bandwidth requirements of the digital signal.

The basic encoding technique that we just described is called **pulse code modulation (PCM)**. Speech encoding often uses PCM, with a sampling rate of 8,000 samples per second and 8 bits per sample, giving a rate of 64 kbps. The audio compact disk (CD) also uses PCM, with a sampling rate of 44,100 samples per second with 16 bits per sample; this gives a rate of 705.6 kbps for mono and 1.411 Mbps for stereo.

A bit rate of 1.411 Mbps for stereo music exceeds most access rates, and even 64 kbps for speech exceeds the access rate for a dial-up modem user. For these reasons, PCM-encoded speech and music are rarely used in the Internet. Instead compression techniques are used to reduce the bit rates of the stream. Popular compression techniques for speech include **GSM** (13 kbps), **G.729** (8 kbps), and **G.723.3** (both 6.4 and 5.3 kbps), and a large number of proprietary techniques, including those used by RealNetworks. A popular compression technique for near CD-quality stereo music is **MPEG 1 layer 3**, more commonly known as **MP3**. MP3 encoders typically compress to rates of 96 kbps, 128 kbps, and 160 kbps, and produce very little sound degradation. When an MP3 file is broken up into pieces, each piece is still playable. This headerless file format allows MP3 music files to be streamed across the Internet (assuming the playback bit rate and speed of the Internet connection are compatible). The MP3 compression standard is complex, using psychoacoustic masking, redundancy reduction, and bit reservoir buffering.

Video Compression in the Internet

A video is a sequence of images, typically being displayed at a constant rate, for example at 24 or 30 images per second. An uncompressed, digitally encoded image consists of an array of pixels, with each pixel encoded into a number of bits to represent luminance and color. There are two types of redundancy in video, both of which can be exploited for compression. Spatial redundancy is the redundancy within a given image. For example, an image that consists of mostly white space can be efficiently compressed. Temporal redundancy reflects repetition from image to subsequent image. If, for example, an image and the subsequent image are exactly the same, there is no reason to re-encode the subsequent image; it is more efficient simply to indicate during encoding that the subsequent image is exactly the same.

The MPEG compression standards are among the most popular compression techniques. These include **MPEG 1** for CD-ROM quality video (1.5 Mbps), **MPEG 2** for high-quality **DVD** video (3–6 Mbps), and **MPEG 4** for object-oriented video compression. The MPEG standard draws heavily on the JPEG standard for image compression by exploiting temporal redundancy across images in addition to the spatial redundancy exploited by JPEG. The **H.261** video compression standards are also very popular in the Internet. In addition there are numerous proprietary schemes, including Apple's QuickTime and Real Networks' encoders.

Readers interested in learning more about audio and video encoding are encouraged to see [Rao 1996] and [Solari 1997]. A good book on multimedia networking in general is [Crowcroft 1999].

7.2 Streaming Stored Audio and Video

In recent years, audio/video streaming has become a popular application and a significant consumer of network bandwidth. This trend is likely to continue for several reasons. First, the cost of disk storage continues to decrease rapidly, making room for storage-hungry multimedia files. Today, terabyte storage facilities are available, capable of holding thousands of MPEG 2 videos. Second, improvements in Internet infrastructure, such as high-speed residential access (that is, cable modems and ADSL, as discussed in Chapter 1), content-distribution techniques such as caching and CDNs (see Section 7.5), and new QoS-oriented Internet protocols (see Sections 7.6–7.9) will greatly facilitate the distribution of stored audio and video. And third, there is an enormous pent-up demand for high-quality video on demand, an application that combines two existing killer communication technologies—television and on-demand Web.

In audio/video streaming, clients request compressed audio/video files that reside on servers. As we'll soon discuss, these servers can be ordinary Web servers or can be special streaming servers tailored for the audio/video streaming application. Upon client request, the server directs an audio/video file to the client by sending the file into a socket. Both TCP and UDP socket connections are used in practice. Before being sent into the network, the audio/video file is segmented, and the segments are typically encapsulated with special headers appropriate for audio/video traffic. The **real-time protocol (RTP),** discussed in Section 7.4, is a public-domain standard for encapsulating such segments. Once the requested audio/video file starts to arrive, the client begins to render the file (typically) within a few seconds. Most existing products also provide for user interactivity, for example, pause/resume and temporal jumps within the audio/video file. This user interactivity also requires a protocol for client/server interaction. The **real-time streaming protocol (RTSP)**, discussed at the end of this section, is a public-domain protocol for providing user interactivity.

Users often request audio/video streaming through a Web client (that is, browser). But because audio/video playout is not integrated directly into today's Web clients, a separate **helper application** is required for playing out the audio/video. Helper applications are often called **media players**, the most popular of which are currently Real-Networks' RealPlayer and the Microsoft Windows Media Player. The media player performs several functions, including the following:

♦ *Decompression.* Audio/video is almost always compressed to save disk storage and network bandwidth. A media player must decompress the audio/video on the fly during playout.

♦ *Jitter removal.* Packet jitter is the variability of source-to-destination delays of packets within the same packet stream. Since audio and video must be played out with the same timing with which it was recorded, a receiver will buffer received packets for a short period of time to remove this jitter. We'll examine this topic in detail in Section 7.3.

♦ *Error correction.* Due to unpredictable congestion in the Internet, a fraction of packets in the packet stream can be lost. If this fraction becomes too large, user-perceived audio/video quality becomes unacceptable. To this end, many streaming systems attempt to recover from losses by either (1) reconstructing lost packets through the transmission of redundant packets, (2) having the client explicitly request retransmission of lost packets, or (3) masking loss by interpolating the missing data from the received data.

The media player has a graphical user interface with control knobs. This is the actual interface that the user interacts with. It typically includes volume controls, pause/resume buttons, sliders for making temporal jumps in the audio/video stream, and so on.

Plug-ins may be used to embed the user interface of the media player within the window of the Web browser. For such embeddings, the browser reserves screen space on the current Web page, and it is up to the media player to manage the screen space. But whether it appears in a separate window or within the browser window (as a plug-in), the media player program is executed separately from the browser.

7.2.1 Accessing Audio and Video Through a Web Server

Stored audio/video can reside either on a Web server that delivers the audio/video to the client over HTTP, or on an audio/video streaming server that delivers the audio/video over non-HTTP protocols (protocols that can be either proprietary or open standards). In this subsection, we examine delivery of audio/video from a Web server; in the next subsection, we examine delivery from a streaming server.

Consider first the case of audio streaming. When an audio file resides on a Web server, the audio file is an ordinary object in the server's file system, just as HTML and JPEG files are. When a user wants to hear the audio file, the user's host establishes a TCP connection with the Web server and sends an HTTP request for the object (see Section 2.2). Upon receiving a request, the Web server encapsulates the audio file in an HTTP response message and sends the response message back into the TCP connection. The case of video can be a little trickier, because the audio and video parts of the video may be stored in two files; that is, they may be two objects in the Web server's file system. In this case, two separate HTTP requests are sent to the server (over two separate TCP connections for HTTP/1.0), and the audio and video files arrive at the client in parallel. It is up to the client to manage the synchronization of the two streams. It is also possible that the audio and video are interleaved in the same file, so that only one object need be sent to the client. To keep our discussion simple, for the case of video we assume that the audio and video are contained in one file.

A naive architecture for audio/video streaming is shown in Figure 7.1. In this architecture:

◆ The browser process establishes a TCP connection with the Web server and requests the audio/video file with an HTTP request message.

◆ The Web server sends the audio/video file to the browser in an HTTP response message.

◆ The content-type header line in the HTTP response message indicates a specific audio/video encoding. The client browser examines the content type of the response message, launches the associated media player, and passes the file to the media player.

◆ The media player then renders the audio/video file.

Although this approach is very simple, it has a major drawback: the media player (that is, the helper application) must interact with the server through a Web browser as an intermediary. This can lead to many problems. In particular, when a browser is an

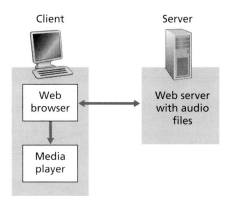

Figure 7.1 ✦ A naive implementation for audio streaming

intermediary, the entire object must be downloaded before the browser passes the object to a helper application. The resulting delay before playout can begin is typically unacceptable for audio/video clips of moderate length. For this reason, audio/video streaming implementations typically have the server send the audio/video file directly to the media player process. In other words, a direct socket connection is made between the server process and the media player process. As shown in Figure 7.2, this is typically done by making use of a **meta file**, a file that provides information (for example, URL or type of encoding) about the audio/video file that is to be streamed.

A direct TCP connection between the server and the media player is obtained as follows:

1. The user clicks on a hyperlink for an audio/video file.
2. The hyperlink does not point directly to the audio/video file, but instead to a meta file. The meta file contains the URL of the actual audio/video file. The HTTP response message that encapsulates the meta file includes a content-type header line that indicates the specific audio/video application.
3. The client browser examines the content-type header line of the response message, launches the associated media player, and passes the entire body of the response message (that is, the meta file) to the media player.
4. The media player sets up a TCP connection directly with the HTTP server. The media player sends an HTTP request message for the audio/video file into the TCP connection.
5. The audio/video file is sent within an HTTP response message to the media player. The media player streams out the audio/video file.

The importance of the intermediate step of acquiring the meta file is clear. When the browser sees the content type of the file, it can launch the appropriate media player, and thereby have the media player contact the server directly.

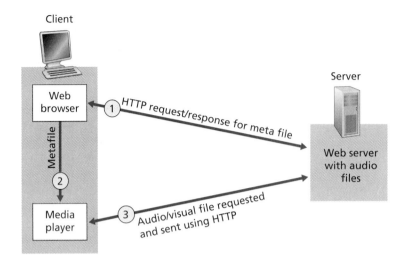

Figure 7.2 ◆ Web server sends audio/video directly to the media player

We have just learned how a meta file can allow a media player to communicate directly with a Web server that stores an audio/video file. Yet many companies that sell products for audio/video streaming do not recommend the architecture we just described. This is because the architecture has the media player communicate with the server over HTTP and hence also over TCP. HTTP is often considered insufficiently rich to allow for satisfactory user interaction with the server; in particular, HTTP does not easily allow a user (through the media player) to send pause/resume, fast-forward, and temporal jump commands to the server.

7.2.2 Sending Multimedia from a Streaming Server to a Helper Application

In order to get around HTTP and/or TCP, audio/video can be stored on and sent from a streaming server to the media player. This streaming server could be a proprietary streaming server, such as those marketed by RealNetworks and Microsoft, or could be a public-domain streaming server. With a streaming server, audio/video can be sent over UDP (rather than TCP) using application-layer protocols that may be better tailored than HTTP to audio/video streaming.

This architecture requires two servers, as shown in Figure 7.3. One server, the HTTP server, serves Web pages (including meta files). The second server, the **streaming server**, serves the audio/video files. The two servers can run on the same end system or on two distinct end systems. The steps for this architecture are similar to those described in the preceding subsection. However, now the media player requests the file from a streaming server rather than from a Web server, and now the media player and streaming server can interact using their own protocols. These protocols can allow for rich user interaction with the audio/video stream.

In the architecture of Figure 7.3, there are many options for delivering the audio/video from the streaming server to the media player. A partial list of the options is given below.

1. The audio/video is sent over UDP at a constant rate equal to the drain rate at the receiver (which is the encoded rate of the audio/video). For example, if the audio is compressed using GSM at a rate of 13 kbps, then the server clocks out the compressed audio file at 13 kbps. As soon as the client receives compressed audio/video from the network, it decompresses the audio/video and plays it back.
2. This is the same as the first option, but the media player delays playout for two to five seconds in order to eliminate network-induced jitter. The client accomplishes this task by placing the compressed media that it receives from the network into a **client buffer**, as shown in Figure 7.4. Once the client has prefetched a few seconds of the media, it begins to drain the buffer. For this, and the previous option, the fill rate $x(t)$ is equal to the drain rate d, except when there is packet loss, in which case $x(t)$ is momentarily less than d.
3. The media is sent over TCP. The server pushes the media file into the TCP socket as quickly as it can; the client (that is, media player) reads from the TCP socket as quickly as it can and places the compressed video into the media player buffer.

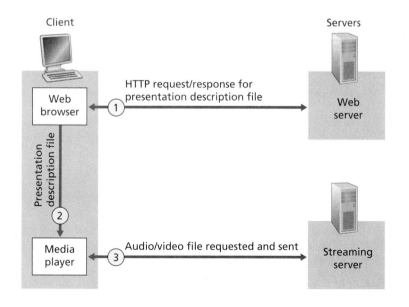

Figure 7.3 ♦ Streaming from a streaming server to a media player

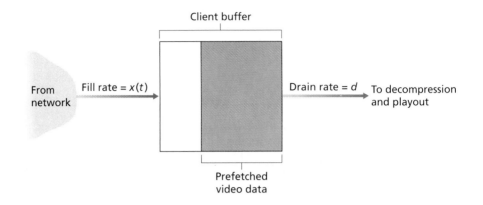

Figure 7.4 ◆ Client buffer being filled at rate x(t) and drained at rate d

After an initial two- to five-second delay, the media player reads from its buffer at a rate d and forwards the compressed media to decompression and playback. Because TCP retransmits lost packets, it has the potential to provide better sound quality than UDP. On the other hand, the fill rate $x(t)$ now fluctuates with time due to TCP congestion control and window flow control. In fact, after packet loss, TCP congestion control may reduce the instantaneous rate to less than d for long periods of time. This can empty the client buffer (a process known as **starvation**) and introduce undesirable pauses into the output of the audio/video stream at the client.

For the third option, the behavior of $x(t)$ will very much depend on the size of the client buffer (which is not to be confused with the TCP receive buffer). If this buffer is large enough to hold all of the media file (possibly within disk storage), then TCP will make use of all the instantaneous bandwidth available to the connection, so that $x(t)$ can become much larger than d. If $x(t)$ becomes much larger than d for long periods of time, then a large portion of media is prefetched into the client, and subsequent client starvation is unlikely. If, on the other hand, the client buffer is small, then $x(t)$ will fluctuate around the drain rate d. Risk of client starvation is much larger in this case.

7.2.3 Real-Time Streaming Protocol (RTSP)

Many Internet multimedia users (particularly those who grew up with a TV remote control in hand) will want to control the playback of continuous media by pausing playback, repositioning playback to a future or past point in time, fast-forwarding playback visually, rewinding playback visually, and so on. This functionality is similar to what a user has with a DVD player when watching a DVD video or with a CD player when listening to a music CD. To allow a user to control playback, the media player and server need a protocol for exchanging playback control information. The real-time streaming protocol (RTSP), defined in RFC 2326, is such a protocol.

Before getting into the details of RTSP, let us first indicate what RTSP does not do.

♦ RTSP does not define compression schemes for audio and video.

♦ RTSP does not define how audio and video are encapsulated in packets for transmission over a network; encapsulation for streaming media can be provided by RTP or by a proprietary protocol. (RTP is discussed in Section 7.4.) For example, RealNetworks' audio/video servers and players use RTSP to send control information to each other, but the media stream itself can be encapsulated in RTP packets or in some proprietary data format.

♦ RTSP does not restrict how streamed media is transported; it can be transported over UDP or TCP.

♦ RTSP does not restrict how the media player buffers the audio/video. The audio/video can be played out as soon as it begins to arrive at the client, it can be played out after a delay of a few seconds, or it can be downloaded in its entirety before playout.

So if RTSP doesn't do any of the above, what does it do? RTSP allows a media player to control the transmission of a media stream. As mentioned above, control actions include pause/resume, repositioning of playback, fast-forward, and rewind. RTSP is an **out-of-band protocol**. In particular, the RTSP messages are sent out-of-band, whereas the media stream, whose packet structure is not defined by RTSP, is considered "in-band." RTSP messages use a different port number, 544, from the media stream. The RTSP specification [RFC 2326] permits RTSP messages to be sent over either TCP or UDP.

Recall from Section 2.3 that the file transfer protocol (FTP) also uses the out-of-band notion. In particular, FTP uses two client/server pairs of sockets, each pair with its own port number: one client/server socket pair supports a TCP connection that transports control information; the other client/server socket pair supports a TCP connection that actually transports the file. The RTSP channel is in many ways similar to FTP's control channel.

Let's now walk through a simple RTSP example, which is illustrated in Figure 7.5. The Web browser first requests a presentation description file from a Web server. The presentation description file can have references to several continuous-media files as well as directives for synchronization of the continuous-media files. Each reference to a continuous-media file begins with the URL method, `rtsp://`. Below we provide a sample presentation file that has been adapted from [Schulzrinne 1997]. In this presentation, an audio and video stream are played in parallel and in lip sync (as part of the same group). For the audio stream, the media player can choose (switch) between two audio recordings, a low-fidelity recording and a high-fidelity recording. (The format of the file is similar to SMIL [SMIL 2004], which is used by many streaming products to define synchronized multimedia presentations.)

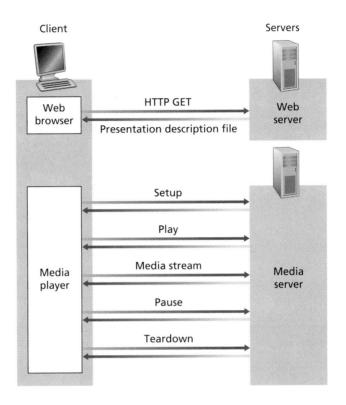

Figure 7.5 ♦ Interaction between client and server using RTSP.

```
<title>Twister</title>
<session>
   <group language=en lipsync>
      <switch>
         <track type=audio
               e="PCMU/8000/1"
               src="rtsp://audio.example.com/twister/audio.en/lofi">
         <track type=audio
               e="DVI4/16000/2" pt="90 DVI4/8000/1"
               src="rtsp://audio.example.com/twister/audio.en/hifi">
         </switch>
         <track type="video/jpeg"
               src="rtsp://video.example.com/twister/video">
   </group>
</session>
```

The Web server encapsulates the presentation description file in an HTTP response message and sends the message to the browser. When the browser receives the HTTP response message, the browser invokes a media player (that is, the helper application) based on the content-type field of the message. The presentation description file includes references to media streams, using the URL method `rtsp://`, as in the sample above. As shown in Figure 7.5, the player and the server then send each other a series of RTSP messages. The player sends an RTSP SETUP request, and the server responds with an RTSP OK message. The player sends an RTSP PLAY request, say, for low-fidelity audio, and the server responds with an RTSP OK message. At this point, the streaming server pumps the low-fidelity audio into its own in-band channel. Later, the media player sends an RTSP PAUSE request, and the server responds with an RTSP OK message. When the user is finished, the media player sends an RTSP TEARDOWN request, and the server confirms with an RTSP OK response.

Now let's take a brief look at the actual RTSP messages. The following is a simplified example of an RTSP session between a client (C:) and a sender (S:).

```
C: SETUP rtsp://audio.example.com/twister/audio RTSP/1.0
   Cseq: 1
   Transport: rtp/udp; compression; port=3056; mode=PLAY
S: RTSP/1.0 200 OK
   Cseq: 1
   Session: 4231
C: PLAY rtsp://audio.example.com/twister/audio.en/lofi RTSP/1.0
   Range: npt=0-
   Cseq: 2
   Session: 4231
S: RTSP/1.0 200 OK
   Cseq: 2
   Session: 4231
C: PAUSE rtsp://audio.example.com/twister/audio.en/lofi RTSP/1.0
   Range: npt=37
   Cseq: 3
   Session: 4231
S: RTSP/1.0 200 OK
   Cseq: 3
   Session: 4231
C: TEARDOWN rtsp://audio.example.com/twister/audio.en/lofi RTSP/1.0
   Cseq: 4
   Session: 4231
S: RTSP/1.0 200 OK
   Cseq: 4
   Session: 4231
```

It is interesting to note the similarities between HTTP and RTSP. All request and response messages are in ASCII text, the client employs standardized methods (SETUP, PLAY, PAUSE, and so on), and the server responds with standardized reply codes. One important difference, however, is that the RTSP server keeps track of the state of the client for each ongoing RTSP session. For example, the server keeps track of whether the client is in an initialization state, a play state, or a pause state (see the programming assignment for this chapter). The session and sequence numbers, which are part of each RTSP request and response, help the server keep track of the session state. The session number is fixed throughout the entire session; the client increments the sequence number each time it sends a new message; the server echoes back the session number and the current sequence number.

As shown in the example, the client initiates the session with the SETUP request, providing the URL of the file to be streamed and the RTSP version. The setup message includes the client port number to which the media should be sent. The setup message also indicates that the media should be sent over UDP using the RTP packetization protocol (to be discussed in Section 7.4). Notice that in this example, the player chose not to play back the complete presentation, but instead only the low-fidelity portion of the presentation.

RTSP is actually capable of doing much more than described in this brief introduction. In particular, RTSP has facilities that allow clients to stream toward the server (for example, for recording). RTSP has been adopted by RealNetworks, one of the industry leaders in audio/video streaming. Henning Schulzrinne makes available a Web page on RTSP [Schulzrinne-RTSP 2004].

At the end of this chapter, you will find a programming assignment for creating a video streaming system (both server and client) that leverages RTSP. This assignment involves writing code that actually constructs and sends RTSP messages at the client. The assignment provides the RTSP server code, which parses the RTSP messages and constructs appropriate responses. Readers interested in obtaining a deeper understanding of RTSP are highly encouraged to work through this interesting assignment.

7.3 Making the Best of the Best-Effort Service: An Internet Phone Example

The Internet's network-layer protocol, IP, provides a best-effort service. That is to say that the service makes its best effort to move each datagram from source to destination as quickly as possible. However, it does not make any promises whatsoever about the extent of the end-to-end delay for an individual packet, or about the extent of packet jitter and packet loss within the packet stream. The lack of guarantees about delay and packet jitter poses significant challenges to the design of real-time multimedia applications such as Internet phone and real-time video conferencing, which are acutely sensitive to packet delay, jitter, and loss. Fortunately, designers of these applications can introduce several useful mechanisms that can preserve good audio and video quality as long as delay, jitter, and loss are not excessive. In this section, we examine some of these mechanisms. To keep the discussion concrete, we discuss these mechanisms in the context of an **Internet phone application**, described below. The situation is similar for real-time video conferencing applications [Bolot 1994].

The speaker in our Internet phone example generates an audio signal consisting of alternating talk spurts and silent periods. In order to conserve bandwidth, our Internet phone application generates packets only during talk spurts. During a talk spurt the sender generates bytes at a rate of 8,000 bytes per second, and every 20 msecs the sender gathers bytes into chunks. Thus, the number of bytes in a chunk is (20 msecs) · (8,000 bytes/sec) = 160 bytes. A special header is attached to each chunk, the contents of which are discussed below. The chunk and its header are encapsulated in a UDP segment, via the call to the socket interface. Thus, during a talk spurt, a UDP segment is sent every 20 msec.

If each packet makes it to the receiver and has a small constant end-to-end delay, then packets arrive at the receiver periodically every 20 msecs during a talk spurt. In these ideal conditions, the receiver can simply play back each chunk as soon as it arrives. But unfortunately, some packets can be lost and most packets will not have the same end-to-end delay, even in a lightly congested Internet. For this reason, the receiver must take more care in determining (1) when to play back a chunk, and (2) what to do with a missing chunk.

7.3.1 The Limitations of a Best-Effort Service

We mentioned that best-effort service can lead to packet loss, excessive end-to-end delay, and packet jitter. Let's examine these issues in more detail.

Packet Loss

Consider one of the UDP segments generated by our Internet phone application. The UDP segment is encapsulated in an IP datagram. As the datagram wanders through the network, it passes through buffers (that is, queues) in the routers in order to access outbound links. It is possible that one or more of the buffers in the route from sender to receiver is full and cannot admit the IP datagram. In this case, the IP datagram is discarded, never to arrive at the receiving application.

Loss could be eliminated by sending the packets over TCP rather than over UDP. Recall that TCP retransmits packets that do not arrive at the destination. However, retransmission mechanisms are often considered unacceptable for interactive real-time audio applications such as Internet phone, because they increase end-to-end delay [Bolot 1996]. Furthermore, due to TCP congestion control, after packet loss the transmission rate at the sender can be reduced to a rate that is lower than the drain rate at the receiver. This can have a severe impact on voice intelligibility at the receiver. For these reasons, almost all existing Internet phone applications run over UDP and do not bother to retransmit lost packets.

But losing packets is not necessarily as disastrous as one might think. Indeed, packet loss rates between 1 and 20 percent can be tolerated, depending on how the voice is encoded and transmitted, and on how the loss is concealed at the receiver. For example, forward error correction (FEC) can help conceal packet loss. We'll see below that with FEC, redundant information is transmitted along with the original information so that some of the lost original data can be recovered from the redundant information. Nevertheless, if one or more of the links between sender and receiver is severely congested, and packet loss exceeds 10 to 20 percent (although these rates are rarely observed in well-provisioned networks [Boutremans 2002]), then there is really nothing that can be done to achieve acceptable audio quality. Clearly, best-effort service has its limitations.

End-to-End Delay

End-to-end delay is the accumulation of transmission, processing, and queuing delays in routers; propagation delays in the links; and end-system processing delays. For highly interactive audio applications, such as Internet phone, end-to-end delays smaller than 150 msecs are not perceived by a human listener; delays between 150 and 400 msecs can be acceptable but are not ideal; and delays exceeding 400 msecs can seriously hinder the interactivity in voice conversations. The receiving side of an Internet phone application will typically disregard any packets that are delayed more than a certain threshold, for example, more than 400 msecs. Thus, packets that are delayed by more than the threshold are effectively lost.

Packet Jitter

A crucial component of end-to-end delay is the random queuing delays in the routers. Because of these varying delays within the network, the time from when a packet is generated at the source until it is received at the receiver can fluctuate from packet to packet. This phenomenon is called **jitter**.

As an example, consider two consecutive packets within a talk spurt in our Internet phone application. The sender sends the second packet 20 msecs after sending the first packet. But at the receiver, the spacing between these packets can become greater than 20 msecs. To see this, suppose the first packet arrives at a nearly empty queue at a router, but just before the second packet arrives at the queue a large number of packets from other sources arrive at the same queue. Because the first packet suffers a small queuing delay and the second packet suffers a large queuing delay at this router, the first and second packets become spaced by more than 20 msecs. The spacing between consecutive packets can also become less than 20 msecs. To see this, again consider two consecutive packets within a talk spurt. Suppose the first packet joins the end of a queue with a large number of packets, and the second packet arrives at the queue before packets from other sources arrive at the queue. In this case, our two packets find themselves one right after the other in the queue. If the time it takes to transmit a packet on the router's outbound link is less than 20 msecs, then the first and second packets become spaced apart by less than 20 msecs.

The situation is analogous to driving cars on roads. Suppose you and your friend are each driving in your own cars from San Diego to Phoenix. Suppose you and your friend have similar driving styles, and that you both drive at 100 km/hour, traffic permitting. Finally, suppose your friend starts out one hour before you. Then, depending on intervening traffic, you may arrive at Phoenix more or less than one hour after your friend.

If the receiver ignores the presence of jitter and plays out chunks as soon as they arrive, then the resulting audio quality can easily become unintelligible at the receiver. Fortunately, jitter can often be removed by using **sequence numbers**, **timestamps**, and a **playout delay**, as discussed below.

7.3.2 Removing Jitter at the Receiver for Audio

For a voice application such as Internet phone or audio-on-demand, the receiver should attempt to provide synchronous playout of voice chunks in the presence of random network jitter. This is typically done by combining the following three mechanisms:

♦ *Prefacing each chunk with a **sequence number**.* The sender increments the sequence number by one for each of the packets it generates.

♦ *Prefacing each chunk with a **timestamp**.* The sender stamps each chunk with the time at which the chunk was generated.

♦ ***Delaying playout*** *of chunks at the receiver*. The playout delay of the received audio chunks must be long enough so that most of the packets are received before their scheduled playout times. This playout delay can either be fixed throughout the duration of the audio session or it may vary adaptively during the audio session lifetime. Packets that do not arrive before their scheduled playout times are considered lost and forgotten; as noted above, the receiver may use some form of speech interpolation to attempt to conceal the loss.

We now discuss how these three mechanisms, when combined, can alleviate or even eliminate the effects of jitter. We examine two playback strategies: fixed playout delay and adaptive playout delay.

Fixed Playout Delay

With the fixed-delay strategy, the receiver attempts to play out each chunk exactly q msecs after the chunk is generated. So if a chunk is timestamped at time t, the receiver plays out the chunk at time $t + q$, assuming the chunk has arrived by that time. Packets that arrive after their scheduled playout times are discarded and considered lost.

What is a good choice for q? Internet telephone can support delays up to about 400 msecs, although a more satisfying interactive experience is achieved with smaller values of q. On the other hand, if q is made much smaller than 400 msecs, then many packets may miss their scheduled playback times due to the network-induced packet jitter. Roughly speaking, if large variations in end-to-end delay are typical, it is preferable to use a large q; on the other hand, if delay is small and variations in delay are also small, it is preferable to use a small q, perhaps less than 150 msecs.

The trade-off between the playback delay and packet loss is illustrated in Figure 7.6. The figure shows the times at which packets are generated and played out for a single talk spurt. Two distinct initial playout delays are considered. As shown by the leftmost staircase, the sender generates packets at regular intervals—say, every 20 msecs. The first packet in this talk spurt is received at time r. As shown in the figure, the arrivals of subsequent packets are not evenly spaced due to the network jitter.

For the first playout schedule, the fixed initial playout delay is set to $p - r$. With this schedule, the fourth packet does not arrive by its scheduled playout time, and the receiver considers it lost. For the second playout schedule, the fixed initial playout delay is set to $p' - r$. For this schedule, all packets arrive before their scheduled playout times, and there is therefore no loss.

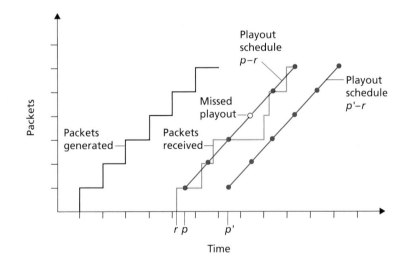

Figure 7.6 ◆ Packet loss for different fixed playout delays.

Adaptive Playout Delay

The example above demonstrates an important delay-loss trade-off that arises when designing a playout strategy with fixed playout delays. By making the initial playout delay large, most packets will make their deadlines and there will therefore be negligible loss; however, for interactive services such as Internet phone, long delays can become bothersome if not intolerable. Ideally, we would like the playout delay to be minimized subject to the constraint that the loss be below a few percent.

The natural way to deal with this trade-off is to estimate the network delay and the variance of the network delay, and to adjust the playout delay accordingly at the beginning of each talk spurt. This adaptive adjustment of playout delays at the beginning of the talk spurts will cause the sender's silent periods to be compressed and elongated; however, compression and elongation of silence by a small amount is not noticeable in speech.

Following [Ramjee 1994], we now describe a generic algorithm that the receiver can use to adaptively adjust its playout delays. To this end, let

t_i = the timestamp of the ith packet = the time the packet was generated by the sender

r_i = the time packet i is received by receiver

p_i = the time packet i is played at receiver

The end-to-end network delay of the ith packet is $r_i - t_i$. Due to network jitter, this delay will vary from packet to packet. Let d_i denote an estimate of the *average* network delay upon reception of the ith packet. This estimate is constructed from the timestamps as follows:

$$d_i = (1 - u)\, d_{i-1} + u\, (r_i - t_i)$$

where u is a fixed constant (for example, $u = 0.01$). Thus d_i is a smoothed average of the observed network delays $r_1 - t_1, \ldots, r_i - t_i$. The estimate places more weight on the recently observed network delays than on the observed network delays of the distant past. This form of estimate should not be completely unfamiliar; a similar idea is used to estimate round-trip times in TCP, as discussed in Chapter 3. Let v_i denote an estimate of the average deviation of the delay from the estimated average delay. This estimate is also constructed from the timestamps:

$$v_i = (1 - u)\, v_{i-1} + u\, |\, r_i - t_i - d_i\, |$$

The estimates d_i and v_i are calculated for every packet received, although they are used only to determine the playout point for the first packet in any talk spurt.

Once having calculated these estimates, the receiver employs the following algorithm for the playout of packets. If packet i is the first packet of a talk spurt, its playout time, p_i, is computed as:

$$p_i = t_i + d_i + Kv_i$$

where K is a positive constant (for example, $K = 4$). The purpose of the Kv_i term is to set the playout time far enough into the future so that only a small fraction of the arriving packets in the talk spurt will be lost due to late arrivals. The playout point for any subsequent packet in a talk spurt is computed as an offset from the point in time when the first packet in the talk spurt was played out. In particular, let

$$q_i = p_i - t_i$$

be the length of time from when the first packet in the talk spurt is generated until it is played out. If packet j also belongs to this talk spurt, it is played out at time

$$p_j = t_j + q_i$$

The algorithm just described makes perfect sense assuming that the receiver can tell whether a packet is the first packet in the talk spurt. If there is no packet loss, then the receiver can determine whether packet i is the first packet of the talk spurt by comparing the timestamp of the ith packet with the timestamp of the $(i - 1)$st packet. Indeed, if $t_i - t_{i-1} > 20$ msecs, then the receiver knows that ith packet starts a new talk spurt. But now suppose there is occasional packet loss. In this case, two successive packets received at the destination may have timestamps that differ by more than 20 msecs when the two packets belong to the same talk spurt. So here is where the sequence numbers are particularly useful. The receiver can use the sequence numbers to determine whether a difference of more than 20 msecs in time-stamps is due to a new talk spurt or to lost packets.

7.3.3 Recovering from Packet Loss

We have discussed in some detail how an Internet phone application can deal with packet jitter. We now briefly describe several schemes that attempt to preserve acceptable audio quality in the presence of packet loss. Such schemes are called **loss recovery schemes**. Here we define packet loss in a broad sense: a packet is lost either if it never arrives at the receiver or if it arrives after its scheduled playout time. Our Internet phone example will again serve as a context for describing loss recovery schemes.

As mentioned at the beginning of this section, retransmitting lost packets is generally not appropriate in an interactive real-time application such as Internet phone. Indeed, retransmitting a packet that has missed its playout deadline serves absolutely no purpose. And retransmitting a packet that overflowed a router queue cannot normally be accomplished quickly enough. Because of these considerations, Internet phone applications often use some type of loss anticipation scheme. Two types of loss anticipation schemes are **forward error correction (FEC)** and **interleaving**.

Forward Error Correction (FEC)

The basic idea of FEC is to add redundant information to the original packet stream. For the cost of marginally increasing the transmission rate of the audio of the stream, the redundant information can be used to reconstruct approximations or exact versions of some of the lost packets. Following [Bolot 1996] and [Perkins 1998], we now outline two FEC mechanisms. The first mechanism sends a redundant encoded chunk after every n chunks. The redundant chunk is obtained by exclusive OR-ing the n original chunks [Shacham 1990]. In this manner if any one packet of the group of $n + 1$ packets is lost, the receiver can fully reconstruct the lost packet. But if two or more packets in a group are lost, the receiver cannot reconstruct the lost packets. By keeping $n + 1$, the group size, small, a large fraction of the lost packets can be recovered when loss is not excessive. However, the smaller the group size, the greater the relative increase of the transmission rate of the audio stream. In particular, the transmission rate increases by a factor of $1/n$; for example, if $n = 3$, then the transmission rate increases by 33 percent. Furthermore, this simple scheme increases the playout delay, as the receiver must wait to receive the entire group of packets before it can begin playout. For more practical details about how FEC works for multimedia transport see [RFC 2733].

The second FEC mechanism is to send a lower-resolution audio stream as the redundant information. For example, the sender might create a nominal audio stream and a corresponding low-resolution, low-bit rate audio stream. (The nominal stream could be a PCM encoding at 64 kbps, and the lower-quality stream could be a GSM encoding at 13 kbps.) The low-bit rate stream is referred to as the redundant stream. As shown in Figure 7.7, the sender constructs the nth packet by taking the nth chunk from the nominal stream and appending to it the $(n - 1)$st chunk from the redundant stream. In this manner, whenever there is nonconsecutive packet loss, the receiver can conceal the loss by playing out the low-bit rate encoded chunk that arrives with the subsequent packet. Of course, low-bit rate chunks give lower quality than the nominal chunks. However, a stream of mostly high-quality chunks, occasional low-quality chunks, and no missing chunks gives good overall audio quality. Note that in this scheme, the receiver only has to receive two packets before playback, so that the increased playout delay is small. Furthermore, if the low-bit rate encoding is much less than the nominal encoding, then the marginal increase in the transmission rate will be small.

In order to cope with consecutive loss, we can use a simple variation. Instead of appending just the $(n - 1)$st low-bit rate chunk to the nth nominal chunk, the sender

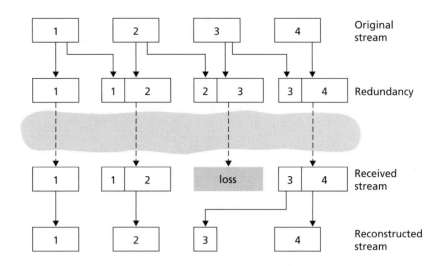

Figure 7.7 ♦ Piggybacking lower-quality redundant information

can append the $(n-1)$st and $(n-2)$nd low-bit rate chunk, or append the $(n-1)$st and $(n-3)$rd low-bit rate chunk, and so on. By appending more low-bit rate chunks to each nominal chunk, the audio quality at the receiver becomes acceptable for a wider variety of harsh best-effort environments. On the other hand, the additional chunks increase the transmission bandwidth and the playout delay.

Free Phone [Freephone 2004] and RAT [RAT 2004] are well-documented Internet phone applications that use FEC. They can transmit lower-quality audio streams along with the nominal audio stream, as described above. Also see [Rosenberg 2000].

Interleaving

As an alternative to redundant transmission, an Internet phone application can send interleaved audio. As shown in Figure 7.8, the sender resequences units of audio data before transmission, so that originally adjacent units are separated by a certain distance in the transmitted stream. Interleaving can mitigate the effect of packet losses. If, for example, units are 5 msecs in length and chunks are 20 msecs (that is, four units per chunk), then the first chunk could contain units 1, 5, 9, and 13; the second chunk could contain units 2, 6, 10, and 14; and so on. Figure 7.8 shows that the loss of a single packet from an interleaved stream results in multiple small gaps in the reconstructed stream, as opposed to the single large gap that would occur in a noninterleaved stream.

Interleaving can significantly improve the perceived quality of an audio stream [Perkins 1998]. It also has low overhead. The obvious disadvantage of interleaving is that it increases latency. This limits its use for interactive applications such as

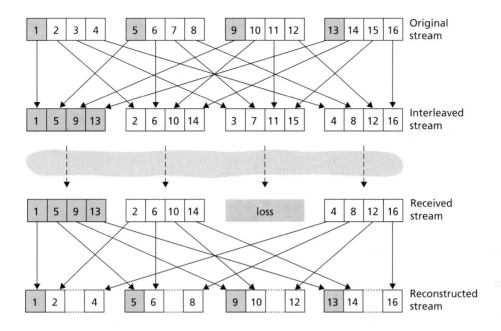

Figure 7.8 ◆ Sending interleaved audio

Internet phone, although it can perform well for streaming stored audio. A major advantage of interleaving is that it does not increase the bandwidth requirements of a stream.

Receiver-Based Repair of Damaged Audio Streams

Receiver-based recovery schemes attempt to produce a replacement for a lost packet that is similar to the original. As discussed in [Perkins 1998], this is possible since audio signals, and in particular speech, exhibit large amounts of short-term self-similarity. As such, these techniques work for relatively small loss rates (less than 15 percent), and for small packets (4–40 msecs). When the loss length approaches the length of a phoneme (5–100 msecs) these techniques break down, since whole phonemes may be missed by the listener.

Perhaps the simplest form of receiver-based recovery is packet repetition. Packet repetition replaces lost packets with copies of the packets that arrived immediately before the loss. It has low computational complexity and performs reasonably well. Another form of receiver-based recovery is interpolation, which uses audio before and after the loss to interpolate a suitable packet to cover the loss. Interpolation performs somewhat better than packet repetition but is significantly more computationally intensive [Perkins 1998].

7.3.4 Streaming Stored Audio and Video

Let us conclude this section with a few words about streaming stored audio and video. Streaming stored audio/video applications also typically use sequence numbers, timestamps, and playout delay to alleviate or even eliminate the effects of network jitter. However, there is an important difference between real-time interactive audio/video and streaming stored audio/video. Specifically, streaming of stored audio/video can tolerate significantly larger delays. Indeed, when a user requests an audio/video clip, the user may find it acceptable to wait five seconds or more before playback begins. And most users can tolerate similar delays after interactive actions such as a temporal jump within the media stream. This greater tolerance for delay gives the application developer greater flexibility when designing stored media applications.

7.4 Protocols for Real-Time Interactive Applications

Real-time interactive applications, including Internet phone and video conferencing, promise to drive much of the future Internet growth. It is therefore not surprising that standards bodies, such as the IETF and ITU, have been busy for many years (and continue to be busy!) at hammering out standards for this class of applications. With the appropriate standards in place for real-time interactive applications, independent companies will be able to create new and compelling products that interoperate with each other. In this section we examine RTP, SIP, and H.323 for real-time interactive applications. All three sets of standards are enjoying widespread implementation in industry products.

7.4.1 RTP

In the previous section we learned that the sender side of a multimedia application appends header fields to the audio/video chunks before passing them to the transport layer. These header fields include sequence numbers and timestamps. Since most multimedia networking applications can make use of sequence numbers and timestamps, it is convenient to have a standardized packet structure that includes fields for audio/video data, sequence number, and timestamp, as well as other potentially useful fields. RTP, defined in RFC 3550, is such a standard. RTP can be used for transporting common formats such as PCM, GSM, and MP3 for sound and MPEG and H.263 for video. It can also be used for transporting proprietary sound and video formats. Today, RTP enjoys widespread implementation in hundreds of products and research prototypes. It is also complementary to other important real-time interactive protocols, including SIP and H.323.

In this section we provide an introduction to RTP and to its companion protocol, RTCP. We also encourage you to visit Henning Schulzrinne's RTP site [Schulzrinne-RTP 2004], which provides a wealth of information on the subject. Also, you may want to visit the Free Phone site [Freephone 2004], which documents an Internet phone application that uses RTP.

RTP Basics

RTP typically runs on top of UDP. The sending side encapsulates a media chunk within an RTP packet, then encapsulates the packet in a UDP segment, and then hands the segment to IP. The receiving side extracts the RTP packet from the UDP segment, then extracts the media chunk from the RTP packet, and then passes the chunk to the media player for decoding and rendering.

As an example, consider the use of RTP to transport voice. Suppose the voice source is PCM-encoded (that is, sampled, quantized, and digitized) at 64 kbps. Further suppose that the application collects the encoded data in 20-msec chunks, that is, 160 bytes in a chunk. The sending side precedes each chunk of the audio data with an **RTP header** that includes the type of audio encoding, a sequence number, and a timestamp. The RTP header is normally 12 bytes. The audio chunk along with the RTP header form the **RTP packet**. The RTP packet is then sent into the UDP socket interface. At the receiver side, the application receives the RTP packet from its socket interface. The application extracts the audio chunk from the RTP packet and uses the header fields of the RTP packet to properly decode and play back the audio chunk.

If an application incorporates RTP—instead of a proprietary scheme to provide payload type, sequence numbers, or timestamps—then the application will more easily interoperate with other networked multimedia applications. For example, if two different companies develop Internet phone software and they both incorporate RTP into their product, there may be some hope that a user using one of the Internet phone products will be able to communicate with a user using the other Internet phone product. In Section 7.4.3 we'll see that RTP is often used in conjunction with the Internet telephony standards.

It should be emphasized that RTP does not provide any mechanism to ensure timely delivery of data or provide other quality-of-service (QoS) guarantees; it does not even guarantee delivery of packets or prevent out-of-order delivery of packets. Indeed, RTP encapsulation is seen only at the end systems. Routers do not distinguish between IP datagrams that carry RTP packets and IP datagrams that don't.

RTP allows each source (for example, a camera or a microphone) to be assigned its own independent RTP stream of packets. For example, for a video conference between two participants, four RTP streams could be opened—two streams for transmitting the audio (one in each direction) and two streams for transmitting the video (again, one in each direction). However, many popular encoding techniques—

including MPEG 1 and MPEG 2—bundle the audio and video into a single stream during the encoding process. When the audio and video are bundled by the encoder, then only one RTP stream is generated in each direction.

RTP packets are not limited to unicast applications. They can also be sent over one-to-many and many-to-many multicast trees. For a many-to-many multicast session, all of the session's senders and sources typically use the same multicast group for sending their RTP streams. RTP multicast streams belonging together, such as audio and video streams emanating from multiple senders in a video conference application, belong to an **RTP session**.

RTP Packet Header Fields

As shown in Figure 7.9, the four main RTP packet header fields are the payload type, sequence number, timestamp, and the source identifier fields.

The payload-type field in the RTP packet is 7 bits long. For an audio stream, the payload-type field is used to indicate the type of audio encoding (for example, PCM, adaptive delta modulation, linear predictive encoding) that is being used. If a sender decides to change the encoding in the middle of a session, the sender can inform the receiver of the change through this payload-type field. The sender may want to change the encoding in order to increase the audio quality or to decrease the RTP stream bit rate. Table 7.1 lists some of the audio payload types currently supported by RTP.

For a video stream, the payload type is used to indicate the type of video encoding (for example, motion JPEG, MPEG 1, MPEG 2, H.261). Again, the sender can change video encoding on the fly during a session. Table 7.2 lists some of the video payload types currently supported by RTP. The other important fields are the following.

♦ *Sequence number field.* The sequence number field is 16 bits long. The sequence number increments by one for each RTP packet sent, and may be used by the receiver to detect packet loss and to restore packet sequence. For example, if the receiver side of the application receives a stream of RTP packets with a gap between sequence numbers 86 and 89, then the receiver knows that packets 87 and 88 are missing. The receiver can then attempt to conceal the lost data.

♦ *Timestamp field.* The timestamp field is 32 bits long. It reflects the sampling instant of the first byte in the RTP data packet. As we saw in the preceding

Figure 7.9 ♦ RTP header fields

Payload-Type Number	Audio Format	Sampling Rate	Rate
0	PCM μ-law	8 kHz	64 kbps
1	1016	8 kHz	4.8 kbps
3	GSM	8 kHz	13 kbps
7	LPC	8 kHz	2.4 kbps
9	G.722	16 kHz	48–64 kbps
14	MPEG Audio	90 kHz	—
15	G.728	8 kHz	16 kbps

Table 7.1 ♦ Audio Payload Types Supported by RTP

section, the receiver can use timestamps in order to remove packet jitter introduced in the network and to provide synchronous playout at the receiver. The timestamp is derived from a sampling clock at the sender. As an example, for audio the timestamp clock increments by one for each sampling period (for example, each 125 μsec for an 8 kHz sampling clock); if the audio application generates chunks consisting of 160 encoded samples, then the timestamp increases by 160 for each RTP packet when the source is active. The timestamp clock continues to increase at a constant rate even if the source is inactive.

♦ *Synchronization source identifier (SSRC).* The SSRC field is 32 bits long. It identifies the source of the RTP stream. Typically, each stream in an RTP session has a distinct SSRC. The SSRC is not the IP address of the sender, but instead is a number that the source assigns randomly when the new stream is started. The probability that two streams get assigned the same SSRC is very small. Should this happen, the two sources pick a new SSRC value.

Payload-Type Number	Video Format
26	Motion JPEG
31	H.261
32	MPEG 1 video
33	MPEG 2 video

Table 7.2 ♦ Some Video Payload Types Supported by RTP

Developing Software Applications with RTP

There are two approaches to developing an RTP-based networked application. The first approach is for the application developer to incorporate RTP by hand, that is, actually to write the code that performs RTP encapsulation at the sender side and RTP unraveling at the receiver side. The second approach is for the application developer to use existing RTP libraries (for C programmers) and Java classes (for Java programmers), which perform the encapsulation and unraveling for the application. Since you may be itching to write your first multimedia networking application using RTP, let us now elaborate a little on these two approaches. (The programming assignment at the end of this chapter will guide you through the creation of an RTP application.) We'll do this in the context of unicast communication (rather than for multicast).

Recall from Chapter 2 that the UDP API requires the sending process to set, for each UDP segment it sends, the destination IP address and the destination port number before popping the packet into the UDP socket. The UDP segment will then wander through the Internet and (if the segment is not lost due to, for example, router buffer overflow) will eventually arrive at the door of the receiving process for the application. This door is fully addressed by the destination IP address and the destination port number. In fact, any IP datagram containing this destination IP address and destination port number will be directed to the receiving process's UDP door. (The UDP API also lets the application developer set the UDP source port number; however, this value has no effect on which process the segment is sent to.) It is important to note that RTP does not mandate a specific port number. When the application developer creates an RTP application, the developer specifies the port numbers for the two sides of the application.

As part of the programming assignment for this chapter, you will write an RTP server that encapsulates stored video frames within RTP packets. You will do this by hand; that is, your application will grab a video frame, add the RTP headers to the frame to create an RTP packet, and then pass the RTP frame to the UDP socket. To do this, you will need to create placeholder fields for the various RTP headers, including a sequence-number field and a timestamp field. And for each RTP packet that is created, you will have to set the sequence number and the timestamp appropriately. You will explicitly code all of these RTP operations into the sender side of your application. As shown in Figure 7.10, your API to the network will be the standard UDP socket API.

An alternative approach (not done in the programming assignment) is to use a Java RTP class (or a C RTP library for C programmers) to implement the RTP operations. With this approach, as shown in Figure 7.11, the application developer is given the impression that RTP is part of the transport layer, with an RTP/UDP API between the application layer and the transport layer. Without getting into the nitty-gritty details (as they are class/library-dependent), when sending a chunk of media into the API, the sending side of the application needs to provide the interface with

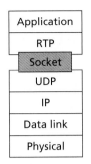

Figure 7.10 ♦ RTP is part of the application and lies above the UDP socket.

the media chunk itself, a payload-type number, an SSRC, and a timestamp, along with a destination port number and an IP destination address. We mention here that the Java Media Framework (JMF) includes a complete RTP implementation.

7.4.2 RTP Control Protocol (RTCP)

RFC 1889 also specifies RTCP, a protocol that a networked multimedia application can use in conjunction with RTP. As shown in the multicast scenario in Figure 7.12, RTCP packets are transmitted by each participant in an RTP session to all other participants in the session using IP multicast. For an RTP session, typically there is a single multicast address and all RTP and RTCP packets belonging to the session use the multicast address. RTP and RTCP packets are distinguished from each other through the use of distinct port numbers. (The RTCP port number is set to be equal to the RTP port number plus one.)

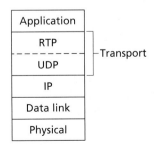

Figure 7.11 ♦ RTP can be viewed as a sublayer of the transport layer.

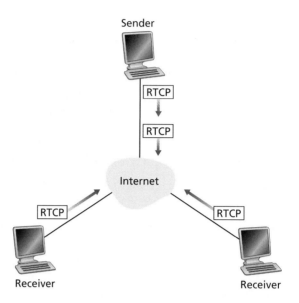

Figure 7.12 ◆ Both senders and receivers send RTCP messages.

RTCP packets do not encapsulate chunks of audio or video. Instead, RTCP packets are sent periodically and contain sender and/or receiver reports that announce statistics that can be useful to the application. These statistics include number of packets sent, number of packets lost, and interarrival jitter. The RTP specification [RFC 3550] does not dictate what the application should do with this feedback information; this is up to the application developer. Senders can use the feedback information, for example, to modify their transmission rates. The feedback information can also be used for diagnostic purposes; for example, receivers can determine whether problems are local, regional, or global.

RTCP Packet Types

For each RTP stream that a receiver receives as part of a session, the receiver generates a reception report. The receiver aggregates its reception reports into a single RTCP packet. The packet is then sent into the multicast tree that connects all the session's participants. The reception report includes several fields, the most important of which are listed below.

◆ The SSRC of the RTP stream for which the reception report is being generated.

◆ The fraction of packets lost within the RTP stream. Each receiver calculates the number of RTP packets lost divided by the number of RTP packets sent as part of the stream. If a sender receives reception reports indicating that the receivers are receiving only a small fraction of the sender's transmitted packets, it can switch to a lower encoding rate, with the aim of decreasing network congestion and improving the reception rate.

♦ The last sequence number received in the stream of RTP packets.

♦ The interarrival jitter, which is a smoothed estimate of the variation in the interarrival time between successive packets in the RTP stream.

For each RTP stream that a sender is transmitting, the sender creates and transmits RTCP sender report packets. These packets include information about the RTP stream, including:

♦ The SSRC of the RTP stream

♦ The timestamp and wall clock time of the most recently generated RTP packet in the stream

♦ The number of packets sent in the stream

♦ The number of bytes sent in the stream

Sender reports can be used to synchronize different media streams within an RTP session. For example, consider a video conferencing application for which each sender generates two independent RTP streams, one for video and one for audio. The timestamps in these RTP packets are tied to the video and audio sampling clocks, and are not tied to the *wall clock time* (i.e., real time). Each RTCP sender report contains, for the most recently generated packet in the associated RTP stream, the timestamp of the RTP packet and the wall clock time when the packet was created. Thus the RTCP sender report packets associate the sampling clock with the real-time clock. Receivers can use this association in RTCP sender reports to synchronize the playout of audio and video.

For each RTP stream that a sender is transmitting, the sender also creates and transmits source description packets. These packets contain information about the source, such as the e-mail address of the sender, the sender's name, and the application that generates the RTP stream. It also includes the SSRC of the associated RTP stream. These packets provide a mapping between the source identifier (that is, the SSRC) and the user/host name.

RTCP packets are stackable; that is, receiver reception reports, sender reports, and source descriptors can be concatenated into a single packet. The resulting packet is then encapsulated into a UDP segment and forwarded into the multicast tree.

RTCP Bandwidth Scaling

You may have observed that RTCP has a potential scaling problem. Consider, for example, an RTP session that consists of one sender and a large number of receivers. If each of the receivers periodically generates RTCP packets, then the aggregate transmission rate of RTCP packets can greatly exceed the rate of RTP packets sent by the sender. Observe that the amount of RTP traffic sent into the multicast tree does not change as the number of receivers increases, whereas the amount of RTCP traffic grows linearly with the number of receivers. To solve this scaling problem, RTCP modifies the rate at which a participant sends RTCP packets into the multicast tree as a function of the number of participants in the session. Also, since each participant sends control packets to everyone else, each participant can estimate the total number of participants in the session [Friedman 1999].

RTCP attempts to limit its traffic to 5 percent of the session bandwidth. For example, suppose there is one sender, which is sending video at a rate of 2 Mbps. Then RTCP attempts to limit its traffic to 5 percent of 2 Mbps, or 100 kbps, as follows. The protocol gives 75 percent of this rate, or 75 kbps, to the receivers; it gives the remaining 25 percent of the rate, or 25 kbps, to the sender. The 75 kbps devoted to the receivers is equally shared among the receivers. Thus, if there are R receivers, then each receiver gets to send RTCP traffic at a rate of 75/R kbps, and the sender gets to send RTCP traffic at a rate of 25 kbps. A participant (a sender or receiver) determines the RTCP packet transmission period by dynamically calculating the average RTCP packet size (across the entire session) and dividing the average RTCP packet size by its allocated rate. In summary, the period for transmitting RTCP packets for a sender is

$$T = \frac{\text{number of senders}}{.25 \cdot .05 \cdot \text{session bandwidth}} (\text{avg. RTCP packet size})$$

And the period for transmitting RTCP packets for a receiver is

$$T = \frac{\text{number of receivers}}{.75 \cdot .05 \cdot \text{session bandwidth}} (\text{avg. RTCP packet size})$$

7.4.3 SIP

Imagine a world in which, when you are working on your PC, your phone calls arrive over the Internet to your PC. When you get up and start walking around, your new phone calls are automatically routed to your PDA. And when you are driving in your car, your new phone calls are automatically routed to some Internet appliance in your car. In this same world, while participating in a conference call, you can access an address book to call and invite other participants into the conference. The other participants may be at their PCs, or walking with their PDAs, or driving their cars—no matter where they are, your invitation is transparently routed to them. In this same world, when you browse an individual's homepage, there will be a link "Call Me"; clicking on this link establishes an Internet phone session between your PC and the owner of the homepage (wherever that person might be).

In this world, there is no longer a circuit-switched telephone network. Instead, all calls pass over the Internet—from end to end. In this same world, companies no longer use private branch exchanges (PBXs), that is, local circuit switches for handling intracompany telephone calls. Instead, the intracompany phone traffic flows over the company's high-speed LAN.

All of this may sound like science fiction. And, of course, today's circuit-switched networks and PBXs are not going to disappear completely in the near future [Jiang 2001]. Nevertheless, protocols and products exist to turn this vision into a reality. Among the most promising protocols in this direction is the Session Initiation Protocol (SIP), defined in [RFC 3261]. SIP is a lightweight protocol that does the following:

♦ It provides mechanisms for establishing calls between a caller and a callee over an IP network. It allows the caller to notify the callee that it wants to start a call. It allows the participants to agree on media encodings. It also allows participants to end calls.

♦ It provides mechanisms for the caller to determine the current IP address of the callee. Users do not have a single, fixed IP addresses because they may be assigned addresses dynamically (using DHCP) and because they may have multiple IP devices, each with a different IP address.

♦ It provides mechanisms for call management, such as adding new media streams during the call, changing the encoding during the call, inviting new participants during the call, call transfer, and call holding.

Setting Up a Call to a Known IP Address

To understand the essence of SIP, it is best to take a look at a concrete example. In this example, Alice is at her PC and she wants to call Bob, who is also working at his PC. Alice's and Bob's PCs are both equipped with SIP-based software for making and receiving phone calls. In this initial example, we'll assume that Alice knows the IP address of Bob's PC. Figure 7.13 illustrates the SIP call-establishment process.

In Figure 7.13, we see that an SIP session begins when Alice sends Bob an INVITE message, which resembles an HTTP request message. This INVITE message is sent over UDP to the well-known port 5060 for SIP. (SIP messages can also be sent over TCP.) The INVITE message includes an identifier for Bob (bob@193.64.210.89), an indication of Alice's current IP address, an indication that Alice desires to receive audio, which is to be encoded in format AVP 0 (PCM encoded μ-law) and encapsulated in RTP, and an indication that she wants to receive the RTP packets on port 38060. After receiving Alice's INVITE message, Bob sends an SIP response message, which resembles an HTTP response message. This response SIP message is also sent to the SIP port 5060. Bob's response includes a 200 OK as well as an indication of his IP address, his desired encoding and packetization for reception, and his port number to which the audio packets should be sent.

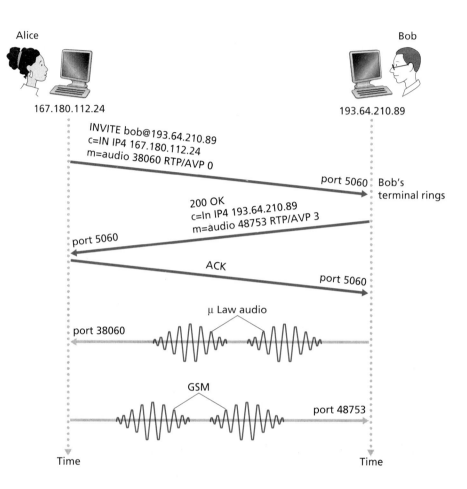

Figure 7.13 ♦ SIP call establishment when Alice knows Bob's IP address

Note that in this example Alice and Bob are going to use different audio-encoding mechanisms: Alice is asked to encode her audio with GSM whereas Bob is asked to encode his audio with PCM μ-law. After receiving Bob's response, Alice sends Bob an SIP acknowledgment message. After this SIP transaction, Bob and Alice can talk. (For visual convenience, Figure 7.13 shows Alice talking after Bob, but in truth they would normally talk at the same time.) Bob will encode and packetize the audio as requested and send the audio packets to port number 38060 at IP address 167.180.112.24. Alice will also encode and packetize the audio as requested and send the audio packets to port number 48753 at IP address 193.64.210.89.

From this simple example, we have learned a number of key characteristics of SIP. First, SIP is an out-of-band protocol: the SIP messages are sent and received in sockets that are different from those used for sending and receiving the media data. Second, the SIP messages themselves are ASCII-readable and resemble HTTP messages. Third, SIP requires all messages to be acknowledged, so it can run over UDP or TCP.

In this example, let's consider what would happen if Bob does not have a PCM μ-law codec for encoding audio. In this case, instead of responding with 200 OK, Bob would likely respond with a 600 Not Acceptable and list in the message all the codecs he can use. Alice would then choose one of the listed codecs and send another INVITE message, this time advertising the chosen codec. Bob could also simply reject the call by sending one of many possible rejection reply codes. (There are many such codes, including "busy," "gone," "payment required," and "forbidden.")

SIP Addresses

In the previous example, Bob's SIP address is sip:bob@193.64.210.89. However, we expect many—if not most—SIP addresses to resemble e-mail addresses. For example, Bob's address might be sip:bob@domain.com. When Alice's SIP device sends an INVITE message, the message would include this e-mail-like address; the SIP infrastructure would then route the message to the IP device that Bob is currently using (as we'll discuss below). Other possible forms for the SIP address could be Bob's legacy phone number or simply Bob's first/middle/last name (assuming it is unique).

An interesting feature of SIP addresses is that they can be included in Web pages, just as people's e-mail addresses are included in Web pages with the mailto URL. For example, suppose Bob has a personal homepage, and he wants to provide a means for visitors to the homepage to call him. He could then simply include the URL sip:bob@domain.com. When the visitor clicks on the URL, the SIP application in the visitor's device is launched and an INVITE message is sent to Bob.

SIP Messages

In this short introduction to SIP, we'll not cover all SIP message types and headers. Instead, we'll take a brief look at the SIP INVITE message, along with a few common header lines. Let us again suppose that Alice wants to initiate an IP phone call to Bob, and this time Alice knows only Bob's SIP address, bob@domain.com, and does not know the IP address of the device that Bob is currently using. Then her message might look something like this:

```
INVITE sip:bob@domain.com SIP/2.0
Via: SIP/2.0/UDP 167.180.112.24
From: sip:alice@hereway.com
To: sip:bob@domain.com
```

```
Call-ID: a2e3a@pigeon.hereway.com
Content-Type: application/sdp
Content-Length: 885

c=IN IP4 167.180.112.24
m=audio 38060 RTP/AVP 0
```

The INVITE line includes the SIP version, as does an HTTP request message. Whenever an SIP message passes through a SIP device (including the device that originates the message), it attaches a Via header, which indicates the IP address of the device. (We'll see soon that the typical INVITE message passes through many SIP devices before reaching the callee's SIP application.) Similar to an e-mail message, the SIP message includes a From header line and a To header line. The message includes a Call-ID, which uniquely identifies the call (similar to the message-ID in e-mail). It includes a Content-Type header line, which defines the format used to describe the content contained in the SIP message. It also includes a Content-Length header line, which provides the length in bytes of the content in the message. Finally, after a carriage return and line feed, the message contains the content. In this case, the content provides information about Alice's IP address and how Alice wants to receive the audio.

Name Translation and User Location

In the example in Figure 7.13, we assumed that Alice's SIP device knew the IP address where Bob could be contacted. But this assumption is quite unrealistic, not only because IP addresses are often dynamically assigned with DHCP, but also because Bob may have multiple IP devices (for example, different devices for his home, work, and car). So now let us suppose that Alice knows only Bob's e-mail address, bob@domain.com, and that this same address is used for SIP-based calls. In this case, Alice needs to obtain the IP address of the device that the user bob@domain.com is currently using. To find this out, Alice creates an INVITE message that begins with INVITE bob@domain.com SIP/2.0 and sends this message to an **SIP proxy**. The proxy will respond with an SIP reply that might include the IP address of the device that bob@domain.com is currently using. Alternatively, the reply might include the IP address of Bob's voicemail box, or it might include a URL of a Web page (that says "Bob is sleeping. Leave me alone!"). Also, the result returned by the proxy might depend on the caller: if the call is from Bob's wife, he might accept the call and supply his IP address; if the call is from Bob's mother-in-law, he might respond with the URL that points to the I-am-sleeping Web page!

Now, you are probably wondering, how can the proxy server determine the current IP address for bob@domain.com? To answer this question, we need to say a few words about another SIP device, the **SIP registrar**. Every SIP user has an associated registrar. Whenever a user launches an SIP application on a device, the application sends an SIP register message to the registrar, informing the registrar of its current

IP address. For example, when Bob launches his SIP application on his PDA, the application would send a message along the lines of:

```
REGISTER sip:domain.com SIP/2.0
Via: SIP/2.0/UDP 193.64.210.89
From: sip:bob@domain.com
To: sip:bob@domain.com
Expires: 3600
```

Bob's registrar keeps track of Bob's current IP address. Whenever Bob switches to a new SIP device, the new device sends a new register message, indicating the new IP address. Also, if Bob remains at the same device for an extended period of time, the device will send refresh register messages, indicating that the most recently sent IP address is still valid. (In the example above, refresh messages need to be sent every 3600 seconds to maintain the address at the registrar server.) It is worth noting that the registrar is analogous to a DNS authoritative name server: the DNS server translates fixed host names to fixed IP addresses; the SIP registrar translates fixed human identifiers (for example, bob@domain.com) to dynamic IP addresses. Often SIP registrars and SIP proxies are run on the same host.

Now let's examine how Alice's SIP proxy server obtains Bob's current IP address. From the preceding discussion we see that the proxy server simply needs to forward Alice's INVITE message to Bob's registrar/proxy. The registrar/proxy could then forward the message to Bob's current SIP device. Finally, Bob, having now received Alice's INVITE message, could send an SIP response to Alice.

As an example, consider Figure 7.14, in which jim@umass.edu, currently working on 217.123.56.89, wants to initiate a voice-over-IP session with keith@upenn.edu, currently working on 197.87.54.21. The following steps are taken: (1) Jim sends an INVITE message to the umass SIP proxy. (2) The proxy does a DNS lookup on the SIP registrar upenn.edu (not shown in diagram) and then forwards the message to the registrar server. (3) Because keith@upenn.edu is no longer registered at the upenn registrar, the upenn registrar sends a redirect response, indicating that it should try keith@eurecom.fr. (4) The umass proxy sends an INVITE to the eurecom SIP registrar. (5) The eurecom registrar knows the IP address of keith@eurecom.fr and forwards the INVITE to the host 197.87.54.21, which is running Keith's SIP client. (6–8). A SIP response is sent back through registrars/proxies to the SIP client on 217.123.56.89. (9) Media is sent directly between the two clients. (There is also an SIP acknowledgment message, which is not shown.)

Our discussion of SIP has focused on call initiation for voice calls. SIP, being a signaling protocol for initiating and ending calls in general, can be used for video conference calls as well as for text-based sessions. In fact, SIP has become a fundamental component in many instant-messaging applications. Readers desiring to learn more about SIP are encouraged to visit Henning Schulzrinne's SIP Web site

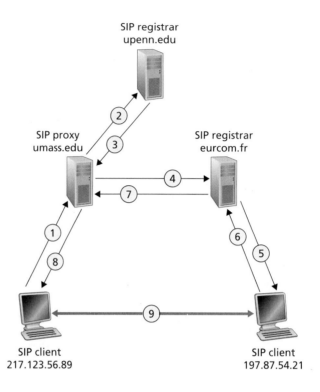

Figure 7.14 ♦ Session initiation, involving SIP proxies and registrars

[Schulzrinne-SIP 2004]. In particular, on this site you will find open source software for SIP clients and servers [SIP Software 2004].

7.4.4 H.323

As an alternative to SIP, H.323 is a popular standard for real-time audio and video conferencing among end systems on the Internet. As shown in Figure 7.15, the standard also covers how end systems attached to the Internet communicate with telephones attached to ordinary circuit-switched telephone networks. (SIP does this as well, although we did not discuss it.) The H.323 gatekeeper is a device similar to an SIP registrar.

The H.323 standard is an umbrella specification that includes the following specifications:

♦ A specification for how endpoints negotiate common audio/video encodings. Because H.323 supports a variety of audio and video encoding standards, a protocol is needed to allow the communicating endpoints to agree on a common encoding.

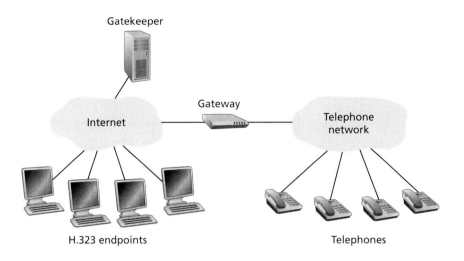

Figure 7.15 ♦ H.323 end systems attached to the Internet can communicate with telephones attached to a circuit-switched telephone network.

♦ A specification for how audio and video chunks are encapsulated and sent over the network. In particular, H.323 mandates RTP for this purpose.

♦ A specification for how endpoints communicate with their respective gatekeepers.

♦ A specification for how Internet phones communicate through a gateway with ordinary phones in the public circuit-switched telephone network.

Minimally, each H.323 endpoint *must* support the G.711 speech compression standard. G.711 uses PCM to generate digitized speech at either 56 kbps or 64 kbps. Although H.323 requires every endpoint to be voice capable (through G.711), video capabilities are optional. Because video support is optional, manufacturers of terminals can sell simpler speech terminals as well as more complex terminals that support both audio and video. Video capabilities for an H.323 endpoint are optional. However, if an endpoint does support video, then it must (at the very least) support the QCIF H.261 (176 x 144 pixels) video standard.

H.323 is a comprehensive umbrella standard, which, in addition to the standards and protocols described above, mandates a H.245 control protocol, a Q.931 signaling channel, and an RAS protocol for registration with the gatekeeper.

We conclude this section by highlighting some of the most important differences between H.323 and SIP.

♦ H.323 is a complete, vertically integrated suite of protocols for multimedia conferencing: signaling, registration, admission control, transport, and codecs.

♦ SIP, on the other hand, addresses only session initiation and management and is a single component. SIP works with RTP but does not mandate it. It works with G.711 speech codecs and QCIF H.261 video codecs but does not mandate them. It can be combined with other protocols and services.

♦ H.323 comes from the ITU (telephony), whereas SIP comes from the IETF and borrows many concepts from the Web, DNS, and Internet e-mail.

♦ H.323, being an umbrella standard, is large and complex. SIP uses the KISS principle: keep it simple, stupid.

For an excellent discussion of H.323, SIP, and voice-over-IP in general, see [Hersent 2000].

7.5 Distributing Multimedia: Content Distribution Networks

With video streaming rates ranging from hundreds of kbps for low-resolution video to several Mbps for DVD video, the task of streaming a stored video, on demand, to a large number of geographically distributed users seems a daunting challenge. The simplest approach would be to store the video in a single server and simply stream the video from a video server (or server farm) to a client for each client request as we discussed in Section 7.2. But there are two obvious problems with this solution. First, because a client may be very far from the server, server-to-client packets may pass through many ISPs, increasing the likelihood of significant delay and loss. Second, if the video is very popular, the video will likely be sent many times through the same ISPs (and over the same communication links), thereby consuming significant bandwidth. In Chapter 2 we discussed how caching can alleviate these problems. Although we discussed caching in terms of traditional Web content, it should be clear that caching is also appropriate for multimedia content such as stored audio and video. In this section we discuss **content distribution networks (CDNs)**, which provide an alternative approach to distributing stored multimedia content (as well as for distributing traditional Web content).

CDNs are based on the philosophy that if the client can't come to the content (because the best-effort path from server-to-client path cannot support streaming video), the content should be brought to the client. CDNs thus use a different model than Web caching. For a CDN, the paying customers are no longer the ISPs but the content providers. A content provider with a video to distribute (such as CNN) pays a CDN company (such as Akamai) to get its video to requesting users with the shortest possible delays.

A CDN company typically provides its content distribution service as follows:

1. The CDN company installs hundreds of **CDN servers** throughout the Internet. The CDN company typically places the CDN servers in a **data center**. A **data center**, owned and run by a third party, is typically a building filled with server hosts. These data centers are often in lower-tier ISPs, close to ISP access networks and the clients.
2. The CDN replicates its customers' content in the CDN servers. Whenever a customer updates its content, the CDN redistributes the fresh content to the CDN servers.
3. The CDN company provides a mechanism so that when a client requests content, the content is provided by the CDN server that can best deliver the content to the specific client. This server may be the closest CDN server to the client (perhaps in the same ISP as the client) or may be a CDN server with a congestion-free path to the client.

It is interesting to note that many independent companies are involved in the CDN paradigm. A content provider (such as CNN) distributes its content through a CDN company (such as Akamai). The CDN company buys CDN servers from a server vendor (such as Cisco or IBM) and installs the servers in hosting centers, owned by a hosting center company (such as AT&T). Thus, not counting the ISPs, there are four independent companies involved in the CDN paradigm!

Figure 7.16 shows the interaction between the content provider and the CDN company. The content provider first determines which of its objects (e.g., videos) it wants the CDN to distribute. (The content provider distributes the remaining objects without intervention from the CDN.) The content provider tags and then pushes this content to a CDN node, which in turn replicates and pushes the content to all its CDN servers. The CDN company may own a private network for pushing the content from the CDN node to the CDN servers. Whenever the content provider modifies a CDN-distributed object, it pushes the fresh version to the CDN node, which again immediately replicates and distributes the object to the CDN servers. It is important to keep in mind that each CDN server typically contains objects from many content providers.

Now comes the interesting question. When a browser in a user's host is instructed to retrieve a specific object (identified with a URL), how does the browser determine whether it should retrieve the object from the origin server or from one of the CDN servers? Typically, CDNs make use of DNS redirection in order to guide browsers to the correct server [Kangasharju 2000].

As an example, suppose the hostname of the content provider is www.foo.com. Suppose the name of the CDN company is cdn.com. Further suppose that the content provider only wants its video mpeg files to be distributed by the CDN; all other objects, including the base HTML pages, are distributed directly by the content provider. To accomplish this, the content provider modifies

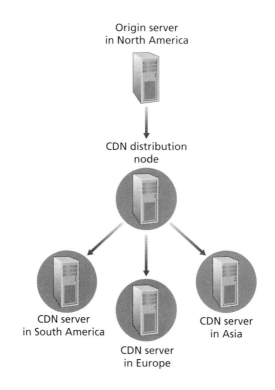

Origin server
in North America

CDN distribution
node

CDN server
in South America

CDN server
in Europe

CDN server
in Asia

Figure 7.16 ♦ The CDN pushes content provider's tagged objects to its CDN servers.

all the HTML objects in the origin server so that the URLs of the video files are prefixed with `http://www.cdn.com`. Thus, if an HTML file at the content provider originally had a reference to `http://www.foo.com/sports/ruth.mpg`, the content provider would tag this object by replacing the reference in the HTML file with `http://www.cdn.com/www.foo.com/sports/ruth.mpg`.

When a browser requests a Web page containing the image ruth.mpg, the following actions occur:

1. The browser sends its request for the base HTML object to the origin server, `www.foo.com`, which sends the requested HTML object to the browser. The browser parses the HTML file and finds the reference to `http://www.cdn.com/www.foo.com/sports/ruth.mpg`.
2. The browser then does a DNS lookup on `www.cdn.com`, which is the hostname for the referenced URL. The DNS is configured so that all queries about `www.cdn.com` that arrive to a root DNS server are sent to an authoritative DNS server for `www.cdn.com`. When the authoritative DNS server receives

the query, it extracts the IP address of the requesting browser. Using an internal network map that it has constructed for the entire Internet, the CDN's DNS server returns the IP address of the CDN server that is likely the best for the requesting browser (often the closest CDN server to the browser).

3. DNS in the requesting client receives a DNS reply with the IP address. The browser then sends its HTTP request to the CDN server with that IP address. The browser obtains ruth.mpg from this CDN server. For subsequent requests from `www.cdn.com`, the client continues to use the same CDN server since the IP address for `www.cdn.com` is in the DNS cache (in the client host or in the local DNS name server).

In summary, as shown in Figure 7.17, the requesting host first goes to the origin Web server to get the base HTML object, then to the CDN's authoritative DNS server to get the IP address of the best CDN server, and finally to that CDN server to get the video. Note that no changes need be made to HTTP, DNS, or the browser to implement this distribution scheme.

What remains to explain is how a CDN company determines the "best" CDN server for the requesting host. Although each CDN company has its own proprietary way of doing this, it is not difficult to get a rough idea of what they do. For every access ISP in the Internet (containing potential requesting clients), the CDN company keeps track of the best CDN server for that access ISP. The CDN company determines the best CDN server based on it knowledge of Internet routing tables (specifically, BGP tables, which we discussed in Chapter 4), roundtrip time estimates, and other measurement data it has from its various servers to various access

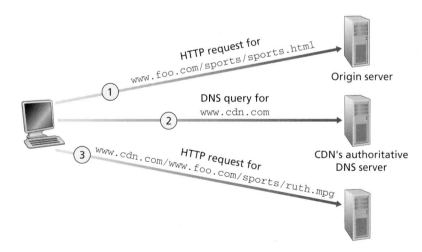

Figure 7.17 ♦ CDNs use DNS to direct requests to nearby CDN server.

networks; see [Verma 2001] for a discussion. In this manner, the CDN estimates which CDN server provides the best best-effort service to the ISP. The CDN does this for a large number of access ISPs in the Internet and uses this information to configure the authoritative DNS server.

CDNs are also often deployed by enterprises that have a large number of regional offices. An enterprise's regional offices are typically connected to the Internet (or to a private network) via relatively low-speed links (e.g., T1 links at 1.544 Mbps). Many such enterprises today need to distribute video e-learning or other corporate video material to their employees. To accomplish this task, an enterprise purchases CDN servers and installs them in its regional offices. When the enterprise has a new video to distribute, it pushes the video to all of its regional offices, and the employees are then served the video by their regional CDN server. In this manner, each video is sent over each regional office's access link only once, thereby not over-burdening the access links with repeated distributions of the same videos. Furthermore, enterprise CDNs often push the video from the central enterprise site to the regional CDN servers when distributing a high-bandwidth video will not interfere with other important traffic, such as at night.

7.6 Beyond Best Effort

In previous sections we learned how sequence numbers, timestamps, FEC, RTP, and H.323 can be used by multimedia applications in today's Internet. CDNs represent a system-wide solution for distributing multimedia content. But are these techniques alone enough to support reliable and robust multimedia applications, such as an IP telephony service that is equivalent to a service in today's telephone network? Before answering this question, let's recall again that today's Internet provides a best-effort service to all of its applications; that is, it does not make any promises about the QoS an application will receive. An application will receive whatever level of performance (for example, end-to-end packet delay and loss) that the network is able to provide at that moment. Recall also that today's public Internet does not allow delay-sensitive multimedia applications to request any special treatment. Because every packet, including delay-sensitive audio and video packets, is treated equally at the routers, all that's required to ruin the quality of an ongoing IP telephone call is enough interfering traffic (that is, network congestion) to noticeably increase the delay and loss seen by an IP telephone call.

In this section, we will identify *new* architectural components that can be added to the Internet architecture to shield an application from such congestion and thus make high-quality networked multimedia applications a reality. Many of the issues that we will discuss in this, and the remaining sections of this chapter, are currently, or recently have been under active discussion in the IETF Diffserv, Intserv, and RSVP working groups.

Figure 7.18 shows a simple network scenario we'll use to illustrate the most important architectural components that have been proposed in order to provide explicit support for the QoS needs of multimedia applications. Suppose that two application packet flows originate on Hosts H1 and H2 on one LAN and are destined for Hosts H3 and H4 on another LAN. The routers on the two LANs are connected by a 1.5 Mbps link. Let's assume the LAN speeds are significantly higher than 1.5 Mbps, and focus on the output queue of router R1; it is here that packet delay and packet loss will occur if the aggregate sending rate of the H1 and H2 exceeds 1.5 Mbps. Let's now consider several scenarios, each of which will provide us with important insight into the underlying principles for providing QoS guarantees to multimedia applications.

7.6.1 Scenario 1: A 1 Mbps Audio Application and an FTP Transfer

Scenario 1 is illustrated in Figure 7.19. Here, a 1 Mbps audio application (for example, a CD-quality audio call) shares the 1.5 Mbps link between R1 and R2 with an FTP application that is transferring a file from H2 to H4. In the best-effort Internet, the audio and FTP packets are mixed in the output queue at R1 and (typically) transmitted in a first-in-first-out (FIFO) order. In this scenario, a burst of packets from the FTP source could potentially fill up the queue, causing IP audio packets to be excessively delayed or lost due to buffer overflow at R1. How should we solve this

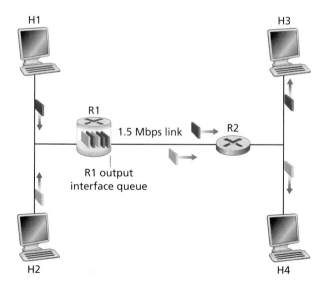

Figure 7.18 ◆ A simple network with two applications

potential problem? Given that the FTP application does not have time constraints, our intuition might be to give strict priority to audio packets at R1. Under a strict priority scheduling discipline, an audio packet in the R1 output buffer would always be transmitted before any FTP packet in the R1 output buffer. The link from R1 to R2 would look like a dedicated link of 1.5 Mbps to the audio traffic, with FTP traffic using the R1-to-R2 link only when no audio traffic is queued.

In order for R1 to distinguish between the audio and FTP packets in its queue, each packet must be marked as belonging to one of these two classes of traffic. Recall from Section 4.4.1 that this was the original goal of the type-of-service (ToS) field in IPv4. As obvious as this might seem, this then is our first principle underlying the provision of QoS guarantees:

> **Principle 1:** Packet marking allows a router to distinguish among packets belonging to different classes of traffic.

7.6.2 Scenario 2: A 1 Mbps Audio Application and a High-Priority FTP Transfer

Our second scenario is only slightly different from scenario 1. Suppose now that the FTP user has purchased "platinum" (that is, high-priced) Internet access from its ISP, while the audio user has purchased cheap, low-budget Internet service that costs only a minuscule fraction of platinum service. Should the cheap user's audio packets be given priority over FTP packets in this case? Arguably not. In this case, it would seem more reasonable to distinguish packets on the basis of the sender's IP

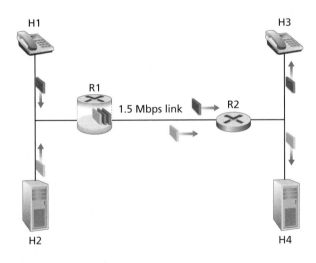

Figure 7.19 ◆ Competing audio and FTP Applications

address. More generally, we see that it is necessary for a router to *classify* packets according to some criteria. This then calls for a slight modification to principle 1:

Principle 1 (modified): Packet classification allows a router to distinguish among packets belonging to different classes of traffic.

Explicit packet marking is one way in which packets may be distinguished. However, the marking carried by a packet does not, by itself, mandate that the packet will receive a given quality of service. Marking is but one *mechanism* for distinguishing packets. The manner in which a router distinguishes among packets by treating them differently is a *policy* decision.

7.6.3 Scenario 3: A Misbehaving Audio Application and an FTP Transfer

Suppose now that somehow (by use of mechanisms that we'll study in subsequent sections) the router knows it should give priority to packets from the 1 Mbps audio application. Since the outgoing link speed is 1.5 Mbps, even though the FTP packets receive lower priority, they will still, on average, receive 0.5 Mbps of transmission service. But what happens if the audio application starts sending packets at a rate of 1.5 Mbps or higher (either maliciously or due to an error in the application)? In this case, the FTP packets will starve, that is, they will not receive any service on the R1-to-R2 link. Similar problems would occur if multiple applications (for example, multiple audio calls), all with the same priority, were sharing a link's bandwidth; one noncompliant flow could degrade and ruin the performance of the other flows. Ideally, one wants a degree of *isolation* among flows, in order to protect one flow from another misbehaving flow. This, then, is a second underlying principle the provision of QoS guarantees.

Principle 2: It is desirable to provide a degree of isolation among traffic flows, so that one flow is not adversely affected by another misbehaving flow.

In the following section, we will examine several specific mechanisms for providing this isolation among flows. We note here that two broad approaches can be taken. First, it is possible to police traffic flows, as shown in Figure 7.20. If a traffic flow must meet certain criteria (for example, that the audio flow not exceed a peak rate of 1 Mbps), then a policing mechanism can be put into place to ensure that these criteria are indeed observed. If the policed application misbehaves, the policing mechanism will take some action (for example, drop or delay packets that are in violation of the criteria) so that the traffic actually entering the network conforms to the criteria. The leaky bucket mechanism that we examine in the following section is perhaps the most widely used policing mechanism. In Figure 7.20, the packet classification and marking mechanism (Principle 1) and the policing mechanism (Principle 2) are co-located at the edge of the network, either in the end system or at an edge router.

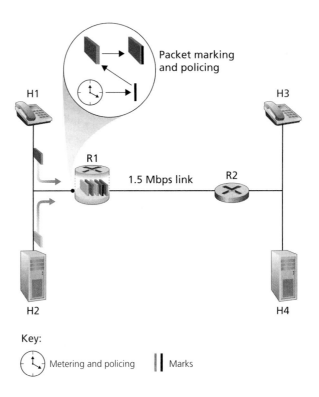

Figure 7.20 ◆ Policing (and marking) the audio and FTP traffic flows

An alternative approach for providing isolation among traffic flows is for the link-level packet-scheduling mechanism to explicitly allocate a fixed amount of link bandwidth to each application flow. For example, the audio flow could be allocated 1Mbps at R1, and the FTP flow could be allocated 0.5 Mbps. In this case, the audio and FTP flows see a logical link with capacity 1.0 and 0.5 Mbps, respectively, as shown in Figure 7.21.

With strict enforcement of the link-level allocation of bandwidth, a flow can use only the amount of bandwidth that has been allocated; in particular, it cannot utilize bandwidth that is not currently being used by the other applications. For example, if the audio flow goes silent (for example, if the speaker pauses and generates no audio packets), the FTP flow would still not be able to transmit more than 0.5 Mbps over the R1-to-R2 link, even though the audio flow's 1 Mbps bandwidth allocation is not being used at that moment. It is therefore desirable to use bandwidth as efficiently as possible, allowing one flow to use another flow's unused bandwidth at any given point in time. This is the third principle underlying the provision of QoS:

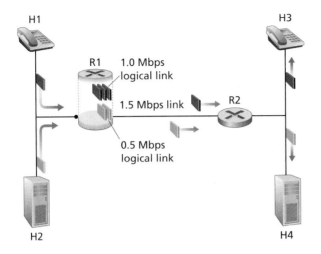

Figure 7.21 ◆ Logical isolation of audio and FTP application flows

Principle 3: While providing isolation among flows, it is desirable to use resources (for example, link bandwidth and buffers) as efficiently as possible.

7.6.4 Scenario 4: Two 1 Mbps Audio Applications over an Overloaded 1.5 Mbps Link

In our final scenario, two 1 Mbps audio connections transmit their packets over the 1.5 Mbps link, as shown in Figure 7.22. The combined data rate of the two flows (2 Mbps) exceeds the link capacity. Even with classification and marking (Principle 1), isolation of flows (Principle 2), and sharing of unused bandwidth (Principle 3), of which there is none, this is clearly a losing proposition. There is simply not enough bandwidth to accommodate the applications' needs. If the two applications equally share the bandwidth, each would receive only 0.75 Mbps. Looked at another way, each application would lose 25 percent of its transmitted packets. This is such an unacceptably low QoS that the application is completely unusable; there's no need even to transmit any audio packets in the first place.

For a flow that needs a minimum QoS in order to be considered usable, the network should either allow or *block* the flow. The telephone network is an example of a network that performs such call blocking—if the required resources (an end-to-end circuit in the case of the telephone network) cannot be allocated to the call, the call is blocked (prevented from entering the network) and a busy signal is returned to the user. In our example, there is no gain in allowing a flow into the network if it will not receive a sufficient QoS to be considered usable. Indeed, there is a *cost* to

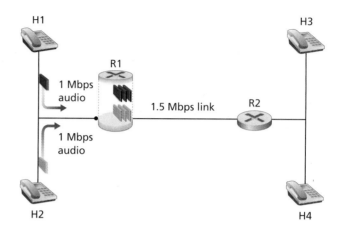

Figure 7.22 ◆ Two competing audio applications overloading the R1-to-R2 link

admitting a flow that does not receive its needed QoS, as network resources are being used to support a flow that provides no utility to the end user.

Implicit with the need to provide a guaranteed QoS to a flow is the need for the flow to declare its QoS requirements. This process of having a flow declare its QoS requirement, and then having the network either accept the flow (at the required QoS) or block the flow is referred to as the **call admission** process. The need for call admission is the fourth underlying principle in the provision of QoS guarantees:

> **Principle 4:** If sufficient resources will not always be available, a call admission process is needed in which flows declare their QoS requirements and are then either admitted to the network (at the required QoS) or blocked from the network (if the required QoS cannot be provided by the network).

In our discussion so far, we have identified four basic principles in providing QoS guarantees for multimedia applications. In the following section, we consider various mechanisms for implementing these principles. In the sections following that, we examine proposed Internet service models for providing QoS guarantees.

7.7 Scheduling and Policing Mechanisms

In the previous section, we identified the important underlying principles in providing QoS guarantees to networked multimedia applications. In this section, we will examine various mechanisms that are used to provide these QoS guarantees.

7.7.1 Scheduling Mechanisms

Recall from our discussion in Section 1.6 and Section 4.3 that packets belonging to various network flows are multiplexed and queued for transmission at the output buffers associated with a link. The manner in which queued packets are selected for transmission on the link is known as the **link-scheduling discipline**. We saw in the previous section that the link-scheduling discipline plays an important role in providing QoS guarantees. Let us now consider several of the most important link-scheduling disciplines in more detail.

First-In-First-Out (FIFO)

Figure 7.23 shows the queuing model abstractions for the FIFO link-scheduling discipline. Packets arriving at the link output queue wait for transmission if the link is currently busy transmitting another packet. If there is not sufficient buffering space to hold the arriving packet, the queue's **packet-discarding policy** then determines whether the packet will be dropped (lost) or whether other packets will be removed from the queue to make space for the arriving packet. In our discussion below we will ignore packet discard. When a packet is completely transmitted over the outgoing link (that is, receives service) it is removed from the queue.

The FIFO (also known as first-come-first-served, or FCFS) scheduling discipline selects packets for link transmission in the same order in which they arrived at the output link queue. We're all familiar with FIFO queuing from bus stops (particularly in England, where queuing seems to have been perfected) or other service centers, where arriving customers join the back of the single waiting line, remain in order, and are then served when they reach the front of the line.

Figure 7.24 shows the FIFO queue in operation. Packet arrivals are indicated by numbered arrows above the upper timeline, with the number indicating the order in which the packet arrived. Individual packet departures are shown below the lower timeline. The time that a packet spends in service (being transmitted) is indicated by the shaded rectangle between the two timelines. Because of the FIFO discipline, packets leave in the same order in which they arrived. Note that after the departure of packet 4, the link remains idle (since packets 1 through 4 have been transmitted and removed from the queue) until the arrival of packet 5.

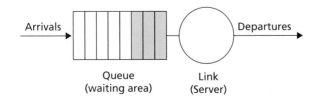

Figure 7.23 ◆ FIFO queuing abstraction

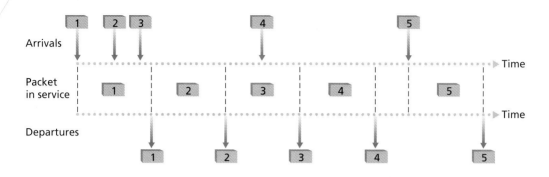

Figure 7.24 ♦ The FIFO queue in operation

Priority Queuing

Under **priority queuing**, packets arriving at the output link are classified into priority classes at the output queue, as shown in Figure 7.25. As discussed in the previous section, a packet's priority class may depend on an explicit marking that it carries in its packet header (for example, the value of the ToS bits in an IPv4 packet), its source or destination IP address, its destination port number, or other criteria. Each priority class typically has its own queue. When choosing a packet to transmit, the priority queuing discipline will transmit a packet from the highest priority class that has a nonempty queue (that is, has packets waiting for transmission). The choice among packets *in the same priority class* is typically done in a FIFO manner.

Figure 7.26 illustrates the operation of a priority queue with two priority classes. Packets 1, 3, and 4 belong to the high-priority class, and packets 2 and 5 belong to the low-priority class. Packet 1 arrives and, finding the link idle, begins

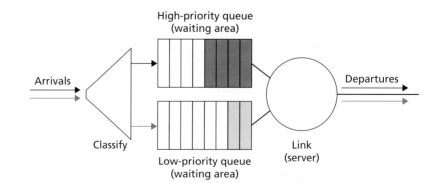

Figure 7.25 ♦ Priority queuing model

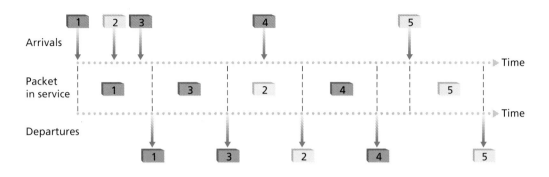

Figure 7.26 ♦ Operation of the priority queue

transmission. During the transmission of packet 1, packets 2 and 3 arrive and are queued in the low- and high-priority queues, respectively. After the transmission of packet 1, packet 3 (a high-priority packet) is selected for transmission over packet 2 (which, even though it arrived earlier, is a low-priority packet). At the end of the transmission of packet 3, packet 2 then begins transmission. Packet 4 (a high-priority packet) arrives during the transmission of packet 2 (a low-priority packet). Under a nonpreemptive priority queuing discipline, the transmission of a packet is not interrupted once it has begun. In this case, packet 4 queues for transmission and begins being transmitted after the transmission of packet 2 is completed.

Round Robin and Weighted Fair Queuing (WFQ)

Under the **round robin queuing discipline**, packets are sorted into classes as with priority queuing. However, rather than there being a strict priority of service among classes, a round robin scheduler alternates service among the classes. In the simplest form of round robin scheduling, a class 1 packet is transmitted, followed by a class 2 packet, followed by a class 1 packet, followed by a class 2 packet, and so on. A so-called work-conserving queuing discipline will never allow the link to remain idle whenever there are packets (of any class) queued for transmission. A **work-conserving round robin discipline** that looks for a packet of a given class but finds none will immediately check the next class in the round robin sequence.

Figure 7.27 illustrates the operation of a two-class round robin queue. In this example, packets 1, 2, and 4 belong to class 1, and packets 3 and 5 belong to the second class. Packet 1 begins transmission immediately upon arrival at the output queue. Packets 2 and 3 arrive during the transmission of packet 1 and thus queue for transmission. After the transmission of packet 1, the link scheduler looks for a class 2 packet and thus transmits packet 3. After the transmission of packet 3, the scheduler looks for a class 1 packet and thus transmits packet 2. After the transmission of packet 2, packet 4 is the only queued packet; it is thus transmitted immediately after packet 2.

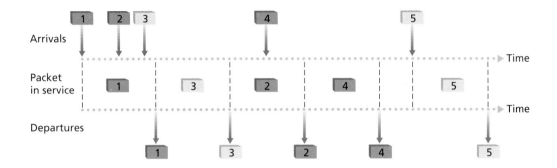

Figure 7.27 ♦ Operation of the two-class round robin queue

A generalized abstraction of round robin queuing that has found considerable use in QoS architectures is the so-called **weighted fair queuing** (WFQ) discipline [Demers 1990; Parekh 1993]. WFQ is illustrated in Figure 7.28. Arriving packets are classified and queued in the appropriate per-class waiting area. As in round robin scheduling, a WFQ scheduler will serve classes in a circular manner—first serving class 1, then serving class 2, then serving class 3, and then (assuming there are three classes) repeating the service pattern. WFQ is also a work-conserving queuing discipline and thus will immediately move on to the next class in the service sequence when it finds an empty class queue.

WFQ differs from round robin in that each class may receive a *differential* amount of service in any interval of time. Specifically, each class, *i*, is assigned a weight, w_i. Under WFQ, during any interval of time during which there are class *i* packets to send, class *i* will then be guaranteed to receive a fraction of service equal to $w_i/(\Sigma w_j)$, where the sum in the denominator is taken over all classes that also

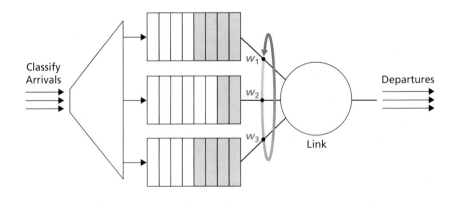

Figure 7.28 ♦ Weighted fair queuing (WFQ)

have packets queued for transmission. In the worst case, even if all classes have queued packets, class i will still be guaranteed to receive a fraction $w_i/(\Sigma w_j)$ of the bandwidth. Thus, for a link with transmission rate R, class i will always achieve a throughput of at least $R \cdot w_i/(\Sigma w_j)$. Our description of WFQ has been an idealized one, as we have not considered the fact that packets are discrete units of data and a packet's transmission will not be interrupted to begin transmission of another packet; [Demers 1990] and [Parekh 1993] discuss this packetization issue. As we will see in the following sections, WFQ plays a central role in QoS architectures. It is also available in today's router products [Cisco QoS 2002]. (Intranets that use WFQ-capable routers can therefore provide QoS to their internal flows.)

7.7.2 Policing: The Leaky Bucket

In Section 7.6 we also identified policing, the regulation of the rate at which a flow is allowed to inject packets into the network, as one of the cornerstones of any QoS architecture. But what aspects of a flow's packet rate should be policed? We can identify three important policing criteria, each differing from the other according to the time scale over which the packet flow is policed:

♦ *Average rate.* The network may wish to limit the long-term average rate (packets per time interval) at which a flow's packets can be sent into the network. A crucial issue here is the interval of time over which the average rate will be policed. A flow whose average rate is limited to 100 packets per second is more constrained than a source that is limited to 6,000 packets per minute, even though both have the same average rate over a long enough interval of time. For example, the latter constraint would allow a flow to send 1,000 packets in a given second-long interval of time (subject to the constraint that the rate be less than 6,000 packets over a minute-long interval containing these 1,000 packets), while the former constraint would disallow this sending behavior.

♦ *Peak rate.* While the average rate constraint limits the amount of traffic that can be sent into the network over a relatively long period of time, a peak-rate constraint limits the maximum number of packets that can be sent over a shorter period of time. Using our example above, the network may police a flow at an average rate of 6,000 packets per minute, while limiting the flow's peak rate to 1,500 packets per second.

♦ *Burst size.* The network may also wish to limit the maximum number of packets (the "burst" of packets) that can be sent into the network over an extremely short interval of time. In the limit, as the interval length approaches zero, the burst size limits the number of packets that can be instantaneously sent into the network. Even though it is physically impossible to instantaneously send multiple packets into the network (after all, every link has a physical transmission rate that cannot be exceeded!), the abstraction of a maximum burst size is a useful one.

The leaky bucket mechanism is an abstraction that can be used to characterize these policing limits. As shown in Figure 7.29, a leaky bucket consists of a bucket that can hold up to b tokens. Tokens are added to this bucket as follows. New tokens, which may potentially be added to the bucket, are always being generated at a rate of r tokens per second. (We assume here for simplicity that the unit of time is a second.) If the bucket is filled with less than b tokens when a token is generated, the newly generated token is added to the bucket; otherwise the newly generated token is ignored, and the token bucket remains full with b tokens.

Let us now consider how the leaky bucket can be used to police a packet flow. Suppose that before a packet is transmitted into the network, it must first remove a token from the token bucket. If the token bucket is empty, the packet must wait for a token. (An alternative is for the packet to be dropped, although we will not consider that option here.) Let us now consider how this behavior polices a traffic flow. Because there can be at most b tokens in the bucket, the maximum burst size for a leaky-bucket-policed flow is b packets. Furthermore, because the token generation rate is r, the maximum number of packets that can enter the network of *any* interval of time of length t is $rt + b$. Thus, the token generation rate, r, serves to limit the long-term average rate at which packets can enter the network. It is also possible to use leaky buckets (specifically, two leaky buckets in series) to police a flow's peak rate in addition to the long-term average rate; see the homework problems at the end of this chapter.

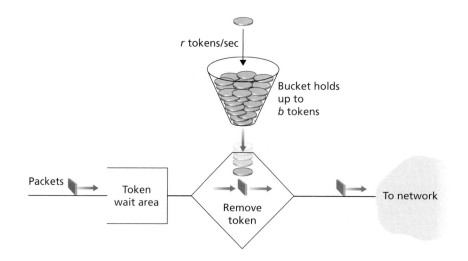

Figure 7.29 ♦ The leaky bucket policer

Leaky Bucket + Weighted Fair Queuing = Provable Maximum Delay in a Queue

In Section 7.8 we'll examine the so-called Intserv and Diffserv approaches for providing quality of service in the Internet. We'll see that both leaky bucket policing and WFQ scheduling can play an important role. Let us thus close this section by considering a router's output link that multiplexes n flows, each policed by a leaky bucket with parameters b_i and r_i, $i = 1, \ldots, n$, using WFQ scheduling. We use the term *flow* here loosely to refer to the set of packets that are not distinguished from each other by the scheduler. In practice, a flow might be comprised of traffic from a single end-to-end connection (as in Intserv) or a collection of many such connections (as in Diffserv), see Figure 7.30.

Recall from our discussion of WFQ that each flow, i, is guaranteed to receive a share of the link bandwidth equal to at least $R \cdot w_i/(\Sigma w_j)$, where R is the transmission rate of the link in packets/sec. What then is the maximum delay that a packet will experience while waiting for service in the WFQ (that is, after passing through the leaky bucket)? Let us focus on flow 1. Suppose that flow 1's token bucket is initially full. A burst of b_1 packets then arrives to the leaky bucket policer for flow 1. These packets remove all of the tokens (without wait) from the leaky bucket and then join the WFQ waiting area for flow 1. Since these b_1 packets are served at a rate of at least $R \cdot w_i/(\Sigma w_j)$ packet/sec, the last of these packets will then have a maximum delay, $d_{max,}$ until its transmission is completed, where

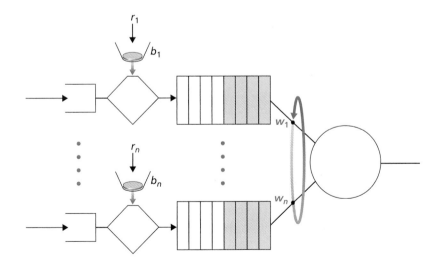

Figure 7.30 ◆ *n* multiplexed leaky bucket flows with WFQ scheduling

$$d_{max} = \frac{b_1}{R \cdot w_1/\Sigma w_j}$$

The rationale behind this formula is that if there are b_1 packets in the queue and packets are being serviced (removed) from the queue at a rate of at least $R \cdot w_1/(\Sigma w_j)$ packets per second, then the amount of time until the last bit of the last packet is transmitted cannot be more than $b_1/(R \cdot w_1/(\Sigma w_j))$. A homework problem asks you to prove that as long as $r_1 < R \cdot w_1/(\Sigma w_j)$, then d_{max} is indeed the maximum delay that any packet in flow 1 will ever experience in the WFQ queue.

7.8 Integrated Services and Differentiated Services

In the previous sections, we identified both the principles and the mechanisms used to provide quality of service in the Internet. In this section, we consider how these ideas are exploited in two architectures that have been proposed for providing quality of service in the Internet—the integrated services (**Intserv**) and differentiated services (**Diffserv**) architecture. As we will see, Intserv is a framework developed within the IETF to provide individualized QoS guarantees to individual application sessions. The goal of Diffserv is to provide the ability to handle different classes of traffic in different ways within the Internet. Although neither Intserv nor Diffserv have taken off and found widespread adoption (for reasons we will discuss), they represent the IETF's current standards for providing quality of service guarantees. Incorporating the principles and mechanisms we've studied in the previous sections, they are thus of interest to us.

7.8.1 Intserv

Two key features lie at the heart of the Intserv architecture:

♦ *Reserved resources.* A router is required to know what amounts of its resources (buffers, link bandwidth) are already reserved for ongoing sessions.

♦ *Call setup.* A session requiring QoS guarantees must first be able to reserve sufficient resources at each network router on its source-to-destination path to ensure that its end-to-end QoS requirement is met. This call setup (also known as call admission) process requires the participation of each router on the path. Each router must determine the local resources required by the session, consider the amounts of its resources that are already committed to other ongoing sessions, and determine whether it has sufficient resources to satisfy the per-hop QoS requirement of the session at this router without violating local QoS guarantees made to an already-admitted session.

Figure 7.31 depicts the call setup process. Let us now consider the steps involved in call admission in more detail:

1. *Traffic characterization and specification of the desired QoS.* In order for a router to determine whether or not its resources are sufficient to meet the QoS requirements of a session, that session must first declare its QoS requirement, as well as characterize the traffic that it will be sending into the network, and for which it requires a QoS guarantee. In the Intserv architecture, the so-called Rspec (R for reservation) defines the specific QoS being requested by a connection; the so-called Tspec (T for traffic) characterizes the traffic the sender will be sending into the network or that the receiver will be receiving from the network. The specific form of the Rspec and Tspec will vary, depending on the service requested, as discussed below. The Tspec and Rspec are defined in part in RFC 2210 and RFC 2215.

2. *Signaling for call setup.* A session's Tspec and Rspec must be carried to the routers at which resources will be reserved for the session. In the Internet, the RSVP protocol, which is discussed in detail shortly, is currently the signaling protocol of choice. RFC 2210 describes the use of the RSVP resource reservation protocol with the Intserv architecture.

3. *Per-element call admission.* Once a router receives the Tspec and Rspec for a session requesting a QoS guarantee, it can determine whether or not it can admit the call. This call admission decision will depend on the traffic specification, the

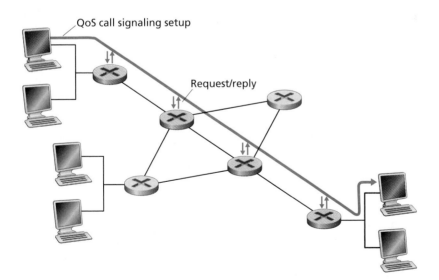

Figure 7.31 ♦ The call setup process

requested type of service, and the existing resource commitments already made by the router to ongoing sessions. Per-element call admission is shown in Figure 7.32.

The Intserv architecture defines two major classes of service: guaranteed service and controlled-load service. We will see shortly that each provides a very different form of a QoS guarantee.

Guaranteed Quality of Service

The guaranteed service specification, defined in RFC 2212, provides firm (mathematically provable) bounds on the queuing delays that a packet will experience in a router. While the details behind guaranteed service are rather complicated, the basic idea is really quite simple. To a first approximation, a source's traffic characterization is given by a leaky bucket (see Section 7.7) with parameters (r, b) and the requested service is characterized by a transmission rate, R, at which packets will be transmitted. In essence, a session requesting guaranteed service is requiring that the bits in its packet be guaranteed a forwarding rate of R bits/sec. Given that traffic is specified using a leaky bucket characterization, and a guaranteed rate of R is being requested, it is also possible to bound the maximum queuing delay at the router. Recall that with a leaky bucket traffic characterization, the amount of traffic (in bits) generated over any interval of length t is bounded by $rt + b$. Recall also from Section 7.7, that when a leaky bucket source is fed into a queue that guarantees that queued traffic will be serviced at least at a rate of R bits per second, the maximum queuing delay experienced by any packet will be bounded by b/R, as long as R is

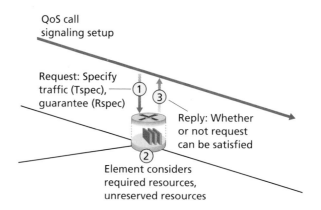

Figure 7.32 ◆ Per-element call behavior

greater than r. The actual delay bound guaranteed under the guaranteed service definition is slightly more complicated, due to packetization effects (the simple b/R bound assumes that data is in the form of a fluid-like flow rather than discrete packets), the fact that the traffic arrival process is subject to the peak-rate limitation of the input link (the simple b/R bound assumes that a burst of b bits can arrive in zero time), and possible additional variations in a packet's transmission time.

Controlled-Load Network Service

A session receiving controlled-load service will receive "a quality of service closely approximating the QoS that same flow would receive from an unloaded network element" [RFC 2211]. In other words, the session may assume that a "very high percentage" of its packets will successfully pass through the router without being dropped and will experience a queuing delay in the router that is close to zero. Interestingly, controlled-load service makes no quantitative guarantees about performance—it does not specify what constitutes a very high percentage of packets nor what quality of service closely approximates that of an unloaded network element.

The controlled-load service targets real-time multimedia applications that have been developed for today's Internet. As we have seen, these applications perform quite well when the network is unloaded, but rapidly degrade in performance as the network becomes more loaded.

7.8.2 Diffserv

The ability to request and reserve per-flow resources, in turn, makes it possible for the Intserv framework to provide QoS guarantees to individual flows. As work on Intserv proceeded, however, researchers involved began to appreciate some of the difficulties associated with the Intserv model and per-flow reservation of resources.

♦ *Scalability.* Per-flow resource reservation implies the need for a router to process resource reservations and to maintain per-flow state for *each* flow passing though the router. Per-flow reservation processing at a backbone router can thus incur a potentially significant overhead in large networks.

♦ *Flexible service models.* The Intserv framework provides for a small number of pre-specified service classes. This particular set of service classes does not allow for more qualitative or relative definitions of service distinctions (for example, "Service class A will receive preferred treatment over service class B."). These more qualitative definitions might better fit our intuitive notion of service distinction (for example, first class versus coach class in air travel; "platinum" versus "gold" versus "standard" credit cards).

These considerations led to the so-called Diffserv activity within the Internet Engineering Task Force. The Diffserv architecture aims to provide *scalable* and *flexible* service differentiation—that is, the ability to handle different "classes" of traffic in different ways within the Internet. The need for *scalability* arises from the fact that hundreds of thousands of simultaneous source-destination traffic flows may be present at a backbone router of the Internet. We will see shortly that this need is met by placing only simple functionality within the network core, with more complex control operations being implemented at the edge of the network. The need for *flexibility* arises from the fact that new service classes may arise and old service classes may become obsolete. The Diffserv architecture is flexible in the sense that it does not define specific services or service classes (for example, as is the case with Intserv). Instead, Diffserv provides the functional components, that is, the pieces of a network architecture, with which such services can be built. Let us now examine these components in detail.

Differentiated Services: A Simple Scenario

To set the framework for defining the architectural components of the differentiated service (Diffserv) model, let's begin with the simple network shown in Figure 7.33. In this section, we describe one possible use of the Diffserv components. Many other variations are possible, as described in RFC 2475. Our goal here is to provide an introduction to the key aspects of Diffserv, rather than to describe the architectural model in exhaustive detail. Readers interested in learning more about Diffserv are encouraged to see the comprehensive book [Kilkki 1999].

The Diffserv architecture consists of two sets of functional elements:

♦ *Edge functions: packet classification and traffic conditioning.* At the incoming edge of the network (that is, at either a Diffserv-capable host that generates traffic or at the first Diffserv-capable router that the traffic passes through), arriving packets are marked. More specifically, the differentiated service (DS) field of the packet header is set to some value. For example, in Figure 7.33, packets being sent from H1 to H3 might be marked at R1, while packets being sent from H2 to H4 might be marked at R2. The mark that a packet receives identifies the class of traffic to which it belongs. Different classes of traffic will then receive different service within the core network.

♦ *Core function: forwarding.* When a DS-marked packet arrives at a Diffserv-capable router, the packet is forwarded onto its next hop according to the so-called **per-hop behavior** associated with that packet's class. The per-hop behavior influences how a router's buffers and link bandwidth are shared among the competing classes of traffic. A crucial tenet of the Diffserv architecture is that a router's per-hop behavior will be based *only* on packet markings, that is, the class of traffic to which a packet belongs. Thus, if packets being sent from H1 to H3 in Figure 7.33 receive the same marking as packets being sent from H2 to H4,

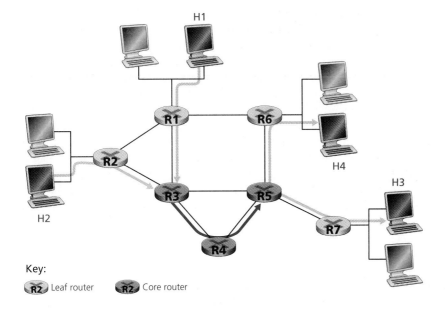

Figure 7.33 ♦ A simple Diffserv network example

then the network routers treat these packets as an aggregate, without distinguishing whether the packets originated at H1 or H2. For example, R3 would not distinguish between packets from H1 and H2 when forwarding these packets on to R4. Thus, the differentiated service architecture obviates the need to keep router state for individual source-destination pairs—an important consideration in meeting the scalability requirement discussed at the beginning of this section.

An analogy might prove useful here. At many large-scale social events (for example, a large public reception, a large dance club or discothèque, a concert, or a football game), people entering the event receive a pass of one type or another: VIP passes for Very Important People; over-21 passes for people who are 21 years old or older (for example, if alcoholic drinks are to be served); backstage passes at concerts; press passes for reporters; even an ordinary pass for the Ordinary Person. These passes are typically distributed upon entry to the event, that is, at the edge of the event. It is here at the edge where computationally intensive operations, such as paying for entry, checking for the appropriate type of invitation, and matching an invitation against a piece of identification, are performed. Furthermore, there may be a limit on the number of people of a given type that are allowed into an event. If there is such a limit, people may have to wait before entering the event. Once inside the event, one's pass allows one to receive differentiated service at many locations around the event—a VIP is provided with free drinks, a better table, free food, entry to exclusive rooms, and fawning service. Conversely, an ordinary person is excluded from certain areas, pays for drinks, and receives only basic service. In both cases, the service received within the event depends solely on the type of one's pass. Moreover, all people within a class are treated alike.

Diffserv Traffic Classification and Conditioning

Figure 7.34 provides a logical view of the classification and marking function within the edge router. Packets arriving to the edge router are first classified. The classifier selects packets based on the values of one or more packet header fields (for example, source address, destination address, source port, destination port, and protocol ID) and steers the packet to the appropriate marking function. A packet's mark is carried within the DS field [RFC 3260] in the IPv4 or IPv6 packet header. The definition of the DS field is intended to supersede the earlier definitions of the IPv4 type of service field and the IPv6 traffic class fields that we discussed in Chapter 4.

In some cases, an end user may have agreed to limit its packet-sending rate to conform to a declared **traffic profile**. The traffic profile might contain a limit on the peak rate, as well as the burstiness of the packet flow, as we saw in Section 7.7 with the leaky bucket mechanism. As long as the user sends packets into the network in a way that conforms to the negotiated traffic profile, the packets receive their priority marking and are forwarded along their route to the destination. On the other hand, if the traffic profile is violated, out-of-profile packets might be marked differently, might be shaped (for example, delayed so that a maximum rate constraint would be observed), or might be dropped at the network edge. The role of the **metering function**, shown in Figure 7.34, is to compare the incoming packet flow with the negotiated traffic profile and to determine whether a packet is within the negotiated traffic profile. The actual decision about whether to immediately remark, forward, delay, or drop a packet is a policy issue determined by network administrator and is *not* specified in the Diffserv architecture.

Per-Hop Behaviors

So far, we have focused on the edge functions in the Diffserv architecture. The second key component of the Diffserv architecture involves the **per-hop behavior** (PHB) performed by Diffserv-capable routers. PHB is rather cryptically, but carefully, defined as "a description of the externally observable forwarding behavior of a Diffserv node applied to a particular Diffserv behavior aggregate" [RFC 2475]. Digging a little deeper into this definition, we can see several important considerations embedded within it:

♦ A PHB can result in different classes of traffic receiving different performance (that is, different externally observable forwarding behaviors).

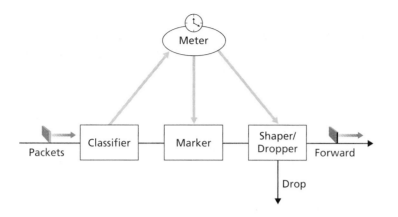

Figure 7.34 ♦ Logical view of packet classification and traffic conditioning at the end router

♦ While a PHB defines differences in performance (behavior) among classes, it does not mandate any particular mechanism for achieving these behaviors. As long as the externally observable performance criteria are met, any implementation mechanism and any buffer/bandwidth allocation policy can be used. For example, a PHB would not require that a particular packet-queuing discipline, for example, a priority queue versus a weighted fair queuing queue versus a first-come-first-served queue, be used to achieve a particular behavior. The PHB is the end, to which resource allocation and implementation mechanisms are the means.

♦ Differences in performance must be observable and hence measurable.

Currently, two PHBs have been defined: an expedited forwarding (EF) PHB [RFC 3246] and an assured forwarding (AF) PHB [RFC 2597].

♦ The **expedited forwarding** PHB specifies that the departure rate of a class of traffic from a router must equal or exceed a configured rate. That is, during any interval of time, the class of traffic can be guaranteed to receive enough bandwidth so that the output rate of the traffic equals or exceeds this minimum configured rate. Note that the EF per-hop behavior implies some form of isolation among traffic classes, as this guarantee is made *independently* of the traffic intensity of any other classes that are arriving to a router. Thus, even if the other classes of traffic are overwhelming router and link resources, enough of those resources must still be made available to the class to ensure that it receives its minimum-rate guarantee. EF thus provides a class with the simple *abstraction* of a link with a minimum guaranteed link bandwidth.

♦ The **assured forwarding** PHB is more complex. AF divides traffic into four classes, where each AF class is guaranteed to be provided with some minimum amount of bandwidth and buffering. Within each class, packets are further partitioned into one of three drop preference categories. When congestion occurs within an AF class, a router can then discard (drop) packets based on their drop preference values. See [RFC 2597] for details. By varying the amount of resources allocated to each class, an ISP can provide different levels of performance to the different AF traffic classes.

Interv and Diffserv Retrospective

For the past 20 years there have been numerous unsuccessful attempts to introduce QoS into packet-switched networks. The various attempts have failed so far more because of economic and legacy reasons than because of technical reasons. These attempts include end-to-end ATM networks and TCP/IP networks deploying Intserv or Diffserv. Will these efforts be successful, or at least partially successful in the long term? Let's take a look at a few of the issues involved.

So far we have assumed that Intserv or Diffserv are deployed within a single administrative domain. The more typical case is where an end-to-end service must be fashioned from multiple ISPs sitting between communicating end systems. In order to provide end-to-end Intserv or Diffserv service, all the ISPs between the end systems not only must provide this service, but most also cooperate and make settlements in order to offer end customers true end-end service. Without this kind of cooperation, ISPs directly selling Intserv or Diffserv service to customers will find themselves repeatedly saying: "Yes, we know you paid extra, but we don't have a service agreement with one of our higher-tier ISPs. I'm sorry that there were many gaps in your voice-over-IP call!"

Another concern with these advanced services is that they need to police and possibly shape traffic, which may turn out to be complex and costly. One also needs to bill the service differently, most likely by volume rather than with a fixed monthly fee as currently done by most ISPs—another costly requirement for the ISP. Finally, if Intserv or Diffserv were actually in place and the network ran at only moderate load, most of the time there would be no perceived difference between a best-effort service and an Intserv/Diffserv service. Indeed, today, end-to-end delay is usually dominated by access rates and router hops rather than by queuing delays in the routers. Imagine the unhappy Intserv/Diffserv customer who has paid for premium service but finds that the best-effort service being provided to others almost always has the same performance as premium service!

7.9 RSVP

We learned in Section 7.8 that in order for a network to provide QoS guarantees, there must be a signaling protocol that allows applications running in hosts to reserve resources in the Internet. The resource ReSerVation Protocol (RSVP) [RFC 2205; Zhang 1993] is such a signaling protocol for the Internet. When people talk about *resources* in the Internet context, they usually mean link bandwidth and router buffers. To keep the discussion concrete and focused, however, we'll assume that the word *resource* is synonymous with *bandwidth*. We note that RSVP has been extended and used as a signaling protocol in other circumstances, perhaps most notably in the form of RSVP-TE [RFC 3209] for MPLS signaling, as discussed in Section 5.8.2. Our focus here, however, will be on the use of RSVP for resource (bandwidth) reservation.

7.9.1 The Essence of RSVP

The RSVP protocol allows applications to reserve bandwidth for their data flows. It is used by a host, on the behalf of an application data flow, to request a specific amount of bandwidth from the network. RSVP is also used by the routers to forward bandwidth reservation requests. To implement RSVP, RSVP software must be present in the receivers, senders, and routers. The two principal characteristics of RSVP are:

1. It provides **reservations for bandwidth in multicast trees** (unicast is handled as a degenerate case of multicast).
2. It is **receiver-oriented**; that is, the receiver of a data flow initiates and maintains the resource reservation used for that flow.

These two characteristics are illustrated in Figure 7.35. The diagram shows a multicast tree with data flowing from the top of the tree to hosts at the bottom of the tree. Although data originates from the sender, the reservation messages originate from the receivers. When a router forwards a reservation message upstream toward the sender, the router may merge the reservation message with other reservation messages arriving from downstream.

Before discussing RSVP in greater detail, we need to consider the notion of a **session**. As with RTP, a session can consist of multiple multicast data flows. Each sender in a session is the source of one or more data flows; for example, a sender might be the source of a video data flow and an audio data flow. Each data flow in a session has the same multicast address. To keep the discussion concrete, we assume that routers and hosts identify the session to which a packet belongs by the packet's multicast address. This assumption is somewhat restrictive; the actual RSVP specification allows for more general methods to identify a session. Within a session, the data flow to which a packet belongs also needs to be identified. This could be done, for example, with the flow identifier field in IPv6.

What RSVP Is Not

We emphasize that the RSVP standard [RFC 2205] does not specify *how* the network provides the reserved bandwidth to the data flows. It is merely a protocol that

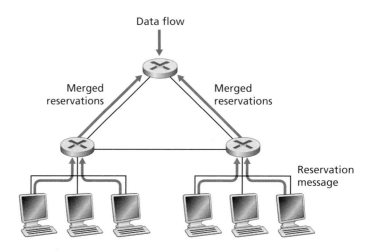

Figure 7.35 ◆ RSVP: multicast- and receiver-oriented

allows the applications to reserve the necessary link bandwidth. Once the reservations are in place, it is up to the routers in the Internet to actually provide the reserved bandwidth to the data flows. This provisioning would likely be done with the scheduling mechanisms (priority scheduling, weighted fair queuing, etc.) discussed in Section 7.7.

It is also important to understand that RSVP is not a routing protocol—it does not determine the links in which the reservations are to be made. Instead it depends on an underlying routing protocol (unicast or multicast) to determine the routes for the flows. Once the routes are in place, RSVP can be used to reserve bandwidth in the links along these routes. (We shall see shortly that when a route changes, RSVP re-reserves resources.) Once the reservations are in place, the routers' packet schedulers must actually provide the reserved bandwidth to the data flows. Thus, RSVP is only one piece—albeit an important piece—in the QoS guarantee puzzle.

RSVP is sometimes referred to as a *signaling protocol.* By this it is meant that RSVP is a protocol that allows hosts to establish and tear down reservations for data flows. The term *signaling protocol* comes from the jargon of the circuit-switched telephony community.

Heterogeneous Receivers

Consider a network in which some receivers can receive a flow at 28.8 kbps, others at 128 kbps, and yet others at 10 Mbps or higher. This heterogeneity of the receivers poses an interesting question. If a sender is multicasting a video to a group of heterogeneous receivers, should the sender encode the video for low quality at 28.8 kbps, for medium quality at 128 kbps, or for high quality at 10 Mbps? If the video is encoded at 10 Mbps, then only the users with 10 Mbps access will be able to watch the video. On the other hand, if the video is encoded at 28.8 kbps, then the 10 Mbps users will have to see a low-quality image when they know they can see something much better.

To resolve this dilemma it is often suggested that video and audio be encoded in layers. For example, a video might be encoded into two layers: a base layer and an enhancement layer. The base layer could have a rate of 20 kbps, whereas the enhancement layer could have a rate of 100 kbps; in this manner receivers with 28.8 kbps access could receive the low-quality base-layer image, and receivers with 128 kbps could receive both layers to construct a high-quality image.

We note that the sender does not need to know the receiving rates of all the receivers. It only needs to know the maximum rate of all its receivers. The sender encodes the video or audio into multiple layers and sends all the layers up to the maximum rate into multicast tree. The receivers pick out the layers that are appropriate for their receiving rates. In order to not excessively waste bandwidth in the network's links, the heterogeneous receivers must communicate to the network the rates they can handle. We'll see that RSVP gives foremost attention to the issue of reserving resources for heterogeneous receivers.

7.9.2 A Few Simple Examples

Let's first describe RSVP in the context of a concrete one-to-many multicast example. Suppose there is a source that is transmitting the video of a major sporting event over the Internet. This session has been assigned a multicast address, and the source stamps all of its outgoing packets with this multicast address. Also suppose that an underlying multicast routing protocol has established a multicast tree from the sender to four receivers as shown in Figure 7.36; the numbers next to the receivers are the rates at which the receivers want to receive data. Let us also assume that the video is layered and encoded to accommodate this heterogeneity of receiver rates.

Roughly speaking, RSVP operates in a two-pass manner, as illustrated in the following simple example. A transmitting source will advertise its content by sending **RSVP path messages** through a multicast tree, indicating the bandwidth required for the content, the soft-state timeout interval (see sidebar on Principle of Soft State), and information about the upstream path to the sender. Each receiver sends an **RSVP reservation message** upstream into the multicast tree. This reservation message specifies the rate at which the receiver would like to receive the data from the source. When the reservation message reaches a router, the router adjusts its packet scheduler to accommodate the reservation. It then sends a reservation upstream. The amount of bandwidth reserved upstream from the router depends on the bandwidths reserved downstream. In the example in Figure 7.36, receivers R1, R2, R3, and R4 reserve 20 kbps, 100 kbps, 3 Mbps, and 3 Mbps, respectively. Thus router D's downstream receivers request a maximum of 3 Mbps. For this one-to-many transmission, router D sends a reservation message to router B requesting that

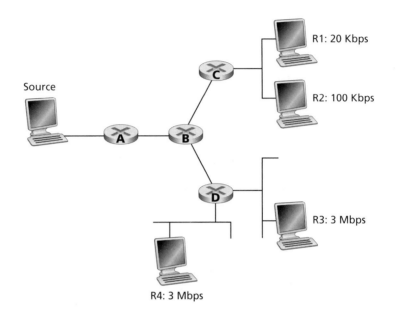

Figure 7.36 ♦ An RSVP example

router B reserve 3 Mbps on the link between the two routers. Note that only 3 Mbps are reserved and not $3 + 3 = 6$ Mbps; this is because receivers R3 and R4 are watching the same sporting event, so their reservations may be merged. Similarly, router C requests that router B reserve 100 kbps on the link between routers B and C; the layered encoding ensures that receiver R1's 20 kbps stream is included in the 100 kbps stream. Once router B receives the reservation message from its downstream routers and passes the reservations to its schedulers, it sends a new reservation message to its upstream router, router A. This message reserves 3 Mbps of bandwidth on the link from router A to router B, which is again the maximum of the downstream reservations.

We see from this first example that RSVP is **receiver-oriented**; that is, the receiver of a data flow initiates and maintains the resource reservation used for that flow. Note that each router receives a reservation message from each of its downstream links in the multicast tree and sends only one reservation message into its upstream link.

As another example, suppose that four persons are participating in a video conference, as shown in Figure 7.37. Each person has three windows open on her computer to look at the other three persons. Suppose that the underlying routing protocol has established the multicast tree among the four hosts. Finally, suppose each person wants to see each of the videos at 3 Mbps. Then on each of the links in this

PRINCIPLES IN PRACTICE

THE PRINCIPLE OF SOFT STATE

RSVP is used to install state (bandwidth reservations) in routers, and is known as a *soft-state* protocol. Broadly speaking, we associate the term *soft-state* with signaling approaches in which installed state times out (and is removed) unless periodically refreshed by the receipt of a signaling message (typically from the entity that initially installed the state) indicating that the state should continue to remain installed. Since unrefreshed state will eventually time out, soft-state signaling requires neither explicit state removal nor a procedure to remove orphaned state should the state-installer crash. Similarly, since state installation and refresh messages will be followed by subsequent periodic refresh messages, reliable signaling is not required. The term *soft state* was coined by Clark [Clark 1988], who described the notion of periodic state refresh messages being sent by an end system, and suggested that with such refresh messages, state could be lost in a crash and then automatically restored by subsequent refresh messages—all transparently to the end system and without invoking any explicit crash-recovery procedures:

> ". . . the state information would not be critical in maintaining the desired type of service associated with the flow. Instead, that type of service would be enforced by the end points, which would periodically send messages to ensure that the proper type of service was being associated with the flow. In this way, the state information associated with the flow could be lost in a crash without permanent disruption of the service features being used. I call this concept "soft state," and it may very well permit us to achieve our primary goals of survivability and flexibility. . ."

Roughly speaking, then, the essence of a soft-state approach is the use of best-effort periodic state-installation/refresh by the state installer and state-removal-by-timeout at the state-holder. Soft state approaches have been taken in numerous protocols, including RSVP , PIM (Section 4.7) , SIP (Section 7.4), and IGMP (Section 4.7), and in forwarding tables in transparent bridges (Section 5.6).

Hard-state signaling takes the converse approach to soft state—installed state remains installed unless explicitly removed by the receipt of a state-teardown message from the state-installer. Since the state remains installed unless explicitly removed, hard-state signaling requires a mechanism to remove an orphaned state that remains after the state-installer has crashed or departed without removing the state. Similarly, since state installation and removal are performed only once (and without state refresh or state timeout), it is important for the state-installer to know when the state has been installed or removed. Reliable (rather than best-effort) signaling protocols are thus typically associated with hard-state protocols. Roughly speaking, then, the essence of a hard-state approach is the reliable and explicit installation and removal of state information. Hard-state approaches have been taken in protocols such as ST-II [Partridge 1992, RFC 1190] and Q.2931 [ITU-T Q.2931 1994].

RSVP has provided for explicit (although optional) removal of reservations since its conception.

(continues)

ACK-based reliable signaling was introduced as an extension to RSVP in [RFC 2961] and was also suggested in [Pan 1997]. RSVP has thus optionally adopted some elements of a hard-state signaling approach. For a discussion and comparison of soft-state versus hard-state protocols, see [Ji 2003].

---

multicast tree, RSVP would reserve 9 Mbps in one direction and 3 Mbps in the other direction. Note that RSVP does not merge reservations in this example, as each person wants to receive three distinct streams.

Now consider an audio conference among the same four persons over the same multicast tree. Suppose b bps are needed for an isolated audio stream. Because in an audio conference it is rare that more than two persons speak at the same time, it is not necessary to reserve $3 \cdot b$ bps into each receiver; $2 \cdot b$ should suffice. Thus, in this last application we can conserve bandwidth by merging reservations.

Call Admission

Just as the restaurant manager from Section 1.3.1 should not accept reservations for more tables than the restaurant has, the amount of bandwidth on a link that a router reserves should not exceed the link's capacity. Thus whenever a router receives a new reservation message, it must first determine if its downstream links on the multicast tree can accommodate the reservation. This **admission test** is performed whenever a router receives a reservation message. If the admission test fails, the

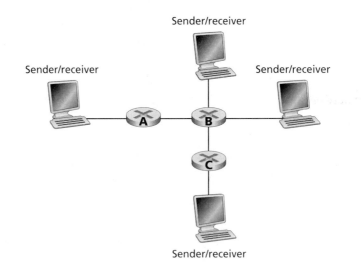

Figure 7.37 ◆ An RSVP video conference example

router rejects the reservation and returns an error message to the appropriate receiver(s).

RSVP does not define the admission test, but it assumes that the routers perform such a test and that RSVP can interact with the test. For addtional material on call admission, you are encouraged to consult [Jamin 1996; Breslau 2000; Roberts 2004].

7.10 Summary

Multimedia networking is one of the most exciting (yet still-to-be-fully-realized) developments in the Internet today. People throughout the world are spending less time in front of their radios and televisions, and are instead turning to the Internet to receive audio and video emissions, both live and prerecorded. As high-speed access penetrates more residences, this trend will continue—couch potatoes throughout the world will access their favorite video programs through the Internet rather than through the traditional broadcast distribution channels. In addition to audio and video distribution, the Internet is also being used to transport phone calls. In fact, over the next 10 years the Internet may render the traditional circuit-switched telephone system nearly obsolete in many countries. The Internet not only will provide phone service for less money, but will also provide numerous value-added services, such as video conferencing, online directory services, voice messaging services, and Web integration.

In Section 7.1 we classified multimedia applications into three categories: streaming stored audio and video, one-to-many transmission of real-time audio and video, and real-time interactive audio and video. We emphasized that multimedia applications are delay-sensitive and loss-tolerant—characteristics that are very different from static-content applications that are delay-tolerant and loss-intolerant. We also discussed some of the hurdles that today's best-effort Internet places before multimedia applications. We surveyed several proposals to overcome these hurdles, including simply improving the existing networking infrastructure (by adding more bandwidth, more network caches, and more CDN nodes, and by deploying multicast), adding functionality to the Internet so that applications can reserve end-to-end resources (and so that the network can honor these reservations), and finally, introducing service classes to provide service differentiation.

In Sections 7.2–7.4 we examined architectures and mechanisms for multimedia networking in a best-effort network. In Section 7.2 we surveyed several architectures for streaming stored audio and video. We discussed user interaction—such as pause/resume, repositioning, and visual fast-forward—and provided an introduction to RTSP, a protocol that provides client-server interaction to streaming applications. In Section 7.3 we examined how interactive real-time applications can be designed to run over a best-effort network. We saw how a combination of client buffers, packet sequence numbers, and timestamps can greatly alleviate the effects of network-induced jitter. In Section 7.4 we explored protocols for real-time interactive multimedia, including RTP, SIP, and H.323. In Section 7.5 we investigated how content distribution networks bring multimedia content to users.

Sections 7.6–7.9 looked at how the Internet can evolve to provide guaranteed QoS to its applications. In Section 7.6 we identified several principles for providing QoS to multimedia applications. These principles include packet marking and classification, isolation of packet flows, efficient use of resources, and call admission. In Section 7.8 we surveyed a variety of scheduling policies and policing mechanisms that can provide the foundation of a QoS networking architecture. The scheduling policies include priority scheduling, round robin scheduling, and weighted fair queuing. We then explored the leaky bucket as a policing mechanism. In Section 7.9 we showed how these principles and mechanisms have led to the definitions of new Intserv and Diffserv standards for providing QoS in the Internet, and an Internet signaling protocol for reservations, namely, RSVP.

Now that we have finished our study of multimedia networking, it is time to move on to another exciting topic: network security. Recent advances in multimedia networking may move the distribution of audio and video information to the Internet. As we'll see in the next chapter, recent advances in network security may well help move the majority of economic transactions to the Internet.

Homework Problems and Questions

Chapter 7 Review Questions

SECTIONS 7.1–7.2

1. What is meant by interactivity for streaming stored audio/video? What is meant by interactivity for real-time interactive audio/video?

2. Three camps were discussed for improving the Internet so that it better supports multimedia applications. Briefly summarize the views of each camp. In which camp do you belong?

3. Figures 7.1, 7.2, and 7.3 present three schemes for streaming stored media. What are the advantages and disadvantages of each scheme?

SECTIONS 7.3–7.4

4. What is the difference between end-to-end delay and packet jitter? What are the causes of packet jitter?

5. Why is a packet that is received after its scheduled playout time considered lost?

6. Section 7.3 describes two FEC schemes. Briefly summarize them. Both schemes increase the transmission rate of the stream by adding overhead. Does interleaving also increase the transmission rate?

7. How are different RTP streams in different sessions identified by a receiver? How are different streams from within the same session identified? How are RTP and RTPC packets (as part of the same session) distinguished?

8. Three RTCP packet types are described in Section 7.4. Briefly summarize the information contained in each of these packet types.

SECTIONS 7.6–7.9

9. In Section 7.6, we discussed nonpreemptive priority queuing. What would be preemptive priority queuing? Does preemptive priority queuing make sense for computer networks?

10. Give an example of a scheduling discipline that is *not* work conserving.

11. What are some of the difficulties associated with the Intserv model and per-flow reservation of resources?

Problems

1. Surf the Web and find two products for streaming stored audio and/or video. For each product, determine:

   a. Whether meta files are used

   b. Whether the audio/video is sent over UDP or TCP

   c. Whether RTP is used

   d. Whether RTSP is used

2. Write a poem, a short story, a description of a recent vacation, or any other piece that takes two to five minutes to recite. Recite and record your piece. Convert your recording to one of the RealNetworks or Microsoft audio formats using one of the free encoders. Upload the file to the same server that holds your personal homepage. Also upload the corresponding meta file to the server. Finally, create a link from your homepage to the meta file.

3. Consider the client buffer shown in Figure 7.4. Suppose that the streaming system uses the third option; that is, the server pushes the media into the socket as quickly as possible. Suppose the available TCP bandwidth $>> d$ most of the time. Also suppose that the client buffer can hold only about one-third of the media. Describe how $x(t)$ and the contents of the client buffer will evolve over time.

4. Are the TCP receive buffer and the media player's client buffer the same thing? If not, how do they interact?

5. In the Internet phone example in Section 7.3, let h be the total number of header bytes added to each chunk, including UDP and IP header.

a. Assuming an IP datagram is emitted every 20 msecs, find the transmission rate in bits per second for the datagrams generated by one side of this application.

b. What is a typical value of h when RTP is used?

6. Consider the procedure described in Section 7.3 for estimating average delay d_i. Suppose that $u = 0.1$. Let $r_1 - t_1$ be the most recent sample delay, let $r_2 - t_2$ be the next most recent sample delay, and so on.

a. For a given audio application suppose four packets have arrived at the receiver with sample delays $r_4 - t_4$, $r_3 - t_3$, $r_2 - t_2$, and $r_1 - t_1$. Express the estimate of delay d in terms of the four samples.

b. Generalize your formula for n sample delays.

For the formula in Part b, let n approach infinity and give the resulting formula. Comment on why this averaging procedure is called an exponential moving average.

7. Repeat Parts a and b in Question 6 for the estimate of average delay deviation.

8. For the Internet phone example in Section 7.3, we introduced an online procedure (exponential moving average) for estimating delay. In this problem we will examine an alternative procedure. Let t_i be the timestamp of the ith packet received; let r_i be the time at which the ith packet is received. Let d_n be our estimate of average delay after receiving the nth packet. After the first packet is received, we set the delay estimate equal to $d_1 = r_1 - t_1$.

a. Suppose that we would like $d_n = (r_1 - t_1 + r_2 - t_2 + \ldots + r_n - t_n)/n$ for all n. Give a recursive formula for d_n in terms of d_{n-1}, r_n, and t_n.

b. Describe why for Internet telephony, the delay estimate described in Section 7.3 is more appropriate than the delay estimate outlined in Part a.

9. Compare the procedure described in Section 7.3 for estimating average delay with the procedure in Section 3.5 for estimating round-trip time. What do the procedures have in common? How are they different?

10. Consider the adaptive playout strategy described in Section 7.3.

a. How can two successive packets received at the destination have time-stamps that differ by more than 20 msecs when the two packets belong to the same talk spurt?

b. How can the receiver use sequence numbers to determine whether a packet is the first packet in a talk spurt? Be specific.

11. Recall the two FEC schemes for Internet phone described in Section 7.3. Suppose the first scheme generates a redundant chunk for every four original chunks. Suppose the second scheme uses a low-bit rate encoding whose transmission rate is 25 percent of the transmission rate of the nominal stream.

a. How much additional bandwidth does each scheme require? How much playback delay does each scheme add?

b. How do the two schemes perform if the first packet is lost in every group of five packets? Which scheme will have better audio quality?

c. How do the two schemes perform if the first packet is lost in every group of two packets? Which scheme will have better audio quality?

12. How is the interarrival time jitter calculated in the RTCP reception report? (*Hint*: Read the RTP RFC.)

13. a. Suppose we send into the Internet two IP datagrams, each carrying a different UDP segment. The first datagram has source IP address A1, destination IP address B, source port P1, and destination port T. The second datagram has source IP address A2, destination IP address B, source port P2, and destination port T. Suppose that A1 is different from A2 and P1 is different from P2. Assuming that both datagrams reach their final destination, will the two UDP datagrams be received by the same socket? Why or why not?

b. Suppose Alice, Bob, and Claire want to have an audio conference call using SIP and RTP. For Alice to send and receive RTP packets to and from Bob and Claire, is only one UDP socket sufficient (in addition to the socket needed for the SIP messages)? If yes, then how does Alice's SIP client distinguish between the RTP packets received from Bob and Claire?

14. Consider an RTP session consisting of four users, all of which are sending and receiving RTP packets into the same multicast address. Each user sends video at 100 kbps.

a. RTCP will limit its traffic to what rate?

b. A particular receiver will be allocated how much RTCP bandwidth?

c. A particular sender will be allocated how much RTCP bandwidth?

15. a. How is RTSP similar to HTTP? Does RTSP have methods? Can HTTP be used to request a stream?

b. How is RTSP different from HTTP? For example, is HTTP in-band or out-of-band? Does RTSP maintain state information about the client (consider the pause/resume function)?

16. What are the current Microsoft products for real-time audio/video conferencing. Do these products use any of the protocols discussed in this chapter (for example, RTP or RTSP)?

17. True or false:

a. If stored video is streamed directly from a Web server to a media player, then the application is using TCP as the underlying transport protocol.

b. When using RTP, it is possible for a sender to change encoding in the middle of a session.

c. All applications that use RTP must use port 87.

d. Suppose an RTP session has a separate audio and video stream for each sender. Then the audio and video streams use the same SSRC.

e. In differentiated services, while per-hop behavior defines differences in performance among classes, it does not mandate any particular mechanism for achieving these performances.

f. Suppose Alice wants to establish an SIP session with Bob. In her INVITE message she includes the line: m=audio 48753 RTP/AVP 3 (AVP 3 denotes GSM audio). Alice has therefore indicated in this message that she wishes to send GSM audio.

g. Referring to the preceding statement, Alice has indicated in her INVITE message that she will send audio to port 48753.

h. SIP messages are typically sent between SIP entities using a default SIP port number.

i. In order to maintain registration, SIP clients must periodically send REGISTER messages.

j. SIP mandates that all SIP clients support G.711 audio encoding.

18. Suppose that the WFQ scheduling policy is applied to a buffer that supports three classes, and suppose the weights are 0.5, 0.25, and 0.25 for the three classes.

   a. Suppose that each class has a large number of packets in the buffer. In what sequence might the three classes be served in order to achieve the WFQ weights? (For round robin scheduling, a natural sequence is 123123123 . . .).

   b. Suppose that classes 1 and 2 have a large number of packets in the buffer, and there are no class 3 packets in the buffer. In what sequence might the three classes be served in to achieve the WFQ weights?

19. Consider the leaky bucket policer (discussed in Section 7.7) that polices the average rate and burst size of a packet flow. We now want to police the peak rate, p, as well. Show how the output of this leaky bucket policer can be fed into a second leaky bucket policer so that the two leaky buckets in series police the average rate, peak rate, and burst size. Be sure to give the bucket size and token generation rate for the second policer.

20. A packet flow is said to conform to a leaky bucket specification (r,b) with burst size b and average rate r if the number of packets that arrive to the leaky bucket is less than $rt + b$ packets in every interval of time of length t for all t. Will a packet flow that conforms to a leaky bucket specification (r,b) ever have to wait at a leaky bucket policer with parameters r and b? Justify your answer.

21. Show that as long as $r_1 < R \, w_1/(\Sigma \, w_j)$, then d_{max} is indeed the maximum delay that any packet in flow 1 will ever experience in the WFQ queue.

Discussion Questions

1. How can a host use RTCP feedback information to determine whether problems are local, regional, or global?

2. Do you think it is better to stream stored audio/video on top of TCP or UDP?

3. Write a report on Cisco's SIP products.

4. Can the problem of providing QoS guarantees be solved simply by throwing enough bandwidth at the problem, that is, by upgrading all link capacities so that bandwidth limitations are no longer a concern?

5. An interesting emerging market is using Internet phone and a company's high-speed LAN to replace the same company's PBX (private branch exchange). Write a one-page report on this issue. Cover the following questions in your report:

   a. What is a traditional PBX? Who would use it?

   b. Consider a call between a user in the company and another user out of the company who is connected to the traditional telephone network. What sort of technology is needed at the interface between the LAN and the traditional telephone network?

   c. In addition to Internet phone software and the interface of Part b, what else is needed to replace the PBX?

6. Consider the four principles for providing QoS support in Section 7.6. Describe the circumstances, if any, under which each of these principles need not be followed.

Programming Assignment

In this lab you will implement a streaming video server and client. The client will use the real-time streaming protocol (RTSP) to control the actions of the server. The server will use the real-time protocol (RTP) to packetize the video for transport over UDP.

You will be given Java code that partially implements RTSP and RTP at the client and server. Your job will be to complete both the client and server code. When you are finished, you will have created a client-server application that does the following:

♦ The client sends SETUP, PLAY, PAUSE, and TEARDOWN RTSP commands, and the server responds to the commands.

♦ When the server is in the playing state, it periodically grabs a stored JPEG frame, packetizes the frame with RTP, and sends the RTP packet into a UDP socket.

♦ The client receives the RTP packets, removes the JPEG frames, decompresses the frames, and renders the frames on the client's monitor.

The code you will be given implements the RTSP protocol in the server and the RTP depacketization in the client. The code also takes care of displaying the transmitted video. You will need to implement RTSP in the client and RTP server.

This programming assignment will significantly enhance the student's understanding of RTP, RTSP, and streaming video. It is highly recommended. The assignment also suggests a number of optional exercises, including implementing the RTSP DESCRIBE command at both client and server. You can find full details of the assignment, as well as important snippets of Java code, at the Web site http://www.awl.com/kurose-ross.

Henning Schulzrinne

Henning Schulzrinne is an associate professor and head of the Internet Real-Time Laboratory at Columbia University. He is the co-author of RTSP, RTP, and SIP—key protocols for audio and video communication over the Internet. Henning received his BS in electrical and industrial engineering at Darmstadt University in Germany, his MS in electrical and computer engineering at the University of Cincinnati, and his PhD in electrical engineering at the University of Massachusetts, Amherst.

What made you decide to specialize in multimedia networking?

This happened almost by accident. As a PhD student, I got involved with DARTnet, an experimental network spanning the United States with T1 lines. DARTnet was used as a proving ground for multicast and Internet real-time tools. That led me to write my first audio tool, NeVoT. Through some of the DARTnet participants, I became involved in the IETF, in the then-nascent Audio Video Transport working group. This group later ended up standardizing RTP.

What was your first job in the computer industry? What did it entail?

My first job in the computer industry was soldering together an Altair computer kit when I was a high school student in Livermore, California. Back in Germany, I started a little consulting company that devised an address management program for a travel agency—storing data on cassette tapes for our TRS-80 and using an IBM Selectric typewriter with a home-brew hardware interface as a printer.

My first real job was with AT&T Bell Laboratories, developing a network emulator for constructing experimental networks in a lab environment.

What are the goals of the Internet Real-Time Lab?

Our goal is to provide pieces for the infrastructure of the Internet as the single future communications platform. This includes the development of protocols, such as SIP and RTSP for signaling or RNAP, YESSIR, and BGRP, for resource reservation, the measurement of performance of Internet protocols and applications, and development of algorithms to increase the quality of service in the Internet. We build prototype applications, such as Internet telephony servers and clients, and have dabbled in hardware, building our own Internet phone.

Recently, we have started to investigate how multimedia and other network services can be located across the Internet. Also, wireless LAN technology offers new opportunities for distributing multimedia content via local replication rather than large-scale peer-to-peer networks or content distribution networks.

What is your vision for the future of multimedia networking?

We are now in a transition phase, just a few years shy of when IP will be the universal platform for multimedia services. We expect radio, telephone, and TV to be up even during snowstorms and earthquakes, so when the Internet takes over the role of these dedicated networks, users will expect the same level of reliability.

To some extent, networking research faces the problem that operating system research has had for a number of years, even more so. While it is still possible to run "boutique" research operating systems in small communities, running a separate network largely defeats its purpose. We will have to learn to design network technologies for an interconnection of competing carriers, with lots of ignorant or malicious end-users.

Visible advances in multimedia networks will largely be driven by factors outside the field itself, namely advances in access and backbone speeds as well as cheap computing power.

Why does SIP have a promising future?

As the current wireless network upgrade to 3G networks proceeds, there is the hope of a single multimedia signaling mechanism spanning all types of networks, from cable modems, to corporate telephone networks and public wireless networks. Together with software radios, this will make it possible in the future that a single device can be used on a home network, as a cordless BlueTooth phone, in a corporate network via 802.11 and in the wide area via 3G networks. Even before we have such a single universal wireless device, the personal mobility mechanisms make it possible to hide the differences between networks. One identifier becomes the universal means of reaching a person, rather than remembering or passing around half a dozen technology- or location-specific telephone numbers.

SIP also breaks apart the provision of voice (bit) transport from voice services. It now becomes technically possible to break apart the local telephone monopoly, where one company provides neutral bit transport, while others provide IP "dial tone" and the classical telephone services, such as gateways, call forwarding, and caller ID.

Beyond multimedia signaling, SIP offers a new service that has been missing in the Internet: event notification. We have approximated such services with HTTP kludges and e-mail, but this was never very satisfactory. Since events are a common abstraction for distributed systems, this may simplify the construction of new services.

Do you have any advice for students entering the networking field?

Networking is almost a classical bridging discipline. It draws from electrical engineering, computer science, operations research, and other disciplines. Thus, networking researchers have to be familiar with subjects well outside their core area.

Work in networks can be immensely satisfying since it is about allowing people to communicate and exchange ideas, one of the essentials of being human. Many areas of engineering have reached a performance plateau; cars, trains, and planes still pretty much work the same as they did 20 or more years ago and probably won't run much faster in another 20. The major change will be in the ability to have these entities communicate and thus improve their performance by making them safer and avoiding gridlock.

8

Security in Computer Networks

Let us introduce Alice and Bob, two people who want to communicate and wish to do so "securely." This being a networking text, we should remark that Alice and Bob could be two routers that want to exchange routing tables securely, a client and server that want to establish a secure transport connection, or two e-mail applications that want to exchange secure e-mail—all case studies that we will consider later in this chapter. Alice and Bob are well-known fixtures in the security community, perhaps because their names are more fun than a generic entity named "A" that wants to communicate securely with a generic entity named "B." Illicit love affairs, wartime communication, and business transactions are the commonly cited human needs for secure communications; preferring the first to the latter two, we're happy to use Alice and Bob as our sender and receiver, and imagine them in this first scenario.

We said that Alice and Bob want to communicate and wish to do so "securely," but what precisely does this mean? As we will see, security (like love) is a many-splendored thing; that is, there are many facets to security. Certainly, Alice and Bob would like for the contents of their communication to remain secret from an eavesdropper (say, a jealous spouse). They probably would also like to make sure that when they are communicating, they are indeed communicating with each other, and that if their communication is tampered with by an eavesdropper, that this tampering is detected. In the first part of this chapter, we'll cover techniques that allow for encrypting/decrypting communication, authenticating the party with whom one is communicating, and ensuring message integrity.

In the second part of this chapter we'll consider the fact that communicating endpoints execute at nodes within an enterprise or home network, in much the same way that Alice and Bob might live in houses from which they communicate by sending postal mail. We'll see that a network (like a house) may be vulnerable to attacks, but can take countermeasures to ensure that the network/house and its entitites/occupants are protected from the "bad guys" who are definitely out there. We'll thus also cover network firewalls, which provide a degree of isolation and protection from those outside of the network. We'll also consider various forms of attacks on the network infrastructure, and the countermeasures taken to foil (or at least mitigate the effects of) these attacks. The chapter concludes with case studies of security at the application, transport, network, and link layers.

8.1 What Is Network Security?

Let's begin our study of network security by returning to our lovers, Alice and Bob, who want to communicate "securely." What precisely does this mean? Certainly, Alice wants only Bob to be able to understand a message that she has sent, even though they are communicating over an insecure medium where an intruder (Trudy, the intruder) may intercept, read, and perform computations on whatever is transmitted from Alice to Bob. Bob also wants to be sure that the message he receives from Alice was indeed sent by Alice, and Alice wants to make sure that the person with whom she is communicating is indeed Bob. Alice and Bob also want to make sure that the contents of their messages have not been altered in transit. They also want to be assured that they can communicate in the first place, i.e., that no one denies them access to the resources needed to communicate. Given these considerations, we can identify the following desirable properties of **secure communication**.

♦ *Confidentiality.* Only the sender and intended receiver should be able to understand the contents of the transmitted message. Because eavesdroppers may intercept the message, this necessarily requires that the message be somehow **encrypted** (its data disguised) so that an intercepted message cannot be **decrypted** (understood) by an interceptor. This aspect of confidentiality is probably the most commonly perceived meaning of the term *secure communication.* Note, however, that this is not only a restricted definition of secure communication (we list additional aspects of secure communication below), but a rather restricted definition of *confidentiality* as well. For example, Alice might also want the mere fact that she is communicating with Bob (or the timing or frequency of her communications) to be a secret. We'll study cryptographic techniques for encrypting and decrypting data in Section 8.2. We'll see that confidential communication often relies on one or more *keys* that are used to encrypt/decrypt communication. We'll cover the topic of key distribution in Section 8.5.

♦ *Authentication.* Both the sender and receiver should be able to confirm the identity of the other party involved in the communication—to confirm that the other party is indeed who or what they claim to be. Face-to-face human communication solves this problem easily by visual recognition. When communicating entities exchange messages over a medium where they cannot see the other party, authentication is not so simple. Why, for instance, should you believe that a received e-mail containing a text string saying that the e-mail came from a friend of yours indeed came from that friend? If someone calls you on the phone claiming to be your bank and asking for your account number, secret personal identification number (PIN), and account balances for verification purposes, would you give that information out over the phone? Hopefully not! We will examine authentication techniques in Section 8.3, including several that, perhaps surprisingly, also rely on the cryptographic techniques from Section 8.2.

♦ *Message integrity and nonrepudiation.* Even if the sender and receiver are able to authenticate each other, they also want to ensure that the content of their communication is not altered, either maliciously or by accident, in transmission. Extensions to the checksumming techniques that we encountered in reliable transport and data link protocols can be used to provide such message integrity, a topic we'll study in Section 8.4. We'll also see how a recipient can prove that a message must have come from the claimed sender. We'll see that both message integrity and nonrepudiation also rely on cryptographic concepts from Section 8.2.

♦ *Availability and access control.* The compelling need for network security has been made painfully obvious over the past several years by numerous denial-of-service (DoS) attacks that have rendered a network, host, or other piece of network infrastructure unusable by legitimate users; perhaps the most notorious of these DoS attacks have been against the Web sites of a number of high-profile companies. Thus a key requirement of secure communication must be that communication can occur in the first place—that the "bad guys" cannot prevent the infrastructure from being used by legitimate users. The fact that some users may be legitimate while others are not naturally leads to the notion of access control, ensuring that entities seeking to gain access to resources are allowed to do so only if they have the appropriate access rights and perform their accesses in a well-defined manner.

Confidentiality, authentication, message integrity, and nonrepudiation have been considered key components of secure communication for quite some time [McCumber 1991]. Availability and access control are more recent extensions to the notion of secure communication [Maconachy 2001, Bishop 2003], no doubt motivated by the very real-world concerns of securing the network infrastructure against a potential onslaught by the "bad guys." One of the surest ways to ensure that "bad guys" can do no harm is to make sure their packets do not enter the network in the first place. A firewall is a device that sits between the network to be protected ("us") and the rest of the world (the "bad guys"—"them"). It controls access to and from the network by regulating which packets can pass into and out of the network. Firewalls have rapidly become a commonplace component in networks ranging from small home networks to networks belonging to the largest corporations on earth. We'll examine how firewalls provide access control (on a per-packet basis and on a per-service basis) in Section 8.6.

Our definition of secure communication has focused primarily on *protecting* communication and network resources. In practice, network security involves not only protection, but also *detecting* breaches of secure communication and attacks on the infrastructure, and then *responding* to these attacks. In many cases, in responding to attacks, a network administrator may deploy additional protection mechanisms. In this sense, network security is achieved through a continuous cycle of protection, detection, and response. (A slightly dated but highly readable book that illustrates aspects of this cycle is [Stoll 1995]).

We'll continue this chapter by covering (in Section 8.7) common types of attacks and the countermeasures that can be taken against them. In Section 8.8 we'll close the chapter with case studies that apply techniques from Sections 8.2 through 8.5 in the application layer, transport layer, network layer, and data link layer.

Having established what we mean by network security, let's next consider exactly what information an intruder may have access to, and what actions can be taken by the intruder. Figure 8.1 illustrates the scenario. Alice, the sender, wants to send data to Bob, the receiver. In order to exchange data securely, while meeting the requirements of confidentiality, authentication, and message integrity, Alice and Bob will exchange control messages and data messages (in much the same way that TCP senders and receivers exchange control segments and data segments). All or some of these messages will typically be encrypted. A passive intruder can potentially perform

♦ *eavesdropping*—listening to and recording control and data messages on the channel.

♦ *modification, insertion,* or *deletion* of messages or message content

As we'll see, unless appropriate countermeasures are taken, these capabilities allow an intruder to mount a wide variety of security attacks: snooping on communication (possibly stealing passwords and data), impersonating another entitty, hijacking an ongoing session, denying service to legitimate network users by overloading system resources, and so on. We'll cover these in Section 8.7. These and other security threats are also discussed in the collection of essays [Denning 1997] and the very readable book by Rubin [Rubin 2001]. A summary of reported attacks is maintained at the CERT Coordination Center [CERT 2004]. See also [Cisco Security 2004; Voydock 1983; Bhimani 1996].

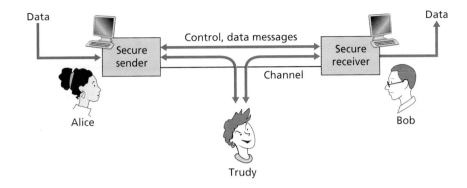

Figure 8.1 ♦ Sender, receiver, and intruder (Alice, Bob, and Trudy)

Having established that there are indeed real threats (Trudy) loose in the Internet, what are the Internet equivalents of Alice and Bob, our friends who need to communicate securely? Certainly, Bob and Alice might be human users at two end systems, for example, a real Alice and a real Bob who really do want to exchange secure e-mail. They might also be participants in an electronic commerce transaction. For example, a real Bob might want to transfer his credit card number securely to a Web server to purchase an item online. Similarly, a real Alice might want to interact with her bank online. As noted in [RFC 1636], however, the parties needing secure communication might themselves also be part of the network infrastructure. Recall that the domain name system (DNS, see Section 2.5) or routing daemons that exchange routing information (see Section 4.6) require secure communication between two parties. The same is true for network management applications, a topic we examine in Chapter 9. An intruder that could actively interfere with, control, or corrupt DNS lookups and updates [RFC 2535, IETF dnsext 2004], routing computations [Murphy 2003], or network management functions [RFC 2574] could wreak havoc in the Internet.

Having now established the framework, a few of the most important definitions, and the need for network security, let us next delve into cryptography. While the use of cryptography in providing confidentiality is self-evident, we'll see shortly that it is also central to providing authentication, message integrity, nonrepudiation, and access control—making cryptography a cornerstone of network security.

8.2 Principles of Cryptography

Although cryptography has a long history dating back at least as far as Julius Caesar, modern cryptographic techniques, including many of those used in the Internet, are based on advances made in the past 30 years. Kahn's book, *The Codebreakers* [Kahn 1967], and Singh's book, *The Code Book: The Science of Secrecy from Ancient Egypt to Quantum Cryptography* [Singh 1999], provide a fascinating look at the long history of cryptography. A detailed (but entertaining and readable) technical discussion of cryptography, particularly from a network standpoint, is [Kaufman 1995]. [Diffie 1998] provides a compelling and up-to-date examination of the political and social (for example, privacy) issues that are now inextricably intertwined with cryptography. A complete discussion of cryptography itself requires a complete book [Kaufman 1995; Schneier 1995] and so we only touch on the essential aspects of cryptography, particularly as they are practiced on the Internet. An excellent online site is the RSA Labs FAQ page [RSA FAQ 2004]. We also note that while our focus in this section will be on the use of cryptography for confidentiality, we'll see shortly that cryptographic techniques are inextricably woven into authentication, message integrity, nonrepudiation, and more.

Cryptographic techniques allow a sender to disguise data so that an intruder can gain no information from the intercepted data. The receiver, of course, must be able to recover the original data from the disguised data. Figure 8.2 illustrates some of the important terminology.

Suppose now that Alice wants to send a message to Bob. Alice's message in its original form (for example, "`Bob, I love you. Alice`") is known as **plaintext**, or **cleartext**. Alice encrypts her plaintext message using an **encryption algorithm** so that the encrypted message, known as **ciphertext**, looks unintelligible to any intruder. Interestingly, in many modern cryptographic systems, including those used in the Internet, the encryption technique itself is *known*—published, standardized, and available to everyone (for example, [RFC 1321; RFC 2437; RFC 2420; NIST 2001]), even a potential intruder! Clearly, if everyone knows the method for encoding data, then there must be some secret information that prevents an intruder from decrypting the transmitted data. This is where keys come in.

In Figure 8.2, Alice provides a **key**, K_A, a string of numbers or characters, as input to the encryption algorithm. The encryption algorithm takes the key and the plaintext message, m, as input and produces ciphertext as output. The notation $K_A(m)$ refers to the ciphertext form (encrypted using the key K_A) of the plaintext message, m. The actual encryption algorithm that uses key K_A will be evident from the context. Similarly, Bob will provide a key, K_B, to the **decryption algorithm** that takes the ciphertext and Bob's key as input and produces the original plaintext as output. That is, if Bob receives an encrypted message $K_A(m)$, he decrypts it by computing $K_B(K_A(m)) = m$. In **symmetric key systems**, Alice's and Bob's keys are identical and are secret. In **public key systems**, a pair of keys is used. One of the keys is known to both Bob and Alice (indeed, it is known to the whole world). The other key is known only by either Bob or Alice (but not both). In the following two subsections, we consider symmetric key and public key systems in more detail.

CASE HISTORY

CODE-BREAKING CONTESTS

First adopted by the US government in 1977, the Data Encryption Standard (DES) 56-bit algorithm is still widely used by financial services and other industries around the world to protect sensitive information. The company RSA Security has been sponsoring a series of DES-cracking contests to emphasize the need for encryption stronger than the current 56-bit standard. The challenge is to decrypt a message that has been encoded with 56-bit DES within a specified amount of time. Code breakers meet the challenge by exhaustively searching over all of the possible secret keys. RSA awards a $10,000 prize to the winners.

The first DES Challenge, in 1997, was won by a team from Colorado that recovered the secret key in less than four months. Since then improved technology has made much faster exhaustive search efforts possible. In February 1998, Distributed.Net won RSA's DES Challenge II-1 with a 41-day effort, and in July, the Electronic Frontier Foundation (EFF) won RSA's DES Challenge II-2 when it cracked the DES message in 56 hours.

In January 1999, Distributed.Net, a worldwide coalition of computer enthusiasts, worked with EFF's Deep Crack, a specially designed supercomputer, and a worldwide network of nearly 100,000 PCs on the Internet, to win RSA Data Security's DES Challenge III in only 22 hours and 15 minutes. EFF's Deep Crack and the Distributed.Net computers were testing 245 billion keys per second when the key was found!

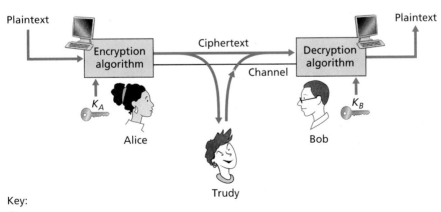

Key:

 Key

Figure 8.2 ♦ Cryptographic components

8.2.1 Symmetric Key Cryptography

All cryptographic algorithms involve substituting one thing for another, for example, taking a piece of plaintext and then computing and substituting the appropriate ciphertext to create the encrypted message. Before studying a modern key-based cryptographic system, let us first get our feet wet by studying a very old, very simple symmetric key algorithm attributed to Julius Caesar, known as the **Caesar cipher** (a cipher is a method for encrypting data).

For English text, the Caesar cipher would work by taking each letter in the plaintext message and substituting the letter that is k letters later (allowing wraparound; that is, having the letter "z" followed by the letter "a") in the alphabet. For example if $k = 3$, then the letter "a" in plaintext becomes "d" in ciphertext; "b" in plaintext becomes "e" in ciphertext, and so on. Here, the value of k serves as the key. As an example, the plaintext message "`bob, i love you. alice`" becomes "`ere, l oryh brx. dolfh`" in ciphertext. While the ciphertext does indeed look like gibberish, it wouldn't take long to break the code if you knew that the Caesar cipher was being used, as there are only 25 possible key values.

An improvement on the Caesar cipher is the **monoalphabetic cipher**, which also substitutes one letter of the alphabet with another letter of the alphabet. However, rather than substituting according to a regular pattern (for example, substitution with an offset of k for all letters), any letter can be substituted for any other letter, as long as each letter has a unique substitute letter, and vice versa. The substitution rule in Figure 8.3 shows one possible rule for encoding plaintext.

The plaintext message "`bob, i love you. alice`" becomes "`nkn, s gktc wky. mgsbc.`" Thus, as in the case of the Caesar cipher, this looks like gibberish. A monoalphabetic cipher would also appear to be better than the Caesar cipher in that there are 26! (on the order of 10^{26}) possible pairings of letters rather than 25 possible pairings. A brute-force approach of trying all 10^{26} possible pairings would require far too much work to be a feasible way of breaking the encryption algorithm and decoding the message. However, by statistical analysis of the plaintext language, for example, knowing that the letters "e" and "t" are the most frequently occurring letters in typical English text (accounting for 13 percent and 9 percent of letter occurrences), and knowing that particular two- and three-letter occurrences of letters appear quite often together (for example, "in," "it," "the," "ion," "ing," and so forth) make it relatively easy to break this code. If the intruder

| Plaintext letter: | a b c d e f g h i j k l m n o p q r s t u v w x y z |
| Ciphertext letter: | m n b v c x z a s d f g h j k l p o i u y t r e w q |

Figure 8.3 ◆ A monoalphabetic cipher

has some knowledge about the possible contents of the message, then it is even easier to break the code. For example, if Trudy the intruder is Bob's wife and suspects Bob of having an affair with Alice, then she might suspect that the names "bob" and "alice" appear in the text. If Trudy knew for certain that those two names appeared in the ciphertext and had a copy of the example ciphertext message above, then she could immediately determine seven of the 26 letter pairings, requiring 10^9 fewer possibilities to be checked by a brute-force method. Indeed, if Trudy suspected Bob of having an affair, she might well expect to find some other choice words in the message as well.

When considering how easy it might be for Trudy to break Bob and Alice's encryption scheme, one can distinguish three different scenarios, depending on what information the intruder has.

♦ *Ciphertext-only attack.* In some cases, the intruder may have access only to the intercepted ciphertext, with no certain information about the contents of the plaintext message. We have seen how statistical analysis can help in a **ciphertext-only attack** on an encryption scheme.

♦ *Known-plaintext attack.* We saw above that if Trudy somehow knew for sure that "bob" and "alice" appeared in the ciphertext message, then she could have determined the (plaintext, ciphertext) pairings for the letters *a, l, i, c, e, b,* and *o*. Trudy might also have been fortunate enough to have recorded all of the ciphertext transmissions and then found Bob's own decrypted version of one of the transmissions scribbled on a piece of paper. When an intruder knows some of the (plaintext, ciphertext) pairings, we refer to this as a **known-plaintext attack** on the encryption scheme.

♦ *Chosen-plaintext attack.* In a **chosen-plaintext attack**, the intruder is able to choose the plaintext message and obtain its corresponding ciphertext form. For the simple encryption algorithms we've seen so far, if Trudy could get Alice to send the message, "The quick brown fox jumps over the lazy dog," she could completely break the encryption scheme. We'll see shortly that for more sophisticated encryption techniques, a chosen-plaintext attack does not necessarily mean that the encryption technique can be broken.

Five hundred years ago, techniques improving on monoalphabetic encryption, known as **polyalphabetic encryption**, were invented. The idea behind polyalphabetic encryption is to use multiple monoalphabetic ciphers, with a specific monoalphabetic cipher to encode a letter in a specific position in the plaintext message. Thus, the same letter, appearing in different positions in the plaintext message, might be encoded differently. An example of a polyalphabetic encryption scheme is shown in Figure 8.4. It has two Caesar ciphers (with $k = 5$ and $k = 19$), shown as rows. We might choose to use these two Caesar ciphers, C_1 and C_2, in the repeating pattern C_1, C_2, C_2, C_1, C_2. That is, the first letter of plaintext is to be encoded using

C_1, the second and third using C_2, the fourth using C_1, and the fifth using C_2. The pattern then repeats, with the sixth letter being encoded using C_1, the seventh with C_2, and so on. The plaintext message "bob, i love you." is thus encrypted "ghu, n etox dhz." Note that the first "b" in the plaintext message is encrypted using C_1, while the second "b" is encrypted using C_2. In this example, the encryption and decryption "key" is the knowledge of the two Caesar keys ($k = 5$, $k = 19$) and the pattern C_1, C_2, C_2, C_1, C_2.

Data Encryption Standard (DES) and Advanced Encryption Standard (AES)

Let us now fast-forward to modern times and examine the Data Encryption Standard (DES) [NIST 1993], a symmetric key encryption standard published in 1977 and updated most recently in 1993 by the US National Bureau of Standards for commercial and nonclassified US government use. DES encodes plaintext in 64-bit chunks using a 64-bit key. Actually, 8 of these 64 bits of the key are odd parity bits (there is one parity bit for each of the 8 bytes), so the DES key is effectively 56 bits long. The National Institute of Standards and Technology (the successor to the National Bureau of Standards) states the goal of DES as follows: "The goal is to completely scramble the data and key so that every bit of the ciphertext depends on every bit of the data and every bit of the key. . . . With a good algorithm, there should be no correlation between the ciphertext and either the original data or key" [NIST 1999].

The basic operation of DES is illustrated in Figure 8.5. In our discussion we will overview DES operation, leaving the nitty-gritty, bit-level details (there are *many*) to other sources [Kaufman 1995; Schneier 1995]. [Schneier 1995] includes a C implementation as well. DES consists of two permutation steps (the first and last steps of the algorithm), in which all 64 bits are permuted, with 16 identical rounds of operation in between. The operation of each round is identical, taking the output of the previous round as input. During each round, the rightmost 32 bits of the input are moved to the left 32 bits of the output. The entire 64-bit input to the ith round and the 48-bit key for the ith round (derived from the larger DES 56-bit key) are taken as input to a function that involves expansion of 4-bit input chunks into 6-bit chunks, exclusive OR-ing with the expanded 6-bit chunks of the 48-bit key Ki, a substitution operation, and further exclusive OR-ing with the leftmost 32 bits of the

Plaintext letter:	a b c d e f g h i j k l m n o p q r s t u v w x y z
$C_1(k = 5)$:	f g h i j k l m n o p q r s t u v w x y z a b c d e
$C_2(k = 19)$:	t u v w x y z a b c d e f g h i j k l m n o p q r s

Figure 8.4 ◆ A polyalphabetic cipher using two Caesar ciphers

input; see [Kaufman 1995; Schneier 1995] for details. The resulting 32-bit output of the function is then used as the rightmost 32 bits of the round's 64-bit output, as shown in Figure 8.5. Decryption works by reversing the algorithm's operations.

How well does DES work? How secure is it? No one can tell for sure [Kaufman 1995]. In 1997, a network security company, RSA Data Security Inc., launched a DES Challenge contest to crack (decode) a short phrase it had encrypted using 56-bit DES. The unencoded phrase ("`Strong cryptography makes the world a safer place.`") was determined in less than four months by a team that used volunteers throughout the Internet to systematically explore the key space. The team claimed the $10,000 prize after testing only a quarter of the key space—about 18 quadrillion keys [RSA Challenge 2002]. The 1999 DES Challenge III was won in a little over 22 hours, with a network of volunteers and a special-purpose

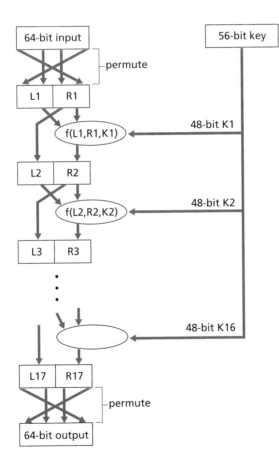

Figure 8.5 ♦ Basic operation of DES

computer that was built for less than $250,000 (nicknamed Deep Crack), a feat that is documented online [EFF 1999].

We should also note that so far we have considered only the encryption of a 64-bit quantity. When longer messages are encrypted, which is typically the case, DES is often used with a technique known as **cipher-block chaining**, in which the encrypted version of the jth 64-bit quantity of data is XOR-ed with the $(j + 1)$st unit of data before the $(j + 1)$st unit of data is encrypted.

If 56-bit DES is considered too insecure, one can simply run the 56-bit algorithm multiple times, taking the 64-bit output from one iteration of DES as the input to the next DES iteration, using a different encryption key each time. For example, **triple-DES (3DES)** is a US government standard [NIST 1999b] that replaces DES, which is being phased out and is permitted only in legacy systems. In one configuration, 3DES first runs the DES encryption algorithm over the data using a first 56-bit key, then runs the DES decryption algorithm over the output of the first round of encryption using a second key, and finally runs the DES encryption algorithm over the output of the second round using a third key. 3DES has been proposed as the encryption standard for the point-to-point (PPP) protocol [RFC 2420] for the data link layer (see Section 5.7). A detailed discussion of key lengths and the estimated time and budget needed to crack DES can be found in [Blaze 1996].

In November 2001, NIST announced the successor to DES: the Advanced Encryption Standard (AES) [NIST 2001, Danielyan 2001], also known as the Rijndael algorithm [Daemen 2000]. AES is a symmetric key algorithm that processes data in 128-bit blocks and can operate with keys that are 128, 192, and 256 bits long. NIST estimates that a machine that could crack 56-bit DES in one second (that is, try 2^{55} keys per second) would take approximately 149 trillion years to crack a 128-bit AES key.

8.2.2 Public Key Encryption

For more than 2,000 years (since the time of the Caesar cipher and up to the 1970s), encrypted communication required that the two communicating parties share a common secret—the symmetric key used for encryption and decryption. One difficulty with this approach is that the two parties must somehow agree on the shared key; but to do so requires (presumably *secure*) communication! Perhaps the parties could first meet and agree on the key in person (for example, two of Caesar's centurions might meet at the Roman baths) and thereafter communicate with encryption. In a networked world, however, communicating parties may never meet and may never converse except over the network. Is it possible for two parties to communicate with encryption without having a shared secret key that is known in advance? In 1976, Diffie and Hellman [Diffie 1976] demonstrated an algorithm (known now as Diffie-Hellman Key Exchange) to do just that—a radically different and marvelously elegant approach toward secure communication that has led to the development of today's public key cryptography systems. We'll see shortly that public key cryptography systems also have several wonderful properties that make them useful not only for encryption, but for authentication and digital signatures as well. Interestingly, it has recently come to light that ideas similar to those in [Diffie 1976] and [RSA 1978] had been independently developed in the early 1970s in a series of secret reports by researchers at the Communications-Electronics Security Group in the United Kingdom [Ellis 1987]. As is often the case, great ideas can spring up independently in many places; fortunately, public key advances took place not only in private, but also in the public view, as well.

The use of public key cryptography is conceptually quite simple. Suppose Alice wants to communicate with Bob. As shown in Figure 8.6, rather than Bob and Alice sharing a single secret key (as in the case of symmetric key systems), Bob (the recipient of Alice's messages) instead has two keys—a **public key** that is available to *everyone* in the world (including Trudy the intruder) and a **private key** that is known only to Bob. We will use the notation K_B^+ and K_B^- to refer to Bob's public and private keys, respectively. In order to communicate with Bob, Alice first fetches Bob's public key. Alice then encrypts her message, m, to Bob using Bob's public key and a known (for example, standardized) encryption algorithm; that is, Alice computes $K_B^+(m)$. Bob receives Alice's encrypted message and uses his private key and a known (for example, standardized) decryption algorithm to decrypt Alice's encrypted message. That is, Bob computes $K_B^-(K_B^+(m))$. We will see below that there are encryption/decryption algorithms and techniques for choosing public and private keys such that $K_B^-(K_B^+(m)) = m$; that is, applying Bob's public key, K_B^+, to a message, m (to get $K_B^+(m)$), and then applying Bob's private key, K_B^-, to the encrypted version of m (that is, computing $K_B^-(K_B^+(m))$) gives back m. This is a remarkable result! In this manner, Alice can use Bob's publicly available key to send a secret

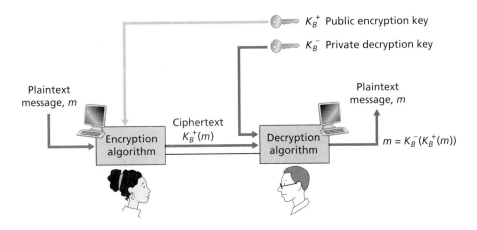

Figure 8.6 ◆ Public key cryptography

message to Bob without either of them having to distribute any secret keys! We will see shortly that we can interchange the public key and private key encryption and get the same remarkable result that is, $K_B^-(K_B^+(m)) = K_B^+(K_B^-(m)) = m$.

The use of public key cryptography is thus conceptually simple. But two immediate worries may spring to mind. A first concern is that although an intruder intercepting Alice's encrypted message will see only gibberish, the intruder knows both the key (Bob's public key, which is available for all the world to see) and the algorithm that Alice used for encryption. Trudy can thus mount a chosen-plaintext attack, using the known standardized encryption algorithm and Bob's publicly available encryption key to encode any message she chooses! Trudy might well try, for example, to encode messages, or parts of messages, that she suspects that Alice might send. Clearly, if public key cryptography is to work, key selection and encryption/decryption must be done in such a way that it is impossible (or at least so hard as to be nearly impossible) for an intruder to either determine Bob's private key or somehow otherwise decrypt or guess Alice's message to Bob. A second concern is that since Bob's encryption key is public, anyone can send an encrypted message to Bob, including Alice or someone *claiming* to be Alice. In the case of a single shared secret key, the fact that the sender knows the secret key implicitly identifies the sender to the receiver. In the case of public key cryptography, however, this is no longer the case since anyone can send an encrypted message to Bob using Bob's publicly available key. A digital signature, a topic we will study in Section 8.4, is needed to bind a sender to a message.

While there may be many algorithms and keys that address these concerns, the **RSA algorithm** (named after its founders, Ron Rivest, Adi Shamir, and Leonard Adleman) has become almost synonymous with public key cryptography. Let's first see how RSA works and then examine why it works. Suppose that Bob wants to receive encrypted messages, as shown in Figure 8.6. There are two interrelated components of RSA:

- The choice of the public key and the private key
- The encryption and decryption algorithm

In order to choose the public and private keys, Bob must perform the following steps.

1. Choose two large prime numbers, p and q. How large should p and q be? The larger the values, the more difficult it is to break RSA, but the longer it takes to perform the encoding and decoding. RSA Laboratories recommends that the product of p and q be on the order of 1024 bits for corporate use and 768 bits for use with "less valuable information" [RSA Key 2004] (which leads one to wonder why corporate use is deemed so much more important than other use!). For a discussion of how to find large prime numbers, see [Caldwell 2004].

2. Compute $n = pq$ and $z = (p - 1)(q - 1)$.
3. Choose a number, e, less than n, which has no common factors (other than 1) with z. (In this case, e and z are said to be relatively prime.) The letter e is used since this value will be used in encryption.
4. Find a number, d, such that $ed - 1$ is exactly divisible (that is, with no remainder) by z. The letter d is used because this value will be used in decryption. Put another way, given e, we choose d such that the integer remainder when ed is divided by z is 1. (The integer remainder when an integer x is divided by the integer n, is denoted $x \bmod n$).
5. The public key that Bob makes available to the world, K_B^+, is the pair of numbers (n,e); his private key, K_B^-, is the pair of numbers (n,d).

The encryption by Alice and the decryption by Bob are done as follows.

♦ Suppose Alice wants to send Bob a bit pattern, or number, m, such that $m < n$. To encode, Alice performs the exponentiation, m^e, and then computes the integer remainder when m^e is divided by n. Thus, the encrypted value, c, of the plaintext message, m, that Alice sends is

$$c = m^e \bmod n$$

♦ To decrypt the received ciphertext message, c, Bob computes

$$m = c^d \bmod n$$

which requires the use of his private key (n,d).

As a simple example of RSA, suppose Bob chooses $p = 5$ and $q = 7$. (Admittedly, these values are far too small to be secure.) Then $n = 35$ and $z = 24$. Bob chooses $e = 5$, since 5 and 24 have no common factors. Finally, Bob chooses $d = 29$, since $5 \cdot 29 - 1$ (that is, $ed - 1$) is exactly divisible by 24. Bob makes the two values, $n = 35$ and $e = 5$, public and keeps the value $d = 29$ secret. Observing these two public values, suppose Alice now wants to send the letters "l," "o," "v," and "e" to Bob. Interpreting each letter as a number between 1 and 26 (with "a" being 1, and "z" being 26), Alice and Bob perform the encryption and decryption shown in Tables 8.1 and 8.2, respectively.

Given that the "toy" example in Tables 8.1 and 8.2 has already produced some extremely large numbers, and given that we know that we saw earlier that p and q should each be several hundred bits long, several practical issues regarding RSA come to mind. How does one choose large prime numbers? How does one then choose e and d? How does one perform exponentiation with large numbers? A discussion of these important issues is beyond the scope of this book; see [Kaufman 1995] and the references therein for details.

Plaintext Letter	m: numeric representation	m^e	ciphertext $c = m^e$ mod n
l	12	248832	17
o	15	759375	15
v	22	5153632	22
e	5	3125	10

Table 8.1 ✦ Alice's RSA encryption, $e = 5$, $n = 35$

Ciphertext c	c^d	$m = c^d$ mod n	Plaintext Letter
17	4819685721067509150914118252230716977	12	l
15	127834039488589391112327557568359375	15	o
22	851643319086537701956194499721106030592	22	v
10	100000000000000000000000000000	5	e

Table 8.2 ✦ Bob's RSA decryption, $d = 29$, $n = 35$

We do note here that the exponentiation required by RSA is a rather time-consuming process. By contrast, DES is at least 100 times faster in software and between 1,000 and 10,000 times faster in hardware [RSA Fast 2004]. As a result, RSA is often used in practice in combination with DES or AES. For example, if Alice wants to send Bob a large amount of encrypted data at high speed, she could do the following. First Alice chooses a DES key that will be used to encode the data itself; this key is sometimes referred to as a **session key**, K_S. Alice must inform Bob of the session key, since this is the shared symmetric key they will use for DES. Alice thus encrypts the session key value using Bob's public RSA key, that is, computes $c = (K_S)^e$ mod n. Bob receives the RSA-encrypted session key, c, and decrypts it to obtain the session key, K_S. Bob now knows the session key that Alice will use for her DES-encrypted data transfer.

Why Does RSA Work?

The RSA encryption/decryption appears rather magical. Why should it be that by applying the encryption algorithm and then the decryption algorithm, one recovers the original message? In order to understand why RSA works, we'll need to perform arithmetic operations using modulo-n arithmetic. In modular arithmetic, one performs the usual operations of addition, multiplication, and exponentiation. However, the result of each operation is replaced by the integer remainder that is left when the result is divided by n. We will take $n = pq$, where p and q are the large prime numbers used in the RSA algorithm.

Recall that under RSA encryption, a message (represented by an integer), m, is first exponentiated to the power e using modulo-n arithmetic to encrypt. Decryption is performed by raising this value to the power d, again using modulo-n arithmetic. The result of an encryption step followed by a decryption step is thus $(m^e)^d$. Let's now see what we can say about this quantity. We have

$$(m^e)^d \bmod n = m^{ed} \bmod n$$

Although we're trying to remove some of the magic about why RSA works, we'll need to use a rather magical result from number theory here. Specifically, we'll need the result that says if p and q are prime, and $n = pq$, then $x^y \bmod n$ is the same as $x^{(y \bmod (p-1)(q-1))} \bmod n$ [Kaufman 1995]. Applying this result, we have

$$(m^e)^d \bmod n = m^{(ed \bmod (p-1)(q-1))} \bmod n$$

But remember that we chose e and d such that $ed - 1$ is exactly divisible (that is, with no remainder) by $(p-1)(q-1)$, or equivalently that ed is divisible by $(p-1)(q-1)$ with a remainder of 1, and thus $ed \bmod (p-1)(q-1) = 1$. This gives us

$$(m^e)^d \bmod n = m^1 \bmod n = m$$

that is, that

$$(m^e)^d \bmod n = m$$

This is the result we were hoping for! By first exponentiating to the power of e (that is, encrypting) and then exponentiating to the power of d (that is, decrypting), we obtain the original value, m. Even *more* wonderful is the fact that if we first exponentiate to the power of d and then exponentiate to the power of e—that is, we reverse the order of encryption and decryption, performing the decryption operation first and then applying the encryption operation—we also obtain the original value, m! (The proof for this result follows the exact same reasoning as above, since $m^{ed} = m^{de}$) We will see shortly that this wonderful property of the RSA algorithm,

$$(m^e)^d \bmod n = m = (m^d)^e \bmod n$$

will be of great use.

The security of RSA relies on the fact that there are no known algorithms for quickly factoring a number, in this case the public value *n,* into the primes *p* and *q*. If one knew *p* and *q,* then given the public value *e,* one could then easily compute the secret key, *d*. On the other hand, it is not known whether or not there *exist* fast algorithms for factoring a number, and in this sense the security of RSA is not guaranteed.

8.3   Authentication

Authentication is the process of proving one's identity to someone else. As humans, we authenticate each other in many ways: we recognize each other's faces when we meet, we recognize each other's voices on the telephone, we are authenticated by the customs official who checks us against the picture on our passport.

In this section we consider how one party can authenticate another party when the two are communicating over a network. We focus here on authenticating a "live" party, at the point in time when communication is actually occurring. This is a subtly different problem from proving that a message received at some point in the past (for example, that may have been archived) did indeed come from that claimed sender. This latter problem is referred to as the **digital signature** problem, which we explore in Section 8.4.

When performing authentication over the network, the communicating parties cannot rely on biometric information, such as a visual appearance or a voiceprint. Indeed, we will see in our later case studies that it is often network elements such as routers and client/server processes that must authenticate each other. Here, authentication must be done solely on the basis of messages and data exchanged as part of an **authentication protocol**. Typically, an authentication protocol would run *before* the two communicating parties run some other protocol (for example, a reliable data transfer protocol, a routing information exchange protocol, or an e-mail protocol). The authentication protocol first establishes the identities of the parties to each other's satisfaction; only after authentication do the parties get down to the work at hand.

As in the case of our development of a reliable data transfer (rdt) protocol in Chapter 3, we will find it instructive here to develop various versions of an authentication protocol, which we will call **ap** (authentication protocol), and poke holes in each version as we proceed. (If you enjoy this stepwise evolution of a design, you might also enjoy [Bryant 1988], which recounts a fictitious narrative between designers of an open-network authentication system, and their discovery of the many subtle issues involved.)

Let's assume that Alice needs to authenticate herself to Bob.

8.3.1 Authentication Protocol *ap1.0*

Perhaps the simplest authentication protocol we can imagine is one where Alice simply sends a message to Bob saying she is Alice. This protocol is shown in Figure

8.7. The flaw here is obvious—there is no way for Bob actually to know that the person sending the message "I am Alice" is indeed Alice. For example, Trudy (the intruder) could just as well send such a message.

8.3.2 Authentication Protocol *ap2.0*

If Alice has a well-known network address (e.g., an IP address) from which she always communicates, Bob could attempt to authenticate Alice by verifying that the source address on the IP datagram carrying the authentication message matches Alice's well-known address. In this case, Alice would be authenticated. This might stop a very network-naive intruder from impersonating Alice, but it wouldn't stop the determined student studying this book, or many others!

From our study of the network and data link layers, we know that it is not that hard (for example, if one had access to the operating system code and could build one's own operating system kernel, as is the case with Linux and several other freely available operating systems) to create an IP datagram, put whatever IP source address we want (for example, Alice's well-known IP address) into the IP datagram, and send the datagram over the link-layer protocol to the first-hop router. From then on, the incorrectly source-addressed datagram would be dutifully forwarded to Bob. This approach, shown in Figure 8.8, is a form of IP spoofing, a well-known security attack that we'll consider in more detail in Section 8.7. IP spoofing can be avoided if Trudy's first-hop router is configured to forward only datagrams containing Trudy's IP source address [RFC 2827]. However, this capability is not universally deployed or enforced. Bob would thus be foolish to assume that Trudy's network manager (who might be Trudy herself) had configured Trudy's first-hop router to forward only appropriately addressed datagrams.

Figure 8.7 ♦ Protocol *ap1.0* and a failure scenario

Figure 8.8 ♦ Protocol *ap2.0* and a failure scenario

8.3.3 Authentication Protocol *ap3.0*

One classic approach to authentication is to use a secret password. We have PINs to identify ourselves to automatic teller machines and login passwords for operating systems. The password is a shared secret between the authenticator and the person being authenticated. We saw in Section 2.2 that HTTP uses a password-based authentication scheme. Telnet and FTP use password authentication as well. In protocol *ap3.0,* Alice thus sends her secret password to Bob, as shown in Figure 8.9.

Since passwords are so widely used, we might suspect that protocol *ap3.0* is fairly secure. If so, we'd be wrong! The security flaw here is clear. If Trudy eavesdrops on Alice's communication, then she can learn Alice's password. Lest you think this is unlikely, consider the fact that when you Telnet to another machine and log in, the login password is sent unencrypted to the Telnet server. Someone connected to the Telnet client or server's LAN can possibly sniff (read and store) all packets transmitted on the LAN and thus steal the login password. In fact, this is a well-known approach for stealing passwords (see, for example, [Jimenez 1997]). Such a threat is obviously very real, so *ap3.0* clearly won't do.

8.3.4 Authentication Protocol *ap3.1*

Our next idea for fixing *ap3.0* is naturally to encrypt the password. By encrypting the password, we can prevent Trudy from learning Alice's password. If we assume that Alice and Bob share a symmetric secret key, K_{A-B}, then Alice can encrypt the password and send her identification message, "I am Alice," and her encrypted password to Bob. Bob then decrypts the password and, assuming the password is correct, authenticates Alice. Bob feels comfortable in authenticating Alice since

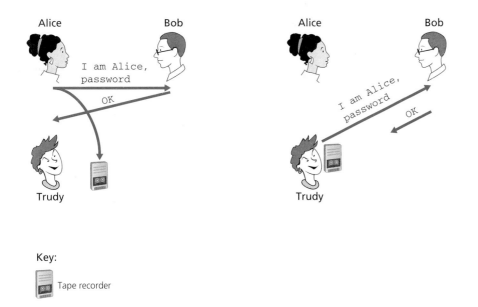

Figure 8.9 ♦ Protocol *ap3.0* and a failure scenario

Alice not only knows the password, but she also knows the shared secret key value needed to encrypt the password. Let's call this protocol *ap3.1*.

While it is true that *ap3.1* prevents Trudy from learning Alice's password, the use of cryptography here does not solve the authentication problem. Bob is subject to a **playback attack**: Trudy need only eavesdrop on Alice's communication, record the encrypted version of the password, and play back the encrypted version of the password to Bob to pretend that she is Alice. The use of an encrypted password in *ap3.1* doesn't make the situation manifestly different from that of protocol *ap3.0* in Figure 8.9.

8.3.5 Authentication Protocol *ap4.0*

The problem with *ap3.1* is that the same password is used over and over again. One way to solve this problem would be to use a different password each time. Alice and Bob could agree on a sequence of passwords (or on an algorithm for generating passwords) and use each password only once, in sequence. This idea is used in the S/KEY system [RFC 1760], adopting an approach due to Lamport [Lamport 1981] for generating a sequence of passwords.

Rather than just stop here with this solution, however, let us consider a more general approach for combatting the playback attack. The failure scenario in Figure

8.9 resulted from the fact that Bob could not distinguish between the original authentication of Alice and the later playback of Alice's original authentication. That is, Bob could not tell if Alice was live (that is, was currently really on the other end of the connection) or whether the messages he was receiving were a recorded playback of a previous authentication of Alice. The very (*very*) observant reader will recall that the three-way TCP handshake protocol needed to address the same problem—the server side of a TCP connection did not want to accept a connection if the received SYN segment was an old copy (retransmission) of a SYN segment from an earlier connection. How did the TCP server side solve the problem of determining whether the client was really live? It chose an initial sequence number that had not been used in a very long time, sent that number to the client, and then waited for the client to respond back with an ACK segment containing that number. We can adopt the same idea here for authentication purposes.

A **nonce** is a number that a protocol will use only once in a lifetime. That is, once a protocol uses a nonce, it will never use that number again. Our *ap4.0* protocol uses a nonce as follows.

1. Alice sends the message "I am Alice" to Bob.
2. Bob chooses a nonce, R, and sends it to Alice.
3. Alice encrypts the nonce using Alice and Bob's symmetric secret key, K_{A-B}, and sends the encrypted nonce, $K_{A-B}(R)$, back to Bob. As in protocol *ap3.1*, it is the fact that Alice knows K_{A-B} and uses it to encrypt a value that lets Bob know that the message he receives was generated by Alice. The nonce is used to ensure that Alice is live.
4. Bob decrypts the received message. If the decrypted nonce equals the nonce he sent Alice, then Alice is authenticated.

Protocol *ap4.0* is illustrated in Figure 8.10. By using the once-in-a-lifetime value, R, and then checking the returned value, $K_{A-B}(R)$, Bob can be sure that Alice is both who she says she is (since she knows the secret key value needed to encrypt R) and live (since she has encrypted the nonce, R, that Bob just created).

8.3.6 Authentication Protocol *ap5.0*

The use of a nonce and symmetric key cryptography formed the basis of our successful authentication protocol, *ap4.0*. A natural question is whether we can use a nonce and public key cryptography (rather than symmetric key cryptography) to solve the authentication problem. The use of a public key approach would obviate a difficulty in any shared key system—worrying about how the two parties learn the secret shared key value in the first place. A protocol that uses public key cryptography in a manner analogous to the use of symmetric key cryptography in protocol *ap4.0* is protocol *ap5.0*.

1. Alice sends the message "I am Alice" to Bob.

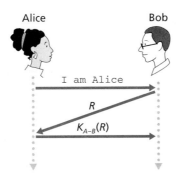

Alice   Bob

I am Alice

R

$K_{A-B}(R)$

Figure 8.10 ♦ Protocol *ap4.0*: no failure scenario

2. Bob chooses a nonce, R, and sends it to Alice. Once again, the nonce will be used to ensure that Alice is live.
3. Alice uses her *private* key, K_A^-, to encrypt the nonce and sends the resulting value $K_A^-(R)$ to Bob. Since only Alice knows her private key, no one except Alice can generate $K_A^-(R)$.
4. Bob applies Alice's public key, K_A^+, to the received message; that is, Bob computes $K_A^+(K_A^-(R))$. Recall from our discussion of RSA public key cryptography in Section 8.2 that $K_A^+(K_A^-(R)) = R$. Thus, Bob computes R and authenticates Alice.

The operation of protocol *ap5.0* is illustrated in Figure 8.11. Is protocol *ap5.0* as secure as protocol *ap4.0*? Both use nonces. Since *ap5.0* uses public key techniques, it requires that Bob retrieve Alice's public key. This leads to an interesting scenario, shown in Figure 8.12, in which Trudy may be able to impersonate Alice to Bob.

1. Trudy sends the message "`I am Alice`" to Bob.
2. Bob chooses a nonce, R, and sends it to Alice, but the message is intercepted by Trudy.
3. Trudy uses her private key, K_T^-, to encrypt the nonce and sends the resulting value, $K_T^-(R)$, to Bob. To Bob, $K_T^-(R)$ is just a bunch of bits and he doesn't know whether the bits represent $K_T^-(R)$ or $K_A^-(R)$.
4. Bob must now get Alice's public key in order to apply K_A^+ to the value he just received. He sends a message to Alice asking her for K_A^+ (Bob might also retrieve Alice's public key from her Web site). Trudy intercepts this message as well and replies to Bob with K_T^+, that is, Trudy's public key. Bob computes $K_T^+(K_T^-(R)) = R$ and thus authenticates Trudy as Alice!

From this scenario it is clear that protocol *ap5.0* is only as secure as the distribution of public keys. Fortunately, there *are* secure ways of distributing public keys, as we'll see in Section 8.5.

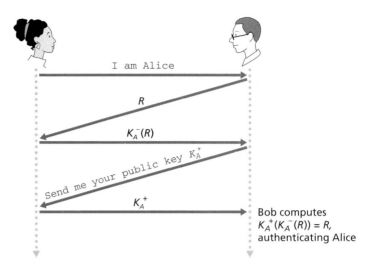

Figure 8.11 ♦ Protocol *ap5.0* working correctly

In the scenario in Figure 8.12, Bob and Alice might together eventually discover that something is amiss, as Bob will claim to have interacted with Alice, but Alice knows that she has never interacted with Bob. There is an even more insidious attack

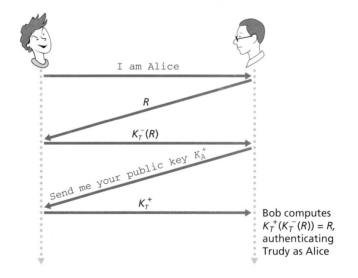

Figure 8.12 ♦ A security hole in protocol *ap5.0*

that would avoid this detection. In the scenario in Figure 8.13, Alice and Bob are talking to each other, but by exploiting the same hole in the authentication protocol, Trudy is able to *transparently* interpose herself between Alice and Bob. In particular, if Bob begins sending encrypted data to Alice using the encryption key he receives from Trudy, Trudy can recover the plaintext of the communication from Bob to Alice. At the same time, Trudy can forward Bob's data to Alice (after reencrypting data using Alice's real public key).

Bob is happy to be sending encrypted data, and Alice is happy to be receiving data encrypted using her own public key; both are unaware of Trudy's presence. Should Bob and Alice meet later and discuss their interaction, Alice will have received exactly what Bob sent, so nothing will be detected as being amiss. This is

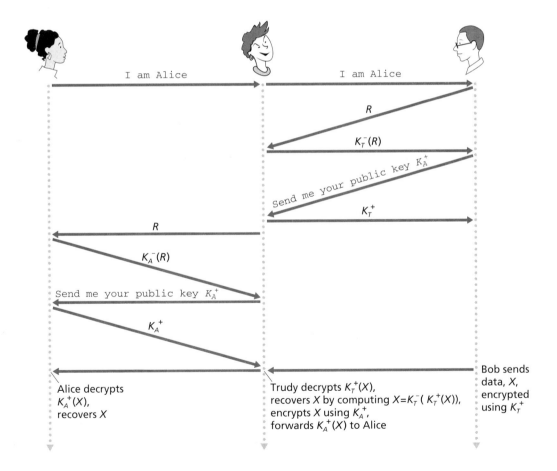

Figure 8.13 ◆ A man-in-the-middle attack

one example of the so-called **man-in-the-middle attack** (more appropriately here, a "woman-in-the-middle" attack). It is also sometimes known as a **bucket-brigade attack**, since Trudy's passing of data between Alice and Bob resembles the passing of buckets of water along a chain of people (a "bucket brigade") who are putting out a fire using a remote source of water.

8.4 Integrity

Think of the number of the times you've signed your name to a piece of paper during the last week. You sign checks, credit card receipts, legal documents, and letters. Your signature attests to the fact that you (as opposed to someone else) have acknowledged and/or agreed with the document's contents. In a digital world, one often wants to indicate the owner or creator of a document, or to signify one's agreement with a document's content. A **digital signature** is a cryptographic technique for achieving these goals in a digital world.

Just as with handwritten signatures, digital signing should be done in a way that is verifiable, nonforgeable, and nonrepudiable. That is, it must be possible to prove that a document signed by an individual was indeed signed by that individual (the signature must be verifiable) and that *only* that individual could have signed the document (the signature cannot be forged, and a signer cannot later repudiate or deny having signed the document). This is easily accomplished using techniques from public key cryptography.

8.4.1 Generating Digital Signatures

Suppose that Bob wants to digitally sign a document, m. We can think of the document as a file or a message that Bob is going to sign and send. As shown in Figure 8.14, to sign this document, Bob simply uses his private key, K_B^-, to compute $K_B^-(m)$. At first, it might seem odd that Bob is using his private key (which we saw in Section 8.2 was used to decrypt a message that had been encrypted with his public key) to sign a document. But recall that encryption and decryption are nothing more than a mathematical operation (exponentiation to the power of e or d in RSA; see Section 8.2) and recall that Bob's goal is not to scramble or obscure the contents of the document, but rather to sign the document in a manner that is verifiable, nonforgeable, and nonrepudiable. Bob has the document, m, and his digital signature of the document is $K_B^-(m)$.

Does the digital signature $K_B^-(m)$ meet our requirements of being verifiable, nonforgeable, and nonrepudiable? Suppose Alice has m and $K_B^-(m)$. She wants to prove in court (being litigious) that Bob had indeed signed the document and was the only person who could have possibly signed the document. Alice takes Bob's public key, K_B^+, and applies it to the digital signature, $K_B^-(m)$, associated with the

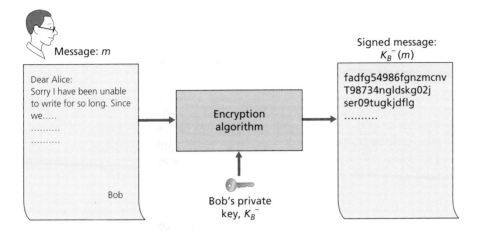

Figure 8.14 ◆ Creating a digital signature for a document

document, m. That is, she computes $K_B^+(K_B^-(m))$, and *voilà*, with a dramatic flurry, she produces m, which exactly matches the original document! Alice then argues that only Bob could have signed the document, for the following reasons.

◆ Whoever signed the message must have used the private key, K_B^-, in computing the signature $K_B^-(m)$, such that $K_B^+(K_B^-(m)) = m$.

◆ The only person who could have known the private key, K_B^-, is Bob. Recall from our discussion of RSA in Section 8.2 that knowing the public key, K_B^+, is of no help in learning the private key, K_B^-. Therefore, the only person who could know K_B^- is the person who generated the pair of keys, (K_B^+, K_B^-), in the first place, Bob. (Note that this assumes, though, that Bob has not given K_B^- to anyone, nor has anyone stolen K_B^- from Bob.)

It is also important to note that if the original document, m, is ever modified to some alternate form, m', the signature that Bob created for m will not be valid for m', since $K_B^+(K_B^-(m))$ does not equal m'.

Thus we see that public key cryptography techniques provide a simple and elegant way to digitally sign documents that is verifiable, nonforgeable, and nonrepudiable, and that protects against later modification of the document.

8.4.2 Message Digests

We have seen that public key technology can be used to create a digital signature. One concern with signing data by encryption is that encryption and decryption are computationally expensive. When you are digitally signing a really important

document, say a merger between two large multinational corporations or an agreement with a child to have her clean her room weekly, computational cost may not be
important. However, many network devices and processes (for example, routers
exchanging routing information and e-mail user agents exchanging e-mail) routinely
exchange data that may not need to be encrypted. Nonetheless, they do want to
ensure that

♦ The sender of the data is as claimed; that is, the sender has signed the data and
this signature can be checked.

♦ The transmitted data has not been changed since the sender created and signed
the data.

Given the overheads of encryption and decryption, signing data via complete
encryption/decryption can be overkill. A more efficient approach, using message
digests, can accomplish these two goals without full message encryption.

A **message digest** is in many ways like a checksum. Message digest algorithms
take a message, m, of arbitrary length and compute a fixed-length "fingerprint" of
the data known as a message digest, $H(m)$. The message digest protects the data in
the sense that if m is changed to m' (either maliciously or by accident) then $H(m)$,
computed for the original data (and transmitted with that data), will not match the
$H(m')$ computed over the changed data, m'. While the message digest provides for
data integrity, how does it help with signing the message m? The goal here is that
rather than having Bob digitally sign the entire message by computing $K_B^-(m)$, he
should be able to sign just the message digest by computing $K_B^-(H(m))$. That is, having m and $K_B^-(H(m'))$ together (note that m is not encrypted) should be just as good
as having a signed complete message, $K_B^-(m)$. This means that m and $K_B^-(H(m))$
together should be nonforgeable, verifiable, and nonrepudiable. Nonforgeability
will require that the message digest algorithm that computes the message digest
have some special properties, as we will see below.

Our definition of a message digest may seem quite similar to the definition of a
checksum (for example, the Internet checksum, see Section 3.3.2) or a more powerful error-detection code such as a cyclic redundancy check (see Section 5.2). Is it
really any different? Checksums, cyclic redundancy checks, and message digests are
all examples of **hash functions**. As shown in Figure 8.15, a hash function takes an
input, m, and computes a fixed-size string known as a hash. The Internet checksum,
CRCs, and message digests all meet this definition. If signing a message digest is
going to be just as good as signing the entire message, in particular if it is going to
satisfy the nonforgeability requirement, then a message digest algorithm must have
the following additional property:

♦ It is computationally infeasible to find any two different messages x and y such
that $H(x) = H(y)$.

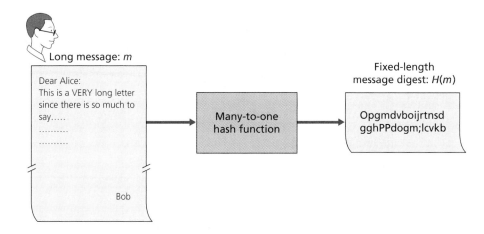

Figure 8.15 ♦ Hash functions are used to create message digests.

Informally, this property means that it is computationally infeasible for an intruder to substitute one message for another message that is protected by a message digest. That is, if $(m,H(m))$ are the message and message digest pair created by the sender, then an intruder cannot forge the contents of another message, y, that has the same message digest value as the original message. When Bob signs m by computing $K_B^-(H(m))$, we know that no other message can be substituted for m. Furthermore, Bob's digital signature of $H(m)$ uniquely identifies Bob as the verifiable, nonrepudiable signer of $H(m)$ (and as a consequence, m as well), as discussed above in Section 8.4.1.

In the context of Bob sending a message to Alice, Figure 8.16 provides a summary of the operational procedure of creating a digital signature. Bob puts his original long message through a hash function to create a message digest. He then digitally signs the message digest with his private key. The original message (in cleartext) along with the digitally signed message digest (henceforth referred to as the digital signature) is then sent to Alice. Figure 8.17 provides a summary of the operational procedure of verifying message integrity. Alice applies the sender's public key to the message to recover the message digest. Alice also applies the hash function to the cleartext message to obtain a second message digest. If the two message digests match, then Alice can be sure about the integrity and author of the message.

8.4.3 Hash Function Algorithms

Let's convince ourselves that a simple checksum, such as the Internet checksum, would make a poor message digest algorithm. Rather than performing 1's complement arithmetic (as in the Internet checksum), let us compute a checksum by

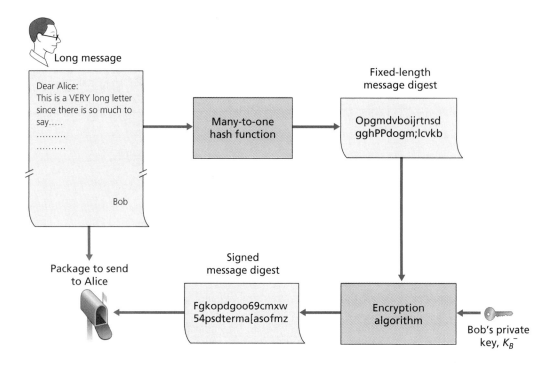

Figure 8.16 ◆ Sending a digitally signed message

treating each character as a byte and adding the bytes together using 4-byte chunks at a time. Suppose Bob owes Alice $100.99 and sends an IOU to Alice consisting of the text string "IOU100.99BOB." The ASCII representation (in hexadecimal notation) for these letters is 49, 4F, 55, 31, 30, 30, 2E, 39, 39, 42, 4F, 42.

Figure 8.18 (top) shows that the 4-byte checksum for this message is B2 C1 D2 AC. A slightly different message (and a much more costly one for Bob) is shown in the bottom half of Figure 8.18. The messages "IOU100.99BOB" and "IOU900.19BOB" have the *same* checksum. Thus, this simple checksum algorithm violates the two requirements above. Given the original data, it is simple to find another set of data with the same checksum. Clearly, for security purposes, we are going to need a more powerful hash function than a checksum.

The MD5 message digest algorithm of Ron Rivest [RFC 1321] is in wide use today. It computes a 128-bit message digest in a four-step process consisting of a padding step (adding a one followed by enough zeros so that the length of the message satisfies certain conditions), an append step (appending a 64-bit representation of the message length before padding), an initialization of an accumulator, and a final looping step in which the message's 16-word blocks are processed (mangled)

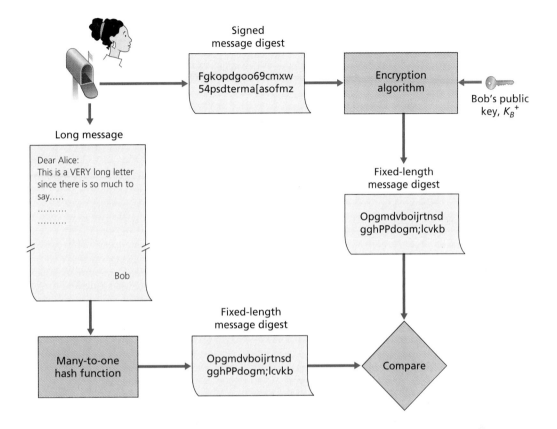

Figure 8.17 ◆ Verifying the integrity of a signed message

in four rounds. It is not known whether MD5 actually satisfies the requirements listed above. Rivest claims, "It is conjectured that the difficulty of coming up with two messages having the same message digest is on the order of 2^{64} operations, and that the difficulty of coming up with any message having a given message digest is on the order of 2^{128} operations." No one has argued with this claim. For a description of MD5 (including a C source code implementation) see [RFC 1321].

The second major message digest algorithm in use today is the Secure Hash Algorithm (SHA-1) [FIPS 1995]. This algorithm is based on principles similar to those used in the design of MD4 [RFC 1320], the predecessor to MD5. SHA-1, a US federal standard, is required for use whenever a secure message digest algorithm is needed for federal applications. It produces a 160-bit message digest. The longer output length makes SHA-1 more secure.

	ASCII				
Message	Representation				
I O U 1	49	4F	55	31	
0 0 . 9	30	30	2E	39	
9 B O B	39	42	4F	42	
	B2	C1	D2	AC	Checksum

	ASCII				
Message	Representation				
I O U 9	49	4F	55	39	
0 0 . 1	30	30	2E	31	
9 B O B	39	42	4F	42	
	B2	C1	D2	AC	Checksum

Figure 8.18 ◆ Initial message and fraudulent message have the same checksum!

8.5 Key Distribution and Certification

In Section 8.2 we saw that a drawback of symmetric key cryptography was the need for the two communicating parties to have agreed upon their secret key ahead of time. With public key cryptography, this *a priori* agreement on a secret value is not needed. However, as we discussed in Section 8.2, public key cryptography has its own difficulties, in particular the problem of obtaining someone's true public key. Both of these problems—determining a shared key for symmetric key cryptography and securely obtaining the public key for public key cryptography—can be solved using a **trusted intermediary**. For symmetric key cryptography, the trusted intermediary is called a **key distribution center (KDC)**, which is a single, trusted network entity with whom one has established a shared secret key. We will see that one can use the KDC to obtain the shared keys needed to communicate securely with *all* other network entities, avoiding some of the pitfalls we uncovered in Section 8.3. For public key cryptography, the trusted intermediary is called a **certification authority (CA)**. A CA certifies that a public key belongs to a particular entity (a person or a network entity). For a certified public key, if you can safely trust the CA that certified the key, then you can be sure about to whom the public key belongs. Once a public key is certified, then it can be distributed from just about anywhere, including a public key server, a personal Web page, or a diskette.

KERBEROS

Kerberos [RFC 1510; Neuman 1994] is an authentication service developed at MIT that uses symmetric key encryption techniques and a key distribution center. Although it is conceptually the same as the generic key distribution center (KDC) we describe in Section 8.5.1, its vocabulary is slightly different. Kerberos also contains several nice variations and extensions of the basic KDC mechanisms. Kerberos was designed to authenticate users accessing network servers and was initially targeted for use within a single administrative domain such as a campus or company. Thus, Kerberos is framed in the language of users who want to access network services (servers) using application-level network programs such as Telnet (for remote login) and NFS (for access to remote files), rather than human-to-human conversants who want to authenticate themselves to each other, as in our earlier examples. Nonetheless, the key (pun intended) underlying techniques remain the same.

The Kerberos authentication server (AS) plays the role of the KDC. The AS is the repository of not only the secret keys of all users (so that each user can communicate securely with the AS) but also information about which users have access privileges to which services on which network servers. When Alice wants to access a service on Bob (who we now think of as a server), the protocol closely follows our example in Figure 8.19.

1. Alice contacts the Kerberos AS, indicating that she wants to use Bob. All communication between Alice and the AS is encrypted using a secret key that is shared between Alice and the AS. In Kerberos, Alice first provides her name and password to her local host. Alice's local host and the AS then determine the one-time secret session key for encrypting communication between Alice and the AS.

2. The AS authenticates Alice, checks that she has access privileges to Bob, and generates a one-time symmetric session key, $R1$, for communication between Alice and Bob. The authentication server (in Kerberos parlance, now referred to as the Ticket Granting Server) sends Alice the value of $R1$, and also a ticket to Bob's services. The ticket contains Alice's name, the Alice–Bob session key, $R1$, and an expiration time, all encrypted using Bob's secret key (known by only Bob and the AS), as in Figure 8.19. Alice's ticket is valid only until its expiration time, and it will be rejected by Bob if presented after that time. For Kerberos V4, the maximum lifetime of a ticket is about 21 hours. In Kerberos V5, the lifetime must expire before the end of year 9999, a definite Y10K problem!

3. Alice then sends her ticket to Bob. She also sends along an $R1$-encrypted timestamp that is used as a nonce. Bob decrypts the ticket using his secret key, obtains the session key, and decrypts the timestamp using the just-learned session key. Bob sends back the nonce to Alice, encrypted using $R1$, thus showing that Bob knows $R1$ and is live.

The most recent version of Kerberos (V5) provides support for multiple authentication servers, delegation of access rights, and renewable tickets. [Kaufman 1995] and [RFC 1510] provide ample details.

8.5.1 The Key Distribution Center

Suppose once again that Bob and Alice want to communicate using symmetric key cryptography. Suppose they have never met and thus have not established a shared secret key in advance. How can they now agree on a secret key, given that they can communicate with each other only over the network? A solution often adopted in practice is to use a trusted KDC.

The KDC is a server that shares a unique secret symmetric key with each registered user. This key might be manually installed at the server when a user first registers. The KDC knows the secret key of each user, and each user can communicate securely with the KDC using this key. Let's see how knowledge of this one key allows a user to obtain a key securely for communicating with any other registered user. Suppose that Alice and Bob are users of the KDC; they know only their individual keys, K_{A-KDC} and K_{B-KDC}, respectively, for communicating securely with the KDC. Alice takes the first step, and they proceed as illustrated in Figure 8.19.

1. Using K_{A-KDC} to encrypt her communication with the KDC, Alice sends a message to the KDC saying she (A) wants to communicate with Bob (B). We denote this message, $K_{A-KDC}(A, B)$.
2. The KDC, knowing K_{A-KDC}, decrypts $K_{A-KDC}(A, B)$. The KDC then generates a random number, $R1$. This is the shared key value that Alice and Bob will use to perform symmetric encryption when they communicate with each other. This key is referred to as a **one-time session key**, because Alice and Bob will use this key for only this one session. The KDC now needs to inform Alice and

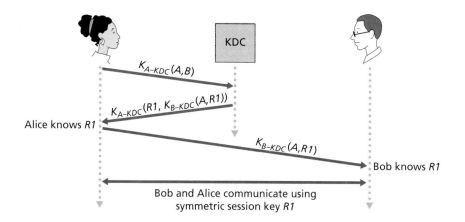

Figure 8.19 ◆ Setting up a one-time session key using a key distribution center

Bob of the value of $R1$. The KDC thus sends back a message to Alice, encrypted using K_{A-KDC}, containing the following.

♦ $R1$, the one-time session key that Alice and Bob will use to communicate.

♦ A pair of values, A and $R1$, encrypted by the KDC using Bob's key, K_{B-KDC}. We denote this $K_{B-KDC}(A, R1)$. It is important to note that KDC is sending Alice not only the value of $R1$ for her own use, but also an encrypted version of $R1$ and Alice's name, encrypted using Bob's key. Alice can't decrypt this pair of values in the message (she doesn't know Bob's encryption key), but then she doesn't really need to. We'll see shortly that Alice will simply forward this encrypted pair of values to Bob, who will be able to decrypt them.

The KDC puts these items into a message, encrypts them using Alice's shared key, and sends them to Alice. The message from the KDC to Alice is thus K_{A-KDC} $(R1, K_{B-KDC}(A, R1))$.

3. Alice receives the message from the KDC, decrypts it, and extracts $R1$ from the message. Alice now knows the one-time session key, $R1$. Alice also extracts $K_{B-KDC}(A, R1)$ and forwards this to Bob.

4. Bob decrypts the received message, $K_{B-KDC}(A, R1)$ using K_{B-KDC} and extracts A and $R1$. Bob now knows the one-time session key, $R1$, and the person with whom he is sharing this key, A. Of course, he takes care to authenticate Alice using $R1$ before proceeding any further.

8.5.2 Public Key Certification

One of the principal features of public key cryptography is that it is possible for two entities to exchange secret messages without having to exchange secret keys. For example, when Alice wants to send a secret message to Bob, she simply encrypts the message with Bob's public key and sends the encrypted message to Bob; she doesn't need to know Bob's private key, nor does Bob need to know her private key. Thus, public key cryptography obviates the need for a KDC infrastructure.

Of course, with public key cryptography, the communicating entities still have to exchange public keys. A user can make its public key publicly available in many ways, for example, by posting the key on the user's personal Web page, by placing the key in a public key server, or by sending the key to a correspondent by e-mail. A Web commerce site can place its public key on its server in a manner such that browsers automatically download the public key when connecting to the site. Routers can place their public keys on public key servers, thereby allowing other network entities to retrieve them.

There is, however, a subtle, yet critical, problem with public key cryptography. To gain insight into this problem, let's consider an Internet commerce example. Suppose that Alice is in the pizza delivery business and she accepts orders over the Internet. Bob, a pizza lover, sends Alice a plaintext message that includes his home address and the type of pizza he wants. In this message, Bob also includes a digital signature (that is, a signed message digest for the original plaintext message). As discussed in Section 8.4, Alice can obtain Bob's public key (from his personal Web page, a public key server, or an e-mail message) and verify the digital signature. In this manner she makes sure that Bob, rather than some adolescent prankster, placed the order.

This all sounds fine until clever Trudy comes along. As shown in Figure 8.20, Trudy decides to play a prank. Trudy sends a message to Alice in which she says she is Bob, gives Bob's home address, and orders a pizza. She also attaches a digital signature, but she attaches the signature by signing the message digest with her (that is, Trudy's) private key. Trudy also masquerades as Bob by sending Alice Trudy's public key but saying that it belongs to Bob. In this example, Alice will apply Trudy's public key (thinking that it is Bob's) to the digital signature and conclude that the plaintext message was indeed created by Bob. Bob will be very surprised when the delivery person brings a pizza with everything on it to his home!

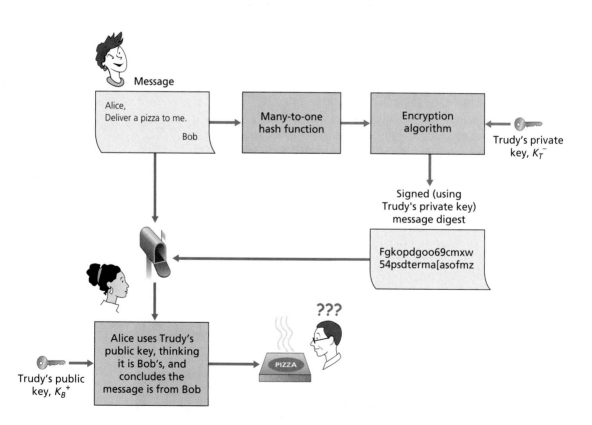

Figure 8.20 ◆ Trudy masquerades as Bob using public key cryptography.

We see from this example that in order for public key cryptography to be useful, entities (users, browsers, routers, and so on) need to know *for sure* that they have the public key of the entity with whom they are communicating. For example, when Alice is communicating with Bob using public key cryptography, she needs to know for sure that the public key that is supposed to be Bob's is indeed Bob's. We had similar concerns in our authentication protocols in Figures 8.12 and 8.13.

Binding a public key to a particular entity is typically done by a CA, whose job is to validate identities and issue certificates. A CA has the following roles.

1. A CA verifies that an entity (a person, a router, and so on) is who it says it is. There are no mandated procedures for how certification is done. When dealing with a CA, one must trust the CA to have performed a suitably rigorous identity verification. For example, if Trudy were able to walk into the Fly-by-Night CA and simply announce "I am Alice" and receive certificates associated with the identity of Alice, then one shouldn't put much faith in public keys certified by the Fly-by-Night certificate authority. On the other hand, one might (or might not!) be more willing to trust a CA that is part of a federal—or state—program (for example, Utah licenses CAs in that state [Utah 2004]). You can trust the identity associated with a public key only to the extent that you can trust a CA and its identity verification techniques. What a tangled web of trust we spin!

2. Once the CA verifies the identity of the entity, the CA creates a **certificate** that binds the public key of the entity to the identity. The certificate contains the public key and globally unique identifying information about the owner of the public key (for example, a human name or an IP address). The certificate is digitally signed by the CA. These steps are shown in Figure 8.21.

Let us now see how certificates can be used to combat pizza-ordering pranksters, like Trudy, and other undesirables. When Alice receives Bob's order, she gets Bob's certificate, which may be on his Web page, in an e-mail message, or in a certificate server. Alice uses the CA's public key to check the validity of Bob's CA-signed certificate. If we assume that the public key of the CA itself is known to all (for example, it could be published in a trusted, public, and well-known place, such as the *New York Times,* so that it is known to all and cannot be spoofed), then Alice can be sure that she is indeed dealing with Bob. Figure 8.21 illustrates the steps involved in CA-mediated public key encryption. You can view the CA certificates stored in your Netscape browser by choosing Communicator, Tools, Security Info, Certificates; in Internet Explorer, choose Tools, Internet Options, Content, Certificates.

Both the International Telecommunication Union (ITU) and the IETF have developed standards for certificate authorities. ITU X.509 [ITU 1993] specifies an authentication service as well as a specific syntax for certificates. [RFC 1422] describes CA-based key management for use with secure Internet e-mail. It is compatible with X.509 but goes beyond X.509 by establishing procedures and

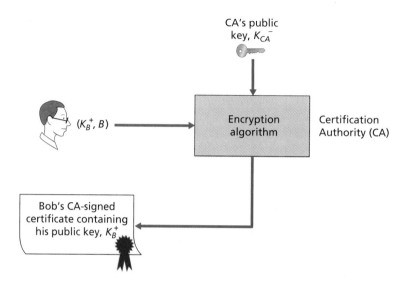

Figure 8.21 ♦ Bob obtains a certificate from the CA.

conventions for a key management architecture. Table 8.3 describes some of the important fields in a certificate.

With the recent boom in e-commerce and the consequent widespread need for secure transactions, there has been increased interest in certificate authorities.

Field Name	Description
Version	Version number of X.509 specification
Serial Number	CA-issued unique identifier for a certificate
Signature	Specifies the algorithm used by CA to sign this certificate
Issuer Name	Identity of CA issuing this certificate, in distinguished name (DN) [RFC 2253] format
Validity period	Start and end of period of validity for certificate
Subject name	Identity of entity whose public key is associated with this certificate, in DN format
Subject public key	The subject's public key as well as an indication of the public key algorithm (and algorithm parameters) to be used with this key

Table 8.3 ♦ Selected fields in a X.509 and RFC 1422 public key

Among the companies providing CA services are Digital Signature Trust Company [Digital Signature 2004] and Verisign [Verisign 2004].

A certificate issued by Thawte Consulting to Netfarmers Enterprises, Inc., as viewed through a Netscape browser, is shown in Figure 8.22.

8.6 Access Control: Firewalls

We've seen throughout this chapter that the Internet is not a very safe place—bad guys are out there, wreaking all sorts of havoc. From a network administrator's point of view, the world divides quite neatly into two camps—the good guys (who belong to the organization administering the network, and who should be able to access resources inside the administrator's network in a relatively unconstrained manner) and the bad guys (everyone else, whose access to network resources must be carefully scrutinized). In many organizations, ranging from medieval castles to modern corporate office buildings, there is a single point of entry/exit where both good guys and bad guys entering and leaving the organization are security-checked. In a castle, this was done at a gate at one end of the drawbridge; in a corporate building, this is done at the security/reception desk. In a computer network, when traffic entering/leaving a network is security-checked, logged, dropped, and/or forwarded, it is done at a device known as a firewall.

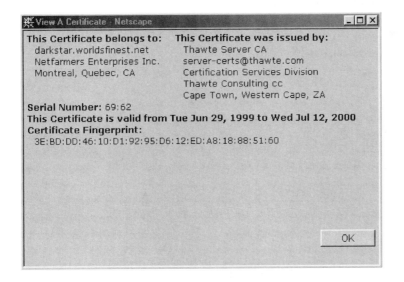

Figure 8.22 ♦ A certificate issued by Thawte Consulting to Netfarmers Enterprises, Inc.

A **firewall** is a combination of hardware and software that isolates an organization's internal network from the Internet at large, allowing some packets to pass and blocking others. A firewall allows a network administrator to control access between the outside world and resources within the administered network by managing the traffic flow to and from these resources. Figure 8.23 shows a firewall, sitting squarely at the boundary between the administered network and the rest of the Internet. While large organizations may use multiple levels of firewalls or distributed firewalls [Ioannidis 2000], locating a firewall at a single access point to the network, as shown in Figure 8.23, makes it easier to manage and enforce a security-access policy.

There are two types of firewalls: **packet-filtering firewalls** (which operate at the network layer) and **application-level gateways** (which operate at the application layer). We'll cover each of these in turn in the following two subsections.

8.6.1 Packet Filtering

As shown in Figure 8.23, an organization typically has a gateway router connecting its internal network to its ISP (and hence to the larger public Internet). All traffic leaving and entering the internal network passes through this router, and it is at this router where **packet filtering** occurs. Packet filters operate by first parsing datagram headers and then applying filtering rules from an administrator-specified rule set to determine whether to drop the datagram or let the datagram pass. Filtering decisions are typically based on

♦ IP source or destination address

♦ TCP or UDP source and destination port

♦ ICMP message type

♦ Connection-initialization datagrams using the TCP SYN or ACK bits

As a simple example, a filter can be set to block all UDP segments and all Telnet connections. Such a configuration prevents outsiders from logging onto internal hosts using Telnet, and insiders from logging onto external hosts using Telnet connections, by blocking all TCP segments (each encapsulated in a datagram) whose source or destination port number is 23 (corresponding to Telnet). Filtering UDP traffic is a popular policy for corporations—much to the chagrin of leading audio- and video-streaming vendors, whose products stream over UDP in the default mode. Filtering Telnet connections is also popular, because it prevents outside intruders from logging onto internal machines. [CERT Filtering 2002] provides a list of recommended port/protocol packet filterings to avoid a number of well-known security holes in existing network applications.

A filtering policy can also be based on the combination of addresses and port numbers. For example, the filtering router can forward all Telnet datagrams (those with a port number of 23) except those going to and coming from a list of specific

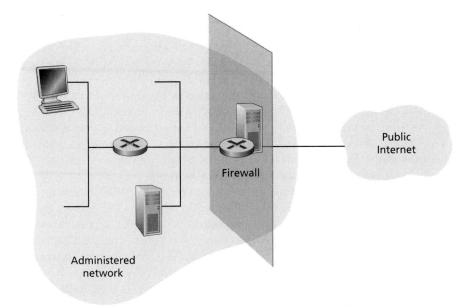

Figure 8.23 ◆ Firewall placement between the administered network and the outside world

IP addresses. This policy permits Telnet connections to and from hosts on the allowed list. Unfortunately, basing the policy on external addresses provides no protection against datagrams that have a source address belonging to a host on the allowed list but that in fact have been sent by another host (most likely belonging to a bad guy who has forged the datagrams' source address). We'll examine such IP spoofing in the following section.

Filtering can also be based on whether or not the TCP ACK bit is set. This trick is quite useful if an organization wants to let its internal clients connect to external servers but to prevent external clients from connecting to internal servers. Recall from Section 3.5 that the first segment in every TCP connection has the ACK bit set to 0, whereas all the other segments in the connection have the ACK bit set to 1. Thus, if an organization wants to prevent external clients from initiating connections to internal servers, it simply filters all incoming segments with the ACK bit set to 0. This policy kills all TCP connections originating from the outside, but permits connections originating internally.

While these examples may make it appear rather easy to specify filtering rules that implement a given security policy, there are actually many subtleties and potential pitfalls involved. To illustrate a few of the issues, let's consider a simple example, adapted from [Chapman 1992]. Packet filtering operates by sequentially checking filtering rules against the datagram being inspected; the first rule matching the datagram determines the action taken. Our scenario is as follows. Suppose Alice administers a company network 222.22.0.0/16 and, in general, wants to disallow access to her network from the public Internet (rule R3 in Table 8.4). However, Alice is collaborating with Bob and his colleagues, who are at a university, and so Alice wants to let users from Bob's university (whose network address is 111.11/16) access a specific subnet, 222.22.22/24 within her company's network (rule R1). A complicating factor is that Trudy, a well-known hacker, is in Bob's university and that Trudy's subnet, 111.11.11/24, is an insecure hacker haven. So Alice doesn't want any traffic from 111.11.11/24 entering anywhere into her network (rule R2). Alice's packet-filtering rules are summarized in Table 8.4.

Table 8.5 shows the handling of selected datagrams by Alice's corporate firewall when the rules are applied in one of two different orders. When rules are applied in the order of most specific source address first: R2, R1, R3 (the next to last column in Table 8.5), we obtain the desired results: datagrams such as P1 that have a source in the hacker subnet and a destination that is within the corporate network but outside of the special subnet are not allowed past the firewall (by rule R2). Similarly, datagrams such as P2 from the hacker subnet that are destined for the special subnet are not allowed past the firewall (by rule R2). Under rule order R2, R1, R3, datagrams from the general university network are allowed into the special subnet (datagram P3) but not into other parts of the corporate network (datagram P4).

Suppose, however, that rules are applied in the order R1, R2, R3 (the last column in Table 8.5). In this case, datagram P2 is mistakenly allowed access to the special subnet under rule R1, since P2's source and destination addresses match the source and destination specification for rule R1, and rule R1 is being applied first. The lesson from this simple three-rule example is clear—*the ordering of evaluation of firewall rules is important*. Clearly, careful thought is required—imagine the difficulties involved in specifying firewalls with thousands of rules! One might be tempted to think that applying more specific rules first might always avoid unanticipated or unwanted behavior arising from ordering issues. However, we'll see in the homework problems at the end of the chapter that this is not necessarily the case.

Rule	Source Address	Destination Address	Action	Comments
R1	111.11/16	222.22.22/24	permit	Let datagrams from Bob's university network into a restricted subnet.
R2	111.11.11/24	222.22/16	deny	Don't let traffic from Trudy's subnet into anywhere within Alice's network.
R3	0.0.0.0/0	0.0.0.0/0	deny	Don't let traffic into Alice's network.

Table 8.4 ◆ Packet-filtering rules

Datagram Number	Source IP Address	Destination IP Address	Desired Action	Action Under R2, R1, R3	Action Under R1, R2, R3
P1	111.11.11.1 (hacker subnet)	222.22.6.6 (corp.net)	deny	deny (R2)	deny (R2)
P2	111.11.11.1 (hacker subnet)	222.22.22.2 (special subnet)	deny	deny (R2)	permit (R1)
P3	111.11.6.6 (univ. net, not the hacker subnet)	222.22.22.2 (special subnet)	permit	permit (R1)	permit (R1)
P4	111.11.6.6 (univ. net, not the hacker subnet)	222.22.6.6 (corp. net)	deny	deny (R3)	deny (R3)

Table 8.5 ◆ Results of packet filtering, according to rule order

8.6.2 Application Gateway

In the examples above, we have seen that packet-level filtering allows an organization to perform coarse-grain filtering on IP and TCP/UDP headers, including IP addresses, port numbers, and acknowledgment bits. For example, we have seen that filtering based on a combination of IP addresses and port numbers can allow internal clients to Telnet outside while preventing external clients from Telneting inside. But what if an organization wants to provide the Telnet service to a restricted set of internal users (as opposed to IP addresses)? And what if the organization wants such privileged users to authenticate themselves first before being allowed to create Telnet sessions to the outside world? Such tasks are beyond the capabilities of a filter. Indeed, information about the identity of the internal users is not included in the IP/TCP/UDP headers, but is instead in the application-layer data.

In order to have finer-level security, firewalls must combine packet filters with application gateways. Application gateways look beyond the IP/TCP/UDP headers and make policy decisions based on application data. An **application gateway** is an application-specific server through which all application data (inbound and outbound) must pass. Multiple application gateways can run on the same host, but each gateway is a separate server with its own processes.

To get some insight into application gateways, let's design a firewall that allows only a restricted set of internal users to Telnet outside and prevents all external clients from Telneting inside. Such a policy can be accomplished by implementing a combination of a packet filter (in a router) and a Telnet application gateway, as shown in Figure 8.24. The router's filter is configured to block all Telnet connections except those that originate from the IP address of the application gateway.

Such a filter configuration forces all outbound Telnet connections to pass through the application gateway. Consider now an internal user who wants to Telnet to the outside world. The user must first set up a Telnet session with the application gateway. An application running in the gateway, which listens for incoming Telnet sessions, prompts the user for a user ID and password. When the user supplies this information, the application gateway checks to see if the user has permission to Telnet to the outside world. If not, the Telnet connection from the internal user to the gateway is terminated by the gateway. If the user has permission, then the gateway (1) prompts the user for the hostname of the external host to which the user wants to connect, (2) sets up a Telnet session between the gateway and the external host, and (3) relays to the external host all data arriving from the user, and relays to the user all data arriving from the external host. Thus the Telnet application gateway not only performs user authorization but also acts as a Telnet server and a Telnet client, relaying information between the user and the remote Telnet server. Note that the filter will permit Step 2 because the gateway initiates the Telnet connection to the outside world.

Internal networks often have multiple application gateways, for example, gateways for Telnet, HTTP, FTP, and e-mail. In fact, an organization's mail server (see Section 2.4) and Web cache are application gateways.

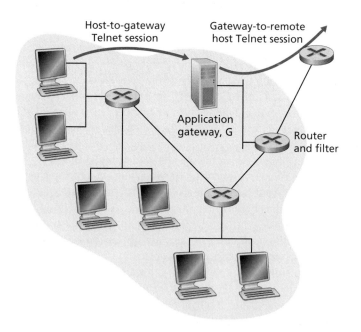

Figure 8.24 ◆ Firewall consisting of an application gateway and a filter

Application gateways do not come without their disadvantages. First, a different application gateway is needed for each application. Second, there is a performance penalty to be paid, since all data will be relayed via the gateway. This becomes a concern particularly when multiple users or applications are using the same gateway machine. Finally, a certain amount of extra configuration effort must be taken; either

♦ The client software must know how to contact the gateway instead of the external server when the user makes a request, and must know how to tell the application gateway what external server to connect to, or

♦ The user must explicitly connect to the external server through the application gateway.

We conclude this section by mentioning that firewalls are by no means a panacea for all security problems. They introduce a trade-off between the degree of communication with the outside world and the level of security. Because filters can't stop spoofing of IP addresses and port numbers, filters often use an all-or-nothing policy (for example, banning all UDP traffic). Gateways can also have software bugs, allowing attackers to penetrate them. Finally, firewalls are even less effective if internally generated communication can reach the outside world without passing through the firewall. Wireless communication and dial-up modems are two such examples.

8.7 Attacks and Countermeasures

Having now examined encryption/decryption, authentication, message integrity, key distribution, and firewalls, let's see how these techniques can be used to combat various network-related attacks that have been launched against a network. Some of the most sensational security attacks, such as the CodeRed [CERT 2001-19], the Melissa virus [CERT 1999-04], and the Slammer worm [CERT 2003-04, Moore 2003] use the Internet to spread themselves but attack operating systems (via buffer overflow in a Microsoft IIS server in the case of CodeRed) or application software (Microsoft Word in the case of the Melissa virus) rather than attacking the network itself. This being a networking book, our focus will be on attacks that exploit, cripple, or involve the network in some special way.

8.7.1 Mapping

In the real world (as opposed to the cyberworld) an attack is often preceded by information gathering. Movie gangsters "case the joint;" soldiers scout the area. The purpose is clear—the more one knows about a target before attacking, the less likely one is to be caught and the higher the probability of success. This is also true in the cyber-world. Before attacking a network, attackers would like to know the IP addresses of machines on the network, the operating systems they use, and the services that they offer. With this information, attacks can be more focused and are less likely to cause alarm. The process of gathering this information is known as **mapping**.

A program such as `ping` can be used to determine the IP addresses of machines on the network by simply observing which addresses respond to a `ping` message. **Port scanning** refers to the technique of sequentially contacting (either via a TCP connection request, or via a simple UDP datagram) port numbers on a machine and seeing what happens in response. These responses, in turn, can be used to determine the services offered (for example, HTTP or FTP) by the machine. Nmap [Nmap 2004] is a widely used, open-source utility for network exploration and security auditing that performs port scanning. Many firewalls, such as those sold by Check-point [Checkpoint 2004], detect mapping and port-scanning, as well as other such malicious activity, and report it to the network manager.

8.7.2 Packet Sniffing

A **packet sniffer** is a program running in a network-attached device that passively receives *all* data link–layer frames passing by the device's network adapter. In a broadcast environment such as an Ethernet LAN, this means that the packet sniffer receives all frames being transmitted from or to all hosts on the LAN. Any host with an Ethernet card can easily serve as a packet sniffer, as the Ethernet adapter needs only be set to **promiscuous mode** to receive all passing Ethernet frames. These frames, in turn, can be passed on to application programs that extract application-level data. For example, in the Telnet scenario shown in Figure 8.25, the login pass-word prompt sent from A to B, as well as the password entered at B, are sniffed at host C. Having obtained passwords to user accounts, attackers can later impersonate these accounts to launch denial-of-service attacks, as discussed below. Thus packet sniffing is a double-edged sword—it can be invaluable to a network administrator for network monitoring and management (see Chapter 9) but can also be used by the unethical hacker.

Packet-sniffing software is freely available at various Web sites and as commercial products. Professors teaching a networking course have been known to assign lab exercises that involve writing a packet-sniffing and application-level data reconstruction program. Indeed, the Ethereal [Ethereal 2004] labs associated with this text (see the introductory Ethereal lab at the end of Chapter 1) use exactly such a packet sniffer!

The key to detecting packet sniffing is to detect network interfaces that are running in promiscuous mode. Within an enterprise, network managers may install software in all the enterprise's computers that will alert the managers when an interface is configured in promiscuous mode. Various tricks can also be performed remotely to detect promiscuous interfaces. For example, a host that replies to an ICMP echo datagram (that is, that elicits an ICMP echo reply; see Figure 4.21) that is correctly

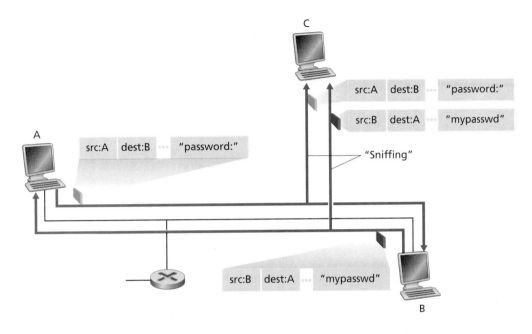

Figure 8.25 ◆ Packet sniffing

addressed in the IP datagram but contains an incorrect MAC (frame-level) address is likely to have its interface configured in promiscuous mode. The key to living with packet sniffing is to encrypt all data (particularly passwords) that cross a network link.

8.7.3 Spoofing

Any Internet-connected device necessarily sends IP datagrams into the network. Recall from Chapter 4 that these datagrams carry the sender's IP address as well as upper-layer data. A user with complete control over that device's software (in particular its operating system) can easily modify the device's protocols to place an arbitrary IP address into a datagram's Source Address field. This is known as **IP spoofing**. A user can thus craft an IP packet containing any payload (upper-layer) data it desires and make it appear as if that data were sent from an arbitrary IP host. IP spoofing is often used in denial-of-service attacks in order to hide the originator(s) of the attack, as discussed below. With a spoofed source IP address on a datagram, it is difficult to find the host that actually sent the datagram.

From a technical standpoint, spoofing can be easily prevented. Routers that perform **ingress filtering** check the IP address of incoming datagrams and determine whether the source address is in the range of network addresses that are known to be reachable via that interface. This check can be easily performed at the edge of a network, for example, at a corporate gateway or firewall, where all hosts within the corporation are known to be within a given address range. Ingress filtering is considered a current best practice [RFC 2827] in the Internet. Although simply from a technical standpoint, ingress filtering cannot be mandated and so is difficult to put in place from a social standpoint. As a result, ingress filtering is not universally deployed.

8.7.4 Denial-of-Service and Distributed Denial-of-Service Attacks

A broad class of security threats can be classified as **denial-of-service (DoS) attacks**. As the name suggests, a DoS attack renders a network, host, or other piece of network infrastructure unusable by legitimate users. Typically, a DoS attack works by creating so much work for the infrastructure under attack that legitimate work cannot be performed. In a **SYN flooding attack** [CERT SYN 1996], the attacker deluges a server with TCP SYN packets, each having a spoofed IP source address. The server, not being able to differentiate between a legitimate SYN and a spoofed SYN, completes the second step of the TCP handshake (see Section 3.5.6) for a spoofed SYN, allocating data structures and state. The third step of the three-way handshake is never completed by the attacker, leaving an ever-increasing number of partially open connections. The load of SYN packets to be processed and depletion of free memory eventually brings the server to its knees. A related form of attack sends IP fragments to a host but never sends enough fragments to complete a datagram. The attacked host continues to accumulate fragments, waiting in vain for fragments that would complete a datagram, consuming an ever-increasing amount of storage over time. A **smurf attack** [CERT Smurf 1998] operates by having a large number of innocent hosts respond to ICMP echo-request packets (see Section 4.4.3) that contain a spoofed source IP address. This results in a large number of ICMP echo-reply packets being sent to the host whose IP address is being spoofed.

In a **distributed denial-of-service (DDoS) attack**, the attacker first gains access to user accounts on numerous hosts across the Internet (for example, by sniffing passwords or by otherwise breaking into a user's account). As shown in Figure 8.26, the attacker then installs and runs a slave program at each compromised site that quietly waits for commands from a master program. Once a large number of such slave programs are running, the master program contacts and instructs each of them to launch a DoS attack directed at the same target host. The resulting coordinated attack is particularly devastating, since it is coming from so many directions at once.

DoS attacks made the headlines in February 2000, when eBay, Yahoo, CNN, and other major Web sites were attacked [Cnet 2000]. It is difficult to protect oneself against DoS and (even more so) DDoS attacks. Packet filtering is difficult because it is difficult to distinguish good datagrams from bad ones. For example, how can a packet-filtering firewall know whether an arriving SYN is for a legitimate connection (for example, a customer who wants to make a purchase at the company's Web site) or a malicious SYN, which will tie up server resources by not subsequently completing the three-way handshake. IP spoofing makes it difficult to locate the true source(s) of the attack(s). A number of recent research efforts [Savage 2000; Snoeren 2001; Adler 2002] have looked at techniques for marking IP headers as they pass through a router in order to trace back a flow of DoS datagrams to their source. Once a compomised source host has been identified, it can be quarantined, although this is usually a slow process, requiring human intervention. Solving a DDoS attack is even more difficult and time-consuming.

8.7.5 Hijacking

Suppose that Alice and Bob have an ongoing connection, and that Trudy is in a position to monitor packets flowing between Bob and Alice. Trudy can take over, or **hijack**, the ongoing connection between Alice and Bob. In particular, Trudy can fool Bob into believing that he continues to communicate with Alice even though he is communicating with Trudy. Trudy first takes Alice out of the picture by launching a DoS attack on her. Having been eavesdropping on Alice and Bob's communication, Trudy knows the full state (for example, sequence number, ACK number, receiver advertsied window) of Alice's TCP connection to Bob. Trudy can thus spoof IP datagrams to Bob (using Alice's address as the source address) containing valid TCP segments and an arbitrary user payload. Imagine the havoc that Trudy can wreak on Bob and Alice's relationship!

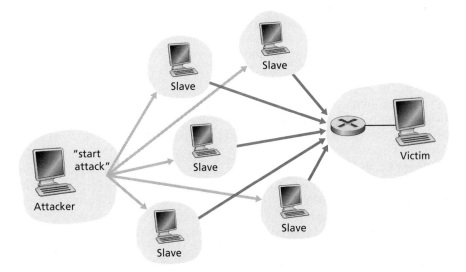

Figure 8.26 ♦ A DDoS attack

Various network attacks and security threats are discussed in the collection of essays [Denning 1997] and the very readable book by Rubin [Rubin 2001]. A summary of reported attacks is maintained at the CERT Coordination Center [CERT 2004]. See also [Cisco Security 2004; Voydock 1983; Bhimani 1996].

8.8 Security in Many Layers: Case Studies

In previous sections we examined fundamental issues in network security, including symmetric key and public key cryptography, authentication, key distribution, message integrity, and digital signatures. We are now going to examine how these tools are being used to provide security in the Internet. Interestingly, it is possible to provide security services in any of the top four layers of the Internet protocol stack]. When security is provided for a specific application-layer protocol, the application using the protocol will enjoy one or more security services, such as confidentiality, authentication, or integrity. When security is provided for a transport-layer protocol, all applications that use that protocol enjoy the security services of the transport protocol. When security is provided at the network layer on a host-to-host basis, all transport-layer segments (and hence all application-layer data) enjoy the security services of the network layer. When security is provided on a link basis, then the data in all frames traveling over the link receive the security services of the link.

In this section we examine how security tools are being used in the application, transport, network, and data link layers. Being consistent with the general structure of this book, we begin at the top of the protocol stack and discuss security at the application layer. Our approach is to use a specific application, e-mail, as a case study for application-layer security. We then move down the protocol stack. We'll examine the SSL protocol (which provides security at the transport layer), IPsec (which provides security at the network layer), and the security of the IEEE 802.11 wireless LAN protocol.

You might be wondering why security functionality is being provided at more than one layer in the Internet. Wouldn't it suffice simply to provide the security functionality at the network layer and be done with it? There are two answers to this question. First, although security at the network layer can offer "blanket coverage" by encrypting all the data in the datagrams (that is, all the transport-layer segments) and by authenticating all the source IP addresses, it can't provide user-level security. For example, a commerce site cannot rely on IP-layer security to authenticate a customer who is purchasing goods at the commerce site. Thus, there is a need for security functionality at higher layers as well as blanket coverage at lower layers. Second, it is generally easier to deploy new Internet services, including security services, at the higher layers of the protocol stack. While waiting for security to be broadly deployed at the network layer, which is probably still many years in the future, many application developers "just do it" and introduce security functionality into their favorite applications. A classic example is Pretty Good Privacy (PGP), which provides secure e-mail (discussed later in this section). Requiring only client and server application code, PGP was one of the first security technologies to be broadly used in the Internet.

8.8.1 Secure E-mail

In this section we use the techniques introduced in the previous section to create a high-level design of a secure e-mail system. We create this high-level design in an incremental manner, at each step introducing new security services. When designing a secure e-mail system, let us keep in mind the racy example introduced in Section 8.1—the love affair between Alice and Bob. Imagine that Alice wants to send an e-mail message to Bob, and Trudy wants to intrude.

Before plowing ahead and designing a secure e-mail system for Alice and Bob, we should consider which security features would be most desirable for them. First and foremost is *confidentiality*. As discussed in Section 8.1, neither Alice nor Bob wants Trudy to read Alice's e-mail message. The second feature that Alice and Bob would most likely want to see in the secure e-mail system is *sender authentication*. In particular, when Bob receives the message "I don't love you anymore. I never want to see you again. Formerly yours, Alice," he would naturally want to be sure that the message came from Alice and not from Trudy. Another feature that the two lovers would appreciate is *message integrity*, that is, assurance that the message Alice sends is not modified while enroute to Bob. Finally, the e-mail system should provide *receiver authentication*; that is, Alice wants to make sure that she is indeed sending the letter to Bob and not to someone else (for example, Trudy) who is impersonating Bob.

So let's begin by addressing the foremost concern, confidentiality. The most straightforward way to provide confidentiality is for Alice to encrypt the message with symmetric key technology (such as DES or AES) and for Bob to decrypt the message on receipt. As discussed in Section 8.2, if the symmetric key is long enough, and if only Alice and Bob have the key, then it is extremely difficult for anyone else (including Trudy) to read the message. Although this approach is straightforward, it has the fundamental difficulty that we discussed in Section 8.2—it is hard to distribute a symmetric key so that only Alice and Bob have copies of it. So we naturally consider an alternative approach—public key cryptography (using, for example, RSA). In the public key approach, Bob makes his public key publicly available (e.g., in a public key server or on his personal Web page), Alice encrypts her message with Bob's public key, and she sends the encrypted message to Bob's e-mail address. (The encrypted message is encapsulated with MIME headers and sent over ordinary SMTP, as discussed in Section 2.4.) When Bob receives the message, he simply decrypts it with his private key. Assuming that Alice knows for sure that the public key is Bob's public key (and that the key is long enough), this approach is an excellent means to provide the desired confidentiality. One problem, however, is that public key encryption is relatively inefficient, particularly for long messages. (Long e-mail messages are now commonplace in the Internet, due to the increasing use of attachments, images, audio, and video.)

To overcome the efficiency problem, let's make use of a session key (discussed in Section 8.5). In particular, Alice (1) selects a symmetric session key, K_S, at random, (2) encrypts her message, m, with the symmetric key, K_S, (3) encrypts the symmetric key with Bob's public key, K_B^+, (4) concatenates the encrypted message and the encrypted symmetric key to form a "package," and (5) sends the package to Bob's e-mail address. The steps are illustrated in Figure 8.27. (In this and the subsequent figures, the circled "+" represents concatenation and the circled "−" represents deconcatenation.) When Bob receives the package, he (1) uses his private key, K_B^-, to obtain the symmetric key, K_s, and (2) uses the symmetric key K_s to decrypt the message m.

Having designed a secure e-mail system that provides confidentiality, let's now design another system that provides both sender authentication and integrity. We'll suppose, for the moment, that Alice and Bob are no longer concerned with confidentiality (they want to share their feelings with everyone!), and are concerned only about sender authentication and message integrity. To accomplish this task, we use digital signatures and message digests, as described in Section 8.4. Specifically, Alice (1) applies a hash function, H (for example, MD5), to her message, m, to obtain a message digest, (2) signs the result of the hash function with her private key, K_A^-, to create a digital signature, (3) concatenates the original (unencrypted) message with the signature to create a package, and (4) sends the package to Bob's e-mail address. When Bob receives the package, he (1) applies Alice's public key, K_A^+, to the signed message digest and (2) compares the result of this operation with his own hash, H, of the message. The steps are illustrated in Figure 8.28. As discussed in Section 8.5, if the two results are the same, Bob can be pretty confident that the message came from Alice and is unaltered.

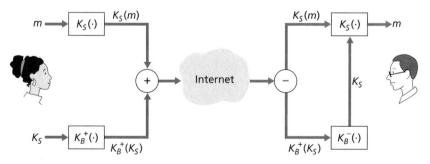

Alice sends e-mail message m Bob receives e-mail message m

Figure 8.27 ◆ Alice uses a symmetric session key, K_S, to send a secret e-mail to Bob.

CASE HISTORY

PHIL ZIMMERMANN AND PGP

Philip R. Zimmermann is the creator of Pretty Good Privacy (PGP). For that, he was the target of a three-year criminal investigation because the government held that US export restrictions for cryptographic software were violated when PGP spread all around the world following its 1991 publication as freeware. After releasing PGP as shareware, someone else put it on the Internet and foreign citizens downloaded it. Cryptography programs in the United States are classified as munitions under federal law and may not be exported.

Despite the lack of funding, the lack of any paid staff, and the lack of a company to stand behind it, and despite government interventions, PGP nonetheless became the most widely used e-mail encryption software in the world. Oddly enough, the US government may have inadvertently contributed to PGP's spread because of the Zimmermann case.

The US government dropped the case in early 1996. The announcement was met with celebration by Internet activists. The Zimmermann case had become the story of an innocent person fighting for his rights against the abuses of big government. The government's giving in was welcome news, in part because of the campaign for Internet censorship in Congress and the push by the FBI to allow increased government snooping.

After the government dropped its case, Zimmermann founded PGP Inc., which was acquired by Network Associates in December 1997. Zimmermann is now an independent consultant in matters cryptographic.

Now let's consider designing an e-mail system that provides confidentiality, sender authentication, *and* message integrity. This can be done by combining the procedures in Figures 8.27 and 8.28. Alice first creates a preliminary package, exactly as in Figure 8.28, that consists of her original message along with a digitally signed hash of the message. She then treats this preliminary package as a message in itself and sends this new message through the sender steps in Figure 8.27, creating a new package that is sent to Bob. The steps applied by Alice are shown in Figure 8.29. When Bob receives the package, he first applies his side of Figure 8.27 and then his side of Figure 8.28. It should be clear that this design achieves the goal of providing confidentiality, sender authentication, and message integrity. Note that, in this scheme, Alice uses public key cryptography twice: once with her own private key and once with Bob's public key. Similarly, Bob also uses public key cryptography twice—once with his private key and once with Alice's public key.

The secure e-mail design outlined in Figure 8.29 probably provides satisfactory security for most e-mail users for most occasions. But there is still one important

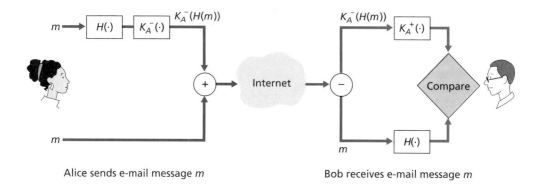

Alice sends e-mail message *m*   Bob receives e-mail message *m*

Figure 8.28 ♦ Using hash functions and digital signatures to provide sender authentication and message integrity

issue that remains to be addressed. The design in Figure 8.29 requires Alice to obtain Bob's public key, and requires Bob to obtain Alice's public key. The distribution of these public keys is a nontrivial problem. For example, Trudy might masquerade as Bob and give Alice her own public key while saying that it is Bob's public key, enabling her to receive the message meant for Bob. As we learned in Section 8.5, a popular approach for securely distributing public keys is to *certify* the public keys using a certificate authority.

PGP

Written by Phil Zimmermann in 1991, **Pretty Good Privacy (PGP)** is an e-mail encryption scheme that has become a *de facto* standard. Its Web site serves more than a million pages a month to users in 166 countries [PGPI 2004]. Versions of PGP are available in the public domain; for example, you can find the PGP software for your favorite platform as well as lots of interesting reading at the International PGP Home Page [PGPI 2004]. (A particularly interesting essay by the author of PGP is [Zimmermann 2004].) PGP is also commercially available and as a plug-in for many e-mail user agents, including Microsoft's Exchange and Outlook, and Qualcomm's Eudora. The PGP design is, in essence, the same as the design shown in Figure 8.29. Depending on the version, the PGP software uses MD5 or SHA for calculating the message digest; CAST, triple-DES, or IDEA for symmetric key encryption; and RSA for the public key encryption. In addition, PGP provides data compression.

When PGP is installed, the software creates a public key pair for the user. The public key can be posted on the user's Web site or placed in a public key server. The private key is protected by the use of a password. The password has to be entered every time the user accesses the private key. PGP gives the user the option of digitally signing the message, encrypting the message, or both digitally signing and encrypting. Figure 8.30 shows a PGP signed message. This message appears after the MIME header. The encoded data in the message is $K_A^-(H(m))$, that is, the digitally signed message digest. As we discussed above, in order for Bob to verify the integrity of the message, he needs to have access to Alice's public key.

Figure 8.31 shows a secret PGP message. This message also appears after the MIME header. Of course, the plaintext message is not included within the secret e-mail message. When a sender (such as Alice) wants both confidentiality and integrity, PGP contains a message like that of Figure 8.31 within the message of Figure 8.30.

PGP also provides a mechanism for public key certification, but the mechanism is quite different from the more conventional certificate authority. PGP public keys are certified by a web of trust. Alice herself can certify any key/username pair when she believes the pair really belong together. In addition, PGP permits Alice to say that she trusts another user to vouch for the authenticity of more keys. Some PGP users sign each other's keys by holding key-signing parties. Users physically gather, exchange floppy disks containing public keys, and certify each other's keys by signing them with their private keys. PGP public keys are also distributed by **PGP public key servers** on the Internet. When a user submits a public key to such a server, the server stores a copy of the key, sends a copy of the key to all the other public key servers, and serves the key to anyone who requests it. Although key-signing parties and PGP public key servers actually exist, by far the most common ways for users to distribute their public keys are by posting them on their personal Web pages and by advertising them in their e-mails.

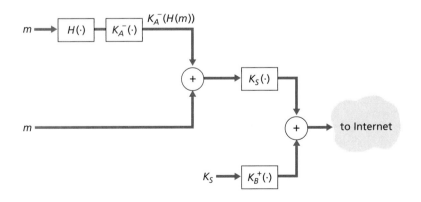

Figure 8.29 ♦ Alice uses symmetric key cryptography, public key cryptography, a hash function, and a digital signature to provide secrecy, sender authentication, and message integrity.

```
-----BEGIN PGP SIGNED MESSAGE-----
Hash:   SHA1
Bob:
Can I see you tonight?
Passionately yours, Alice
-----BEGIN PGP SIGNATURE-----
Version: PGP for Personal Privacy 5.0
Charset:  noconv
yhHJRHhGJGhgg/12EpJ+lo8gE4vB3mqJhFEvZP9t6n7G6m5Gw2
-----END PGP SIGNATURE-----
```

Figure 8.30 ◆ A PGP signed message

```
-----BEGIN PGP MESSAGE-----
Version: PGP for Personal Privacy 5.0
u2R4d+/jKmn8Bc5+hgDsqAewsDfrGdszX68liKm5F6Gc4sDfcXyt
RfdS10juHgbcfDssWe7/K=lKhnMikLo0+1/BvcX4t==Ujk9PbcD4
Thdf2awQfgHbnmKlok8iy6gThlp
-----END PGP MESSAGE
```

Figure 8.31 ◆ A secret PGP message

8.8.2 Secure Sockets Layer (SSL) and Transport Layer Security (TLS)

In the previous section, we considered how the application-layer can use (in secure e-mail) the various security mechanisms that we studied earlier in this chapter: encryption, authentication, key distribution, message integrity, and digital signatures. In this section, we'll continue our case study of various security mechanisms by dropping down a layer in the protocol stack and covering secure sockets and a secure transport layer. We'll take Internet commerce as a motivating application, since business and financial transactions are an important driving force for Internet security.

Let's walk through a typical Internet commerce scenario. Bob is surfing the Web and arrives at the Alice Incorporated site, which is selling a product. The Alice Incorporated site displays a form in which Bob is supposed to enter the quantity desired, his address, and his payment card number. Bob enters this information, clicks on submit, and expects to receive (say, via ordinary mail) the product; he also expects to receive a charge for the product in his next payment card statement. This all sounds good, but if no security measures are taken—such as encryption or authentication—Bob could be in for a few surprises.

♦ An intruder could intercept the order and obtain Bob's payment card information. The intruder could then make purchases at Bob's expense.

♦ The site could display Alice Incorporated's famous logo but actually be a site maintained by Trudy, who is masquerading as Alice Incorporated. Trudy could take Bob's money and run. Or Trudy could make her own purchases and have them billed to Bob's account.

Many other surprises are possible, and we will discuss a few of these in the next subsection. but these are two of the most serious problems. Internet commerce using the SSL protocol can address both these problems.

Secure sockets layer (SSL), originally developed by Netscape (see also [Woo 1994]), is a protocol designed to provide data encryption and authentication between a Web client and a Web server. The protocol begins with a handshake phase that negotiates an encryption algorithm (for example, DES or IDEA) and keys, and authenticates the server to the client. Optionally, the client can also be authenticated to the server. Once the handshake is complete and the transmission of application data begins, all data is encrypted using session keys negotiated during the handshake phase. SSL is widely used in Internet commerce, being implemented in almost all popular browsers and Web servers. Furthermore, it is also the basis of the Transport Layer Security (TLS) protocol [RFC 2246].

SSL and TLS are not limited to the Web application; for example, they can similarly be used for authentication and data encryption for IMAP (Internet Mail Access Protocol) mail access. SSL can be viewed as a layer that sits between the application layer and the transport layer. On the sending side, SSL receives data (such as an HTTP or IMAP message from an application), encrypts the data, and directs the encrypted data to a TCP socket. On the receiving side, SSL reads from the TCP socket, decrypts the data, and directs the data to the application. Although SSL can be used with many Internet applications, we'll discuss it in the context of the Web, where it is being used today principally for Internet commerce.

SSL provides the following features:

♦ *SSL server authentication,* allowing a user to confirm a server's identity. An SSL-enabled browser maintains a list of trusted certification authorities (CAs) along with the public keys of the CAs. When the browser wants to do business with an SSL-enabled Web server, it obtains a certificate from the server containing the server's public key. The certificate is issued (that is, digitally signed) by a CA listed in the client's list of trusted CAs. This feature allows the browser to authenticate the server before the user submits a payment card number. In the context of the earlier example, this server authentication enables Bob to verify that he is indeed sending his payment card number to Alice Incorporated, and not to someone else who might be masquerading as Alice Incorporated.

♦ *SSL client authentication,* allowing a server to confirm a user's identity. Analogous to server authentication, client authentication makes use of client certificates, which have also been issued by CAs. This authentication is important if the server, for example, is a bank sending confidential financial information to a customer and it wants to check the recipient's identity. Client authentication, although supported by SSL, is optional. To keep our discussion focused, we will henceforth ignore it.

♦ *An encrypted SSL session,* in which all information sent between browser and server is encrypted by the sending software (browser or Web server) and decrypted by the receiving software (browser or Web server). This confidentiality may be important to both the customer and the merchant. Also, SSL provides a mechanism for detecting tampering with the information by an intruder.

How SSL Works

A user, say Bob, surfs the Web and clicks on a link that takes him to a secure page housed by Alice's SSL-enabled server. The protocol part of the URL for this page is https, rather than the ordinary http. The browser and server then run the SSL handshake protocol, which (1) authenticates the server and (2) generates a shared symmetric key. Both of these tasks make use of RSA public key technology. The main flow of events in the handshake phase is shown in Figure 8.32. During this phase, Alice sends Bob her certificate, from which Bob obtains Alice's public key. Bob then creates a random symmetric key, encrypts it with Alice's public key, and sends the encrypted key to Alice. Bob and Alice now share a symmetric session key. Once this handshake protocol is complete, all data sent between the browser and server (over TCP connections) is encrypted using the symmetric session key.

Having given a high-level overview of SSL, let's take a closer look at some of the more important details. The SSL handshake performs the following steps:

1. The browser sends the server the browser's SSL version number and cryptographic preferences. The browser sends its cryptographic preferences because the browser and server negotiate which symmetric key algorithm they are going to use.
2. The server sends the browser the server's SSL version number, cryptographic preferences, and its certificate. Recall that the certificate includes the server's RSA public key and is certified by some CA; that is, the certificate has been signed with the CA's private key.
3. The browser has a list of trusted CAs and a public key for each CA on the list. When the browser receives the certificate from the server, it checks to see whether the CA is on the list. If not, the user is warned of the problem and informed that an encrypted and authenticated connection cannot be established. If the CA is on the list, the browser uses the CA's public key to validate the certificate and obtain the server's public key.

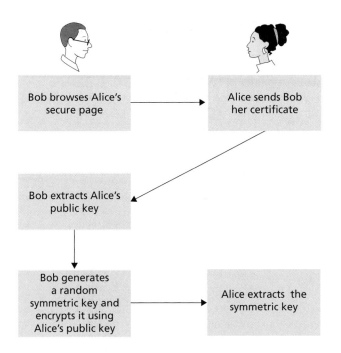

Figure 8.32 ◆ High-level overview of the handshake phase of SSL

4. The browser generates a symmetric session key, encrypts it with the server's public key, and sends the encrypted session key to the server.
5. The browser sends a message to the server informing it that future messages from the client will be encrypted with the session key. It then sends a separate (encrypted) message indicating that the browser portion of the handshake is finished.
6. The server sends a message to the browser informing it that future messages from the server will be encrypted with the session key. It then sends a separate (encrypted) message indicating that the server portion of the handshake is finished.
7. The SSL handshake is now complete, and the SSL session has begun. The browser and the server use the session keys to encrypt and decrypt the data they send to each other and to validate its integrity.

The SSL handshake actually has many more steps than listed above. You can find more information about SSL at [Netscape SSL 1998]. In addition to payment card purchases, we point out here that SSL can be (and is) used for other financial transactions such as online banking and stock trading.

The Limitations of SSL in Internet Commerce

Thanks to its simplicity and early development, SSL is widely implemented in browsers, servers, and Internet commerce products. These SSL-enabled servers and browsers provide a popular platform for payment card transactions. Nevertheless, we should keep in mind that SSL was not specifically tailored for payment card transactions, but instead for generic secure communication between a client and server. Because of this generic design, SSL lacks many features that the payment card industry would like to see in an Internet commerce protocol.

Consider once again what happens when Bob makes a purchase from Alice Incorporated over SSL. The signed certificate that Bob receives from Alice assures Bob that he is really dealing with Alice Incorporated, and that Alice Incorporated is a bona fide company. However, the generic certificate does not indicate whether Alice Incorporated is authorized to accept payment card purchases nor if the company is a reliable merchant. This opens the door for merchant fraud. And there is a similar problem for client authorization. Even if SSL client authentication is used, the client certificate does not tie Bob to a specific authorized payment card; thus, Alice Incorporated has no assurance that Bob is authorized to make a payment card purchase. This opens the door to all kinds of fraud, including purchases with stolen credit cards and customer repudiation of purchased products.

8.8.3 Network-Layer Security: IPsec

The **IP security** protocol, more commonly known as **IPsec**, is a suite of protocols that provides security at the network layer. IPsec is a rather complex animal—parts of it are described in more than a dozen RFCs. In this section, we will discuss IPsec in a specific context, namely, in the context that *all* hosts in the Internet support IPsec. Although this is many years away, the context will simplify the discussion and help us understand the key features of IPsec. Two key RFCs are RFC 2401, which describes the overall IP security architecture, and RFC 2411, which provides an overview of the IPsec protocol suite and the documents describing it.

Before getting into the specifics of IPsec, let us step back and consider what it means to provide security at the network layer. Consider first what it means to provide **network-layer confidentiality**. The network layer would provide confidentiality if all the data carried by all IP datagrams were encrypted. This means that whenever a host wants to send a datagram, it encrypts the data field of the datagram before shipping it out into the network. In principle, the encryption could be done with symmetric key encryption, public key encryption, or with session keys that are negotiated using public key encryption. The data field could be a TCP segment, a UDP segment, an ICMP message, and so on. If such a network-layer service were in place, all data sent by hosts—including e-mail, Web pages, control messages, and management messages (such as ICMP and SNMP)—would be hidden from any third party that was wire tapping the network. Thus, such a service would provide a certain blanket coverage for all Internet traffic, thereby giving all of us a certain sense of security.

In addition to confidentiality, one might also want the network layer to also provide **source authentication**. When a destination host receives an IP datagram with a particular IP source address, it authenticates the source by making sure that the IP datagram was indeed generated by the host with that IP source address. Such a service prevents datagrams with spoofed IP addresses from being authenticated.

In the IPsec protocol suite there are two principal protocols: the **Authentication Header (AH) protocol** and the **Encapsulation Security Payload (ESP) protocol**. When a source host sends secure datagrams to a destination host, it does so with either the AH protocol or the ESP protocol. The AH protocol provides source authentication and data integrity but does not provide confidentiality. The ESP protocol provides authentication, data integrity, and confidentiality. Providing more services, the ESP protocol is naturally more complicated and requires more processing than the AH protocol.

In both the AH and the ESP protocols, before secured datagrams are sent from a source host to a destination host, the source and network hosts handshake and create a network-layer logical connection. This logical channel is called a **security association (SA)**. Thus, IPsec transforms the traditional connectionless network layer of the Internet to a layer with logical connections. The logical connection defined by an SA is a *simplex connection*; that is, it is unidirectional. If both hosts want to send secure datagrams to each other, then two SAs (that is, logical connections) need to be established, one in each direction. An SA is uniquely identified by a three-tuple consisting of

♦ A security protocol (AH or ESP) identifier
♦ The source IP address for the simplex connection
♦ A 32-bit connection identifier called the Security Parameter Index (SPI)

For a given SA (that is, a given logical connection from source host to destination host), each IPsec datagram will have a special field for the SPI. All of the datagrams in the SA will use the same SPI value in this field.

Authentication Header (AH) Protocol

As mentioned above, the AH protocol provides source host authentication and data integrity but not confidentiality. When a particular source host wants to send one or more datagrams to a particular destination, it first establishes an SA with the destination. After having established the SA, the source can send secure datagrams to the destination host. The secure datagrams include the AH header, which is inserted between the original IP datagram data (for example, a TCP or UDP segment) and the IP header, as shown in Figure 8.33. Thus the AH header augments the original data field, and this augmented data field is encapsulated as a standard IP datagram. For the protocol field in the IP header, the value 51 is used to indicate that the datagram includes an AH header. When the destination host receives the IP datagram, it takes note of the 51 in the protocol field and processes the datagram using the AH protocol. (Recall that the protocol field in the IP datagram is used to determine the upper-layer protocol—for example, UDP, TCP, or ICMP—that will be passed the data portion of an IP datagram.) Intermediate routers process the datagrams just as they always have—they examine the destination IP address and forward the datagrams accordingly.

The AH header includes several fields:

♦ *Next Header* field, which has the role that the protocol field has for an ordinary datagram. It indicates whether the data following the AH header is a TCP segment, UDP segment, ICMP segment, and so on. (Recall that the protocol field in the IP datagram is now being used to indicate the AH protocol, so it can no longer be used to indicate the transport-layer protocol.)

♦ *Security Parameter Index (SPI)* field, an arbitrary 32-bit value that, in combination with the destination IP address and the security protocol, uniquely identifies the SA for the datagram.

♦ *Sequence Number* field, a 32-bit field containing a sequence number for each datagram. It is initially set to 0 at the establishment of an SA. The AH protocol uses the sequence numbers to prevent playback and man-in-the-middle attacks (see Section 8.3).

♦ *Authentication Data* field, a variable-length field containing a signed message digest (that is, a digital signature) for this datagram. The message digest is calculated over the original IP datagram, thereby providing source host authentication and IP datagram integrity. The digital signature is computed using the algorithm specified by the SA, such as MD5 or SHA.

When the destination host receives an IP datagram with an AH header, it determines the SA for the datagram and then authenticates the datagram's integrity by processing the authentication data field. The IPsec authentication scheme (for both the AH and ESP protocols) uses a scheme called HMAC, which is an encrypted

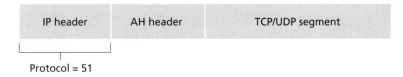
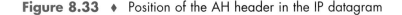

Figure 8.33   ♦   Position of the AH header in the IP datagram

message digest described in [RFC 2104]. HMAC uses a shared secret key between two parties rather than public key methods for message authentication. Further details about the AH protocol can be found in [RFC 2402].

The ESP Protocol

The ESP protocol provides network-layer confidentiality as well as source host authentication and data integrity. Once again, it all begins with a source host establishing an SA with a destination host. Then the source host can send secured datagrams to the destination host. As shown in Figure 8.34, a secured datagram is created by surrounding the original IP datagram data with header and trailer fields, and then inserting this encapsulated data into the data field of an IP datagram. For the protocol field in the header of the IP datagram, the value 50 is used to indicate that the datagram includes an ESP header and trailer. When the destination host receives the IP datagram, it takes note of the 50 in the protocol field and processes the datagram using the ESP protocol. As shown in Figure 8.34, the original IP datagram data along with the ESP Trailer field are encrypted. Confidentiality is provided with DES-CBC encryption [RFC 2405]. The ESP header consists of a 32-bit field for the SPI and a 32-bit field for the sequence number, which have exactly the same role as in the AH protocol. The trailer includes the Next Header field, which also has exactly the same role as in AH. Note that because the Next Header field is encrypted along with the original data, an intruder will not be able to determine the transport protocol that is being used. Following the trailer there is the Authentication Data field, which again serves the same role as in the AH protocol. Further details about the ESP protocol can be found in [RFC 2406].

SA and Key Management

For successful deployment of IPsec, a scalable and automated SA and key management scheme is necessary. Several protocols have been defined for these tasks.

♦ The **Internet Key Exchange (IKE)** algorithm [RFC 2409] is the default key management protocol for IPsec.

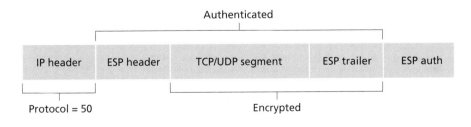

Figure 8.34 ♦ The ESP fields in the IP datagram

♦ The **Internet Security Association and Key Management Protocol (ISKMP)** defines procedures for establishing and tearing down SAs [RFC 2407; RFC 2408]. ISKMP's security association is completely separate from IKE key exchange.

This wraps up our summary of IPsec. We have discussed IPsec in the context of IPv4 and the transport mode. IPsec also defines a tunnel mode, in which routers introduce the security functionality rather than the hosts. Finally, IPsec describes encryption procedures for IPv6 as well as IPv4.

8.8.4 Security in IEEE 802.11

Security is a particularly important concern in wireless networks, where radio waves carrying frames can propagate far beyond the building containing the wireless base station(s) and hosts. An eye-opening reminder of this fact is the 18-month "war-driving" effort undertaken by Peter Shipley, who drove around the San Francisco Bay area with a laptop and 802.11 card looking for wireless networks that were "visible" from outside the building [Shipley 2001]. He recorded more than 9,000 such networks; one street corner in San Francisco offered six different available networks! Perhaps even more alarming, Shipley noted that 85 percent of these 9,000 networks do not even utilize the (rather weak, as we'll see) security mechanisms in the original 802.11 standard.

The issue of security in 802.11 has attracted considerable attention in both technical circles and in the media. While there has been considerable discussion, there has been little debate—there seems to be universal agreement that the original 802.11 specification contains a number of serious security flaws. Indeed, public domain software can now be downloaded that exploits these holes, making those who use the vanilla 802.11 security mechanisms as open to security attacks as the 85 percent of the Bay area wireless network users who use no security features at all.

In the following, we discuss the security mechanisms initially standardized in the 802.11 specification, known collectively as **Wired Equivalent Privacy (WEP)**. As the name suggests, WEP is meant to provide a level of security similar to that found in wired networks. We'll then discuss a few of the security holes in WEP and discuss the 802.11i standard, a fundamentally more secure version of 802.11 adopted in 2004.

Wired Equivalent Privacy (WEP)

The IEEE 802.11 WEP protocol [IEEE 802.11 1999] provides authentication and data encryption between a host and a wireless access point (that is, base station) using a symmetric shared key approach. WEP does not specify a key management algorithm, so it is assumed that the host and wireless access point have somehow agreed on the key via an out-of-band method. Authentication is carried out as in the *ap4.0* protocol that we developed in Section 8.3. Four steps are involved:

1. A wireless host requests authentication by an access point.
2. The access point responds to the authentication request with a 128-byte nonce value.
3. The wireless host encrypts the nonce using the symmetric key that it shares with the access point.
4. The access point decrypts the host-encrypted nonce.

If the decrypted nonce matches the nonce value originally sent to the host, then the host is authenticated by the access point.

The WEP data encryption algorithm is illustrated in Figure 8.35. A secret 40-bit symmetric key, K_S, is assumed to be known by both a host and the access point. In addition, a 24-bit Initialization Vector (IV) is appended to the 40-bit key to create a 64-bit key that will be used to encrypt a single frame. The IV will change from one frame to another, and hence each frame will be encrypted with a different 64-bit key. Encryption is performed as follows. First a 4-byte CRC value (see Section 5.2) is computed for the data payload. The payload and the four CRC bytes are then encrypted using the RC4 stream cipher. We will not cover the details of RC4 here (see [Schneier 1995] for details). For our purposes, it is enough to know that when presented with a key value (in this case, the 64-bit (K_S, IV) key), the RC4 algorithm produces a stream of key values, $k_1^{IV}, k_2^{IV}, k_3^{IV}, \ldots$ that are used to encrypt the data and CRC value in a frame. For practical purposes, we can think of these operations being performed a byte at a time. Encryption is performed by XOR-ing the ith byte of data, d_i, with the ith key, k_i^{IV}, in the stream of key values generated by the (K_S, IV) pair to produce the ith byte of ciphertext, c_i:

$$c_i = d_i \text{ XOR } k_i^{IV}$$

The IV value changes from one frame to the next and is included *in plaintext* in the header of each WEP-encrypted 802.11 frame, as shown in Figure 8.35. The receiver takes the secret 40-bit symmetric key that it shares with the sender, appends the IV, and uses the resulting 64-bit key (which is identical to the key used by the sender to perform encryption) to decrypt the frame.

$$d_i = c_i \text{ XOR } k_i^{IV}$$

Proper use of the RC4 algorithm requires that the same 64-bit key value *never* be used more than once. Recall that the WEP key changes on a frame-by-frame basis. For a given K_S (which changes rarely, if ever), this means that there are only 2^{24} unique keys. If these keys are chosen randomly, we can show [Walker 2000] that the probability of having chosen the same IV value (and hence used the same 64-bit key) is more than 99 percent after only 12,000 frames. With 1 K frame sizes and a data transmission rate of 11 Mbps, only a few seconds are needed before 12,000 frames are transmitted. Furthermore, since the IV is transmitted in plaintext in the frame, an eavesdropper will know whenever a duplicate IV value is used.

To see one of the several problems that occur when a duplicate key is used, consider the following chosen-plaintext attack taken by Trudy against Alice. Suppose that Trudy (possibly using IP spoofing) sends a request (for example, an HTTP or FTP request) to Alice to transmit a file with known content, $d_1, d_2, d_3, d_4, \ldots$. Trudy also observes the encrypted data $c_1, c_2, c_3, c_4 \ldots$. Since $d_i = c_i$ XOR k_i^{IV}, if we XOR c_i with each side of this equality we have

$$d_i \text{ XOR } c_i = k_i^{IV}$$

With this relationship, Trudy can use the known values of d_i and c_i to compute k_i^{IV}. The next time Trudy sees the same value of IV being used, she will know the key sequence $k_1^{IV}, k_2^{IV}, k_3^{IV}, \ldots$ and will thus be able to decrypt the encrypted message.

There are several additional security concerns with WEP as well. [Fluhrer 2001] described an attack exploiting a known weakness in RC4 when certain weak keys are chosen. [Stubblefield 2002] discusses efficient ways to implement and exploit this attack. Another concern with WEP involves the CRC bits shown in Figure 8.35 and transmitted in the 802.11 frame to detect altered bits in the payload However, an attacker who changes the encrypted content (e.g., substituting gibberish for the original encrypted data), computes a CRC over the substituted gibbersish and places the CRC into a WEP frame can produce a 802.11 frame that will be accepted by the receiver. What is needed here are message integrity techniques such as those we studied in Section 8.4 to detect content tampering or substitution. For

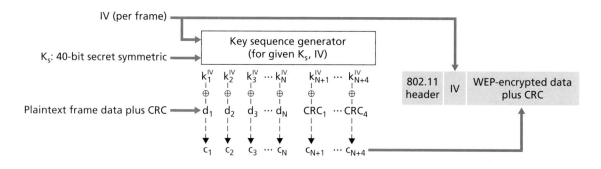

Figure 8.35 ◆ 802.11 WEP protocol

more details of WEP security, see [Walker 2000; Weatherspoon 2000, 802.11 Security 2004] and the references therein.

IEEE802.11i

Soon after the 1999 release of IEEE 802.11, work began on developing a new and improved version of 802.11 with stronger security mechanisms. The new standard, known as 802.11i, is undergoing final ratification and is due to be approved in early 2004. As we'll see, while WEP provided relatively weak encryption, only a single way to perform authentication, and no key-distribution mechanisms, IEEE 802.11i provides for much stronger forms of encryption, an extensible set of authentication mechanisms, and a key distribution mechanism. In the following, we present an overview of 802.11i; an excellent (streaming audio) technical overview of 802.11i is [TechOnline 2004].

Figure 8.36 overviews the 802.11i framework. In addition to the wireless client and access point, 802.11i defines an authentication server with which the AP can communicate. Separating the authentication server from the AP allows one authentication server to serve many APs, centralizing the (often sensitive) decisions

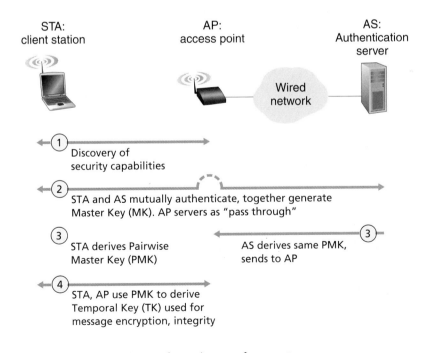

Figure 8.36 ◆ 802.11i: four phases of operation

regarding authentication and access within the single server, and keeping AP costs and complexity low. 802.11i operates in four phases:

1. *Discovery.* In the discovery phase, the AP advertises its presence and the forms of authentication and encryption that can be provided to the wireless client node. The client then requests the specific forms of authentication and encryption that it desires. Although the client and AP are already exchanging messages, the client has not yet been authenticated nor does it have an encryption key, and so several more steps will be required before the client can communicate with an arbitrary remote host over the wireless channel.

2. *Mutual Authentication and Master Key (MK) Generation.* Authentication takes place between the wireless client and the authentication server. In this phase, the access point acts essentially as a relay, forwarding messages between the client and the authentication server. The **Extensible Authentication Protocol (EAP)** [RFC 2284] defines the end-to-end message formats used in a simple request/response mode of interaction between the client and authentication server. As shown in Figure 8.37 EAP messages are encapsulated using **EAPoL** (EAP over LAN, [IEEE 802.1X]) and sent over the 802.11 wireless link. These EAP messages are then decapsulated at the access point, and then re-encapsulated using the **RADIUS** protocol for transmission over UDP/IP to the authentication server. While the RADIUS server and protocol [RFC 2138] are not required by the 802.11i protocol, they are *de facto* standard components for

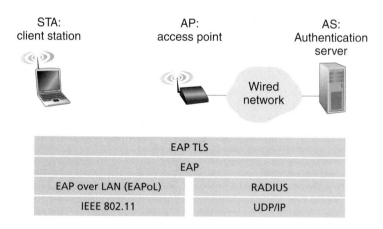

Figure 8.37 ♦ EAP is an end-end protocol. EAP messages are encapsulated using EAPoL over the wireless link between the client and the access point, and using RADIUS over UDP/IP between the access point and the authentication server.

802.11i. The recently standardized **DIAMETER** protocol [RFC 3588] is likely to replace RADIUS in the near future.

With EAP, the authentication server can choose one of a number of ways to perform authentication. While 802.11i does not mandate a particular authentication method, the EAP-TLS authentication scheme [RFC 2716] is often used. EAP-TLS uses public key techniques (including nonce encryption and message digests) similar to those we studied in Sections 8.3, 8.4, and 8.5 to allow the client and the authentication server to mutually authenticate each other, and to derive an Master Key (MK) that is known to both parties.

3. *Pairwise Master Key (PMK) Generation.* The MK is a shared secret known only to the client and the authentication server, which they each use to generate a second key, the Pairwise Master Key (PMK). The authentication server then sends the PMK to the AP. This where we wanted to be! The client and AP now have a shared key (recall that in WEP, the problem of key distribution was not addressed at all) and have mutually authenticated each other. They're just about ready to get down to business.

4. *Temporal Key (TK) Generation.* With the PMK, the wireless client and AP can now generate additional keys that will be used for communication. Of particular interest is the Temporal Key (TK), which will be used to perform the link-level encryption of data sent over the wireless link and to an arbitrary remote host.

802.11i provides several forms of encryption, including an AES-based encryption scheme and a strengthened version of WEP encryption.

8.9 Summary

In this chapter, we've examined the various mechanisms that our secret lovers, Bob and Alice, can use to communicate securely. We've seen that Bob and Alice are interested in confidentiality (so they alone are able to understand the contents of a transmitted message), authentication (so they are sure that they are talking with each other), and message integrity (so they are sure that their messages are not altered in transit). Of course, the need for secure communication is not confined to secret lovers. Indeed, we saw in Sections 8.6 through 8.8 that security is needed at various layers in a network architecture to protect against bad guys who have a large arsenal of possible attacks at hand.

The first part of this chapter presented various principles underlying secure communication. In Section 8.2 we covered cryptographic techniques for encrypting and decrypting data, including symmetric key cryptography and public key cryptography. DES and RSA were examined as specific case studies of these two major classes of cryptographic techniques in use in today's networks. In Section 8.3 we turned our attention to authentication and developed a series of increasingly sophisticated authentication protocols to ensure that a conversant is indeed who he or she claims to be, and is live. We saw that both symmetric key cryptography and public key cryptography can play an important role not only in disguising data (encryption/decryption), but also in performing authentication. Techniques for signing a digital document in a manner that is verifiable, nonforgeable, and nonrepudiable were covered in Section 8.4. Once again, the application of cryptographic techniques proved essential. We examined digital signatures and message digests, the latter being a shorthand way of signing a digital document. In Section 8.5 we examined key distribution protocols. We saw that for symmetric key encryption, a key distribution center—a single trusted network entity—can be used to distribute a shared symmetric key among communicating parties. For public key encryption, a certification authority distributes certificates to validate public keys.

Armed with the techniques covered in Sections 8.2 through 8.5, Bob and Alice can communicate securely. (One can only hope that they are networking students who have learned this material and can thus avoid having their tryst uncovered by Trudy!) But, increasingly, confidentiality is only a small part of the network security picture. Increasingly, the focus in network security has been on securing the network infrastructure against a potential onslaught by the bad guys. In the latter part of this chapter, we thus covered firewalls (which regulate access to and from a protected network) and a range of attacks that can be mounted against the network by outsiders as well as the countermeasures that can be taken against them. We concluded the chapter with case studies that apply techniques from Sections 8.2 through 8.5 in the application layer, transport layer, network layer, and link layer.

Homework Problems and Questions

Chapter 8 Review Questions

1. What are the differences between message confidentiality and message integrity? Can you have one without the other? Justify your answer.

2. What is the difference between an active and a passive intruder?

3. What is an important difference between a symmetric key system and a public key system?

4. Suppose that an intruder has an encrypted message as well as the decrypted version of that message. Can the intruder mount a ciphertext-only attack, a known-plaintext attack, or a chosen-plaintext attack?

5. Suppose N people want to communicate with each of $N - 1$ other people using symmetric key encryption. All communication between any two people, i and j, is visible to all other people in this group of N, and no other person in this group should be able to decode their communication. How many keys are

required in the system as a whole? Now suppose that public key encryption is used. How many keys are required in this case?

6. What is the purpose of a nonce in an authentication protocol?

7. What does it mean to say that a nonce is a once-in-a-lifetime value? In whose lifetime?

8. What is the man-in-the-middle attack? Can this attack occur when symmetric keys are used?

9. What does it mean for a signed document to be verifiable, nonforgeable, and nonrepudiable?

10. In what way does a message digest provide a better message integrity check than a checksum such as the Internet checksum?

11. In what way does a public-key encrypted message digest provide a better digital signature than using the public-key encrypted message?

12. Is the message associated with a message digest encrypted? Explain your answer.

13. What is a key distribution center? What is a certificate authority?

14. Summarize the key differences in the services provided by the Authentication Header (AH) protocol and the Encapsulation Security Payload (ESP) protocol in IPsec.

Problems

1. Using the monoalphabetic cipher in Figure 8.3, encode the message "`This is an easy problem.`" Decode the message "`rmij'u uamu xyj.`"

2. Show that Trudy's known-plaintext attack, in which she knows the (ciphertext, plaintext) translation pairs for seven letters, reduces the number of possible substitutions to be checked in the example in Section 8.2.1 by approximately 10^9.

3. Consider the polyalphabetic system shown in Figure 8.4. Will a chosen-plaintext attack that is able to get the plaintext encoding of the message, "`The quick brown fox jumps over the lazy dog`" be sufficient to decode all messages? Why or why not?

4. Using RSA, choose $p = 3$ and $q = 11$, and encode the word "`hello.`" Apply the decryption algorithm to the encrypted version to recover the original plaintext message.

5. Consider our authentication protocol *ap4.0*, in which Alice authenticates herself to Bob, which we saw works well (i.e., we found no flaws in it.). Now suppose that while Alice is authenticating herself to Bob, Bob must authenticate

himself to Alice. Give a scenario by which Trudy, pretending to be Alice, can now authenticate herself to Bob as Alice. (*Hint*: Consider that the sequence of operations of *ap4.0*, one with Trudy initiating and one with Bob initiating, can be arbitrarily interleaved. Pay particular attention to the fact that both Bob and Alice will use a nonce, and that if care is not taken, the same nonce can be used maliciously.)

6. In the man-in-the-middle attack in Figure 8.13, Alice has not authenticated Bob. If Alice were to require Bob to authenticate himself using *ap5.0*, would the man-in-the-middle attack be avoided? Explain your reasoning.

7. The Internet BGP routing protocol uses the MD5 message digest rather than public key encryption to sign BGP messages. Why do you think MD5 was chosen over public key encryption?

8. Compute a third message, different from the two messages in Figure 8.18, that has the same checksum as the messages in Figure 8.18.

9. In the protocol and discussion of Figure 8.19, why doesn't Alice have to authenticate Bob explicitly?

10. Why is there no explicit authentication in the protocol in Figure 8.19? Is authentication needed? Why?

11. Consider the KDC and the CA servers. Suppose a KDC goes down. What is the impact on the ability of parties to communicate securely; that is, who can, and cannot, communicate? Justify your answer. Suppose now that a CA goes down. What is the impact of this failure?

12. Consider the following variation of the packet-filtering firewall discussed in Section 8.6. Suppose Alice wants to disallow access to her network 222.22.0.0/16 from the public Internet (rule R3 in the first table below). Alice is again collaborating with Bob and his colleagues, who are at a university, and so Alice wants to let users from Bob's university (whose network address is 111.11/16) access a specific subnet, 222.22.22/24, within her company's network (rule R1 below). Alice knows that Trudy, a well-known hacker, is in Bob's university and that Trudy's subnet, 111.11.11/24, is an insecure hacker haven. So Alice doesn't want any traffic from 111.11.11/24 entering anywhere into her network (rule R2) *except* into the special subnet 222.22.22/24 (allowed under rule R1; this exception is the important difference from our example in Section 8.6). Alice's packet-filtering rules are summarized in the table below.

Rule	Source Address	Destination Address	Action	Comments
R1	111.11/16	222.22.22/24	permit	Let datagrams from Bob's university network (including Trudy's hacker subnet) into a restricted subnet.

R2	111.11.11/24	222.22/16	deny	Don't let traffic from Trudy's subnet into Alice's network; but see R1.
R3	0.0.0.0/0	0.0.0.0/0	deny	Don't let traffic into Alice's network.

- ◆ Fill in the table below for the actions taken for this scenario under ordering R1, R2, and R3, and under ordering R2, R1, R3.
- ◆ For packets P1, P2, P3, and P4, what would be the result of removing rule R2?

Datagram Number	Source IP Address	Destination IP Address	Desired Action	Action Under R2, R1, R3	Action Under R1, R2, R3
P1	111.11.11.1 (hacker subnet)	222.22.6.6 (corp.net)	deny		
P2	111.11.11.1 (hacker subnet)	222.22.22.2 (special subnet)	permit		
P3	111.11.6.6 (univ. net, not the hacker subnet)	222.22.22.2 (special subnet)	permit		
P4	111.11.6.6 (univ. net, not the hacker subnet)	222.22.6.6 (corp. net)	deny		

13. Figure 8.29 shows the operations that Alice must perform to provide confidentiality, authentication, and integrity. Diagram the corresponding operations that Bob must perform on the package received from Alice.

 # Discussion Questions

1. Suppose that an intruder could insert DNS messages into and remove DNS messages from the network. Give three scenarios showing the problems that such an intruder could cause.

2. No one has formally proven that 3DES or RSA are secure. Given this, what evidence do we have that they are indeed secure?

3. If IPsec provides security at the network layer, why is it that security mechanisms are still needed at layers above IP?

4. Go to the international PGP homepage (http://www.pgpi.org/). What version of PGP are you legally allowed to download, given the country you are in?

AN INTERVIEW WITH...

Steven M. Bellovin

Steven M. Bellovin is an AT&T Fellow in the Network Services Research Lab at AT&T Labs Research in Florham Park, New Jersey. His focus is on networks, security, and why the two are incompatible. In 1995, he was awarded the Usenix Lifetime Achievement Award for his work in the creation of Usenet, the first newsgroup exchange network that linked two or more computers and allowed users to share information and join in discussions. Steve is also an elected member of the National Academy of Engineering. He received his BA from Columbia University and his PhD from the University of North Carolina at Chapel Hill.

What led you to specialize in the networking security area?

This is going to sound odd, but the answer is simple: it was fun. My background was in systems programming and systems administration, which leads fairly naturally to security. And I've always been interested in communications, ranging back to part-time systems programming jobs when I was in college.

My work on security continues to be motivated by two things—a desire to keep computers useful, which means that their function can't be corrupted by attackers, and a desire to protect privacy.

What was your vision for Usenet at the time that you were developing it? And now?

We originally viewed it as a way to talk about computer science and computer programming around the country, with a lot of local use for administrative matters, for sale ads, and so on. In fact, my original prediction was one to two messages per day, from 50–100 sites at the most—ever. But the real growth was in people-related topics, including—but not limited to—human interactions with computers. My favorite newsgroups, over the years, have been things like rec.woodworking, as well as sci.crypt.

To some extent, netnews has been displaced by the Web. Were I to start designing it today, it would look very different. But it still excels as a way to reach a very broad audience that is interested in the topic, without having to rely on particular Web sites.

Has anyone inspired you professionally? In what ways?

Professor Fred Brooks—the founder and original chair of the computer science department at the University of North Carolina at Chapel Hill, the manager of the team that developed the IBM S/360 and OS/360, and the author of *The Mythical Man-Month*—was a tremendous influence on my career. More than anything else, he taught outlook and trade-offs—how to look at problems in the context of the real world (and how much messier the real world is than a theorist would like), and how to balance competing interests in designing a solution. Most computer work is engineering—the art of making the right trade-offs to satisfy many contradictory objectives.

What is your vision for the future of networking and security?

Thus far, much of the security we have has come from isolation. A firewall, for example, works by cutting off access to certain machines and services. But we're in an era of increasing connectivity—it's gotten harder to isolate things. Worse yet, our production systems require far more separate pieces, interconnected by networks. Securing all that is one of our biggest challenges.

Could you tell us about any special projects you're working on right now?

I'm focusing a lot on operational issues. It's not enough for a system to be secure; it has to be usable, too. That in turn means that network operators have to be able to monitor things. But monitoring can conflict with security—security tends to hide and protect computers and information, but operators need to see certain things. In addition, systems need to keep functioning even when crucial components are down. How do we share information to the right parties, without letting the bad guys in? This is a question I'm involved in answering right now.

What would you say have been the greatest advances in security? How much further do we have to go?

At least scientifically, we know how to do cryptography. That's been a big help. But most security problems are due to buggy code, and that's a much harder problem. In fact, it's the oldest unsolved problem in computer science, and I think it will remain that way. The challenge is figuring out how to secure systems when we have to build them out of insecure components. We can already do that for reliability in the face of hardware failures; can we do the same for security?

Do you have any advice for students about the Internet and networking security?

Learning the mechanisms is the easy part. Learning how to "think paranoid" is harder. You have to remember that probability distributions don't apply—the attackers can and will find improbable conditions. And the details matter—a lot.

9

Network Management

Having made our way through the first eight chapters of this text, we're now well aware that a network consists of *many* complex, interacting pieces of hardware and software—from the links, switches, routers, hosts, and other devices that comprise the physical components of the network to the many protocols (in both hardware and software) that control and coordinate these devices. When hundreds or thousands of such components are cobbled together by an organization to form a network, it is not surprising that components will occasionally malfunction, that network elements will be misconfigured, that network resources will be overutilized, or that network components will simply "break" (for example, a cable will be cut or a can of soda will be spilled on top of a router). The network administrator, whose job it is to keep the network "up and running," must be able to respond to (and better yet, avoid) such mishaps. With potentially thousands of network components spread out over a wide area, the network administrator in a network operations center (NOC) clearly needs tools to help monitor, manage, and control the network. In this chapter, we'll examine the architecture, protocols, and information base used by a network administrator in this task.

9.1 What Is Network Management?

Before diving in to network management itself, let's first consider a few illustrative "real-world" non-networking scenarios in which a complex system with many interacting components must be monitored, managed, and controlled by an administrator. Electrical power-generation plants (at least as portrayed in the popular media in such movies as *The China Syndrome*) have a control room where dials, gauges, and lights monitor the status (temperature, pressure, flow) of remote valves, pipes, vessels, and other plant components. These devices allow the operator to monitor the plant's many components, and may alert the operator (with the famous flashing red warning light) when trouble is imminent. Actions are taken by the plant operator to control these components. Similarly, an airplane cockpit is instrumented to allow a pilot to monitor and control the many components that make up an airplane. In these two examples, the "administrator" *monitors* remote devices and *analyzes* their data to ensure that they are operational and operating within prescribed limits (for example, that a core meltdown of a nuclear power plant is not imminent, or that the plane is not about to run out of fuel), *reactively controls* the system by making adjustments in response to the changes within the system or its environment, and *proactively manages* the system (for example, by detecting trends or anomalous behavior, allowing action to be taken before serious problems arise). In a similar sense, the network administrator will actively monitor, manage, and control the system with which she or he is entrusted.

In the early days of networking, when computer networks were research artifacts rather than a critical infrastructure used by millions of people a day, "network management" was unheard of. If one encountered a network problem, one might run a few pings to locate the source of the problem and then modify system settings, reboot hardware or software, or call a remote colleague to do so. (A very readable discussion of the first major "crash" of the ARPAnet on October 27, 1980, long before network management tools were available, and the efforts taken to recover from and understand the crash is [RFC 789].) As the public Internet and private intranets have grown from small networks into a large global infrastructure, the need to manage the huge number of hardware and software components within these networks more systematically has grown more important as well.

In order to motivate our study of network management, let's begin with a simple example. Figure 9.1 illustrates a small network consisting of three routers and a number of hosts and servers. Even in such a simple network, there are many scenarios in which a network administrator might benefit tremendously from having appropriate network management tools:

♦ *Detecting failure of an interface card at a host or a router.* With appropriate network management tools, a network entity (for example router A) may report to the network administrator that one of its interfaces has gone down. (This is

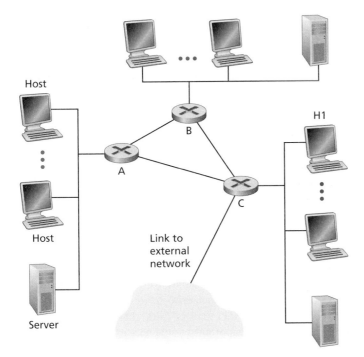

Figure 9.1 ◆ A simple scenario illustrating the uses of network management

certainly preferable to a phone call to the NOC from an irate user who says the network connection is down!) A network administrator who actively monitors and analyzes network traffic may be able to *really* impress the would-be irate user by detecting problems in the interface ahead of time and replacing the interface card before it fails. This might be done, for example, if the administrator noted an increase in checksum errors in frames being sent by the soon-to-die interface.

◆ *Host monitoring.* Here, the network administrator might periodically check to see if all network hosts are up and operational. Once again, the network administrator may really be able to impress a network user by proactively responding to a problem (host down) before it is reported by a user.

◆ *Monitoring traffic to aid in resource deployment.* A network administrator might monitor source-to-destination traffic patterns and notice, for example, that by switching servers between LAN segments, the amount of traffic that crosses multiple LANs could be significantly decreased. Imagine the happiness all around (especially in higher administration) when better performance is achieved with no new equipment costs. Similarly, by monitoring link utilization, a network administrator might determine that a LAN segment or the external link to the outside world is overloaded and that a higher-bandwidth link should thus be provisioned (alas, at an increased cost). The network administrator might also want to be notified automatically when congestion levels on a link exceed a given threshold value, in order to provision a higher-bandwidth link before congestion becomes serious.

♦ *Detecting rapid changes in routing tables.* Route flapping—frequent changes in the routing tables—may indicate instabilities in the routing or a misconfigured router. Certainly, the network administrator who has improperly configured a router would prefer to discover the error him- or herself, before the network goes down.

♦ *Monitoring for SLAs.* With the advent of **Service Level Agreements (SLAs)**—contracts that define specific performance metrics and acceptable levels of network provider performance with respect to these metrics—interest in traffic monitoring has increased significantly over the past few years [Larsen 1997; Huston 1999a]. MCI and Sprint are just two of the many network providers that guarantee SLAs [MCI 2004; Sprint 2004] to their customers. These SLAs include service availability (outage), latency, throughput, and outage notification requirements. Clearly, if performance criteria are to be part of a service agreement between a network provider and its users, then measuring and managing performance will be of great importance to the network administrator.

♦ *Intrusion detection.* A network administrator may want to be notified when network traffic arrives from, or is destined for, a suspicious source (for example, host or port number). Similarly, a network administrator may want to detect (and in many cases filter) the existence of certain types of traffic (for example, source-routed packets, or a large number of SYN packets directed to a given host) that are known to be characteristic of the types of security attacks that we considered in Chapter 8.

The International Organization for Standardization (ISO) has created a network management model that is useful for placing the anecdotal scenarios above in a more structured framework. Five areas of network management are defined:

♦ *Performance management.* The goal of performance management is to quantify, measure, report, analyze, and control the performance (for example, utilization and throughput) of different network components. These components include individual devices (for example, links, routers, and hosts) as well as end-to-end abstractions such as a path through the network. We will see shortly that protocol standards such as the Simple Network Management Protocol (SNMP) [RFC 3410] play a central role in Internet performance management.

♦ *Fault management.* The goal of fault management is to log, detect, and respond to fault conditions in the network. The line between fault management and performance management is rather blurred. We can think of fault management as the immediate handling of transient network failures (for example, link, host, or router hardware or software outages), while performance management takes the longer-term view of providing acceptable levels of performance in the face of varying traffic demands and occasional network device failures. As with perform-ance management, the SNMP protocol plays a central role in fault management.

♦ *Configuration management.* Configuration management allows a network man-ager to track which devices are on the managed network and the hardware and software configurations of these devices. An overview of configuration manage-ment and requirements for IP-based networks can be found in [RFC 3139].

♦ *Accounting management.* Accounting management allows the network manager to specify, log, and control user and device access to network resources. Usage quotas, usage-based charging, and the allocation of resource-access privileges all fall under accounting management.

♦ *Security management.* The goal of security management is to control access to network resources according to some well-defined policy. The key distribution centers and certification authorities that we studied in Section 8.5 are compo-nents of security management. The use of firewalls to monitor and control exter-nal access points to one's network, a topic we studied in section 8.6, is another crucial component.

In this chapter, we'll cover only the rudiments of network management. Our focus will be purposefully narrow—we'll examine only the *infrastructure* for net-work management—the overall architecture, network management protocols, and information base through which a network administrator keeps the network up and running. We'll *not* cover the decision-making processes of the network administra-tor, who must plan, analyze, and respond to the management information that is con-veyed to the NOC. In this area, topics such as fault identification and management [Katzela 1995; Medhi 1997; Steinder 2002], proactive anomaly detection [Thottan 1998], alarm correlation [Jakobson 1993], and more come into consideration. Nor will we cover the broader topic of service management [Saydam 1996; RFC 3052; AT&T SLM 2004]—the provisioning of resources such as bandwidth, server capac-ity, and the other computational/communication resources needed to meet the mis-sion-specific service requirements of an enterprise. In this latter area, standards such as TMN [Glitho 1995; Sidor 1998] and TINA [Hamada 1997] are larger, more encompassing (and arguably much more cumbersome) standards that address this larger issue. TINA, for example, is described as "a set of common goals, principles, and concepts that cover the management of services, resources, and parts of the Dis-tributed Processing Environment" [Hamada 1997]. Clearly, each of these topics is enough for a separate text and would take us a bit far afield from the more technical aspects of computer networking. So, as noted above, our more modest goal here will be to cover the important "nuts and bolts" of the infrastructure through which the network administrator keeps the bits flowing smoothly.

An often-asked question is "What is network management?" Our discussion above has motivated the need for, and illustrated a few of the uses of, network management. We'll conclude this section with a single-sentence (albeit a rather long run-on sentence) definition of network management from [Saydam 1996]:

"Network management includes the deployment, integration, and coordination of the hardware, software, and human elements to monitor, test, poll, configure, analyze, evaluate, and control the network and element resources to meet the real-time, operational performance, and Quality of Service requirements at a reasonable cost."

It's a mouthful, but it's a good workable definition. In the following sections, we'll add some meat to this rather bare-bones definition of network management.

9.2 The Infrastructure for Network Management

We've seen in the preceding section that network management requires the ability to "monitor, test, poll, configure, . . . and control" the hardware and software components in a network. Because the network devices are distributed, this will, at a minimum, require that the network administrator be able to gather data (for example, for monitoring purposes) from a remote entity and be able to effect changes at that remote entity (for example, control it). A human analogy will prove useful here for understanding the infrastructure needed for network management.

Imagine that you're the head of a large organization that has branch offices around the world. It's your job to make sure that the pieces of your organization are operating smoothly. How will you do so? At a minimum, you'll periodically gather data from your branch offices in the form of reports and various quantitative measures of activity, productivity, and budget. You'll occasionally (but not always) be explicitly notified when there's a problem in one of the branch offices; the branch manager who wants to climb the corporate ladder (perhaps to get your job) may send you unsolicited reports indicating how smoothly things are running at his or her branch. You'll sift through the reports you receive, hoping to find smooth operations everywhere but no doubt finding problems in need of your attention. You might initiate a one-on-one dialogue with one of your problem branch offices, gather more data in order to understand the problem, and then pass down an executive order ("Make this change!") to the branch office manager.

Implicit in this very common human scenario is an infrastructure for controlling the organization—the boss (you), the remote sites being controlled (the branch offices), your remote agents (the branch office managers), communication protocols (for transmitting standard reports and data, and for one-on-one dialogues), and data (the report contents and the quantitative measures of activity, productivity, and budget). Each of these components in human organizational management has a counterpart in network management.

The architecture of a network management system is conceptually identical to this simple human organizational analogy. The network management field has its own specific terminology for the various components of a network management architecture, and so we adopt that terminology here. As shown in Figure 9.2, there are three principal components of a network management architecture: a managing entity (the boss in our analogy above—you), the managed devices (the branch office), and a network management protocol.

The **managing entity** is an application, typically with a human in the loop, running in a centralized network management station in the network operations center (NOC). The managing entity is the locus of activity for network management; it controls the collection, processing, analysis, and/or display of network management information. It is here that actions are initiated to control network behavior and here that the human network administrator interacts with the network devices.

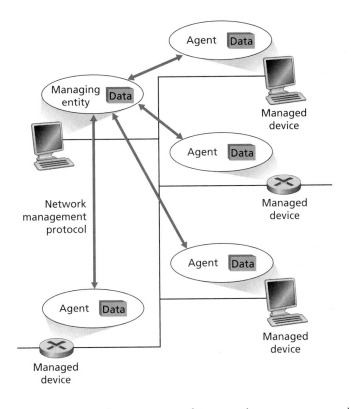

Figure 9.2 ♦ Principal components of a network management architecture

A **managed device** is a piece of network equipment (including its software) that resides on a managed network. This is the branch office in our human analogy. A managed device might be a host, router, bridge, hub, printer, or modem. Within a managed device, there may be several so-called **managed objects.** These managed objects are the actual pieces of hardware within the managed device (for example, a network interface card), and the sets of configuration parameters for the pieces of hardware and software (for example, an intradomain routing protocol such as RIP). In our human analogy, the managed objects might be the departments within the branch office. These managed objects have pieces of information associated with them that are collected into a **Management Information Base (MIB);** we'll see that the values of these pieces of information are available to (and in many cases able to be set by) the managing entity. In our human analogy, the MIB corresponds to quantitative data (measures of activity, productivity, and budget, with the latter being settable by the managing entity!) exchanged between the branch office and the main office. We'll study MIBs in detail in Section 9.3. Finally, also resident in each managed device is a **network management agent,** a process running in the managed device that communicates with the managing entity, taking local actions at the managed device under the command and control of the managing entity. The network management agent is the branch manager in our human analogy.

The third piece of a network management architecture is the **network management protocol.** The protocol runs between the managing entity and the managed devices, allowing the managing entity to query the status of managed devices and indirectly take actions at these devices via its agents. Agents can use the network management protocol to inform the managing entity of exceptional events (for example, component failures or violation of performance thresholds). It's important to note that the network management protocol does not itself manage the network. Instead, it provides a tool with which the network administrator can manage ("monitor, test, poll, configure, analyze, evaluate, and control") the network. This is a subtle, but important, distinction.

Although the infrastructure for network management is conceptually simple, one can often get bogged down with the network-management-speak vocabulary of "managing entity," "managed device," "managing agent," and "management information base." For example, in network-management-speak, in our simple host-monitoring scenario, "managing agents" located at "managed devices" are periodically queried by the "managing entity"—a simple idea, but a linguistic mouthful! With any luck, keeping in mind the human organizational analogy and its obvious parallels with network management will be of help as we continue through this chapter.

Our discussion of network management architecture above has been generic, and broadly applies to a number of the network management standards and efforts that have been proposed over the years. Network management standards began maturing in the late 1980s, with OSI **CMISE/CMIP** (the **Common Management Information Services Element/Common Management Information Protocol**) [Piscatello 1993; Stallings 1993; Glitho 1998] and the Internet **SNMP (Simple**

SPRINTLINK'S NETWORK OPERATIONS CENTER

Networks come in all sizes, and from the smallest home network to the largest tier-1 ISP, it is the job of the network operator(s) to ensure that the network is operating smoothly. But what happens in a network operations center (NOC), and what does a network operator actually do?

With a global IP network (known as Sprintlink, http://www.sprintlink.net/) of approximately 65 IP-level PoPs (Points of Presence, locations containing Sprintlink IP routers) and 700 routers, Sprint is one of the planet's largest tier-1 ISPs. Sprintlink's NOC is located in Reston VA. Sprint also maintains NOCs for its ATM network, frame-relay network, and underlying fiber plant. At any one time, a small team of four network operators manages the core of the Sprintlink IP network, with another dozen or so individuals working in IP service assurance. Automation – in monitoring, configuration management, ticket (reported problem) generation and management, alarm correlation, fault-identification, and service restoration – make it possible for this remarkably small group of operators to manage such a large and complex network.

Sprint technicians monitor the health of the network in operations centers such as the one pictured above.

(continues)

When problems do occur, a Sprintlink operator's principal focus in on maintaining, or quickly restoring, service to customers. NOC operators perform triage, diagnosis, and restoration, following a well-defined/documented set of procedures in response to a known set of problems and/or symptoms. Problems that are not immediately diagnosable, or can not be fixed by operators within a level-of-severity-specific time frame (e.g., 15 minutes) are referred to on-call members of Sprint's National Technical Assistance Center (NTAC). NTAC members are responsible for diving deeper into the root causes of problems; they also write procedures for the NOC operators, and work with equipment suppliers (e.g., router vendors) to diagnose and fix equipment-related problems, as needed. Approximately 70% of problems are handled directly by NOC operators. NOC and NTAC staff interact with other individuals as well, including staff in the NOCs of Sprint customer networks, Sprint staff in field locations who provide on-site "eyes, hands, and ears," and staff in the NOCs of peer networks.

As discussed earlier in this chapter, "network management" within Sprintlink (as well as other ISPs) has evolved from fault management to performance management to service management, with an increasing emphasis on customer needs. While focusing on customer needs, Sprint operators also take great pride in operational excellence and their role in maintaining and safeguarding the global network infrastructure of one of the world's largest ISPs.

Network Management Protocol) [RFC 3410; Stallings 1999; Rose 1996] emerging as the two most important standards [Miller 1997; Subramanian 2000]. Both are designed to be independent of vendor-specific products or networks. Because SNMP was quickly designed and deployed at a time when the need for network management was becoming painfully clear, SNMP found widespread use and acceptance. Today, SNMP has emerged as the most widely used and deployed network management framework. We'll cover SNMP in detail in the following section.

9.3 The Internet-Standard Management Framework

Contrary to what the name SNMP (Simple Network Management Protocol) might suggest, network management in the Internet is much more than just a protocol for moving management data between a management entity and its agents, and has grown to be much more complex than the word "simple" might suggest. The current Internet-Standard Management Framework traces its roots back to the Simple Gateway Monitoring Protocol, SGMP [RFC 1028]. SGMP was designed by a group of university network researchers, users, and managers, whose experience with SGMP allowed them to design, implement, and deploy SNMP in just a few months [Lynch

1993]—a far cry from today's rather drawn-out standardization process. Since then, SNMP has evolved from SNMPv1 through SNMPv2 to the most recent version, SNMPv3 [RFC 3410], released in April 1999 and updated in December 2002.

When describing any framework for network management, certain questions must inevitably be addressed:

♦ What (from a semantic viewpoint) is being monitored? And what form of control can be exercised by the network administrator?

♦ What is the specific form of the information that will be reported and/or exchanged?

♦ What is the communication protocol for exchanging this information?

Recall our human organizational analogy from the previous section. The boss and the branch managers will need to agree on the measures of activity, productivity, and budget used to report the branch office's status. Similarly, they'll need to agree on the actions the boss can take (for example, cut the budget, order the branch manager to change some aspect of the office's operation, or fire the staff and shut down the branch office). At a lower level of detail, they'll need to agree on the form in which this data is reported. For example, in what currency (dollars, euros?) will the budget be reported? In what units will productivity be measured? While these may seem like trivial details, they must be agreed upon, nonetheless. Finally, the manner in which information is conveyed between the main office and the branch offices (that is, their communication protocol) must be specified.

The Internet-Standard Management Framework addresses the questions posed above. The framework consists of four parts:

♦ Definitions of *network management objects* known as MIB objects. In the Internet network management framework, management information is represented as a collection of managed objects that together form a virtual information store, known as the Management Information Base (MIB). An MIB object might be a counter, such as the number of IP datagrams discarded at a router due to errors in an IP datagram header, or the number of carrier sense errors in an Ethernet interface card; descriptive information such as the version of the software running on a DNS server; status information such as whether a particular device is functioning correctly; or protocol-specific information such as a routing path to a destination. MIB objects thus define the management information maintained by a managed device. Related MIB objects are gathered into **MIB modules.** In our human organization analogy, the MIB defines the information conveyed between the branch office and the main office.

♦ A *data definition language,* known as SMI (Structure of Management Information) that defines the data types, an object model, and rules for writing and revising management information. MIB objects are specified in this data definition language. In our human organizational analogy, the SMI is used to define the details of the *format* of the information to be exchanged.

♦ A *protocol, SNMP,* for conveying information and commands between a managing entity and an agent executing on behalf of that entity within a managed network device.

♦ *Security and administration capabilities.* The addition of these capabilities represents the major enhancement in SNMPv3 over SNMPv2.

The Internet network management architecture is thus modular by design, with a protocol-independent data definition language and MIB, and an MIB-independent protocol. Interestingly, this modular architecture was first put in place to ease the transition from an SNMP-based network management to a network management framework being developed by the International Organization for Standardization (ISO), the competing network management architecture when SNMP was first conceived—a transition that never occurred. Over time, however, SNMP's design modularity has allowed it to evolve through three major revisions, with each of the four major parts of SNMP discussed above evolving independently. Clearly, the right decision about modularity was made, even if for the wrong reason!

In the following subsections, we cover the four major components of the Internet-standard management framework in more detail.

9.3.1 Structure of Management Information: SMI

The **Structure of Management Information, SMI** (a rather oddly named component of the network management framework whose name gives no hint of its functionality), is the language used to define the management information residing in a managed-network entity. Such a definition language is needed to ensure that the syntax and semantics of the network management data are well defined and unambiguous. Note that the SMI does not define a specific instance of the data in a managed-network entity, but rather the language in which such information is specified. The documents describing the SMI for SNMPv3 (which rather confusingly, is called SMIv2) are [RFC 2578; RFC 2579; RFC 2580]. Let's examine the SMI in a bottom-up manner, starting with the base data types in the SMI. We'll then look at how managed objects are described in SMI, then how related managed objects are grouped into modules.

SMI Base Data Types

RFC 2578 specifies the basic data types in the SMI MIB module-definition language. Although the SMI is based on the ASN.1 (Abstract Syntax Notation One) [ISO 1987; ISO X.680 1998] object-definition language (see Section 9.4), enough SMI-specific data types have been added that SMI should be considered a data definition language in its own right. The 11 basic data types defined in RFC 2578 are shown in Table 9.1. In addition to these scalar objects, it is also possible to impose a tabular structure on an ordered collection of MIB objects using the SEQUENCE OF construct; see RFC 2578 for details. Most of the data types in Table 9.1 will be familiar (or self-explanatory) to most readers. The one data type we will discuss in more detail shortly is the OBJECT IDENTIFIER data type, which is used to name an object.

SMI Higher-Level Constructs

In addition to the basic data types, the SMI data definition language also provides higher-level language constructs.

The OBJECT-TYPE construct is used to specify the data type, status, and semantics of a managed object. Collectively, these managed objects contain the management data that lie at the heart of network management. There are more than 10,000 defined objects in various Internet RFCs [RFC 3410]. The OBJECT-TYPE construct has four clauses. The SYNTAX clause of an OBJECT-TYPE definition specifies the basic data type associated with the object. The MAX-ACCESS clause

Data type	Description
INTEGER	32-bit integer, as defined in ASN.1, with a value between -2^{31} and $2^{31} - 1$ inclusive, or a value from a list of possible named constant values.
Integer32	32-bit integer with a value between -2^{31} and $2^{31} - 1$ inclusive.
Unsigned32	Unsigned 32-bit integer in the range 0 to $2^{32} - 1$ inclusive.
OCTET STRING	ASN.1-format byte-string representing arbitrary binary or textual data, up to 65535 bytes long.
OBJECT IDENTIFIER	ASN.1-format administratively assigned (structured name); see Section 9.3.2
IPaddress	32-bit Internet address, in network-byte order.
Counter32	32-bit counter that increases from 0 to $2^{32} - 1$ and then wraps around to 0.
Counter64	64-bit counter.
Gauge32	32-bit integer that will not count above $2^{32} - 1$ nor decrease beyond 0 when increased or decreased.
TimeTicks	Time, measured in 1/100ths of a second since some event.
Opaque	Uninterpreted ASN.1 string, needed for backward compatibility.

Table 9.1 ◆ Basic data types of the SMI

specifies whether the managed object can be read, be written, be created, or have its value included in a notification. The STATUS clause indicates whether the object definition is current and valid, obsolete (in which case it should not be implemented, as its definition is included for historical purposes only), or deprecated (obsolete, but implementable for interoperability with older implementations). The DESCRIP-TION clause contains a human-readable textual definition of the object; this "docu-ments" the purpose of the managed object and should provide all the semantic information needed to implement the managed object.

As an example of the OBJECT-TYPE construct, consider the `ipInDelivers` object-type definition from RFC 2011. This object defines a 32-bit counter that keeps track of the number of IP datagrams that were received at the managed device and were successfully delivered to an upper-layer protocol. The final line of this definition is concerned with the name of this object, a topic we'll consider in the following subsection.

```
ipInDelivers OBJECT-TYPE
    SYNTAX          Counter32
    MAX-ACCESS      read-only
    STATUS          current
    DESCRIPTION
            "The total number of input datagrams
            successfully delivered to IP user-protocols
            (including ICMP)."
    ::= { ip 9 }
```

The MODULE-IDENTITY construct allows related objects to be grouped together within a "module." For example, RFC 2011 specifies the MIB module that defines managed objects (including `ipInDelivers`) for managing implementa-tions of the Internet Protocol (IP) and its associated Internet Control Message Proto-col (ICMP). RFC 2012 specifies the MIB module for TCP, and RFC 2013 specifies the MIB module for UDP. RFC 2021 defines the MIB module for RMON remote monitoring. In addition to containing the OBJECT-TYPE definitions of the man-aged objects within the module, the MODULE-IDENTITY construct contains clauses to document contact information of the author of the module, the date of the last update, a revision history, and a textual description of the module. As an exam-ple, consider the module definition for management of the IP protocol:

```
ipMIB MODULE-IDENTITY
    LAST-UPDATED "9411010000Z"
    ORGANIZATION "IETF SNMPv2 Working Group"
    CONTACT-INFO
            "           Keith McCloghrie
            Postal: Cisco Systems, Inc.
```

```
                170 West Tasman Drive
                San Jose, CA 95134-1706
                US
        Phone:  +1 408 526 5260
        E-mail: kzm@cisco.com"
DESCRIPTION
        "The MIB module for managing IP and ICMP
        implementations, but excluding their
        management of IP routes."
REVISION "9103310000Z"
DESCRIPTION
        "The initial revision of this MIB module
        was part of MIB-II."
::= { mib-2 48}
```

The NOTIFICATION-TYPE construct is used to specify information regarding "SNMPv2-Trap" and "InformationRequest" messages generated by an agent, or a managing entity; see Section 9.3.3. This information includes a textual DESCRIPTION of when such messages are to be sent, as well as list of values to be included in the message generated; see [RFC 2578] for details. The MODULE-COMPLIANCE construct defines the set of managed objects within a module that an agent must implement. The AGENT-CAPABILITIES construct specifies the capabilities of agents with respect to object- and event-notification definitions.

9.3.2 Management Information Base: MIB

As noted above, the **Management Information Base, MIB,** can be thought of as a virtual information store, holding managed objects whose values collectively reflect the current "state" of the network. These values may be queried and/or set by a managing entity by sending SNMP messages to the agent that is executing in a managed device on behalf of the managing entity. Managed objects are specified using the OBJECT-TYPE SMI construct discussed above and gathered into **MIB modules** using the MODULE-IDENTITY construct.

The IETF has been busy standardizing the MIB modules associated with routers, hosts, and other network equipment. This includes basic identification data about a particular piece of hardware, and management information about the device's network interfaces and protocols. As of 2004 there were more than 100 standards-based MIB modules and an even larger number of vendor-specific (private) MIB modules. With all of these standards, the IETF needed a way to identify and name the standardized modules as well as the specific managed objects within a module. Rather than start from scratch, the IETF adopted a standardized object identification (naming) framework that had already been put in place by the International Organization for Standardization (ISO). As is the case with many standards bodies, the ISO had "grand plans" for their standardized object identification framework—to identify every possible standardized object (for example, data format, protocol, or piece of information) in any network, regardless of the network standards organization (for example, Internet IETF, ISO, IEEE, or ANSI), equipment manufacturer, or network owner. A lofty goal indeed! The object identification framework adopted by ISO is part of the ASN.1 (Abstract Syntax Notation One) [ISO 1987; ISO X.680 1998] object definition language that we'll discuss in Section 9.4. Standardized MIB modules have their own cozy corner in this all-encompassing naming framework, as discussed below.

As shown in Figure 9.3, objects are named in the ISO naming framework in a hierarchical manner. Note that each branch point in the tree has both a name and a number (shown in parentheses); any point in the tree is thus identifiable by the sequence of names or numbers that specify the path from the root to that point in the identifier tree. A fun, but incomplete and unofficial, Web-based utility for traversing part of the object identifier tree (using branch information contributed by volunteers) may be found in [Alvestrand 1997].

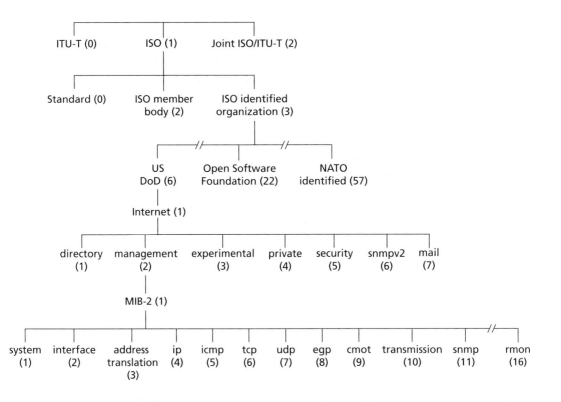

Figure 9.3 ♦ ASN.1 Object identifier tree

At the top of the hierarchy are the ISO and the Telecommunication Standardization Sector of the International Telecommunication Union (ITU-T), the two main standards organizations dealing with ASN.1, as well as a branch for joint efforts by these two organizations. Under the ISO branch of the tree, we find entries for all ISO standards (1.0) and for standards issued by standards bodies of various ISO-member countries (1.2). Although not shown in Figure 9.3, under (ISO member body, a.k.a. 1.2) we would find USA (1.2.840), under which we would find a number of IEEE, ANSI, and company-specific standards. These include RSA (1.2.840.11359) and Microsoft (1.2.840.113556), under which we find the Microsoft File Formats (1.2.840.113556.4) for various Microsoft products, such as Word (1.2.840.113556.4.2). But we are interested here in networking (*not* Microsoft Word files), so let us turn our attention to the branch labeled 1.3, the standards issued by bodies recognized by the ISO. These include the U.S. Department of Defense (6) (under which we will find the Internet standards), the Open Software Foundation (22), the airline association SITA (69), and NATO-identified bodies (57), as well as many other organizations.

Under the `Internet` branch of the tree (1.3.6.1), there are seven categories. Under the `private` (1.3.6.1.4) branch, we find a list [IANA 2004b] of the names and private enterprise codes of more than 4,000 private companies that have registered with the Internet Assigned Numbers Authority (IANA) [IANA 2004]. Under the `management` (1.3.6.1.2) and `MIB-2` branches (1.3.6.1.2.1) of the object identifier tree, we find the definitions of the standardized MIB modules. Whew—it's a long journey down to our corner of the ISO name space!

Standardized MIB Modules

The lowest level of the tree in Figure 9.3 shows some of the important hardware-oriented MIB modules (`system` and `interface`) as well as modules associated with some of the most important Internet protocols. RFC 3600 lists all of the standardized MIB modules. While MIB-related RFCs make for rather tedious and dry reading, it is instructive (that is, like eating vegetables, it is "good for you") to consider a few MIB module definitions to get a flavor for the type of information in a module.

The managed objects falling under `system` contain general information about the device being managed; all managed devices must support the system MIB objects. Table 9.2 defines the objects in the system group, as defined in RFC 1213. Table 9.3 defines the managed objects in the MIB module for the UDP protocol at a managed entity.

9.3.3 SNMP Protocol Operations and Transport Mappings

The Simple Network Management Protocol version 2 (SNMPv2) [RFC 3416] is used to convey MIB information among managing entities and agents executing on

Object Identifier	Name	Type	Description (from RFC 1213)
1.3.6.1.2.1.1.1	`sysDescr`	OCTET STRING	"Full name and version identification of the system's hardware type, software operating-system, and networking software."
1.3.6.1.2.1.1.2	`sysObjectID`	OBJECT IDENTIFIER	Vendor-assigned object ID that "provides an easy and unambiguous means for determining 'what kind of box' is being managed."
1.3.6.1.2.1.1.3	`sysUpTime`	TimeTicks	"The time (in hundredths of a second) since the network management portion of the system was last re-initialized."
1.3.6.1.2.1.1.4	`sysContact`	OCTET STRING	"The contact person for this managed node, together with information on how to contact this person."
1.3.6.1.2.1.1.5	`sysName`	OCTET STRING	"An administratively assigned name for this managed node. By convention, this is the node's fully qualified domain name."
1.3.6.1.2.1.1.6	`sysLocation`	OCTET STRING	"The physical location of this node."
1.3.6.1.2.1.1.7	`sysServices`	Integer32	A coded value that indicates the set of services available at this node: physical (for example, a repeater), data link/subnet (for example, bridge), Internet (for example, IP gateway), end-end (for example, host), applications.

Table 9.2 ♦ Managed objects in the MIB-2 system group

behalf of managing entities. The most common usage of SNMP is in a **request-response mode** in which an SNMPv2 managing entity sends a request to an SNMPv2 agent, who receives the request, performs some action, and sends a reply to the request. Typically, a request will be used to query (retrieve) or modify (set) MIB object values associated with a managed device. A second common usage of SNMP is for an agent to send an unsolicited message, known as a **trap message,** to a managing entity. Trap messages are used to notify a managing entity of an exceptional situation that has resulted in changes to MIB object values. We saw earlier in Section 9.1 that the network administrator might want to receive a trap message, for example, when an interface goes down, congestion reaches a predefined level on a link, or some other noteworthy event occurs. Note that there are a number of important trade-offs between polling (request-response interaction) and trapping; see the homework problems.

SNMPv2 defines seven types of messages, known generically as protocol data units—PDUs, as shown in Table 9.4. The format of the PDU is shown in Figure 9.4.

Object Identifier	Name	Type	Description (from RFC 2013)
1.3.6.1.2.1.7.1	`udpInDatagrams`	Counter32	"total number of UDP datagrams delivered to UDP users"
1.3.6.1.2.1.7.2	`udpNoPorts`	Counter32	"total number of received UDP datagrams for which there was no application at the destination port"
1.3.6.1.2.1.7.3	`udpInErrors`	Counter32	"number of received UDP datagrams that could not be delivered for reasons other than the lack of an application at the destination port"
1.3.6.1.2.1.7.4	`udpOutDatagrams`	Counter32	"total number of UDP datagrams sent from this entity"
1.3.6.1.2.1.7.5	`udpTable`	SEQUENCE of UdpEntry	"a sequence of UdpEntry objects, one for each port that is currently open by an application, giving the IP address and the port number used by application"

Table 9.3 ♦ Managed objects in the MIB-2 udp module

SNMPv2 PDU Type	Sender-receiver	Description
`GetRequest`	manager-to-agent	get value of one or more MIB object instances
`GetNextRequest`	manager-to-agent	get value of next MIB object instance in list or table
`GetBulkRequest`	manager-to-agent	get values in large block of data, for example, values in a large table
`InformRequest`	manager-to-manager	inform remote managing entity of MIB values remote to its access
`SetRequest`	manager-to-agent	set value of one or more MIB object instances
`Response`	agent-to-manager or	generated in response to
	manager-to-manager	`GetRequest`,
		`GetNextRequest`,
		`GetBulkRequest`,
		`SetRequest PDU`, or
		`InformRequest`
`SNMPv2-Trap`	agent-to-manager	inform manager of an exceptional event

Table 9.4 ♦ SNMPv2 PDU types

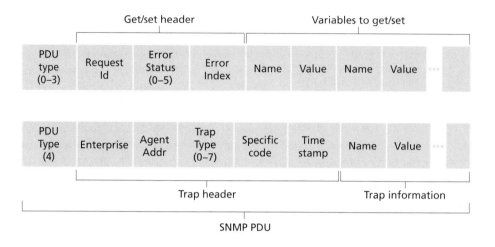

Figure 9.4 ♦ SNMP PDU format

♦ The GetRequest, GetNextRequest, and GetBulkRequest PDUs are all sent from a managing entity to an agent to request the value of one or more MIB objects at the agent's managed device. The object identifiers of the MIB objects whose values are being requested are specified in the variable binding portion of the PDU. GetRequest, GetNextRequest, and GetBulkRequest differ in the granularity of their data requests. GetRequest can request an arbitrary set of MIB values; multiple GetNextRequests can be used to sequence through a list or table of MIB objects; GetBulkRequest allows a large block of data to be returned, avoiding the overhead incurred if multiple GetRequest or GetNextRequest messages were to be sent. In all three cases, the agent responds with a Response PDU containing the object identifiers and their associated values.

♦ The SetRequest PDU is used by a managing entity to set the value of one or more MIB objects in a managed device. An agent replies with a Response PDU with the "noError" error status to confirm that the value has indeed been set.

♦ The InformRequest PDU is used by a managing entity to notify another managing entity of MIB information that is remote to the receiving entity. The receiving entity replies with a Response PDU with the "noError" error status to acknowledge receipt of the InformRequest PDU.

♦ The final type of SNMPv2 PDU is the trap message. Trap messages are generated asynchronously; that is, they are *not* generated in response to a received request but rather in response to an event for which the managing entity requires notification. RFC 1907 defines well-known trap types that include a cold or warm start by a device, a link going up or down, the loss of a neighbor, or an authentication failure event. A received trap request has no required response from a managing entity.

Given the request-response nature of SNMPv2, it is worth noting here that although SNMP PDUs can be carried via many different transport protocols, the SNMP PDU is typically carried in the payload of a UDP datagram. Indeed, RFC 1906 states that UDP is "the preferred transport mapping." Since UDP is an unreliable transport protocol, there is no guarantee that a request, or its response, will be received at the intended destination. The Request ID field of the PDU is used by the managing entity to number its requests to an agent; an agent's response takes its Request ID from that of the received request. Thus, the Request ID field can be used by the managing entity to detect lost requests or replies. It is up to the managing entity to decide whether to retransmit a request if no corresponding response is received after a given amount of time. In particular, the SNMP standard does not mandate any particular procedure for retransmission, or even if retransmission is to be done in the first place. It only requires that the managing entity "needs to act responsibly in respect to the frequency and duration of retransmissions." This, of course, leads one to wonder how a "responsible" protocol should behave!

9.3.4 Security and Administration

The designers of SNMPv3 have said that "SNMPv3 can be thought of as SNMPv2 with additional security and administration capabilities" [RFC 3410]. Certainly, there are changes in SNMPv3 over SNMPv2, but nowhere are those changes more evident than in the area of administration and security. The central role of security in SNMPv3 was particularly important, since the lack of adequate security resulted in SNMP being used primarily for monitoring rather than control (for example, `SetRequest` is rarely used in SNMPv1).

As SNMP has matured through three versions, its functionality has grown but so too, alas, has the number of SNMP-related standards documents. This is evidenced by the fact that there is even now an RFC [RFC 3411] that "describes an architecture for describing SNMP Management Frameworks"! While the notion of an "architecture" for "describing a framework" might be a bit much to wrap one's mind around, the goal of RFC 3411 is an admirable one—to introduce a common language for describing the functionality and actions taken by an SNMPv3 agent or managing entity. The architecture of an SNMPv3 entity is straightforward, and a tour through the architecture will serve to solidify our understanding of SNMP.

So-called **SNMP applications** consist of a command generator, notification receiver, and proxy forwarder (all of which are typically found in a managing entity); a command responder and notification originator (both of which are typically found in an agent); and the possibility of other applications. The command generator generates the `GetRequest`, `GetNextRequest`, `GetBulkRequest`, and `SetRequest` PDUs that we examined in Section 9.3.3 and handles the received responses to these PDUs. The command responder executes in an agent and receives, processes, and replies (using the `Response` message) to received `GetRequest`, `GetNextRequest`, `GetBulkRequest`, and `SetRequest` PDUs. The notification originator application in an agent generates `Trap` PDUs; these PDUs are eventually received and processed in a notification receiver application at a managing entity. The proxy forwarder application forwards request, notification, and response PDUs.

A PDU sent by an SNMP application next passes through the SNMP "engine" before it is sent via the appropriate transport protocol. Figure 9.5 shows how a PDU generated by the command generator application first enters the dispatch module, where the SNMP version is determined. The PDU is then processed in the message-processing system, where the PDU is wrapped in a message header containing the SNMP version number, a message ID, and message size information. If encryption or authentication is needed, the appropriate header fields for this information are included as well; see [RFC 3411] for details. Finally, the SNMP message (the application-generated PDU plus the message header information) is passed to the

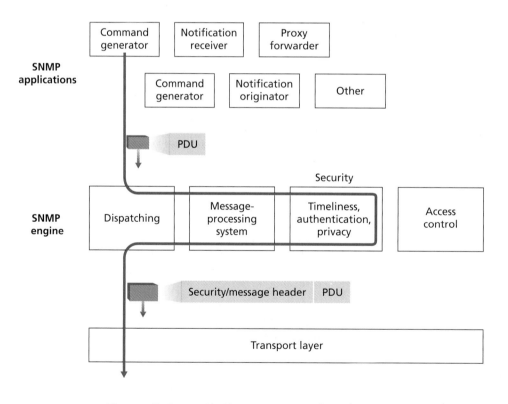

Figure 9.5 ◆ SNMPv3 engine and applications

appropriate transport protocol. The preferred transport protocol for carrying SNMP messages is UDP (that is, SNMP messages are carried as the payload in a UDP datagram), and the preferred port number for the SNMP is port 161. Port 162 is used for trap messages.

We have seen above that SNMP messages are used not just to monitor, but also to control (for example, through the `SetRequest` command) network elements. Clearly, an intruder that could intercept SNMP messages and/or generate its own SNMP packets into the management infrastructure could wreak havoc in the network. Thus, it is crucial that SNMP messages be transmitted securely. Surprisingly, it is only in the most recent version of SNMP that security has received the attention that it deserves. SNMPv3 security is known as **user-based security** [RFC 3414] in that there is the traditional concept of a user, identified by a username, with which security information such as a password, key value, or access privileges are associated. SNMPv3 provides for encryption, authentication, protection against playback attacks (see Sections 8.2 and 8.3), and access control.

PRINCIPLES IN PRACTICE

There are hundreds (if not thousands) of network management products available today, all embodying to some extent the network management framework and SNMP foundation that we have studied in this section. A survey of these products is well beyond the scope of this text and (no doubt) the reader's attention span. Thus, we provide here pointers to a few of the more prominent products. A good starting point for an overview of the breadth of network management tools is Chapter 12 in [Subramanian 2000].

Network management tools can be divided broadly into those from network equipment vendors that specialize in the management of the vendor's equipment, and those aimed at managing networks with heterogeneous equipment. Among the vendor-specific offerings is CiscoWorks2000 [Cisco CiscoWorks 2000], for the management of LANs and WANs built on a Cisco device foundation. Nortel's Optivity Network Management System [Nortel 2004] provides for network management, service management, and policy management (bandwidth management, QoS, application-level security, and IP/address).

Among the popular tools for managing heterogeneous networks are Hewlett-Packard's OpenView [OpenView 2004], Aprisma's Spectrum [Aprisma 2004], and Sun's Solstice network management system [Sun 2004]. All three of these systems adopt a distributed system architecture in which multiple servers gather network management information from their managed domain. The network management station can then gather results from these servers, display information, and take control actions. All three products support the SNMP and CMIP protocols and provide automated assistance for event/alarm correlation.

♦ *Encryption.* SNMP PDUs can be encrypted using the Data Encryption Standard (DES) in cipher-block chaining mode; see Section 8.2 for a discussion of DES. Note that since DES is a shared-key system, the secret key of the user encrypting data must be known by the receiving entity that must decrypt the data.

♦ *Authentication.* SNMP combines the use of a hash function, such as the MD5 algorithm that we studied in Section 8.4, with a secret key value to provide both authentication and protection against tampering. The approach, known as HMAC (Hashed Message Authentication Codes) [RFC 2104], is conceptually simple. Suppose the sender has an SNMP PDU, m, that it wants to send to the receiver. This PDU may have already been encrypted. Suppose also that both the sender and receiver know a shared secret key, K, which need not be the same key used for encryption. The sender will send m to the receiver. However, rather than sending along a simple message digest (see Section 8.4.2) or Message Integrity Code (MIC), $MIC(m)$, that has been computed over m to protect against tampering, the sender appends the shared secret key to m and computes a MIC, $MIC(m,K)$ over the combined PDU and key. The value $MIC(m,K)$ (but not the secret key!) is then transmitted along with m. When the receiver receives m, it appends the secret key, K, and computes $MIC(m,K)$. If this computed value matches the transmitted value of $MIC(m,K)$, then the receiver knows not only that the message has not been tampered with, but also that the message was sent by someone who knows the value of K, that is, by a trusted, and now authenticated, sender. In operation, HMAC actually performs the append-and-hash operation twice, using a slightly modified key value each time; see [RFC 2104] for details.

♦ *Protection against playback.* Recall from our discussion in Chapter 8 that nonces can be used to guard against playback attacks. SNMPv3 adopts a related approach. In order to ensure that a received message is not a replay of some earlier message, the receiver requires that the sender include a value in each message that is based on a counter in the *receiver.* This counter, which functions as a nonce, reflects the amount of time since the last reboot of the receiver's network management software and the total number of reboots since the receiver's network management software was last configured. As long as the counter in a received message is within some margin of error of the receiver's actual value, the message is accepted as a nonreplay message, at which point it may be authenticated and/or decrypted. See [RFC 3414] for details.

♦ *Access control.* SNMPv3 provides a view-based access control [RFC 3415] that controls which network management information can be queried and/or set by which users. An SNMP entity retains information about access rights and policies in a Local Configuration Datastore (LCD). Portions of the LCD are themselves accessible as managed objects, defined in the View-based Access Control Model Configuration MIB [RFC 3415], and thus can be managed and manipulated remotely via SNMP.

9.4 ASN.1

In this book we have covered a number of interesting topics in computer networking. This section on ASN.1, however, may not make the top-ten list of interesting topics. Like vegetables, knowledge about ASN.1 and the broader issue of presentation services is something that is "good for you." ASN.1 is an ISO-originated standard that is used in a number of Internet-related protocols, particularly in the area of network management. For example, we saw in Section 9.3 that MIB variables in SNMP were inextricably tied to ASN.1. So while the material on ASN.1 in this section may be rather dry, we hope the reader will take it on faith that the material *is* important.

In order to motivate our discussion here, consider the following thought experiment. Suppose one could reliably copy data from one computer's memory directly into a remote computer's memory. If one could do this, would the communication problem be "solved"? The answer to the question depends on one's definition of "the communication problem." Certainly, a perfect memory-to-memory copy would exactly communicate the bits and bytes from one machine to another. But does such an exact copy of the bits and bytes mean that when software running on the receiving computer accesses this data, it will see the same values that were stored into the sending computer's memory? The answer to this question is "not necessarily"! The crux of the problem is that different computer architectures, different operating systems, and different compilers have different conventions for storing and representing data. If data is to be communicated and stored among multiple computers (as it is in every communication network), this problem of data representation must clearly be solved.

As an example of this problem, consider the simple C code fragment below. How might this structure be laid out in memory?

```
struct {
   char code;
   int x;
   } test;
test.x = 259;
test.code = 'a';
```

The left side of Figure 9.6 shows a possible layout of this data on one hypothetical architecture: there is a single byte of memory containing the character 'a', followed by a 16-bit word containing the integer value 259, stored with the most significant byte first. The layout in memory on another computer is shown in the right half of Figure 9.6. The character 'a' is followed by the integer value stored with the least significant byte stored first and with the 16-bit integer aligned to start on a 16-bit word boundary. Certainly, if one were to perform a verbatim copy

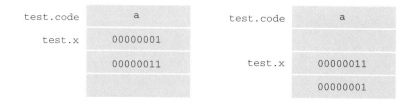

Figure 9.6 ✦ Two different data layouts on two different architectures

between these two computers' memories and use the same structure definition to access the stored values, one would see very different results on the two computers!

The fact that different architectures have different internal data formats is a real and pervasive problem. The particular problem of integer storage in different formats is so common that it has a name. "Big-endian" order for storing integers has the most significant bytes of the integer stored first (at the lowest storage address). "Little-endian" order stores the least significant bytes first. Sun SPARC and Motorola processors are big-endian, while Intel and DEC/Compaq Alpha processors are little-endian. As an aside, the terms "big-endian" and "little-endian" come from the book, *Gulliver's Travels,* by Jonathan Swift, in which two groups of people dogmatically insist on doing a simple thing in two different ways (hopefully, the analogy to the computer architecture community is clear). One group in the land of Lilliput insists on breaking their eggs at the larger end ("the big-endians"), while the other insists on breaking them at the smaller end. The difference was the cause of great civil strife and rebellion.

Given that different computers store and represent data in different ways, how should networking protocols deal with this? For example, if an SNMP agent is about to send a Response message containing the integer count of the number of received UDP datagrams, how should it represent the integer value to be sent to the managing entity—in big-endian or little-endian order? One option would be for the agent to send the bytes of the integer in the same order in which they would be stored in the managing entity. Another option would be for the agent to send in its own storage order and have the receiving entity reorder the bytes, as needed. Either option would require the sender or receiver to learn the other's format for integer representation.

A third option is to have a machine-independent, OS-independent, language-independent method for describing integers and other data types (that is, a data-definition language) and rules that state the manner in which each of the data types is to be transmitted over the network. When data of a given type is received, it is received in a known format and can then be stored in whatever machine-specific format is required. Both the SMI that we studied in Section 9.3 and ASN.1 adopt this third option. In ISO parlance, these two standards describe a **presentation service**—the service of transmitting and translating information from one machine-specific format to another. Figure 9.7 illustrates a real-world presentation problem; neither receiver understands the essential idea being communicated—that the speaker likes something. As shown in Figure 9.8, a presentation service can solve this problem by translating the idea into a commonly understood (by the presentation service), person-independent language, sending that information to the receiver, and then translating into a language understood by the receiver.

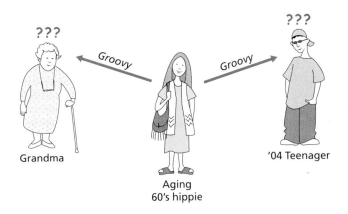

Figure 9.7 ♦ The presentation problem

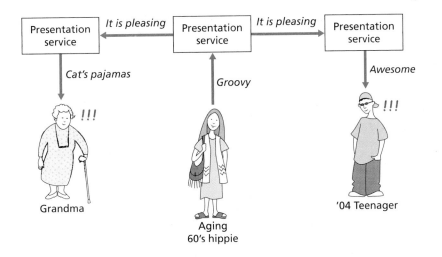

Figure 9.8 ♦ The presentation problem solved

Table 9.5 shows a few of the ASN.1-defined data types. Recall that we encountered the INTEGER, OCTET STRING, and OBJECT IDENTIFIER data types in our earlier study of the SMI. Since our goal here is (mercifully) not to provide a complete introduction to ASN.1, we refer the reader to the standards or to the printed and online book [Larmouth 1996] for a description of ASN.1 types and constructors, such as SEQUENCE and SET, that allow for the definition of structured data types.

In addition to providing a data definition language, ASN.1 also provides **Basic Encoding Rules (BER)** that specify how instances of objects that have been defined using the ASN.1 data definition language are to be sent over the network. The BER adopts a so-called **TLV (Type, Length, Value) approach** to encoding data for transmission. For each data item to be sent, the data type, the length of the data item, and then the actual value of the data item are sent, in that order. With this simple convention, the received data is essentially self-identifying.

Figure 9.9 shows how the two data items in a simple example would be sent. In this example, the sender wants to send the character string "smith" followed by the value 259 decimal (which equals 00000001 00000011 in binary, or a byte value of 1 followed by a byte value of 3), assuming big-endian order. The first byte in the transmitted stream has the value 4, indicating that the type of the following data item is an OCTET STRING; this is the "T" in the TLV encoding. The second byte in the stream contains the length of the OCTET STRING, in this case 5. The third byte in the transmitted stream begins the OCTET STRING of length 5; it contains the ASCII representation of the letter "s." The T, L, and V values of the next data item are 2 (the INTEGER type tag value), 2 (that is, an integer of length 2 bytes), and the two-byte big-endian representation of the value 259 decimal.

In our discussion above, we have only touched on a small and simple subset of ASN.1. Resources for learning more about ASN.1 include the ASN.1 standards

Tag	Type	Description
1	BOOLEAN	value is "true" or "false"
2	INTEGER	can be arbitrarily large
3	BITSTRING	list of one or more bits
4	OCTET STRING	list of one or more bytes
5	NULL	no value
6	OBJECT IDENTIFIER	name, in the ASN.1 standard naming tree, see Section 9.2.2
9	REAL	floating point

Table 9.5 ♦ Selected ASN.1 data types

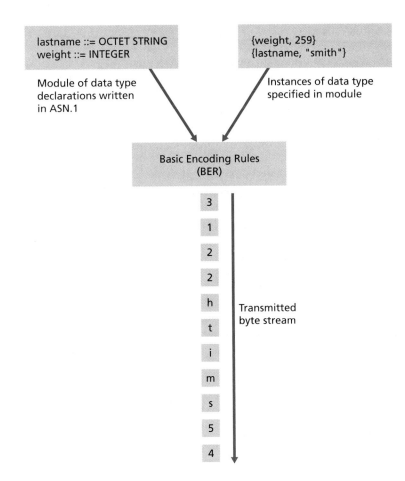

Figure 9.9 ♦ BER encoding example

document [ISO 1987; ISO X.680 1998], the online OSI-related book [Larmouth 1996], and [OSS 2004].

9.5 Conclusion

Our study of network management, and indeed of all of networking, is now complete!

In this final chapter on network management, we began by motivating the need for providing appropriate tools for the network administrator—the person whose job it is to keep the network "up and running"—for monitoring, testing, polling, configuring, analyzing, evaluating, and controlling the operation of the network. Our analogies with the management of complex systems such as power plants, airplanes, and human organization helped motivate this need. We saw that the architecture of network management systems revolves around five key components: (1) a network manager, (2) a set of managed remote (from the network manager) devices, (3) the Management Information Bases (MIBs) at these devices, containing data about the devices' status and operation, (4) remote agents that report MIB information and take action under the control of the network manager, and (5) a protocol for communication between the network manager and the remote devices.

We then delved into the details of the Internet network management framework, and the SNMP protocol in particular. We saw how SNMP instantiates the five key components of a network management architecture and spent considerable time examining MIB objects, the SMI—the data definition language for specifying MIBs, and the SNMP protocol itself. Noting that the SMI and ASN.1 are inextricably tied together, and that ASN.1 plays a key role in the presentation layer in the ISO/OSI seven-layer reference model, we then briefly examined ASN.1. Perhaps more important than the details of ASN.1 itself was the noted need to provide for translation between machine-specific data formats in a network. While some network architectures explicitly acknowledge the importance of this service by having a presentation layer, this layer is absent in the Internet protocol stack.

It is also worth noting that there are many topics in network management that we chose *not* to cover—topics such as fault identification and management, proactive anomaly detection, alarm correlation, and the larger issues of service management (for example, as opposed to network management). While important, these topics would form a text in their own right, and we refer the reader to the references noted in Section 9.1.

Homework Problems and Questions

Chapter 9 • Review Questions

SECTION 9.1

1. Why would a network manager benefit from having network management tools? Describe five scenarios.

2. What are the five areas of network management defined by the ISO?

3. What is the difference between network management and service management?

SECTION 9.2

4. Define the following terms: managing entity, managed device, management agent, MIB, network management protocol.

SECTION 9.3

5. What is the role of the SMI in network management?

6. What is an important difference between a request-response message and a trap message in SNMP?

7. What are the seven message types used in SNMP?

9. What is meant by an "SNMP engine"?

SECTION 9.4

9. What is the purpose of the ASN.1 object identifier tree?

10. What is the role of ASN.1 in the ISO/OSI reference model's presentation layer?

11. Does the Internet have a presentation layer? If not, how are concerns about differences in machine architectures—for example, the different representation of integers on different machines—addressed?

12. What is meant by TLV encoding?

Problems

1. Consider the two ways in which communication occurs between a managing entity and a managed device: request-response mode and trapping. What are the pros and cons of these two approaches, in terms of (1) overhead, (2) notification time when exceptional events occur, and (3) robustness with respect to lost messages between the managing entity and the device?

2. In Section 9.3 we saw that it was preferable to transport SNMP messages in unreliable UDP datagrams. Why do you think the designers of SNMP chose UDP rather than TCP as the transport protocol of choice for SNMP?

3. What is the ASN.1 object identifier for the ICMP protocol (see Figure 9.3)?

4. Suppose you worked for a U.S.-based company that wanted to develop its own MIB for managing a product line. Where in the object identifier tree (Figure 9.3) would it be registered? (Hint: You'll have to do some digging through RFCs or other documents to answer this question.)

5. Suppose Microsoft developed a new file format for a new software product. Where in the object identifier tree would it be registered?

6. Consider Figure 9.9. What would be the BER encoding of {`weight`, `271`} {`lastname`, `"Jackson"`}

7. Consider Figure 9.9. What would be the BER encoding of {`weight`, `296`} {`lastname`, `"Browne"`}?

 **Discussion Questions**

1. Besides a power plant or an airplane cockpit, what is an analogy of a complex distributed system that needs to be controlled?

2. Consider the motivating scenario in Section 9.1. What other activities do you think a network administrator might want to monitor? Why?

3. Read RFC 789. How might the ARPAnet crash of 1980 have been avoided (or its recovery simplified) if the ARPAnet's managers had today's network management tools?

Jeff Case

Jeff Case is the founder and chief technical officer at SNMP Research, Inc. SNMP (Simple Network Management Protocol) is a leading producer of Internet standards and standards-based products for network management. Jeff received two bachelor's degrees (industrial education, electrical engineering technology) and two master's degrees (industrial education, electrical engineering) at Purdue University. He received his PhD in technical education at the University of Illinois, Urbana-Champaign.

Why did you decide to specialize in networking?

I have had a fascination with hooking things together ever since sticking hair pins in power outlets as a toddler. This progressed to an interest in audio equipment during my teen years—making sound systems for rock bands seemingly strong enough to pulverize concrete. While working my way through college as a TV and radio repairman (mostly audio equipment), I got bit by the computer bug, with an interest in everything digital, including both computer hardware and computer software. I became interested in interfacing weird stuff to other weird stuff. First, it was interfacing peripherals to processors. Later, it was interfacing systems to systems. Networking is the ultimate interface. To date, the Internet is the ultimate network.

What was your first job in the computer industry? What did it entail?

Most of my early professional years were at Purdue University. At one time or another, I taught nearly every course in the curriculum for undergraduate electrical and computer engineering technology students. This included creating new courses on the then-emerging topics of microprocessor hardware and software. One semester our class would design a computer from chips, constructing it in the laboratory portion of the course, with one team doing the CPU, another the memory subsystem, and yet another the I/O subsystem, and so on. The next semester we would write the system software for the hardware we had built.

It was during this same time that I began working in a leadership role in campus-wide computing, eventually reporting to the chancellor as the director of academic computer user services.

What is the most challenging part of your job?

Staying up to date with all the changes, both technical and business. I am a very technical manager, and it is increasingly difficult to stay up to date on the technical advances in our industry. My role also requires me to track changes in the business space, such as mergers and acquisitions.

What do you see for the future of networking and the Internet?

More, more, more. More speed. More ubiquity. More content. More tension between anarchy and governance. More spam. More anti-spam. More security problems. More security solutions. Finally, we should expect the unexpected.

What people have inspired you professionally?

My late father, who was a successful businessman; Dilbert; Dr. Vint Cerf, Dr. Jon Postel, Dr. Marshall Rose, and Chuck Davin, who are well-known Internet industry figures; Bill Seifert, now a VC partner; Dr. Rupert Evans, my dissertation professor; my wife, who works with me in the business; and last, but not least, Jesus.

I've read that you have a remarkable collection of "sayings." When you were a CS professor, did you have any sayings you offered students?

"One example is worth two books" (from Gauss, I think).

"Sometimes there is a gap between theory and practice. The gap between theory and practice in theory is not as large as the gap between theory and practice in practice." (I have no idea where this came from.)

What have been the greatest obstacles in creating Internet standards?

Money. Politics. Egos. Leadership failures.

What has been the most surprising use of SNMP technology?

All of them. I really got involved in Internet management to meet my own survival needs. I needed to have some decent tools to manage my organization's networking infrastructure. The widespread success that came from lots of other folks needing to solve similar problems was serendipity, good luck, and lots of hard work. The important thing is that we got the architecture right early on.

References

A URL for the reference is provided wherever possible. While all URLs provided below were valid (and tested) in April 2004. Unfortunately, URLs can become out of date. Please consult the online version of this book (http://www.awl.com/kurose-ross) for an up-to-date bibliography.

A note on Internet Request for Comments (RFCs): Copies of Internet RFCs are maintained at multiple sites. The RFC URLs below all point into the RFC archive at the Information Sciences Institute (ISI), maintained at the RFC Editor of the Internet Society (the body that oversees the RFCs). Other RFC sites include http://www.faqs.org/rfcs, and http://www.csl.sony.co.jp/rfc/ (located in Japan). Internet RFCs can be updated or obsoleted by later RFCs. We encourage you to check the sites listed above for the most up-to-date information. The RFC search facility at ISI, http://www.rfc-editor.org/rfc.html, will allow you to search for an RFC and show updates to that RFC.

[3Com 2004] 3Com Corporation, "Network Interface Cards," http://www.3com.com/products/nics.html

[3GPP 2004] Third Generation Partnership Project, http://www.3gpp.org/

[802.11 Security] The Unofficial 802.11 Security Web Page, http://www.drizzle.com/~aboba/IEEE/

[Abitz 1993] P. Albitz and C. Liu, *DNS and BIND,* O'Reilly & Associates, Petaluma, CA, 1993.

[Abramson 1970] N. Abramson, "The Aloha System—Another Alternative for Computer Communications," *Proceedings of Fall Joint Computer Conference, AFIPS Conference,* p. 37, 1970.

[Abramson 1985] N. Abramson, "Development of the Alohanet," *IEEE Transactions on Information Theory,* Vol. IT-31, No. 3 (Mar. 1985), pp. 119–123.

[Adler 2002] M. Adler, "Tradeoffs in Probabilistic Packet Marking for IP Traceback,*"* *Proceedings of 34th ACM Symposium on Theory of Computing (STOC),* May 2002. http://www.cs.umass.edu/~micah/pubs/traceback.ps

[Adya 2004] A. Adya, W. J. Bolosky, M. Castro, G. Cermak, R. Chaiken, J. R. Douceur, J. Howell, J. R. Lorch, M. Theimer, R. P. Wattenhofer, "FARSITE: Federated, Available, and Reliable Storage for an Incompletely Trusted Environment." *Proceedings of the 5th OSDI,* December 2002. http://research.microsoft.com/~adya/pubs/osdi2002.pdf

[Ahn 1995] J. S. Ahn, P. B. Danzig, Z. Liu, and Y. Yan, "Experience with TCP Vegas: Emulation and Experiment," *Proceedings of ACM SIGCOMM '95* (Boston, MA, Aug. 1995), pp. 185–195. http://www.acm.org/sigcomm/sigcomm95/papers/ahn.html

[Akamai 2004] Akamai homepage, http://www.akamai.com

[Alvestrand 1997] H. Alvestrand, "Object Identifier Registry," http://www.alvestrand.no/harald/objectid/top.html

[Aprisma 2004] Aprisma homepage, http://www.aprisma.com/

[ARIN 1996] ARIN, "IP allocation report," ftp://rs.arin.net/netinfo/ip_network_allocations

[ASO-ICANN 2004] The Address Supporting Organization home page, http://www.aso.icann.org

[Ash 1998] G. R. Ash, *Dynamic Routing in Telecommunications Networks,* McGraw Hill, NY, NY, 1998.

[AT&T SLM 2004] AT&T Business, "AT&T Enterprise Hosting Services Service Guide," http://www.att.com/abs/serviceguide/docs/eh_sg.pdf

[ATM Forum 2004] The ATM Forum Web site, http://www.atmforum.com/

[Ayanoglu 1995] E. Ayanoglu, S. Paul, T. F. La Porta, K. K. Sabnani, R. D. Gitlin, "AIR-MAIL: A Link-Layer Protocol for Wireless Networks," *ACM ACM/Baltzer Wireless Networks Journal*, 1: 47–60, February 1995. http://www.bell-labs.com/user/sanjoy/airmail.ps.Z

[Bakre 1995] A. Bakre, B. R. Badrinath, "I-TCP: Indirect TCP for Mobile Hosts," *Proceedings of the 15th International Conf. on Distributed Computing Systems (ICDCS)*, May 1995, pp. 136–143. ftp://paul.rutgers.edu/pub/badri/itcp-tr314.ps.Z

[Balakrishnan 1995] H. Balakrishnan, S. Seshan, R. H. Katz, "Improving Reliable Transport and Handoff Performance in Cellular Wireless Networks," *ACM Wireless Networks*, 1, no. 4 (December 1995). http://nms.lcs.mit.edu/~hari/papers/winet.ps

[Balakrishnan 1997] H. Balakrishnan, V. Padmanabhan, S. Seshan, R. Katz, "A Comparison of Mechanisms for Improving TCP Performance over Wireless Links," *IEEE/ACM Transactions on Networking* 5, no. 6 (December 1997). http://nms.lcs.mit.edu/~hari/papers/ton.ps

[Baptista 2003] A. Baptista, T. Leen, Y. Zhang, A. Chawla, D. Maier, W. Feng, W. Feng, J. Walpole, C. Silva, J. Freire, # "Environmental Observation and Forecasting Systems: Vision, Challenges and Successes of a Prototype," *Encyclopedia of Physical Science and Technology* (R. A. Meyers, Ed.), Academic Press, Third Edition, Vol. 5., pp 565-581.

[Baran 1964] P. Baran, "On Distributed Communication Networks," *IEEE Transactions on Communication Systems,* Mar. 1964. Rand Corporation Technical report with the same title (Memorandum RM-3420-PR, 1964). http://www.rand.org/publications/RM/RM3420/

[BBC 2001] BBC news online "A Small Slice of Design," April 2001, http://news.bbc.co.uk/1/low/sci/tech/1264205.stm

[Berners-Lee 1989] T. Berners-Lee, CERN, "Information Management: A Proposal," Mar. 1989, May 1990. http://www.w3.org/History/1989/proposal.html

[Berners-Lee 1994] T. Berners-Lee, R. Cailliau, A. Luotonen, H. Frystyk Nielsen, and A. Secret, "The World-Wide Web," *Communications of the ACM,* Vol. 37, No. 8 (Aug. 1994), Pages 76–82

[Bertsekas 1991] D. Bertsekas and R. Gallagher, *Data Networks, 2nd Ed.,* Prentice Hall, Englewood Cliffs, NJ, 1991.

[Bhagwat 2003] P. Bhagwat, B. Raman, D. Sanghi, "Turning 802.11 Inside Out," *Proceedings of the 2003 ACM Hotnets II Workshop*, Cambridge, MA (November 2003). http://nms.lcs.mit.edu/HotNets-II/papers/inside-out.pdf

[Bhimani 1996] Anish Bhimani: "Securing the Commercial Internet," *Communications of the ACM,* Vol. 39 No. 6: 29–35; March 1996

[Biddle 2003] P. Biddle, P. England, M. Peinado, B. Willman, "The Darknet and the Future of Content Distribution." 2002 ACM Workshop on Digital Rights Management, (Nov. 2002, Washington, D.C.) http://crypto.stanford.edu/DRM2002/darknet5.doc

[Biersack 1992] E. W. Biersack, "Performance evaluation of forward error correction in ATM networks," *Proceedings of ACM SIGCOMM '92* (Baltimore, MD 1992), pp. 248–257. http://www.acm.org/pubs/articles/proceedings/comm/144179/p248-biersack/p248-biersack.pdf

[BIND 2004] Internet Software Consortium page on BIND, http://www.isc.org/bind.html

[Bisdikian 2001] C. Bisdikian, "An Overview of the Bluetooth Wireless Technology," *IEEE Communications Magazine*, No. 12 (December 2001): 86–94.

[Bishop 2003] M. Bishop, *Computer Security: Art and Science,* Boston: Addison Wesley, Boston MA, 2003

[Black 1995] U. Black, *ATM Volume I: Foundation for Broadband Networks*, Prentice Hall, 1995.

[Black 1997] U. Black, ATM, Volume II: Signaling in Broadband Networks, Prentice Hall, 1997.

[Blaze 1996] M. Blaze, W. Diffie, R. Rivest, B. Schneier, T. Shimomura, E. Thompson, and M. Weiner, "Minimal Key Lengths for Symmetric Ciphers to Provide Adequate Commercial Security," http://www.counterpane.com/keylength.html

[Bluetooth 2002] R. Morrow, *Bluetooth: Operation and Use*, New York: McGraw-Hill, 2002.

[Bochman 1984] G. V. Bochmann and C. A. Sunshine, "Formal methods in communication protocol design," *IEEE Transactions on Communications,* Vol. COM-28, No. 4 (Apr. 1980), pp. 624–631.

[Bolot 1994] J-C. Bolot and T. Turletti, "A rate control scheme for packet video in the Internet," *Proceedings of IEEE Infocom,* 1994, pp. 1216–1223. ftp://ftp-sop.inria.fr/rodeo/bolot/94.Video_control.ps.gz

[Bolot 1996] J-C. Bolot and Andreas Vega-Garcia, "Control Mechanisms for Packet Audio in the Internet," *Proceedings of IEEE Infocom,* 1996, pp. 232–239. ftp://ftp-sop.inria.fr/rodeo/bolot/96.Audio_ctl.ps.gz

[Boutremans 2002] C. Boutremans, G. Iannaccone, C. Diot, "Impact of Link Failures on VoIP Performance," *12th International Workshop on Network and Operating Systems Support for Digital Audio and Video (NOSSDAV),* Miami, May 2002. http://ipmon.sprint.com/pubs_trs/pubs/gianluca/voip.pdf

[Bradner 1996] S. Bradner, A. Mankin, *IPng: Internet Protocol Next Generation,* Addison-Wesley, Reading, MA, 1996.

[Brakmo 1995] L. Brakmo and L. Peterson, "TCP Vegas: End to End Congestion Avoidance on a Global Internet," *IEEE Journal of Selected Areas in Communications,* Vol. 13, No. 8, pp. 1465–1480, Oct. 1995. ftp://ftp.cs.arizona.edu/xkernel/Papers/jsac.ps.Z

[Brodnik 1997] A. Brodnik, S. Carlsson, M. Degemark, S. Pink, "Small Forwarding Tables for Fast Routing Lookups," *Proceedings of ACM SIGCOMM '97* (Cannes, France, Oct. 1997), pp. 3–15. http://www.acm.org/sigs/sigcomm/sigcomm97/papers/p192.html

[Brown 1997] K. Brown, S. Singh, "M-TCP: TCP for Mobile Cellular Networks," *ACM CCR* 27, no. 5 (1997). http://www.cs.pdx.edu/~singh/ftp/mtcp.ps.gz

[Bryant 1988] B. Bryant, "Designing an Authentication System: A Dialogue in Four Scenes," http://web.mit.edu/kerberos/www/dialogue.html

[Bush 1945] V. Bush, "As We May Think," *The Atlantic Monthly,* July 1945. http://www.theatlantic.com/unbound/flashbks/computer/bushf.htm

[Byers 1998] J. Byers, M. Luby, M. Mitzenmacher, A Rege, "A digital fountain approach to reliable distribution of bulk data," *Proceedings of ACM SIGCOMM '98* (Vancouver, 1998, Aug. 1998), pp. 56–67. http://www.acm.org/sigcomm/sigcomm98/tp/abs_05.html

[Cablelabs 2004] CableLabs homepage, http://www.cablelabs.com

[Caldwell 2004] C. Caldwell, The Prime Pages, http://www.utm.edu/research/primes/prove

[Cardwell 2000] N. Cardwell, S. Savage, T. Anderson, "Modeling TCP Latency," *Proceedings of the 2000 IEEE Infocom Conference*, (Tel-Aviv, Israel), March, 2000. http://www.cs.ucsd.edu/users/savage/papers/Infocom2000tcp.ps

[CASA 2004] Center for Collaborative Adaptive Sensing of the Atmosphere, http://www.casa.umass.edu

[Casner 1992] Casner, S., Deering, S., "First IETF Internet Audiocast," *ACM SIGCOMM Computer Communications Review,* Vol. 22, No. 3 (July 1992), pp. 92–97. http://citeseer.nj.nec.com/casner92first.html

[Ceiva 2004] Ceiva homepage, http://www.ceiva.com/

[CENS 2004] Center for Embedded Network Sensing, http://www.cens.ucla.edu/

[Cerf 1974] V. Cerf and R. Kahn, "A Protocol for Packet Network Interconnection," *IEEE Transactions on Communications Technology,* Vol. COM-22, No. 5, pp. 627–641.

[CERT 1999-04] CERT, "Advisory CA-1999-04: Melissa Macro Virus," http://www.cert.org/advisories/CA-1999-04.html

[CERT 2001-09] CERT, "Advisory 2001-09: Statistical Weaknesses in TCP/IP Initial Sequence Numbers," http://www.cert.org/advisories/CA-2001-09.html

[CERT 2001-19] CERT, "Advisory CA-2001-19: "Code Red"Worm Exploiting Buffer Overflow In IIS Indexing Service DLL," http://www.cert.org/advisories/CA-2001-19.html

[CERT 2003-04] CERT, "CERT Advisory CA-2003-04 MS-SQL Server Worm," http://www.cert.org/advisories/CA-2003-04.html

[CERT 2004] CERT Coordination Center, http://www.cert.org/advisories

[CERT Filtering 2002] CERT, "Packet Filtering for Firewall Systems," http://www.cert.org/tech_tips/packet_filtering.html

[CERT Smurf 1998] CERT(r) Advisory CA-98.01, "smurf IP Denail-of-Service Attacks," http://www.cert.org/advisories/CA-1998-01.html

[Cert SYN 1996] CERT, "Advisory CA-96.21: TCP SYN Flooding and IP Spoofing Attacks," http://www.cert.org/advisories/CA-1998-01.html

[CERT 2004 Summaries] CERT, "CERT Summaries," http://www.cert.org/summaries/

[Chao 2001] H. J. Chao, C. Lam, E. Oki, Broadband Packet Switching Technologies—A Practical Guide to ATM Switches and IP Routers, John Wiley & Sons, 2001.

[Chapman 1992] B. Chapman, "Network (In)Security Through Packet Filtering," *Third UNIX Security Symposium, sponsored by USENIX Association*, (Baltimore, MD), 1992, http://www.greatcircle.com/pkt_filtering.html

[Checkpoint 2004] Checkpoint Web site, http://www.checkpoint.com

[Chen 2000] G. Chen, D. Kotz, "A Survey of Context-Aware Mobile Computing Research," *Technical Report TR2000-381*, Dept. of Computer Science, Dartmouth College, November, 2000. http://www.cs.dartmouth.edu/~dfk/papers/chen:survey-tr.pdf

[Cheswick 2000] Bill Cheswick, Hal Burch, Steve Branigan, "Mapping and Visualizing the Internet," *Proc. 2000 Usenix Conference* (June 2000, San Diego) http://www.usenix.org/publications/library/proceedings/usenix2000/general/full_papers/cheswick/cheswick_html/mapping.html

[Chiu 1989] D. Chiu and R. Jain, "Analysis of the Increase and Decrease Algorithms for Congestion Avoidance in Computer Networks," *Computer Networks and ISDN Systems,* Vol. 17, No. 1, pp. 1–14. http://www.cis.ohio-state.edu/~jain/papers/cong_av.htm

[Christiansen 2001] M. Christiansen, K. Jeffay, D. Ott, F. D. Smith, "Tuning Red for Web Traffic," *IEEE/ACM Transactions on Networking*, Vol. 9, No. 3 (June 2001), pp. 249–264, http://www.cs.unc.edu/~jeffay/papers/IEEE-ToN-01.pdf

[Chu 2000] Y Chu, S. Rao, H. Zhang, "The Case for End System Multicast," *Proceedings of ACM SIGMETRICS 2000,* (Santa Clara, CA, Aug. 2000). http://www.cs.cmu.edu/~sanjay/Papers/sigmetrics-2000.ps.gz

[Cisco 12000 1998] Cisco Systems, "Cisco 12000 Series Gigabit Switch Routers," http://www.cisco.com/univercd/cc/td/doc/pcat/12000.htm

[Cisco 8500 1999] Cisco Systems Inc., "Catalyst 8500 Campus Switch Router Architecture," http://www.cisco.com/univercd/cc/td/doc/product/l3sw/8540/rel_12_0/w5_6f/softcnfg/1cfg8500.pdf

[Cisco CiscoWorks 2000] Cisco Systems, Cisco Works2000 homepage, http://www.cisco.com/warp/public/cc/pd/wr2k/index.shtml

[Cisco NAT 2004] Cisco Systems Inc, "How NAT Works," http://www.cisco.com/warp/public/556/nat-cisco.shtml

[Cisco QoS 2002] Cisco Systems Inc, "Advanced QoS Services for the Intelligent Internet," http://www.cisco.com/warp/public/cc/pd/iosw/ioft/ioqo/tech/qos_wp.htm

[Cisco Queue 1995] Cisco Systems Inc., "Interface Queue Management," http://www.cisco.com/warp/public/614/16.html

[Cisco Security 2004] Cisco Systems Inc., "Why You Need a Firewall," http://www.cisco.com/en/US/products/sw/secursw/ps743/products_user_guide_chapter09186a008007f303.html

[Cisco Switches 1999] Cisco Systems Inc, "Cisco Catalyst 1900/2820 - Affordable Switching Solutions" http://www.cisco.com/warp/public/cc/pd/si/index.shtml

[Cisco Switches 2004] Cisco Systems Inc., "Cisco Switches," http://www.cisco.com/warp/public/cc/pd/si/index.shtml

[CISN 2004] California Integrated Seismic Network, http://www.cisn.org/

[Claffy 1998] K. Claffy, G. Miller, and K. Thompson, "The Nature of the Beast: Recent Traffic Measurements from an Internet Backbone," *Proceedings of Inet '98,* (Geneva, Switzerland, July 1998), http://www.caida.org/outreach/papers/1998/Inet98/

[Clark 1988] D. Clark, " The Design Philosophy of the DARPA Internet Protocols, *Proceedings of ACM SIGCOMM'88,* (Stanford, CA), Aug. 1988, Vol. 18, No. 4, http://www.acm.org/sigcomm/ccr/archive/1995/jan95/ccr-9501-clark.html

[Clarke 2002] I. Clarke, T. W. Hong, S. G. Miller, O. Sandberg, B. Wiley, "Protecting Free Expression Online with Freenet," *IEEE Internet Computing*, January–February 2002, pp. 40–49. http://freenet.sourceforge.net/papers/freenet-ieee.pdf

[Cnet 2000] Cnet news.com, "Leading Web Sites Under Attack," http://news.com.com/2100-1017-236683.html

[Cohen 1977] D. Cohen, "Issues in Transnet Packetized Voice Communication," *Proceedings of the Fifth Data Communications Symposium*, (Snowbird, Utah, September 1977) pp. 6-13.

[Cookie Central 2004] Cookie Central homepage, http://www.cookiecentral.com

[Cormen 2001] T. H. Cormen, *Introduction to Algorithms, 2nd Ed.,* MIT Press, Cambridge, MA, 2001.

[Crow 1997] B. Crow, I. Widjaja, J. Kim, P. Sakai, "IEEE 802.11 Wireless Local Area Networks," *IEEE Communications Magazine,* Sept. 1997, pp. 116–126.

[Crowcroft 1995] J. Crowcroft, Z. Wang, A. Smith, J. Adams, *"A Comparison of the IETF and ATM Service Models,"* *IEEE Communications Magazine,* Nov./ Dec. 1995, pp. 12–16. http://citeseer.nj.nec.com/crowcroft95rough.html

[Crowcroft 1999] J. Crowcroft, M. Handley, and I. Wakeman, *Internetworking Multimedia,* Morgan-Kaufman, San Francisco, 1999.

[Cusumano 1998] M.A. Cusumano and D.B. Yoffie, *Competing on Internet Time: Lessons from Netscape and its Battle with Microsoft,* Free Press, NY, NY, 1998

[Daemen 2000] J. Daemen, V. Rijmen, "The Block Cipher Rijndael," in *Smart Card Research and Applications, LNCS 1820,* (J. J. Quisquater, B. Schneier, eds.), Springer-Verlag, 2000, pp. 288–296.

[Daigle 1991] J. N. Daigle, *Queuing Theory for Telecommunications,* Addison-Wesley, Reading, MA, 1991.

[Dalal 1978] Y. Dalal, R. Metcalfe, "Reverse Path Forwarding of Broadcast Packets," *Communications of the ACM*, Vol. 21, No. 12, (Dec. 1978), pp. 1040-1048.

[Danielyan 2001] E. Danielyan, *"Goodbye DES, Welcome AES,"* *Internet Protocol Journal* 4(2), June 2001. http://www.cisco.com/en/US/about/ac123/ac147/ac174/about_cisco_ipj _archive_issues_list.html

[DEC 1990] Digital Equipment Corporation, "In Memoriam: J. C. R. Licklider 1915–1990," SRC Research Report 61, Aug. 1990. http://www.memex.org/licklider.pdf

[DeClercq 2002] J. DeClercq, O. Paridaens, "Scalability Implications of Virtual Private Networks," *IEEE Communications Magazine*, 40(5), May 2002, pp. 151–157.

[Deering 1990] S. Deering, D. Cheriton, "Multicast routing in datagram internetworks and extended LANs," *ACM Transactions on Computer Systems,* Vol. 8, No. 2 (1990), pp. 85–110.

[Deering 1996] S. Deering, D. Estrin, D. Faranacci, V. Jacobson, C. Liu, L. Wei, "The PIM Architecture for Wide Area Multicasting," *IEEE/ACM Transactions on Networking,* Vol. 4, No. 2 (Apr. 1996), pp. 153–162.

[Demers 1990] A. Demers, S. Keshav, and S. Shenker, "Analysis and Simulation of a Fair Queuing Algorithm," *Internetworking: Research and Experience,* Vol. 1, No. 1, pp. 3–26, 1990.

[Denning 1997] D. Denning (Editor), P. Denning (Preface), *Internet Besieged: Countering Cyberspace Scofflaws,* Addison-Wesley, Reading, MA, 1997.

[dhc 2004] IETF Dynamic Host Configuration working group, http://www.ietf.org/html.charters/dhc-charter.html

[Dialpad 2004] Dialpad homepage, http://www.dialpad.com

[Diffie 1976] W. Diffie and M. E. Hellman, "New Directions in Cryptography," *IEEE Transactions on Information Theory,* Vol IT-22 (1976), pp. 644–654.

[Diffie 1998]W. Diffie and S. Landau, *Privacy on the Line, The Politics of Wiretapping and Encryption,* MIT Press, Cambridge MA, 1998.

[Digital Signature 2004] Digital Signature Trust Company, http://www.trustdst.com/

[Diot 2000] C. Diot, B. N. Levine, B. Lyles, H. Kassem, D. Balensiefen, "Deployment Issues for the IP Multicast Service and Architecture," *IEEE Network,* Vol. 14, No. 1 (Jan./Feb. 2000), pp. 78–88, http://signl.cs.umass.edu/pubs/brian.ieeenetwork00.ps.gz

[Dodge 2004] M. Dodge, "An Atlas of Cyberspaces," http://www.cybergeography.org/atlas/isp_maps.html

[Donahoo 2000] M. Donahoo, K. Calvert, *TCP/IP Sockets in C: Practical Guide for Programmers*, Morgan Kaufman, 2000.

[Dornan 2001] A. Dornan, *The Essential Guide to Wireless Communications Applications: From Cellular Systems to WAP and M-Commerce,* Prentice Hall, Upper Saddle River, N.J., 2001.

[Droms 1999] R. Droms, T. Lemon, *The DHCP Handbook*, Macmillan Technical Publishing, Indianapolis, IN, 1999.

[DSL 2004] DSL Forum, http://www.dslforum.org/

[EFF 1999] Electronic Frontier Foundation, "Frequently Asked Questions (FAQ) About the Electronic Frontier Foundation's DES Cracker Machine," http://www.eff.org/pub/Privacy/Crypto/Crypto_misc/DESCracker/HTML/19980716_eff_des_faq.html

[Elgamal 2001] A. Elgamal, F. Seible, F. Vernon, M. Trivedi, M. Fraser, "On-Line Structural Monitoring and Data Management," *Proceedings, 6th Seismic Research Workshop,* California Department of Transportation, Sacramento, California, June 12–13, 2001. http://www.calit2.net/eci/caltrans_health_monitoring_paper.pdf

[Ellis 1987] H. Ellis, "The Story of Non-Secret Encryption," http://www.cesg.gov.uk/site/publications/media/ellis.pdf

[Ericsson EDGE 2004] Ericsson, "EDGE: Introduction of High-Speed Data in GSM/GPRS Networks." http://www.ericsson.com/products/white_papers_pdf/edge_wp_technical.pdf

[Estrin 1997] D. Estrin, M. Handley, A. Helmy, P. Huang, D. Thaler, "A Dynamic Bootstrap Mechanism for Rendezvous-based Multicast Routing," *Proceedings of IEEE Infocom '98,* (New York, NY, April 1998). http://ceng.usc.edu/~helmy/infocom-bootstrap-99.pdf

[Estrin 1998b] Deborah Estrin, V. Jacobson, D. Farinacci, L. Wei, Steve Deering, Mark Handley, David Thaler, Ching-Gung Liu, Puneet Sharma, A. Helmy, "Protocol Independent Multicast-Sparse Mode (PIM-SM): Motivation and Architecture," work in progress, http://netweb.usc.edu/pim/pimsm/PIM-Arch.ps.gz

[Estrin 2002] D. Estrin, D. Culler, K. Pister, "Connecting the Physical World with Pervasive Networks," *IEEE Pervasive Computing*, 1,1 (Jan.–March 2002).

[Ethereal 2004] Ethereal homepage, http://www.ethereal.com

[Faloutsos 1999] C. Faloutsos, M. Faloutsos, P. Faloutsos, "What Does the Internet Look Like? Empirical Laws of the Internet Topology," *Proceedings of ACM SIGCOMM 1999*, Boston, MA, September 1999.

[Feamster 2004] N. Feamster, J. Winick, J. Rexford, "A Model for BGP Routing for Network Engineering," *Proceedings of 2004 ACM Sigmetrics*, NY, NY (June 2004). http://www.research.att.com/~jrex/papers/whatifatron.pdf

[Feldmeier 1988] D. Feldmeier, "Improving Gateway Performance with a Routing Table Cache," *Proc. 1988 IEEE Infocom Conference* (New Orleans LA, Mar. 1988).

[Feldmeier 1995] D. Feldmeier, "Fast Software Implementation of Error Detection Codes," *IEEE/ACM Transactions on Networking*, Vol. 3., No. 6 (Dec. 1995), pp. 640–652.

[FIPS 1995] Federal Information Processing Standard, "Secure Hash Standard," FIPS Publication 180-1. http://www.itl.nist.gov/fipspubs/fip180-1.htm

[FIPS-46-1 1988] US National Bureau of Standards, "Data Encryption Standard," Federal Information Processing Standard (FIPS) Publication 46-1, Jan. 1988. http://www.itl.nist.gov/fipspubs/fip46-2.htm

[Fletcher 1982] J. G. Fletcher, "An Arithmetic Checksum for Serial Transmissions," *IEEE Transactions on Communications*, Vol. 30, No. 1 (Jan. 1982), pp. 247–253.

[Floyd 1999] S. Floyd and K. Fall, "Promoting the Use of End-to-End Congestion Control in the Internet," *IEEE/ACM Transactions on Networking*, Vol. 6, No. 5 (Oct. 1998), pp. 458–472. http://www.icir.org/floyd/end2end-paper.html

[Floyd 2000] S. Floyd, M. Handley, J. Padhye, J. Widmer, "Equation-Based Congestion Control for Unicast Applications," Proceedings 2000 ACM Sigcomm Conference, (Stockholm, Sweden, Aug. 2000). http://www.icir.org/tfrc/tcp-friendly.pdf

[Floyd 2001] S. Floyd, "A Report on Some Recent Developments in TCP Congestion Control," *IEEE Communications Magazine* (April 2001), http://www.aciri.org/floyd/papers/report_Jan01.pdf

[Floyd 2004] S. Floyd, "References on RED (Random Early Detection) Queue Management," http://www.icir.org/floyd/red.html

[Floyd Synchronization 1994] S. Floyd, V. Jacobson, "Synchronization of Periodic Routing Messages," *IEEE/ACM Transactions on Networking*, Vol. 2, No. 2 (Apr. 1997), pp. 122–136. http://www.aciri.org/floyd/papers/sync_94.ps.Z

[Floyd TCP 1994] S. Floyd, "TCP and Explicit Congestion Notification," *ACM Computer Communication Review*, Vol. 24, No. 5, pp. 10–23, Oct. 1994. http://www.aciri.org/floyd/papers/tcp_ecn.4.ps.Z

[Fluhrer 2001] S. Fluhrer, I. Mantin, A. Shamir, "Weaknesses in the Key Scheduling Algorithm of RC4," *Eighth Annual Workshop on Selected Areas in Cryptography*, Toronto, August 2002. http://www.drizzle.com/~aboba/IEEE/rc4_ksaproc.pdf

[Fortz 2000] B. Fortz, M. Thorup, "Internet Traffic Engineering by Optimizing OSPF Weights," *Proceedings of 2000 IEEE Infocom*. http://www.ieee-infocom.org/2000/papers/165.ps

[Fortz 2002] B. Fortz, J. Rexford, M. Thorup, "Traffic Engineering with Traditional IP Routing Protocols," *IEEE Communication Magazine,* October 2002. http://www.research.att.com/~jrex/papers/ieeecomm02.ps

[Foster 2002] I. Foster, "The Grid: A New Infrastructure for 21st Century Science," *Physics Today,* 55(2):42–47, 2002, http://www.aip.org/pt/vol-55/iss-2/p42.html.

[Freephone 2004] "Freephone: Why use the Plain Old Telephone when you can get so much better on the Internet?" http://www-sop.inria.fr/rodeo/fphone/

[Friedman 1999] T. Friedman, D. Towsley "Multicast Session Membership Size Estimation," *Proc. IEEE Infocom '99* (New York, USA, March 1999) ftp://gaia.cs.umass.edu/pub/Friedman99_Infocom99.ps.gz

[Frost 1994] J. Frost, "BSD Sockets: A Quick and Dirty Primer," http://world.std.com/~jimf/papers/sockets/sockets.html

[Gallager 1983] R. G. Gallager, P. A. Humblet, P. M. Spira, "A Distributed Algorithm for Minimum Weight-Spanning Trees," *ACM Trans. on Programming Languages and Systems,* 1(5), (January 1983), pp. 66–77.

[Gao 2001] L. Gao, J. Rexford, "Stable Internet Routing Without Global Coordination," *IEEE/ACM Trans. Networking,* 9(6), pp. 681–692, December 2001. http://www.research.att.com/~jrex/papers/sigmetrics00.long.pdf

[Garces-Erce 2003] L. Garces-Erce, K. W. Ross, E. Biersack, P. Felber, G. Urvoy-Keller, "TOPLUS: Topology Centric Lookup Service," *Fifth International Workshop on Networked Group Communications (NGC'03)*, Munich, September 2003. http://cis.poly.edu/~ross/papers/TOPLUS.pdf

[Gartner 2003] F. C. Gartner, "A Survey of Self-Stabilizing Spanning-Tree Construction Algorithms," *Technical Report IC/2003/38*, Swiss Federal Institute of Technology (EPFL), School of Computer and Communication Sciences, June 10, 2003. http://ic2.epfl.ch/publications/documents/IC_TECH_REPORT_200338.pdf.

[Gauthier 1999] L. Gauthier, C. Diot, and J. Kurose, "End-to-end Transmission Control Mechanisms for Multiparty Interactive Applications on the Internet," *Proceedings of IEEE Infocom '99,* (New York, NY, Apr. 1999). ftp://ftp.sprintlabs.com/diot/infocom99-mimaze.zip

[Giacopelli 1990] J. Giacopelli, M. Littlewood,W. D. Sincoskie "Sunshine: A high performance self-routing broadband packet switch architecture," *1990 International Switching Symposium.* An extended version of this paper appeared in *IEEE J. Sel. Areas in Commun.,* Vol. 9, No. 8 (Oct. 1991), pp. 1289–1298.

[Girard 1990] A. Girard, *Routing and Dimensioning in Circuit-Switched Networks,* Addison-Wesley, Reading, MA, 1990.

[Glitho 1995] R. Glitho and S. Hayes (eds.), special issue on Telecommunications Management Network, *IEEE Communications Magazine,* Vol. 33, No. 3 (Mar. 1995).

[Glitho 1998] R. Glitho, "Contrasting OSI Systems Management to SNMP and TMN," *Journal of Network and Systems Management,* Vol. 6, No. 2 (June 1998), pp. 113–131.

[Gnutella 2004] "The Gnutella Protocol Specification, v0.4" http://www9.limewire.com/developer/gnutella_protocol_0.4.pdf

[Goodman 1997] David J. Goodman, *Wireless Personal Communications Systems,* Prentice-Hall, 1997

[Goodman 1997b] D. Goodman (Chair), *The Evolution of Untethered Communications,* National Academy Press,Washington DC, Dec. 1997. http://www.nap.edu/readingroom/books/evolution/index.html

[Goralski 1999]W. Goralski, *Frame Relay for High-Speed Networks,* John Wiley, New York, 1999.

[Goralski 2001]W. Goralski, *Optical Networking and WDM,* Osborne/McGraw-Hill, Berkeley, CA, 2001.

[Griffin 2002] T. Griffin, "Interdomain Routing Links," http://www.research.att.com/~griffin/interdomain.html

[Gummadi 2003] K. P. Gummadi, R. J. Dunn, S. Saroiu, S. D. Gribble, H. M. Levy, J. Zahorjan, "Measurement, Modeling, and Analysis of a Peer-to-Peer File-Sharing Workload,"*Proceedings of the 19th ACM Symposium on Operating Systems Principles (SOSP-19),* October 2003.
http://www.cs.washington.edu/homes/tzoompy/publications/sosp/2003/abstract.html

[Gupta 1998] P. Gupta, S. Lin, N. McKeown. "Routing lookups in hardware at memory access speeds," *Proc. IEEE Infocom 1998* (San Francisco, CA, April 1998), pp. 1241–1248. http://tiny-tera.stanford.edu/~nickm/papers/Infocom98_lookup.pdf

[Gupta 2001] P. Gupta, N. McKeown, "Algorithms for Packet Classification," *IEEE Network Magazine,* Vol. 15, No. 2 (Mar./Apr. 2001), pp. 24–32, http://klamath.stanford.edu/~pankaj/paps/ieeenetwork_tut_01.pdf

[Halabi 2000] S. Halabi, *Internet Routing Architectures, 2nd Ed.*, Cisco Press, 2000.

[Hamada 1997] T. Hamada, H. Kamata, S. Hogg, "An Overview of the TINA Management Architecture," *Journal of Network and Systems Management,* Vol. 5. No. 4 (Dec. 1997). pp. 411–435.

[Heidemann 1997] J. Heidemann, K. Obraczka, and J. Touch, "Modeling the Performance of HTTP over Several Transport Protocols," *IEEE/ACM Transactions on Networking,* Vol. 5, No. 5 (Oct. 1997), pp. 616–630. http://www.isi.edu/~johnh/PAPERS/Heidemann96a.html

[Held 2001] G. Held, *Data Over Wireless Networks: Bluetooth, WAP, and Wireless LANs*, McGraw-Hill, 2001.

[Hersent 2000] O. Hersent, D. Gurle, J-P Petit, *IP Telephony: Packet-Based Multimedia Communication Systems*," Pearson Education Limited, Edinburgh, 2000.

[Hinden 2004] R. Hinden, "IP Next Generation (IP ng)," http://playground.sun.com/pub/ipng/html/ipng-main.html

[Holbrook 1999] H. Holbrook, D. Cheriton, "IP Multicast Channels: EXPRESS Support for Large-Scale Single-Source Applications," *Proceedings of ACM SIGCOMM '99* (Boston, MA, Aug. 1999). http://www.acm.org/sigs/sigcomm/sigcomm99/papers/session2-3.html

[Hollot 2002] C.V. Hollot, V. Misra, D. Towsley, W. Gong, "Analysis and design of controllers for AQM routers supporting TCP flows," IEEE Transactions on Automatic Control, Vol. 47, No. 6 (June 2002), pp. 945-959. http://www1.cs.columbia.edu/~misra/pubs/TAC_special.pdf

[Huang 2002] C. Haung, V. Sharma, K. Owens, V. Makam, "Building Reliable MPLS Networks Using a Path Protection Mechanism," *IEEE Communications Magazine,* 40(3), March 2002, pp. 156–162.

[Huitema 1998] C. Huitema, *IPv6: The New Internet Protocol, 2nd Ed.,* Prentice Hall, Englewood Cliffs, NJ, 1998.

[Huston 1999a] G. Huston, "Interconnection, Peering, and Settlements—Part I," *The Internet Protocol Journal,* Vol. 2, No. 1, (March 1999). http://www.cisco.com/warp/public/759/ipj_2-1/ipj_2-1_ps1.html

[Huston 1999b] G. Huston, "Interconnecting, Peering, and Settlements—Part II," *The Internet Protocol Journal,* Vol. 2, No. 2 (June 1999). http://www.cisco.com/warp/public/759/ipj_2-2/ipj_2-2_ps1.html

[Huston 2001] G. Huston, "Analyzing the Internet BGP Routing Table," *The Internet Protocol Journal*, Vol. 4, No. 1 (Mar. 2001), http://www.cisco.com/warp/public/759/ipj_4-1/ipj_4-1_bgp.html

[IAB 2004] Internet Architecture Board, http://www.iab.org/iab/

[IANA 2004] Internet Assigned Number Authority homepage, http://www.iana.org/

[ICANN 2004] The Internet Corporation for Assigned Names and Numbers, http://www.icann.org

[IEC Optical 2003] IEC Online Education, "Optical Access," http://www.iec.org/online/tutorials/opt_acc/

[IEEE 802 2004] "IEEE 802 LAN/MAN Standards Committee," http://www.ieee802.org/

[IEEE 802.11 1999] IEEE 802.11, 1999 Edition (ISO/IEC 8802-11: 1999) IEEE Standards for Information Technology—Telecommunications and Information Exchange Between Systems—Local and Metropolitan Area Network—Specific Requirements—Part 11: Wireless LAN Medium Access Control (MAC) and Physical Layer (PHY) Specification, http://standards.ieee.org/getieee802/download/802.11-1999.pdf

[IEEE 802.15 2004] IEEE 802.15 Working Group for WPAN. http://grouper.ieee.org/groups/802/15/.

[Kaaranen 2001] H. Kaaranen, S. Naghian, L. Laitinen, A. Ahtiainen, Valtteri Niemi, *UMTS Networks: Architecture, Mobility and Services,* New York: John Wiley & Sons, 2001

[IEEE 802.1X] IEEE Std 802.1X-2001 Port-Based Network Access Control, http://standards.ieee.org/reading/ieee/std_public/description/lanman/802.1x-2001_desc.html

[IETF 2004] Internet Engineering Task Force homepage, http://www.ietf.org

[IETF dnsext 2004] IETF DNS Extensions Working Group, http://www.ietf.org/html.charters/dnsext-charter.html

[Interlinknetworks 2004] Interlinknetworks, "Introduction to 802.1x for Wireless Local Area Networks," http://www.interlinknetworks.com/resource/wp5-1-1.htm

[IMAP 2002] The IMAP Connection, http://www.imap.org/

[Interlinknetworks 2004] Internlinknetworks, "Introduction to 802.1x for Wireless Local Area Networks," http://www.interlinknetworks.com/resource/wp5-1-1.htm

[Ioannidis 2000] S. Ioannidis, A. Keromytis, S. Bellovin, J. M. Smith, "Implementing a Distributed Firewall," *Proceedings of the ACM Computer and Communications Security (CCS)* 2000, (Athens, Greece), pp. 190–199, http://www.cis.upenn.edu/~strongman/Papers/df.pdf

[Iren 1999] S. Iren, P. Amer, P. Conrad, "The Transport Layer: Tutorial and Survey," *ACM Computing Surveys,* Vol 31, No 4, (Dec 1999). http://www.cis.udel.edu/~amer/PEL/survey/

[ISC 2004] Internet Systems Consortium, http://www.isc.org

[ISO 1987] International Organization for Standardization, "Information processing systems —Open Systems Interconnection—," International Standard 8824 (Dec. 1987). http://asn1.elibel.tm.fr/en/standards/index.htm

[ISO X.680 1998] International Organization for Standardization, "X.680: ITU-T Recommendation X.680 (1997) | ISO/IEC 8824-1:1998, Information Technology—Abstract Syntax Notation One (ASN.1): Specification of Basic Notation." http://asn1.elibel.tm.fr/en/standards/index.htm

[ITU 2000] International Telecommunication Union, "Recommendation X.509 (11/93) Information technology - Open Systems Interconnection - The Directory: Public-key and attribute certificate frameworks" http://www.itu.int/rec/recommendation.asp?type= items&lang=e&parent=T-REC-X.509-200003-I

[ITU 2004] The ITU Web site, http://www.itu.int/

[ITU Statistics 2004] International Telecommunication Union, "Key Global Telecom Indicators for the World Telecommunication Service Sector," http://www.itu.int/ITU-D/ict/ statistics/at_glance/KeyTelecom99.html

[ITU-T Q.2931 1994] "Broadband Integrated Service Digital Network (B-ISDN) Digital Subscriber Signaling System no.2 (DSS2) User Network Interface Layer 3 Specification for Basic Call/Connection Control," *ITU-T Recommendation Q.2931*, Geneva: International Telecommunication Union, 1994.

[Iyer 2002] S. Iyer, R. Zhang, N. McKeown, "Routers with a Single Stage of Buffering," *Proceedings 2002 ACM Sigcomm Conference,* http://www.acm.org/sigs/sigcomm/ sigcomm2002/papers/routersingle.pdf.

[Jacobson 1988] V. Jacobson, "Congestion Avoidance and Control," *Proceedings of ACM SIGCOMM '88,* (Stanford, CA, Aug. 1988), pp. 314–329, ftp://ftp.ee.lbl.gov/papers/ congavoid.ps.Z

[Jain 1989] R. Jain, "A Delay-Based Approach for Congestion Avoidance in Interconnected Heterogeneous Computer Networks," *ACM Computer Communications Review,* Vol. 19, No. 5 (1989), pp. 56–71. http://www.cis.ohio-state.edu/~jain/papers/delay.htm

[Jain 1994] R. Jain, *FDDI Handbook: High-Speed Networking Using Fiber and Other Media,* Addison-Wesley, Reading, MA, 1994.

[Jain 1996] R. Jain. S. Kalyanaraman, S. Fahmy, R. Goyal, and S. Kim, "Tutorial Paper on ABR Source Behavior," *ATM Forum*/96-1270, Oct. 1996. http://www.cis.ohio-state.edu/ ~jain/atmf/a96-1270.htm

[Jaiswal 2003] S. Jaiswal, G. Iannaccone, C. Diot, J. Kurose, D. Towsley, "Measurement and Classification of Out-of-Sequence Packets in a Tier-1 IP backbone," *Proceedings of 2003 INFOCOM,* ftp://gaia.cs.umass.edu/pub/Jaiswal03_oos.pdf.

[Jakobson 1993] G. Jacobson and M. Weissman, "Alarm Correlation," *IEEE Network Magazine,* 1993, pp. 52–59.

[Ji 2003] P. Ji, Z. Ge, J. Kurose, D. Towsley, "A Comparison of Hard-state and Soft-state Signaling Protocols," *Proceedings of 2003 ACM SIGCOMM,* http://www.acm.org/sigs/ sigcomm/sigcomm2003/papers/p251-ji.pdf

[Jiang 2001] W. Jiang, J. Lennox, H. Schulzrinne, K. Singh, "Towards Junking the PBX: Deploying IP Telephony," *NOSSDAV'01* (Port Jefferson, NY, June 2001). http://www.cs.columbia.edu/~hgs/papers/Jian0106_Junking.pdf

[Jimenez 1997] D. Jimenez, "Outside Hackers Infiltrate MIT Network, Compromise Security," *The Tech,* Vol. 117, No. 49 (Oct. 1997), p. 1. http://www-tech.mit.edu/V117/N49/hackers.49n.html

[Jin 2004] C. Jin, D. X. We, S. Low, "FAST TCP: Motivation, architecture, algorithms, performance," *Proc. IEEE Infocom,* Hong Kong, March 2004, http://netlab.caltech.edu/pub/papers/FAST-csreport2003.pdf.

[Kaaranen 2001] H. Kaaranen, S. Naghian, L. Laitinen, A. Ahtiainen, Valtteri Niemi, *UMTS Networks, Architecture, Mobility and Services,* John Wiley &Sons, 2001.

[Kahn 1967] D. Kahn, *The Codebreakers, the Story of Secret Writing,* The Macmillan Company, 1967.

[Kahn 1978] R. E. Kahn, S. Gronemeyer, J. Burchfiel, R. Kunzelman, "Advances in Packet Radio Technology," *Proc. of the IEEE,* 66, 11 (November 1978).

[Kangasharju 2000] J. Kangasharju, K. W. Ross, and J. W. Roberts, "Performance Evaluation of Redirection Schemes in Content Distribution Networks," *Proceedings of 5th Web Caching and Content Distribution Workshop, Lisbon,* Portugal, May 2000, Lisbon, Portugal. http://www.terena.nl/conf/wcw/Proceedings/S4/S4-2.ps

[Kapoor 1997] H. Kapoor, "CoreBuilder 5000 Switch Module Architecture," 3 Corporation, white paper, number 500645.

[Kar 2000] K. Kar, M. Kodialam, T. V. Lakshman, "Minimum Interference Routing of Bandwidth Guaranteed Tunnels with MPLS Traffic Engineering Applications," *IEEE J. Selected Areas in Communications,* December, 2000.

http://www.bell-labs.com/org/11347A/paper/minint_jsac.pdf

[Karol 1987] M. Karol, M. Hluchyj, A. Morgan, "Input Versus Output Queuing on a Space-Division Packet Switch," *IEEE Transactions on Communications,* Vol. COM-35, No. 12 (Dec. 1987), pp. 1347–1356.

[Katzela 1995] I. Katzela, and M. Schwartz. "Schemes for Fault Identification in Communication Networks," *IEEE/ACM Transactions on Networking,* Vol. 3, No. 6 (Dec. 1995), pp. 753–764.

[Kaufman 1995] C. Kaufman, R. Perlman, M. Speciner, *Network Security, Private Communication in a Public World,* Prentice Hall, Englewood Cliffs, NJ, 1995.

[KaZaA 2004] KaZaA homepage, http://www.kazaa.com

[Kelly 2003] T. Kelly, *Scalable TCP: Improving Performance in Highspeed Wide Area Networks,* http://www-lce.eng.cam.ac.uk/~ctk21/papers/scalable_improve_hswan.pdf.

[Kende 2000] M. Kende, "The Digital Handshake: Connecting Internet Backbones," FCC Report, 2000, http://www.fcc.gov/Bureaus/OPP/working_papers/oppwp32.pdf

[Keshav 1998] S. Keshav, R. Sharma, "Issues and Trends in Router Design," *IEEE Communications Magazine,* Vol. 36, No. 5 (May 1998), pp. 144–151.

[Kilkki 1999] K. Kilkki, *Differentiated Services for the Internet,* Macmillan Technical Publishing, Indianapolis, IN, 1999.

[Kleinrock 1961] L. Kleinrock, "Information Flow in Large Communication Networks," RLE Quarterly Progress Report, July 1961.

[Kleinrock 1964] L. Kleinrock, *1964 Communication Nets: Stochastic Message Flow and Delay,* McGraw-Hill, NY, NY, 1964.

[Kleinrock 1975] L. Kleinrock, *Queuing Systems, Vol. 1,* John Wiley, New York, 1975.

[Kleinrock 1975b] L. Kleinrock and F. A. Tobagi, "Packet Switching in Radio Channels: Part I—Carrier Sense Multiple-Access Modes and Their Throughput-Delay Characteristics," *IEEE Transactions on Communications,* Vol. COM-23, No. 12 (Dec. 1975), pp. 1400–1416.

[Kleinrock 1976] L. Kleinrock, *Queuing Systems, Vol. 2,* John Wiley, New York, 1976.

[Kleinrock 2004] L. Kleinrock, "The Birth of the Internet," http://www.lk.cs.ucla.edu/LK/Inet/birth.html

[Kohler 2004] E. Kohler, M. Handley, S. Floyd, J. Padhye, DCCP homepage, http://www.icir.org/kohler/dccp/

[Korhonen 2003] J. Korhonen, *Introduction to 3G Mobile Communications*, 2nd ed., Artech House, 2003.

[Krishnamurthy 2001] B. Krishnamurthy, and J. Rexford, *Web Protocols and Practice: HTTP/1.1, Networking Protocols, and Traffic Measurement*, Addison-Wesley, Boston, MA, 2001.

[Kurose 1996] J. F. Kurose, Unix Network Programming, http://manic.cs.umass.edu/~amldemo/courseware/intro.html

[Labovitz 1997] C. Labovitz, G. R. Malan, F. Jahanian, "Internet Routing Instability," *Proceedings of ACM SIGCOMM '97* (Cannes, France, 1997), Pages 115–126. http://www.acm.org/sigcomm/sigcomm97/papers/p109.html

[Labrador 1999] M. Labrador, S. Banerjee, "Packet Dropping Policies for ATM and IP Networks," *IEEE Communications Surveys*, Vol. 2, No. 3 (Third Quarter 1999), pp. 2–14, http://www.comsoc.org/livepubs/surveys/public/3q99issue/banerjee.html

[Lakshman 1997] T. V. Lakshman, U. Madhow, "The Performance of TCP/IP for Networks with High Bandwidth-Delay Products and Random Loss," *IEEE/ACM Transactions on Networking,* Vol. 5 No. 3 (1997). pp. 336–350. http://citeseer.ist.psu.edu/lakshman96 performance.html

[Lam 1980] S. Lam, "A Carrier Sense Multiple Access Protocol for Local Networks," *Computer Networks,* Vol. 4 (1980), pp. 21–32, 1980.

[Lamport 1981] L. Lamport, "Password Authentication with Insecure Communication", *Communications of the ACM,* Vol. 24, No. 11 (Nov. 1981), pp. 770–772.

[Larmouth 1996] J. Larmouth, *Understanding OSI,* International Thomson Computer Press 1996. Chapter 8 of this book deals with ASN.1 and is available on-line at http://www.salford.ac.uk/iti/books/osi/all.html#head8

[Larsen 1997] A. Larsen, "Guaranteed Service: Monitoring Tools," *Data Communications,* June 1997, pp. 85–94.

[Lawton 2001] G. Lawton, "Is IPv6 Finally Gaining Ground?" *IEEE Computer Magazine* (Aug. 2001), pp. 11–15.

[Leiner 1998] B. Leiner, V. Cerf, D. Clark, R. Kahn, L. Kleinrock, D. Lynch, J. Postel, L. Roberts, and S. Woolf, "A Brief History of the Internet," http://www.isoc.org/internet/history/brief.html

[Liang 2004] J. Liang, R. Kumar, K.W. Ross, "Understanding KaZaA", http://cis.poly.edu/~ross/papers/

[Lin 2001] Y. Lin, I. Chlamtac, *Wireless and Mobile Network Architectures*, John Wiley and Sons, New York, NY, 2001.

[Liu 2002] B. Liu, D. Goeckel, D. Towsley, "TCP-Cognizant Adaptive Forward Error Correction in Wireless Networks," *Proceedings of Globe Internet 2002.* ftp://gaia.cs.umass.edu/pub/wirelessTCPtech.pdf

[Luotonen 1998] A. Luotonen, *Web Proxy Servers,* Prentice Hall, Englewood Cliffs, New Jersey, 1998.

[Lynch 1993] D. Lynch, M. Rose, *Internet System Handbook,* Addison-Wesley, Reading, MA, 1993.

[Macedonia 1994] Macedonia, M. R., Brutzman, D. P., "MBone Provides Audio and Video Across the Internet," *IEEE Computer Magazine,* Vol. 27, No. 4 (Apr. 1994), pp. 30–36. ftp://taurus.cs.nps.navy.mil/pub/mbmg/mbone.html

[Maconachy 2001] W.V. Maconachy, C. Schou, D. Ragsdale, D. Welch, "A Model for Information Assurance: an Integrated Approach," *Proceedings of the 2001 IEEE Workshop on Information Assurance and Security*, (West Point, NY), 2001, http://www.itoc.usma.edu/Documents/Workshop2001/paperW2C3(55).pdf

[Maennel 2002] O. Maennel, A. Feldmann, "Realistic BGP Traffic for Test Labs," *Proceedings. of 2002 ACM Sigcomm*, http://www.acm.org/sigs/sigcomm/sigcomm2002/papers/bgplab.pdf.

[Mahdavi 1997] J. Mahdavi and S. Floyd, "TCP-Friendly Unicast Rate-Based Flow Control," unpublished note, Jan. 1997. http://www.psc.edu/networking/papers/tcp_friendly.html

[Mainwaring 2002] A.Mainwaring, R. Szewczyk, D. Culler, J. Anderson "Wireless Sensor Networks for Habitat Monitoring" *ACM International Workshop on Wireless Sensor Networks and Applications (WSNA)*, 2002. http://citeseer.ist.psu.edu/mainwaring02wireless.html

[Manelli 2001] T. Manelli, "What Happened to Internet Appliances?" *PC World,* (April 2001), http://www.pcworld.com/news/article/0,aid,47184,00.asp

[manet 2004] IETF Mobile Ad-hoc Networks (manet) Working Group, http://www.ietf.org/html.charters/manet-charter.html

[Maymounkov 2002] P. Maymounkov and D. Mazières. "Kademlia: A Peer-to-Peer Information System Based on the XOR Metric." *Proceedings of the 1st International Workshop on Peer-to-Peer Systems (IPTPS '02)*, pp. 53–65, March 2002.

[McAuley 1994] A. McAuley, "Weighted Sum Codes for Error Detection and Their Comparison with Existing Codes," *IEEE/ACM Transactions on Networking,* Vol. 2, No. 1 (Feb. 1994), pp. 16–22.

[McCumber 1991] J. McCumber, "Information Systems Security: A Comprehensive Model," *Proceedings of the 14th National Computer Security Conference*, (Baltimore, MD), 1991.

[MCI 2004] MCI, "Terms and Conditions: Service Level Agreement," http://global.mci.com/terms/sla/

[McKeown 1997a] N. McKeown, M. Izzard, A. Mekkittikul,W. Ellersick, M. Horowitz, "The Tiny Tera: A Packet Switch Core," *IEEE Micro Magazine,* Jan.–Feb. 1997. http://tiny-tera.stanford.edu/~nickm/papers/HOTI_96.ps

[McKeown 1997b] N. McKeown, "A Fast Switched Backplane for a Gigabit Switched Router," *Business Communications Review,* Vol. 27, No. 12. http://www.bcr.com/bcrmag/12/mckeown.htm

[McKusik 1996] M. K. McKusick, K. Bostic, M. Karels, and J. Quarterman, *The Design and Implementation of the 4.4BSD Operating System,* Addison-Wesley, Reading, MA, 1996.

[McQuillan 1980] J. McQuillan, I. Richer, E. Rosen, "The New Routing Algorithm for the Arpanet," *IEEE Transactions on Communications,* COM-28(5) (May 1980), pp. 711–719.

[Medhi 1997] D. Medhi and D. Tipper (eds.), Special Issue: Fault Management in Communication Networks, *Journal of Network and Systems Management,* Vol. 5. No. 2 (June 1997).

[Metcalfe 1976] R. M. Metcalfe and D. R. Boggs. "Ethernet: Distributed Packet Switching for Local Computer Networks," *Communications of the Association for Computing Machinery,* Vol. 19, No. 7, (July 1976), pp. 395–404. http://www.acm.org/classics/apr96/

[Microsoft Player Media 2004] Microsoft Windows Media homepage, http://www.microsoft.com/windows/windowsmedia/

[Miller 1997] M.A. Miller, *Managing Internetworks with SNMP,* 2nd ed., M & T Books, New York, 1997.

[Mockapetris 1988] P. V. Mockapetris, K. J. Dunlap, "Development of the Domain Name System," *Proceedings of SIGCOMM '88*, Stanford, CA, 1988. http://citeseer.nj.nec.com/mockapetris88development.html

[Molinero-Fernandez 2002] P. Molinaro-Fernandez, N. McKeown, H. Zhang, "Is IP Going to Take Over the World (of Communications)?" *Proc. 2002 ACM Hotnets*, http://www.acm.org/sigcomm/HotNets-I/papers/fernandez.pdf

[Molle 1987] M. L. Molle, K. Sohraby, and A. N. Venetsanopoulos, "Space-Time Models of Asynchronous CSMA Protocols for Local Area Networks," *IEEE Journal on Selected Areas in Communications,* Vol. 5, No. 6, (1987) pp. 956–968.

[Molva 1999] R. Molva, "Internet Security Architecture," Computer Networks and ISDN Systems, Vol. 31, No. 8 (1999), pp. 787-804.

[Moore 2003] D. Moore, V. Paxson, S. Savage, C. Shannon, S. Staniford, N. Weaver, "Inside the Slammer Worm," http://www.caida.org/outreach/papers/2003/sapphire2/

[Mouly 1992] M. Mouly, M. Pautet, *The GSM System for Mobile Communications*, Cell and Sys, Palaiseau, France, 1992.

[Moy 1998] J. Moy, *OSPF: Anatomy of An Internet Routing Protocol*, Addison-Wesley, Reading, MA, 1998.

[mrouted 1996] "mrouted," v3.8 of DVMRP routing software for various workstation routing platforms, ftp://parcftp.xerox.com/pub/net-research/ipmulti

[Mukherjee 1997] B. Mukherjee, Optical Communication Networks, McGraw-Hill, 1997.

[Murphy 2003] S. Murphy, "BGP Security Vulnerabilities Analysis," draft-ietf-idr-bgp-vuln-00.txt, June 2003, ftp://ftp.rfc-editor.org/in-notes/internet-drafts/draft-ietf-idr-bgp-vuln-00.txt

[Nahum 2002] E. Nahum, T. Barzilai, D. Kandlur, "Performance Issues in WWW Servers," *IEEE/ACM Transactions on Networking*, 10(1), February 2002, http://www.research.ibm.com/people/n/nahum/publications/ton02-www-camera.pdf.

[Nesbitt 2002] S. Nesbitt, "Network Appliances," Jan. 2002, About.com, http://netappliances.about.com/cs/settopboxes/

[Net2Phone 2004] http://www.net2phone.com/

[Netcraft 2004] The Netcraft Web Server Survey, Netcraft Web Site, http://www.netcraft.com/survey/

[Netscape Cookie 1999] Netscape Communications Corp., "Persistent Client State http Cookies," http://home.netscape.com/newsref/std/cookie_spec.html

[Netscape SSL 1998] Netscape Communications Corps, "Introduction to SSL," http://developer.netscape.com/docs/manuals/security/sslin/

[Neuman 1994] B. Neuman and T. Tso, "Kerberos: An Authentication Service for Computer Networks," *IEEE Communication Magazine,* Vol. 32, No. 9 (Sept. 1994), pp. 33–38.

[Neumann 1997] R. Neumann, "Internet Routing Black Hole," *The Risks Digest: Forum on Risks to the Public in Computers and Related Systems,* Vol. 19, No. 12 (May 1997). http://catless.ncl.ac.uk/Risks/19.12.html#subj1.1

[Nielsen 1997] H. F. Nielsen, J. Gettys, A. Baird-Smith, E. Prud'hommeaux, H. W. Lie, and C. Lilley, "Network Performance Effects of HTTP/1.1, CSS1, and PNG," *W3C Document,* 1997 (also appears in *Proceedings of ACM SIGCOMM '97,* Cannes, France, pp. 155–166). http://www.acm.org/sigcomm/sigcomm97/papers/p102.html

[NIST 1993] National Institute of Standards and Technology, "Federal Information. Data Encryption Standard," Processing Standards Publication 46-2, 1993. http://www.itl.nist.gov/fipspubs/fip46-2.htm

[NIST 1999] National Institute of Standards and Technology, "Data Encryption Standard Fact Sheet," http://csrc.nist.gov/cryptval/des/des.txt

[NIST 1999b] National Institute of Standards and Technology, "Draft Federal Information Processing Standard (FIPS) 46-3, Data Encryption Standard (DES), and Request for Comments," http://csrc.nist.gov/cryptval/des/fr990115.htm

[NIST 2001] National Institute of Standards and Technology, "Advanced Encryption Standard (AES)," Federal Information Processing Standards 197, Nov. 2001, http://csrc.nist.gov/publications/fips/fips197/fips-197.pdf

[Nmap 2004] Nmap homepage, http://www.insecure.com/nmap

[Nonnenmacher 1998] J. Nonnenmacher, E. Biersak, D. Towsley, "Parity-Based Loss Recovery for Reliable Multicast Transmission," *IEEE/ACM Transactions on Networking,* Vol. 6, No. 4 (Aug. 1998), pp. 349–361. ftp://gaia.cs.umass.edu/pub/NBT97:fec.ps.gz

[Nortel 2004] Nortel Networks, Optivity Portfolio, http://www.nortelnetworks.com/products/01/optivity

[NTIA 1998] National Telecommunications and Information Administration (NTIA), U.S. Department of Commerce, "Management of Internet names and addresses," Docket Number: 980212036-8146-02. http://www.ntia.doc.gov/ntiahome/domainname/6_5_98dns.htm

[Odlyzko 2003] A. Odlyzko, "Internet Traffic Growth: Sources and Implications," A. M. Optical Transmission Systems and Equipment for WDM Networking II, *Proc. SPIE,.* 5247, 2003, pp. 1–15. http://www.dtc.umn.edu/~odlyzko/doc/itcom.internet.growth.pdf.

[OpenView2004] HP OpenView homepage, http://www.openview.hp.com/

[OSS 2004] OSS Nokalva, "ASN.1 Resources," http://www.oss.com/asn1/

[Overpeer 2004] Overpeer Inc., http://www.overpeer.com.

[Padhye 2000] J. Padhye, V. Firoiu, D. Towsley, J. Kurose, "Modeling TCP Reno Performance: A Simple Model and its Empirical Validation," *IEEE/ACM Transactions on Networking,* Vol. 8 No. 2 (April 2000). pp. 133–145.

[Padhye 2001] J. Padhye, S. Floyd, "On Inferring TCP Behavior," In *Proceedings of ACM SIGCOMM,* 2001, (San Diego, CA), 2001v. http://www.aciri.org/floyd/papers/tbit.pdf

[Pan 1997] P. Pan and H. Schulzrinne, "Staged Refresh Timers for RSVP," In *2nd* Global Internet Conference, Phoenix, 1997. http://www.cs.columbia.edu/~pingpan/papers/timergi.pdf

[Parekh 1993] A. Parekh and R. Gallager, "A generalized processor sharing approach to flow control in integrated services networks: the single-node case," *IEEE/ACM Transactions on Networking,* Vol. 1, No. 3 (June 1993), pp. 344–357.

[Partridge 1992] C. Partridge, S. Pink, "An Implementation of the Revised Internet Stream Protocol (ST-2)," *Journal of Internetworking: Research and Experience* 3(1), March 1992. http://www.sics.se/cna/publications/ST-2.ps

[Partridge 1998] C. Partridge, et al. "A Fifty Gigabit per second IP Router," *IEEE/ACM Transactions on Networking,* Vol. 6, No. 3 (Jun. 1998), pp. 237–248.

[Paxson 1997] V. Paxson, "End-to-end Internet packet dynamics," *Proceedings of ACM SIGCOMM '97,* (Sept. 1997, Cannes, France). http://www.acm.org/sigcomm/sigcomm97/papers/p086.html

[Perkins 1994] A. Perkins, "Networking with Bob Metcalfe," *The Red Herring Magazine,*Nov. 1994. http://www.herring.com/mag/issue15/bob.html

[Perkins 1998a] C. Perkins, O. Hodson and V. Hardman, "A Survey of Packet Loss Recovery Techniques for Streaming Audio," *IEEE Network Magazine,* Sept./ Oct. 1998, pp. 40–47.

[Perkins 1998b] C. Perkins, *Mobile IP: Design Principles and Practice*, Addison-Wesley, Reading, MA, 1998.

[Perkins 2000] C. Perkins, *Ad Hoc Networking*, Addison-Wesley, Reading, MA, 2000.

[Perlman 1999] R. Perlman, *Interconnections: Bridges, Routers, Switches, and Internetworking Protocols,* 2nd ed., Addison-Wesley Professional Computing Series, Reading, MA, 1999.

[PGPI 2004] The International PGP Home Page, http://www.pgpi.org

[Phifer 2000] L. Phifer, "The Trouble with NAT*,*" *The Internet Protocol Journal,* Vol. 3, No.4 (Dec. 2000), http://www.cisco.com/warp/public/759/ipj_3-4/ipj_3-4_nat.html

[Pickholtz 1982] R. Pickholtz, D. Schilling, L. Milstein, "Theory of Spread Spectrum Communication—a Tutorial," *IEEE Transactions on Communications,* Vol. COM-30, No. 5 (May 1982), pp. 855–884.

[Piscatello 1993] D. Piscatello and A. Lyman Chapin, *Open Systems Networking,* Addison-Wesley, Reading, MA, 1993.

[Point Topic 2003] Point Topic Ltd., *World Broadband Statistics*, Sept. 2003, http://www.point-topic.com

[QuickTime 2004] QuickTime homepage, http://www.apple.com/quicktime

[Quittner 1998] J. Quittner, M. Slatalla, *Speeding the Net: The Inside Story of Netscape and How it Challenged Microsoft,* Atlantic Monthly Press, 1998.

[Ramakrishnan 1990] K. K. Ramakrishnan and Raj Jain, "A Binary Feedback Scheme for Congestion Avoidance in Computer Networks," *ACM Transactions on Computer Systems,* Vol. 8, No. 2 (May 1990), pp. 158–181.

[Raman 1999] S. Raman, S. McCanne, "A Model, Analysis, and Protocol Framework for Soft State-based Communication," *Proceedings of ACM SIGCOMM '99* (Boston, MA, Aug. 1999). http://www.acm.org/sigs/sigcomm/sigcomm99/papers/session1-2.html

[Ramaswami 1998] R. Ramaswami, K. Sivarajan, *Optical Networks: A Practical Perspective,* Morgan Kaufman Publishers, 1998

[Ramjee 1994] R. Ramjee, J. Kurose, D. Towsley, and H. Schulzrinne, "Adaptive Playout Mechanisms for Packetized Audio Applications in Wide-Area Networks," *Proceeding IEEE Infocom 94.* ftp://gaia.cs.umass.edu/pib/ Ramj94:Adaptive.ps.Z

[Ratnasamy 2001] S. Ratnasamy, P. Francis, M. Handley, R. Karp, and S. Shenker, "A Scalable Content-Addressable Network," *In Proceedings of ACM SIGCOMM,* 2001, (San Diego, CA), 2001. http://www.acm.org/sigcomm/sigcomm2001/p13.html

[Rao 1996] K. R. Rao and J. J. Hwang, *Techniques and Standards for Image, Video and Audio Coding,* Prentice Hall, Englewood Cliffs, NJ, 1996.

[RAT 2004] Robust Audio Tool, http://www-mice.cs.ucl.ac.uk/multimedia/software/rat/

[RealNetworks 2004] RealNetworks homepage, http://www.realnetworks.com

[Reid 2003] N. Reid and R. Seide, *802.11 (Wi-Fi) Networking Handbook*, McGraw-Hill/Osborne, New York, 2003.

[RFC 001] S. Crocker, "Host Software," RFC 001 (the *very first* RFC!). http://www.rfc-editor.org/rfc/rfc1.txt

[RFC 741] D. Cohen, "Specifications for the Network Voice Protocol NVP", RFC 741, Nov. 1977. ftp://ftp.rfc-editor.org/in-notes/rfc741.txt

[RFC 768] J. Postel, "User Datagram Protocol," RFC 768, Aug. 1980. http://www.rfc-editor.org/rfc/rfc768.txt

[RFC 789] E. Rosen, "Vulnerabilities of Network Control Protocols," RFC 789. http://www.rfc-editor.org/rfc/rfc789.txt

[RFC 791] J. Postel, "Internet Protocol: DARPA Internet Program Protocol Specification," RFC 791, Sept. 1981. http://www.rfc-editor.org/rfc/rfc791.txt

[RFC 792] J. Postel, "Internet Control Message Protocol," RFC 792, Sept. 1981. http://www.rfc-editor.org/rfc/rfc792.txt

[RFC 793] J. Postel, "Transmission Control Protocol," RFC 793, Sept. 1981. http://www.rfc-editor.org/rfc/rfc793.txt

[RFC 801] J. Postel, "NCP/TCP Transition Plan," RFC 801 Nov. 1981. http://www.rfc-editor.org/rfc/rfc801.txt

[RFC 821] J. Postel, "Simple Mail Transfer Protocol," RFC 821, Aug. 1982. http://www.rfc-editor.org/rfc/rfc211.txt obsoleted by RFC 2821.

[RFC 822] D. H. Crocker, "Standard for the Format of ARPA Internet Text Messages," RFC 822, Aug. 1982. http://www.rfc-editor.org/rfc/rfc822.txt

[RFC 826] D. C. Plummer, "An Ethernet Address Resolution Protocol—or—Converting Network Protocol Addresses to 48.bit Ethernet Address for Transmission on Ethernet Hardware," RFC 826, Nov. 1982. http://www.rfc-editor.org/rfc/rfc826.txt

[RFC 829] V. Cerf, "Packet Satellite Technology Reference Sources," *RFC 829*, November 1982. http://www.rfc-editor.org/rfc/rfc829.txt

[RFC 854] J. Postel and J. Reynolds, "TELNET Protocol Specification," RFC 854. May 1993. http://www.rfc-editor.org/rfc/rfc854.txt

[RFC 904] D. Mills, "Exterior Gateway Protocol Formal Specification," RFC 904, Apr. 1984. http://www.rfc-editor.org/rfc/rfc904.txt

[RFC 950] J. Mogul, J. Postel, "Internet Standard Subnetting Procedure," RFC 950, Aug. 1985. http://www.rfc-editor.org/rfc/rfc904.txt.

[RFC 959] J. Postel and J. Reynolds, "File Transfer Protocol (FTP)," RFC 959, Oct. 1985. http://www.rfc-editor.org/rfc/rfc959.txt

[RFC 977] B. Kantor and P. Lapsley, "Network News Transfer Protocol," RFC 977, Feb. 1986. http://www.rfc-editor.org/rfc/rfc977.txt

[RFC 1028] J. Davin, J.D. Case, M. Fedor, M. Schoffstall, "A Simple Gateway Monitoring Protocol," RFC 1028, Nov. 1987, http://www.rfc-editor.org/rfc/rfc1028.txt.

[RFC 1034] P. V. Mockapetris, "Domain Names—Concepts and Facilities," RFC 1034, Nov. 1987. http://www.rfc-editor.org/rfc/rfc1034.txt

[RFC 1035] P. Mockapetris, "Domain Names—Implementation and Specification," RFC 1035, Nov. 1987. http://www.rfc-editor.org/rfc/rfc1035.txt

[RFC 1058] C. L. Hendrick, "Routing Information Protocol," RFC 1058, June 1988. http://www.rfc-editor.org/rfc/rfc1058.txt

[RFC 1071] R. Braden, D. Borman, and C. Partridge, "Computing The Internet Checksum," RFC 1071, Sept. 1988. http://www.rfc-editor.org/rfc/rfc1071.txt

[RFC 1075] D. Waitzman, C. Partridge ,S. Deering, "Distance Vector Multicast Routing Protocol," RFC 1075, Nov. 1988. http://www.rfc-editor.org/rfc/rfc1071.txt.

[RFC 1112] S. Deering, "Host Extension for IP Multicasting," RFC 1112, Aug. 1989. http://www.rfc-editor.org/rfc/rfc1112.txt

[RFC 1122] R. Braden, "Requirements for Internet Hosts—Communication Layers," RFC 1122, Oct. 1989. http://www.rfc-editor.org/rfc/rfc1122.txt

[RFC 1123] R. Braden, ed., "Requirements for Internet Hosts—Application and Support," *RFC-1123*, October 1989. ftp://ftp.rfc-editor.org/in-notes/rfc1123.txt.

[RFC 1142] D. Oran, "OSI IS-IS Intra-domain Routing Protocol," RFC 1142, Feb. 1990, ftp://ftp.rfc-editor.org/in-notes/rfc1142.txt

[RFC 1180] T. Socolofsky and C. Kale, "A TCP/IP Tutorial," RFC 1180, Jan. 1991. http://www.rfc-editor.org/rfc/rfc1180.txt

[RFC 1190] C. Topolcic, "Experimental Internet Stream Protocol: Version 2 (ST-II)," RFC 1190, October 1990. ftp://ftp.rfc-editor.org/in-notes/rfc1190.txt

[RFC 1191] J. Mogul, S. Deering, "Path MTU Discovery," RFC 1191, November 1990, ftp://ftp.rfc-editor.org/in-notes/rfc1191.txt

[RFC 1213] K. McCloghrie, M. T. Rose, "Management Information Base for Network Management of TCP/IP-based internets: MIB-II," RFC 1213, Mar. 1991. http://www.rfc-editor.org/rfc/rfc1213.txt

[RFC 1256] S. Deering, "ICMP Router Discovery Messages," RFC 1256, Sept. 1991. http://www.rfc-editor.org/rfc/rfc1256.txt

[RFC 1320] R. Rivest, "The MD4 Message-Digest Algorithm," RFC 1320, Apr. 1992. http://www.rfc-editor.org/rfc/rfc1320.txt

[RFC 1321] R. Rivest, "The MD5 Message-Digest Algorithm," RFC 1321, Apr. 1992. http://www.rfc-editor.org/rfc/rfc1321.txt

[RFC 1323] V. Jacobson, S. Braden, and D. Borman, "TCP Extensions for High Performance," RFC 1323, May 1992. http://www.rfc-editor.org/rfc/rfc1323.txt

[RFC 1332] G. McGregor, "The PPP Internet Protocol Control Protocol (IPCP)," RFC 1332, May 1992. http://www.rfc-editor.org/rfc/rfc1332.txt

[RFC 1378] B. Parker, "The PPP AppleTalk Control Protocol (ATCP)," RFC 1378, Nov. 1992. http://www.rfc-editor.org/rfc/rfc1378.txt

[RFC 1422] S. Kent, "Privacy Enhancement for Internet Electronic Mail: Part II: Certificate-Based Key Management," RFC 1422, Feb. 1993. http://www.rfc-editor.org/rfc/rfc1422.txt

[RFC 1510] J. Kohl, C. Neuman, "The Kerberos Network Authentication Service (V5)," RFC 1510, Sept. 1993. http://www.rfc-editor.org/rfc/rfc1510.txt

[RFC 1519] V. Fuller, T. Li, J. Yu, K. Varadhan, "Classless inter-domain routing (CIDR)," RFC 1519, Sept. 1993. http://www.rfc-editor.org/rfc/rfc1519.txt

[RFC 1542]W. Wimer, "Clarifications and Extensions for the Bootstrap Protocol," RFC 1542, Oct. 1993. http://www.rfc-editor.org/rfc/rfc1542.txt

[RFC 1547] D. Perkins, "Requirements for an Internet Standard Point-to-Point Protocol," RFC 1547, Dec. 1993. http://www.rfc-editor.org/rfc/rfc1547.txt

[RFC 1584] J. Moy, "Multicast Extensions to OSPF," RFC 1584, Mar. 1994. http://www.rfc-editor. org/rfc/rfc1584.txt

[RFC 1631] K. Egevang, P. Francis, "The IP Network Address Translator (NAT)," RFC 1631, May 1994. http://www.rfc-editor.org/rfc/rfc1631.txt

[RFC 1633] R. Braden, D. Clark, S. Shenker, "Integrated Services in the Internet Architecture: an Overview," RFC 1633, June 1994. http://www.rfc-editor.org/rfc/rfc1633.txt

[RFC 1636] R. Braden, D. Clark, S. Crocker, C. Huitema, "Report of IAB Workshop on Security in the Internet Architecture," RFC 1636, Nov. 1994. http://www.rfc-editor.org/rfc/rfc1636.txt

[RFC 1661]W. Simpson (ed.), "The Point-to-Point Protocol (PPP)," RFC 1661, July 1994. http://www.rfc-editor.org/rfc/rfc1661.txt

[RFC 1662]W. Simpson (ed.), "PPP in HDLC-like framing," RFC 1662, July 1994. http://www.rfc-editor.org/rfc/rfc1662.txt

[RFC 1700] J. Reynolds and J. Postel, "Assigned Numbers," RFC 1700, Oct. 1994. http://www.rfc-editor.org/rfc/rfc1700.txt

[RFC 1730] M. Crispin, "Internet Message Access Protocol—Version 4," RFC 1730, Dec. 1994. http://info.internet.isi.edu/in-notes/rfc/files/rfc1730.txt.. Obsoleted by RFC 2060.

[RFC 1752] S. Bradner, A. Mankin, "The Recommendations for the IP Next Generation Protocol," RFC 1752, Jan. 1995. http://www.rfc-editor.org/rfc/rfc1752.txt

[RFC 1760] N. Haller, "The S/KEY One-Time Password System," RFC 1760, Feb. 1995. http://www.rfc-editor.org/rfc/rfc1760.txt

[RFC 1762] S. Senum, "The PPP DECnet Phase IV Control Protocol (DNCP)," RFC 1762, Mar. 1995. http://www.rfc-editor.org/rfc/rfc1762.txt

[RFC 1771] Y. Rekhter and T. Li, "A Border Gateway Protocol 4 (BGP-4)," RFC 1771, Mar. 1995. http://www.rfc-editor.org/rfc/rfc1771.txt

[RFC 1772] Y. Rekhter and P. Gross, "Application of the Border Gateway Protocol in the Internet," RFC 1772, Mar. 1995. http://www.rfc-editor.org/rfc/rfc1772.txt

[RFC 1773] P. Traina, "Experience with the BGP-4 protocol," RFC 1773, Mar. 1995. http://www.rfc-editor.org/rfc/rfc1773.txt.

[RFC 1779] S. Kille, "A String Representation of Distinguished Names," RFC 1779, Mar. 1995. http://www.rfc-editor.org/rfc/rfc1779.txt. Obsoleted by RFC 2253

[RFC 1810] J. Touch, "Report on MD5 Performance," RFC 1810, June 1995. http://www.rfc-editor.org/rfc/rfc1810.txt

[RFC 1812] F. Baker, ed., "Requirements for IP Version 4 Routers*," RFC-1812*, June 1995. ftp://ftp.rfc-editor.org/in-notes/rfc1812.txt.

[RFC 1884] R. Hinden, S. Deering, "IP Version 6: addressing architecture," RFC 1884, Dec. 1995. http://www.rfc-editor.org/rfc/rfc1884.txt. Obsoleted by RFC 2373

[RFC 1906] J. Case, K. McCloghrie, M. Rose, S. Waldbusser, "Transport Mappings for Version 2 of the Simple Network Management Protocol (SNMPv2)," RFC 1906, Jan. 1996. http://www.rfc-editor.org/rfc/rfc1906.txt

[RFC 1907] J. Case, K. McCloghrie, M. Rose, and S. Waldbusser, "Management Information Base for Version 2 of the Simple Network Management Protocol (SNMPv2)," RFC 1907, Jan. 1996. http://www.rfc-editor.org/rfc/rfc1907.txt

[RFC 1911] G. Vaudreuil, "Voice Profile for Internet Mail," RFC 1911, Feb. 1996. http://www.rfc-editor.org/rfc/rfc1911.txt. Obsoleted by RFC 2421.

[RFC 1918] Y. Rekhter, B. Moskowitz, D. Karrenberg, G. J. de Groot, E. Lear, "Address Allocation for Private Internets," RFC 1918, February 1996. ftp://ftp.rfc-editor.org/in-notes/rfc1918.txt

[RFC 1930] J. Hawkinson, T. Bates, "Guidelines for Creation, Selection, and Registration of an Autonomous System (AS)," RFC 1930, March 1996. ftp://ftp.rfc-editor.org/in-notes/rfc1930.txt

[RFC 1938] N. Haller, C. Metz, "A One-Time Password System," RFC 1938, May 1996, ftp://ftp.rfc-editor.org/in-notes/rfc1938.txt

[RFC 1939] J. Myers and M. Rose, "Post Office Protocol—Version 3," RFC 1939, May 1996. http://www.rfc-editor.org/rfc/rfc1939.txt

[RFC 1945] T. Berners-Lee, R. Fielding, H. Frystyk, "Hypertext Transfer Protocol—HTTP/1.0," RFC 1945, May 1996 http://www.rfc-editor.org/rfc/rfc1945.txt

[RFC 1994] W., Simpson, "PPP Challenge Handshake Authentication Protocol (CHAP)," RFC 1994, Aug. 1996, ftp://ftp.rfc-editor.org/in-notes/rfc1994.txt

[RFC 2001] W. Stevens, "TCP Slow Start, Congestion Avoidance, Fast Retransmit, and Fast Recovery Algorithms," RFC 2001, Jan. 1997. http://www.rfc-editor.org/rfc/rfc2001.txt. Obsoleted by RFC 2581.

[RFC 2003] C. Perkins, "IP Encapsulation within IP," RFC 2003, Oct. 1996. http://www.rfc-editor.org/rfc/rfc2003.txt

[RFC 2004] C. Perkins, "Minimal Encapsulation within IP," RFC 2004, Oct. 1996. http://www.rfc-editor.org/rfc/rfc2004.txt

[RFC 2011] K. McCloghrie, "SNMPv2 Management Information Base for the Internet Protocol using SMIv2," RFC 2011, Nov. 1996. http://www.rfc-editor.org/rfc/rfc2011.txt

[RFC 2012] K. McCloghrie, "SNMPv2 Management Information Base for the Transmission Control Protocol using SMIv2," RFC 2012, Nov. 1996. http://www.rfc-editor.org/rfc/rfc2012.txt

[RFC 2013] K. McCloghrie, "SNMPv2 Management Information Base for the User Datagram Protocol using SMIv2," RFC 2013, Nov. 1996. http://www.rfc-editor.org/rfc/rfc2013.txt

[RFC 2018] M. Mathis, J. Mahdavi, S. Floyd, and A. Romanow, "TCP Selective Acknowledgment Options," RFC 2018, Oct. 1996. http://www.rfc-editor.org/rfc/rfc2018.txt

[RFC 2021] S. Waldbusser, "Remote Network Monitoring Management Information Base Version 2 using SMIv2," RFC 2021, Jan. 1997. http://www.rfc-editor.org/rfc/rfc2021.txt

[RFC 2045] N. Freed, N. Borenstein, "Multipurpose Internet Mail Extensions (MIME) Part One: Format of Internet Message Bodies," RFC 2045, Nov. 1996. http://www.rfc-editor.org/rfc/rfc2045.txt

[RFC 2046] N. Freed, N. Borenstein, "Multipurpose Internet Mail Extensions (MIME) Part Two: Media Types," RFC 2046, Nov. 1996. http://www.rfc-editor.org/rfc/rfc2046.txt

[RFC 2048] N. Freed, J. Klensin, J. Postel "Multipurpose Internet Mail Extensions (MIME) Part Four: Registration Procedures," RFC 2048, Nov. 1996. http://www.rfc-editor.org/rfc/rfc2048.txt

[RFC 2050] K. Hubbard, M. Kosters, D. Conrad, D. Karrenberg, J. Postel, "Internet Registry IP Allocation Guidelines," RFC 2050, Nov. 1996. http://www.rfc-editor.org/rfc/rfc2050.txt

[RFC 2060] R. Crispin, "Internet Message Access Protocol—Version 4rev1," RFC 2060, Dec. 1996. http://www.rfc-editor.org/rfc/rfc2060.txt

[RFC 2068] R. Fielding, J. Gettys, J. Mogul, H. Frystyk, and T. Berners-Lee, "Hypertext Transfer Protocol—HTTP/1.1," RFC 2068, Jan. 1997. http://www.rfc-editor.org/rfc/rfc2068.txt. Obsoleted by RFC 2616.

[RFC 2104] H. Krawczyk, M. Bellare, R. Canetti, "HMAC: Keyed-Hashing for Message Authentication," RFC 2104, Feb. 1997. http://www.rfc-editor.org/rfc/rfc2104.txt

[RFC 2109] D. Kristol and L. Montulli, "HTTP State Management Mechanism," RFC 2109, Feb. 1997. http://www.rfc-editor.org/rfc/rfc2109.txt

[RFC 2131] R. Droms, "Dynamic Host Configuration Protocol," RFC 2131, Mar. 1997. http://www.rfc-editor.org/rfc/rfc2109.txt

[RFC 2136] P. Vixie, S. Thomson,Y. Rekhter, and J. Bound, "Dynamic Updates in the Domain Name System," RFC 2136, Apr. 1997. http://www.rfc-editor.org/rfc/rfc2136.txt

[RFC 2153]W. Simpson, "PPP Vendor Extensions," RFC 2153, May 1997. http://www.rfc-editor.org/rfc/rfc2153.txt

[RFC 2186] K. Claffy and D. Wessels, "Internet Caching Protocol (ICP), version 2," RFC 2186, Sept. 1997. http://www.rfc-editor.org/rfc/rfc2186.txt

[RFC 2189] A. Ballardie, "Core Based Trees (CBT version 2) Multicast Routing: Protocol Specification," RFC 2189, Sept. 1997. http://www.rfc-editor.org/rfc/rfc2189.txt

[RFC 2201] A. Ballardie, "Core Based Trees (CBT) Multicast Routing Architecture," RFC 2201, Sept. 1997. http://www.rfc-editor.org/rfc/rfc2201.txt

[RFC 2205] R. Braden, Ed., L. Zhang, S. Berson, S. Herzog, S. Jamin, "Resource ReSerVation Protocol (RSVP)—Version 1 Functional Specification," RFC 2205, Sept. 1997. http://www.rfc-editor.org/rfc/rfc2205.txt

[RFC 2210] J. Wroclawski, "The Use of RSVP with IETF Integrated Services," RFC 2210, Sept. 1997. http://www.rfc-editor.org/rfc/rfc2210.txt

[RFC 2211] J. Wroclawski, "Specification of the Controlled-Load Network Element Service," RFC 2211, Sept. 1997. http://www.rfc-editor.org/rfc/rfc2211.txt

[RFC 2212] S. Shenker, C. Partridge, R. Guerin, "Specification of Guaranteed Quality of Service," RFC 2212, Sept. 1997. http://www.rfc-editor.org/rfc/rfc2212.txt

[RFC 2215] S. Shenker, J. Wroclawski, "General Characterization Parameters for Integrated Service Network Elements," RFC 2215, Sept. 1997. http://www.rfc-editor.org/rfc/rfc2215.txt

[RFC 2225] M Laubach, J. Halpern, "Classical UP and ARP over ATM," RFC 2225, April 1998. http://www.rfc-editor.org/rfc/rfc2225.txt

[RFC 2246] T. Dierks and C. Allen, "The TLS Protocol," RFC 2246, Jan. 1998. http://www.rfc-editor.org/rfc/rfc2246.txt

[RFC 2253] M. Wahl, S. Kille, T. Howes, "Lightweight Directory Access Protocol (v3)," RFC 2253, Dec. 1997. http://www.rfc-editor.org/rfc/rfc2253.txt

[RFC 2284] L. Blunk, J. Vollbrecht, "PPP Extensible Authentication Protocol (EAP," RFC 2284, March 1998, ftp://ftp.rfc-editor.org/in-notes/rfc2284.txt

[RFC 2326] H. Schulzrinne, A. Rao, R. Lanphier, "Real Time Streaming Protocol (RTSP)," RFC 2326, Apr. 1998. http://www.rfc-editor.org/rfc/rfc2326.txt

[RFC 2328] J. Moy, "OSPF Version 2," RFC 2328, Apr. 1998. http://www.rfc-editor.org/rfc/rfc2328.txt

[RFC 2362] D. Estrin, D. Farinacci, A. Helmy, D. Thaler, S. Deering, M. Handley, V. Jacobson, C. Liu, P. Sharma, L. Wei, "Protocol Independent Multicast-Sparse Mode (PIM-SM): Protocol Specification," RFC 2362, June 1998. http://www.rfc-editor.org/rfc/rfc2362.txt

[RFC 2373] R. Hinden, S. Deering, "IP Version 6 Addressing Architecture," RFC 2373, July 1998. http://www.rfc-editor.org/rfc/rfc2373.txt

[RFC 2400] J. Postel, J. Reynolds, "Internet Official Protocol Standards," RFC 2400, Sept. 1998. http://www.rfc-editor.org/rfc/rfc2400.txt. Obsoleted by RFC 2500.

[RFC 2401] S. Kent, R. Atkinson, "Security Architecture for the Internet Protocol," RFC 2401, Nov. 1998. http://www.rfc-editor.org/rfc/rfc2401.txt

[RFC 2402] S. Kent and R. Atkinson, "IP Authentication Header," RFC 2402, Nov. 1998. http://www.rfc-editor.org/rfc/rfc2402.txt

[RFC 2405] C. Madson and N. Doraswamy, "The ESP DES-CBC Cipher Algorithm with Explicit IV," RFC 2405, Nov. 1998. http://www.rfc-editor.org/rfc/rfc2405.txt

[RFC 2406] S. Kent, R. Atkinson, "IP Encapsulating Security Payload (ESP)," RFC 2406, Nov. 1998. http://www.rfc-editor.org/rfc/rfc2406.txt

[RFC 2407] D. Piper, "The Internet IP Security Domain of Interpretation for ISAKMP," RFC 2407, Nov. 1998. http://www.rfc-editor.org/rfc/rfc2407.txt

[RFC 2408] D. Maughan, M. Schertler, M. Schneider, J. Turner, "Internet Security Association and Key Management Protocol (ISAKMP)," RFC 2408, Nov. 1998. http://www.rfc-editor. org/rfc/rfc2408.txt

[**RFC 2409**] D. Harkins, D. Carrel, "The Internet Key Exchange (IKE)," RFC 2409, Nov. 1998. http://www.rfc-editor.org/rfc/rfc2409.txt

[**RFC 2411**] R. Thayer, N. Doraswamy, R. Glenn, "IP Security Document Road Map," RFC 2411, Nov. 1998. http://www.rfc-editor.org/rfc/rfc2411.txt

[**RFC 2420**] H. Kummert, "The PPP Triple-DES Encryption Protocol (3DESE)," RFC 2420, Sept. 1998. http://www.rfc-editor.org/rfc/rfc2420.txt

[**RFC 2421**] G. Vaudreuil, G. Parsons, "Voice Profile for Internet Mail—version 2," RFC 2421, Sept. 1998. http://www.rfc-editor.org/rfc/rfc2421.txt

[**RFC 2427**] C. Brown, A. Malis, "Multiprotocol Interconnect over Frame Relay," RFC 2427, Sept. 1998. http://www.rfc-editor.org/rfc/rfc2427.txt

[**RFC 2437**] B. Kaliski, J. Staddon, "PKCS #1: RSA Cryptography Specifications, Version 2," RFC 2437, Oct. 1998. http://www.rfc-editor.org/rfc/rfc2437.txt

[**RFC 2453**] G. Malkin, "RIP Version 2," RFC 2453, Nov. 1998. http://www.rfc-editor.org/rfc/rfc2453.txt.

[**RFC 2460**] S. Deering, R. Hinden, "Internet Protocol, Version 6 (IPv6) Specification," RFC 2460, Dec. 1998. http://www.rfc-editor.org/rfc/rfc2460.txt

[**RFC 2463**] A. Conta, S. Deering, "Internet Control Message Protocol (ICMPv6) for the Internet Protocol Version 6 (IPv6)," RFC 2463, Dec. 1998. http://www.rfc-editor.org/rfc/rfc2463.txt

[**RFC 2474**] K. Nicols, S. Blake, F. Baker, D. Black, "Definition of the Differentiated Services Field (DS Field) in the IPv4 and IPv6 Headers," RFC 2474, Dec. 1998. http://www.rfc-editor.org/rfc/rfc2473.txt

[**RFC 2475**] S. Blake, D. Black, M. Carlson, E. Davies, Z. Wang,W. Weiss, "An Architecture for Differentiated Services," RFC 2475, Dec. 1998. http://www.rfc-editor.org/rfc/rfc2475.txt

[**RFC 2481**] K. K. Ramakrishnan and S. Floyd, "A Proposal to Add Explicit Congestion Notification (ECN) to IP," RFC 2481, Jan. 1999. http://www.rfc-editor.org/rfc/rfc2481.txt

[**RFC 2500**] J. Reynolds, R. Braden, "Internet Official Protocol Standards," RFC 2500, June 1999. http://www.rfc-editor.org/rfc/rfc2500.txt.

[**RFC 2535**] D. Eastlake, "Domain Name System Security Extensions," RFC 2535, Mar. 1999, ftp://ftp.rfc-editor.org/in-notes/rfc2535.txt

[**RFC 2578**] K. McCloghrie, D. Perkins, J. Schoenwaelder, "Structure of Management Information Version 2 (SMIv2)," RFC 2578, Apr. 1999. http://www.rfc-editor.org/rfc/rfc2578.txt

[**RFC 2579**] K. McCloghrie, D. Perkins, J. Schoenwaelder, "Textual Conventions for SMIv2," RFC 2579, Apr. 1999. http://www.rfc-editor.org/rfc/rfc2579.txt

[**RFC 2580**] K. McCloghrie, D. Perkins, J. Schoenwaelder, "Conformance Statements for SMIv2," RFC 2580, Apr. 1999. http://www.rfc-editor.org/rfc/rfc2580.txt

[**RFC 2581**] M. Allman, V. Paxson,W. Stevens, " TCP Congestion Control," RFC 2581, Apr. 1999. http://www.rfc-editor.org/rfc/rfc2581.txt

[**RFC 2582**] S. Floyd, T. Henderson, "The NewReno Modification to TCP's Fast Recovery Algorithm," RFC 2582, April 1999.. ftp://ftp.isi.edu/in-notes/rfc2582.txt

[**RFC 2597**] J. Heinanen, F. Baker,W. Weiss, J. Wroclawski, "Assured Forwarding PHB Group," RFC 2597, June 1999. http://www.rfc-editor.org/rfc/rfc2597.txt

[RFC 2598] V. Jacobson, K. Nichols, K. Poduri, "An Expedited Forwarding PHB," RFC 2598, June 1999. http://www.rfc-editor.org/rfc/rfc2598.txt

[RFC 2616] R. Fielding, J. Gettys, J. Mogul, H. Frystyk, L. Masinter, P. Leach, T. Berners-Lee, R. Feilding, "Hypertext Transfer Protocol—HTTP/1.1," RFC 2616, June 1999. http://www.rfc-editor.org/rfc/rfc2616.txt

[RFC 2638] K. Nichols, V. Jacobson, L. Zhang, "A Two-bit Differentiated Services Architecture for the Internet," RFC 2638, July 1999. http://www.rfc-editor.org/rfc/rfc2638.txt

[RFC 2644] D. Senie, "Changing the Default for Directed Broadcasts in Router," RFC 2644, Aug. 1999. http://www.rfc-editor.org/rfc/rfc2644.txt

[RFC 2663] P. Srisuresh, M. Holdrege, "IP Network Address Translator (NAT) Terminology and Considerations," RFC 2663.

[RFC 2715] D. Thaler, "Interoperability Rules for Multicast Routing Protocols," RFC 2715, Oct. 1999. http://www.rfc-editor.org/rfc/rfc2715.txt

[RFC 2716] B. Aboba, D. Simon, "PPP EAP TLS Authentication Protocol," RFC 2716, Oct. 1999, ftp://ftp.rfc-editor.org/in-notes/rfc2716.txt

[RFC 2733] J. Rosenberg, H. Schulzrinne, "An RTP Payload Format for Generic Forward Error Correction," RFC 2733, Dec. 1999. http://www.rfc-editor.org/rfc2733.txt

[RFC 2821] J. Klensin, Eed., "Simple Mail Transfer Protocol," RFC 2821, April 2001, http://www.rfc-editor.org/rfc/rfc2821.txt

[RFC 2827] P. Ferguson, D. Senie, "Network Ingress Filtering: Defeating Denial of Service Attacks which Employ IP Source Address Spoofing," RFC 2827. May 2000. http://www.rfc-editor.org/rfc/rfc2827.txt

[RFC 2893] R. Gilligan, E. Nordmark "Transition Mechanisms for IPv6 Hosts and Routers," RFC 2893, Aug. 2000. http://www.rfc-editor.org/rfc/rfc2893.txt

[RFC 2961] L. Berger, D. Gan, G. Swallow, P. Pan, F. Tommasi, S. Molendini, "RSVP Refresh Overhead Reduction Extensions," RFC 2961, April 2001, ftp://ftp.rfc-editor.org/in-notes/rfc3260.txt

[RFC 2988] V. Paxson, M. Allman, "Computing TCP's Retransmission Timer," RFC 2988, Nov., 2000. ftp://ftp.isi.edu/in-notes/rfc2988.txt

[RFC 3022] P. Srisuresh, K. Egevang, "Traditional IP Network Address Translator (Traditional NAT)," RFC 3022, Jan. 2001. http://www.rfc-editor.org/rfc/rfc3022.txt

[RFC 3031] E. Rosen, A. Viswanathan, R. Callon, "Multiprotocol Label Switching Architecture," RFC 3031, Jan. 2001. ftp://ftp.rfc-editor.org/in-notes/rfc3031.txt.

[RFC 3032] E. Rosen, D. Tappan, G. Fedorkow, Y. Rekhter, D. Farinacci, T. Li, A. Conta, "MPLS Label Stack Encoding," RFC 3032, Jan. 2001. ftp://ftp.rfc-editor.org/in-notes/rfc3032.txt

[RFC 3052] M. Eder, S. Nag, "Service Management Architectures Issues and Review," RFC 3052, Jan. 2001, http://www.rfc-editor.org/rfc/rfc3139.txt

[RFC 3139] L. Sanchez, K. McCloghrie, J. Saperia, "Requirements for Configuration Management of IP-Based Networks, RFC 3139, June 2001, http://www.rfc-editor.org/rfc/rfc3139.txt

[RFC3209] D. Awduche, L. Berger, D. Gan, T. Li, V. Srinivasan, G. Swallow, "RSVP-TE: Extensions to RSVP for LSP Tunnels," RFC 3209, Dec. 2001. ftp://ftp.rfc-editor.org/in-notes/rfc3209.txt

[RFC 3221] G. Huston, "Commentary on Inter-Domain Routing in the Internet," RFC 3221, December 2001. ftp://ftp.rfc-editor.org/in-notes/rfc3221.txt

[RFC 3232] J. Reynolds, "Assigned Numbers: RFC 1700 is Replaced by an On-line Database," RFC 3232, January 2002, http://www.rfc-editor.org/rfc/rfc3232.txt

[RFC 3260] D. Grossman, "New Terminology and Clarifications for Diffserv," RFC 3260, April 2002. ftp://ftp.rfc-editor.org/in-notes/rfc3260.txt

[RFC 3261] J. Rosenberg, H. Schulzrinne, G. Carmarillo, A. Johnston, J. Peterson, R. Sparks, M. Handley, E. Schooler, "SIP: Session Initiation Protocol," RFC 3261, July 2002. http://www.rfc-editor.org/rfc/rfc3261.txt

[RFC 3344] C. Perkins, ed., "IP Mobility Support for IPv4," *RFC 3344*, October 2002. ftp://ftp.rfc-editor.org/in-notes/rfc3344.txt

[RFC 3346] J. Boyle, V. Gill, A. Hannan, D. Cooper, D. Awduche, B. Christian, W. S. Lai, "Applicability Statement for Traffic Engineering with MPLS," RFC 3346, Aug. 2002. ftp://ftp.rfc-editor.org/in-notes/rfc3346.txt

[RFC 3376] B. Cain, S. Deering, I. Kouvelas, B. Fenner, A. Thyagarajan, "Internet Group Management Protocol, Version 3," RFC 3376, October 2002. ftp://ftp.rfc-editor.org/in-notes/rfc3376.txt

[RFC 3390] M. Allman, S. Floyd, C. Partridge, "Increasing TCP's Initial Window," RFC 3390, October 2002, ftp://ftp.rfc-editor.org/in-notes/rfc3390.txt.

[RFC 3410] J. Case, R. Mundy, D. Partain, D. Partain, "Introduction and Applicability Statements for Internet Standard Management Framework," RFC 3410, December, 2002, ftp://ftp.rfc-editor.org/in-notes/rfc3410.txt

[RFC 3411] D. Harrington R. Presuhn B. Wijnen, "An Architecture for Describing Simple Network Management Protocol (SNMP) Management Frameworks," RFC 3411, December 2002, ftp://ftp.rfc-editor.org/in-notes/rfc3411.txt

[RFC 3414] U. Blumenthal, U. Blumenthal, "User-based Security Model (USM) for version 3 of the Simple Network Management Protocol (SNMPv3)," RFC 3414, December 2002,

[RFC 3415] B. Wijnen, R. Presuhn, K. McCloghrie, "View-based Access Control Model (VACM) for the Simple Network Management Protocol (SNMP)," RFC 3415, December 2002. ftp://ftp.rfc-editor.org/in-notes/rfc3415.txt

[RFC 3416] R. Presuhn, J. Case, K. McCloghrie, M. Rose, S. Waldbusser, "Version 2 of the Protocol Operations for the Simple Network Management Protocol (SNMP)," December 2002, ftp://ftp.rfc-editor.org/in-notes/rfc3416.txt

[RFC 3468] L. Andersson, G. Swallow, "The Multiprotocol Label Switching (MPLS) Working Group Decision on MPLS Signaling Protocols," RFC 3468, Feb. 2003. ftp://ftp.rfc-editor.org/in-notes/rfc3468.txt

[RFC 3469] V. Sharma, Ed., F. Hellstrand, Ed, "Framework for Multi-Protocol Label Switching (MPLS)-based Recovery," RFC 3469, Feb. 2003. ftp://ftp.rfc-editor.org/in-notes/rfc3469.txt

[RFC 3550] H. Schulzrinne, S. Casner, R. Frederick, V. Jacobson, "RTP: A Transport Protocol for Real-Time Applications," RFC 3550, July 2003, ftp://ftp.rfc-editor.org/in-notes/rfc3550.txt

[RFC 3569] S. Bhattacharyya (ed.), "An Overview of Source-Specific Multicast (SSM)," RFC 3569, July 2003, ftp://ftp.rfc-editor.org/in-notes/rfc3569.txt

[RFC 3588] P. Calhoun, J. Loughney, E. Guttman, G. Zorn, J. Arkko, "Diameter Base Protocol," Sept. 2003, ftp://ftp.rfc-editor.org/in-notes/rfc2716.txt

[RFC 3600] J. Reynolds, 6 S. Ginoza, 6, "Internet Official Protocol Standards," RFC 3600, November 2003, ftp://ftp.rfc-editor.org/in-notes/rfc3600.txt

[RFC 3649] S. Floyd, "HighSpeed TCP for Large Congestion Windows," RFC 3649, December 2003, ftp://ftp.rfc-editor.org/in-notes/rfc3649.txt.

[Rhee 1998] I. Rhee, "Error Control Techniques for Interactive Low-bit Rate Video Transmission over the Internet," *Proceedings ACM SIGCOMM'98,* Vancouver BC, (Aug. 31–Sept. 4, 1998). http://www.acm.org/sigcomm/sigcomm98/tp/abs_24.html

[Roberts 1967] L. Roberts, T. Merril, "Toward a Cooperative Network of Time-Shared Computers," *AFIPS Fall Conference,* Oct. 1966.

[Rom 1990] R. Rom, M. Sidi, *Multiple Access Protocols: Performance and Analysis,* Springer-Verlag, New York, 1990.

[Root Servers 2004] http://www.root-servers.org/

[Rose 1996] M. Rose, *The Simple Book: An Introduction to Internet Management, Revised Second Edition,* Prentice Hall, Englewood Cliffs, NJ, 1996.

[Rosenberg 2000] J. Rosenberg, L. Qiu, H. Schulzrinne, "Integrating Packet FEC into Adaptive Playout Buffer Algorithms on the Internet," *IEEE INFOCOM 2000* (Tel Aviv, 2000).

[Ross 1995] K. W. Ross, *Multiservice Loss Models for Broadband Telecommunication - Networks,* Springer, Berlin, 1995.

[Ross 2003] K. W. Ross, "Asynchronous Voice: A Personal Account," *IEEE Multimedia,* pp. 70–74, April/June 2003.

[Rowston 2001] A. Rowston, and P. Druschel, "Pastry: Scalable, Distributed Object Location and Routing for Large-Scale Peer-to-Peer Systems," in *Proceedings of IFIP/ACM Middleware 2001,* 2001, Heidelberg, Germany, 2001.

[RSA 1978] R. L. Rivest, A. Shamir, and L. M. Adleman, "A method for obtaining digital signatures and public-key cryptosystems," *Communications of the ACM,* Vol. 21, No. 2, pp. 120–126, Feb. 1978.

[RSA Challenge 2002] RSA Data Security Inc., "What is the RSA Secret Key Challenge?" http://www.rsasecurity.com/rsalabs/faq/2-4-4.html

[RSA FAQ 2004] RSA Inc., "RSA Laboratories' Frequently Asked Questions About Today's Cryptography, Version 4.1," http://www.rsasecurity.com/rsalabs/faq

[RSA Fast 2004] RSA Laboratories, "How fast is RSA?" http://www.rsasecurity.com/rsalabs/faq/3-1-2.html

[RSA Key 2004] RSA Laboratories, "How large a key should be used in the RSA Crypto system?" http://www.rsasecurity.com/rsalabs/faq/3-1-5.html

[Rubenstein 1998] D. Rubenstein, J. Kurose, D. Towsley "Real-Time Reliable Multicast Using Proactive Forward Error Correction," *Proceedings of NOSSDAV '98* (Cambridge, UK, July 1998). http://gaia.cs.umass.edu/pub/Rubenst98:proact.ps.gz

[Rubin 2001] A. Rubin, White-Hat Security Arsenal: Tackling the Threats, Addison-Wesley, 2001.

[Saltzer 1984] J. Saltzer, D. Reed, D. Clark, "End-to-End Arguments in System Design," *ACM Transactions on Computer Systems (TOCS),* 2(4) (November 1984).

[Saroiu 2002] S. Saroiu, K. Gummadi, R. Dunn, S. Gribble, H. Levy, "An Analysis of Internet Content Delivery Systems," *Proc. Usenix OSDI 2002*, pp. 315–328. http://www.usenix.org/events/osdi02/tech/saroiu/saroiu_html/index.html

[Savage 1999] S. Savage, A. Collins, E. Hoffman, J. Snell, T. Anderson, "The End-to-End Effects of Internet Path Selection," in *Proceedings of 1999 ACM SIGCOMM*, Boston, MA, September 1999

[Savage 2000] S. Savage, D. Wetherall, A. Karlin, T. Anderson, "Practical Network Support for IP Traceback, *Proceedings of the 2000 ACM SIGCOMM Conference*, (Stockholm, Sweden), August 2000, pp. 295–306, http://www.cs.washington.edu/homes/savage/papers/Sigcomm00.pdf

[Saydam 1996] T. Saydam and T. Magedanz, "From Networks and Network Management into Service and Service Management," *Journal of Networks and System Management,* Vol. 4, No. 4 (Dec. 1996), pp. 345–348.

[Schneier 1995] B. Schneier, *Applied Cryptography: Protocols, Algorithms, and Source Code in C,* John Wiley and Sons, 1995.

[Schulzrinne 1997] H. Schulzrinne, "A Comprehensive Multimedia Control Architecture for the Internet," N*OSSDAV'97 (Network and Operating System Support for Digital Audio and Video),* St. Louis, Missouri; May 19, 1997. http://www.cs.columbia.edu/~hgs/papers/Schu9705_Comprehensive.ps.gz

[Schulzrinne-RTP 2004] Henning Schulzrinne's RTP site, http://www.cs.columbia.edu/~hgs/rtp

[Schulzrinne-RTSP 2004] Henning Schulzrinne's RTSP site, http://www.cs.columbia.edu/~hgs/rtsp

[Schulzrinne-SIP 2004] Henning Schulzrinne's SIP site, http://www.cs.columbia.edu/~hgs/sip

[Schurmann 1996] G. Schurmann, "Multimedia Mail," *ACM Multimedia Systems,* Oct. 1996, pp. 281–295.

[Schwartz 1977] M. Schwartz, *Computer-Communication Network Design and Analysis*, Prentice-Hall, Englewood Cliffs, N.J., 1997.

[Schwartz 1980] M. Schwartz, *Information, Transmission, Modulation, and Noise,* McGraw Hill, NY, NY 1980.

[Schwartz 1982] M. Schwartz, "Performance Analysis of the SNA Virtual Route Pacing Control," *IEEE Transactions on Communications,* Vol. COM-30, No. 1, (Jan. 1982), pp. 172–184.

[Schwiebert 2001] L. Schwiebert, S. Gupta, J. Weinmann, "Research Challenges in Wireless Networks of Biomedical Sensors," *ACM Mobicom 2001*, 2001, pp. 151-165. http://citeseer.ist.psu.edu/schwiebert01research.html

 [Scourias 2001] J. Scourias, T. Farley, "Overview of the Global System for Mobile Communications: GSM." http://www.privateline.com/PCS/GSM0.html

[Segaller 1998] S. Segaller, *Nerds 2.0.1, A Brief History of the Internet,* TV Books, New York, 1998.

[Semeria 1996] C. Semeria, "Understanding IP addressing: Everything you ever wanted to know," http://www.3com.com/nsc/501302s.html

[Shacham 1990] N. Shacham, P. McKenney, "Packet Recovery in High-Speed Networks Using Coding and Buffer Management," *Proc. IEEE Infocom Conference* (San Francisco, 1990), pp. 124–131.

[Sharma 1997] Puneet Sharma, Deborah Estrin, Sally Floyd, Van Jacobson, "Scalable Timers for Soft State Protocols," *Proc. IEEE Infocom '97 Conference,* Apr. 1997 (Kobe, Japan).

[Shipley 2001] P. Shipley, "Open WLANS: The Early Results of War Driving," http://www.dis.org/filez/openlans.pdf

[Sidor 1998] D. Sidor, "TMN Standards: Satisfying Today's Needs While Preparing for Tomorrow," *IEEE Communications Magazine,* Vol. 36, No. 3 (Mar. 1998), pp. 54–64.

[Singh 1999] S. Singh, *The Code Book: The Evolution of Secrecy from Mary, Queen of Scots to Quantum Cryptography,* Doubleday Press, 1999.

[SIP Software 2004] H. Schulzrinne Software Package site, http://www.cs.columbia.edu/IRT/software

[SMIL 2004] W3C Synchronized Multimedia homepage, http://www.w3.org/AudioVideo

[Snoeren 2001] A. Snoeren, C. Partridge, L. Sanchez, C. Jones, F. Tchakountio, S. Kent, W. T. Strayer, "Hash-Based IP Traceback," *Proceedings of the 2001 ACM Sigcomm,* http://www.acm.org/sigcomm/sigcomm2001/p1-snoeren.pdf

[Solari 1997] S. J. Solari, *Digital Video and Audio Compression,* McGraw Hill, NY, NY, 1997.

[Solensky 1996] F. Solensky, "IPv4 Address Lifetime Expectations," in *IPng: Internet Protocol Next Generation* (S. Bradner, A. Mankin, ed), Addison-Wesley, Reading, MA, 1996.

[Spragins 1991] J. D. Spragins, *Telecommunications Protocols and Design,* Addison-Wesley, Reading, MA, 1991.

[Sprint 2004] Sprint, "Network Overview: SLAs," http://www.sprintbiz.com/about/network_slas.html

[Spurgeon 2002] C. Spurgeon, "Charles Spurgeon's Ethernet Web Site," http://wwwhost.ots.utexas.edu/ethernet/ethernet-home.html

[Srinivasan 1999] V. Srinivasan and G. Varghese, "Fast Address Lookupp Using Controlled Prefix Expansion," *ACM Transactions Computer Sys.,* Vol 17, No. 1 (Feb 1999), pp. 1–40.

[Stallings 1993] W. Stallings, *SNMP, SNMP v2, and CMIP The Practical Guide to Network Management Standards,* Addison-Wesley, Reading, MA, 1993.

[Stallings 1999] W. Stallings, *SNMP, SNMPv2, SNMPv3, and RMON 1 and 2,* Addison-Wesley, Reading, MA, 1999.

[Steinder 2002] M. Steinder, A. Sethi, "Increasing robustness of fault localization through analysis of lost, spurious, and positive symptoms," in *Proc. IEEE INFOCOM,* 2002. http://www.ieee-infocom.org/2002/papers/665.pdf

[Stevens 1990] W. R. Stevens, *Unix Network Programming,* Prentice-Hall, Englewood Cliffs, NJ.

[Stevens 1994] W. R. Stevens, *TCP/IP Illustrated, Vol. 1: The Protocols,* Addison-Wesley, Reading, MA, 1994.

[Stevens 1997] W.R. Stevens, *Unix Network Programming, Volume 1: Networking APIs-Sockets and XTI,* 2nd edition, Prentice-Hall, Englewood Cliffs, NJ, 1997.

[Stewart 1999] J. Stewart, *BGP4: Interdomain Routing in the Internet,* Addison-Wesley, 1999.

[Stoica 2001] I. Stoica, R. Morris, D. Karger, M.F. Kaashoek, H. Balakrishnan, "Chord: A Scalable Peer-to-Peer Lookup Service for Internet Applications," In *Proceedings of ACM SIGCOMM,* 2001, (San Diego, CA), 2001. http://www.acm.org/sigcomm/sigcomm2001/p12.html

[Stoll 1995] C. Stoll, The Cuckoo's Egg: Tracking a Spy Through the Maze of Computer Espionage, Pocket Books, 1995.

[Stone 1998] J. Stone, M. Greenwald, C. Partridge, and J. Hughes, "Performance of Checksums and CRC's Over Real Data," *IEEE/ACM Transactions on Networking,* Vol. 6, No. 5 (Oct. 1998), pp 529–543

[Stone 2000] J. Stone, C. Partridge, "When Reality and the Checksum Disagree," *Proceedings of ACM SIGCOMM '00,* (Stockholm, Sweden, Aug. 2000).

[Strayer 1992] W. T. Strayer, B. Dempsey, A. Weaver, *XTP: The Xpress Transfer Protocol,* Addison-Wesley, Reading, MA, 1992.

[Stubblefield 2002] A. Stubblefield, J. Ioannidis, A. Rubin, "Using the Fluhrer, Mantin, and Shamir Attack to Break WEP," *Proceedings of the 2002 Network and Distributed Systems Security Symposium* (2002), 17–22. http://www.cs.rice.edu/~astubble/wep/wep_attack.pdf

[Subramanian 2000] M. Subramanian, *Network Management: Principles and Practice,* Addison-Wesley, Reading, MA, 2000.

[Subramanian 2002] L. Subramanian, S. Agarwal, J. Rexford, R. Katz, "Characterizing the Internet Hierarchy from Multiple Vantage Points," *Proc. 2002 IEEE Infocom.*

[Sun 2004] Sun Microsystems, "System and Network Management," http://www.sun.com/products-n-solutions/software/management/

[Sunshine 1978] C. Sunshine and Y. K. Dalal, "Connection Management in Transport Protocols," *Computer Networks,* North-Holland, Amsterdam, 1978.

[T-Mobile 2004] T-Mobile HotSpot US Location Map, http://locations.hotspot.t-mobile.com

[Tangmunarunkit 2001] H. Tangmunarunkit, R. Govindan, D. Estrin, S. Shenker, "The Impact of Routing Policy on Internet Paths," *Proceedings 2001 IEEE INFOCOM*, Alaska, April 2001. http://www.isi.edu/~hongsuda/publication/info2001.ps

[TechnOnLine 2004] TechOnLine, "Protected Wireless Networks," online webcast tutorial, http://www.techonline.com/community/tech_topic/internet/21752

[Teleography 2002] Teleography—a research division of Pirmetrica, "WorldCom Controls the Most Internet Bandwidth, Connections, and Revenue," http://www.telegeography.com/press/releases/2002/10-jul-2002.html.

[Thaler 1997] D. Thaler and C. Ravishankar, "Distributed Center-Location Algorithms," *IEEE Journal on Selected Areas in Communications,* Vol. 15, No. 3, (Apr. 1997), pp. 291–303.

[Think 2002] Technical History of Network Protocols, "Cyclades," http://www.cs.utexas.edu/users/jeffo/cs370/CYCLADES/jeffo/cyclades/index.htm

[Thinplanet 2002] Thinplanet homepage, http://www.thinplanet.com/

[Thottan 1998] M. Thottan and C. Ji, "Proactive Anomaly Detection Using Distributed Intelligent Agents," *IEEE Network Magazine,* Vol. 12, No. 5 (Sept./ Oct. 1998), pp. 21–28.

[Tobagi 1990] F. Tobagi, "Fast Packet Switch Architectures for Broadband Integrated Networks," *Proc. of the IEEE,* Vol. 78, No. 1 (Jan. 1990), pp. 133–167.

[Turner 1986] J. Turner, "New Directions in Communications (or Which Way to the Information Age?)," *Proceedings of the Zürich Seminar on Digital Communication,* (Zurich, Switzerland, Mar. 1986), pp. 25–32.

[Turner 1988] J. S. Turner "Design of a Broadcast packet switching network," *IEEE Transactions on Communications,* Vol. 36, No. 6 (June 1988), pp. 734–743.

[Utah 2004] Utah Division of Corporations and Commercial Codes, Digital Signature Licensing Information, http://www.commerce.state.ut.us/corporat/dsmain.htm

[Varghese 1997] G. Varghese and A. Lauck, "Hashed and Hierarchical Timing Wheels: Efficient Data Structures for Implementing a Timer Facility," *IEEE/ACM Transactions on Networking,* Vol. 5, No. 6, (Dec. 1997), pp. 824–834.

[Verisign 2004] http://www.verisign.com

[Verizon 2004] Verizon Communication, *Verizon Broadband Anytime.* http://www.verizon.net/wifi/

[Verma 2001] D.C. Verma, *Content Distribution Networks: An Engineering Approach,* John Wiley, 2001

[Viterbi 1995] A. Viterbi, *CDMA: Principles of Spread Spectrum Communication,* Addison-Wesley, Reading, MA, 1995.

[VON 2004] Voice on the Net, http://www.von.com

[von Lohmann 2003] F. von Lohmann, "Peer-to-Peer File Sharing and Copyright Law: A Primer for Developers," *2nd International Workshop on Peer-to-Peer Systems (IPTPS '03),* Berkeley, 2003. http://iptps03.cs.berkeley.edu/final-papers/copyright.pdf

[Voydock 1983] V.L. Voydock, and S.T. Kent, "Security Mechanisms in High-Level Network Protocols," *ACM Computing Surveys* Vol. 15, No. 2 (June 1983), pp. 135–171.

[W3C 1995] The World Wide Web Consortium, "A Little History of the World Wide Web," 1995. http://www.w3.org/History.html

[WAP 2004] WAP Forum, "WAP 2.0 Technical White Paper," http://www.wapforum.org/what/whitepapers.htm.

[Wakeman 1992] Ian Wakeman, Jon Crowcroft, Zheng Wang, and Dejan Sirovica, "Layering Considered Harmful," *IEEE Network,* Jan. 1992, pp. 20–24.

[Waldvogel 1997] M. Waldvogel et al., "Scalable High Speed IP Routing Lookup," *Proceedings of ACM SIGCOMM '97* (Cannes, France, Sept. 1997). http://www.acm.org/sigs/sigcomm/sigcomm97/papers/p182.html

[Walker 2000] J. Walker, "IEEE P802.11 Wireless LANs, Unsafe at Any Key Size; An Analysis of the WEP Encapsulation," Oct. 2000, http://www.drizzle.com/~aboba/IEEE/0-362.zip

[Weatherspoon 2000] S. Weatherspoon, "Overview of IEEE 802.11b Security," *Intel Technology Journal,* (2nd Quarter 2000), http://developer.intel.com/technology/itj/q22000/articles/art_5.htm

[Web ProForum 1999] Web ProForum, "Tutorial on H.323," 1999. http://www.webproforum.com/h323/index.html

[Wei 2004] W. Wei, B. Wang, J. Kurose, D. Towsley, "Detecting and Distinguishing Wired and Wireless Packet Losses in an End-End Connection," *Technical Report,* Dept. Computer Science, University of Massachusetts, 2004

[Weinstein 2002] S. Weinstein, "The Mobile Internet:Wireless LAN vs. 3G Cellular Mobile*," IEEE Communications Magazine* (February 2002). pp. 26–28.

[Weiser 1991] M. Weiser, "The Computer for the Twenty-First Century," *Scientific American* (September 1991): 94–10. http://www.ubiq.com/hypertext/weiser/SciAmDraft3.html

[Wessels 2001] D. Wessels, *Web Caching*, O'Reilly, Sebastopol, CA, 2001.

[Wimba 2004] Wimba homepage, http://www.wimba.com

[Woo 1994] T. Woo, R. Bindignavle, S. Su, and S. Lam. SNP: an interface for secure network programming. In Proceedings of 1994 Summer USENIX, pages 45—58, Boston, MA, June 1994. http://www.cs.utexas.edu/users/lam/Vita/Cpapers/WBSL94.pdf

[Wood 2004] L. Wood, "Lloyds Satellites Constellations," http://www.ee.surrey.ac.uk/Personal/L.Wood/constellations/iridium.html

[Xiao 2000] X. Xiao, A. Hannan, B. Bailey, L. Ni, "Traffic Engineering with MPLS in the Internet," *IEEE Network*, March/April 2000.
http://www.cse.msu.edu/~xiaoxipe/papers/mplsTE/mpls.te.pdf

[Yahoo-MIME 1999]Yahoo MIME WWW page, http://dir.yahoo.com/Computers_and_Internet/Multimedia/MIME/

[Yeager 1996] N. J. Yeager and R. E. McGrath, *Web Server Technology,* Morgan Kaufmann Publishers, San Francisco, 1996.

[Zegura 1997] E. Zegura, K. Calvert, M. Donahoo, "A Quantitative Comparison of Graph-based Models for Internet Topology," *IEEE/ACM Transactions on Networking,* Vol. 5, No. 6, (Dec. 1997). http://www.cc.gatech.edu/fac/ Ellen.Zegura/papers/ton-model.ps.gz. See also http://www.cc.gatech.edu/ projects/gtim for a software package that generates networks with realistic structure.

[Zhang 1991] L. Zhang, S. Shenker, and D. D. Clark, "Observations on the Dynamics of a Congestion Control Algorithm: The Effects of Two Way Traffic," *Proceedings of ACM SIGCOMM '91,* Zürich, 1991. http://www1.acm.org/pubs/citations/proceedings/comm/115992/p133-zhang/

[Zhang 1993] L. Zhang, S. Deering, D. Estrin, S. Shenker, D. Zappala, "RSVP: A New Resource Reservation Protocol," *IEEE Network Magazine,* Vol. 7, No. 9 (Sept. 1993), pp. 8–18.

[Zhang 1998] L. Zhang, R. Yavatkar, Fred Baker, Peter Ford, Kathleen Nichols, M. Speer, Y. Bernet, "A Framework for Use of RSVP with Diff-serv Networks," <draft-ietf-diffservrsvp-01.txt>, 11/20/1998. Work in progress.

[Zhao 2004] B. Y. Zhao, L. Huang, J. Stribling, S. C. Rhea, A. D. Joseph, J. Kubiatowicz, "Tapestry: A Resilient Global-scale Overlay for Service Deployment," *IEEE Journal on Selected Areas in Communications,* January 2004, 22(1).
http://www.cs.berkeley.edu/~adj/publications/paper-files/tapestry_jsac.pdf

[Ziff-Davis 1998] Ziff-Davis Publishing, "Ted Nelson: Hypertext pioneer," 1998. http://www.zdnet.com/zdtv/screensavers_story/0,3656,2127396-2102293,00.html

[Zimmermann 2004] P. Zimmermann, "Why do you need PGP?" http://www.pgpi.org/doc/whypgp/en/

Index